Irene C. Fountas **&** Gay Su Pinnell

# The Reading
# Minilessons
## Book

## Your Every Day Guide for Literacy Teaching

## GRADE 4

**HEINEMANN**
Portsmouth, NH

**Heinemann**
361 Hanover Street
Portsmouth, NH 03801–3912
www.heinemann.com

*Offices and agents throughout the world*

The author and publisher wish to thank those who have generously given permission to reprint borrowed material: Please see the Credits section beginning on page 635.

Library of Congress Cataloging-in-Publication Data is on file at the Library of Congress.
ISBN: 978-0-325-09865-4

*Editor:* Sue Paro
*Production:* Cindy Strowman
*Cover and interior designs:* Ellery Harvey
*Illustrator:* Sarah Snow
*Typesetter:* Sharon Burkhardt
*Manufacturing:* Erin St. Hilaire

Printed in the United States of America on acid-free paper

1  2  3  4  5  6  7  WC  24  23  22  21  20  19
June 2019 Printing

# CONTENTS

# 2 Literary Analysis

## Fiction and Nonfiction

### General

## Messages and Themes

## Style and Language

## Illustrations

## Book and Print Features

## Nonfiction

### Genre

## Book and Print Features

## Fiction

### Genre

## Style and Language

# 3   Strategies and Skills

# 4 Writing About Reading

Chapter **1**

# The Role of Reading Minilessons in Literacy Learning

THE GOAL OF ALL READING is the joyful, independent, and meaningful processing of a written text. As a competent reader, you become immersed in a fiction or nonfiction text; you read for a purpose; you become highly engaged with the plot, the characters, or the content. Focused on the experience of reading the text, you are largely unconscious of the thousands of actions happening in your brain that support the construction of meaning from the print that represents language. And, this is true whether the print is on a piece of paper or an electronic device. Your purpose may be to have vicarious experiences via works of fiction that take you to places far distant in time and space—even to worlds that do not and cannot exist! Or, your purpose may be to gather fuel for thinking (by using fiction or nonfiction) or it may be simply to enjoy the sounds of human language via literature and poetry. Most of us engage in the reading of multiple texts every day—some for work, some for pleasure, and some for practical guidance—but what we all have in common as readers is the ability to independently and simultaneously apply in-the-head systems of strategic actions that enable us to act on written texts.

Young readers are on a journey toward efficient processing of any texts they might like to attempt, and it is important every step of the way that they have successful experiences in independently reading those texts that are available at each point in time. In a literacy-rich classroom with a multitext approach, readers have the opportunity to hear written texts read aloud through interactive read-aloud, and so they build a rich treasure chest of known stories and nonfiction books that they can share as a classroom community. They understand and talk about these shared texts in ways that extend comprehension, vocabulary, and knowledge of the ways written texts are presented and organized. They participate with their classmates in the shared or performance reading of a common text so that they understand more and know how to act on written language. They experience tailored instruction in small guided reading groups using leveled texts precisely matched to their current abilities and needs for challenge. They stretch their thinking as they discuss a variety of complex texts in book clubs. They process fiction and nonfiction books with expert teacher support—always moving in the direction of more complex texts that will lift their reading abilities. *But it is in independent reading that they apply everything they have learned across all of those instructional contexts.* So the goal of all the reading instruction is to enable the reader to engage in effective, efficient, and meaningful processing of written text *every day* in the classroom. This is what it means to grow up literate in our schools.

Independent reading involves choices based on interests and tastes. Competent, independent readers are eager to talk and write about the books they have chosen and read on their own. They are gaining awareness of themselves as readers with favorite authors, illustrators, genres, and topics; their capacity for self-regulation is growing. The key to this kind of independent reading is making an explicit connection between all other instructional contexts—interactive read-aloud, shared reading, guided reading, and book clubs—and the reader's own independent work. Making these explicit links is the goal of minilessons. All teaching, support, and confirmation lead to the individual's successful, independent reading.

## Making Learning Visible Through Minilessons

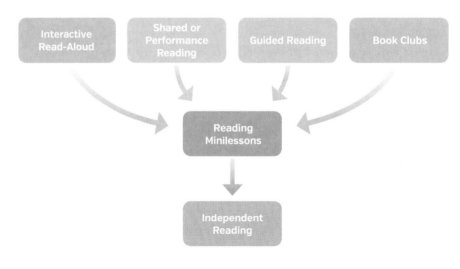

**Figure 1-1:** Various reading experiences supported by explicit instruction in reading minilessons lead to independent reading.

## What Is a Reading Minilesson?

A reading minilesson is a concise and focused lesson on any aspect of effective reading that is important for students to explicitly understand at a particular point in time. It is an opportunity to build on all of the students' literacy experiences, make one important understanding visible, and hold learners accountable for applying it consistently in reading. These explicit minilessons place a strong instructional frame around independent reading.

A minilesson takes only a few minutes and usually involves the whole class. Because it builds on shared literary experiences that the students in your class have experienced prior to the lesson, you can quickly bring these shared texts to mind as powerful examples. Usually, you will teach only one focused lesson each day, but minilessons are logically organized to build on each other. Each minilesson is designed to engage your students in an inquiry process that leads to the discovery and understanding of a general principle that they can immediately apply. Most of the time, interactive read-aloud books and shared or performance reading texts that students have already heard serve as mentor texts from which they generalize the understanding. In this way, the reading minilesson provides a link between students' previous experience and their own independent reading (see Figure 1-1). The reading minilesson plays a key role in systematic, coherent teaching, all of which is directed toward each reader's developing competencies.

To help students connect ideas and develop deep knowledge and broad application of **principles**, related reading minilessons are grouped under **umbrella** concepts (see Chapter 3). An umbrella is the broad category within which several lessons are linked to each other and all of which contribute to the understanding of the umbrella concept. Within each umbrella, the lessons build on each other (see Figure 1-2). In each lesson, you will create an **anchor chart** with the students. This visual representation of the principle will be a useful reference tool as students learn new routines, encounter new texts, and draw and write about their reading in a reader's notebook.

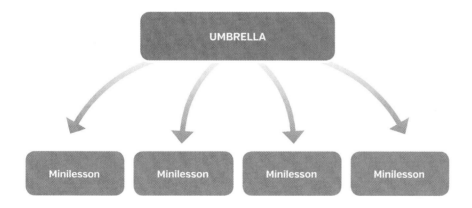

**Figure 1-2:** Each minilesson focuses on a different aspect of the larger umbrella concept.

# Four Types of Reading Minilessons

In this book, you will find 225 minilessons that are organized into four types:

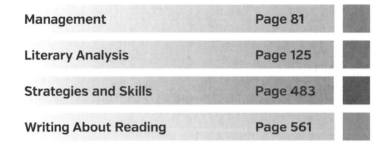

| | |
|---|---|
| Management | Page 81 |
| Literary Analysis | Page 125 |
| Strategies and Skills | Page 483 |
| Writing About Reading | Page 561 |

**Management Minilessons.** These lessons include routines that are essential to the smooth functioning of the classroom and student-centered, independent literacy learning. The Management minilessons are designed to support students' development of independence and self-regulatory behavior. The Management minilessons for fourth graders help students learn to be respectful members of a classroom community of readers who share book recommendations, talk together about books, and write about reading on a regular basis. You'll also find minilessons that support students in reading independently at school and at home and that prepare them for living a reading life by developing their reading interests and preferences, challenging themselves to stretch and grow as readers and dedicating time to read at home. Most of your minilessons at the beginning of the school year will focus on management. You will want to repeat any of the lessons as needed across the year. A guiding principle: teach a minilesson on anything that prevents the classroom from running smoothly and feeling like a strong community.

**Literary Analysis Minilessons.** These lessons build students' awareness of the characteristics of various genres and of the elements of fiction and nonfiction texts. Most of the mentor texts used to illustrate the principles are interactive read-aloud books that you have read previously to the class. However, a few mentor texts are independent reading books or guided reading books. When using these books, make sure that you have read them aloud to the whole class before the minilesson. Through these lessons, students learn how to apply new thinking to their independent reading; they also learn how to share their thinking with others.

**Strategies and Skills Minilessons.** Readers need to develop a robust body of in-the-head strategic actions for the efficient processing of texts. For example, they need to monitor their reading for accuracy and understanding, solve words (simple and complex), read fluently with phrasing, and constantly construct meaning. And, as they encounter more complex books in fourth grade, they need to use a variety of effective techniques when approaching texts that are difficult for them to read. The lessons not only support your students in monitoring their comprehension but also address the importance of focus and persistence in reading difficult texts. Teaching related to processing texts (decoding words, parsing language, and reading with accuracy and fluency) will best take place in guided reading and independent reading conferences. The general lessons included in this volume reinforce broad principles that every reader in your class may need to be reminded of from time to time. Included in Section Three: Strategies and Skills is Umbrella 7: Reading in Digital Environments, which is designed to help you teach students to effectively find online the information they need, evaluate its relevance and credibility, and stay focused while doing so. At fourth grade, when many students begin to spend more time reading in digital environments, these lessons provide essential teaching for the digital age.

**Writing About Reading Minilessons.** Throughout the fourth-grade year, students will have opportunities to use a reader's notebook to respond

**Figure 1-4:** Characteristics of effective minilessons

## Characteristics of Effective Minilessons

### Effective Minilessons . . .

- have a **clear rationale and a goal** to focus meaningful teaching
- are **relevant to the specific needs of readers** so that your teaching connects with the learners
- are **brief, concise, and to the point** for immediate application
- use **clear and specific language** to avoid talk that clutters learning
- stay **focused on a single idea** so students can apply the learning and build on it day after day
- **build one understanding on another** across several days instead of single isolated lessons
- use an **inquiry approach** whenever possible to support constructive learning
- often include **shared, high-quality mentor texts** that can be used as examples
- are **well paced** to engage and hold students' interest
- are **grouped into umbrellas** to foster depth in thinking and coherence across lessons
- provide time for students to **"try out" the new concept** before independent application
- engage students in **summarizing the new learning** and thinking about its application to their own work
- build **academic vocabulary** appropriate to the grade level
- help students become **better readers and writers**
- **foster community** through the development of shared language
- **can be assessed** as you observe students in authentic literacy activities to provide feedback on your teaching
- help **students understand what they are learning** how to do and how it helps them as readers

to what they read. These lessons introduce *Reader's Notebook: Intermediate* (Fountas and Pinnell 2011) and help students use this important tool for independent literacy learning. Fourth graders will use a reader's notebook to keep track of their reading and writing (which will include new genres and forms of writing), keep a record of the principles taught in minilessons, write a weekly letter about the books they are reading, and write regularly about the thinking they do while reading.

The goal of all minilessons is to help students to think and act like readers and to build effective processing strategies while reading continuous text independently. Whether you are teaching Management lessons, Literary Analysis lessons, Strategies and Skills lessons, or Writing About Reading lessons, the characteristics of effective minilessons, listed in Figure 1-4, apply.

## Constructing Anchor Charts for Effective Minilessons

Anchor charts are an essential part of each minilesson in this book (see Figure 1-5). They provide a way for you to capture the students' thinking during the lesson and reflect on the learning at the end. When you think about a chart, it helps you think through the big, important ideas and the language you will use in the minilesson. It helps you think about the sequence and your efficiency in getting down what is important.

Each minilesson in this book provides guidance for adding information to the chart. Read through each lesson carefully to know whether any parts of the chart should be prepared ahead or whether the chart is constructed during the lesson or at the end. After the lesson, the charts become resources for your students to use for reference throughout the day and on following days. They can revisit these charts as they apply the principles in reading, talking, and writing about books, or as they try out new routines in the classroom. You can refer to them during interactive read-aloud, shared and performance reading, reading conferences, guided reading, and book clubs. Anchor charts are a resource for students who need a visual representation of their learning.

Though your charts will be unique because they are built from the ideas your students share, you will want to consider some of the common characteristics among the charts we have included in this book. We have created one example in each lesson, but vary it as you see fit. When you create charts with students, consider the following:

> ▶ **Make your charts simple, clear, and organized.** The charts you create with your students should be clearly organized. Regardless of grade, it is important to keep them simple without a lot of dense text. Provide white space and write in dark, easy-to-read colors. You will notice that some of the sample charts are more conceptual. The idea is conveyed through a few words and a visual representation. Others use a grid to show how the principle is applied specifically across several texts.

▶ **Make your charts visually appealing and useful.** Many of the minilesson charts for fourth grade contain visual support, and this is especially helpful to English language learners. For example, you will see book covers, symbols, and drawings. Some students will benefit from the visuals to help them in reading the words on the chart and in understanding the concept. The drawings are intentionally simple to give you a quick model to draw yourself. English language learners might need to rely heavily on a graphic representation of the principle ideas. You might find it helpful to prepare these drawings on separate pieces of paper or sticky notes ahead of the lesson and tape or glue them on the chart as the students construct their understandings. This time-saving tip can also make the charts look more interesting and colorful, because certain parts stand out for the students.

▶ **Make your charts colorful.** Though the sample minilesson charts are colorful for the purpose of engagement or organization, be careful about the amount and types of color that you use. You may want to use color for specific purposes. For example, color can help you point out particular parts of the chart ("Look at the purple word on the chart") or support English language learners by providing a visual link to certain words or ideas. However, color can also be distracting if overused. Be thoughtful about when you choose to use colors to highlight an idea or a word on a chart so that students are supported in reading continuous text. Text that is broken up by a lot of different colors can be very distracting for readers. You will notice that the minilesson principle is usually written in black or another dark color across the top of the chart so that it stands out and is easily recognized as the focus of the lesson.

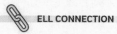
**ELL CONNECTION**

**Figure 1-5:** Constructing anchor charts with your students provides verbal and visual support for all learners.

**Illustrators create art to add to the meaning of the text.**

| Title | What the Illustrations Help You Understand | |
|---|---|---|
| THESE HANDS | • a character's actions | Example: The illustrations show that people march together to change unfair laws. |
| TEA with MILK | • a character's feelings | Examples: Large empty space around May shows loneliness. The stiffness of the two characters shows shyness and discomfort. |
| The Other Side | • what is not in the words | Examples: The words say "everyone ... seemed far away" but the illustration shows that the girls don't want to be far away from each other. |

Anchor charts support language growth in all students, and especially in English language learners. Conversation about the minilesson develops oral language and then connects that oral language to print when you write words on the chart and provide picture support. By constructing an anchor chart with your students, you provide print that is immediately accessible to them because they helped create it and have ownership of the language. After a chart is finished, revisit it as often as needed to reinforce not only the ideas but also the printed words.

## Balancing Time and Inquiry

Most minilessons in this book follow an inquiry-based approach in which students discover and construct understandings of the minilesson principle. Constructing ideas through inquiry can take a lot of time if not properly structured and supported. Notice that most of the minilessons in this book start right away with focused examples from mentor texts rather than a general review of the books. Time can be lost by reviewing each mentor text used in a minilesson. Avoid starting the lesson by asking "Do you remember what this book is about?" or "What happened in this story?" Instead, choose examples from books your students know really well. Following are some helpful time-saving tips:

▶ Teach students to listen to one another to avoid wasting time by repeating the same information during the minilesson.

▶ Avoid repeating every student response yourself. Repeat (or ask the student to repeat) only if clarification is needed.

▶ Take a few responses and move on; you don't need to hear from everyone who has raised a hand. Over time, assure everyone has a chance to respond.

▶ Don't be afraid to ask a student to hold a thought for another time if it is not related or is only tangentially related. A lot of time can be lost when students share personal stories or go far away from the focus. Stay focused on building understanding of the minilesson principle and invite the sharing of personal experiences only when it is applicable to understanding the principle.

▶ Make sure the mentor text examples you choose are short and to the point. Usually you will not need to read more than a paragraph or a few sentences out of the mentor texts to conduct the inquiry.

▶ Assess your students' talk as they participate in the inquiry and omit examples you do not need. Each minilesson section generally has two or three examples. They are there if you need them, but you should judge from your students' participation whether you need to share every example or whether you can simply move on and ask students to have a try.

# Using Reading Minilessons with Fourth-Grade Students

A minilesson brings to students' conscious attention a focused principle that will assist them in developing an effective, independent literacy processing system. It provides an opportunity for students to do the following:

- Respond to and act on a variety texts
- Become aware of and be able to articulate understandings about texts
- Engage in further inquiry to investigate the characteristics of texts
- Search for and learn to recognize patterns and characteristics of written texts
- Build new ideas on known ideas
- Learn how to think about effective actions as they process texts
- Learn to manage their own reading lives
- Learn how to work together well in the classroom
- Learn to talk to others to share their thinking about books
- Learn how to write to communicate their thinking about books

Reading minilessons help readers build in-the-head processing systems. In the following chapters, you will explore how minilessons support students in using integrated systems of strategic actions for thinking *within*, *beyond*, and *about* many different kinds of texts and also how to use minilessons to build a community of readers who demonstrate a sense of agency and responsibility. You will also look in more depth at how minilessons fit within a design for literacy learning and within a multitext approach.

We conclude this chapter with some key terms we will use as we describe minilessons in the next chapters (see Figure 1-6). Keep these in mind so you can develop a common language to talk about the minilessons you teach.

**Figure 1-6:** Important terms used in *The Reading Minilessons Book*

## Key Terms When Talking About Reading Minilessons

| | |
|---|---|
| Umbrella | A group of minilessons, all of which are directed at different aspects of the same larger understanding. |
| Principle | A concise statement of the understanding students will need to learn and apply. |
| Mentor Text | A fiction or nonfiction text that offers a clear example of the principle toward which the minilesson is directed. Students will have previously heard and discussed the text. |
| Text Set | A group of fiction or nonfiction texts or a combination of fiction and nonfiction texts that, taken together, support a theme or exemplify a genre. Students will have previously heard all the texts referenced in a minilesson and had opportunities to make connections between them. |
| Anchor Chart | A visual representation of the lesson concept, using a combination of words and images. It is constructed by the teacher and students to summarize the learning and is used as a reference tool by the students. |

# Chapter 2

## Using *The Literacy Continuum* to Guide the Teaching of Reading Minilessons

WE BELIEVE SCHOOLS SHOULD BE places where students read, think, talk, and write every day about relevant content that engages their hearts and minds. Learning deepens when students engage in thinking, talking, reading, and writing about texts across many different learning contexts and in whole-group, small-group, and individual instruction. Students who live a literate life in their classrooms have access to multiple experiences with texts throughout a day. As they participate in interactive read-aloud, shared and performance reading, guided reading, book clubs, and independent reading, they engage in the real work of reading and writing. They build a network of systems of strategic actions that allow them to think deeply within, beyond, and about text.

The networks of in-the-head strategic actions are inferred from observations of proficient readers, writers, and speakers. We have described these networks in *The Fountas & Pinnell Literacy Continuum: A Tool for Assessment, Planning, and Teaching* (Fountas and Pinnell 2017b). This volume presents detailed text characteristics and behaviors and understandings to notice, teach, and support for prekindergarten through middle school across eight instructional reading, writing, and language contexts. In sum, *The Literacy Continuum* describes proficiency in reading, writing, and language as it changes over grades and over levels.

**Figure 2-1:** Minilesson principles are drawn from the observable behaviors of proficient students as listed in *The Literacy Continuum.*

| | INSTRUCTIONAL CONTEXT | BRIEF DEFINITION | DESCRIPTION OF THE CONTINUUM |
|---|---|---|---|
| 1 | Interactive Read-Aloud and Literature Discussion | Students engage in discussion with one another about a text that they have heard read aloud or one they have read independently. | • Year by year, grades PreK–8<br>• Genres appropriate to grades PreK–8<br>• Specific behaviors and understandings that are evidence of thinking within, beyond, and about the text |
| 2 | Shared and Performance Reading | Students read together or take roles in reading a shared text. They reflect the meaning of the text with their voices. | • Year by year, grades PreK–8<br>• Genres appropriate to grades PreK–8<br>• Specific behaviors and understandings that are evidence of thinking within, beyond, and about the text |
| 3 | Writing About Reading | Students extend their understanding of a text through a variety of writing genres and sometimes with illustrations. | • Year by year, grades PreK–8<br>• Genres/forms for writing about reading appropriate to grades PreK–8<br>• Specific evidence in the writing that reflects thinking within, beyond, and about the text |
| 4 | Writing | Students compose and write their own examples of a variety of genres, written for varying purposes and audiences. | • Year by year, grades PreK–8<br>• Genres/forms for writing appropriate to grades PreK–8<br>• Aspects of craft, conventions, and process that are evident in students' writing, grades PreK–8 |
| 5 | Oral and Visual Communication | Students present their ideas through oral discussion and presentation. | • Year by year, grades PreK–8<br>• Specific behaviors and understandings related to listening and speaking, presentation |
| 6 | Technological Communication | Students learn effective ways of communicating and searching for information through technology; they learn to think critically about information and sources. | • Year by year, grades PreK–8<br>• Specific behaviors and understandings related to effective and ethical uses of technology |
| 7 | Phonics, Spelling, and Word Study | Students learn about the relationships of letters to sounds as well as the structure and meaning of words to help them in reading and spelling. | • Year by year, grades PreK–8<br>• Specific behaviors and understandings related to nine areas of understanding related to letters, sounds, and words, and how they work in reading and spelling |
| 8 | Guided Reading | Students read a teacher-selected text in a small group; the teacher provides explicit teaching and support for reading increasingly challenging texts. | • Level by level, A to Z<br>• Genres appropriate to grades PreK–8<br>• Specific behaviors and understandings that are evidence of thinking within, beyond, and about the text<br>• Specific suggestions for word work (drawn from the phonics and word analysis continuum) |

**Figure 2-2:** From *The Literacy Continuum* (Fountas and Pinnell 2017b, 3)

## Systems of Strategic Actions

The systems of strategic actions are represented in the wheel diagram shown in Figure 2-3 and on the inside back cover of this book. This model helps us think about the thousands of in-the-head processes that take place simultaneously and largely unconsciously when a competent reader processes a text. When the reader engages the neural network, he builds a literacy processing system over time that becomes increasingly sophisticated. Teaching in each instructional context is directed toward helping every reader expand these in-the-head networks across increasingly complex texts.

Four sections of *The Literacy Continuum* (Fountas and Pinnell 2017b)—Interactive Read-Aloud and Literature Discussion, Shared and Performance Reading, Guided Reading, and Writing About Reading—describe the specific competencies or goals of readers, writers, and language users:

**Within** the Text   (literal understanding achieved through searching for and using information, monitoring and self-correcting, solving words, maintaining fluency, adjusting, and summarizing) The reader gathers the important information from the fiction or nonfiction text.

**Beyond** the Text   (predicting; making connections with personal experience, content knowledge and other texts; synthesizing new information; and inferring what is implied but not stated) The reader brings understanding to the processing of a text, reaching for ideas or concepts that are implied but not explicitly stated.

**About** the Text   (analyzing or critiquing the text) The reader looks at a text to analyze, appreciate, or evaluate its construction, logic, literary elements, or quality.

*The Literacy Continuum* is the foundation for all the minilessons. The minilesson principles come largely from the behaviors and understandings in the Interactive Read-Aloud continuum, but some are selected from the Shared and Performance Reading; Oral and Visual Communication; Phonics, Spelling, and Word Study; Technological Communication; Writing About Reading; and Guided Reading continua. In addition, we have included minilessons related to working together in a classroom community to assure that effective literacy instruction can take place. In most lessons, you will see a direct link to the goals from *The Literacy Continuum* called Continuum Connection.

As you ground your teaching in support of each reader's development of the systems of strategic actions, it is important to remember that these actions are never applied one at a time. A reader who comprehends a text engages these actions rapidly and simultaneously and largely without conscious attention. Your intentional talk and conversations in the various instructional contexts should support students in engaging and building their processing systems while they respond authentically as readers and enjoy the text.

**Figure 2-3:** All of your teaching will be grounded in support of each reader's development of the systems of strategic actions (see the inside back cover for a larger version of the Systems of Strategic Actions wheel).

## Relationship of Intentional Talk to Reading Minilessons

*Intentional talk* refers to the language you use that is consciously directed toward the goal of instruction. We have used the term *facilitative talk* to refer to the language that the teacher uses to support student learning in specific ways. When you plan for intentional talk in your interactive read-aloud and shared and performance reading experiences, think about the meaning of the text and what your students will need to think about to fully understand and enjoy the story. You might select certain pages where you want to stop and have students turn and talk about their reading so they can engage in sharing their thinking with each other. The interactive read-aloud and shared and performance reading sections of *The Literacy Continuum* can help you plan what to talk about. For example, when you read a book like *The Royal Bee*, you would likely invite talk about the character's traits and motivations, make predictions about the ending, and notice and discuss the details in the illustrations (see Figure 2-4). When you read a text set of biographies, you might invite students to comment on why the author wrote a book about the subject, how the author gives information, and what they think is the author's message.

As you talk about texts together, embed brief and specific teaching in your read-aloud lessons while maintaining a focus on enjoyment and support for your students in gaining the meaning of the whole text. In preparation, mark a few places with sticky notes and a comment or question to invite thinking. Later, when you teach explicit minilessons about concepts such as theme, writer's craft, and text organization, your students will already have background knowledge to bring to the minilesson and will be ready to explore how the principle works across multiple texts.

In reading minilessons, you explicitly teach the principles you have already embedded in the students' previous experiences with text in these different instructional contexts. Intentional talk within each context prepares a foundation for this explicit focus.

Through each interactive read-aloud and shared or performance reading experience, you build a large body of background knowledge, academic vocabulary, and a library of shared texts to draw on as you explore specific literary principles. You will read more about this multitext approach in Chapter 9.

**Figure 2-4:** Mark a few pages to invite students to think about during interactive read-aloud. Later, you might teach an explicit minilesson on one of the concepts introduced during the interactive read-aloud..

# Chapter 3

## Understanding the Umbrellas and Minilessons

MINILESSONS IN THIS BOOK ARE organized into conceptual groups, called "umbrellas," in which groups of principles are explored in sequence, working toward larger concepts. Within each section (Management, Literary Analysis, etc.), the umbrellas are numbered in sequence and are often referred to by *U* plus the number, for example, U1 for the first umbrella. A suggested sequence of umbrellas is presented in Figure 8-2 to assist you in planning across the year, but the needs of your students always take priority.

## Umbrella Front Page

Each umbrella has an introductory page on which the minilessons in the umbrella are listed and directions are provided to help you prepare to present the minilessons within the umbrella (see Figure 3-1). The introductory page is designed to provide an overview of how the umbrella is organized and the texts from *Fountas & Pinnell Classroom™ Interactive Read-Aloud Collection, Independent Reading Collection, Guided Reading Collection,* and *Book Clubs Collection* that are suggested for the lessons (Fountas and Pinnell 2020). In addition, we provide types of texts you might select if you are not using the books referenced in the lessons. Understanding how the umbrella is designed and how the minilessons fit together will help you keep your lessons focused, concise, and brief. Using familiar mentor texts that you have previously read and enjoyed with your students will help you streamline the lessons in the umbrella. You will not need to spend a lot of time rereading large sections of the texts because the students will already know them well.

When you teach lessons in an umbrella, you help students make connections between concepts and texts and help them develop deeper understandings. A rich context such as this one is particularly helpful for English language learners. Grouping lessons into umbrellas supports English language learners in developing shared vocabulary and language around a single and important area of knowledge.

Following the umbrella front page, you will see a series of two-page lesson spreads that include several parts.

A list of minilessons is organized under the umbrella.

Prepare to present the minilessons in this umbrella with these suggestions.

Use these suggested mentor texts as examples in the minilessons in this umbrella or use books that have similar characteristics.

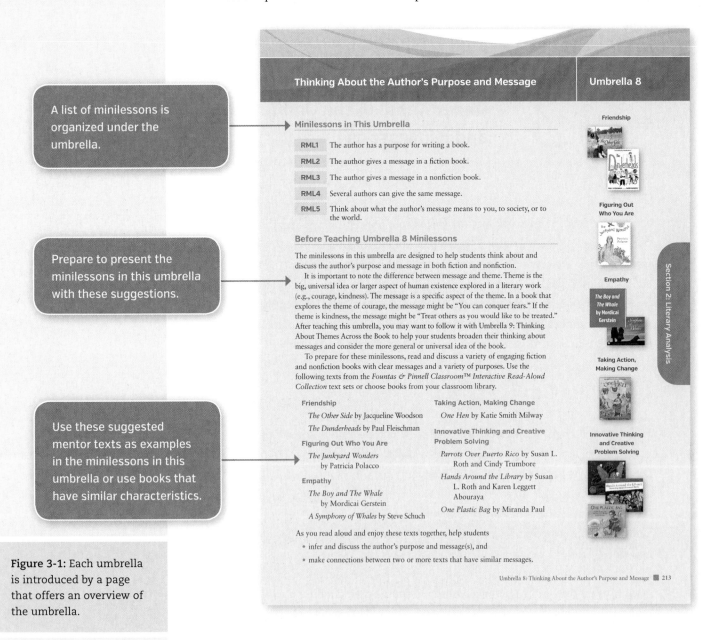

**Figure 3-1:** Each umbrella is introduced by a page that offers an overview of the umbrella.

# Two-Page Minilesson Spread

Each minilesson includes a two-page spread that consists of several parts (see Figure 3-2). The section (for example, Literary Analysis), umbrella number (for example, U1), and minilesson number (for example, RML1) are listed at the top to help you locate the lesson you are looking for. Accordingly, the code LA.U1.RML1 identifies the first minilesson in the first umbrella of the Literary Analysis section.

## Principle, Goal, Rationale

The **Principle** describes the understanding the students will need to learn and apply. The idea of the principle is based on *The Literacy Continuum* (Fountas and Pinnell 2017b), but the language of the principle has been carefully crafted to be precise, focused on a single idea, and accessible to students. We have placed the principle at the top of the lesson on the left-hand page so you have a clear idea of the understanding you will help students construct through the example texts used in the lesson. Although we have crafted the language to make it appropriate for the age group, you may shape the language in a slightly different way to reflect the way your students use language. Be sure that the principle is stated simply and clearly and check for understanding. Once that is accomplished, say it the same way every time.

The **Goal** of the minilesson is stated in the top section of the lesson, as is the **Rationale,** to help you understand what this particular minilesson will do and why it may be important for the students in your classroom. In this beginning section, you will also find suggestions for specific behaviors and understandings to observe as you assess students' learning during or after the minilesson.

## Minilesson

In the **Minilesson** section of the lesson, you will find an example lesson for teaching the understanding, or principle. The example includes suggestions for teaching and the use of precise language and open-ended questions to engage students in a brief, focused inquiry. Effective minilessons include, when possible, the process of inquiry so students can actively construct their understanding from concrete examples, because *telling* is not *teaching.* Instead of simply being told what they need to know, students get inside the understanding by engaging in the thinking themselves. In the inquiry process, invite students to look at a group of texts that were read previously (for example, stories in which characters change). Choose the books carefully so they represent the characteristics students are learning about. They will have knowledge of these texts because they have previously experienced them. Invite them to talk about what they notice across all the books. As students

# A Closer Look at a Reading Minilesson

The **Goal** of the minilesson is clearly identified, as is the **Rationale**, to support your understanding of what this particular minilesson is and why it may be important for the students in your classroom.

The **Reading Minilesson Principle**—a brief statement that describes the understanding students will need to learn and apply.

This code identifies this minilesson as the fourth reading minilesson (RML4) in the eighth umbrella (U8) in the Literary Analysis (LA) section.

Specific behaviors and understandings to observe as you assess students' learning after presenting the minilesson.

**Academic Language** and **Important Vocabulary** that students will need to understand in order to access the learning in the minilesson.

Suggested language to use when teaching the minilesson principle.

**Figure 3-2:** All the parts of a single minilesson are contained on a two-page spread.

---

## RML4
### LA.U8.RML4

**Reading Minilesson Principle**
### Several authors can give the same message.

Thinking About the Author's Purpose and Message

### You Will Need

▸ two sets of two books that share a similar message, such as the following:

- *The Boy and The Whale* by Mordicai Gerstein and *A Symphony of Whales* by Steve Schuch, from Text Set: Empathy
- *One Hen* by Katie Smith Milway, from Text Set: Taking Action, Making Change and *One Plastic Bag* by Miranda Paul, from Text Set: Innovative Thinking and Creative Problem Solving

▸ chart paper and markers

### Academic Language / Important Vocabulary

▸ message
▸ author

### Continuum Connection

▸ Think across texts to derive larger messages, themes, or ideas [p. 59]
▸ Infer the larger ideas and messages in a nonfiction text [p. 63]

### Goal

Think across works of fiction and nonfiction to derive larger messages.

### Rationale

When you teach students that sometimes different authors give the same or very similar messages in their books, they build an understanding of universal ideas and the recognition that people are connected by common ideas.

### Assess Learning

Observe students when they talk about author's message and notice if there is evidence of new learning based on the goal of this minilesson.

▸ Do students notice when two or more books have the same or a very similar message?
▸ Do they use the terms *message* and *author*?

### Minilesson

To help students think about the minilesson principle, use familiar fiction and nonfiction texts to help students identify the author's message. Here is an example.

▸ Show the cover of *The Boy and the Whale*.

   When we discussed *The Boy and the Whale*, you noticed that one of the author's messages is "It is important to help animals that are in danger."

▸ Write the message on chart paper.

   Now let's think about the author's message in another book you have read.

▸ Show the cover of *A Symphony of Whales* and read the title. Briefly review some of the pages to remind students of the story.

   What happens in this story?

   What do you think the author wants you to learn or understand from this story? What is his message?

▸ Record students' responses on the chart.

   What do you notice about the author's message in both these books?

   Sometimes more than one author gives the same message or very similar messages in their books.

## RML**4**

LA.U8.RML4

### Have a Try

Invite the students to talk with a partner about the author's message in *One Plastic Bag*.

▶ Show the cover of *One Hen* and read the title.

You noticed that one of the author's messages in this book is "One person can make change happen."

▶ Write the author's message on the chart. Then show the cover of *One Plastic Bag*. Briefly review some pages.

Turn and talk to your partner about the author's message in *One Plastic Bag*. What big idea does the author want you to understand?

▶ Invite a few students to share their thinking, and record students' responses on the chart.

What do you notice about the author's message in both these books?

### Summarize and Apply

Summarize the learning and remind students to think about the author's message when they read.

What did you notice about the authors' messages in the books we discussed today?

▶ Write the principle at the top of the chart.

When you read today, think about the author's message and be ready to share it when we come back together. We'll see if any of your books have the same message.

### Share

Following independent reading time, gather students together in the meeting area to talk about their reading.

Who would like to share the author's message in the book you read today?

Did anyone else read a book with the same or a similar message?

### Extend the Lesson (Optional)

After assessing students' understanding, you might decide to extend the learning.

▶ As students read books and discover the same or similar messages among them, keep a list or organize baskets of books that have the same or similar messages.

▶ Discuss how two authors teach the same message in similar or different ways.

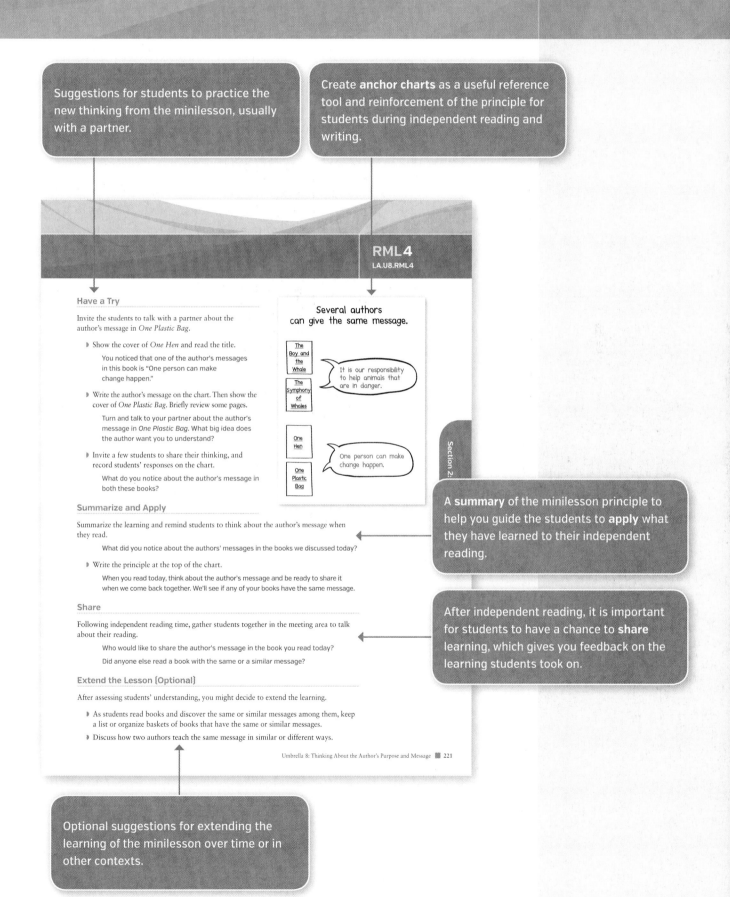

Several authors can give the same message.

| The Boy and the Whale | It is our responsibility to help animals that are in danger. |
| The Symphony of Whales | |

| One Hen | One person can make change happen. |
| One Plastic Bag | |

Section 2:

Umbrella 8: Thinking About the Author's Purpose and Message ■ 221

explore the text examples using your questions and supportive comments as a guide, co-construct the anchor chart, creating an organized and visual representation of the students' noticings and understandings. (See the section on anchor charts in Chapter 1 for more information on chart creation.) From this exploration and the discussion surrounding it, students derive the principle, which is then written at the top of the chart.

Throughout this book, you will find models and examples of the anchor charts you will co-construct with students. Of course, the charts you create will be unique because they reflect your students' thinking. Learning is more powerful and enjoyable for students when they actively search for the meaning, find patterns, talk about their understandings, and share in the co-construction of the chart. Students need to form networks of understanding around the concepts related to literacy and to be constantly looking for connections for themselves.

ELL CONNECTION

Creating a need to produce language is an important principle in building language, and reading minilessons provide many opportunities for students to express their thoughts in language and to communicate with others. The inquiry approach found in these lessons invites more student talk than teacher talk, and that can be both a challenge and an opportunity for you as you work with English language learners. In our previous texts, we have written that Marie Clay (1991) urges us to be "strong minded" about holding meaningful conversations even when they are difficult. In *Becoming Literate,* she warns us that it is "misplaced sympathy" to do the talking for those who are developing and learning language. Instead, she recommends "concentrating more sharply, smiling more rewardingly and spending more time in genuine conversation." Building talk routines, such as turn and talk, into your reading minilessons can be very helpful in providing these opportunities for English language learners in a safe and supportive way.

When you ask students to think about the minilesson principle across several texts that they have previously listened to and discussed, they are more engaged and able to participate because they know these texts and can shift their attention to a new way of thinking about them. Using familiar texts is particularly important for English language learners. When you select examples for a reading minilesson, choose texts that you know were particularly engaging for the English language learners in your classroom. Besides choosing accessible, familiar texts, it is important to provide plenty of wait and think time. For example, you might say, "Let's think about that for a minute" before calling for responses.

When working with English language learners, value partially correct responses. Look for what the child knows about the concept instead of focusing on faulty grammar or language errors. Model appropriate language use in your responses, but do not correct a child who is attempting to use language to learn it. You might also provide an oral sentence frame to get the student response started. Accept variety in pronunciation and intonation, remembering that the more students speak, read, and write, the more they will take on the understanding of grammatical patterns and the complex intonation patterns that reflect meaning in English.

## Have a Try

Because students will be asked to apply the new thinking on their own during independent literacy work, it is important to give students a chance to apply it with a partner or a small group while still in the whole-group setting. **Have a Try** is designed to be brief, but it offers you an opportunity to gather information on how well students understand the minilesson principle. In many minilessons, students are asked to apply the new thinking to another concrete example from a familiar book. In Management lessons, students quickly practice the new routine that they will be asked to do independently. You will often add further thinking to the chart after the students have had the chance to try out their new learning.

The Have a Try portion of the reading minilesson is particularly important for English language learners. Besides providing repetition and allowing for the gradual release of responsibility, it gives English language learners a safe place to try out the new idea before sharing it with the whole group. These are a few suggestions for how you might support students during the Have a Try portion of the lesson:

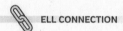 **ELL CONNECTION**

- ▶ Pair students with specific partners in a way that will allow for a balance of talk between the two.

- ▶ Spend time teaching students how to turn and talk. (In Section One: Management, the second minilesson in Umbrella 2: Getting Started with Independent Reading, addresses the turn and talk routine.) Teach students how to provide wait time for one another, invite the other partner into the conversation, and take turns.

- ▶ Provide concrete examples to discuss so that students are clear about what they need to talk about and are able to stay grounded in the text. English language learners will feel more confident if they are able to talk about a text that they know really well.

- ▶ Observe partnerships involving English language learners and provide support as needed.

- ▶ When necessary, you might find it helpful to provide the oral language structure or language stem for how you want your students to share. For example, ask them to start with the phrase "I think the character feels . . ." and to rehearse the language structure a few times before turning and talking.

## Summarize and Apply

This part of the lesson consists of two parts: summarizing the learning and applying the learning to independent reading.

The **summary** is a brief but essential part of the lesson. It provides a time to bring together all of the learning that has taken place through the inquiry and to help students think about its application and relevance to their own learning. It is best to involve the students in constructing the minilesson principle with you. Ask them to reflect on the chart you have created together and talk about what they have learned that day. In simple, clear language, shape the suggestions. Other times, you may decide to help summarize the new learning to keep the lesson short and allow enough time for the students to apply it independently. Whether you state the principle or co-construct it with your students, summarize the learning in a way that makes the principle generative and applicable to future texts the students will read.

After the summary, the students **apply** their new understandings to their independent reading. However, before students begin their independent reading, let them know what you expect them to discuss or bring for the group sharing session so they can think about it as they read. This way, they know they are accountable for trying out the new thinking in their own books and are expected to share upon their return.

Students engaged in independent reading will choose books from the classroom library. These are genuine choices based on their interests and previous experiences. Book levels are not used in the classroom library. Some teachers choose to have students shop for books in the library at specific times and have them keep selected books in their personal literacy boxes. When you designate certain times for browsing, you maximize students' time spent on reading and are able to carve out time to assist with book selection. When needed, plan to supply independent reading books that will provide opportunities to apply the principle. For example, if you teach the umbrella on studying biographies, make sure students have access to biographies. You will notice that in some of the lessons, students are invited to read from a certain basket of books in the classroom library to ensure that there are opportunities to apply their new learning.

We know that when students first take on new learning, they often overgeneralize or overapply the new learning at the exclusion of some of the other things they have learned. The best goal when students are reading any book is to enjoy it, process it effectively, and gain its full meaning. Always encourage meaningful and authentic engagement with text. You don't want students so focused and determined to apply the minilesson principle that they make superficial connections to text that actually distract from their understanding of the book. You will likely find the opportunity in many reading conferences, guided reading lessons, or book club meetings to reinforce the minilesson understanding.

In our professional book, *Teaching for Comprehending and Fluency: Thinking, Talking, and Writing About Reading, K–8* (Fountas and Pinnell 2006), we write, "Whenever we instruct readers, we mediate (or change) the meaning they derive from their reading. Yet we must offer instruction that helps readers expand their abilities. There is value in drawing readers' attention to important aspects of the text that will enrich their understanding, but we need to understand that using effective reading strategies is not like exercising one or two muscles at a time. The system must always work together as an integrated whole." The invitation to apply the new learning must be clear enough to have students try out new ways of thinking, but "light" enough to allow room for readers to expand and express their own thinking. The application of the minilesson principle should not be thought of as an exercise or task that needs to be completed but instead as an invitation to a deeper, more meaningful response to the events or ideas in a text.

While students are reading independently, you may be meeting with small groups for guided reading or book clubs, rotating to observe students working independently, or conferring with individuals. If you have a reading conference, you can take the opportunity to reinforce the minilesson principle. We have provided two conferring record sheets (choose whichever form suits your purpose) for you to download from the online resources (see Figure 3-3) so that you can make notes about your individual conferences with students. You can use your notes to plan the content of future minilessons.

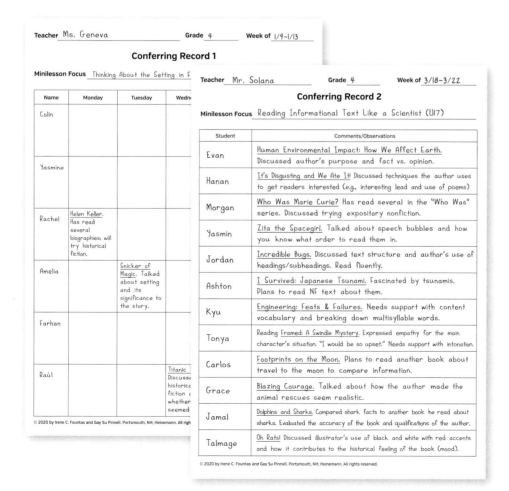

**Figure 3-3:** Choose one of these downloadable forms to record your observations of students' behaviors and understandings during reading conferences. Visit **resources.fountasandpinnell.com** to download this and all other online resources.

## Share

At the end of the independent work time, students come together and have the opportunity to **share** their learning with the entire group. Group share provides an opportunity for you to revisit, expand, and deepen understanding of the minilesson principle as well as to assess learning. In Figure 3-2, you will notice that in the Share section we provide suggestions for how to engage students in sharing their discoveries. Often, students are asked to bring a book to share and to explain how they applied the minilesson principle in their independent reading. Sometimes we suggest sharing with the whole group, but other times we suggest that sharing take place among pairs, triads, or quads. As you observe and talk to students engaged in independent reading, shared and performance reading, guided reading, or book clubs, you can assess whether they are easily able to apply the minilesson principle. Use this information to inform how you plan to share. If only a few students were able to apply the minilesson to their reading (for example, if the minilesson applies to a particular book feature or genre characteristic that not all students came across in their books during independent reading), you might ask only a few students to share. Whereas if you observe most of the class applying the principle, you might have them share in pairs or small groups.

As a general guideline, in addition to revisiting the reading minilesson principle at the end of independent reading time, you might also ask students to share what they thought or wrote about their reading that day. For example, a student might share part of a letter he wrote about his reading. Another student might share a memorable line from a book or celebrate reaching the goal of trying a book in a different genre. The Share is a wonderful way to bring the community of readers and writers back together to expand their understandings and celebrate their learning at the end of the workshop time.

There are some particular accommodations you might want to consider to support English language learners during sharing:

▶ Ask English language learners to share in pairs before sharing with the whole group.

▶ Use individual conferences and guided reading to help students rehearse the language structure they might use to share their application of the minilesson principle to the text they have read.

▶ Teach the entire class respectful ways to listen to peers and model how to give their peers time to express their thoughts. Many of the minilessons in the Management section will be useful for developing a peaceful, safe and supportive community of readers and writers.

### Extending the Lesson

At the end of each lesson we offer suggestions for **extending** the learning of the principle. Sometimes extending the learning involves repeating the lesson over time with different examples. Fourth graders might need to experience some of the concepts more than once before they are able to transfer actions to their independent reading. Using the questions in the Assess Learning section will help you to determine if you need to repeat the lesson, move on, or revisit the lesson (perhaps in a slightly different way) in the future. Other suggestions for extending the lesson include applying the minilesson concept within other contexts, performing readers' theater, or writing and drawing in response to reading. In several cases, the suggestions will refer to a reader's notebook (see Chapter 7 for more information about writing about reading and Section Four: Writing About Reading for minilessons that teach ways to use a reader's notebook).

## Umbrella Back Page

### Assessment and Link to Writing

Following the minilessons in each umbrella, you will see the final umbrella page that includes **Assessment**, sometimes **Link to Writing**, and **Reader's Notebook**. The last page of each umbrella, shown in Figure 3-4, provides suggestions for assessing the learning that has taken place through the minilessons in the entire umbrella. The information you gain from observing what the students can already do, almost do, and not yet do will help inform the selection of the next umbrella you teach. (See Chapter 8 for more information about assessment and the selection of umbrellas.) In many umbrellas, this last page also provides a Link to Writing. In some cases, this section provides further suggestions for writing about reading in a reader's notebook. However, in most cases, the Link to Writing provides ideas for how students might try out some of the new learning in their own writing. For example, after learning about text features in nonfiction, you might want to teach students how to include one or more of the features, such as a table of contents or sidebar, in their own nonfiction writing.

You will also find a section titled Reader's Notebook, which describes how to access and print a copy of the minilesson principles for your students to glue in a reader's notebook to refer to as needed.

Gain important information by **assessing** students' understandings as they apply and share their learning of a minilesson principle. Observe and then follow up with individuals or address the principle during guided reading.

## Assessment

After you have taught the minilessons in this umbrella, observe students as they talk and write about their reading across instructional contexts: interactive read-aloud, independent reading, guided reading, shared reading, and book club. Use *The Literacy Continuum* (Fountas and Pinnell 2017) to guide the observation of students' reading and writing behaviors.

▶ What evidence do you have of new understandings related to the author's purpose and message?

- Can the students infer the author's purpose and message in both fiction and nonfiction books?
- Do they understand that a book can have more than one purpose and message?
- Do they notice when two or more books have the same or a very similar message?
- Do they talk about ways to apply an author's message to real life?
- Do they use academic vocabulary, such as *purpose* and *message*?

▶ In what other ways, beyond the scope of this umbrella, are students talking about fiction and nonfiction books?

- Are they talking about the theme of books?
- Are they noticing and talking about illustrations?
- Are they noticing different genres of fiction and nonfiction?

Use your observations to determine the next umbrella you will teach. You may also consult Minilessons Across the Year (pp. 59–61) for guidance.

## Link to Writing

After teaching the minilessons in this umbrella, help students link the new learning to their own writing:

▶ When students write both fiction and nonfiction texts, remind them to think about their purpose for writing, the message they want to convey to readers, and how they want to convey it.

## Reader's Notebook

When this umbrella is complete, provide a copy of the minilesson principles (see resources.fountasandpinnell.com) for students to glue in the reader's notebook (in the Minilessons section if using *Reader's Notebook: Intermediate* [Fountas and Pinnell 2011]), so they can refer to the information as needed.

Wrap up the umbrella by engaging students in an activity that uses their expanded understanding of the umbrella concept.

**Figure 3-4**: The final page of each umbrella offers ways to wrap up new learning from the umbrella: questions to use in assessing students' learning, suggestions for linking new learning to writing, and a reference to online resources for downloading the umbrella's principles.

## Online Resources for Planning

We have provided examples in this book of how to engage your fourth-grade students in developing the behaviors and understandings of competent readers, as described in *The Literacy Continuum* (Fountas and Pinnell 2017b). Remember that you can modify the suggested lesson to fit your students and construct new lessons using the goals of the continuum as needed for your particular students. The form shown in Figure 3-5 will help you plan each part of a new minilesson. For example, you can design a minilesson that uses a different set of example texts from the ones suggested in this book or you can teach a concept in a way that fits the current needs of your students. The form shown in Figure 3-6 will help you plan which minilessons to teach over a period of time so as to address the goals that are important for your students. You can find both forms at **resources.fountasandpinnell.com**.

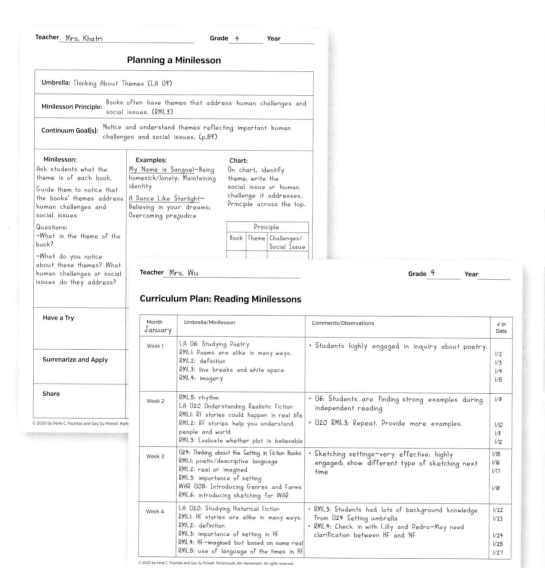

**Figure 3-5:** Use this downloadable form to plan your own minilessons.

**Figure 3-6:** Use this downloadable form to make notes about specific minilessons for future planning.

# Chapter 4

## Management Minilessons: Building a Literacy Community

MANAGEMENT MINILESSONS FOCUS ON ROUTINES for thinking and talking about reading and working together in the classroom. Good management allows you to teach effectively and efficiently; use these lessons to create an orderly, busy classroom in which students know what is expected as well as how to behave responsibly and respectfully in a community of learners. They learn how the classroom library is organized, how to choose books and return them, how to use their voices in the classroom, and how to engage in independent reading. You can use these minilessons to teach your students the routines for independent reading, how to use and return materials, and how to solve problems independently. Classroom management is important in implementing a multitext approach to literacy learning. You want your students to grow in the ability to regulate their own behavior and to sustain reading and writing for increasing periods of time.

Altogether, there are eighteen minilessons in the Management section for your use. Teach the Management minilessons in the order that fits your class, or consult the suggested sequence in Figure 8-2. You may need to reteach some Management minilessons across the year, especially as students encounter more complex situations and routines. Sometimes when there is a schedule change or other disruption in classroom operations, a refresher Management minilesson will be needed. Any management problem in your classroom should be addressed through a Management minilesson.

# The Physical Space

Before students enter your classroom, prepare the physical space in a way that provides maximum support for learning. Remember that this relatively small room must support the productive work of some 20 to 30 people, 6 or 7 hours a day, 180-plus days a year. Each Management umbrella will help your students become acquainted with different parts of the classroom, which will make them feel secure and at home. Make sure that the classroom is:

▶ **Welcoming and Inviting.** Pleasing colors and a variety of furniture will help. There is no need for commercially published posters or slogans. The room can be filled with the work that students have produced beginning on day one. The classroom library should be as inviting as a bookstore or a public library. Place books in baskets and tubs on shelves to make the front covers of books visible and accessible for easy browsing. Clear out old, dated, poor-quality, inaccurate, or tattered books that students never choose. Clearly label (or, even better, have students label) the tub or basket with the topic, author, series, genre, or illustrator (see Figure 4-1). Add new books to the library all year and retire books that are no longer of interest or that perpetuate stereotypes and inaccuracies.

▶ **Organized for Easy Use.** The first thing you might want to do is to take out everything you do not need. Clutter increases stress and noise. Using scattered and hard-to-find materials increases student dependence on the teacher. Consider keeping supplies for reading, writing, and word study in designated areas. For example, some teachers designate a writing area where they keep paper, highlighters, staplers, etc. Every work area should be clearly organized with necessary, labeled materials and nothing else. The work that takes place in each area should be visible at a glance; all materials needed for the particular activity should be available. See Figure 4-2 for a list of some suggested materials to keep accessible in the different areas in your classroom.

▶ **Designed for Whole-Group, Small-Group, and Individual Instruction.** Minilessons are generally provided as whole-class instruction and typically take place at an easel in a meeting space that is comfortable and large enough to accommodate all students in a group or circle. It will be helpful to have a colorful rug with some way of helping students find an individual space to sit without crowding one another. Often, the meeting space is adjacent to the classroom library so books are handy. The teacher usually has a larger chair or seat next to an easel or two so that he

**Figure 4-1:** Whenever possible, involve the students in making the classroom their own.

can display the mentor texts, make anchor charts, do shared writing, or place materials for shared or performance reading. This space is available for all whole-group instruction; for example, the students come back to it for group share. In addition to the group meeting space, there should be designated tables and spaces in the classroom for small-group reading instruction. The guided reading table is best located in a quiet corner of the room that keeps the group focused on reading, talking, and listening and at the same time allows you to scan the room to identify students who may need help staying on task independently. The table (round or horseshoe) should be positioned so the students in the group are turned away from the activity in the classroom. You might also designate a place to meet with book clubs. Provide a space that allows everyone to comfortably see one another and engage in conversation (ideally a circle of chairs). Students also need tables and spaces throughout the classroom where they can work independently and where you can easily set a chair next to a student for a brief, individual conference.

▶ **Respectful of personal space.** Fourth-grade students do not necessarily need an individual desk. Desks can be pushed together to make tables. But they do need a place to keep a personal box, including items such as their book of choice (or several that they plan to read) and a reader's notebook. These containers can be placed on a shelf and labeled for each student. A writer's notebook, writing folder, and word study folder may be stored in the same place or in groups by themselves to be retrieved easily. If students have personal poetry books (colorfully decorated by them and growing out of the shared reading of poetry and poetry workshop), they can be placed face out on a rack for easy retrieval. Artifacts like these add considerably to the aesthetic quality of the classroom.

**Figure 4-2:** Adapted from *Guided Reading: Responsive Teaching Across the Grades* (Fountas and Pinnell 2017c)

| Classroom Areas | Materials |
| --- | --- |
| Classroom Library | Organize books by topic, author, illustrator, genre, and series. Spaces for students to read comfortably and independently. |
| Writing Materials | Pencils, different types of paper for first and final drafts, markers, stapler, scissors, glue, sticky notes, colored pencils, and highlighters. |
| Word Work Materials | Blank word cards; magnetic letters; games; folders for Look, Cover, Write, Check; word study principles; place for students' individualized lists. |
| Listening Area or Media Center | Player (e.g., iPod®, iPhone®, tablet), clear set of directions with picture clues, multiple copies of books organized in boxes or plastic bags. |

## A Peaceful Atmosphere for a Community of Readers and Writers

The minilessons in this book will help you establish a classroom environment where students can become confident, self-determined, and kind members of the community. They are designed to contribute to an ambiance of peaceful activity and shared responsibility in the fourth-grade classroom. Through the Management minilessons, students will make agreements, or set norms, about working together as a community of readers and writers. They will learn how to find help when the teacher is busy, listen to and show empathy for one another, and make everyone feel included. The lessons in this section are designed to help you develop a community of readers and writers who use multiple resources to find interesting and enjoyable books, are excited to share book recommendations, and challenge themselves and one another to stretch and grow in their reading tastes, preferences, and goals. The overall tone of every classroom activity is respectful. Fourth-grade students who enter your classroom for the first time will benefit from learning your expectations and being reminded of how to work with twenty to thirty others in a small room day after day. These minilessons are designed to help you establish the atmosphere you want. Everything in the classroom reflects the students who work there; it is their home for the year.

## Getting Started with Independent Reading: A Readers' Workshop Structure

Many of the minilessons in the Management section will be the ones that you address early in the year to establish routines that students will use to work at their best with one another and independently. In Umbrella 2: Getting Started with Independent Reading, you will teach students the routines and structure for independent reading. We recommend a readers' workshop structure for grade 4 in which students move from a whole-class meeting, to individual reading and small-group work, and back to a whole-class meeting (see Figure 4-3). The minilessons in this book are designed with this structure in mind, providing a strong instructional frame around independent reading

**Figure 4-3:** A readers' workshop structure as shown in *Guided Reading: Responsive Teaching Across the Grades* (Fountas and Pinnell 2017c, 565)

| Structure of Readers' Workshop | | |
|---|---|---|
| Book Talks and Minilessons | | 5–15 minutes |
| **Students:**<br>• Independent Reading<br>• Writing in a Reader's Notebook | **Teacher:**<br>• Guided Reading Groups (about 20–25 minutes each)<br>• Book Clubs (about 20–25 minutes each)<br>• Individual Conferences (3–5 minutes each) | 45–50 minutes |
| Group Share | | 5 minutes |

and regular opportunities for students to share their thinking with each other. Your use of time will depend on the amount of time you have for the entire class period. As we explain in Chapter 23 of *Guided Reading: Responsive Teaching Across the Grades*, ideally you will have seventy-five to ninety minutes, though many teachers have only sixty minutes. You will need to adjust accordingly. The minilessons in this umbrella are focused on promoting independence and supporting students in making good book choices for independent reading, including knowing when to abandon a book. Students also learn how to keep their materials for independent reading organized and ready to use. It is possible that you will spend several days reviewing the minilessons in this umbrella until you feel students are able to choose books and read independently for a sustained period of time. It's worth the effort and will benefit the learning community all year. At the beginning of the year, make independent reading time relatively short and circulate around the room to help students select books, write about their reading, and stay engaged. As students become more self-directed, you can increase independent reading time, and this should happen quickly with fourth graders. When you determine that students can sustain productive independent behavior, you can begin to meet with guided reading groups.

## Book Talks and Minilessons

The minilessons in the Management section will help you establish routines for your students that they will use throughout the year. In addition to these lessons, you will want to teach the students to sit in a specific place during book talks and reading minilessons. They might sit on a carpet or in chairs. Be sure everyone can see the chart and hear you and each other. Teachers with larger classes sometimes find it helpful to have a smaller circle sitting on the carpet and the remaining students sitting behind them in chairs. Be sure each student has sufficient personal space. Everyone should have enough space so as not to distract others. Most importantly, make it a comfortable place to listen, view, and talk.

**Figure 4-4:** Readers' workshop begins with a minilesson and, often, a book talk.

Teachers often start readers' workshop with a few short book talks. Book talks are an effective way to engage students' interest in books, enriching independent reading. Consider giving two or three very short book talks before your reading minilesson a few times a week. Students can write titles in their notebooks for later reference (see Writing About Reading minilessons). Book talks are an important part of creating a community of readers and writers who talk about and share books. Once you have set the routines for book talks, you can turn this responsibility over to the students. Minilessons in Management Umbrella 3: Living a Reading Life are designed to teach students how to craft an interesting book talk.

Whether you are engaging your students in a reading minilesson, a book talk, or another whole-group instruction, you will need to teach them how to listen and talk when the entire class is meeting. Management minilessons lay the foundation for this whole-group work.

## Independent Reading, Individual Conferences, and Small-Group Work

After the reading minilesson, work with students individually and in small groups (e.g., in guided reading and book clubs) while other students are engaged in independent reading and writing in the reader's notebook. To establish this as productive independent time, spend time on the minilessons in Management Umbrella 1: Being a Respectful Member of the Classroom Community and Umbrella 2: Getting Started with Independent Reading. Independent reading and the reader's notebook, while highly beneficial in themselves, also act as your management system. Students are engaged in reading and writing for a sustained period of time, freeing you to have individual conferences and to meet with small groups. You will find minilessons in Section Four: Writing About Reading to help you introduce and use the reader's notebook.

**Figure 4-5:** While some students read and write independently, you can work with small groups or hold individual conferences.

During this independent reading time, you will want students to maintain a "0" voice level (see MGT.U1.RML4). Students will have plenty of time during the share and small-group work to express their thinking about books. During independent reading time, there should be limited opportunity for distraction. The only voices heard should be your individual conferences with students and your work with small groups. You may have to repeat the minilesson on voice level more than once for students to remember which voice level is appropriate for a particular activity.

Consider the space in your classroom and position yourself during small-group work in a way that you can scan the room frequently. This thoughtful positioning will allow you to identify problems that arise and make notes to use in individual conferences. However, if you spend the time to set and practice these routines and expectations, students will learn to self-regulate and change inappropriate behavior with little intervention. When they are taught to make good book choices and are members of a community that share and recommend books with one another, they look forward to this quiet time of the day to read books of their own choosing.

When you first start readers' workshop, you will spend all or most of your time engaging in individual conferences to get to know your students. Conferences allow you time to evaluate whether they are making good book choices and help them become self-managed. Students who have persistent difficulty in selecting books might benefit from working with a limited selection of just-right books, which you can assemble in a temporary basket for this purpose.

In fourth grade, you may have some or even many students who are still developing the ability to sustain attention to texts and have less experience than others in managing themselves independently. If this is the case, structure the independent work period around three independent tasks so that you have enough time to meet with individuals and small groups. Here are suggestions for the three tasks:

- Reading books of their choice

- Writing in the reader's notebook

- Completing a carefully designed word study/phonics activity with a partner (linked to the phonics and word study minilesson you teach at another part of the day)

This kind of transition will not be needed long because students will build stamina for reading as well as writing about their reading. The more time you invest in teaching the Management minilessons to establish the foundation for a strong and independent learning environment, the quicker you will be able to make this transition.

## Sharing Time

The readers' workshop ends with the community of readers and writers coming together for a short time to share discoveries made during independent reading time. Whatever is taught in the minilesson (management routines, literary analysis, strategies and skills, or writing about reading) guides the independent work time and is revisited during group share. Besides using sharing time to revisit the minilesson principle, you can use this time for your students to self-evaluate how the whole class is working together. The charts you create together during Management minilessons can be a source for self-evaluation. For example, you might ask students to review the list of agreements they made for working together and evaluate the class's behavior based on the chart criteria.

In addition to evaluating independent work time, you might also ask students to evaluate the quality of their sharing time. Is everyone able to see and hear each other? Does everyone transition well from turning and talking with a partner back to the whole group? Is everyone using an appropriate voice level? Do enough students have an opportunity to share their thinking?

In *Guided Reading: Responsive Teaching Across the Grades* (Fountas and Pinnell 2017c), we wrote the following: "The readers' workshop brings together both individual interests and the shared experiences of a literate community. Students read at a sharper edge when they know they will be sharing their thoughts with peers in their classroom. They are personally motivated because they have choice. In addition to providing an excellent management system, the workshop engages students in massive amounts of daily reading and in writing about reading" (p. 571). The Management minilessons in this book are designed to set a management system in motion in which choice and independence are guiding principles. Students develop into a community of readers and writers that respect and look forward to listening to and responding to each other's ideas.

# Chapter 5

## Literary Analysis Minilessons: Thinking and Talking About Books

LITERARY ANALYSIS MINILESSONS SUPPORT STUDENTS in a growing awareness of the elements of literature and the writer's and illustrator's craft. Use these lessons to help students learn how to think analytically about texts and identify the characteristics of fiction and nonfiction genres. Invite them to notice characters and how they change, critique whether a story's plot is believable, and analyze how nonfiction writers present and organize information as well as how they use graphics and other nonfiction features. Prior to each Literary Analysis minilesson, students will have listened to texts read aloud or will have experienced them through shared or performance reading. You will have read the texts aloud and taught specific lessons that encourage students to discuss and explore concepts and to respond in writing, art, or drama. This prior knowledge will be accessed as they participate in the minilesson and will enable them to make the understanding explicit. They then can apply the concepts to their own reading and share what they have learned with others.

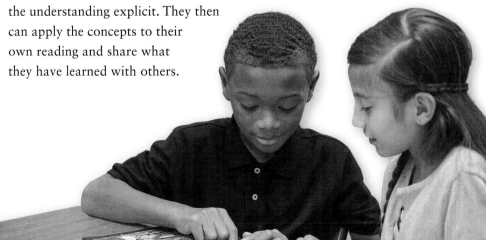

## Organization of Literary Analysis Umbrellas and the Link to *The Literacy Continuum*

There are 150 Literary Analysis minilessons in Section Two of this book. These minilessons are divided into categories according to *The Literacy Continuum* (Fountas and Pinnell 2017b), and the order of presentation in this book follows that of *The Literacy Continuum*. The categories of fiction and nonfiction are listed below.

▶ Fiction and Nonfiction
- General
- Genre
- Messages and Themes
- Style and Language
- Illustrations
- Book and Print Features

▶ Nonfiction
- Genre
- Organization
- Topic
- Illustration/Graphics
- Book and Print Features

▶ Fiction
- Genre
- Setting
- Plot
- Character
- Style and Language

As you can tell from the suggested sequence in Minilessons Across the Year (Figure 8-2), you will want to use simpler concepts (such as characters have feelings and motivations) before more sophisticated concepts (such as recognizing that characters can be complex and change).

Echoes of the Literary Analysis minilessons reverberate across all the instruction for the year in instructional contexts for reading (interactive read-aloud, shared and performance reading, guided reading, book clubs, and independent reading) as well as for writing. The students continue to develop their understanding of the characteristics of fiction and nonfiction texts.

# Genre Study

Within the Literary Analysis section you will find six umbrellas that bring students through a process of inquiry-based study of the characteristics of a particular genre. Genre study gives students the tools they need to navigate a variety of texts with deep understanding. When readers understand the characteristics of a genre, they know what to expect when they begin to read a text. They use their knowledge of the predictable elements within a genre as a road map to anticipate structures and elements of the text. They make increasingly more sophisticated connections between books within the same genre and build on shared language for talking about genre. In our professional book *Genre Study: Teaching with Fiction and Nonfiction Books* (Fountas and Pinnell 2012c), we designed a six-step approach for learning about a variety of genres. The six broad steps are described in Figure 5-1. For this book, we have designed specific minilessons based on our *Genre Study* book to help you engage your students in the powerful process of becoming knowledgeable about a range of genres.

The first two steps of the genre study process take place before and during interactive read-aloud. Steps 3–5 are accomplished through reading minilessons. Step 6 is addressed on the last page of each genre study umbrella. In fourth grade, we suggest six genre studies to help students expand their understanding of genre. Figure 5-3 is an overview of how we categorize various fiction and nonfiction genres. As students progress through the grades, they will revisit some genres to gain a deeper understanding and be introduced to new genres. In grade 4, we feature genre studies about poetry, memoir, biography, fantasy, fairy tales, and historical fiction. Though poetry is a form of writing, not a genre, we think it is important for students to become deeply familiar with its characteristics. One genre study introduces students to the

**Figure 5-1:** Adapted from *Genre Study* (Fountas and Pinnell 2012c)

| Steps in the Genre Study Process |
| --- |

| 1 | Collect books in a text set that represent good examples of the genre you are studying. |
| 2 | Immerse. Read aloud each book using the lesson guidelines. The primary goal should be enjoyment and understanding of the book. |
| 3 | Study. After you have read these mentor texts, have students analyze characteristics or "noticings" that are common to the texts, and list the characteristics on chart paper. |
| 4 | Define. Use the list of characteristics to create a short working definition of the genre. |
| 5 | Teach specific minilessons on the important characteristics of the genre. |
| 6 | Read and Revise. Expand students' understanding by encouraging them to talk about the genre in appropriate instructional contexts (book club, independent reading conferences, guided reading lessons, and shared or performance reading lessons) and revise the definition. |

## Fairy Tales

**Noticings:**

| Always | Often |
|---|---|
| • Come from all different cultures | • Good wins over evil. |
| • Characters and events can't exist in real life. | • Goodness rewarded and evil punished |
| • Same types of characters appear. | • Characters simple—either good or bad |
| • Magic or the supernatural in the stories. | • Happy ending |
| | • Romance and adventure |
| | • Lesson or outcome reflects the values of the culture. |
| | • Repetition |
| | • Similar language, such as "once upon a time" or "long ago" |

**Figure 5-2:** On this anchor chart, the teacher has recorded what the students noticed was always or often true about several fairy tales that they had read.

fantasy genre in a general way, but the genre has two distinct branches: traditional literature and modern fantasy. Fairy tales are a type of traditional literature. They share characteristics with all fantasy stories but also have specific characteristics of their own.

Modern fantasy is rooted in traditional literature. The same themes, ideas, or subjects, called motifs (e.g., the struggle between good and evil, the presence of magic), are found in both. These motifs are often embedded in one's mind as part of a cultural experience, so students who are not familiar with traditional European motifs may be familiar with others.

It is important to make connections between straightforward traditional literature and the more challenging literature that students will be expected to understand later on. Early experiences with these motifs in traditional literature provide a strong foundation for understanding the more complex types of fantasy, such as high fantasy and science fiction. The steps in the genre study process allow students to discover these characteristics through inquiry.

The first step in the genre study process, **Collect**, involves collecting a set of texts. The genre study minilessons in this book draw on texts sets from the

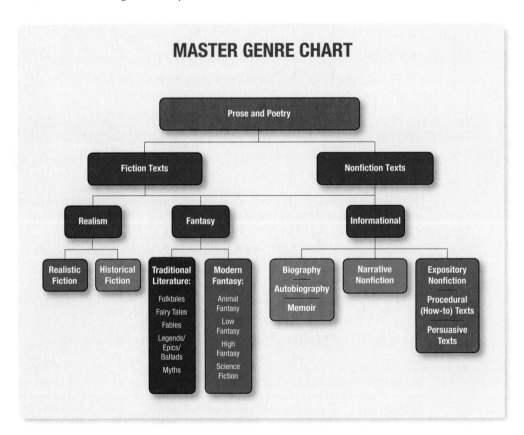

**Figure 5-3:** Master Genre Chart from *Genre Study: Teaching with Fiction and Nonfiction Books* (Fountas and Pinnell 2012c)

*Fountas & Pinnell Classroom™ Interactive Read-Aloud Collection* (Fountas and Pinnell 2020). Use these texts if you have them, but we encourage you to collect additional texts within each genre to immerse your students in as many texts as possible. Students will enjoy additional examples of the genre placed in a bin in the classroom library. You can use the texts listed in the Before Teaching section of each umbrella as a guide to making your own genre text set if you do not have access to the *Interactive Read-Aloud Collection.*

As you engage students in step 2 of the genre study process, **Immerse,** be sure that the students think and talk about the meaning of each text during the interactive read-aloud. The imperative is for students to enjoy a wonderful book, so it is important for them to respond to the full meaning of the text before focusing their attention on the specific characteristics of the genre.

After immersing students in the books through interactive read-aloud, it is time to teach minilessons in the appropriate genre study umbrella. The first minilesson in each genre study umbrella addresses step 3 in the process, **Study.** During this initial minilesson, help students notice characteristics that are common across all of the texts. As students discuss and revisit books in the genre, list their noticings on chart paper. Distinguish between what is *always* true about the genre and what is *often* true about the genre.

The second minilesson in each genre study umbrella addresses step 4 in the process, **Define.** Use shared writing to co-construct a working definition of the genre based on the students' previous noticings. Help students understand that you will revisit and revise this definition as they learn more about the genre over the next few days.

Next, as part of step 5, **Teach,** provide specific minilessons related to each of your students' noticings about the genre. In each genre study umbrella, we offer minilessons that we think would develop out of most fourth graders' noticings. Pick and choose the lessons that match your own students' noticings or use these lessons as a model to develop your own minilessons. In the minilessons and throughout a genre study, support your teaching with prompts for thinking, talking, and writing about reading. Prompts and definitions for each genre are included in *Fountas & Pinnell Genre Prompting Guide for Fiction* (2012a) and *Fountas & Pinnell Genre Prompting Guide for Nonfiction, Poetry, and Test Taking* (2012b).

At the end of the umbrella, work with the students to **Read and Revise** the class definition of the genre based on the minilessons that have been taught. Using shared writing, make changes to the definition so it reflects your students' understanding of the genre.

## Allen Say

### Noticings:

| Always | Often |
|---|---|
| • Allen Say is both the author and the illustrator. | • The story is told in first person. |
| • The dialogue moves the story along. | • The main character(s) is on a journey. |
| • He writes fiction stories. | • The story involves family. |
| | • He uses details from his life (biographical). |
| | • He wants you to learn about a culture that might be different from your own. |

**Figure 5-4**: This chart shows what students noticed about the work of author and illustrator Allen Say.

**Figure 5-5**: Minilessons address step 3 of an author/illustrator study.

# Author and Illustrator Studies

Section Two: Literary Analysis also includes two umbrellas of minilessons for conducting inquiry-based author and illustrator studies. They are Umbrella 3: Studying Authors and Their Processes and Umbrella 11: Studying Illustrators and Analyzing an Illustrator's Craft. Author and illustrator studies allow students to make connections to the people behind the books they love. For an author or illustrator study, be sure that the students think and talk about the full meaning of each text in interactive read-aloud before identifying characteristics specific to the author or illustrator.

Students will need plenty of opportunity to explore the texts during read-aloud time, on their own, or in groups or pairs. As they become more familiar with the steps in an author or illustrator study, they learn how to notice characteristics common to a particular author's or illustrator's work. The steps in an author/illustrator study are described in Figure 5-5.

In the first minilesson in Umbrella 3: Studying Authors and Their Processes, you provide a demonstration of step 3 by working with your students to create a chart of "noticings" about an author or illustrator. In this lesson, we model a study of Allen Say from the *Fountas & Pinnell Classroom™ Interactive Read-Aloud Collection* (Fountas and Pinnell 2020). For this author study, we have chosen to study an author who is also the illustrator of his books. You might choose to study authors and illustrators you and your students are familiar with and love. The other minilessons in this umbrella address how some writers use their own lives as inspiration; how authors write about the same themes, topics, or settings; and how authors engage in research. We recommend teaching the lessons in this umbrella across the year, as you conduct author or illustrator studies, instead of consecutively (see Minilessons Across the Year, Figure 8-2). Simply collect books by a particular author or illustrator and follow the steps listed in Figure 5-5. Use the same language and process modeled in the minilessons in these umbrellas but substitute the authors and illustrators of your choice.

## Steps in an Author/Illustrator Study

1   Gather a set of books and read them aloud to the class over several days. The goal is for students to enjoy the books and discuss the full meaning.

2   Take students on a quick tour of all the books in the set. As you reexamine each book, you might want to have students do a brief turn and talk with a partner about what they notice.

3   Have students analyze the characteristics of the author's or illustrator's work, and record their noticings on chart paper.

4   You may choose to read a few more books by the author and compare them to the books in this set, adding to the noticings as needed.

# Chapter 6

## Strategies and Skills Minilessons: Teaching for Effective Processing

STRATEGIES AND SKILLS minilessons will help students continue to strengthen their ability to process print by searching for and using information from the text, self-monitoring their reading, self-correcting their errors, and solving multisyllable words. You'll notice the students engaging in these behaviors in your interactive read-aloud, shared or performance reading, and guided reading lessons. Strategies and skills are taught in every instructional context for reading, but guided reading is the most powerful one. The text is just right to support the learning of all the readers in the group, enabling them to learn how to solve words and engage in the act of problem solving across a whole text.

The Strategies and Skills minilessons in this book may serve as reminders and be helpful to the whole class. They can be taught any time you see a need. For example, as students engage in independent reading, they may need to realize that a reader

- uses context to understand vocabulary,

- breaks apart a new word to read it,

- understands how connectives work in sentences, and

- applies different techniques to monitor comprehension when reading a difficult text.

The minilessons in Section Three: Strategies and Skills are designed to bring a few important strategies to temporary, conscious attention so that students are reminded to think in these ways as they problem solve in independent reading. By the time students participate in these minilessons, they should have engaged these strategic actions successfully in shared or guided reading. In the minilessons, they will recognize the strategic actions; bring them to brief, focused attention; and think about applying them consistently in independent reading. Some Strategies and Skills minilessons require students to see the print from a page of text. For these lessons, we recommend you use a document camera or write the word, sentence, or phrase from the text on a piece of chart paper.

Through the reading of continuous text, students develop an internal sense of in-the-head actions; for example, monitoring and checking, searching for and using information, and using multiple sources of information to solve words. They have a sense of how to put words together in phrases and use intonation to convey meaning. They are thinking more deeply about how a character would speak the dialogue. And, they are learning to check their comprehension by summarizing the most important parts and the big ideas and messages of a fiction or nonfiction text. The minilesson, the application, and the share help them better understand what they do and internalize effective and efficient reading behaviors.

**Figure 6-1:** Strategies and Skills minilessons strengthen students' ability to process print. They serve as reminders for the whole class but are most powerful when taught during guided reading lessons.

## Reading in Digital Environments

Fourth graders increasingly use the internet to research topics they are investigating, read reviews, participate in online communities, and compare information from multiple sources. A 2015 report by Common Sense Media, (https://www.commonsensemedia.org/sites/default/files/uploads/research/census_researchreport.pdf, 21) found that eight- to twelve-year-old children spend an average of two and a half hours per day using digital media (e.g., computers, tablets, and smart phones) outside of school. It is important for students to learn to navigate digital environments safely and critically. Umbrella 7: Reading in Digital Environments is designed to provide an overview of some of these crucial skills; however, we encourage you to become informed about the safety features and policies that your school district uses to safeguard students as they navigate the digital world. The minilessons in this umbrella help students learn how to use search engines efficiently and effectively, evaluate the credibility and sources of the information they find, and stay focused in a reading environment that provides link after link to related and sometimes unrelated information. Students need to learn to be critical readers of *all* information, but the seemingly anonymous nature of many websites requires students to be active in seeking out, identifying, and evaluating the sources of the digital information they are reading.

Students also need teaching to efficiently use search engines to find information and evaluate the results of their searches. In a study at the University of Maryland, a team of researchers found that children (ages seven through eleven) in their sample group showed an inability to construct queries requiring more than one search step (http://www.cs.umd.edu/hcil/trs/2009-04/2009-04.pdf). This limitation created frustration for students

involved in the search process because they couldn't find exactly what they were looking for. The study also showed that when students *did* successfully execute a search, they focused primarily on the first few items on the results page and ignored the rest of the information. The first two lessons in Umbrella 7 offer techniques for searching effectively and evaluating which search results seem relevant and worthy of further investigation. We hope this umbrella will get you started in establishing critical reading within a digital environment and inspire you and your students to learn more about navigating this challenging, yet rewarding, world of information.

# Chapter 7

## Writing About Reading Minilessons: The Reading-Writing Connection

THROUGH DRAWING/WRITING ABOUT READING, students reflect on their understanding of a text. For example, a story might have a captivating character or characters or a humorous sequence of events. A nonfiction text might have interesting information or call for an opinion. Two kinds of writing about reading are highly effective with fourth-grade students.

▶ **Shared Writing.** In shared writing (see Figure 7-1) you offer the highest level of support to the students. You act as scribe while the students participate fully in the composition of the text. You help shape the text, but the students supply the language and context.

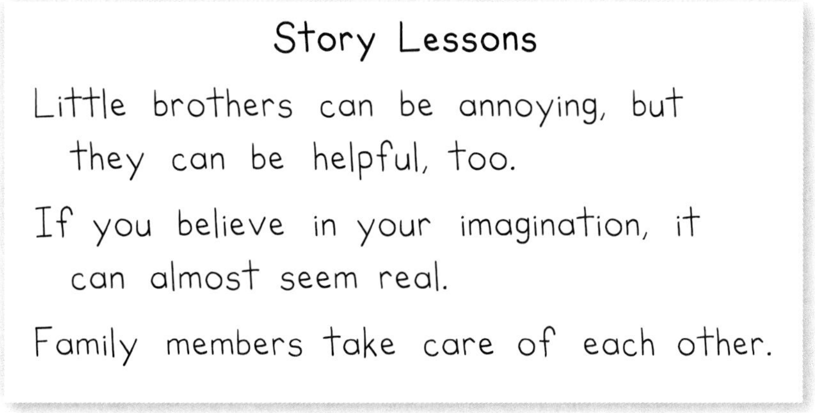

---

### Story Lessons

Little brothers can be annoying, but they can be helpful, too.

If you believe in your imagination, it can almost seem real.

Family members take care of each other.

---

**Figure 7-1:** In shared writing, the teacher acts as scribe.

▶ **Independent Writing.** For fourth graders, the first independent writing responses might involve just a simple paragraph, but these responses increase in complexity over time with students eventually writing multiple paragraphs about their reading (see Figure 7-2). After you have introduced and modeled different forms of writing about reading, fourth graders begin trying these different ways independently. Occasionally, it may be helpful to teach students how to use graphic organizers to bring structure to their writing about both fiction and nonfiction books (see Umbrella 4: Using Graphic Organizers to Share Thinking About Books in the Writing About Reading section). Fourth graders also enjoy writing independently about their reading in a weekly letter to you (see Figure 7-6). Keep good examples of different writing on hand (possibly in a scrapbook) for students to use as models.

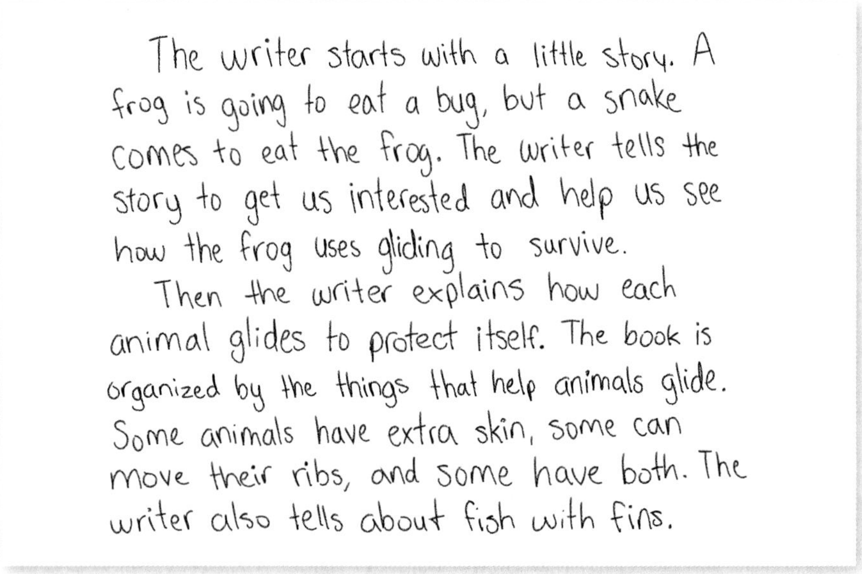

**Figure 7-2:** The independent writing in response to reading minilessons will reflect students' thinking about their reading.

> The writer starts with a little story. A frog is going to eat a bug, but a snake comes to eat the frog. The writer tells the story to get us interested and help us see how the frog uses gliding to survive.
> Then the writer explains how each animal glides to protect itself. The book is organized by the things that help animals glide. Some animals have extra skin, some can move their ribs, and some have both. The writer also tells about fish with fins.

In most Literary Analysis lessons, you will find a suggestion for extending the learning using shared or independent writing. In whatever way students write, they are exposed to different ways of thinking about their reading. Because students are encouraged to write about their thinking and integrate new vocabulary and content words from their reading, the independent writing of your students will not be entirely standard spelling. They are continuing to develop systems for writing words through approximation, and their risk-taking attempts are still critical to their success. You can expect fourth graders to accurately spell a significant number of high-frequency words as well as words with patterns that you have introduced in phonics and word study lessons; however, they will try many others using their growing vocabulary and knowledge about the way words work. You will notice that in Umbrella 3: Writing Letters to Share Thinking About Books, we have provided a lesson for students to evaluate the qualities of a good dialogue letter. In this lesson, students learn to proofread and evaluate the use of standard conventions as one aspect of writing quality letters.

The students' independent writing about reading will be in a reader's notebook. The first two umbrellas in Section Four provide inquiry-based lessons for exploring the reader's notebook and establish routines for writing about reading. Some of these routines include keeping lists of books read and books "to be read," maintaining a section of minilesson notes, and tallying the types of writing about reading that have been attempted and completed. This section also includes inquiry-based lessons to help students learn different genres and forms for responding to their reading in independent writing. The minilessons in Umbrella 5: Introducing Different Genres and Forms for Responding to Reading provide examples of how to use a particular genre or form to explore an aspect of literary analysis. For example, in RML2, students participate in analyzing an example of a short write in which the writer critiques the author's and illustrator's craft choices in a particular book. The extension to the lesson provides a list of other types of literary analysis that might also be addressed using a short write. Other suggestions for using the form or genre are included in online resources. You can find a comprehensive list of different genres and forms for fourth grade in the Writing About Reading section of *The Literacy Continuum* (Fountas and Pinnell 2017b).

Like Management minilessons, the lessons in the Writing About Reading umbrellas need not be taught consecutively within the umbrella; instead, they can be paired with the Literary Analysis lessons that support the concept students are being asked to write about. For example, if you have just completed Literary Analysis minilessons about plot (Umbrella 25: Understanding Plot), you might decide it would be an appropriate time to teach students how write a summary of a fiction book. After writing a few summaries as a whole class through shared writing and teaching the summary lesson in Writing About Reading (WAR.U5.RML4), students will be able to write a summary independently. Through this gradual release of responsibility, students learn how to transition to writing about their reading independently as they learn how to use each section of the notebook. A reader's notebook is an important tool to support student independence and response to books. It becomes a rich collection of thinking across the years.

Figure 7-3: Occasionally ask students to reflect on their understanding of a text by writing independently about their reading.

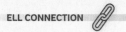

For English language learners, a reader's notebook is a safe place to practice a new language. It eventually becomes a record of their progress not only in content and literary knowledge but in acquiring a new language. However, they may do as much drawing as writing depending on where they are in acquiring English. Drawing is key because it provides a way to rehearse ideas. Use this opportunity to ask students to talk about what they have drawn, and then help them compose labels for their artwork so they begin to attach meaning to the English words. In some cases, you might choose to pull together small groups of students and engage them in interactive writing, in which the teacher and students compose together and share the pen. This might be particularly helpful with English language learners who might still be learning English letter and sound correlations. Students who struggle with spelling and phonics can also benefit from interactive writing in small groups.

Eventually, the students will do more writing, but you can support the writing by providing a chance for them to rehearse their sentences before writing them and encouraging students to borrow language from the texts they are writing about. The writing in a reader's notebook is a product they can read because they have written it. It is theirs. They can read and reread it to themselves and to others, thereby developing their confidence in the language.

## Using a Reader's Notebook in Fourth Grade

A reader's notebook is a place where students can collect their thinking about books. They draw and write to tell about themselves and respond to books and to keep a record of their reading lives. A reader's notebook includes

**Figure 7-4:** Students write to share their thinking about reading in a reader's notebook.

- a section for students to list the title, author, and genre of the books they have read and whether the books were easy, just right, or challenging,

- a section for helping students choose and recommend books, including a place to list books to read in the future,

- a section to glue in reading minilesson principles to refer to as needed (see Figure 7-5), and

- a section for students to respond to books they have read or listened to.

Grade 4
Section Two: Literary Analysis
Umbrella 13 Reading Minilesson Principles (RML1–RML6)

**Studying Memoir**

Memoirs are alike in many ways.

The definition of memoir is what is always true about it.

Writers tell about a memory of a time, place, person, or event in their lives and why it was important to them.

Most memoirs are written in the first person.

A memoir often has a turning point, or a point when an important decision is made.

The writer usually expresses new insight or a larger message.

© 2020 by Irene C. Fountas and Gay Su Pinnell. Portsmouth, NH; Heinemann. All rights reserved.

**Figure 7-5:** At the end of each umbrella, download the umbrella's principles, like the sample shown here. Students can glue the principles in the reader's notebook to refer to as needed. Encourage students to make notes or sketches to help remember the principles. To download the principles, go to **resources.fountasandpinnell.com.**

With places for students to make a record of their reading and respond to books in a variety of ways using different kinds of writing (including charts, webs, short writes, and letters), a reader's notebook thus represents a rich record of progress. To the student, the notebook represents a year's work to reflect on with pride and share with family. Students keep their notebooks in their personal boxes, along with their bags of book choices for independent reading time. We provide a series of minilessons in Section Four: Writing About Reading for teaching students how to use a reader's notebook. As described previously, reading minilessons in the Writing About Reading section focus on writing in response to reading.

If you do not have access to the preprinted *Reader's Notebook: Intermediate* (Fountas and Pinnell 2011), simply give each student a plain notebook (bound if possible). Glue in sections and insert tabs yourself to make a neat, professional notebook that can be cherished.

## Writing Letters About Reading: Moving from Talk to Writing

In fourth grade, we continue the routine of having students write a weekly letter about their reading in the past week. In most cases, they address these letters to you, the teacher, although occasionally they may write to other readers in the classroom or school. Letter writing is an authentic way to transition from oral conversation to written conversation about books. Students have had rich experiences talking about books during interactive read-aloud, guided reading, book clubs, and reading conferences. Writing letters in a reader's notebook allows them to continue this dialogue in writing and provides an opportunity to increase the depth of reader response.

By using the Writing About Reading section of *The Literacy Continuum* (Fountas and Pinnell 2017b) and carefully analyzing students' letters, you can systematically assess students' responses to the texts they are reading independently. The *Fountas & Pinnell Prompting Guide, Part 2, for Comprehension: Thinking, Talking, and Writing* (2009b) is a useful resource for choosing the language to prompt the thinking you want to see in a student's response. A weekly letter from you offers the opportunity to respond in a timely way to address students individually, differentiating instruction by asking specific questions or making comments targeted at the strengths and needs of each student's individual processing system.

Letters about reading also provide you with the opportunity to model your own thinking about reading. This reader-to-reader dialogue helps students learn more about what readers do when they actively respond to a text. The depth of their oral discussions will increase as students experience writing letters over time. Just as the discussions in your classroom set the stage for readers to begin writing letters, the writing of letters about reading will in turn enrich the discussions in your classroom.

Umbrella 3: Writing Letters to Share Thinking About Books, in Section Four, provides minilessons for getting dialogue letters started in your classroom. Through inquiry-based lessons, students learn the format of a letter, the routines involved in writing a weekly letter, and the qualities of a strong response. They learn to identify the different types of thinking they might include in a letter and how to integrate evidence to support their thinking.

We recommend that you teach these minilessons over two or three weeks. For example, you might teach the first two minilessons in this umbrella in the first week to introduce the format and content of a letter. You can then ask students to apply these new understandings to writing their first letter. After responding to their letters, use RML3 to introduce the second round of writing letters. This minilesson teaches students how to respond to your questions in their next letter. As students work on their second letter, choose

**Figure 7-6:** Weekly letters about reading allow you and your students to participate in a written dialogue to share thinking about the books the class has read together or books the students have read on their own.

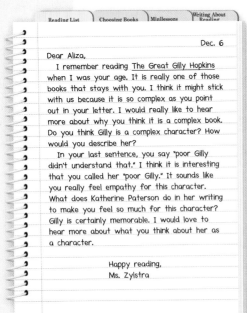

to teach RML4, which helps them learn how to add voice to their letters and make them interesting. Lastly, you may decide to wait until the third week as students embark on the third letter to provide an inquiry lesson on the qualities of a good letter (RML5). They can use these characteristics to evaluate the quality of their own reading letters. When you teach these minilessons over time, you give students the opportunity to gain experience writing letters about their reading before introducing another new principle.

## Managing Letters About Reading

Before introducing dialogue letters, think about how you will manage to read and respond to your students in a timely way. Some teachers assign groups of students to submit their letters on particular days of the week as shown in Figure 7-7. Many teachers find it more manageable to respond to five or six letters a day versus responding to the whole class at once. As the students write letters about reading, collect samples of quality letters that you might be able to share as examples in subsequent years to launch the writing of letters in your classroom.

We recommend that students work on their weekly letters during independent reading time. They can write their letters all at one time or over the course of two or three days. Monitor how long students are spending on writing versus reading to make sure they are dedicating enough time to both. However you choose to organize and manage this system, you will want to make sure it is feasible for both you and your students. It is critical that you are able to respond to the letters in a timely manner because students will quickly move on to new books and ask new questions about their reading.

You will find several other suggestions for helping students write thoughtful letters in Chapter 27 of *Teaching for Comprehending and Fluency* (Fountas and Pinnell 2006).

**Figure 7-7:** To make reading and responding to students' letters manageable, set up a schedule so that only a few letters are due each day.

## Letters Due

| Monday | Tuesday | Wednesday | Thursday |
|--------|---------|-----------|----------|
| Carlos | Lily | Charlotte | Elijah |
| Nora | Mason | Abdul | Riley |
| Darius | Ethan | Lanona | Caden |
| Jackson S. | Sophia M. | Alonzo | Jackson B. |
| Sophia T. | Mia | Kiara | Anh |
| Harper | Logan | Oliver | Noah |

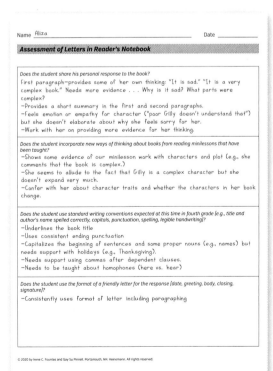

**Figure 7-8:** Use questions such as these to evaluate students' letters about their reading. To download the questions, visit resources.fountasandpinnell.com.

# Chapter 8

## Putting Minilessons into Action: Assessing and Planning

As NOTED IN CHAPTER 2, the minilessons in this book are examples of teaching that address the specific bullets that list the behaviors and understandings to notice, teach for, and support in *The Literacy Continuum* (Fountas and Pinnell 2017b) for fourth grade. We have drawn from the sections on Interactive Read-Aloud, Shared and Performance Reading, Guided Reading, Writing About Reading, Technological Communication, and Oral and Visual Communication to provide a comprehensive vision of what students need to become aware of, understand, and apply to their own literacy and learning. With such a range of important goals, how do you decide what to teach and when?

## Deciding Which Reading Minilessons to Teach

To decide which reading minilessons to teach, first look at the students in front of you. Teach within what Vygotsky (1978) called the "zone of proximal development"—the zone between what the students can do independently and what they can do with the support of a more expert other. Teach on the cutting edge of students' competencies. Select topics for minilessons that address the needs of the majority of students in your class.

Think about what will be helpful to most readers based on your observations of their reading and writing behaviors. Here are some suggestions and tools to help you think about the students in your classroom:

- **Use *The Literacy Continuum*** (Fountas and Pinnell 2017b) to assess your students and observe how they are thinking, talking, and writing/drawing about books. Think about what they can already do, almost do, and not yet do to select the emphasis for your teaching. Look at the Selecting Goals pages in each section to guide your observations.

- **Use the Interactive Read-Aloud and Literature Discussion section.** Scan the Selecting Goals in this section and think about the ways you have noticed students thinking and talking about books.

- **Use the Writing About Reading section** to analyze how students are responding to texts in their drawing and writing. This analysis will help you determine possible next steps. Talking and writing about reading provides concrete evidence of students' thinking.

- **Use the Oral and Visual Communication continuum** to help you think about some of the routines your students might need for better communication between peers. You will find essential listening and speaking competencies to observe and teach.

- **Use the Technological Communication section** to help you assess your students' technological skills and plan teaching that will help them improve their computer literacy and their ability to read digital texts.

- **Look for patterns in your anecdotal records.** Review the anecdotal notes you take during reading conferences, shared and performance reading, guided reading, and book clubs to notice trends in students' responses and thinking. Use *The Literacy Continuum* to help you analyze the records and determine strengths and areas for growth across the classroom. Your observations will reveal what students know and what they need to learn next as they build knowledge over time. Each goal becomes a possible topic for a minilesson.

- **Consult district and state standards as a resource.** Analyze the skills and areas of knowledge specified in your local and state standards. Align these standards with the minilessons suggested in this text to determine which might be applicable within your frameworks (see fountasandpinnell.com/resourcelibrary for an alignment of *The Literacy Continuum* with Common Core Standards).

- **Use the Assessment section after each umbrella.** Take time to assess student learning after the completion of each umbrella. Use the guiding questions on the last page of each umbrella to determine strengths and next steps for your students. This analysis can help you determine what minilessons to reteach if needed and what umbrella to teach next.

## A Suggested Sequence

The suggested sequence of umbrellas, Minilessons Across the Year, shown in Figure 8-2 (also downloadable from the online resources for record keeping), is intended to help you establish a community of independent readers and writers early in the year and work toward more sophisticated concepts across the year. Learning in minilessons is applied in many different situations and so is reinforced daily across the curriculum. Minilessons in this sequence are timed so they occur after students have had sufficient opportunities to build some explicit understandings as well as a great deal of implicit knowledge of aspects of written texts through interactive read-aloud and shared and performance reading texts. In the community of readers, they have acted on texts through talk, writing, and extension through writing and art. These experiences have prepared them to fully engage in the reading minilesson and move from this shared experience to the application of the concepts in their independent reading.

The sequence of umbrellas in Minilessons Across the Year follows the suggested sequence of text sets in *Fountas & Pinnell Classroom™ Interactive Read-Aloud Collection* (Fountas and Pinnell 2020). If you are using this collection, you are invited to follow this sequence of texts. If you are not using it, the first page of each umbrella describes the types of books students will need to have read before you teach the minilessons. The text sets are grouped together by theme, topic, author, and genre, not by skill or concept. Thus, in many minilessons, you will use books from several different text sets, and you will see the same books used in more than one umbrella.

We have selected the most concrete and instructive examples from the recommended books. The umbrellas draw examples from text sets that have been read and enjoyed previously. In most cases, the minilessons draw on text sets that have been introduced within the same month or at least in close proximity to the umbrella. However, in some cases, minilessons taught later, for example in month eight, might draw on texts introduced earlier in the year. Most of the time, students will have no problem recalling the events of these early books because you have read and discussed them thoroughly as a class, and sometimes students have responded to them through writing or art. However, in some cases, you might want to quickly reread a book or a portion of it before teaching the umbrella so it is fresh in the students' minds.

If you are new to these minilessons, you may want to follow the suggested sequence, but remember to use the lessons flexibly to meet the needs of the students you teach:

▷ Omit lessons that you think are not necessary for your students (based on assessment and your experiences with them in interactive read-aloud).

Repeat some lessons that you think need more time and instructional attention (based on observation of students across reading contexts).

Repeat some lessons using different examples for a particularly rich experience.

Move lessons around to be consistent with the curriculum that is adopted in your school or district.

The minilessons are here for your selection according to the instructional needs of your class, so do not be concerned if you do not use them all within the year. Record or check the minilessons you have taught so that you can reflect on the work of the semester and year. You can do this simply by downloading the minilessons record form (see Figure 8-1) from online resources (resources.fountasandpinnell.com).

**Figure 8-1:** Download this record-keeping form to record the minilessons that you have taught and to make notes for future reference.

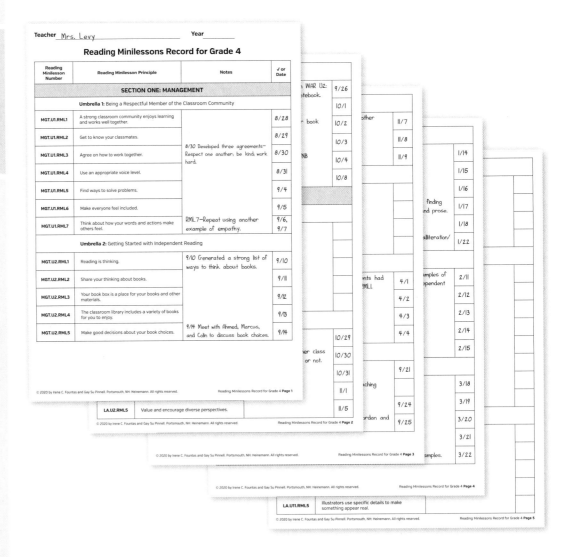

## MINILESSONS ACROSS THE YEAR

| Month | Recommended Umbrellas | Approximate Time |
|---|---|---|
| Month 1 | **MGT U1:** Being a Respectful Member of the Classroom Community | 1 week |
| | **MGT U2:** Getting Started with Independent Reading | 1 week |
| | **WAR U1:** Introducing a Reader's Notebook | 1 week |
| | **MGT U3:** Living a Reading Life | 1 week |
| Month 2 | **WAR U2:** Using a Reader's Notebook | 1 week |
| | **WAR U3:** Writing Letters to Share Thinking About Books (RML1–RML2) | 2 days |
| | **LA U13:** Studying Memoir | 1 week |
| | **LA U5:** Understanding Fiction and Nonfiction Genres | 4 days |
| | **WAR U3:** Writing Letters to Share Thinking About Books (RML3) | 1 day |
| | **LA U3:** Studying Authors and Their Processes (RML1) | 1 day |
| | *Note: We recommend teaching this minilesson as part of an author study. The lesson can be repeated each time an author is studied. If you are using the* Fountas & Pinnell Classroom™ Interactive Read-Aloud Collection, *the first author study is Allen Say.* | |
| | **LA U1:** Getting Started with Book Clubs | 1 week |
| | **WAR U3:** Writing Letters to Share Thinking About Books (RML4–RML5) | 2 days |
| Month 3 | **SAS U1:** Solving Multisyllable Words | 1 week |
| | **LA U11:** Studying Illustrators and Analyzing an Illustrator's Craft | 1 week |
| | *Note: We recommend teaching this minilesson as part of an illustrator study. The first minilesson in this umbrella can be repeated each time an illustrator is studied. If you are using the* Fountas & Pinnell Classroom™ Interactive Read-Aloud Collection, *the first illustrator study is Floyd Cooper.* | |
| | **LA U3:** Studying Authors and Their Processes (RML1) | 1 day |
| | *Note: We recommend teaching this minilesson as part of an author study. The lesson can be repeated each time an author is studied. If you are using the* Fountas & Pinnell Classroom™ Interactive Read-Aloud Collection, *the second author study is Doug Florian.* | |
| | **LA U2:** Learning Conversational Moves in Book Club | 1.5 weeks |

**KEY**

| | | |
|---|---|---|
| **MGT** | **Section One** | Management Minilessons |
| **LA** | **Section Two** | Literary Analysis Minilessons |
| **SAS** | **Section Three** | Strategies and Skills Minilessons |
| **WAR** | **Section Four** | Writing About Reading Minilessons |

**Figure 8-2:** Use this chart as a guideline for planning your year with minilessons.

| Month | Recommended Umbrellas | Approximate Time |
|-------|----------------------|------------------|
| Month 4 | **SAS U4:** Maintaining Fluency | **0.5 week** |
| | **LA U25:** Understanding Plot | **1 week** |
| | **LA U26:** Understanding Characters' Feelings, Motivations, and Intentions | **1 week** |
| | **WAR U5:** Introducing Different Genres and Forms for Responding to Reading (RML1–RML3) | **0.5 week** |
| | **SAS U5:** Summarizing (RML1) | **1 day** |
| | **WAR U5:** Introducing Different Genres and Forms for Responding to Reading (RML4–RML5) | **0.5 week** |
| | **SAS U2:** Using Context and Word Parts to Understand Vocabulary | **1 week** |
| Month 5 | **SAS U3:** Understanding Connectives | **1 week** |
| | **LA U6:** Studying Poetry | **1.5 weeks** |
| | **LA U20:** Understanding Realistic Fiction | **0.5 week** |
| | **LA U24:** Thinking About the Setting in Fiction Books | **0.5 week** |
| | **WAR U5:** Introducing Different Genres and Forms for Responding to Reading (RML6) | **1 day** |
| | **LA U23:** Studying Historical Fiction | **1 week** |
| Month 6 | **LA U10:** Reading Like a Writer: Analyzing the Writer's Craft | **1.5 weeks** |
| | **LA U27:** Understanding a Character's Traits and Development | **1 week** |
| | **WAR U5:** Introducing Different Genres and Forms for Responding to Reading (RML7–RML8) | **0.5 week** |
| | **LA U14:** Studying Biography | **1.5 weeks** |
| | **SAS U5:** Summarizing (RML2) | **1 day** |
| | **LA U7:** Exploring Different Kinds of Poetry | **1 week** |
| Month 7 | **SAS U6:** Monitoring Comprehension of Difficult Texts | **1 week** |
| | **LA U4:** Reading Graphic Texts | **1 week** |
| | **LA U8:** Thinking About the Author's Purpose and Message | **1 week** |
| | **LA U12:** Noticing Book and Print Features | **1 week** |
| | **SAS U7:** Reading in Digital Environments | **1 week** |

| Month | Recommended Umbrellas | Approximate Time |
|---|---|---|
| Month 8 | **LA U17:** Reading Informational Text Like a Scientist | 1 week |
| | **LA U16:** Noticing How Nonfiction Authors Choose to Organize Information | 1.5 weeks |
| | **WAR U4:** Using Graphic Organizers to Share Thinking About Books (RML1) | 1 day |
| | **LA U19:** Using Text Features to Gain Information | 1 week |
| | **LA U18:** Learning Information from Illustrations/Graphics | 1 week |
| | **WAR U4:** Using Graphic Organizers to Share Thinking About Books (RML2) | 1 day |
| Month 9 | **SAS U5:** Summarizing (RML3) | 1 day |
| | **LA U3:** Studying Authors and Their Processes (RML 1–4) | 1 week |
| | *Note: We recommend teaching this minilesson as part of an author study. The lesson can be repeated each time an author/illustrator is studied. If you are using the* Fountas & Pinnell Classroom™ Interactive Read-Aloud Collection, *the last author study is Patricia McKissack.* | |
| | **LA U15:** Exploring Persuasive Texts | 0.5 week |
| | **WAR U5:** Introducing Different Genres and Forms for Responding to Reading (RML9) | 1 day |
| | **LA U28:** Analyzing the Writer's Craft in Fiction Books | 1 week |
| | **LA U9:** Thinking About Themes | 1 week |
| | **WAR U4:** Using Graphic Organizers to Share Thinking About Books (RML3) | 1 day |
| Month 10 | **LA U21:** Studying Fantasy | 1.5 weeks |
| | **LA U22:** Studying Fairy Tales | 1.5 weeks |
| | **WAR U4:** Using Graphic Organizers to Share Thinking About Books (RML4–RML5) | 2 days |

*Note: Minilessons Across the Year offers general guidance as to the time of year you might teach a particular umbrella and is aligned with the *Fountas & Pinnell Classroom™ Interactive Read-Aloud Collection* sequence. However, because there are 225 reading minilessons in *The Reading Minilessons, Grade 4,* it would not be possible to teach every one of these lessons in a normal 180-day school year. You will need to make choices about which minilessons will benefit your students. The minilessons are designed for you to pick and choose what your students need at a particular point in time based on your careful observation of students' reading behaviors.

# Chapter 9

## Reading Minilessons Within a Multitext Approach to Literacy Learning

THIS COLLECTION OF 225 LESSONS for fourth grade is embedded within an integrated set of instructional approaches that build an awareness of classroom routines, literary characteristics, strategies and skills, and ways of writing about texts. In Figure 9-8, this comprehensive, multitext approach is represented, along with the central role of minilessons. Note that students' processing systems are built across instructional contexts so that students can read increasingly complex texts independently. *The Literacy Quick Guide: A Reference Tool for Responsive Literacy Teaching* (Fountas and Pinnell 2018) provides concise descriptions of these instructional contexts. In this chapter, we will look at how the reading minilessons fit within this multitext approach and provide a balance between implicit and explicit teaching that allows for authentic response and promotes the enjoyment of books.

Throughout this chapter we describe how to build the shared literary knowledge of your classroom community, embedding implicit and explicit teaching with your use of intentional conversation and specific points of instructional value to set a foundation for explicit teaching in reading minilessons. All of the teaching in minilessons is reinforced in shared and performance reading, guided reading, and book clubs, with all pathways leading to the goal of effective independent reading.

Let's look at the range of research-based instructional contexts that constitute an effective literacy design.

# Interactive Read-Aloud

Interactive read-aloud provides the highest level of teacher support for students as they experience a complex, grade-appropriate text. In this instructional context, you carefully select sets of high-quality student literature, fiction and nonfiction, and read them aloud to students. We use the word *interactive* because talk is a salient characteristic of this instructional context. You do the reading but pause to invite student discussion in pairs, in triads, or as a whole group at selected points. After the reading, students engage in a lively discussion. Finally, you invite students to revisit specific points in the text for deeper learning and may provide further opportunities for responding to the text through writing, drama, movement, or art.

We recommend that you read aloud from high-quality, organized text sets that you use across the year. A text set contains several titles that are related in some conceptual way, such as the following categories:

- Author
- Illustrator
- Genre
- Topic
- Theme or big idea
- Format (such as graphic texts)

ELL CONNECTION

When you use books organized in text sets, you can support students in making connections across a related group of texts and in engaging in deeper thinking about texts. All students benefit from the use of preselected sets, but these connected texts are particularly supportive for English language learners. Text sets allow students to develop vocabulary around a particular theme, genre, or topic. This shared collection of familiar texts and the shared vocabulary developed through the talk provide essential background knowledge that all students will be able to apply during subsequent reading minilessons.

**Figure 9-1:** Interactive read-aloud in a fourth-grade class

The key to success with reading minilessons is providing the intentional instruction in interactive read-aloud that will, first, enable the students to enjoy and come to love books and, second, build a foundation of shared understandings about texts within a community of readers and writers.

If you are using *Fountas & Pinnell Classroom™* (Fountas and Pinnell 2020), you will notice that we have used examples from the *Interactive Read-Aloud Collection* as the mentor texts in the minilessons. If you do not have the texts from *Fountas & Pinnell Classroom™*, select read-aloud texts with the same characteristics (described at the beginning of each umbrella) to read well ahead of the minilessons and then use the lessons as organized and presented in this book. Simply substitute the particular texts you selected. You can draw on any texts you have already read and discussed with your students as long as the genre is appropriate for the set of minilessons and the ideas can be connected. For example, if you are going to teach a set of minilessons about characters, pull examples from fiction stories rather than nonfiction books and include engaging characters. If you are reading rich literature in various genres to your students, the chances are high that many of the types of reading behaviors or understandings you are teaching for in reading minilessons can be applied to those texts.

At the beginning of each umbrella (set of related minilessons), you will find a section titled Before Teaching Minilessons that offers guidance in the use of interactive read-aloud as a prelude to teaching the explicit minilessons in the umbrella. It is important to note that the texts in a text set can be used for several different umbrellas. In general, text sets are connected with each other in particular ways so students can think about concepts across texts and notice literary characteristics during read-aloud lessons. But the texts have multiple uses. When you have finished reading the books in a set, you will have provided students with a rich, connected set of literacy

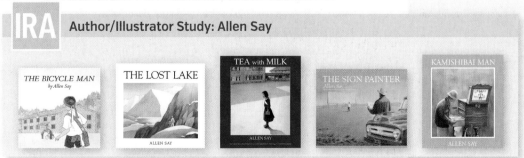

Figure 9-2: Examples of preselected text sets from *Fountas & Pinnell Classroom™ Interactive Read-Aloud Collection*

**Books We Have Shared**

- The Other Side by Jacqueline Woodson
- Better Than You by Trudy Ludwig
- A Boy and a Jaguar by Alan Rabinowitz
- Heroes by Ken Mochizuki
- La Mariposa by Francisco Jimenez
- A Symphony of Whales by Steve Schuch
- The Boy and the Whale by Mordicai Gerstein
- The Crane Wife by Odds Bodkin
- Giant Squid by Candace Fleming
- Eye to Eye: How Animals See the World by Steve Jenkins
- Meet Danitra Brown by Nikki Grimes
- These Hands by Margaret H. Mason

**Figure 9-3**: Keep a list of books that you have shared with your students as a record of shared literary knowledge.

experiences that include both explicitly taught and implicitly understood concepts. Then, you have a rich resource from which you can select examples to use as mentor texts in minilessons. We have selected examples across sets. Rich literary texts can be used for multiple types of lessons, so you will see many of the same familiar texts referenced throughout the reading minilessons. Each time a text is used for a different focus, students have a chance to view it with new eyes and see it differently. Usually, texts are not reread in entirety during a minilesson. They are already known because of the rich and deep experiences in your classroom. The result is shared literary knowledge for the class. In minilessons, they are revisited briefly with a particular focus. It is most powerful to select examples from texts that students have heard in their *recent* experience. But, you can always revisit favorites that you read at the very beginning of the year. In fact, reading many picture books at the beginning of the year will quickly build your students' repertoire of shared texts, providing you with a variety of choices for mentor texts for your minilessons. When texts have been enjoyed and loved in interactive read-aloud, students know them deeply and can remember them over time. It is helpful to keep an ongoing list of books read during interactive read-aloud so you and your students can refer to them throughout the year (see Figure 9-3). Some of the books in the *Interactive Read-Aloud Collection* are novels, and you are apt to include novels in text sets you assemble yourself as well. This is appropriate for readers in fourth grade. It is important to remember the power of shorter picture books to expose students to a wide variety of genres, authors, and themes. When you continue to read aloud age-appropriate picture books while working through a longer novel, you expose your students to different authors and genres while developing some of the deeper understandings a novel can offer. It is also important to note that you can use familiar novels as mentor texts in your minilesson examples in the same way that you use picture books.

Here are some steps to follow for incorporating your own texts into the minilessons:

1. Identify a group of read-aloud texts that will be valuable resources for use in the particular minilesson. (These texts may be from the same text set, but usually they are drawn from several different sets. The key is their value in teaching routines, engaging in literary analysis, building particular strategies and skills, or writing about reading.)

2. The mentor texts you select will usually be some that you have already read to and discussed with the students, but if not, read and discuss them with the goal of enjoyment and understanding. The emphasis in interactive read-aloud is not on the minilesson principle but on enjoying and deeply understanding the text, appreciating the illustrations and design, and constructing an understanding of the deeper messages of the text.

3. Teach the reading minilesson as designed, substituting the texts you have chosen and read to the students.

Interactive read-aloud will greatly benefit your English language learners. In *Fountas & Pinnell Classroom*™ (Fountas and Pinnell 2020), we have selected the texts with English language learners in mind and recommend that you do the same if you are selecting texts from your existing resources. In addition to expanding both listening and speaking vocabularies, interactive read-aloud provides constant exposure to English language syntax. Stories read aloud provide "ear print" for the students. Hearing grammatical structures of English over and over helps English language learners form an implicit knowledge of the rules. Here are some other considerations for your English language learners:

ELL CONNECTION

▶ Increase the frequency of your interactive read-alouds.

▶ Choose books that have familiar themes and concepts and take into account the cultural backgrounds of all the students in your classroom.

▶ Be sure that students can "see themselves" as well as the diversity of the world in a good portion of the texts you read.

▶ Reread texts that your English language learners enjoy. Rereading texts that students especially enjoy will help them acquire and make use of language that goes beyond their current understanding.

▶ Choose texts that are simple and have high picture support. This will allow you to later revisit concrete examples from these texts during reading minilessons.

▶ Seat English language learners in places where they can easily see, hear, and participate in the text.

▶ Preview the text with English language learners by holding a small-group discussion before reading the book to the entire class. As they hear it the second time, they will understand more and will have had the experience of talking. This will encourage the students to participate more actively during the discussion.

When you provide a rich and supportive experience through interactive read-aloud, you prepare English language learners for a successful experience in reading minilessons. They will bring the vocabulary and background knowledge developed in interactive read-aloud to the exploration of the reading minilesson principle. These multiple layers of support will pave the road to successful independent reading.

## Shared and Performance Reading

In the early grades, shared reading of big books and enlarged texts plays a vital role in helping students understand how to find and use information from print—directional movement, one-to-one correspondence, words and letters, and the whole act of reading and understanding a story or nonfiction text. As readers become more proficient, shared reading and performance reading (see Figure 9-4) continue to offer opportunities for more advanced reading work than students can do independently. In fact, a form of shared reading can be used at every grade level and is especially supportive to English language learners, who can benefit greatly from working with a group of peers.

For students in grade 4 and above, you can use the level of support that shared reading affords to develop readers' competencies in word analysis, vocabulary, fluency, and comprehension. You'll want to provide regular opportunities for shared and performance reading not only of fiction and nonfiction books but of poems, readers' theater scripts, plays, speeches, and primary source documents as well. Select a page or pages from a text and use a document camera to enlarge it so that students can see the features you are asking them to discuss. If you have a class set of novels, distribute them to focus on a particular section or chapter as a shared reading experience. Of course, you would want to choose a section that would be meaningful on its own without having to have the context of the entire novel.

Like the books read aloud, the texts you select for shared and performance reading should offer students the opportunity to discuss characters, events, concepts, and ideas. Read the text to the students and then invite them to read all or a portion of it in unison. Having students reread the text several times until they know it well gives you the option of revisiting it for different purposes; for example, to locate content words, practice fluency, or use inflection to convey the author's meaning. If you want, you can then extend the meaning through writing, art, or drama.

Here are some steps to follow for incorporating shared and performance reading as part of your classroom activities:

1. Display an enlarged text or provide individual copies if available. The text may be one that the students have previously read.

2. Engage students in a shared reading of the text. Plan to reread it several times. (Use your own judgment. Sometimes two or three readings are

sufficient.) Remember, the focus at this point is on understanding and enjoying the text, not on teaching a specific principle.

3. Revisit the text to do some specific teaching toward any of the systems of strategic actions listed in *The Literacy Continuum* (Fountas and Pinnell 2017b). If the text you've selected is a choral reading, script, poem, or speech, encourage students to perform it, using their voices and inflection to convey the writer's meaning.

4. If you plan to use a shared reading text in a reading minilesson, implement the lesson as designed using the texts you have used in teaching.

On the occasions that you use a shared reading text in a minilesson, students will have had opportunities to notice print and how it works and to practice fluent reading. They will have located individual words and noticed the use of bold and sound words. They will have learned how to use the meaning, language, and print together to process the text fluently and may have used performance techniques to amplify the writer's intent. In addition, here, too, they will have noticed characteristics of the genre, the characters, and the message anchors.

Shared and performance reading can also be important in reinforcing students' ability to apply understandings from the minilesson. You can revisit the texts to remind students of the minilesson principle and invite them to notice text characteristics or engage strategic actions to process them. When you work across texts, you help students apply understandings in many contexts.

Figure 9-4: Performance reading (readers' theater) in a fourth-grade class

Shared and performance reading provide a supportive environment for English language learners to both hear and produce English language structures and patterns. Familiar shared reading texts often have repeated or rhythmic text, which is easy to learn. Using shared reading texts to teach Strategies and Skills minilessons can be particularly supportive for English language learners because they have had the opportunity to develop familiarity with the meaning, the vocabulary, and the language structures of the text. They can focus on exploring the minilesson principle because they are not working so hard to read and understand the text. Shared reading gives them the background and familiarity with text that makes it possible to easily learn the minilesson principle.

Shared reading is a context that is particularly supportive to English language learners because of the enjoyable repetition and opportunity to "practice" English syntax with the support of the group. Shared reading can be done in a whole-group or small-group setting. Following are some suggestions you can use to support English language learners:

- Use enlarged texts, projected texts, or, if available, an individual copy of the text for every student.

- Select texts with easy-to-say refrains, often involving rhyme and repeating patterns.

- Reread the text as much as needed to help students become confident in joining in.

- Use some texts that lend themselves to inserting students' names or adding repetitive verses.

## Guided Reading

Guided reading is small-group instruction using an appropriately selected leveled text that is at students' instructional level. This means that the text is more complex than the students can process independently, so it offers appropriate challenge.

Supportive and precise instruction with the text enables the students to read it with proficiency, and in the process they develop in-the-head strategic actions that they can apply to the reading of other texts. Guided reading involves several steps:

1. Assess students' strengths through the analysis of oral reading behaviors as well as the assessment of comprehension—thinking within, beyond, and about the text. This knowledge enables you to determine an appropriate reading level for instruction.

2. Bring together a small group of students who are close enough to the same level that it makes sense to teach them together. (Ongoing assessment takes place in the form of running records or reading records

so that the information can guide the emphasis in lessons and groups may be changed and reformed as needed.)

3. Based on assessment, select a text that is at students' instructional level and offers opportunities for new learning.

4. Introduce the text to the students in a way that will support reading and engage them with the text.

5. Have students read the text individually. (In fourth grade, this usually means reading silently. You may choose to hear several students read softly to you so you can check on their processing.) Support reading through quick interactions that use precise language to support effective processing.

6. Invite students to engage in an open-ended discussion of the text and use some guiding questions or prompts to help them extend their thinking.

7. Based on previous assessment and observation during reading, select a teaching point.

8. Engage students in quick word work that helps them flexibly apply principles for solving words that have been selected based on information gained from the analysis of oral reading behaviors and reinforcement of principles explored in phonics minilessons (see *The Fountas & Pinnell Comprehensive Phonics, Spelling, and Word Study Guide* [2017a] and *Fountas & Pinnell Word Study System, Grade 4* [2020]).

9. As an option, you may have students engage in writing about the book to extend their understanding, but it is not necessary—or desirable—to write about every book.

Guided reading texts are not usually used as examples in minilessons because they are not texts that are shared by the entire class. However, on occasion, you might find a guided reading book that perfectly illustrates a minilesson

**Figure 9-5:** Guided reading in a fourth-grade class

principle. In this case, you will want to introduce the book to the entire class as an interactive read-aloud before using it as a mentor text. You can also take the opportunity to reinforce the minilesson principle across the guided reading lesson at one or more points:

▶ In the introduction to the text, refer to a reading minilesson principle as one of the ways that you support readers before reading a new text.

▶ In your interactions with students during the reading of the text, remind them of the principle from the reading minilesson.

▶ In the discussion after the text, reinforce the minilesson principle when appropriate.

▶ In the teaching point, reinforce the minilesson principle.

In small-group guided reading lessons, students explore aspects of written texts that are similar to the understandings they discuss in interactive read-aloud and shared and performance reading. They notice characters and character change, talk about where the story takes place, talk about the problem in the story and the ending, and discuss the lesson or message of the story. They talk about information they learned and questions they have, they notice genre characteristics, and they develop phonics knowledge and word-solving strategies. So, guided reading also gives readers the opportunity to apply what they have learned in reading minilessons.

ELL CONNECTION

When you support readers in applying the minilesson principle within a guided reading lesson, you give them another opportunity to talk about text with this new thinking in mind. It is particularly helpful to English language learners to have the opportunity to try out this new thinking in a small, safe setting. Guided reading can provide the opportunity to talk about the minilesson principle before the class comes back together to share. Often, students feel more confident about sharing their new thinking with the whole group because they have had this opportunity to practice talking about their book in the small-group setting.

## Book Clubs

For a book club meeting, bring together a small group of students who have chosen the same book to read and discuss with their classmates. The book can be one that you have read to the group or one that the students can either read independently or listen to and understand from an audio recording.

The implementation of book clubs follows these steps:

1. Preselect about four books that offer opportunities for deep discussion. These books may be related in some way (for example, they might be by the same author or feature stories around a theme). Or, they might just be a group of titles that will give students good choices.

2. Give a book talk about each of the books to introduce them to students. A book talk is a short "commercial" for the book.

3. Have students read and prepare for the book club discussion. (If the student cannot read the book, prepare an audio version that can be used during independent reading time.) Each reader marks a place or places that he wants to discuss with a sticky note.

4. Convene the group and facilitate the discussion.

5. Have the students self-evaluate the discussion.

Book clubs provide students the opportunity for deep, enjoyable talk with their classmates about books. Minilessons in two umbrellas are devoted to teaching the routines of book clubs. Literary Analysis Umbrella 1: Getting Started with Book Clubs focuses on the routines for getting started and takes students through the process of choosing books, marking pages they want to discuss, and participating in the discussion in meaningful ways. Umbrella 2: Learning Conversational Moves in Book Club teaches students how to enter a conversation, invite others to participate, build on other people's ideas, and change the focus when necessary.

A discussion among four or five diverse fourth-grade students can go in many directions, and you want to hear all of their ideas! *Prompting Guide, Part 2, for Comprehension: Thinking, Talking, and Writing* (Fountas and Pinnell 2009b) is a helpful tool. The section on book discussions contains precise teacher language for getting a discussion started, asking for thinking, affirming thinking, agreeing and disagreeing, changing thinking, clarifying thinking, extending thinking, focusing on the big ideas, making connections, paraphrasing, questioning and hypothesizing, redirecting, seeking evidence, sharing thinking, and summarizing.

Figure 9-6: Book club in a fourth-grade class

Before teaching several of the book club minilessons, we suggest holding a fishbowl observation of a book club discussion. To do this, prepare a small book group ahead of time and help them mark pages in the book they want to discuss. Have the small group sit in a circle with the remaining students sitting outside the circle to observe. Lead the conversation as needed, having book club members talk about their thinking for a few minutes. Encourage them to invite others in the group to talk, ask each other questions, and agree or disagree with one another in a respectful way. In some cases, you will ask students to observe through a particular lens. In others, they will be asked to make general observations. In either case, the prepared group models what a book club meeting should look like. The minilessons in the book club umbrellas offer suggestions for how to conduct these fishbowl observations prior to teaching the lesson.

 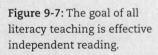

Book clubs offer English language learners the unique opportunity to enter into conversations about books with other students. If they have listened to an audio recording many times, they are gaining more and more exposure to language. The language and content of the book lifts the conversation and gives them something to talk about. They learn the conventions of discourse, which become familiar because they do it many times. They can hear others talk and respond with social language, such as "I agree with _____ because _____."

## Independent Reading

In independent reading, students have the opportunity to apply all they have learned in minilessons. To support independent reading, assemble a well-organized classroom library with a range of engaging fiction and nonfiction books. Although you will take into account the levels students can read independently to assure a range of options, we do *not* suggest that you arrange the books by level. It is not productive and can be destructive

**Figure 9-7:** The goal of all literacy teaching is effective independent reading.

for the students to choose books by "level." Instead, create tubs or baskets by author, topic, genre, and so forth. There are minilessons in Section One: Management to help you teach fourth graders how to choose books for their own reading (see MGT.U2.RML5). Consider the following as you prepare students to work independently.

▶ **Personal Book Boxes.** A personal book box is where students keep their materials (e.g., reader's notebook, writer's notebook, writing folder, books to read) all together and organized. A magazine holder or cereal box works well. Students can label the boxes with their names and decorate them. Management minilesson MGT.U2.RML3 provides guidance on setting up the box and keeping it organized. Keep these boxes in a central place so that students can retrieve them during independent reading time.

▶ **Classroom Library.** The classroom library is filled with baskets or tubs of books that fourth-grade students will love. Books are organized by topic, theme, genre, series, or author. Management minilesson MGT. U2.RML4 provides guidance for how to organize and introduce your classroom library. Have students help you organize the books so that they share some ownership of the library. In some minilessons, there is a direction to guide students to read from a particular basket in the classroom library so that they have the opportunity to apply the reading minilesson to books that include the characteristics addressed in the minilesson. For example, you might have them read from a basket of fantasy books or a basket of graphic texts.

In some cases, you may find it helpful to compile browsing boxes for some students as an alternative source for independent reading. This might be particularly important for students who find it difficult to choose appropriate books from the classroom library. A browsing box can include previously read guided reading books or books at lower levels. The box or basket can be identified by a color or other means. During independent reading, students select books from a browsing box that has books to suit their needs. The book choices should change along with students' progress.

Becoming independent as a reader is an essential life skill for all students. English language learners need daily opportunities to use their systems of strategic actions on text that is accessible, meaningful, and interesting to them. Here are some suggestions for helping English language learners during independent reading:

 **ELL CONNECTION**

▶ Make sure your classroom library has a good selection of books at a range of levels. If possible, provide books in the first language of your students as well as books with familiar settings and themes.

- During individual conferences, help students prepare—and sometimes rehearse—something that they can share with others about the text during group share. When possible, ask them to think about the minilesson principle.

- Provide opportunities for English language learners to share with partners before being asked to share with the whole group.

## Combining Implicit and Explicit Teaching for Independent Reading

You are about to embark on a highly productive year of literacy lessons. We have prepared these lessons as tools for your use as you help students engage with texts, making daily shifts in learning. When students participate in a classroom that provides a multitext approach to literacy learning, they are exposed to textual elements in a variety of instructional contexts. As described in Figure 9-8, all of these instructional contexts involve embedding literary and print concepts into authentic and meaningful experiences with text. A powerful combination of many concepts is implicitly understood as students engage with books, but the explicit teaching brings them to conscious awareness and supports students' ability to articulate the concepts using academic language.

**Figure 9-8:** Text experiences are supported and developed by implicit and explicit teaching in all instructional contexts, including interactive read-aloud, shared reading, guided reading, book clubs, and independent reading conferences. Reading minilessons provide explicit teaching that makes learning visible and is reinforced in the other contexts.

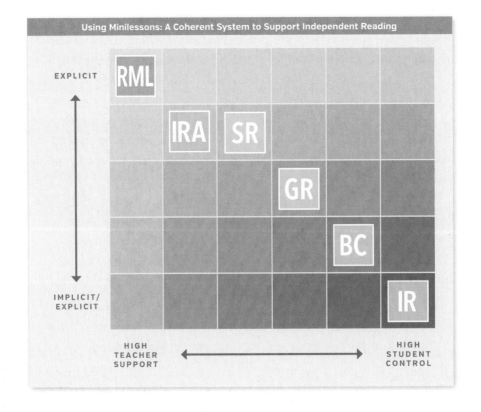

In interactive read-aloud, students are invited to respond to text as they turn and talk and participate in lively discussions after a text is read. You will be able to support your students in thinking within, beyond, and about the text because you will have used *The Literacy Continuum* (Fountas and Pinnell 2017b) to identify when you will pause and invite these conversations and how you will ask questions and model comments to support the behaviors you have selected. In response, your students will experience and articulate deeper thinking about texts.

In shared and performance reading, students learn from both implicit and explicit teaching. For example, when they work on performing a reader's theater script, they read and discuss the text several times, enjoying the story and discussing aspects of the text that support their thinking within, beyond, and about the text. As they prepare to perform the script, the teacher might provide explicit teaching for fluency (e.g., interpreting a character's dialogue using appropriate intonation and stress). The embedded, implicit teaching, as well as some of the more explicit teaching that students experience in shared and performance reading, lays the groundwork for the explicit teaching that takes place in reading minilessons. Reading minilessons become the bridge from these shared and interactive whole-group reading experiences to independent reading.

Guided reading and book clubs scaffold the reading process through a combination of implicit and explicit teaching that helps students apply the reading minilesson principles across a variety of instructional-level texts. The group share reinforces the whole process. Reading minilessons do not

**Figure 9-9:** A rich array of books provides the basis of shared literary knowledge for the community of readers in your classroom.

function in the absence of these other instructional contexts; rather, they all work in concert to build processing systems for students to grow in their ability to independently read increasingly complex texts over time.

The minilessons in this book serve as a guide to a meaningful, systematic approach to joyful literacy learning across multiple reading contexts. Students acquire a complex range of understandings. Whole-class minilessons form the "glue" that connects all of this learning, makes it explicit, and turns it over to the students to apply to their own independent reading and writing. You will find that the talk and learning in those shared experiences will bring your class together as a community with a shared knowledge base. We know that you and your students will enjoy the rich experiences as you engage together in thinking, talking, and responding to a treasure chest of beautiful books. Students deserve these rich opportunities— every child, every day.

## Works Cited

Clay, Marie. 2015 [1991]. *Becoming Literate: The Construction of Inner Control*. Auckland, NZ: Global Education Systems.

Fountas, Irene C., and Gay Su Pinnell. 2006. *Teaching for Comprehending and Fluency: Thinking, Talking, and Writing About Reading, K–8*. Portsmouth, NH: Heinemann.

———. 2009a. *Fountas & Pinnell Prompting Guide, Part 1, for Oral Reading and Early Writing*. Portsmouth, NH: Heinemann.

———. 2009b. *Fountas & Pinnell Prompting Guide, Part 2, for Comprehension: Thinking, Talking, and Writing*. Portsmouth, NH: Heinemann.

———. 2011. *Reader's Notebook: Intermediate*. Portsmouth, NH: Heinemann.

———. 2012a. *Fountas & Pinnell Genre Prompting Guide for Fiction*. Portsmouth, NH: Heinemann.

———. 2012b. *Fountas & Pinnell Genre Prompting Guide for Nonfiction, Poetry, and Test Taking*. Portsmouth, NH: Heinemann.

———. 2012c. *Genre Study: Teaching with Fiction and Nonfiction Books*. Portsmouth, NH: Heinemann.

———. 2017a. *The Fountas & Pinnell Comprehensive Phonics, Spelling, and Word Study Guide*. Portsmouth, NH: Heinemann.

———. 2017b. *The Fountas & Pinnell Literacy Continuum: A Tool for Assessment, Planning, and Teaching*. Portsmouth, NH: Heinemann.

———. 2017c. *Guided Reading: Responsive Teaching Across the Grades*. Portsmouth, NH: Heinemann.

———. 2018. *The Literacy Quick Guide: A Reference Tool for Responsive Literacy Teaching*. Portsmouth, NH: Heinemann.

———. 2020. *Fountas & Pinnell Classroom*, Grade 4. Portsmouth, NH: Heinemann.

———. 2020. *Fountas & Pinnell Word Study System*, Grade 4. Portsmouth, NH: Heinemann.

Park, Francis, and Ginger Park. 2000. *The Royal Bee*. Honesdale, PA: Boyds Mills Press.

Vygotsky, Lev. 1978. *Mind in Society: The Development of Higher Psychological Processes*. Cambridge, MA: Harvard University Press.

# Section 1 | Management

Management minilessons focus on routines for thinking and talking about reading and working together in the classroom. These lessons allow you to teach effectively and efficiently. They are directed toward the creation of an orderly, busy classroom in which students know what is expected as well as how to behave responsibly and respectfully within a community of learners. Most of the minilessons at the beginning of the school year will focus on management.

# 1 Management

## Minilessons in This Umbrella

| RML1 | A strong classroom community enjoys learning and works well together. |
| RML2 | Get to know your classmates. |
| RML3 | Agree on how to work together. |
| RML4 | Use an appropriate voice level. |
| RML5 | Find ways to solve problems. |
| RML6 | Make everyone feel included. |
| RML7 | Think about how your words and actions make others feel. |

## Before Teaching Umbrella 1 Minilessons

The purpose of this umbrella is to communicate to students that they are a community of readers and writers who work and learn together. You can support this notion by creating a warm, inviting, well-organized, and uncluttered classroom in which students can take ownership of their space and materials, and by giving students plenty of opportunities to choose, read, and talk about books.

Read books about friendship, inclusivity, and fitting in to help students understand what it means to be part of a caring and considerate community. The minilessons in this umbrella use books from the following *Fountas & Pinnell Classroom™ Interactive Read-Aloud Collection* text sets, but you can use books from your own classroom library. You will want to select books based on your own students' experiences and interests.

### Friendship

*The Other Side* by Jacqueline Woodson

*Better Than You* by Trudy Ludwig

### Figuring Out Who You Are

*The Junkyard Wonders* by Patricia Polacco

*Heroes* by Ken Mochizuki

**Friendship**

**Figuring Out Who You Are**

**Section 1: Management**

## Reading Minilesson Principle
# A strong classroom community enjoys learning and works well together.

### Being a Respectful Member of the Classroom Community

#### You Will Need

- classroom set up with areas to support students in reading and writing activities (e.g., classroom library; writing-supply area; areas for small-group, whole-group, and independent work)
- chart paper and markers

#### Academic Language / Important Vocabulary

- community

#### Continuum Connection

- Actively participate in conversation during whole- and small-group discussion (p. 337)

## Goal

Discuss what a community of readers and writers is and does.

## Rationale

To create a healthy and positive classroom community, all students must take responsibility for treating each other with respect and doing what they can to support each other. In addition to social and emotional responsibility, students also need to care for the environment, the materials, and other physical aspects of the communal space.

## Assess Learning

Observe students when they work and learn together and notice if there is evidence of new learning based on the goal of this minilesson.

- ▶ Do students understand what it means to be a good classroom community?
- ▶ Do they treat each other and the classroom respectfully?
- ▶ Do they understand and use the term *community*?

## Minilesson

To help students think about the minilesson principle, engage them in a discussion about what responsibilities the members of a community have in creating a positive place for working and learning together. Here is an example.

> In our classroom, we are a community that will work and learn together every day. What is important about how the members of a community need to work together? Turn and talk about that.

- ▶ As needed, discuss the meaning of *community* and use the following prompts:
  - *How can the members of a community make everyone feel included?*
  - *How can the members of a community support each other in their reading and writing work?*
- ▶ After time for discussion, ask students to share their thinking about the classroom community. Create a chart with examples of how the community works together to learn.

## Have a Try

Invite the students to talk with a partner about being a member of the classroom community.

> What will your role be as a member of our classroom community?

▶ After time for discussion, ask students to share.

## Summarize and Apply

Summarize the learning by reviewing the chart.

▶ Write the principle at the top of the chart.

> You can start building a strong community right away by practicing some of the items we listed on the chart. Be ready to share how you strengthened our community when we come back together after independent reading time.

## Share

Following independent reading time, gather students together in the meeting area to talk about how they worked on building a community.

> Who would like to share what you did to help build a strong community?

## Extend the Lesson (Optional)

After assessing students' understanding, you might decide to extend the learning.

▶ Have regular whole-class meetings to discuss how well the class is functioning as a community of readers and writers and to allow students to voice concerns or suggest ways to improve.

---

**A strong classroom community enjoys learning and works well together.**

- Treat everyone with respect and kindness.

- Make sure everyone feels included.

- Listen to what everyone has to say.

- Share ideas honestly.

- Ask for and give help to each other.

- Work well independently or in a group.

community

---

**Reading Minilesson Principle**
# Get to know your classmates.

## Being a Respectful Member of the Classroom Community

### You Will Need

- chart paper prepared with a sketch or photo of yourself and a web of details to help students get to know you
- chart paper and markers

### Academic Language / Important Vocabulary

- classroom community
- conversation
- unique
- diverse

### Continuum Connection

- Actively participate in conversation by listening and looking at the person speaking (p. 337)

## Goal

Learn to value one another's unique identities.

## Rationale

When you encourage students to value the unique identities of others and embrace diversity, you create a rich, interesting classroom community.

## Assess Learning

Observe students when they share about themselves with classmates and notice if there is evidence of new learning based on the goal of this minilesson.

- ▶ Do students talk about how each person is unique and diversity is something to be valued?
- ▶ Are they able to hold a conversation with a classmate?
- ▶ Do they understand the terms *classroom community, conversation, unique,* and *diverse*?

# Minilesson

To help students think about the minilesson principle, engage them in a discussion about getting to know one another using a web with a sketch or photograph of yourself. Here is an example.

- ▶ Display the prepared chart.

    What do you notice about this web?

    This web gives details that tell you something about me. What kinds of things did I write?

- ▶ As students respond, write general categories on a clean sheet of chart paper.

    How can you use my web to get to know me?

    How does getting to know one another build a good community for working and reading?

    By getting to know one another our community becomes stronger. We learn to value and enjoy the uniqueness of each of our community members.

## Have a Try

Invite pairs of students to get to know one another.

> Choose one of the topics on the chart to talk about with your partner.

▶ After time for conversation, ask a few students to share something they learned about their partners.

## Summarize and Apply

Summarize the learning and remind students to get to know one another by talking about the ways they are unique and diverse.

> Today you learned ways to get to know your classmates so you can enjoy and appreciate their uniqueness.

▶ Write the minilesson principle at the top of the chart.

> During independent reading time, make a web about yourself with details that tell about who you are. Bring your web when we meet so you can share something special about yourself with a partner.

## Share

Following independent reading time, have students gather in pairs to get to know one another.

> Share your web with a partner. Is there something the same on your two webs? How are you different?

## Extend the Lesson (Optional)

After assessing students' understanding, you might decide to extend the learning.

▶ Post the webs in the classroom so that students can refer to them and add further details.

Introducing Mr. Gray

Spanish speaker (a little) · husband, father, son · hiker · sports fan · country music lover · gardener · reader of spy thrillers

Get to know your classmates.

Things you can talk about:

- where your name comes from
- languages you speak
- family members
- favorite music, games, or sports
- pets
- favorite foods
- books you like to read
- family traditions

**Reading Minilesson Principle**
## Agree on how to work together.

**Being a Respectful Member of the Classroom Community**

### You Will Need

▶ chart paper and markers

### Academic Language / Important Vocabulary

▶ classroom community

▶ agreement

### Continuum Connection

▶ Speak at an appropriate volume (p. 337)

▶ Use respectful turn-taking conventions (p. 337)

## Goal

Understand that members of a community agree on how to work together.

## Rationale

When students understand that a community works together, they will realize that everyone needs to come to an agreement on how they want to work together. Coming up with an agreement of classroom norms is one way for students to take ownership of their classroom and behaviors so that a positive classroom environment can be created and maintained.

## Assess Learning

Observe students when they construct and follow a classroom agreement and notice if there is evidence of new learning based on the goal of this minilesson.

▶ Do students understand that they are a community?

▶ Do they contribute to ideas for the ways they can work and learn together?

▶ Do they understand the terms *classroom community* and *agreement*?

## Minilesson

To help students think about the minilesson principle, engage them in discussing and creating classroom norms or a community agreement. Here is an example.

> Think about our classroom community. What are some things we can agree upon together that will make it possible for everyone to enjoy working and learning together in our classroom? Let's make a list so that we all understand how to be a respectful member of this community.

▶ As needed, offer prompts to keep the ideas flowing:

  • *When you are reading or writing, how can you do your best work?*

  • *How can you make the classroom a place where everyone can learn?*

▶ Record students' ideas. For each one, ask students to talk about how it will help build and maintain the community.

> How will this idea help you work together, support each other, and enjoy learning?

▶ When students run out of things to say, ask them whether they will agree to implement these ideas.

> This chart will remind us of how we have agreed to work and learn together.

## Have a Try

Invite the students to talk with a partner about the community agreement.

> Do you have any additional ideas for the chart? Turn and talk to your partner about that. You can also talk about why some of the ideas we have written on the chart are important.

▶ After time for discussion, ask a few students to share ideas. Discuss whether any new items should be added to the classroom agreement.

## Summarize and Apply

Summarize the learning and remind students to think about the community agreement.

> Today you made a community agreement. Why is this important for our classroom?

> When you read today, take a moment to think about our agreement and how it will help you as a reader and writer. Why is it important to you?
> What things will you do to follow each part of the agreement? After you have thought about these things, come up and sign the agreement at the bottom. Be ready to share your thinking when we come back together.

## Share

Following independent reading time, gather students together in the meeting area to discuss the classroom agreement.

> Take a look at our community agreement. What do you think? Is there anything we should change or add?

## Extend the Lesson (Optional)

After assessing students' understanding, you might decide to extend the learning.

▶ Keep the agreement posted in the classroom and have new discussions from time to time to evaluate whether any changes should be made.

▶ Encourage students to write about how the classroom agreement helps them enjoy themselves and do their best learning.

---

### Our Classroom Agreement

- Be kind and respectful to each other.
- Be inclusive of others.
- Use an appropriate voice level.
- Take turns.
- Focus on your work.
- Help each other feel safe taking risks.
- Keep the classroom organized.
- Take good care of materials.
- Help each other learn.

Mia   Ava   Hasan   JACK   Logan
Jacob   Tom   Jenny   Aika   Clara
Kris   Owen   Dom   Anh   Petra
Anita   Filip   Minh   Abdul   Miguel
Kaito   Salvatore   Alex   Lee   Yasmin

---

**Reading Minilesson Principle**
# Use an appropriate voice level.

Being a Respectful Member of the Classroom Community

## You Will Need

▸ chart paper and markers

## Academic Language / Important Vocabulary

▸ classroom community
▸ appropriate
▸ voice level

**Continuum Connection**

▸ Speak at an appropriate volume (p. 337)

▸ Adjust speaking volume for different contexts (p. 337)

## Goal

Learn to manage voice levels.

## Rationale

When students identify different voice levels that are appropriate for different settings, they can determine the applicable level and modulate their voices accordingly.

## Assess Learning

Observe students when they talk about voice levels and use their voices, noticing if there is evidence of new learning based on the goal of this minilesson.

▸ Do students participate in creating a voice level chart?

▸ Can they identify the appropriate voice level for a particular situation?

▸ Are they able to adjust their voices to different situations?

▸ Do they understand the terms *classroom community, appropriate,* and *voice level*?

## Minilesson

To help students think about the minilesson principle, engage them in discussing and creating a chart that shows appropriate voice levels. Here is an example.

> When we made our classroom agreement chart, one of the things we discussed was voice level. Why are appropriate voice levels important at school?

▸ Encourage students to talk about the variety of voice levels they think are necessary. Then create a chart with four columns numbered 0 to 3, explaining that the 0 means silence and the 3 means an outside voice.

> Can you show what a silent voice would sound like?
>
> How would you describe this voice level?
>
> What are some examples of activities you do with the 0 voice level?

▸ As students make suggestions, add them under the first voice level number on the chart.

> Now think about the next type of voice level. How does level 1 sound?
>
> How can you describe this voice level?
>
> What are some activities you do at school when you should use this voice level?

▸ Add to the chart. Continue the conversation to complete the chart.

## Have a Try

Invite the students to talk with a partner about voice levels.

> Turn and talk with your partner about the voice levels you use in the classroom. Practice each type of voice level with your partner.

▶ After students turn and talk, ask a couple of pairs to share with the class any new ideas they discussed.

## Summarize and Apply

Summarize the learning and remind students to use a voice level that is appropriate for the situation.

> What type of voice do you think you might use most often?
>
> What type of voice do you have to remind yourself to use?

▶ Write the minilesson principle at the top of the chart paper.

> When you read today, take a moment to think about the appropriate voice level to use while reading independently. Check if you are using that volume.

## Share

Following independent reading time, gather students together in the meeting area to discuss voice level.

> What voice level did you use during reading today?
>
> Did you notice others using an appropriate voice too?
>
> What voice level should you be using right now?

## Extend the Lesson (Optional)

After assessing students' understanding, you might decide to extend the learning.

▶ Extend the conversation by asking students to talk about appropriate voice levels in other places (e.g., bus, home, after-school activities).

▶ Post the voice level chart and have students add other examples and ideas. Have students support a positive learning environment by gently reminding others of the chart as needed.

### Use an appropriate voice level.

| 0 | 1 | 2 | 3 |
|---|---|---|---|
| Silent | Soft Voice | Strong Voice | Outside Voice |
| Independent reading | Guided reading | Speaking to the whole class | Recess |
| Independent work | Small group work | Reading aloud | Physical Education (sometimes) |
| Independent Writing | Partner work | | |
| Taking tests | Lunchroom | | |

Section 1: Management

**Reading Minilesson Principle**
# Find ways to solve problems.

**Being a Respectful Member of the Classroom Community**

### You Will Need

▸ chart paper and markers

### Academic Language / Important Vocabulary

▸ classroom community
▸ problem
▸ solution

## Goal

Learn how to solve problems independently.

## Rationale

When you teach students problem-solving strategies, they become independent and confident, allowing time for you to work with small groups or individual students.

## Assess Learning

Observe students when they try to solve problems and notice if there is evidence of new learning based on the goal of this minilesson.

▸ Can students talk about ways to solve problems?

▸ Do they try to solve common problems on their own?

▸ Do they use the terms *classroom community, problem,* and *solution*?

## Minilesson

To help students think about the minilesson principle, engage them in a discussion about how to problem solve independently. Here is an example.

▸ Have students sit in the meeting area.

> Think about the different problems you might have while working in our classroom. Once in a while you may need my help, but most of the time you can solve problems on your own.

> What are some problems you might have as you work together in the classroom?

▸ As students provide ideas, write them on the left side of a chart, creating a column for problems.

> Now think about some solutions to these problems. Turn and talk about your ideas.

▸ After time for discussion, ask students to share ideas. Write them on the right side of the chart, creating a column for solutions. Encourage students to consider multiple solutions for each type of problem.

> Why is it important for you to solve problems on your own?

▸ Encourage a conversation about why independent problem solving is important. As needed, prompt the conversation with ideas, for example, when the teacher is busy working with small groups, it is important to know how to solve problems on your own.

## Have a Try

Invite the students to talk with a partner about problem solving.

> What is another problem you might have in class? How would you solve it? Turn and talk to your partner about that.

▶ After students turn and talk, ask a couple of pairs to share their ideas with the class. Add new ideas to the chart.

## Summarize and Apply

Summarize the learning and remind students to try to solve problems independently.

> How can solving problems independently help create a positive classroom community?

▶ Write the minilesson principle at the top of the chart paper.

> When you have a problem, try to solve it on your own first before you ask for help, unless it is an emergency. Refer to the chart if you are unsure of a possible solution.

## Find ways to solve problems.

| Problem | Solution |
|---|---|
| Finish work early | • Review your work.<br>• Read a book.<br>• Finish other work. |
| Having a problem with someone in class | • Talk directly and kindly to the person and try to find a solution.<br>• Compromise. |
| Don't understand directions | • Reread directions.<br>• Think about how you have done a similar assignment.<br>• Ask someone in the class. |
| Run out of something like paper, staples, glue, pencils | • Look in the class writing area.<br>• Ask another student if you can borrow an extra. |
| Book is too difficult | • Select a different book. |
| Emergency such as a sick, bleeding, or injured person | • Tell the teacher right away. |

## Share

Following independent reading time, gather students together in the meeting area to discuss problem solving.

> Did anyone have a problem today?

> How did you solve it?

> What might be another way to solve this problem?

## Extend the Lesson (Optional)

After assessing students' understanding, you might decide to extend the learning.

▶ Post the chart in the classroom so students can refer to it when they are looking to solve a problem in the classroom.

▶ Talk about problem solving from time to time and add new ideas to the chart.

▶ Recognize when students solve problems independently and provide positive reinforcement for their efforts.

### Being a Respectful Member of the Classroom Community

#### You Will Need

- several fiction books that emphasize friendship and inclusion, such as the following:
  - *The Junkyard Wonders* by Patricia Polacco, from Text Set: Figuring Out Who You Are
  - *The Other Side* by Jacqueline Woodson, from Text Set: Friendship
- chart paper and markers
- sticky notes

#### Academic Language / Important Vocabulary

- classroom community
- inclusive

### Goal

Learn how to use language and take actions to make others feel included.

### Rationale

When students learn words and actions that invite others to join in, they create an environment in which all classroom community members feel included and valued.

### Assess Learning

Observe students as they discuss inclusion and interact with classmates and notice if there is evidence of new learning based on the goal of this minilesson.

- ) Do students understand why it is important to include others?
- ) Are they able to discuss ways to include others?
- ) Do they understand the terms *classroom community* and *inclusive*?

## Minilesson

To help students think about the minilesson principle, provide an inquiry-based lesson using familiar texts about friendship to help students notice words and actions that show inclusiveness. Here is an example.

- ) Show pages 3–4 of *The Junkyard Wonders*.

  Remember in *The Junkyard Wonders* when the girl was new to the school and Thom asked her to sit next to him on the first day?

  Why is it important to make people feel included, especially when they are new?

- ) Show page 5–6 of *The Other Side*.

  Do you remember when the girl on the fence asked if she could play and the other kids said no?

  How did that make the girl feel?

- ) Read page 16.

  How did the girl feel when Annie responded in a different way than the other girls?

  What are some things you could say that would make someone feel included here in the classroom?

  What could you say outside the classroom?

  Have you ever felt like the girl on the fence?

- ) Ask students to share a few ideas. Write the ideas on chart paper.

## Have a Try

Invite the students to talk with a partner about being inclusive.

> What other things could you say to include others in a classroom discussion, at lunch, or at recess? Turn and talk about that.

▶ After time for discussion, briefly discuss new ideas. Add responses to the chart.

## Summarize and Apply

Summarize the learning and remind students to think about ways they can include others.

> Think about the different ideas posted on the chart and try to use these ideas in the classroom or around the school.

▶ Write the minilesson principle at the top of the chart paper.

> When you read today, notice examples of when characters include others or when a character makes others feel left out. Place a sticky note on the page with the example. Bring the book when we meet so you can share.

## Share

Following independent reading time, gather students together in pairs to discuss examples of inclusiveness.

> Did you find any examples of characters that included others or did not include others? First, share what you noticed. Then turn and talk to another set of partners.

## Extend the Lesson (Optional)

After assessing students' understanding, you might decide to extend the learning.

▶ Notice when students show inclusiveness in the classroom and point out how that is helping build a positive community of learners, readers, and writers.

▶ **Writing About Reading** Have students write about examples of characters who made other characters feel included or excluded. Encourage them to also write about how they felt when they read that part of the book.

> **Make everyone feel included.**
>
> ### In the Classroom
>
> - What do you think about that?
> - What is your opinion?
> - Can I help you with anything?
>
> ### Outside the Classroom
>
> - Would you like to join us?
> - Do you want to sit with me/us at lunch?
> - Do you want to join our game?

Section 1: Management

**Reading Minilesson Principle**
# Think about how your words and actions make others feel.

### You Will Need

- several familiar fiction books that encourage thinking about empathy, such as the following:
  - *Heroes* by Ken Mochizuki, from Text Set: Figuring Out Who You Are
  - *Better Than You* by Trudy Ludwig, from Text Set: Friendship
- chart paper and markers
- sticky notes

### Academic Language / Important Vocabulary

- classroom community
- empathy

### Continuum Connection

- Learn from vicarious experiences with characters [p. 59]

## Goal

Learn how to feel and show empathy toward others.

## Rationale

When students reflect on how their words and actions affect classmates, they develop empathy and concern for others, which contributes to a positive learning environment.

## Assess Learning

Observe students as they discuss empathy and interact with others. Notice evidence of new learning based on the goal of this minilesson.

- ▶ Do students talk about how someone's words or actions make another person feel?
- ▶ Are they able to infer how their own words and actions make others feel?
- ▶ Do they understand the terms *classroom community* and *empathy*?

# Minilesson

To help students think about the minilesson principle, provide an inquiry-based lesson using familiar texts about friendship to help them engage in thinking about empathy. Here is an example.

- ▶ Show pages 1–2 of *Heroes*.

    Think about the boy's feelings as I reread this page from *Heroes*.

- ▶ Read page 2.

    What do you notice about how the words and actions of the other boys made him feel?

- ▶ As students share ideas, create a two-column chart. On one side, write things that the boys say and do. On the other side, write how those words or actions make the main character feel.

    Think about two examples from another book you know.

- ▶ Read pages 4 and 9 from *Better Than You*.

    What did you notice about how the words and actions of one character made another character feel?

- ▶ Add examples to the chart.

    Trying to understand how others feel is called empathy. Thinking about how your words and actions make others feel is one part of empathy.

## Have a Try

Invite the students to talk with a partner about empathy.

> Think of a time when someone's words or actions made you feel good or feel bad. Turn and talk to your partner about that.

▶ After students turn and talk, ask a couple of pairs to share their ideas with the class. Add ideas to the chart.

## Summarize and Apply

Summarize the learning and remind students to think about how their words and actions affect others.

> Think about the different ideas on the chart and how you can use words and actions that make others feel good.

▶ Write the minilesson principle at the top of the chart paper.

> When you read today, notice examples of characters who show empathy toward others or notice when one character understands how another character feels. Place a sticky note on any pages with examples. Bring the book when we meet so you can share.

## Share

Following independent reading time, gather students together in the meeting area to discuss examples of empathy.

> Did you find any examples of characters who used words or actions to make others feel good or bad? Share what you noticed.

## Extend the Lesson (Optional)

After assessing students' understanding, you might decide to extend the learning.

▶ Have students write about examples from their own lives of how the words or actions of others made them feel. Encourage them to also write about what others could have said or done to show more empathy. They can also write about examples of times when they were empathetic toward another person.

▶ Notice when students practice empathy in the classroom and point out how that is helping build a positive community of learners, readers, and writers. Using specific classroom examples that you notice, ask students how they think their words or actions made others feel.

### Think about how your words and actions make others feel.

| | What Someone Said or Did | How That Made Others Feel |
|---|---|---|
| | Kids stared, pointed, and pretended that the boy was the bad guy. | The boy felt sad and discriminated against. |
| | Jake bragged and always had to be better than Tyler. | Tyler felt like he was never good enough. |
| | Uncle Kevin asked Tyler to play the guitar. | Tyler felt a little better. |
| | Someone asked me to play basketball at recess. | I felt happy and included. |
| | Nobody wanted me to play at recess. | I felt sad and alone. |

## Assessment

After you have taught the minilessons in this umbrella, observe students as they learn and interact with others in the classroom.

▶ What evidence do you have of new understandings related to being respectful members of the classroom community?

- Are students developing skills to work and learn together as a community?
- Do they take care of the classroom and the materials they use?
- Do they use ways to get to know one another?
- Do they participate in making and honoring classroom agreements?
- Do students use an appropriate voice level in the classroom?
- Can they find ways to solve problems on their own?
- Are they inclusive of others?
- Do they think about how their words and actions make others feel?
- Do they use terms such as *agreement, problem, solution, and unique* when they talk about the classroom community?

▶ What other minilessons might you teach to help students grow and function as members of a community of readers and writers?

- Are students able to find books to read and books to recommend to others?
- Are they able to share their thinking with others during turn and talk or during a book club meeting?

Use your observations to determine the next umbrella you will teach. You may also consult Minilessons Across the Year (pp. 59–61) for guidance.

## Reader's Notebook

When this umbrella is complete, provide a copy of the minilesson principles (see resources.fountasandpinnell.com) for students to glue in the reader's notebook (in the Minilessons section if using *Reader's Notebook: Intermediate* [Fountas and Pinnell 2011]), so they can refer to the information as needed.

## Minilessons in This Umbrella

| RML1 | Reading is thinking. |
| RML2 | Share your thinking about books. |
| RML3 | Your book box is a place for your books and other materials. |
| RML4 | The classroom library includes a variety of books for you to enjoy. |
| RML5 | Make good decisions about your book choices. |

## Before Teaching Umbrella 2 Minilessons

The purpose of the minilessons in this umbrella is to help students learn what to do during classroom time set aside for independent reading and writing. Students learn that reading and writing are both important parts of independent reading, discover the importance of keeping their personal materials organized, and explore how the classroom library system makes finding books easier. Before teaching the minilessons in this umbrella, decide where students will be during the time for independent reading. Also decide whether you will organize the library ahead of time or whether you will engage students in the process of categorizing the books. Following are some suggestions to prepare for introducing independent reading time:

▶ Organize (or have students help you organize) books in the classroom library into baskets in a way that allows students to see the front covers and provides easy access for browsing.

▶ In each basket, display high-quality, diverse, and interesting books that offer a range of difficulty levels.

▶ Label (or have students label) baskets with the topic, author, illustrator, series, genre, or theme.

▶ Give each student a personal book box for keeping books and other literacy materials.

**Getting Started with Independent Reading**

**You Will Need**

▸ chart paper and markers

**Academic Language / Important Vocabulary**

▸ independent reading

**Continuum Connection**

▸ Give reasons (either text-based or from personal experience) to support thinking (pp. 58, 62)

## Goal

Understand that reading is thinking and that most people do their best thinking when it's quiet.

## Rationale

During independent reading time, students will read independently and write about their thinking in a reader's notebook. This minilesson prepares students to equate reading with thinking and helps them understand that a quiet atmosphere is beneficial for reading. Once students learn the routines of independent reading, you will be able to work with small groups or individuals.

## Assess Learning

Observe students during independent reading and notice if there is evidence of new learning based on the goal of this minilesson.

▸ Do students understand that reading is thinking?

▸ Do they read independently and silently?

▸ Do they use the term *independent reading*?

## Minilesson

To help students think about the minilesson principle, engage them in a discussion about reading as thinking. Here is an example.

> When you read, what aspects of the book do you think about?

▸ Prompt them as necessary and list responses on chart paper.

> There are plenty of things to think about when you read, such as the characters and new information you learned, though you may not think about everything while you read a single book.

> What does the classroom have to be like to do your best thinking while you read?

▸ Ask several volunteers to share their thoughts about the conditions in the classroom that are conducive for independent reading.

> What can you do to help your classmates do their best thinking?

> Reading silently and not interrupting your classmates while they are reading will help everyone do their best reading.

## Have a Try

Invite the students to talk about what they can think about as they read.

> Think of a book you have read or are reading. Choose one item from the chart to talk about in relation to your book.

▶ Ask several students to share what they thought about when they read a book.

## Summarize and Apply

Summarize the learning and remind students to think while they read.

> What did you learn about reading today?

▶ Write the principle at the top of the chart.

> During independent reading today, enjoy a book. Notice what aspect of the book you think about. Bring your book when we meet to share.

## Share

Following independent reading time, gather students together in the meeting area to talk about their reading.

> Turn and talk to your partner about what you were thinking about the book you read today.

## Extend the Lesson (Optional)

After assessing students' understanding, you might decide to extend the learning.

▶ When you meet with individuals to talk about their reading, ask them to tell you what the book makes them think about.

**Reading is thinking.**

### When you read, think about . . .

- characters
- setting
- message
- author's writing
- how it's like my life
- what you wonder
- something that surprised you
- something you learned
- an interesting fact

# RML2
## MGT.U2.RML2

**Reading Minilesson Principle**
# Share your thinking about books.

## Getting Started with Independent Reading

### You Will Need

- chart from MGT.U2.RML1 (optional)
- chart paper and markers
- reader's notebook (optional)

### Academic Language / Important Vocabulary

- independent reading
- reader's notebook
- turn and talk

### Continuum Connection

- Give reasons (either text-based or from personal experience) to support thinking (pp. 58, 62)
- Engage actively in conversational routines: e.g., turn and talk (p. 337)

## Goal

Learn ways to share thinking about reading.

## Rationale

This minilesson establishes that independent reading involves not just thinking about what you read but also sharing that thinking. When students have many opportunities to read books they have chosen themselves and to write and talk about their reading, they are more likely to enjoy reading and become lifelong readers.

## Assess Learning

Observe students during independent reading and notice if there is evidence of new learning based on the goal of this minilesson.

- Do students know ways to share their thinking after reading?
- Do they understand the routine of turn and talk?
- Do they use the terms *independent reading, reader's notebook,* and *turn and talk?*

## Minilesson

To help students think about the minilesson principle, engage them in a discussion about how to share their thinking about reading. Here is an example.

> You know that you think about many different things when you read.

- If you taught MGT.U2.RML1, review the chart with the students.

> After you read during independent reading time, you will share your thinking about your reading. One way to share is to talk about your thinking.

- Add *Turn and Talk* to the chart.

> What are some guidelines for when you turn and talk to a partner?

- Add student ideas to the Turn and Talk section of the chart.
- Show or sketch a page from a reader's notebook on the chart paper to remind students that they can share their thinking by writing about it.

> Another way to share your thinking is by writing about your reading. You can write about any of the aspects of the book that you think about when you read.

> Think about all of the different kinds of things you can write in your notebook. What are some?

## Have a Try

Invite the students to talk with a partner about their reading.

> Turn to your partner, both of you sitting with your legs crisscross and facing one another. Look at what we wrote on the chart under Turn and Talk. Now think about a book you are reading. Turn and talk about the book.

▶ After students turn and talk, invite several students to evaluate their discussion, using the chart for guidance.

## Summarize and Apply

Summarize the learning and remind students to read silently and to share their thinking.

> During independent reading, you will read and then share your thinking.

▶ Write the principle at the top of the chart.

> During independent reading today, read a book silently. When you share, you will have the chance to talk about your reading. You can also write about your thinking in your reader's notebook.

## Share

Following independent reading time, gather students together in the meeting area to talk about their reading.

> Turn and talk to your partner to share your thinking about the book you read today. If you also wrote about your thinking, read what you wrote to your partner.

## Extend the Lesson (Optional)

After assessing students' understanding, you might decide to extend the learning.

▶ Use the turn and talk routine often to engage students in discussion and as a way for them to rehearse their responses in a low-stress situation before sharing with the larger group.

---

**Share your thinking about books.**

| Turn and Talk | Write About Your Reading |
|---|---|
| • Listen carefully.<br><br>• Ask questions to clarify.<br><br>• Look at your partner.<br><br>• Give reasons for your thinking. | Reader's Notebook |

**Reading Minilesson Principle**
# Your book box is a place for your books and other materials.

Getting Started with
Independent Reading

### You Will Need

- for each student, a book box prepared with literacy materials (such as a book from the classroom library, a reader's notebook, a writer's notebook, a writing folder, and a word study folder, in that order)
- chart paper and markers

### Academic Language / Important Vocabulary

- book box
- personal materials
- organized
- reader's notebook
- writer's notebook
- writing folder
- poetry notebook

## Goal

Keep books and materials organized for use during independent reading time.

## Rationale

When students understand that a book box is a place for personal literacy materials, know where to find it, and know how to keep it organized, they spend less time searching for materials and more time reading, writing, and learning.

## Assess Learning

Observe students when they use their book boxes and notice if there is evidence of new learning based on the goal of this minilesson.

- Can students explain the purpose of a book box and the importance of keeping it organized?
- Do they keep their book boxes organized?
- Do they use the terms *book box*, *personal materials*, *organized*, *reader's notebook*, *writer's notebook*, *writing folder*, and *poetry notebook*?

## Minilesson

To help students think about the minilesson principle, help them become familiar with their personal book boxes and engage them in a discussion about how to organize materials in it. Here is an example.

- Before beginning this minilesson, have students retrieve their personal book boxes and bring them to their tables.

  Take a minute to look through your book box and discover what's inside.

- After students have examined the contents of their book boxes, use questions such as the following to prompt discussion:

  - *What did you notice about your personal book box?*
  - *What's inside your book box?*

- Discuss the organization of the materials in the book boxes.

  How are the materials in your book box organized?

  Compare your box and the materials to a partner's. What do you notice?

- Write the order of the materials on chart paper.

  Why do you think the materials are organized in this way?

  Why is it important to keep the materials in your book box organized?

## Have a Try

Invite the students to talk with a partner about the purpose of their book boxes.

> Why is it a good idea for each of you to have your own book box? How will your book box help you learn? Turn and talk to your partner about what you think.

▶ After students turn and talk, invite several pairs to share their thinking with the whole class.

## Summarize and Apply

Summarize the learning and remind students to keep their book boxes organized and to pick them up at the beginning of independent reading.

> What did you learn today about your book box?
>
> When do you think you will use your book box the most?

▶ Write the principle at the top of the chart paper.

> During independent reading today, read the book in your book box. If you want a different book, you can choose one from the classroom library. After you read, remember to put everything back in your box in the same order.

▶ If students have been introduced to a reader's notebook, you can provide an option for writing about their reading.

## Share

Following independent reading time, gather students together in the meeting area to talk about their book boxes.

> How did you use your book box today?

## Extend the Lesson (Optional)

After assessing students' understanding, you might decide to extend the learning.

▶ You might have students add items to their book boxes throughout the school year. As you introduce each new item, discuss its purpose and remind students to keep their boxes organized.

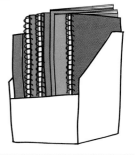

**Your book box is a place for your books and other materials.**

1. A book from the classroom library

2. Reader's notebook

3. Writer's notebook

4. Writing folder

5. Word study folder

6. Poetry notebook

Section 1: Management

**Reading Minilesson Principle**
# The classroom library includes a variety of books for you to enjoy.

## Getting Started with Independent Reading

### You Will Need

▸ an organized, inviting classroom library

▸ several selected books from your classroom library (see Have a Try)

▸ sticky notes

▸ chart paper and markers

### Academic Language / Important Vocabulary

▸ organized

▸ topic

▸ illustrator

▸ author

▸ genre

▸ series

## Goal

Understand how the classroom library is organized to make finding books easier.

## Rationale

When you teach students how the classroom library is organized, they are better able to find and select books to enjoy reading. As an alternative to the process suggested in this lesson, you could have your students sort books, create categories, and label the baskets with you.

## Assess Learning

Observe students when they select books from the classroom library and notice if there is evidence of new learning based on the goal of this minilesson.

▸ Can students explain how and why the classroom library is organized?

▸ Do they use their understanding of the organization of the classroom library to choose books to read?

▸ Do they use the terms *organized, topic, illustrator, author, genre,* and *series*?

## Minilesson

To help students think about the minilesson principle, have them gather in the classroom library to discuss the organization of the books. Here is an example.

> Take a look around and see what you notice about our classroom library.

▸ Use questions such as the following to prompt discussion:

- *What do you notice about how the books in our classroom library are organized?*

- *How will the way the library is organized help you find books to read?*

▸ Help students notice the specific ways the books are organized by using questions such as the following. Alter these questions to reflect the specific categories of books available in your own classroom library, but try to include all the ways the books are organized (e.g., by author, illustrator, genre, series, theme, topic).

- *Where should I look if I want to read a book by Allen Say?*

- *What kind of books are in this basket?* [Point to a basket of books about overcoming obstacles, for example.]

- *Can you help me find the next book in the Poppy series?*

- *Where can I look for books about science?*

▸ Record each category of books that students notice (and an example of that category) on the chart paper.

## Have a Try

Invite the students to talk within small groups about how to organize books in the classroom library.

▸ Divide students into small groups. Give each group a small stack of books. Each book should clearly correspond with a basket in the classroom library. For example, if you have a basket of Allen Say books, you might give one group a book by Allen Say.

Turn and talk to your group about where you think each of your books should go. Then write where it should go on a sticky note, and stick the note on the front cover of the book.

▸ After students turn and talk, invite groups to share their thinking.

## Summarize and Apply

Summarize the learning and remind students to use the organization of the classroom library to help them find and select books to read.

What did you notice today about our classroom library?

▸ Write the principle at the top of the chart.

Before you choose a book to read, think about what kind of book you want to read. Use what you learned today to find a book.

## Share

Following independent reading time, gather students together in the meeting area to talk about the books they chose for independent reading.

Turn and talk to your partner about the book you chose today and how you knew where to find it.

## Extend the Lesson (Optional)

After assessing students' understanding, you might decide to extend the learning.

▸ Regularly rotate the books and categories of books in the classroom library. Involve students in choosing new categories and in organizing new books.

▸ Give regular book talks about books you are adding or want to highlight in the classroom library.

The classroom library includes a variety of books for you to enjoy.

| Author | Illustrator | Genre |
| Allen Say | Floyd Cooper | Historical Fiction |
| Series | Theme | Topic |
| Poppy | Overcoming Obstacles | Endangered Species |

**Reading Minilesson Principle**
## Make good decisions about your book choices.

**You Will Need**

- chart paper and markers

**Academic Language / Important Vocabulary**

- choice
- decision
- independent reading
- recommendation
- genre
- abandon

**Continuum Connection**

- Express tastes and preferences in reading and support choices with descriptions and examples of literary elements: e.g., genre, setting, plot, theme, character, style and language (pp. 528, 539, 548)

### Goal

Make good book choices for independent reading.

### Rationale

When you teach students to be aware of the ways they choose books and to make good decisions about their reading, they spend more time reading books they enjoy. They also become more independent and confident and develop their interests and identities as readers. They are more likely to love reading and to become lifelong readers.

### Assess Learning

Observe students when they choose books and talk about books they have chosen. Notice if there is evidence of new learning based on the goal of this minilesson.

- Do students choose books that interest them and that are just right for them?
- Can they explain why they chose a particular book?
- Do they vary their book choices in terms of genre, topic, and difficulty level?
- Do they understand the terms *choice, decision, independent reading, recommendation, genre,* and *abandon*?

## Minilesson

To help students think about the minilesson principle, engage them in a discussion about how to choose books. Here is an example.

> Sometimes it can be hard to choose a book you want to read. One of the ways I choose books is by asking for recommendations from friends. What are some of the ways you choose books to read?

- Record students' responses on chart paper.

> These are all good ways to make book choices. Another thing to think about is whether a book is easy, just right, or difficult for you. Most of the time it is a good idea to choose a book that you can read with some challenges, but not so many that you can't enjoy it.

- Add *Difficulty level* to the chart as something to think about when choosing books.

> How do you know when you have picked a book that is just right for you?

> Sometimes readers choose to read books that are easy or a bit difficult. When might you decide to read an easy book?

> When might you choose a book that is difficult?

> Sometimes you might choose an easy book to enjoy reading. Sometimes you might choose a book that is difficult because it is about something you really want to learn about.

## Have a Try

Invite the students to talk with a partner about a book they chose recently.

> Think about either the book you're reading now or the last book you read. Turn and talk to your partner about why you chose that book.

▶ After students turn and talk, invite a few students to share. Add responses to the chart.

> Now turn and talk about whether the book you chose was a good choice for you.

## Summarize and Apply

Summarize the learning and remind students to make good decisions about book choices.

> Making good decisions about books sometimes means choosing a book that is different from what you normally read or that may be a bit challenging. But, you might surprise yourself by liking it! Sometimes, though, the book might not be a good choice. If that happens, you can abandon it after you give it a good try.

▶ Write the minilesson principle at the top of the chart.

> If you choose a new book to read today, look for one that you'll enjoy and that is just right for you. Be ready to share why you chose your book when we come back together.

## Share

Following independent reading time, gather students together in the meeting area to discuss their reading choices.

> Who chose a new book to read today? Based on what you've read so far, do you think that book was a good choice for you? Why or why not?

## Extend the Lesson (Optional)

After assessing students' understanding, you might decide to extend the learning.

▶ **Writing About Reading** Have students keep a list in a reader's notebook of books they have read and assess whether each book was a good choice for them (see Umbrella 1: Introducing a Reader's Notebook in Section Four: Writing About Reading).

---

### Make good decisions about your book choices.

**Ways to Choose Books**

- Recommendations from others
- Favorite author or illustrator
- Good reviews
- Award winning
- Part of a series that I like
- Interesting title
- Interesting front cover
- Favorite genre
- Loved the movie version
- Topic I am researching
- Difficulty level

## Assessment

After you have taught the minilessons in this umbrella, observe students as they use classroom spaces and materials. Use *The Literacy Continuum* (Fountas and Pinnell 2017) to guide observation of students' reading and writing behaviors.

▶ What evidence do you have of new understandings related to independent reading?

- Are the students able to find and select books?

- Do students read and write independently during independent reading time?

- Are they making good decisions about book choices?

- Do they return books and other materials to where they belong?

- Do they understand that a personal book box is a place for their books and other materials?

- How well do they keep their personal materials organized in their book boxes?

- Do they use terms such as *community, book box, organized,* and *classroom library*?

▶ What other minilessons might you teach to help students grow and function as readers and as members of the classroom community?

- Do students treat each other respectfully and inclusively?

- Do they incorporate reading into their daily lives and make good choices about their reading?

Use your observations to determine the next umbrella you will teach. You may also consult Minilessons Across the Year (pp. 59–61) for guidance.

## Reader's Notebook

When this umbrella is complete, provide a copy of the minilesson principles (see resources.fountasandpinnell.com) for students to glue in the reader's notebook (in the Minilessons section if using *Reader's Notebook: Intermediate* [Fountas and Pinnell 2011]), so they can refer to the information as needed.

## Minilessons in This Umbrella

| RML1 | Find out about good books to read. |
| RML2 | Recommend a book by giving a book talk. |
| RML3 | Learn how to give a good book talk. |
| RML4 | Think about your reading interests and preferences. |
| RML5 | Challenge yourself to grow or stretch as a reader. |
| RML6 | Find time to read outside of school. |

## Before Teaching Umbrella 3 Minilessons

The importance of literacy instruction extends far beyond the classroom. It is not enough to simply teach students the skills to comprehend what they read. Students who love reading, dedicate time to reading, and consider themselves readers have the greatest chance of success in school and beyond. The purpose of this umbrella is to help students develop lifelong reading habits. The minilessons guide students to dedicate time to reading both in school and outside of school, to make good decisions about the books they read, and to develop their identities and preferences as readers. Before teaching this umbrella, provide students with several opportunities to choose, read, enjoy, share, and talk about books. Use the following books from *Fountas & Pinnell Classroom™ Independent Reading Collection* or other books that your students will find interesting and accessible.

### Independent Reading Collection

*Amazon Rainforest* by William B. Rice

*The Thing About Georgie* by Lisa Graff

*Who Was Jackie Robinson?* by Gail Herman

*Helen Keller: A New Vision* by Tamara Leigh Hollingsworth

*A Snicker of Magic* by Natalie Lloyd

**Section 1: Management**

**Reading Minilesson Principle**
# Find out about good books to read.

### You Will Need

▶ chart paper and markers

### Academic Language / Important Vocabulary

▶ resources
▶ recommendation
▶ online reading community

## Goal

Learn resources for finding books inside and outside the classroom.

## Rationale

When students learn about the many resources for finding books, they expand the book choices that they have available to them.

## Assess Learning

Observe students when finding and recommending books and notice if there is evidence of new learning based on the goal of this minilesson.

▶ Are students able to talk about different resources for locating books they want to read?

▶ Do they understand that resources for finding books can be both inside and outside the classroom?

▶ Do they use the terms *resources, recommendation,* and *online reading community*?

## Minilesson

To help students think about the minilesson principle, engage them in generating a list of ways they can find books to read. Here is an example.

▶ Have students sit so they can all see the chart.

> Think about the different ways that you can get ideas for finding a book you want to read. What are some of those ways?

▶ As students share ideas, create a list on chart paper.

> What are some other places in the school that you can find books you might like to read?

▶ Prompt students to be specific, such as a suggested reading shelf that the librarian puts up in the school library. Add ideas to the chart.

> What about outside the school? What are some places you can look to find ideas for books you want to read?

▶ Continue adding students' ideas to the chart, prompting student thinking to keep the conversation going.

## Have a Try

Invite the students to talk with a partner about finding and recommending books.

> Think about the different places you can learn about books. How can you use these ideas to find a book to read? Which sources have you already used? Talk about that with a partner.

## Summarize and Apply

Summarize the learning and remind students to think about places to find and recommend books.

> Today we made a list of different ways to find books.

▶ Write the minilesson principle at the top of the chart paper.

> During independent reading time today, make a list of places you can look to find a book. You can use ideas we talked about in class and add new ideas of your own.

▶ If students are using a reader's notebook, they can make the list in the notebook.

## Share

Following independent reading time, gather students in pairs.

> With a partner, share the list you made about resources for finding books.

## Extend the Lesson (Optional)

After assessing students' understanding, you might decide to extend the learning.

▶ From time to time, ask students to share the resources they have used to find books to read.

▶ Guide students in navigating appropriate online reading communities to find book recommendations.

---

**Find out about good books to read.**

- classroom library
- book talks by the teacher or classmates
- book shelf in classroom with recommendations
- school library
- school librarian's suggestions
- suggestions from friends
- suggestions from family
- public library
- displays by librarians at public library
- bookstore
- staff picks list in bookstore
- list of books that have won special awards
- online reading communities

**Reading Minilesson Principle**
# Recommend a book by giving a book talk.

## Living a Reading Life

### You Will Need

- several books that students have not read yet, such as the following from *Independent Reading Collection*:
  - *Amazon Rainforest* by William B. Rice
  - *The Thing About Georgie* by Lisa Graff
  - *Who Was Jackie Robinson?* by Gail Herman
- chart paper and markers
- book talks for *The Thing About Georgie* and *Who Was Jackie Robinson?*
- To download the following online resources for this lesson, visit **resources.fountasandpinnell.com**: Book Talks 1

### Academic Language / Important Vocabulary

- book talk
- recommend

### Continuum Connection

- Recall important details about setting, problem and resolution, and characters after a story is read (p. 58)
- Present information in ways that engage listeners' attention (p. 338)

## Goal

Learn that a book talk is a short talk about a book (or series of books) and can be a source for finding a book to read.

## Rationale

When students experience book talks, they learn about books they might enjoy reading.

## Assess Learning

Observe students when they discuss book talks, noticing if there is evidence of new learning based on the goal of this minilesson.

- ▶ Do students understand the purpose of a book talk?
- ▶ Do they use the terms *book talk* and *recommend*?

## Minilesson

To help students think about the minilesson principle, engage them in noticing the qualities of a book talk.

- ▶ Show the cover of *Amazon Rainforest*.

  Do you want to take a trip to an amazing place, full of plants and animals that you may have never seen before? Come along to the Amazon rainforest!

- ▶ Show pages 10–11.

  This book has beautiful photographs, such as this picture of a tamarin, and the author shows you where the rainforest is located. Look how enormous it is! If you want to learn lots of interesting facts about the rainforest, read this book, *Amazon Rainforest*, by William B. Rice.

  Turn and talk about my book talk. What did you notice about the information I shared and how it sounded?

- ▶ After time for discussion, ask a few students to share. Using their comments, make a list on chart paper of what to include in a book talk.

- ▶ Give book talks for a fiction book, such as *The Thing About Georgie*, and for a book in a series, such as *Who Was Jackie Robinson?*

  Turn and talk about some things you can listen for to decide if you want to read a book.

- ▶ After time for discussion, use students' suggestions to make a list on chart paper of the different ways a book talk can help them decide what to read.

## Have a Try

Invite the students to discuss book talks with a partner.

> What information will you include when you are giving a book talk? What will you listen for in a book talk to decide what book to read? Turn and talk about those things.

## Summarize and Apply

Summarize the learning and remind students that book talks are one way to find new books to read.

> What information does a book talk include?

> What can you listen for in a book talk? How can listening help you learn about books you might like to read?

▶ Write the minilesson principle at the top of the chart paper.

> Today if you heard about a book from my book talks that you want to read, write the title and author's name on the Books I Want to Read page in your reader's notebook so that you will remember the book. Think about what made you want to read the book and share that when we meet.

## Share

Following independent reading time, gather students together in the meeting area.

> Did anyone choose a book to read from one of today's book talks? Why did you want to read that book?

## Extend the Lesson (Optional)

After assessing students' understanding, you might decide to extend the learning.

▶ If you haven't already, you might introduce the use of a reader's notebook. *Reader's Notebook: Intermediate* (Fountas and Pinnell 2011) has a section called Books to Read, in which students record the titles and authors of books they want to read.

---

### Recommend a book by giving a book talk.

A book talk . . .

- is short
- includes the title and author
- gives some information about the book without giving too much
- gets others interested in the book

Listen for . . .

- topics you might be interested in
- characters that sound interesting
- genres you might enjoy
- plots that sound enjoyable (for example, funny, exciting, scary)

---

## RML3
**MGT.U3.RML3**

Reading Minilesson Principle
# Learn how to give a good book talk.

## Living a Reading Life

### You Will Need

- several books that students have not read yet, such as the following from *Independent Reading Collection:*
  - *Helen Keller: A New Vision* by Tamara Leigh Hollingsworth
  - *A Snicker of Magic* by Natalie Lloyd
- chart paper and markers
- books marked with sticky notes for a book talk
- book talks for *Helen Keller: A New Vision* and *A Snicker of Magic*
- To download the following online resources for this lesson, visit **resources.fountasandpinnell.com**: Book Talks 2

### Academic Language / Important Vocabulary

- book talk
- prepare
- present

### Continuum Connection

- Speak at an appropriate volume (p. 337)
- Present information in ways that engage listeners' attention (p. 338)
- Speak directly to the audience, making eye contact with individuals (p. 338)

## Goal

Prepare and present the book talk confidently, clearly, and enthusiastically.

## Rationale

When students learn to prepare and present an effective book talk, they learn to express opinions about books in a way that gets others interested in reading.

## Assess Learning

Observe students when they prepare and practice book talks and notice if there is evidence of new learning based on the goal of this minilesson.

- ▶ Are students thinking and talking about characteristics of effective book talks?
- ▶ Do they reflect on book talks they have given and try to improve upon them for next time?
- ▶ Do they use the terms *book talk, prepare,* and *present?*

# Minilesson

To help students think about the minilesson principle, engage them in thinking about how to prepare for and present an effective book talk. Here is an example.

- ▶ Prior to this lesson, prepare a book talk on a nonfiction book, such as *Helen Keller: A New Vision,* and a fiction book, such as *A Snicker of Magic,* or use the prepared book talks in the online resources. Make a few sticky notes to remember important ideas and place other sticky notes on a few pages you want to talk about in the book talks.

  As I give two book talks, think about how I prepared and notice how I get you interested in the books.

- ▶ Give the book talks, modeling your use of prepared sticky notes, your organized manner, and other behaviors so students can observe examples of a good book talk and think about how you prepared for them.

- ▶ After you have given the book talks, have a conversation about what students noticed.

  How did I prepare for these book talks?

  What did you notice about how I presented the book talks?

- ▶ Make a two-column graph on chart paper, and label one column *Prepare* and one column *Present.* As students provide ideas, add to the columns. As needed, prompt the conversation to stimulate student thinking.

## Have a Try

Invite students to talk with a partner about preparing for and presenting a book talk.

> Turn and talk about the book you will be using to prepare and present a book talk. Talk about which ideas you will use from the chart.

## Summarize and Apply

Summarize the learning and remind students to use the ideas on the chart when preparing for a book talk.

> How will you prepare to give the book talk?

> What are some things you will remember to do when you present your book talk?

▶ Write the minilesson principle at the top of the chart paper.

> During independent reading time, prepare for and practice presenting a book talk. Bring your book when we meet so you can practice with a small group.

## Share

Following independent reading time, gather students in the meeting area.

> Who would like to present the book talk you prepared?

## Extend the Lesson (Optional)

After assessing students' understanding, you might decide to extend the learning.

▶ Create a schedule for students to sign up to give book talks throughout the year. The time can be scheduled at the beginning of readers' workshop.

| Learn how to give a good book talk. | |
|---|---|
| **Prepare** | **Present** |
| • Practice holding the book so people can see it. | • Look at audience. |
| • Plan a captivating lead and closing. | • Tell the title and author. |
| • Use sticky notes to write important words or phrases. | • Speak clearly. |
| • Mark places in the book to talk about with sticky notes. | • Use enthusiastic voice. |
| • Think about why people should read the book. | • Use good volume. |
| • Think about what will make others excited to read the book. | • Give reasons why people should read the book. |
| | • Tell just a little but not too much. |
| | • Keep it short. |

**Living a Reading Life**

## You Will Need

- chart paper and markers

## Academic Language / Important Vocabulary

- interest
- preference
- author
- series
- genre

### Continuum Connection

- Express tastes and preferences in reading and support choices with descriptions and examples of literary elements: e.g., genre, setting, plot, theme, character, style and language (pp. 528, 539, 548)

## Goal

Develop reading interests and preferences.

## Rationale

When students develop an understanding of their reading interests and preferences, they are better equipped to choose books that align with those preferences. They are more likely to enjoy what they read and therefore to become lifelong readers. When you understand your students' reading interests and preferences, you can make book recommendations to them.

## Assess Learning

Observe students when they talk about their reading interests and preferences and notice if there is evidence of new learning based on the goal of this minilesson.

- Can students talk confidently about their reading interests and preferences?
- Can they explain why they prefer certain authors or types of books?
- Do they use their reading interests and preferences to help them select books to read?
- Do they use the terms *interest, preference, author, series,* and *genre*?

## Minilesson

To help students think about the minilesson principle, engage them in a discussion about their reading interests and preferences. Here is an example.

> Every reader has personal reading interests and preferences. A preference is something that you like more than something else. For example, I have a preference for realistic fiction books over fantasy books. Does anyone else have a preference for a certain genre or type of book?

- As students discuss their reading preferences, record each one mentioned on chart paper along with the name of the student who suggested it.

> You might also have a preference for a certain author. Who has a favorite author?

- Again, record students' responses on the chart paper.

> Does anyone have a preference for reading books in a series? Why do you like reading a series of books?
>
> What series do you like in particular?

- Continue recording students' responses.

## Have a Try

Invite the students to talk with a partner about their reading preferences.

> Turn and talk to your partner about whether you prefer fiction or nonfiction. Be sure to explain the reasons for your choice.

▶ After students turn and talk, invite a few students to share their thinking. Record their responses on the chart.

## Summarize and Apply

Summarize the learning and remind students to think about their reading interests and preferences.

> Today we talked about reading interests and preferences. What is a reading preference?

> Why do you think it's important to know your own reading interests and preferences?

▶ Write the minilesson principle at the top of the chart.

> Today during independent reading time, spend some time thinking about yourself as a reader. Think about your reading interests and preferences. Write a few sentences in your reader's notebook about the kind of books you like to read and why. Be ready to share your thinking when we come back together.

▶ If students are not (or not yet) using a reader's notebook, have them write on plain paper.

## Share

Following independent reading time, gather students together in pairs to discuss their reading interests and preferences.

> Turn and talk to your partner about what you like to read. After the two of you have shared, turn and talk to another set of partners.

## Extend the Lesson (Optional)

After assessing students' understanding, you might decide to extend the learning.

▶ Use your knowledge of your students' reading interests and preferences to recommend books to them. Recommend books that are in line with their interests but that will also help them stretch and grow as readers. For example, if you know that one of your students often reads stories about aliens but rarely reads nonfiction, you might recommend a nonfiction book about outer space.

---

**Think about your reading interests and preferences.**

### Our Reading Preferences

**Genre**
- realistic fiction – Emma, Joy, Isaiah, Trinity
- fantasy – Logan, Ava, Alex, Isaiah, Silas,
- science fiction – Joy, Conner, Silas, Adnon

**Author**
- Roald Dahl – Zoey, Joy, Isaiah, Aaliyah
- Sharon Creech – Joshua, Adnon, Emma

**Series**
- Chet Gecko Mysteries – Noah, Trinity, Davie, Aaliyah
- Wayside School books – Emma, Silas, Catrina, Isabella, Maria
- Who Was (biography series) – Conner, Davie, Emma, Ava, Alex, Hunter, Carlos

**Fiction or Nonfiction**
- fiction – Isabella, Jacob, Carlos
- nonfiction – Maria, Aaliyah, Hunter

---

Section 1: Management

## RML 5
### MGT.U3.RML5

**Reading Minilesson Principle**
## Challenge yourself to grow or stretch as a reader.

**You Will Need**

- chart paper and markers
- reader's notebook

**Academic Language / Important Vocabulary**

- reading plan
- goal
- challenge

## Goal

Make reading plans and goals to stretch and grow as a reader.

## Rationale

When students make plans for their reading, they are more likely to maintain their reading habits and develop their competencies and identities as readers. Examples of reading plans include reading more books, spending more time reading at home, reading more challenging books, reading different genres of books, reading other authors, reading on a topic, reading a series, etc. As part of their reading plans, students should set specific goals, such as reading a certain number of books or reading daily for a certain length of time.

## Assess Learning

Observe students when they set, work toward, and discuss their reading plans and notice if there is evidence of new learning based on the goal of this minilesson.

- ▶ Do students carry out their reading plans?
- ▶ Do they stay committed to their reading plans? If not, do they reflect on the reasons and adjust their reading plans as appropriate?
- ▶ Do they use the terms *reading plan, goal,* and *challenge*?

## Minilesson

To help students think about the minilesson principle, engage them in a discussion about their reading plans and goals. Here is an example.

> There are so many wonderful books that it can be hard to decide what to read next. One thing that I like to do is to keep a list of all the books that I want to read. When I finish a book on my list, I cross it off and choose another one. Does anyone else keep a list of books you'd like to read?

> Making sure that you have a list of books to read next is part of a plan to help yourself grow as a reader. You might make a reading plan to read more often or to stretch your reading interests. A reading plan has specific goals, such as how many books to read or exactly which books to read, that help you carry out your plan. What goals can you set to grow yourself as a reader?

- ▶ Record students' responses on chart paper. Prompt the conversation as needed. Some suggestions are below.

  - *If I feel that I don't read enough at home, what goal could I set that would help change this?*

  - *If I only read fantasy books, what goal could help me read different genres of books?*

  - *If the books I read are too easy for me and I'm getting bored with them, what reading goal could I set for myself?*

## Have a Try

Invite the students to talk with a partner about the book they would like to read next.

> Turn and talk to your partner about one book or type of book that you would like to read soon. Check the Books to Read and Reading Requirements pages in your reader's notebook for ideas.

▷ After students turn and talk, invite a few students to share their thinking.

## Summarize and Apply

Summarize the learning and remind students to always have goals for challenging themselves as readers.

> Having some reading goals will help you grow and learn more as a reader. It will also help keep your reading exciting because you will always have something to look forward to in your reading future!

▷ Write the minilesson principle at the top of the chart.

> Today during independent reading time, I would like you to take about ten minutes to think about how you are going to challenge yourself to grow or stretch as a reader this year. What goals would you like to set for yourself? In your reader's notebook, write at least one way that you are going to challenge yourself this year.

▷ If students are not (or not yet) using a reader's notebook, have them write on plain paper.

## Share

Following independent reading time, gather students together in the meeting area to discuss their reading goals.

> Who made some goals for yourself that you would like to share?

## Extend the Lesson (Optional)

After assessing students' understanding, you might decide to extend the learning.

▷ During individual reading conferences with students, help them set personalized reading goals. Meet regularly to help them reflect on their progress and adapt their goals as needed.

---

### Challenge yourself to grow or stretch as a reader.

Examples of reading goals:

- Read The Witches by Roald Dahl next.
- Read more nonfiction books.
- Read 100 books this year.
- Read for 30 minutes every night.
- Read 5 books that are more challenging than those I normally read.
- Read all the books in the Magic Tree House series.
- Read 10 books of poetry this year.

Section 1: Management

**Reading Minilesson Principle**
# Find time to read outside of school.

## Living a Reading Life

### You Will Need

- chart paper and markers
- reader's notebook or writing paper

### Academic Language / Important Vocabulary

- classroom library
- independent reading
- reader's notebook

## Goal

Find more time to read outside of school.

## Rationale

Students who spend time reading outside of school on a regular basis do better in school and are more likely to love reading and become lifelong readers. Many people, both adults and children, find it hard to make the time to read, and this minilesson offers suggestions for carving out more time to read.

## Assess Learning

Observe students when they talk about their reading habits and notice if there is evidence of new learning based on the goal of this minilesson.

- Do students report that they read outside of school on a regular basis?
- Do they talk about the books that they have read outside of school?
- Do they use the terms *classroom library, independent reading,* and *reader's notebook*?

## Minilesson

To help students think about the minilesson principle, engage them in a discussion about reading outside of school. Here is an example.

> We've been talking a lot lately about all the wonderful books we have in our classroom library and the time that you get to spend reading during the school day. Reading at school is great, but school is not the only place for reading! The more you read the better reader you will become and you will enjoy it more and learn more.

> Does anyone have a special place at home or another place where you like to read? Why do you like that place?

> I like to read for a while every night before going to sleep. Outside of school, what time of the day is your favorite time to read?

- Record students' responses on chart paper.

> Sometimes I find it hard to find enough time to read. Raise your hand if you wish you had more time to read outside of school.

> One way that I've found to have more time to read is to bring a book with me everywhere I go! For example, when I have a dentist appointment, I read my book in the waiting room.

> If you always have a book with you, you can spend a few minutes reading whenever you have a little bit of spare time. Does anyone else have a tip for finding time to read that you would like to share?

## Have a Try

Invite the students to talk in pairs about their reading habits.

> Is finding time to read outside of school easy or hard for you? Why? Turn and talk to your partner about this question.

▶ After students turn and talk, invite several students to share their thinking. If some students express obstacles to reading, collectively brainstorm ways to overcome them.

## Summarize and Apply

Summarize the learning and remind students to dedicate time to reading outside of school.

> Today we talked about finding places and time to read. You can read just about anywhere you are comfortable and you can see. What are some of the ways we talked about?

▶ Write the principle at the top of the chart.

> Today during independent reading time, take about ten minutes to write in your reader's notebook about your reading time outside of school. You might write about your favorite time and place to read at home. You may also write about ways that you could find time to read more.

▶ If students are not (or not yet) using a reader's notebook, have them write on plain paper.

## Share

Following independent reading time, gather students together in the meeting area to discuss their plans for reading at home more.

> Who thought about ways to find more time to read outside of school?

> What ideas do you have for how you could find more time to read?

## Extend the Lesson (Optional)

After assessing students' understanding, you might decide to extend the learning.

▶ Make casual conversations with students about the books they read outside of school part of the classroom culture.

▶ During individual reading conferences with students, discuss their reading habits outside of school and, if applicable, make a plan for overcoming obstacles to reading at home.

---

### Find time to read outside of school.

| Where? | When? |
|---|---|
| • "in my room" – Alex | • "before bedtime" – Maya |
| • "in the car" – Brooklyn | • "as soon as I wake up" – Eli |
| • "on the sofa in the living room" – Gabriel | • "when I'm waiting for dinner to be ready" – Kaylee |
| • "at my grandma's" – Sunil | |

Section 1: Management

## Assessment

After you have taught the minilessons in this umbrella, observe students when they give book talks and when they talk about their reading plans and preferences.

▶ What evidence do you have of new understandings related to living a reading life?

- Do students take steps to find out what books they want to read?
- Do students recommend books to classmates?
- Are students learning how to give good book talks?
- Do they sometimes choose books that challenge them or that vary from their usual reading choices?
- Can they make reading plans that help them stretch and grow as readers?
- What is their understanding of their own reading interests and preferences?
- Do they view themselves as readers?
- Are they spending time reading outside of school?
- Do they use terms such as *classroom library, independent reading, choice, preferences,* and *decision* when they talk about living a reading life?

▶ What other minilessons might you teach to maintain and grow independent reading habits?

- Do students know how to find books that interest them in your classroom library?
- Do they keep their personal literacy materials organized?

Use your observations to determine the next umbrella you will teach. You may also consult Minilessons Across the Year (pp. 59–61) for guidance.

## Reader's Notebook

When this umbrella is complete, provide a copy of the minilesson principles (see resources.fountasandpinnell.com) for students to glue in the reader's notebook (in the Minilessons section if using *Reader's Notebook: Intermediate* [Fountas and Pinnell 2011]), so they can refer to the information as needed.

# Section 2 | Literary Analysis

Literary Analysis minilessons support students' growing awareness of the elements of literature and the writer's and illustrator's craft. The minilessons help students learn how to think analytically about texts and to identify the characteristics of fiction and nonfiction genres. The books that you read during interactive read-aloud can serve as mentor texts when applying the principles of literary analysis.

# 2 Literary Analysis

## Minilessons in This Umbrella

**RML1**  Choose a book you would like to read and talk about.

**RML2**  Mark places you want to talk about.

**RML3**  Talk about your thinking in book clubs.

**RML4**  Ask questions to clarify understanding.

**RML5**  Give directions to help everyone get to a specific place in the book quickly.

## Before Teaching Umbrella 1 Minilessons

The minilessons in this umbrella are designed to help you introduce and teach procedures and routines to establish book clubs in your classroom. Book clubs (pp. 72–74) are meetings facilitated by the teacher with about six students of varying reading abilities who come together to discuss a common text. The goal is for students to share their thinking with each other and build a richer meaning than one reader could gain alone. You may want to conduct a fishbowl lesson to demonstrate how a book club discussion works, either before selected minilessons as a model or afterward as a reflection. This umbrella will take students through the first set in the book club collection. Based on RML1, students will choose a book club book. Then, after each lesson, you can meet with a different book club. The minilessons in this umbrella use the following books from the *Fountas and Pinnell Classroom™ Book Clubs Collection* and *Interactive Read-Aloud Collection* text sets; however, you can use other book sets from your classroom. Refer to the *Book Clubs Collection* cards for book summaries to use for book talks and additional discussion ideas.

### Book Clubs Collection

#### Friendship

*The Mystery of Meerkat Hill* by Alexander McCall Smith

*The Midnight War of Mateo Martinez* by Robin Yardi

*Click* by Kayla Miller

*A Boy Called Bat* by Elana K. Arnold

### Interactive Read-Aloud Collection

#### Friendship

*The Other Side* by Jacqueline Woodson

**Book Clubs**
**Friendship**

*Interactive Read-Aloud*
**Friendship**

Section 2: Literary Analysis

# RML1
## LA.U1.RML1

## Choose a book you would like to read and talk about.

### Getting Started with Book Clubs

### You Will Need

- prepared book talks for four books students have not read or heard, such as the following from the *Book Clubs Collection:* Text Set: Friendship:
  - *The Mystery of Meerkat Hill* by Alexander McCall Smith
  - *The Midnight War of Mateo Martinez* by Robin Yardi
  - *Click* by Kayla Miller
  - *A Boy Called Bat* by Elana K. Arnold
- chart paper and markers
- sticky notes
- a slip of paper for each student that has the four book club titles written on it
- To download the following online resources for this lesson, visit **resources.fountasandpinnell.com**: Book Talks 3

### Academic Language / Important Vocabulary

- book club
- title
- author
- illustrator
- choice
- preference

### Continuum Connection

- Form and express opinions about a text and support with rationale and evidence [pp. 58, 62]

### Goal

Learn how to make a good book choice for book club meetings.

### Rationale

When students make their own choices about what to read, they are more engaged and motivated to read. This contributes to a positive book club experience and increases the possibility for a lifelong love of reading.

### Assess Learning

Observe students when they choose books for book club meetings and notice if there is evidence of new learning based on the goal of this minilesson.

- Are students able to identify information that will help them select a book they want to read?
- Do they express and reflect on the reasons they choose particular books to read?
- Do they use the terms *book club, title, author, illustrator, choice,* and *preference*?

## Minilesson

To help students think about the minilesson principle, demonstrate the process of choosing a book for a book club meeting. Here is an example.

> Think about your interest in each of these four books as I tell you a little about them.

- Show the cover of *The Mystery of Meerkat Hill.*

  > When a family cow disappears, aspiring detective Precious is on the case. Her interest in the lives of others and her question-asking abilities are useful in her detective work, but this time, she will need some extra help. See how Precious and new students Teb and Pontsho look for clues in this missing cow mystery.

- Turn through a few pages.

  > Do you think you would like to read about this clever detective, Precious Ramotswe? Why?

- Continue giving short book talks for the other three books (use your own book talks or the prepared book talks in online resources).

  > You have now listened to a book talk about four different books. Think about which ones you would enjoy reading.

## Have a Try

Invite the students to talk with a partner about which book interests them.

> Turn and talk to a partner about your first and second choices.

> After time for discussion, ask students to share their thinking.

## Summarize and Apply

Summarize the learning for students.

> We talked about different reasons you might choose a book for your book club meeting.

> During independent reading today, fill out the slip of paper to show your preferences for a book club book. Number the books in the order you want to read them. Number one will be your first choice. Be sure to put your name on the paper.

> While students are reading, collect the numbered slips of paper and create four book clubs. Make a chart to show when each club will meet.

## Share

Following independent reading time, gather students in the meeting area.

> This chart shows which group you will be in for the first book club of the year. It also shows when your book club will meet. Right now, turn and talk to a partner about what you think you will enjoy about the book.

## Extend the Lesson (Optional)

After assessing students' understanding, you might decide to extend the learning.

> After the first round of book club meetings, use the same set of books for a second round of book club meetings, asking students to choose a different book this time. Use the opportunity to explain that not everyone will get to read their first choice every time.

**Book Club Groups**

**Monday**
Yasmin
Angel
Nicole
Joshua
Roman
Jake

**Tuesday**
Diego
Carlos
Olivia
Michael M.
Alex
Iris

**Wednesday**
Ameelah
Grace
Liam
Oliver
Sophia
Michael R.

**Thursday**
Charlotte
Mia
Lakeesha
Madison
Ava
Daniel

Section 2: Literary Analysis

# RML2
## LA.U1.RML2

Reading Minilesson Principle
## Mark places you want to talk about.

## Getting Started with Book Clubs

### You Will Need

- a familiar book, such as the following:
  - *The Other Side* by Jacqueline Woodson, from *Interactive Read-Aloud Collection* Text Set: Friendship
- chart paper and markers
- prepared sticky notes containing page numbers from the book and a few words indicating discussion topics, placed on corresponding pages in *The Other Side*
- document camera (optional)
- set of book club books

### Academic Language / Important Vocabulary

- book club
- sticky notes

### Continuum Connection

- Form and express opinions about a text and support with rationale and evidence (pp. 58, 62)

## Goal

Identify the important information to discuss in preparation for a book club.

## Rationale

When students learn to note parts of a book they want to discuss, they think critically about the book and develop a process for preparing for a discussion.

## Assess Learning

Observe students when they discuss characters and notice if there is evidence of new learning based on the goal of this minilesson.

- Do students understand the purpose of noting pages in a book?
- Are they able to identify and mark relevant pages in a book to prepare for a book club meeting?
- Do they understand the terms *book club* and *sticky notes*?

## Minilesson

To help students think about the minilesson principle, use a familiar book to model how to prepare for a book club meeting by marking pages with sticky notes. Here is an example.

- Show the cover of *The Other Side* with the sticky notes showing.

  Imagine that this book you know, *The Other Side*, is the book I am reading for book club. While I was reading the book, I thought of some things I'd like to talk about in a book club meeting.

- Show page 2 with the first sticky note.

  On page 2, I placed a sticky note on which I wrote *Page 2: the fence.* I wrote this note to remember to talk about how the fence is an important symbol in the book. The note helps me remember the page and what I want to talk about on the page.

- Place the sticky note on the left side of chart paper. On the right side of the chart, start a list of reasons to mark a page. Write *symbols* to show that this is the information that the sticky note is helping you remember.

- Continue discussing the other sticky notes in the book, placing them on the chart, and adding terms on the right side of the chart to remind students of the types of items that can be noted.

## Have a Try

Invite the students to talk with a partner about using sticky notes to prepare for book club meetings.

> Turn and talk about what kind of information a sticky note can help you remember in a book.

▶ After time for discussion, ask students to share ideas. Add new ideas to the chart list.

## Summarize and Apply

Summarize the learning and remind students to use sticky notes to prepare for book club discussions.

> What did you learn about preparing for a book club discussion?

▶ Add the principle to the top of the chart.

> When you read today, use a few sticky notes to prepare for your book club meeting. Remember to add the page number in case the sticky note falls off. Write just a few words on the note, like the examples you see on the chart. Bring the book when we meet so you can share.

▶ Meet with one of the book club groups.

## Share

Following independent reading time, gather students in pairs.

> Share the pages that you marked with a sticky note. Tell your partner why you wanted to remember that page.

## Extend the Lesson (Optional)

After assessing students' understanding, you might decide to extend the learning.

▶ As an alternative to using sticky notes, teach the students how to use a Thinkmark. Students may fill in a Thinkmark for books they read and want to talk about in a book club or a conference. (Visit resources.fountasandpinnell.com to download a Thinkmark.)

---

**Mark places you want to talk about.**

| | |
|---|---|
| Page 2 the fence | • symbols |
| | • details in illustrations |
| Page 4 girls far away from each other | • questions |
| | • message |
| | • theme |
| Page 8 Why do girls seem different from moms? | • interesting parts |
| | • character change |
| | • turning point |
| Page 16 smiles | • author's craft |
| | • word choice or language |

Section 2: Literary Analysis

# RML3
## LA.U1.RML3

### Reading Minilesson Principle
### Talk about your thinking in book clubs.

## Getting Started with Book Clubs

### You Will Need

- students' book club books
- a book that you are reading yourself
- chart paper and markers

### Academic Language / Important Vocabulary

- author
- illustrator
- book club
- discussion

### Continuum Connection

- Use evidence from the text to support a wide range of predictions (pp. 58, 62)
- Form and express opinions about a text and support with rationale and evidence (pp. 58, 62)
- Express opinions and support arguments with evidence (p. 337)

### Goal

Learn how to identify different ways of talking about books during book club.

### Rationale

When students learn to share ideas in a book club, it expands comprehension, creates enthusiasm for reading, and contributes to a rich conversation. You may wish to have one group of students model how to hold a book club by staging a fishbowl discussion (p. 74).

### Assess Learning

Observe students when they meet for book club and notice if there is evidence of new learning based on the goal of this minilesson.

- Are students expressing opinions about books?
- Are they trying out new ways to talk about books?
- Do they use the terms *author, illustrator, book club,* and *discussion*?

## Minilesson

To help students think about the minilesson principle, help them think about what they might want to talk about in book club. Here is an example.

- Show a book that you are reading yourself.

    Here is the book that I am reading. I really enjoy the characters and the setting. If I meet with other friends who are reading this book, what do you think I might talk about?

- Create a chart to write ideas about what to talk about in book club. Add the ideas you shared.

    Think about the book you have been reading for your book club. What are some of the things you find interesting to talk about in book club about the book?

- As students share ideas, add to the list. Prompt the conversation as needed.

## Have a Try

Invite the students to talk with a partner about book club discussion ideas.

> Turn and talk about the book you are reading for your book club. What types of things would you like to talk about with your book club members?

▶ After time for discussion, ask students to share. Add new ideas to the chart.

## Summarize and Apply

Summarize the learning and remind students to think about what they might talk about in book club meetings.

> Today you talked about a range of topics you might discuss in book club meetings.

> As you read your book club book today, think about what you would like to talk about with your classmates. I will be meeting with one book club, and those students will be sharing about their book during our class meeting.

▶ Meet with one of the book club groups.

## Share

Following independent reading time, gather students in the meeting area. Have the book club members you met with share the things they discussed in their book club. Then, invite the class to talk about new ideas.

> Is there anything that you want to add to the chart based on what the book club members shared with you?

## Extend the Lesson (Optional)

After assessing students' understanding, you might decide to extend the learning.

▶ **Writing About Reading** Have students glue a list of items they can reflect on into a reader's notebook as a reference for thinking and writing about books. (Visit resources.fountasandpinnell.com for a copy of the list of items from this lesson. )

### Talk about your thinking in book clubs.

- characters' behaviors and thoughts
- the setting
- the topic
- the title
- the author
- the illustrator
- dialogue
- the plot

- the high point
- flashbacks
- an illustration
- a part that is interesting, funny, confusing, exciting, or surprising
- the genre
- words or phrases that you like
- symbolism
- predictions

I noticed that the author ...

**Section 2: Literary Analysis**

**Reading Minilesson Principle**
## Ask questions to clarify understanding.

### You Will Need

- four students who are prepared to share questions they might raise in a book club meeting
- the book club selection that students will be sharing, such as the following:
  - *A Boy Called Bat* by Elana K. Arnold, from the *Book Clubs Collection:* Text Set: Friendship
- students' book club selections
- sticky notes
- chart paper and markers

### Academic Language / Important Vocabulary

- book club
- questions
- phrase
- clarify

### Continuum Connection

- Ask questions for clarification or to gain information [p. 337]

## Goal

Learn how to ask genuine questions to clarify understandings about the book and about one another's thinking.

## Rationale

When students learn to ask questions to clarify understanding, they learn how to engage in rich conversations about books and learn to converse with each other to understand what others are thinking.

## Assess Learning

Observe students during book club meetings and notice if there is evidence of new learning based on the goal of this minilesson.

- Are students asking relevant, thoughtful questions during book club meetings?
- Are they making comments and posing questions to each other?
- Do they understand why questions are an important part of book club discussions?
- Do they understand the terms *book club, questions, phrase,* and *clarify*?

## Minilesson

To help students think about the minilesson principle, engage them in a discussion about how to ask questions to clarify their classmates' understanding and interpretation of a book. Here is an example.

- Have students who will be sharing questions write each of their questions about the book on a separate sticky note.
- Gather students in the meeting area so they can all view the chart.

  Today, several book club members are going to share the questions they prepared for their book club selection.

- Have the book club members read their questions aloud one at a time, and as they do, add the sticky note with the question on the left side of the chart.

  What do you notice about the book club members' questions?

  These are some interesting questions to help everyone understand the book better. Book club members will have a lot to talk about from these questions.

## Have a Try

Invite the students to talk in small groups about questions they could ask during book club meetings.

> Turn and talk about any questions, confusions, or wonderings you have about your book.

▶ After time for discussion, ask students to share what they talked about with their partners. Write their responses in a generalized way on the right side of the chart.

## Summarize and Apply

Summarize the learning and remind students to think about questions they want to ask during book club meetings.

> As you were sharing your questions, I wrote some of the ways you were starting your questions. Can you think of any other ways you might ask each other questions to try to clarify an understanding about the book or about the discussion?

▶ Add the principle to the top of the chart. Add any new ideas to the right side of the chart.

> If you are reading your book club selection today and you get confused or wonder about something, write it on a sticky note to bring to your book club meeting. If you are meeting with me today for book club, bring any questions you have about the book so we can talk about them and you can understand the book better.

▶ Meet with one of the book club groups.

## Share

Following independent reading time, gather students in the meeting area. Ask the students who met in book club to talk about whether they had any questions answered in book club today.

> Why is book club a good place to talk about questions you might have?

▶ Guide the conversation so students understand the value of getting multiple perspectives.

## Extend the Lesson (Optional)

After assessing students' understanding, you might decide to extend the learning.

▶ Introduce higher-level questions as students become more proficient with asking questions during book club. If you have *Fountas & Pinnell Prompting Guide, Part 2, for Comprehension: Thinking, Talking, and Writing* (Fountas and Pinnell 2009), refer to Section IV: Prompts for Book Discussions.

### Ask questions to clarify understanding.

| Book Club Questions from <u>A Boy Called Bat</u> | What You Can Say or Ask in Book Club |
|---|---|
| "Why does it seem like Bat's mom cares more about the animals than about him?" | Did anyone else wonder about_____? <br><br> Why do you think ____? <br><br> I didn't understand _____. |
| "Could someone really have a skunk for a pet?" | What was interesting to you about_____? <br><br> Why did the writer ____? |
| "Isn't the nickname <u>Bat</u> kind of mean, since it came from kids making fun of him?" | Can you say more about that? <br><br> Do you agree that____? |

**Reading Minilesson Principle**

# Give directions to help everyone get to a specific place in the book quickly.

## You Will Need

- chart paper prepared with a sketch of an open book or a book and document camera
- markers
- students' book club books

## Academic Language / Important Vocabulary

- directions
- exact place
- line
- paragraph
- caption
- panel

## Goal

Understand how to give directions for everyone to locate the same section of a text.

## Rationale

When students learn to use precise language to ensure that everyone can locate the same section of a text, they improve their conversational skills and their ability to talk about books with specific evidence.

## Assess Learning

Observe students when they talk about books to notice evidence of new learning based on the goal of this minilesson.

- Can students follow and use specific language to identify sections of a text?
- Do they use the terms *directions*, *exact place*, *line*, *paragraph*, *caption*, and *panel*?

## Minilesson

To help students think about the minilesson principle, help them practice using directional language to ensure they can locate a specific place in a book quickly. Here is an example.

- Display the prepared chart or use a document camera to project the pages of a book. (If you use a book and document camera, make a list of the specific language on chart paper.)

  Today we are going to talk about how you can get everyone to a specific place in the book you are talking about.

- Point to page 2.

  If I want to talk about this specific part or page, how can I tell you the exact place?

- Write the label *page 2* on the sketch.
- Point to the third sentence.

  How can I tell you how to find this exact place?

- Add a label based on students' responses.
- Repeat the activity with pages that show other features (e.g., words, paragraphs, captions, graphic panels) and ask students to talk about words they could use to help others locate that feature. Add ideas to the chart.

## Have a Try

Invite the students to talk with a partner about ways to help others find an exact place in a book.

▸ Have students work with a partner from their book club. Each person in the group should have a copy of the same book.

  Practice using directions to help each other find a specific place in your book.

▸ After time for discussion, ask students to share directional words they used. Add new ideas to the chart.

## Summarize and Apply

Summarize the learning and remind students to think about how to be sure that everyone is in the exact place during book club meetings.

  What did you learn today about how to help your peers get to the specific place you want to talk about quickly?

▸ Add the principle to the top of the chart.

  During book club, use words to make sure everyone is at the specific place in the book. I will meet with a book club today and they will be able to try this out. Then they will share what they noticed when we meet for our class meeting.

▸ Meet with a book club group.

## Share

Following independent reading time, gather students in the meeting area. Ask the group that met in book club to share.

  What words did you use to make sure everyone was in the specific place when you talked about the book?

▸ Add new ideas to the chart.

## Extend the Lesson (Optional)

After assessing students' understanding, you might decide to extend the learning.

▸ **Writing About Reading** Have students glue a book club reflection chart into a reader's notebook that they can use to think and write more about their experiences in book clubs. (Visit resources.fountasandpinnell.com to download the resource Thinking About Our Book Club Discussion.)

Give directions to help everyone get to a specific place in the book quickly.

second paragraph on page 2

last word in the first sentence

first sentence on page 3

third line from the bottom

caption on page 3

page 2

Poem: third line of the poem

Graphic text: second panel in the bottom row

Section 2: Literary Analysis

## Assessment

After you have taught the minilessons in this umbrella, observe students as they talk and write about their reading across instructional contexts: interactive read-aloud, independent reading, guided reading, shared reading, and book club. Use *The Literacy Continuum* (Fountas and Pinnell 2017) to observe students' reading and writing behaviors.

▶ What evidence do you have of new understandings related to the way students engage with book clubs?

  • Are students able to choose an appropriate book for book club and explain why they chose it?

  • Do they mark the pages and make a note about what they want to talk about?

  • Can they articulate their thinking in book clubs?

  • Are they asking questions to clarify understanding?

  • Do they use clear directions to make sure everyone is at the same place in the book they are discussing?

  • Do they understand terms such as *book club, choice, clarify,* and *discussion*?

▶ In what other ways, beyond the scope of this umbrella, are students talking about books?

  • Are students showing an interest in specific authors or illustrators?

  • Do they notice elements of an author's craft?

Use your observations to determine the next umbrella you will teach. You may also consult Minilessons Across the Year (pp. 59–61) for guidance.

## Link to Writing

After teaching the minilessons in this umbrella, help students link the new learning to their own writing:

▶ Encourage students to write book reviews and recommendations that can be displayed in the classroom and used by others when choosing books.

## Reader's Notebook

When this umbrella is complete, provide a copy of the minilesson principles (see resources.fountasandpinnell.com) for students to glue in the reader's notebook (in the Minilessons section if using *Reader's Notebook: Intermediate* [Fountas and Pinnell 2011]), so they can refer to the information as needed.

## Minilessons in This Umbrella

| | |
|---|---|
| **RML1** | Be a strong listener and a strong speaker. |
| **RML2** | Recognize appropriate times to take a turn. |
| **RML3** | Monitor your participation and encourage others to participate. |
| **RML4** | Invite each other to provide evidence. |
| **RML5** | Value and encourage diverse perspectives. |
| **RML6** | Add on to important ideas to extend the thinking of the group. |
| **RML7** | Change the topic or refocus the discussion as needed. |
| **RML8** | Reflect on and evaluate your book club discussion. |

## Before Teaching Umbrella 2 Minilessons

Once students have begun to participate in book club meetings, you can teach these minilessons to help them learn conversational moves that will improve the quality of the discussions. During book clubs, the teacher plays a key role in facilitating the group to assure new levels of understanding, so even if students are taught to start the discussion, you are still part of the group to lift the conversation as needed. These lessons take students through one set of book club meetings, and Umbrella 1: Getting Started with Book Clubs does this also.

Several lessons suggest doing a fishbowl observation (p. 74) in which you prepare one group to model a book club discussion while the rest of the class observes.

For additional prompts and to learn more, please see *Fountas & Pinnell Prompting Guide, Part 2, for Comprehension: Thinking, Talking, Writing* (Fountas and Pinnell 2009, Section IV: Prompts for Book Discussions, pp. 61–78), as this umbrella reflects some of the language from those sections. To start the discussion, a few language prompts are suggested below.

- *Who wants to get us started?*
- *What does this book make you wonder about?*
- *What is important about this story (or book)?*
- *Let's think together about _____.*
- *Turn and talk to your neighbor and share your first thoughts about this book.*

**Reading Minilesson Principle**

# Be a strong listener and a strong speaker.

## Learning Conversational Moves in Book Club

### You Will Need

- chart paper prepared with two columns: *Strong Listener, Strong Speaker*
- markers
- students' book club books

### Academic Language / Important Vocabulary

- book club
- listener
- speaker

### Continuum Connection

- Actively participate in conversation by listening and looking at the person speaking (p. 337)
- Refrain from speaking over others (p. 337)
- Use conventions of respectful conversation (p. 337)
- Listen to and speak to a partner about a given idea, and make a connection to the partner's idea (p. 337)

## Goal

Understand the verbal and nonverbal ways to demonstrate committed listening and strong, clear speaking skills.

## Rationale

When students think about what it means to be a strong listener and a strong speaker during a book club meeting, they learn to attend to their interactions with other classmates, notice what messages their body language is sending, and learn more about the text through balanced, rich discussions. This lays the foundation for becoming a good communicator and an engaged member of the class.

## Assess Learning

Observe students when they communicate with classmates and notice if there is evidence of new learning based on the goal of this minilesson.

- Do students actively listen to their classmates by making eye contact and turning their bodies toward the speaker?
- Do they speak at an appropriate level, refrain from speaking over others, and take turns talking?
- Do they use the terms *book club, listener,* and *speaker*?

## Minilesson

To help students think about the minilesson principle, help them notice verbal and nonverbal cues and the kind of behaviors they might demonstrate as strong listeners and speakers. Here is an example.

- Before teaching this lesson, conduct a fishbowl demonstration (p. 74) of one book club holding its book club meeting.
- Ask students to reflect on what they noticed about the conversations during the fishbowl demonstration.

  What does it look like to be a strong listener?

  What does it sound like?

- Prompt students' thinking by asking about where their eyes are looking, how their bodies are positioned, or how they might respond when they are the listener. Record students' responses on chart paper.

  What does it look like to be a strong speaker?

  What does it sound like?

- Prompt students' thinking by asking about what they are doing and how their voices sound when they are the speaker. Record responses on the chart.

## Have a Try

Invite the students to talk in a small group and demonstrate what it means to be a strong listener and speaker.

> Talk in your group about the book club book you are reading. When you listen, show what it looks like and sounds like to be a strong listener. When you speak, show what it looks like and sounds like to be a strong speaker. Take turns being the speaker in the group while the other two listen.

▶ After time for discussion, ask students to share what they noticed. Add new ideas to the chart.

## Summarize and Apply

Summarize the learning and remind students to be a strong listener and a strong speaker during book club meetings.

> You learned some ways to be a strong listener and a strong speaker during book club.

▶ Add the principle to the top of the chart.

> Today I will meet with one book club group. Later when we all meet to share, I will ask the book club members to share what they noticed about listening and speaking.

## Share

Following independent reading time, gather students in the meeting area. Ask the group that met in book club to share.

> What did you notice about listening and speaking when you met in book club today?

▶ After book club members respond, ask the whole group to reflect.

> Why is it important to be a strong listener and speaker?

## Extend the Lesson (Optional)

After assessing students' understanding, you might decide to extend the learning.

▶ If you have *Fountas & Pinnell Prompting Guide, Part 2, for Comprehension: Thinking, Talking, and Writing* (Fountas and Pinnell 2009), refer to the prompts that support strong listening and thinking in Section IV: Book Discussion (Change Thinking, Clarify Thinking, Extend Thinking, Paraphrase).

### Be a strong listener and a strong speaker.

| Strong Listener  | • Makes eye contact with the speaker<br>• Body is turned toward the speaker<br>• Might nod at the speaker<br>• Might ask the speaker to say something in a different way<br>• Responds to ideas before changing the subject<br>• Doesn't talk over the speaker |
|---|---|
| Strong Speaker  | • Makes eye contact with everyone in the group<br>• Takes turns<br>• Might nod or gesture to someone in the group<br>• Uses appropriate volume<br>• Asks questions<br>• Adds on to comments |

Section 2: Literary Analysis

# RML2
## LA.U2.RML2

Reading Minilesson Principle
## Recognize appropriate times to take a turn.

**Learning Conversational Moves in Book Club**

### You Will Need

- chart paper and markers
- students' book club books

### Academic Language / Important Vocabulary

- book club
- lull
- respect
- appropriate

### Continuum Connection

- Use turn-talking with courtesy in small group discussion [p. 337]
- Refrain from speaking over others [p. 337]
- Enter a conversation appropriately [p. 337]
- Use conventions of respectful conversation [p. 337]
- Understand the role of nonverbal language and use it effectively [p. 337]

### Goal

Understand verbal and nonverbal cues for knowing when to enter a conversation at the appropriate time.

### Rationale

When students learn how to take turns speaking during book club discussions by looking for verbal and nonverbal cues, they can share their ideas, comment on and extend one another's thoughts, and learn more about the text they are reading. This skill extends beyond book clubs to other conversations and discussions inside and outside of the classroom.

### Assess Learning

Observe students when they converse with classmates and notice if there is evidence of new learning based on the goal of this minilesson.

- Can students recognize appropriate times to speak during a discussion?
- Do they invite others to share their thinking?
- Do they use nonverbal cues to signal that they have something to say?
- Do they understand the terms *book club, lull, respect,* and *appropriate*?

## Minilesson

To help students think about taking turns in a book club discussion, engage them in an interactive lesson on how to look for verbal and nonverbal clues. Here is an example.

- Before teaching this lesson, be sure that students have had a recent book club experience to reflect on, whether it is a fishbowl demonstration (p. 74) or their own book club meeting.

  Think about the book club discussions you have seen or participated in. What did you notice about how everyone took turns speaking? Turn and talk about that.

- As needed, provide several prompts to encourage the conversation.

  - *What did people do when they had something to add to the conversation?*
  - *How did you know when it was your turn to speak?*
  - *Did you, or anyone else, say something to encourage others to take a turn sharing?*

- After time for discussion, bring the group back together and ask students to share their thinking about how to know when it is an appropriate time to speak. Make a list of responses on chart paper.

## Have a Try

Invite the students to talk in a small group about identifying when it is time to take a turn speaking.

> Talk in your group about a book you are currently reading. Take turns sharing and adding on to what your classmates have said.

▶ After time for discussion, ask students to share what they noticed about taking turns. Add new ideas to the chart.

> Why is it important for you to know how to respectfully take turns in a conversation?

## Summarize and Apply

Summarize the learning and remind students to think about book club discussions.

> What did you learn about taking turns speaking during a discussion?

▶ Add the principle to the top of the chart.

> Today I will meet with one book club group. Later when we come together to share, I will ask them to talk about what they observed about taking turns in a discussion.

## Share

Following independent reading time, gather students in the meeting area. Ask the group that met in book club to share.

> What are some examples of how you took turns talking?

> What did you remember to do when you wanted to add to the conversation?

## Extend the Lesson (Optional)

After assessing students' understanding, you might decide to extend the learning.

▶ If you have *Fountas & Pinnell Prompting Guide, Part 2, for Comprehension: Thinking, Talking, and Writing* (Fountas and Pinnell 2009), refer to the prompts that support turn taking in Section IV: Book Discussion (Redirect).

---

### Recognize appropriate times to take a turn.

- Wait for a natural break, pause, or lull in the conversation or when no one has anything to say.

- Make eye contact with the speaker.

- Notice if the speaker is looking around for someone to add to the conversation.

- Lean in to show you have something to say.

---

**Reading Minilesson Principle**

# Monitor your participation and encourage others to participate.

Learning Conversational Moves in Book Club

## You Will Need

- chart paper and markers
- several blank cutouts of speech balloons
- several blank cutouts of thought balloons
- glue stick or tape

## Academic Language / Important Vocabulary

- book club
- participation
- monitor
- encourage

## Continuum Connection

- Use conventional techniques that encourage others to talk: e.g., "What do you think?" "Do you agree? Why or why not?" [p. 337]
- Evaluate one's own part in a group discussion as well as the effectiveness of the group [p. 337]
- Facilitate a group discussion by ensuring that everyone has a chance to speak [p. 337]

## Goal

Monitor your own participation and learn language for encouraging others to participate.

## Rationale

When students are aware of their own level of participation in a book club discussion, they are better prepared to adjust their behavior to either add more to the conversation or contribute less so that others have an opportunity to share.

## Assess Learning

Observe students when they are participating in a book club discussion and notice if there is evidence of new learning based on the goal of this minilesson.

- ▶ Do students participate in the discussion in a balanced way?
- ▶ Can they evaluate whether they are talking too much or too little?
- ▶ Do they use the terms *book club, participation, monitor,* and *encourage*?

## Minilesson

To help students think about the minilesson principle, engage them in a discussion about how to self-monitor in a book club meeting. Here is an example.

- ▶ Before teaching this lesson, be sure that students have had a recent book club experience to reflect on, whether it is a fishbowl demonstration as described at the opening of this umbrella or their own book club meeting.

  What does it mean to monitor your participation in a book club discussion? It means to check how you are taking part in the group. Turn and talk to a partner about what questions you can ask yourself to monitor your participation.

- ▶ After time for discussion, invite students to share. Prompt the conversation as needed. Record student ideas on the prepared thought balloons and place them on the chart under *Questions to Ask Yourself*.

  Now think about how you can invite others to talk during a book club meeting. What are some ways you could encourage someone to participate?

- ▶ Write student ideas on the prepared speech balloons and add them to the chart under *Questions to Invite Others*.

  Look back at the questions on the chart. Why is it important to check your participation and include others during a book club discussion?

- ▶ Prompt the conversation as needed.

## Have a Try

Invite the students to talk with a small group about how they can invite others to participate.

> Turn and talk about any other questions you might ask yourself and language you might use to monitor your participation during book clubs.

▶ After a short time for discussion, ask students to share. Add new ideas to the chart.

## Summarize and Apply

Summarize the learning and remind students to check in on themselves and to invite others to talk during book club discussions.

> What did you learn about monitoring yourself during book club discussions?

▶ Add the principle to the top of the chart. Ask a volunteer to read the questions on the chart.

> Use the chart when you meet with your book club. The book club that meets with me today will share about their book club when we have our class meeting.

## Share

Following independent reading time, gather students in the meeting area. Have the book club members you met with share with the whole group.

> How well did you monitor your own participation and support the participation of other book club members?

## Extend the Lesson (Optional)

After assessing students' understanding, you might decide to extend the learning.

▶ If you have *Fountas & Pinnell Prompting Guide, Part 2, for Comprehension: Thinking, Talking, and Writing* (Fountas and Pinnell 2009), refer to the prompts that support participation in Section IV: Book Discussion (Ask for Thinking, Question/ Hypothesize).

Section 2: Literary Analysis

**Reading Minilesson Principle**
# Invite each other to provide evidence.

## Learning Conversational Moves in Book Club

### You Will Need

- chart paper and markers
- students' book club books

### Academic Language / Important Vocabulary

- book club
- clarify
- evidence

### Continuum Connection

- Use evidence from the text to support statements about the text (pp. 58, 62)

## Goal

Develop language to give evidence and invite others to provide evidence for their thinking.

## Rationale

When students learn to provide evidence for their thinking, they learn to clarify their thinking, clear up potential misconceptions, develop more sophisticated conversation skills, monitor their understanding, and share new insights with classmates.

## Assess Learning

Observe students during book club meetings to notice evidence of new learning based on the goal of this minilesson.

- Do students provide evidence for their thinking during book club from personal experience or from the book?
- Can they identify when more information is needed and know how to ask for it?
- Do they use the terms *book club*, *clarify*, and *evidence*?

## Minilesson

To help students think about the minilesson principle, engage them in a discussion about using evidence during book clubs. Here is an example.

- Right before teaching this minilesson, conduct a fishbowl observation (p. 74) of a book club meeting. Ask students to focus on how the group members provide evidence for their thinking or ask each other for evidence for their opinions. (You may want to prepare the book club members being observed beforehand with some of the language represented in the chart, and you can also model this language.) Ask students to record their observations. Once the observation is complete, engage children in a reflective discussion to help them think about the minilesson principle.

  > What did you notice about some of the ways group members invited each other to add evidence?

- As students share ideas, generalize their thinking to create two lists, one titled *Give Evidence* and the other *Ask for Evidence*. Add responses to the appropriate section. Prompt the conversation as needed. For example:

  - *Why is it important to provide evidence for your thinking during book club?*

  - *How can you make sure you are specific with your evidence?*

  > Sometimes you want to be sure that you understand the point that a book club member is making. If so, you can ask for evidence.

## Have a Try

Invite the students to talk about how they might give evidence or ask for evidence during book club.

▶ Have students sit with one or more members of their current book club. Each person in the group should have a copy of the same book.

> Practice giving evidence or asking for evidence about your book club book.

▶ After a brief time for practice, ask students to share the types of things they said to give or ask for evidence. Add new ideas to the chart.

## Summarize and Apply

Summarize the learning and remind students to think about how to give or ask for evidence during book club meetings.

> Today you learned about giving evidence for your thinking and asking others for theirs.

▶ Add the principle to the top of the chart.

> Think about using the chart when you have book club discussions. Today I will meet with one book club. Later when we have our class meeting, the book club members will share how they provided evidence in their discussion.

## Share

Following independent reading time, gather students in the meeting area. Ask the group that met in book club to share.

> In what ways did you give evidence or ask for evidence?

▶ Add new ideas to the chart. After the group members have shared, ask others in the class to reflect on providing evidence during book club meetings.

> Why is it important to share evidence for your thinking and to ask others to share evidence for their thinking?

## Extend the Lesson (Optional)

After assessing students' understanding, you might decide to extend the learning.

▶ If you have *Fountas & Pinnell Prompting Guide, Part 2, for Comprehension: Thinking, Talking, and Writing* (Fountas and Pinnell 2009), refer to the prompts for giving and seeking evidence in Section IV: Book Discussion (Seek Evidence).

---

**Invite each other to provide evidence.**

| | |
|---|---|
| Give Evidence | • An example of that is on page ____ .<br><br>• I think ____ because ____ .<br><br>• On page ____ , paragraph ____ , the writer says ____ , so ____ .<br><br>• I used this quote because ____ . |
| Ask for Evidence | • What makes you think that?<br><br>• Can you provide some details?<br><br>• What part of the story led you to that conclusion?<br><br>• Help us understand why you thought that. |

Section 2: Literary Analysis

Learning Conversational Moves in Book Club

## You Will Need

▸ chart paper and markers

## Academic Language / Important Vocabulary

▸ book club
▸ diverse
▸ perspective

### Continuum Connection

▸ Use conventions of respectful conversation (p. 337)

▸ Use appropriate conventions in small-group discussion (e.g., "I agree with _____ because . . ."; "I'd like to change the subject . . .") (p. 337)

## Goal

Learn to share different perspectives, agree and disagree respectfully, and provide reasons for opinions.

## Rationale

When students share new and different ideas about a text, they are expanding and deepening their classmates' understandings of the text and working to ensure that a book club discussion is a safe place for everyone to share ideas.

## Assess Learning

Observe students during book club discussions to notice evidence of new learning based on the goal of this minilesson.

▸ Do students show that they value perspectives that differ from their own by respectfully responding to their classmates?

▸ Are they sharing a variety of ideas during book club meetings?

▸ Do they use the terms *book club, diverse,* and *perspective*?

## Minilesson

To help students think about the minilesson principle, engage them in a discussion about how to encourage and value diverse opinions. Here is an example.

▸ Right before teaching this lesson, conduct a fishbowl observation (p. 74) of one book club group discussing their book. Ask students to notice ways they show that they are valuing each other's opinions. Prepare students in the book club with some of the language in the chart.

  Think about a time during a book club discussion when people had different, or diverse, ideas about aspects of the book. Why is it important to hear a variety of ideas, or diverse perspectives?

▸ Prompt the conversation as needed.

  Now think about respectful language you can use when you hear an idea that is different from yours or when you disagree with an idea. Also think about ways you can invite others to share ideas that might be different from yours. Turn and talk about that.

▸ After time for discussion, ask volunteers to suggest ways to discuss diverse ideas. Create two lists on chart paper, one for ways to respond to diverse ideas and one for ways to ask for diverse ideas.

## Have a Try

Invite the students to talk in a small group about what they can say to share or encourage diverse perspectives during book club meetings.

> Think about a book we have recently read aloud together in class. Have a conversation about the book and practice sharing opinions using words that show you are listening. You can look to the chart for ideas if you wish.

▶ After time for a brief discussion, ask students to share about the experience. Add new ideas to the chart.

## Summarize and Apply

Summarize the learning and remind students to think how to share and ask for diverse perspectives.

> Today you learned how to respond to classmates who have new or different ideas. You also learned how to ask your classmates to share different ideas.

▶ Add the principle to the top of the chart.

> Use the chart when you meet with your book club. Today I will meet with one book club. When we have our class meeting, they will share their thinking about the book club discussion.

## Share

Following independent reading time, gather students in the meeting area. Ask the group that met in book club to share.

> Think about your book club. In what ways did you respond to your classmates' ideas? How did you show that you value their ideas? How did you invite others to share their perspective? Talk about that.

## Extend the Lesson (Optional)

After assessing students' understanding, you might decide to extend the learning.

▶ If you have *Fountas & Pinnell Prompting Guide, Part 2, for Comprehension: Thinking, Talking, and Writing* (Fountas and Pinnell 2009), refer to the prompts for supporting diverse viewpoints in Section IV: Book Discussion (Affirm Thinking and Agree/Disagree).

---

### Value and encourage diverse perspectives.

**Respond Respectfully**

- I agree with what you are saying because _____ .
- That seems possible because _____ .
- That's interesting. I hadn't thought of that.
- That makes sense to me, but _____ .
- That helps me understand this in a different way.
- I understand, but I looked at this a different way.

**Invite Others to Share Different Ideas**

- Does anyone see it another way?
- What is everyone else thinking?
- What is another way to think about that?

---

Section 2: Literary Analysis

**Reading Minilesson Principle**
# Add on to important ideas to extend the thinking of the group.

## Learning Conversational Moves in Book Club

### You Will Need

▸ chart paper and markers

### Academic Language / Important Vocabulary

▸ book club

▸ focus

▸ restate

### Continuum Connection

▸ Listen and respond to a partner by agreeing, disagreeing or adding on, and explaining reasons [p. 337]

▸ Sustain a discussion by staying on the main topic and requesting or signaling a change of topic [p. 337]

## Goal

Add on to important ideas to build a deeper understanding.

## Rationale

When students learn how to add on to an important idea and invite others to extend their thinking, they gain a deeper understanding of the text. Some teachers have students use hand signals to indicate when they plan to add on to a topic versus changing the subject. This lesson is designed to move students past using hand signals and to recognize language they can use to have an extended discussion on one idea.

## Assess Learning

Observe students in book club discussions to notice evidence of new learning based on the goal of this minilesson.

▸ Can students identify the important ideas in a discussion?

▸ Can they determine how to appropriately refocus or add on?

▸ Do they use the terms *book club, focus,* and *restate*?

## Minilesson

To help students think about the minilesson principle, engage them in a discussion about how to focus on main ideas and move on. Here is an example.

▸ Right before you plan to teach this minilesson, have your students participate in a fishbowl observation of a book club group. You can prepare the book club members ahead of time by teaching them some of the language on this chart and by modeling it yourself. Ask students to record some of the things the book club members say to stay focused and add on to an important idea. After they have conducted this fishbowl, engage them in reflective discussion about how to add on to an idea to extend the group's thinking.

> What did you notice about some of the ways group members added on to each other's ideas?

▸ Support the conversation as needed. Some suggested prompts are below.

  • *What are some other ways you might add on to a conversation?*

  • *Did you notice the book club members inviting each other to add on to the conversation?*

  • *What were some of the ways they invited each other to add on to an idea?*

▸ Write a list of questions on the chart under the headings *Add On* and *Invite Others to Add On.*

> When you feel that an idea has been fully discussed, then it is time to move on.

## Have a Try

Invite the students to talk with a partner about book club discussions.

> Look back at the chart. Turn and talk about any other ways you add on to a discussion or invite others in.

▶ After time for discussion, ask students to share. Add new ideas to chart.

## Summarize and Apply

Summarize the learning and remind students to think about how to focus, add on to, and restate ideas during book club meetings.

> Why is it important to add on to the conversation in a respectful way?

▶ Add the principle to the top of the chart.

> Use the chart when you meet with your book club. Today I will meet with one book club. When we have our class meeting, they will share what they learned about their book club discussion.

## Share

Following independent reading time, gather students in the meeting area. Ask the group that met in book club to share.

> Share what you noticed about your book club discussion. How did group members add on to or restate what others said?

▶ Add new ideas to the chart. After book club members have responded, ask the class to reflect on book club discussions and provide any new ideas for the chart.

## Extend the Lesson (Optional)

After assessing students' understanding, you might decide to extend the learning.

▶ If you have *Fountas & Pinnell Prompting Guide, Part 2, for Comprehension: Thinking, Talking, and Writing* (Fountas and Pinnell 2009), refer to the prompts for adding on and restating in Section IV: Book Discussion (Make Connections, Paraphrase, Share Thinking).

---

**Add on to important ideas to extend the thinking of the group.**

__Add On__ ✚

- I would like to add that_____.
- Building on what_____ said, I think_____.
- To add on,_____.
- I also think_____.
- Now I'm thinking_____.
- I'm changing my thinking because you_____.
- And this part of the text makes me think_____.

__Invite Others to Add On__

Say more about that

- Say more about that.
- Does anyone else want to add to that?
- What else does that make you think of?
- Say more about what you mean about_____.
- Did anyone else notice that?
- What do others think about that?
- Can anyone add on to_____'s comment/idea?
- Let's reread that paragraph to notice more.

---

**Reading Minilesson Principle**
# Change the topic or refocus the discussion as needed.

## Learning Conversational Moves in Book Club

### You Will Need

▸ chart paper and markers

### Academic Language / Important Vocabulary

▸ book club
▸ refocus
▸ discussion

### Continuum Connection

▸ Use appropriate conventions in small-group discussion (e.g., "I agree with _____ because . . ."; "I'd like to change the subject . . .") (p. 337)

▸ Suggest new lines of discussion when appropriate (p. 337)

▸ Play the role of group leader when needed (p. 337)

## Goal

Learn language to change or refocus a discussion and identify when it is appropriate to use it.

## Rationale

The teacher plays a key role in facilitating the group to ensure new levels of understanding. When students learn to change or refocus a book club discussion, they learn to take responsibility for themselves by keeping a conversation moving forward and gain opportunities to think more deeply about the text. You may eventually teach students to start the discussion, but that doesn't mean you won't be part of the group to observe and lift the conversation as needed.

## Assess Learning

Observe students when they are in book club meetings and notice if there is evidence of new learning based on the goal of this minilesson.

▸ Do students recognize when the discussion needs to be changed or refocused and use appropriate language to do so?

▸ Do they use the terms *book club, refocus,* and *discussion*?

## Minilesson

To help students think about the minilesson principle, engage them in a discussion about noticing when a book club discussion needs to change or be refocused. Here is an example.

▸ Right before you plan to teach this minilesson, have students participate in a fishbowl observation of a book club group. Prepare the members ahead of time by teaching them some of the language on this chart. Ask students to record some of the things the book club members say to change and refocus the discussion. After they have conducted this fishbowl, engage them in reflective discussion.

> Some ways to get the conversation in book club started might be to ask: Who wants to get us started? Or, what do you think would be important to talk about today? But what about when you want to move the discussion in a new direction? What are some ways you noticed the book club group members doing that?

▸ As needed, provide prompts to support the conversation.

- *What might you say to the group to respectfully change the topic?*

- *If a conversation gets off course, what could you say to bring the conversation back to the topic?*

▸ After time for discussion, have students share ideas. On chart paper, make a list of ideas for changing and refocusing the discussion.

## Have a Try

Invite the students to talk with a partner about book club discussions.

> When you feel that an idea has been fully discussed, then it is time to move on. Turn and talk about what else you could say to change or refocus a discussion during a book club meeting.

▶ After a brief time for discussion, ask students to share ideas. Add responses to the chart.

## Summarize and Apply

Summarize the learning and remind students to think about ways to start, change, or refocus the conversation during book club meetings.

> Why is it important to talk about more than one idea during a book club discussion?

▶ Add the principle to the top of the chart.

> Use the chart when you meet with your book club. Today I will meet with one book club. When we meet later to share, they will share their thinking about their discussion.

## Share

Following independent reading time, gather students in the meeting area. Ask the group that met in book club to share.

> How did your book club discussion go? What did you do to have a good discussion?

▶ Add new ideas to the chart. After book club members have responded, ask the class to reflect on book club discussions.

> Why is it important to notice when a book club conversation needs to change or be refocused?

## Extend the Lesson (Optional)

After assessing students' understanding, you might decide to extend the learning.

▶ Use the lesson format to engage students in a discussion about how to start a book club discussion. Some of the language on the chart could be helpful.

▶ If you have *Fountas & Pinnell Prompting Guide, Part 2, for Comprehension: Thinking, Talking, and Writing* (Fountas and Pinnell 2009), refer to the prompts for changing or refocusing the topic in Section IV: Book Discussion (Focus on Big Ideas, Get the Discussion Started/Focus Thinking, Summarize).

---

### Change the topic or refocus the discussion as needed.

| Change | • If everyone is finished with that idea, I'd like to change the topic. <br> • Who has another idea they want us to think about? <br> • What else would be important for us to talk about? <br> • Take us to another part of the story you want us to think about. |
|---|---|
| **Refocus** | • Another way to say that is _____. <br> • I'd like to return to our discussion of_____. <br> • Where are we now with this idea? <br> • We were talking about _____. <br> • We're getting far away from the book. |

**Section 2: Literary Analysis**

**Reading Minilesson Principle**
## Reflect on and evaluate your book club discussion.

### Learning Conversational Moves in Book Club

### You Will Need

- chart paper and markers
- charts from previous minilessons

### Academic Language / Important Vocabulary

- book club
- reflect
- assess
- evaluate

### Continuum Connection

- Evaluate one's own part in a group discussion as well as the effectiveness of the group (p. 337)

### Goal

Develop guidelines to self-assess book club meetings.

### Rationale

When students reflect on a book club meeting, they begin to consider how their preparation and participation help the group better understand the text. Their evaluation process improves their self-assessment skills and increases their ownership and engagement of their work.

### Assess Learning

Observe students during book club meetings to notice evidence of new learning based on the goal of this minilesson.

- Do students reflect on their participation so that they can identify what went well and what they can improve upon?
- Do they use the terms *book club*, *reflect*, *assess*, and *evaluate*?

## Minilesson

To help students think about the minilesson principle, engage them in a reflection of a recent book club discussion. Here is an example.

- Before teaching this lesson, all students should have participated in at least one book club meeting. Post the charts from the previous minilessons in this umbrella.

    Here are the charts we made about ways to have a good book club meeting.

- Ask them to quickly review the charts.

    At the end of a book club meeting, you can reflect on what went well for you and your peers and what things you would like to work on so that your next book club meeting is even better.

    Let's create a list of what you can do to ensure a good book club meeting.

- Ask students for suggestions. As they respond, generalize their thinking and write statements on the chart paper. Prompt the conversation as needed.

    After your next meeting, you can use the list to evaluate how well your meeting went.

## Have a Try

Invite the students to talk with a partner about ways to reflect on and evaluate a book club discussion.

> Turn and talk with a partner about something on the list that went well in your last book club meeting. What made it go well?

▶ After time for discussion, ask students to share ideas. Add to chart.

## Summarize and Apply

Summarize the learning and remind students to reflect after book club meetings.

> Today you created a list to help you think about your book club meetings.

▶ Add the principle to the top of the chart.

> Think about the things on this list after your next book club meeting. Think about what went well and decide on something that you can make better the next time.

▶ Meet with a book club while the other students engage in independent reading.

## Share

Following independent reading time, gather students in the meeting area. Ask the group that met in book club to share.

> What went well in your book club discussion?

> What is something you would like to improve for next time?

> How did the checklist help you evaluate your book club meeting?

## Extend the Lesson (Optional)

After assessing students' understanding, you might decide to extend the learning.

▶ Have students write in a reader's notebook an idea to improve their next book club discussion and how to do it.

▶ Make copies of the checklist (see resources.fountasandpinnell.com) for students to use at the end of a book club meeting.

---

### Reflect on and evaluate your book club discussion.

- ☐ We came prepared with pages marked and ideas to talk about.
- ☐ We took turns talking.
- ☐ We added on to each other's ideas.
- ☐ We invited others to participate.
- ☐ We stayed on topic.
- ☐ We supported our ideas with evidence from the text or personal experience.
- ☐ We respected everyone's ideas, including those we didn't agree with.
- ☐ We asked questions when we wanted to know more or didn't understand something.

## Assessment

After you have taught the minilessons in this umbrella, observe students as they listen and speak about their reading across instructional contexts: interactive read-aloud, independent reading, guided reading, shared reading, and book club. Use *The Literacy Continuum* (Fountas and Pinnell 2017) to observe students' reading and writing behaviors.

▶ What evidence do you have of new understandings related to the way students engage with book clubs?

- Are students effectively using conversation skills and effective language in book club discussions?
- Do they know when to continue addressing one topic or when to move the discussion in a new direction?
- Do they demonstrate that they value everyone's ideas and opinions?
- Are they monitoring their own participation and encouraging others to share?
- Do they use terms such as *book club, listener, speaker, respect, discussion,* and *reflect*?

▶ In what other ways, beyond the scope of this umbrella, are students talking about books?

- Are students talking about author's craft?
- Do they write in response to what they have read?

Use your observations to determine the next umbrella you will teach. You may also consult Minilessons Across the Year (pp. 59–61) for guidance.

## Link to Writing

After teaching the minilessons in this umbrella, help students link the new learning to their own writing:

▶ Encourage students to write in a reader's notebook about ways in which the book club discussion has enhanced and deepened their understanding.

## Reader's Notebook

When this umbrella is complete, provide a copy of the minilesson principles (see resources.fountasandpinnell.com) for students to glue in the reader's notebook (in the Minilessons section if using *Reader's Notebook: Intermediate* [Fountas and Pinnell 2011]), so they can refer to the information as needed.

## Minilessons in This Umbrella

**RML1**   Study authors to learn about their craft.

**RML2**   Authors get ideas for their books from their own lives.

**RML3**   Authors engage in research for their writing.

**RML4**   Authors often write about the same themes, topics, or settings in their books.

## Before Teaching Umbrella 3 Minilessons

During an author study (see p. 42), students learn that authors constantly make decisions as part of the book-writing process. Author study supports students in noticing and appreciating elements of an author's craft and also the kind of research an author engages in to create an authentic and accurate book. Teach one or more of these lessons throughout the year as you conduct an author study or as students think about the decisions authors make in creating their books.

The first step in studying authors is to collect a set of mentor texts. Use the following books from the *Fountas & Pinnell Classroom™ Interactive Read-Aloud Collection* text sets along with the complete Author/Illustrator: Douglas Florian and Author Study: Patricia McKissack text sets, or choose texts by a single author or illustrator whose books your students have read.

**Author/Illustrator Study: Allen Say**

*Kamishibai Man*

*The Sign Painter*

*Tea with Milk*

**Author/Illustrator Study: Douglas Florian**

*Insectlopedia*

*Lizards, Frogs, and Polliwogs*

*Mammalabilia*

*In the Swim*

*On the Wing*

**The Idea of Home**

*Grandfather's Journey* by Allen Say

**Figuring Out Who You Are**

*The Junkyard Wonders* by Patricia Polacco

**Genre Study: Biography (Individuals Making a Difference)**

*Fly High! The Story of Bessie Coleman* by Louise Borden and Mary Kay Kroeger

*Six Dots: A Story of Young Louis Braille* by Jen Bryant

**Genre Study: Historical Fiction**

*Dad, Jackie, and Me* by Myron Uhlberg

As you read aloud and enjoy these texts together, help students

• look across texts to learn more about authors and their craft, and

• think about the research that the author did to make the book authentic.

**Allen Say**

**Douglas Florian**

**The Idea of Home**

**Figuring Out Who You Are**

**Biography (Individuals Making a Difference)**

**Historical Fiction**

**Section 2: Literary Analysis**

**Reading Minilesson Principle**
# Study authors to learn about their craft.

## Studying Authors and Their Processes

### You Will Need

- multiple books by the same author, such as the following:
  - *Grandfather's Journey* by Allen Say, from Text Set: The Idea of Home
  - *Tea with Milk*, *The Sign Painter*, and *Kamishibai Man* by Allen Say, from Text Set: Author/Illustrator Study: Allen Say
- chart paper and markers
- large sticky notes

### Academic Language / Important Vocabulary

- characteristics
- recognize
- style
- author's message
- structure
- craft

### Continuum Connection

- Connect texts by a range of categories: e.g., content, theme, message, genre, author/illustrator, character, setting, special forms, text structure, or organization (pp. 58, 62)
- Analyze texts to determine aspects of a writer's style: e.g., use of language, choice of setting, plot, characters, themes and ideas (p. 60)
- Recognize some authors by the topics they choose or the style of their illustrations (p. 64)

## Goal

Understand that an author usually writes several books and that there are often recognizable characteristics of the writing across books.

## Rationale

When students analyze the characteristics of an author's work, they begin to appreciate that writing is a process of decision making and that artistry is involved. Recognizing an author's patterns or style can heighten anticipation, enjoyment, and depth of understanding because familiarity has been established. Note that this lesson format can be used for future author studies.

## Assess Learning

Observe students when they talk about authors and notice if there is evidence of new learning based on the goal of this minilesson.

- ▶ Do students recognize similar characteristics across books by the same author (e.g., topic, ideas, message, style, point of view, structure)?
- ▶ Are they able to distinguish whether the characteristics they notice are *always* or *often* present in books by the same author?
- ▶ Do they use the terms *characteristics, recognize, style, author's message, structure,* and *craft*?

## Minilesson

To help students think about the minilesson principle, engage them in recognizing an author's style. Here is an example.

- ▶ Show the covers of multiple books by the same author, such as Allen Say.

  You have been enjoying books written by Allen Say. What do you remember about his writing?

- ▶ On chart paper, write the author's name at the top, with the heading *Noticings* underneath. Create separate columns for *Always* and *Often*.

  Would you say that the things you remember are always true of Allen Say's books? Are they often true?

- ▶ Record students' responses in the Always or Often section of the chart. If you wish, use sticky notes for the responses so that you can move them from one column to the other as students determine where they ultimately belong.

- ▶ Read or show pages from *Grandfather's Journey, Tea with Milk,* and *The Sign Painter* to prompt the conversation and make further additions to the chart.

## Have a Try

Invite the students to talk with a partner about Allen Say's books.

▶ Show the cover of *Kamishibai Man* and read a few pages.

> Turn and talk about what you noticed about Allen Say's writing in this book. Do you see any of the characteristics on the chart? Is there anything else that should be added to the chart?

▶ After time for discussion, ask students to share. Add new ideas to chart.

## Summarize and Apply

Summarize the learning and remind students to think about the author when they read independently.

> Today you learned that if you study several books by the same author you begin to notice the kinds of decisions that an author makes about what to include in a book. You learn to recognize how the author writes, and that is called the author's craft.

> During independent reading today, you can read a book by Allen Say if you like. As you read, look for the things we talked about and see if you notice anything new. Bring the book when we meet so you can share.

## Share

Following independent reading time, gather students in the meeting area.

> Did anyone read a book by Allen Say? Share what you noticed.

> Did anyone read a book by an author whose books you have read before? Did you notice something that is always or often true about the author's books?

## Extend the Lesson (Optional)

After assessing students' understanding, you might decide to extend the learning.

▶ Extend the lesson by focusing on the illustrations and doing an illustrator study on Allen Say.

▶ Engage the students in an author study using a nonfiction author.

▶ **Writing About Reading** After conducting several author studies, students can use a reader's notebook to compare and contrast different authors.

---

### Allen Say

**Noticings:**

| Always | Often |
|---|---|
| • Allen Say is both the author and the illustrator. | • The story is told in first person. |
| • The dialogue moves the story along. | • The main character(s) is on a journey. |
| • He writes fiction stories. | • The story involves family. |
| | • He uses details from his life (biographical). |
| | • He wants you to learn about a culture that might be different from your own. |

*Section 2: Literary Analysis*

**Reading Minilesson Principle**

# Authors get ideas for their books from their own lives.

**Studying Authors and Their Processes**

**You Will Need**

- several familiar fiction books in which authors get ideas from their own lives, such as the following:

  - *The Junkyard Wonders* by Patricia Polacco, from Text Set: Figuring Out Who You Are

  - *Dad, Jackie, and Me* by Myron Uhlberg, from Text Set: Historical Fiction

  - *Grandfather's Journey* by Allen Say, from Text Set: Idea of Home

- chart paper and markers

- document camera (optional)

**Academic Language / Important Vocabulary**

- author

- ideas

- author's note

- dedication page

**Continuum Connection**

- Use evidence from the text to support statements about the text (pp. 58, 62)

## Goal

Understand that authors sometimes get writing ideas from their own life experiences.

## Rationale

When you teach students to use parts of a book (e.g., author's note, dedication page) to learn about an author, they realize that many times an author bases all or parts of a story on real-life experiences. Students learn to make a strong connection between the author, the story, and the author's purpose, as well as learn where they can get their own ideas for writing.

## Assess Learning

Observe students when they talk about where authors get ideas for books and notice if there is evidence of new learning based on the goal of this minilesson.

- ▶ Is there evidence that students are reading beyond the body of the text to learn more about authors (e.g., dedication page, author's note, online resources)?

- ▶ Do students understand where authors get ideas for their writing?

- ▶ Do they use the terms *author, ideas, author's note,* and *dedication page*?

# Minilesson

To help students think about the minilesson principle, engage them in discovering how authors use their life experiences in their books. Here is an example.

- ▶ Show the cover of *The Junkyard Wonders*.

    Where do you think Patricia Polacco got her idea to write this book?

    If you don't know, where could you look?

- ▶ Guide students to think about places to find out about an author. Then show (or project) and read the inside covers, the dedication page, and the last page of the book.

    What information do you learn about Patricia Polacco and where she found ideas for this book?

- ▶ As students share ideas, create a chart that shows where they can find information about an author and how the information shows up in a story.

    Now that you know something about Patricia Polacco, how do you see that information used in the story?

- ▶ Add responses to the chart.

- ▶ Repeat the process with *Dad, Jackie, and Me*.

## Have a Try

Invite the students to talk with a partner about where another author got his ideas.

> Turn and talk about how Allen Say got his idea to write *Grandfather's Journey*.

▶ After time for discussion, ask students to share. Add responses to the chart.

## Summarize and Apply

Summarize the learning and remind students to think about where authors get ideas.

> What did you learn about authors today?

▶ Add the principle to the top of the chart.

> When you read today, look for places where you might find additional information about where the author found ideas for the book you are reading. Bring the book when we meet so you can share.

## Share

Following independent reading time, gather students in the meeting area.

> Did anyone read a book and learn where the author got the idea for the book? Talk about that and how it adds to your experience as a reader.

## Extend the Lesson (Optional)

After assessing students' understanding, you might decide to extend the learning.

▶ Talk about how knowing where the author got ideas for writing a book helps in appreciating the book (e.g., develops empathy for characters, the story seems more authentic, the story becomes more engaging).

▶ Encourage students to use ideas from their own lives as they write stories.

### Authors get ideas for their books from their own lives.

| Author | Where can you find out about the author's life? | How do you see the author's life in the story? |
|---|---|---|
| Patricia Polacco | • inside covers<br>• dedication page<br>• last page of book<br>• other books<br>• author website<br>• author interviews | • She had a hard time learning to read like some of her characters.<br>• She had a teacher like the character in her stories. |
| Myron Uhlberg | • author's note<br>• back cover<br>• online resources<br>• book reviews<br>• book summaries | • His dad was deaf like the character in the book.<br>• His dad felt connected to Jackie Robinson. |
| Allen Say | • the story ("my grandfather")<br>• back cover<br>• book reviews<br>• author website | • He tells the story of his grandfather.<br>• His grandfather loved both Japan and the United States. |

**Reading Minilesson Principle**
# Authors engage in research for their writing.

## Studying Authors and Their Processes

### You Will Need

▶ several familiar historical fiction or nonfiction books, such as the following:

- *Fly High!* by Louise Borden and Mary Kay Kroeger and *Six Dots* by Jen Bryant, from Text Set: Genre Study: Biography [Individuals Making a Difference]

- *Dad, Jackie, and Me* by Myron Uhlberg, from Text Set: Historical Fiction

▶ document camera [optional]

▶ chart paper and markers

▶ sticky notes

### Academic Language / Important Vocabulary

▶ author

▶ research

▶ authentic

### Continuum Connection

▶ Think critically about the authenticity and appeal of a narrator's voice (p. 60)

## Goal

Understand that writers engage in research for their writing.

## Rationale

When you teach students to think about how a book has been researched, they learn to evaluate the authenticity and accuracy of the writing. They understand that research is an essential part of writing most books.

## Assess Learning

Observe students when they talk about how an author researches a topic before writing and notice if there is evidence of new learning based on the goal of this minilesson.

▶ Are students thinking critically about how authors gain expertise on a topic?

▶ Do they use the terms *author, research,* and *authentic*?

## Minilesson

To help students think about the minilesson principle, engage them in discussing how authors conduct research prior to writing. Here is an example.

▶ Show the cover of *Fly High*.

> Louise Borden and Mary Kay Kroeger wrote a whole book about Bessie Coleman. What specific types of information would the authors need to find out before writing this book?

▶ As needed, turn through a few pages and prompt the conversation. Create a chart and add student ideas.

> Why is it important for an author to learn about a topic before writing?

> How does an author find out the information needed to write a book?

▶ Read and show (or project) the text in blue on the copyright page and the authors' note on the last page.

> What information does this book give about the authors' research?

▶ As students respond, fill in the chart.

> What would the author need to find out about before writing *Six Dots*?

▶ Add responses to the chart.

▶ Read and show (or project) the page at the end with the acknowledgments and the page that shows where to learn more about Louis Braille and Braille.

> What information does the book give about the author's research?

▶ Add responses to the chart.

## Have a Try

Invite the students to talk with a partner about an author's research.

▶ Read (and project) the second paragraph under the Acknowledgments heading at the end of *Dad, Jackie, and Me*.

> Think about *Dad, Jackie, and Me*. What did the author need to find out for this book? Where did the author find the information?

▶ After time for discussion, ask students to share. Add responses to the chart.

## Summarize and Apply

> What does the chart show you about how an author goes about writing a book?

> Authors need to search for, or research, sources to learn accurate information before writing a book.

▶ Add the principle to the top of the chart.

> During independent reading today, look at the front and back covers and other information that is outside the main part of the book to see if there is information about the author's research. Mark any pages you want to remember with a sticky note. Bring the book when we meet so you can share.

## Share

Following independent reading time, gather students in small groups.

> Share with your group any information you found about the research the author did. Talk about how that research is helpful to you as a reader.

## Extend the Lesson (Optional)

After assessing students' understanding, you might decide to extend the learning.

▶ **Writing About Reading** Have students use a reader's notebook to write about the research the author had to do before writing a book. The book could be fiction or nonfiction.

### Authors engage in research for their writing.

| Title | What did the author need to find out for this book? | Resources the author used |
|---|---|---|
| *Fly High!* | • Details about Bessie's accomplishments<br>• Details about Bessie as a flight student<br>• Information about Bessie's family | **Publications** (Newspapers from the time she lived)<br>**Places of Education** (Bessie's flight school in France)<br>**Relatives or Friends** (Marion Coleman, Bessie's niece) |
| *SIX DOTS* | • Information about reading for people who are blind<br>• What it is like to live when you cannot see<br>• Details of Louis Braille's life | **Specialists** (ophthalmologist)<br>**Organizations** (National Federation for the Blind, The National Braille Press)<br>**Books** (about Louis Braille) |
| *Dad, Jackie, and Me* | • Information about Jackie Robinson's life<br>• Baseball information | **Libraries** (Auburn Avenue Research Library)<br>**Museums** (National Baseball Hall of Fame Museum) |

**Reading Minilesson Principle**

# Authors often write about the same themes, topics, or settings in their books.

## Studying Authors and Their Processes

### You Will Need

- several sets of books by the same author, such as the following:
  - Text Set: Author/Illustrator Study: Douglas Florian
  - Text Set: Author Study: Patricia McKissack
- chart paper and markers
- sticky notes

### Academic Language / Important Vocabulary

- topic
- theme
- similarities
- characteristics
- style

### Continuum Connection

- Recognize some authors by the style of their illustrations, their topics, characters they use, or typical plots [p. 60]
- Recognize some authors by the topics they choose or the style of their illustrations [p. 64]

## Goal

Understand that writers often revisit the same themes, topics, and settings across their books.

## Rationale

When you teach students to see patterns across texts written by the same author, they learn to think in depth about an author's style, interests, values, and ideas, as well as to anticipate similarities as they read books by the same author.

## Assess Learning

Observe students when they talk about similarities across books written by the same author and notice if there is evidence of new learning based on the goal of this minilesson.

- Can students discuss similarities across books by the same author?
- Do they understand that authors can be identified by their style?
- Do they use the terms *topic, theme, similarities, characteristics,* and *style*?

## Minilesson

To help students think about the minilesson principle, engage them in noticing similarities across texts written by the same author. Here is an example.

- Ahead of time, gather the books by Douglas Florian and Patricia McKissack. Cover the author's names with sticky notes and display the covers.
- Hold up *Insectlopedia*. Read and show the illustrations from several pages.

    **Based on what you have noticed in other books, who do you think wrote this book? How do you know?**

- Reveal the author.

    **Think about these other books by Douglas Florian.**

- Show and read several pages from the other books by Douglas Florian.

    **The similarities help you recognize the writing style of Douglas Florian.**

    **What are some similarities found in all these books by Douglas Florian?**

- As needed, prompt students to think about similarities (e.g., settings, topics, themes). Begin filling in a chart with students' responses.
- Repeat the process with two of the books by Patricia McKissack.

## Have a Try

Invite the students to talk with a partner about the style of authors.

❯ Share a few pages from the other two books by Patricia McKissack.

Think about the similarities that these two books by Patricia McKissack have. What other characteristics of her style as an author could be added to the chart? Turn and talk about that.

❯ After time for discussion, ask students to share their thinking. Add responses to the chart.

## Summarize and Apply

Summarize the learning and remind students to notice an author's style when they read.

Today we talked about how you can look for similarities in books by the same author to learn about the author's writing.

❯ Add the principle to the top of the chart.

During independent reading today, you might choose a book by an author you have read before. If you do, use a sticky note to write similarities between the books. Bring the book when we meet so you can share.

## Share

Following independent reading time, gather students in the meeting area.

Did anyone read a book written by an author you have read before? How is it helpful to think about things that are similar across books by the same author? Share your thoughts.

## Extend the Lesson (Optional)

After assessing students' understanding, you might decide to extend the learning.

❯ **Writing About Reading** Have students compare books by the same illustrator and write their observations about the illustrator's style in a reader's notebook.

| Authors often write about the same themes, topics, or settings in their books. | | |
|---|---|---|
| | Douglas Florian | Patricia McKissack |
| Settings | nature | some historical settings |
| Topics | animals, birds, insects, reptiles written about in the form of poetry | character thoughts and feelings<br><br>lessons usually reflecting cultural values<br><br>realistic |
| Themes | sometimes giving advice or warning<br><br>can be informative and imaginative at the same time | older people teaching a lesson |

**Section 2: Literary Analysis**

## Assessment

After you have taught the minilessons in this umbrella, observe students as they talk and write about authors across instructional contexts: interactive read-aloud, independent reading, guided reading, shared reading, and book club. Use *The Literacy Continuum* (Fountas and Pinnell 2017) to guide the observation of students' reading and writing behaviors.

> ❱ What evidence do you have of new understandings related to authors and their work?
>
> > • Do students understand that they can learn about an author's writing by reading many of their books?
> >
> > • Do they understand that authors often get ideas for their stories from their own lives?
> >
> > • Can they recognize books that are written by the same author?
> >
> > • Can they search for important information and learn about the research an author engages in by looking beyond the body of the text?
> >
> > • Do they use terms such as *characteristics, style, craft, author's note,* and *research?*
>
> ❱ In what other ways, beyond the scope of this umbrella, are students thinking about authors and illustrators?
>
> > • Are students noticing the illustrator's craft?

Use your observations to determine the next umbrella you will teach. You may also consult Minilessons Across the Year (pp. 59–61) for guidance.

## Link to Writing

After teaching the minilessons in this umbrella, help students link the new learning to their own writing:

> ❱ Students can write books using the style of an author they enjoy.
>
> ❱ Students can incorporate into their writing one or more of the kinds of writing beyond the body of the text. This might include an author's note, timeline, foreword, or afterword.

## Reader's Notebook

When this umbrella is complete, provide a copy of the minilesson principles (see resources.fountasandpinnell.com) for students to glue in the reader's notebook (in the Minilessons section if using *Reader's Notebook: Intermediate* [Fountas and Pinnell 2011]), so they can refer to the information as needed.

## Minilessons in This Umbrella

**RML1**    Study the illustrations closely to understand what is happening.

**RML2**    Notice the text features the author/illustrator uses to help you follow the action.

**RML3**    Notice the text features the author/illustrator uses to create narration, sound, and dialogue.

**RML4**    Notice how the author/illustrator uses color and lines.

## Before Teaching Umbrella 4 Minilessons

Though not a genre, graphic texts are a popular text format that can be fiction or nonfiction. Reading a graphic text is quite different from reading a book in standard format, and students will benefit from a close look at the techniques used by each author/illustrator to convey story action or information. When reading fiction graphic texts together, encourage students to pay close attention to the illustrations because they carry much of the action. Describe various features of graphic texts, for example, that the panels in graphic texts function like paragraphs and are read left to right and top to bottom. They hold the illustrations, contain the narration, and carry the content. Gutters are the spaces between the panels that sometimes show time passing, meaning that the reader must infer action between panels. Other text features in graphic texts are narrative boxes, speech bubbles, thought bubbles, and sound words, all of which help the reader understand the text.

Before introducing this umbrella, begin to share graphic texts in book talks and create baskets for independent reading. Ask the students to select a graphic text to read for the week. Resources used in these minilessons are from the *Fountas & Pinnell Classroom™ Independent Reading Collection* and are listed below. Collect other graphic texts from your own library that engage students' intellectual curiosity and emotions, making sure the texts have content, themes, and ideas that are appropriate for your students' cognitive development, emotional maturity, and life experience.

### Independent Reading Collection

*Robin Hood: A Graphic Novel* by Aaron Shepard and Anne L. Watson

*Pecos Bill: Colossal Cowboy* by Sean Tulien

*Pigling: A Cinderella Story* by Dan Jolley

*Zita the Spacegirl: Far from Home* by Ben Hatke

As you read aloud and enjoy these texts together, help students

- notice and understand the illustrations,

- discuss text features and read the text for meaning, and

- notice an author/illustrator's color and line choices.

# RML1
**LA.U4.RML1**

Reading Minilesson Principle
## Study the illustrations closely to understand what is happening.

## Reading Graphic Texts

### You Will Need

- two or three graphic texts students are reading, or choose the following from the *Independent Reading Collection*:
  - *Robin Hood* by Aaron Shepard and Anne L. Watson
  - *Pecos Bill* by Sean Tulien
  - *Pigling* by Dan Jolley
- document camera [optional]
- chart paper and markers
- sticky notes prepared with words for the chart, e.g., *Action, Character's feelings, Setting, Problem, Character, Time passing*
- basket of graphic texts

### Academic Language / Important Vocabulary

- graphic texts
- action

### Continuum Connection

- Notice how illustrations and graphics go together with the text in a meaningful way [p. 61]
- Notice how illustrations and graphics help to communicate the writer's message [p. 65]

## Goal

Study the illustrations closely to understand the meaning of the text.

## Rationale

Graphic texts have more illustration than text. Students must learn to follow the story and infer character feelings and traits or other information from the illustrations. This will ensure they gain understanding and meaning from the text.

## Assess Learning

Observe students when they read graphic texts. Notice if there is evidence of new learning based on the goal of this minilesson.

- Can students infer the action of the story from the illustrations?
- Are they using language such as *graphic texts* and *action*?

## Minilesson

To help students understand the role of illustrations in a graphic text, engage them in noticing the details in them. Use a document camera, if available, to support close viewing of the illustrations. Here is an example.

- Show the cover of *Robin Hood*. Display a few pages, stopping on page 9.

  *Robin Hood* is an example of a graphic text. Look at the illustrations on this page while I read it to you.

  What do you see in the illustrations?

  What do the illustrations help you understand about the story?

- Record noticings on a chart. Have a student select a sticky note to tell what the illustrations help readers understand and add it to the chart.
- Repeat this process with page 13.
- If time allows, introduce *Pecos Bill*, and repeat the process using pages 6–7.

  How is reading a graphic text different from reading a book that has no illustrations?

## Have a Try

Invite the students to talk with a partner about another graphic text, *Pigling*.

▶ Display and read pages 8–9.

> Turn and talk to your partner. What do the illustrations show? What do they help you to understand in the story?

▶ After time to turn and talk, ask a few students to share. Record responses on the chart.

## Summarize and Apply

Summarize the learning and remind students to notice the illustrations in a graphic text.

> What is something you need to do when you read a graphic text?

▶ Review the chart and write the principle at the top.

> When you read today, if you are ready to choose a new book, choose a fiction or nonfiction text in graphic format from this basket. As you read, use a sticky note to mark an illustration that helps you understand what is happening. Bring the book when we meet so you can share what you marked.

## Share

Following independent reading time, gather students in groups of three or four to talk about their reading.

> If you read a graphic text—fiction or nonfiction—today, how did the illustrations help you to understand the story or information better?

> Some of you might have read a different kind of book. Did the illustrations help you in a similar way?

## Extend the Lesson (Optional)

After assessing students' understanding, you might decide to extend the learning.

▶ Many graphic texts are fiction, but some are nonfiction. Find examples of nonfiction graphic texts to share with your students.

▶ **Writing About Reading** Encourage students to write in a reader's notebook about a graphic text they have read.

**Study the illustrations closely to understand what is happening.**

| Graphic Text | What do you see in the illustrations? | What do they help you understand in the story? |
|---|---|---|
| ROBIN HOOD | Deer is fine. Deer has been killed by the arrow. | Action |
| | Expression on Robin's face and the look in his eyes show worry. | Character's feelings |
| | Cows in a corral Cowboys Mountain Sun shining | Setting |
| | Cows running or staying in place | Problem |
| PIGLING | Pear Blossom and her mother | Character |
| | Clothing worn in old-time Korea | Setting |
| | Pear tree at different points in time | Time passing |

## RML 2
### LA.U4.RML2

**Reading Minilesson Principle**
## Notice the text features the author/illustrator uses to help you follow the action.

## Reading Graphic Texts

### You Will Need

- two or three graphic texts students are familiar with, or choose the following from the *Independent Reading Collection:*
  - *Robin Hood* by Aaron Shepard and Anne L. Watson
  - *Pigling* by Dan Jolley
- document camera (optional)
- chart paper and markers
- basket of graphic texts

### Academic Language / Important Vocabulary

- panels
- gutters
- pictures

### Continuum Connection

- Notice how illustrations and graphics go together with the text in a meaningful way (p. 61)

## Goal

Notice and understand the function of the panels, gutters, and pictures in a graphic text and the author/illustrator's craft in creating them.

## Rationale

Studying the function of panels and gutters within graphic texts and how an author/illustrator uses these text features, allows students to read graphic texts with strong comprehension and appreciate the author/illustrator's craft.

## Assess Learning

Observe students when they read graphic texts. Notice if there is evidence of new learning based on the goal of this minilesson.

- ▶ Can students talk about how panels and gutters help them understand a story?
- ▶ Are they using language such as *panels, gutters,* and *pictures*?

## Minilesson

Engage the students in noticing the writer's decisions related to panels and gutters and what meaning they communicate. Use a document camera, if available, to support viewing the text features. Here is an example.

- ▶ Show the cover of *Robin Hood*. Display a few pages, stopping on pages 8–9.

  Follow along as I read aloud from *Robin Hood*. Notice how the pictures are organized on the page.

  How does the placement of the pictures help you read this graphic text?

- ▶ Read pages 8–9, pointing to the panels as you read.

  These boxes are called panels.

  The blank spaces between the boxes are called gutters.

- ▶ Point to the two bottom panels on page 9.

  Why is having this blank space here important?

  Why did the authors and illustrator use gutters?

- ▶ Record noticings on a chart. As necessary, prompt students to expand upon their thinking:

  - *Why did the authors and illustrator use boxes?*
  - *What did they include in the boxes?*
  - *How do you know in what order to read the boxes?*

## Have a Try

Invite the students to talk with a partner about pages 16–17 from *Pigling*.

> Turn and talk to your partner. How do the panels and gutters help you to read and understand this part of the story? Why did the illustrator choose to make the pictures like that?

▸ After time to turn and talk, ask a few students to share. Record responses on the chart.

## Summarize and Apply

Summarize the learning and remind students to use the panels and gutters to understand the action of the text.

> What do you need to notice to understand that time has passed?

▸ Review the chart and write the principle at the top.

> When you read today, choose a graphic text from this basket. As you read, notice how the panels and gutters help you to understand what is happening in the story. Bring the book when we meet today so you can share.

## Share

Following independent reading time, gather students in groups of three or four to talk about their reading.

> Talk to your group about how the panels and gutters helped you follow the action of the story.

▸ Display a page from a student's example and ask them to share with the class.

## Extend the Lesson (Optional)

After assessing students' understanding, you might decide to extend the learning.

▸ Use this lesson as a model for teaching students to use text features to gather information in nonfiction graphic texts, including graphic text biographies.

▸ **Writing About Reading** Encourage students to write a response letter about their reading to explain how panels and gutters help them understand the action in a graphic text.

---

**Notice the text features the author/illustrator uses to help you follow the action.**

### Panels

- Help the reader follow the action
- Are read left to right and top to bottom
- Come in different sizes
- Contain speech bubbles
- Panels within panels change the reader's focus.

### Gutters

- Blank spaces between panels
- Help you follow the story
- Come in different sizes
- Show that time has passed between boxes

**Section 2: Literary Analysis**

# Notice the text features the author/illustrator uses to create narration, sound, and dialogue.

## Reading Graphic Texts

### You Will Need

- a graphic text students are familiar with, or choose one of the following from the *Independent Reading Collection:*
  - *Robin Hood* by Aaron Shepard and Anne L. Watson
  - *Pecos Bill* by Sean Tulien
  - *Pigling* by Dan Jolley
  - *Zita the Spacegirl* by Ben Hatke
- document camera (optional)
- chart paper and markers
- sticky notes
- basket of graphic texts

### Academic Language / Important Vocabulary

- features
- speech bubbles
- thought bubbles
- narrative boxes
- sound words

### Continuum Connection

- Notice how illustrations and graphics help communicate the writer's message (p. 61)

## Goal

Notice and understand the use of speech and thought bubbles, lettering, narrative boxes, and sound words to create narration, sound, and dialogue in a graphic text.

## Rationale

Students need to understand why authors and illustrators use text features in a graphic text (e.g., speech and thought bubbles, lettering, narrative boxes, and sound words) and be able to interpret their meaning so that they can follow the story.

## Assess Learning

Observe students when they read graphic texts. Notice if there is evidence of new learning based on the goal of this minilesson.

- Do students read all the narrative boxes to follow the action in the story?
- Do they use text features to understand narration, sound, and dialogue?
- Do students notice and use sound words and lettering to understand where to place emphasis while reading?
- Are they using language such as *features, speech bubbles, thought bubbles, narrative boxes,* and *sound words*?

## Minilesson

To demonstrate the minilesson principle, choose an age-appropriate graphic text your students are reading, such as one from the *Independent Reading Collection,* to engage them in noticing how to use the text features. Use a document camera, if available. Here is an example.

- Read aloud and display the pages from a portion of a graphic text.

  **What features does the author use to tell the story? For example, how do you know what the characters are saying?**

- Record noticings on a chart. As students list the features they notice, ask how to title the category if they have not already named what they see.
- Prompt students to expand upon their noticings using the following:
  - *How does the author or illustrator let you know who is talking? And what they are thinking?*
  - *Besides dialogue, how does the author let you know what is happening?*
  - *How does the size and shape of the lettering help you hear how a character is saying something?*
  - *How does the author convey sound?*

## Have a Try

Invite the students to talk with a partner about a graphic text. Prompt as in the minilesson.

> Look for the features that we talked about. Do you notice any other features?

▶ After time to turn and talk, ask a few students to share. Record responses on the chart.

## Summarize and Apply

Summarize the learning and remind students to notice text features when they read graphic texts.

> What should you look for in a graphic text so you can understand what is going on?

▶ Review the chart and write the principle at the top.

> When you read today, you may choose a graphic text from this basket. As you read, mark with a sticky note a few text features that the author/illustrator uses to create narration, sound, and/or dialogue. Bring the book when we meet so you can share.

| Notice the text features the author/illustrator uses to create narration, sound, and dialogue. | |
|---|---|
| Speech Bubble  Stop! | • Tells what characters are saying  • Pointer shows the character who is talking |
| Thought Bubble  I wonder... | • Tells what characters are thinking  • Cloud-like shapes with small circles that point to the character who is thinking |
| Narrative Box  Meanwhile, Sheila waited for Tom to arrive. | • Tells what is happening  • Written in third person  • Acts like a narrator in a play |
| Lettering  • ALL CAPITAL  • BIG, BOLD  • Small | • Lets you know how to read the words  • Draws your attention, can mean say it a little LOUDER  • Can mean yelling  • Can mean whispering |
| Sound Word  BOOM | • Tells the sound you would hear if it were a movie  • Size tells how loud or soft the sound should be |

## Share

Following independent reading time, gather students in groups of three or four to talk about their reading. Make sure at least one student in each group read a graphic novel.

> What text features did you notice in your reading? How did they help you understand that part of the story?

▶ Ask a few students to share with the class and add to the chart as necessary.

## Extend the Lesson (Optional)

After assessing students' understanding, you might decide to extend the learning.

▶ Continue collecting and offering graphic texts to students for independent reading. Add to the chart as necessary.

▶ Some students might wish to create their own graphic texts. Once they come up with a storyline, remind them of the features they can use to convey the story.

**Reading Minilesson Principle**
# Notice how the author/illustrator uses color and lines.

### You Will Need

- a graphic text students are familiar with, or choose one of the following from the *Independent Reading Collection:*
  - *Pecos Bill* by Sean Tulien
  - *Pigling* by Dan Jolley
- document camera (optional)
- chart paper and markers
- basket of graphic texts

### Academic Language / Important Vocabulary

- motion
- mood

### Continuum Connection

- Notice how the tone of a book is created by the illustrator's choice of colors (p. 61)
- Notice how illustrations and graphics go together with the text in a meaningful way (p. 61)

## Goal

Notice how the author/illustrator uses color and lines.

## Rationale

Encouraging students to notice and understand how authors and illustrators use and make decisions about colors and lines in graphic texts supports students in gaining deeper meaning from their reading.

## Assess Learning

Observe students when they read graphic texts. Notice if there is evidence of new learning based on the goal of this minilesson.

- Do students notice an illustrator's use of color in a graphic text?
- Are they able to discuss why an illustrator might make a certain color choice?
- Can they talk about how lines give more information about the action in a story?
- Are they using language such as *motion* and *mood*?

## Minilesson

To demonstrate the minilesson principle, choose an age-appropriate graphic text your students are reading, with strong use of color and lines, such as one from the *Independent Reading Collection.* Use a document camera, if available. Here is an example.

- Read aloud and display the pages from a portion of *Pigling.*

  What do you notice about the illustrator's use of color?

  Why do you think the illustrator might have chosen that color?

- Record noticings on a chart.

  Now take a look at the way the illustrator uses lines.

  Why do you think the illustrator used those lines? How do they help you understand this part of the story?

- Record noticings on the chart.

## Have a Try

Invite the students to work with a partner to compare pages 9 and 44 from *Pecos Bill*.

> What do you notice about the illustrator's use of color?

▶ After time to turn and talk, ask a few students to share. Record responses on the chart. Then turn to page 31 and repeat this process.

> How did the illustrator use lines on this page?

## Summarize and Apply

Summarize the learning and remind students to notice how authors/illustrators use color and lines in graphic texts.

> Take a look at our chart. What decisions do illustrators make about the colors and lines they use?

▶ Review the chart, add notes to indicate what the colors and lines help show, and write the principle at the top.

> When you read today, choose a graphic text from this basket. Notice the author/illustrator's use of color and lines. Bring the book when we meet so you can share.

## Share

Following independent reading time, gather students in groups of three or four to talk about their reading.

> What did you notice about color and lines in your reading today? Why do you think the author/illustrator made these choices?

▶ Ask a few students to share with the class and add to the chart as necessary.

## Extend the Lesson (Optional)

After assessing students' understanding, you might decide to extend the learning.

▶ Continue collecting and offering graphic texts to students for independent reading. Add to the chart when students find new examples of how an author/illustrator uses color and line.

Notice how the author/illustrator uses color and lines.

| Color | • Shows the time period – a different color can indicate something took place in the past | • Setting |
| | • Shows the location – brown and beige for a story in a desert | |
| | • Pale colors – mother passed away | • Character's feelings |
| | • Bright colors – beautiful wedding day | • Mood |
| Lines | • Show hissing sounds | • Sound |
| | • Show speed of the horse | • Speed, movement |
| | • Show the speed of Pecos running across the desert | |
| | • Curved lines show a tornado | • Motion, movement |

Section 2: Literary Analysis

## Assessment

After you have taught the minilessons in this umbrella, observe students as they talk and write about their reading across instructional contexts: interactive read-aloud, independent reading, guided reading, shared reading, and book club. Use *The Literacy Continuum* (Fountas and Pinnell 2017) to guide the observation of students' reading and writing behaviors.

▶ What evidence do you have of new understandings related to graphic texts?

- Can students understand and discuss how the illustrations support the text?

- Do they read panels and text from left to right and top to bottom?

- Do they understand and use text features to follow the action in the text (e.g., panels, gutters, narrative boxes, speech bubbles, thought bubbles, sound words)?

- Do they notice and discuss an illustrator's decisions around color and lines?

- Are they using vocabulary such as *graphic texts*, *illustrations*, *panels*, *gutters*, *narrative boxes*, *speech bubbles*, *thought bubbles*, *lettering*, and *sound words*?

▶ In what other ways, beyond the scope of this umbrella, are students talking about fiction and nonfiction books?

- Do students study the illustrator's craft moves?

- Are they discussing how illustrations help them understand more about the setting and the characters?

Use your observations to determine the next umbrella you will teach. You may also consult Minilessons Across the Year (pp. 59–61) for guidance.

## Link to Writing

After teaching the minilessons in this umbrella, help students link the new learning to their own writing:

▶ Provide students with time to work on writing their own graphic texts. Remind them to include text features.

## Reader's Notebook

When this umbrella is complete, provide a copy of the minilesson principles (see resources.fountasandpinnell.com) for students to glue in the reader's notebook (in the Minilessons section if using *Reader's Notebook: Intermediate* [Fountas and Pinnell 2011]), so they can refer to the information as needed.

## Minilessons in This Umbrella

**RML1**   There are different genres of fiction books.

**RML2**   There are several types of traditional literature.

**RML3**   There are different genres of nonfiction books.

**RML4**   Hybrid books have fiction and nonfiction parts.

## Before Teaching Umbrella 5 Minilessons

Before teaching Umbrella 5, read and discuss fiction and nonfiction books from a range of genres. Make a Books We Have Shared chart (see p. 66) and add to it as you read books together.

The minilessons in this umbrella support students in understanding that there are different kinds, or genres, of books and that each one has specific characteristics. You may decide to teach this umbrella early in the year to provide students with a framework for thinking about fiction and nonfiction texts or later in the year when students have a deeper understanding of genre. Use the following suggested books from the *Fountas & Pinnell Classroom™ Interactive Read-Aloud Collection* and the *Fountas & Pinnell Classroom™ Independent Reading Collection*, or choose fiction and nonfiction books from your classroom library. For RML2, gather several familiar fables (e.g., "The Boy Who Cried Wolf," "The Lion and the Mouse").

### Interactive Read-Aloud Collection

**Illustration Study: Craft**

*Gecko* by Raymond Huber

*Dingo* by Claire Saxby

*Magnificent Birds* by Narisa Togo

*Giant Squid* by Candace Fleming

**Genre Study: Biography (Individuals Making a Difference)**

*Fly High! The Story of Bessie Coleman* by Louise Borden and Mary Kay Kroeger

**Genre Study: Memoir**

*The Upside Down Boy* by Juan Felipe Herrera

**Series: Vanishing Cultures**

*Himalaya* by Jan Reynolds

**Cinderella Stories**

*The Persian Cinderella* by Shirley Climo

**Empathy**

*The Crane Wife* by Odds Bodkin

**Friendship**

*Better Than You* by Trudy Ludwig

**Author/Illustrator Study: Allen Say**

*Kamishibai Man*

### Independent Reading Collection

*My Son, the Time Traveler* by Dan Greenburg

As you read aloud and enjoy these texts together, help students notice defining characteristics of the different types of fiction and nonfiction.

**Interactive Read-Aloud**

**Craft**

**Biography**

**Memoir**

**Vanishing Cultures**

**Cinderella Stories**

**Empathy**

**Friendship**

**Allen Say**

**Independent Reading**

Section 2: Literary Analysis

**Reading Minilesson Principle**
# There are different genres of fiction books.

## Understanding Fiction and Nonfiction Genres

### You Will Need

- familiar books from a variety of fiction genres, such as the following:
  - *Better Than You* by Trudy Ludwig, from Text Set: Friendship
  - *Kamishibai Man* by Allen Say, from Text Set: Author/Illustrator Study: Allen Say
  - *The Crane Wife* by Odds Bodkin, from Text Set: Empathy
- science fiction books, such as *My Son, the Time Traveler* by Dan Greenburg, from *Independent Reading Collection*
- chart paper and markers
- sticky notes

### Academic Language / Important Vocabulary

- realistic, historical, and science fiction
- traditional literature
- fantasy
- realism
- genre

### Continuum Connection

- Connect texts by a range of categories: e.g., content, theme, message, genre, author/illustrator, character, setting, special forms, text structure, or organization (p. 58)
- Understand that there are different types of texts and that they have different characteristics (p. 58)

## Goal

Understand that there are different genres of fiction texts that fall within the broader categories of realism or fantasy.

## Rationale

Studying the characteristics of fiction genres—realistic, historical, traditional, fantasy, and science fiction—helps students know what to expect when reading and increases their comprehension.

## Assess Learning

Observe students when they talk about fiction books. Notice if there is evidence of new learning based on the goal of this minilesson.

- ❯ Are students able to name different fiction genres?
- ❯ Do they use academic language, such as *realistic fiction, historical fiction, science fiction, traditional literature, fantasy, realism,* and *genre*?

## Minilesson

To help students think about the minilesson principle, engage them in noticing the characteristics of different genres of fiction. Here is an example.

- ❯ Hold up *Better Than You* and read a few pages.

  A story like this could happen in real life, but the author made up the story. What is the genre, or type of book?

  What characteristics show that it is realistic fiction?

- ❯ Write *Realistic Fiction* on chart paper. Record responses.

- ❯ Repeat the process with the historical fiction book, *Kamishibai Man.*

  Realistic fiction and historical fiction are types, or genres, of fiction. These two genres are called realism. The stories are imagined by the author, yet they have characters, places, and events that are true to life.

- ❯ Write *Realism* on the chart.

- ❯ Repeat this process with the traditional literature book, *The Crane Wife.* Read a few pages and then read the author's note opposite the dedication. Write *Traditional Literature* on the chart. Record responses.

- ❯ Repeat this process with a science fiction book, such as *My Son, the Time Traveler.* Write the words *Science Fiction* on the chart. Record responses.

- ❯ Summarize by explaining that traditional literature and science fiction are types of fantasy.

## Have a Try

Invite the students to work in pairs to discuss fiction books they have read.

> Turn and talk to your partner about a fiction book you read recently. Does it fit on this chart? Where? Which type of fiction—or genre—is your book?

▶ After they turn and talk, invite a few pairs to share. Use sticky notes to add book titles to the chart.

## Summarize and Apply

Summarize the learning and remind students to think about which genre of fiction they are reading.

> What does the chart show you about fiction books?

▶ Review the chart and write the principle at the top.

> You can understand books better when you understand their genres.

> Today during independent reading, think about what kind of fiction book you are reading. Bring the book when we come together so you can share your thinking.

## Share

Following independent reading time, gather students together in the meeting area to talk about their reading with the group.

> What kind of fiction book did you read today? How did you know that?

## Extend the Lesson (Optional)

After assessing students' understanding, you might decide to extend the learning.

▶ During interactive read-aloud, talk about characteristics of fiction books and add them to the chart.

▶ Teach students how to record the genre code on a reading list in the reader's notebook (see Umbrella 1: Introducing a Reader's Notebook, in Section Four: Writing About Reading, for more about genre coding).

▶ Add specific genre codes to the Books We Have Shared chart (see p. 66).

▶ **Writing About Reading** Invite students to write in a reader's notebook about a fiction text they read.

There are different genres of fiction books.

| | Book | Genre of Fiction | Characteristic |
|---|---|---|---|
| **R E A L I S M** | BETTER THAN YOU | Realistic Fiction | • Story could happen in real life |
| | KAMISHIBAI MAN | Historical Fiction | • Problem based on real events of the past<br>• Story and characters imagined<br>• Setting in the past |
| **F A N T A S Y** | THE CRANE WIFE | Traditional Literature | • Stories very old<br>• Can't happen in the real world<br>• Some characters not real<br>• Sometimes they trick each other |
| | THE ZACK FILES | Science Fiction | • Technology not yet invented<br>• Time travel<br>• Alien characters |

Section 2: Literary Analysis

**Reading Minilesson Principle**
# There are several types of traditional literature.

## Understanding Fiction and Nonfiction Genres

### You Will Need

- familiar traditional literature books, such as the following:
  - *The Persian Cinderella* by Shirley Climo, from Text Set: Cinderella Stories
  - *The Crane Wife* by Odds Bodkin, from Text Set: Empathy
- a fable students have not read but may be familiar with (e.g., "The Boy Who Cried Wolf," "The Lion and the Mouse")
- chart from RML1 (optional)
- chart paper and markers
- sticky notes
- basket of traditional literature texts, including fables, one for each student

### Academic Language / Important Vocabulary

- traditional literature
- fairy tales
- fables
- folktales

### Continuum Connection

- Understand that there are different types of texts and that they have different characteristics (p. 58)
- Notice and understand the characteristics of some specific fiction genres: e.g., realistic fiction, historical fiction, folktale, fairy tale, fractured fairy tale, fable, myth, legend, epic, ballad, fantasy, including science fiction, hybrid text (p. 58)

## Goal

Understand that there are different types of traditional literature.

## Rationale

Studying the characteristics of traditional literature helps students know what to expect when reading and increases comprehension.

## Assess Learning

Observe students when they choose to read traditional literature. Notice if there is evidence of new learning based on the goal of this minilesson.

- ▶ Are students able to identify different genres of traditional literature?
- ▶ Do they use academic language, such as *traditional literature, fairy tales, fables,* and *folktales*?

## Minilesson

To help students thinks about the minilesson principle, engage them in noticing the characteristics of traditional literature. Here is an example.

- ▶ If you taught RML1 and made the chart, display it. Review or summarize characteristics of traditional literature.
- ▶ Hold up *The Persian Cinderella*.

  This book is a special kind of traditional literature called a fairy tale. How do you know this book is a fairy tale?

- ▶ Write *Fairy Tale* on the chart. Prompt students to identify elements that make a fairy tale a fairy tale. Record responses.
- ▶ Hold up *The Crane Wife*.

  This book is another kind of traditional literature called a folktale. What do you notice about the characters in this book?

  How are characters in a folktale different from characters in a fairy tale?

  What do you notice about the plot?

- ▶ Write *Folktale* on the chart. Record responses.

  Fables are a third kind of traditional literature. You might be familiar with some fables, like "The Boy Who Cried Wolf" or "The Lion and the Mouse."

- ▶ Write *Fable* on the chart. Coach students to analyze defining elements of a fable, including the types of characters and the moral (lesson) at the end. Record responses.

## Have a Try

Invite the students to talk about traditional literature they have read.

> Think about a traditional literature book you read recently. Does it fit on the chart? Where? Why?

▶ Use sticky notes to add book titles to the chart.

## Summarize and Apply

Summarize the learning and remind students to think about kinds of traditional literature.

> What does this chart show about traditional literature?

▶ Review the chart and write the principle at the top.

> Today during independent reading, everyone will choose a book from this basket of traditional literature books. Think about whether the book you are reading is a fable, a folktale, or a fairy tale. Bring the book when we come back together so you can share your thinking.

## Share

Following independent reading time, gather students together in the meeting area to talk about their reading with the group.

> What kind of traditional literature did you read today? What genre characteristics did you notice?

## Extend the Lesson (Optional)

After assessing students' understanding, you might decide to extend the learning.

▶ As students become more confident in understanding the characteristics of traditional literature, you might decide to introduce additional types of traditional literature, such as myths, ballads, legends, and epics.

▶ Teach students how to record the genre code on their reading list in a reader's notebook (see WAR.U1.RML2 for more about genre coding).

▶ Add specific genre codes to the Books We Have Shared chart (see p. 66).

There are several types of traditional literature.

| Book | Type of Traditional Literature | Characteristics |
|---|---|---|
| The PERSIAN CINDERELLA | Fairy Tale | • Retold many times<br>• Characters and events cannot exist in the real world<br>• Magical things happen<br>• Good wins over evil |
| The Crane Wife | Folktale | • Retold many times<br>• Ordinary people, or "folk"<br>• Do things typical people do<br>• Setting could be real<br>• Sometimes repetition |
| The Boy Who Cried Wolf | Fable | • Retold many times<br>• Story is imagined<br>• Cannot happen in real life<br>• Teaches a moral or a lesson |

Section 2: Literary Analysis

## RML3
### LA.U5.RML3

**Reading Minilesson Principle**
# There are different genres of nonfiction books.

## Understanding Fiction and Nonfiction Genres

### You Will Need

- familiar books from a variety of nonfiction genres, such as the following:
  - *Magnificent Birds* by Narisa Togo and *Giant Squid* by Candace Fleming, from Text Set: Illustration Study: Craft
  - *Fly High! The Story of Bessie Coleman* by Louise Borden and Mary Kay Kroeger, from Text Set: Genre Study: Biography (Individuals Making a Difference)
  - *The Upside Down Boy* by Juan Felipe Herrera, from Text Set: Genre Study: Memoir
  - *Himalaya* by Jan Reynolds, from Text Set: Series: Vanishing Cultures
- chart paper and markers

### Academic Language / Important Vocabulary

- biography
- autobiography
- memoir
- expository
- narrative nonfiction
- subject

### Continuum Connection

- Notice and understand the characteristics of some specific nonfiction genres: e.g., expository, narrative procedural and persuasive texts, biography, autobiography, memoir, hybrid text (p. 62)

## Goal

Understand that there are different genres of nonfiction texts (e.g., biography, autobiography, memoir, expository, and narrative nonfiction).

## Rationale

When students understand there are different genres of nonfiction, and the characteristics and organization of each, they are better prepared to read and gain information.

## Assess Learning

Observe students when they talk about nonfiction books. Notice if there is evidence of new learning based on the goal of this minilesson.

- Can students describe the characteristics of different genres of nonfiction texts?
- Do they use academic language, such as *biography, autobiography, memoir, expository, narrative nonfiction,* and *subject*?

## Minilesson

To help students think about the minilesson principle, engage them in noticing the characteristics of different kinds of nonfiction. Here is an example.

- Show some pages from the book *Magnificent Birds*.

  What type of book is this? How do you know?

- Make three columns on the chart paper and write *Book, Genre of Nonfiction,* and *Characteristics*. Leave space above to add the principle later.

  There are different genres of fiction, and the same is true for nonfiction. This book is called expository nonfiction. What do you notice about how this book is written?

- Write *Expository* on the chart. Record responses. If students respond with specific information about birds, reframe their answers to be more general, such as "The book gives information about one overall topic."

- Repeat the process for a narrative nonfiction book, such as *Giant Squid*.

  How is this book different from the expository nonfiction book?

- Repeat the process for a biography, such as *Fly High! The Story of Bessie Coleman*.

  A biography is written by one person about another. An autobiography is like a biography, but the author and the subject are the same. If you were to write about your life, you would be both the author and the subject.

- Repeat this process for a memoir, such as *The Upside Down Boy*, reading the author's note and pages 4 and 7.

## Have a Try

Invite the students to talk about persuasive text in small groups.

❱ Read the introduction and show a few pages from a persuasive text, such as *Himalaya*.

This is another genre of nonfiction called a persuasive text. Discuss in your group what you notice about the book *Himalaya*.

❱ Write *Persuasive* on the chart. Invite each group to share. Add responses to the chart.

## Summarize and Apply

Summarize the learning and remind students to think about the genre of nonfiction they are reading.

When you think about the genre, or kind, of nonfiction you are reading, you will understand the book better.

❱ Write the principle at the top of the chart.

Today during independent reading time, you may want to choose a nonfiction book if you finish the book you are reading. Notice what genre of nonfiction it is and bring the book when we come back together so you can share your thinking.

## Share

Following independent reading time, gather students together in the meeting area to talk about their reading in groups of two or three.

If you read nonfiction today, discuss with your group what genre of nonfiction you think it is. What makes you think that?

## Extend the Lesson (Optional)

After assessing students' understanding, you might decide to extend the learning.

❱ Teach students how to record the genre code on their reading list in a reader's notebook (see WAR.U1.RML2 for more about genre coding).

❱ Add specific genre codes to the Books We Have Shared chart (see p. 66).

**There are different genres of nonfiction books.**

| Book | Genre of Nonfiction | Characteristics |
|---|---|---|
| MAGNIFICENT BIRDS | Expository | • Information about one topic<br>• Categories to organize information |
| GIANT SQUID | Narrative | • Gives information about a topic<br>• Told as a story, or narrative |
| Fly High! | Biography | • About a person's life<br>• Important events or accomplishments<br>• Author and subject are different (third person) |
| The Upside Down Boy | Memoir | • Author and subject are the same (first person)<br>• Important memories<br>• True |
| HIMALAYA | Persuasive | • True information<br>• Convinces you to think a certain way or do something |

Section 2: Literary Analysis

**Reading Minilesson Principle**
# Hybrid books have fiction and nonfiction parts.

## Understanding Fiction and Nonfiction Genres

### You Will Need

- familiar hybrid books, such as the following from Text Set: Illustration Study: Craft:
  - *Gecko* by Raymond Huber
  - *Dingo* by Claire Saxby
- chart paper and markers
- basket of nonfiction and hybrid books
- sticky notes

### Academic Language / Important Vocabulary

- fiction
- nonfiction
- hybrid

### Continuum Connection

- Connect texts by a range of categories: e.g., content, message, genre, author/illustrator, special form, text structure, or organization (p. 62)
- Notice and understand the characteristics of some specific nonfiction genres: e.g., expository, narrative procedural and persuasive texts, biography, autobiography, memoir, hybrid text (p. 62)

## Goal

Notice and understand the characteristics of hybrid books.

## Rationale

Before teaching this minilesson, assess students' understanding of the characteristics of fiction and nonfiction genres to ensure they have a deep understanding of both. Authors layer genres into hybrid books to engage students in a topic—often using a narrative structure—and to help them consider a topic from different points of view.

## Assess Learning

Observe students when they discuss books. Notice if there is evidence of new learning based on the goal of this minilesson.

- Can students describe what a hybrid text is?
- Do they use their knowledge of hybrid books to support their understanding of their reading?
- Do they use academic language, such as *fiction, nonfiction,* and *hybrid*?

## Minilesson

To help students think about the minilesson principle, engage them in noticing the characteristics of books. Here is an example.

- Hold up the book *Gecko*.

  As I read, think about what the authors share and how they share it.

- Read only the larger print from page 14.

  What kind of information did the author give on this page? Is that fiction or nonfiction? How do you know?

- Draw three columns on a piece of chart paper. Label one column *Fiction* and record students' responses in that column. Then read only the small print from the same page.

  What kind of information did the author give in the smaller print? Is that information fiction or nonfiction? How do you know?

- Record responses under *Nonfiction* on the chart.

- Repeat this process with another page from the text.

## Have a Try

Invite the students to talk with a partner about another hybrid book, *Dingo*.

▶ Hold up *Dingo*. Read all of the print on pages 12–17.

What do you notice about the kind of information the author gives in this book? Is it fiction or nonfiction?

▶ After they turn and talk, invite students to share with the class, prompting as necessary. Add responses to the chart.

## Summarize and Apply

Summarize the learning and remind students to notice that some books have fictional and nonfictional parts.

Look at the chart. What do you notice about both of these books?

▶ Write the principle at the top of the chart.

Some books have fiction parts and nonfiction parts. These books are called hybrid books. In a hybrid book, the author includes a story, with characters and events, alongside true information.

▶ Provide a basket of nonfiction and hybrid books for the students to choose from during independent reading.

Today for independent reading, if you finish your book you may choose a book from this basket. As you read, notice if your book is a hybrid book and think about what makes it so. Mark what you notice with a sticky note so that you can share.

## Share

Following independent reading time, gather students together in the meeting area to talk about their reading.

Did you read a hybrid book today? Tell us how you know that.

## Extend the Lesson (Optional)

After assessing students' understanding, you might decide to extend the learning.

▶ **Writing About Reading** Invite students to build a chart to show the fiction and nonfiction parts of hybrid books (download from resources.fountasandpinnell.com). Students can glue the grid into a reader's notebook.

### Hybrid books have fiction and nonfiction parts.

| Book | Fiction | Nonfiction |
|------|---------|-----------|
| Gecko | • The character, Gecko, is an animal hunting for food. <br> • Gecko catches the cockroach and eats it. | • Geckos eat insects, worms, fruit, and other small lizards. <br> • Geckos have many tiny teeth. |
| Dingo | • The character, Dingo, is an animal hunting for food. <br> • Dingo runs quietly through the snow. <br> • Dingo catches a lizard. | • Dingoes eat insects, eggs, plants, and meat. <br> • Meat gives dingoes energy. <br> • Dingoes travel far each day. |

Section 2: Literary Analysis

## Assessment

After you have taught the minilessons in this umbrella, observe students as they talk and write about their reading across instructional contexts: interactive read-aloud, independent reading, guided reading, shared reading, and book club. Use *The Literacy Continuum* (Fountas and Pinnell 2017) to guide the observation of students' reading and writing behaviors.

▶ What evidence do you have of new understandings related to the genres of fiction and nonfiction?

- Are students able to describe the characteristics of fiction genres, such as realistic fiction, historical fiction, science fiction, and fantasy?
- Can students describe the characteristics of traditional literature, such as fairy tales, fables, and folktales?
- Are students able to describe the characteristics of nonfiction genres, such as biography, autobiography, memoir, expository, and narrative nonfiction?
- Can they correctly identify the fiction and nonfiction parts of hybrid books?
- Do they use academic language, such as *fiction, nonfiction, folktales,* and *memoir*?

▶ In what other ways, beyond the scope of this umbrella, are students talking about fiction and nonfiction genres?

- Can students determine the author's message or the author's purpose for writing a fiction or nonfiction book?
- Do students notice the different text features of nonfiction?

Use your observations to determine the next umbrella you will teach. You may also consult Minilessons Across the Year (pp. 59–61) for guidance.

## Link to Writing

After teaching the minilessons in this umbrella, help students link the learning to their own writing:

▶ When students write fiction or nonfiction in writers' workshop, encourage them to incorporate the characteristics of the particular genre they use to write their own pieces.

## Reader's Notebook

When this umbrella is complete, provide a copy of the minilesson principles (see resources.fountasandpinnell.com) for students to glue in the reader's notebook (in the Minilessons section if using *Reader's Notebook: Intermediate* [Fountas and Pinnell 2011]), so they can refer to the information as needed.

## Minilessons in This Umbrella

**RML1**  Poems are alike in many ways.

**RML2**  The definition of poetry is what is always true about it.

**RML3**  Poets use line breaks and white space to show you how to read the poem.

**RML4**  Poets use imagery to make you see, hear, and feel things.

**RML5**  Poets use rhythm so you can enjoy the language.

**RML6**  Poets repeat words with the same sounds.

**Poetry**

## Before Teaching Umbrella 6 Minilessons

Poetry is not a genre, but a "broad, overarching category of language of writing that can appear in any genre. . . . Poetry is compact writing characterized by imagination and artistry and imbued with intense meaning" (Fountas and Pinnell 2012c, 19). Studying poetry through the lens of genre study, even though it is not a single genre, allows students to understand the characteristics of poetry and to think about the role poetry plays in their lives as readers.

In a genre study (see pp. 39–41), students learn what to expect when beginning to read a text, enabling them to comprehend it more deeply. Before beginning this genre study, give students the opportunity to hear, read, and enjoy many different poems. Read poems that encompass a variety of forms (lyrical, free verse, haiku, limerick, etc.) and topics. Read poems that tell stories, poems that convey information, and poems that explore emotions and ideas. Read poems that play with sound and language. Use the following books from the *Fountas & Pinnell Classroom*™ *Interactive Read-Aloud Collection* text set listed below or choose poetry texts from your own library.

**Genre Study: Poetry**

*On the Wing* by David Elliott

*Shape Me a Rhyme* by Jane Yolen

*A Place to Start a Family: Poems About Creatures That Build* by David L. Harrison

As you read aloud and enjoy these texts together, help students

- think and talk about the meaning of each poem, and

- notice and discuss characteristics of poetry, such as line breaks, imagery, rhythm, and repetition.

**Reading Minilesson Principle**
## Poems are alike in many ways.

## Studying Poetry

### You Will Need

- for each group of students, a book of familiar poems, such as those from Text Set: Genre Study: Poetry
- chart paper and markers
- another familiar poem
- document camera (optional)

### Academic Language / Important Vocabulary

- poetry
- poem
- poet
- rhythm
- white space
- line break

### Continuum Connection

- Connect texts by a range of categories: e.g., content, theme, message, genre, author/illustrator, character, setting, special forms, text structure, or organization (pp. 58, 62)
- Understand that there are different types of texts and that they have different characteristics (p. 58)

### Goal

Notice and understand the elements of poetry.

### Rationale

When you teach students to analyze the characteristics of poetry, they know what to expect when they read a poem. They are prepared to see the images that poets create, learn the information poets share, follow the stories poets tell, and feel the emotions that poetry evokes. Understanding the characteristics of poetry also helps students write poems of their own.

### Assess Learning

Observe students when they read and discuss poetry and notice if there is evidence of new learning based on the goal of this minilesson.

- Can students talk about the characteristics of poetry?
- Do they understand that some characteristics are always evident and that some characteristics are evident only sometimes in poetry?
- Do they use vocabulary such as *poetry, poem, poet, rhythm, white space,* and *line break* when talking about poetry?

## Minilesson

To help students think about the minilesson principle, use familiar poems to engage them in noticing the characteristics of poetry. Here is an example.

- Divide students into small groups. Give each group a book of poems they have previously read and discussed.

    With your group, take a look at the poems I've given you. Think about what makes a poem a poem. What do you notice about your poems? What do some or all of your poems have in common? Discuss what you notice with your group.

- After students talk in their small groups, invite each group to share their thinking with the class. Help students decide whether each characteristic mentioned is always, often, or sometimes a characteristic of poetry. Record responses on chart paper. If students need more guidance, prompt discussion with questions such as the following:

    - *What do you notice about how your poems are written?*
    - *What do you notice about how your poems sound when you read them aloud?*
    - *What do you notice about the lines of the poems?*
    - *What do you notice about how poets describe people, places, or things?*
    - *Does anyone have a poem that has an interesting shape?*

## Have a Try

Invite the students to talk with a partner about the characteristics of a poem.

▶ Put students into pairs. Read aloud or display another familiar poem (use a document camera if available).

> Think about the characteristics of poetry we listed on our chart. Which of these characteristics do you notice in this poem? Do you notice anything about this poem that is not on our chart? Turn and talk with your partner about what you notice.

▶ After students turn and talk, invite several pairs to share their thinking. Discuss whether any new noticings are always, often, or sometimes a characteristic of poetry. Add them to the chart if appropriate.

## Summarize and Apply

Summarize the learning and remind students to think about the characteristics of poetry when they read poems.

> What did you notice about poetry today?

> Today during independent reading, choose a poetry book to read. Use our chart to think about your noticings. Bring one poem you like with you when we come back together and be ready to share the characteristics you noticed in it.

## Share

Following independent reading time, gather students together in the meeting area to talk about poetry.

▶ Have students turn and read their poem to a partner.

> Talk to your partner about what characteristics of poetry you noticed in your poem.

## Extend the Lesson (Optional)

After assessing students' understanding, you might decide to extend the learning.

▶ Encourage students to think about the characteristics of poetry when they write their own poems.

---

### Poems

**Noticings:**

**Always**
- Poets use few words to tell about an idea or to express a feeling.
- Poets use rhythm so you can enjoy the language.
- Poets use white space and line breaks to show you how to read the poem.

**Often**
- The poet's words make you see, hear, smell, or feel things.
- Poets repeat words and phrases.

**Sometimes**
- The poem has print in a shape that tells you about the meaning.
- Poets use rhyme.
- The poet compares one thing to another (metaphors and similes).
- Poets repeat the same sounds in a poem.

---

Section 2: Literary Analysis

**Reading Minilesson Principle**
## The definition of poetry is what is always true about it.

**Studying Poetry**

### You Will Need

- a familiar poem, such as "California Trapdoor Spider" from *A Place to Start a Family* by David L. Harrison, from Text Set: Genre Study: Poetry
- chart from RML1
- chart paper and markers
- document camera (optional)

### Academic Language / Important Vocabulary

- poetry
- poet
- definition

### Continuum Connection

- Notice and understand some elements of poetry: e.g., figurative language, rhyme, repetition, onomatopoeia, layout/line breaks (shape), imagery, alliteration, assonance (p. 58)
- Notice and understand some elements of poetry when they appear in nonfiction: e.g., figurative language, rhyme, repetition, onomatopoeia, layout/line breaks (shape), imagery, alliteration, assonance (p. 62)

## Goal

Create a working definition for poetry.

## Rationale

When students create a definition, they synthesize their understandings about poetry to arrive at a more complete understanding of its essence. As they become more familiar with poetry, they can revise the definition.

## Assess Learning

Observe students when they talk about poetry and notice if there is evidence of new learning based on the goal of this minilesson.

- Can students define poetry?
- Can they explain how a particular poem fits their definition of poetry?
- Do they use vocabulary such as *poetry, poet,* and *definition*?

## Minilesson

To help students think about the minilesson principle, engage them in constructing a definition of poetry. Here is an example.

- Divide students into small groups.
- Display the chart you created during RML1.

  Here's the list of our noticings about poetry. You noticed characteristics that are always, often, or sometimes present in poems. Now let's use what you noticed to write a definition of poetry. The definition of poetry is a sentence or a few sentences that tell what is always true about it.

- Write the words *Poetry is* on a separate sheet of chart paper.

  Think about how you would complete this sentence. How would you describe what poetry is to someone who has never read a poem? Turn and talk to share your ideas with a partner.

- After time for discussion, invite the students to share their best ideas. Discuss how to combine everyone's ideas to create a whole-class definition of poetry. Write the definition on the chart paper.

## Have a Try

Invite the students to talk with a partner about "California Trapdoor Spider."

> Display "California Trapdoor Spider," or another familiar poem, where everyone can see it. Read it aloud.
>
> > Does this poem fit our definition of poetry? Turn and talk to your partner about what you think and why.

> After students turn and talk, invite a few students to share their thinking.

## Summarize and Apply

Summarize the learning and remind students to think about the definition of poetry when they read poems.

> We wrote a definition of poetry together. As you read more poems, you may notice more things about poetry. We can revise our definition of poetry as you learn more about poetry.

> You may want to read a poetry book during independent reading today. If so, think about whether the poems you read fit our definition of poetry. Choose one poem to share when we come back together.

## Share

Following independent reading time, gather students together in the meeting area to discuss poetry.

> Who read a poem today that they would like to share with us?

> Does your poem fit our definition of poetry? If so, how? If not, why not?

## Extend the Lesson (Optional)

After assessing students' understanding, you might decide to extend the learning.

> Revisit and revise the definition as students gain new understandings about poetry (see Read and Revise on p. 200).

> Challenge students to write a poem that defines poetry ("Poetry is . . .").

---

### Poetry

Poetry is a kind of writing that uses few words to describe an idea in an imaginative or artistic way. The poet uses line breaks and white space.

**Section 2: Literary Analysis**

**Reading Minilesson Principle**

# Poets use line breaks and white space to show you how to read the poem.

### You Will Need

- two familiar poems with multiple stanzas, such as the following from Text Set: Genre Study: Poetry:
  - "California Trapdoor Spider" from *A Place to Start a Family* by David L. Harrison
  - "Circle" from *Shape Me a Rhyme* by Jane Yolen
- chart paper and markers
- document camera (optional)

### Academic Language / Important Vocabulary

- poem
- poet
- line break
- white space

### Continuum Connection

- Notice and understand some elements of poetry: e.g., figurative language, rhyme, repetition, onomatopoeia, layout/line breaks (shape), imagery, alliteration, assonance (p. 58)
- Notice and understand some elements of poetry when they appear in nonfiction: e.g., figurative language, rhyme, repetition, onomatopoeia, layout/ line breaks (shape), imagery, alliteration, assonance (p. 62)

## Goal

Learn how to read the line breaks and white space of a poem.

## Rationale

Poets intentionally use line breaks and white space to construct the rhythm of a poem and to group ideas thematically. When you teach students to notice this, they are better able to think about the structure and meaning of poetry.

## Assess Learning

Observe students when they read and talk about poetry and notice if there is evidence of new learning based on the goal of this minilesson.

- When students read poetry aloud, do they pause at appropriate points?
- Can they talk about how and why poets use line breaks and white space?
- Do they use vocabulary such as *poem, poet, line break,* and *white space,* when talking about poetry?

## Minilesson

To help students think about the minilesson principle, use a familiar poem to help them notice line breaks and white space. Here is an example.

- Display the poem "California Trapdoor Spider" so all students can see it.
- Read the poem aloud. Reread the poem emphasizing the line breaks.

  What did you notice about how I read these lines?

  How did I know when to pause?

  How would I read these sentences differently if this were a paragraph instead of a poem?

  When you're reading a paragraph, you always pause when you reach the end of a sentence. When you're reading a poem, you pause slightly when you reach the end of a line. The end of a line in a poem is called a line break. Poets choose where to put the line breaks. How do you think poets decide where to put line breaks?

  How do line breaks help you when you read poetry?

- Point to the space between the two stanzas of the poem.

  When I was reading the poem aloud, what did I do when I got to this part?

  This is called white space. White space is a place in a poem where there are no words. Why do you think the poet put white space here?

  How will the white space help you read the poem?

## Have a Try

Invite the students to talk with a partner about the poem "Circle."

▶ Display another familiar poem, such as "Circle."

Read this poem aloud with your partner. Remember to pay attention to the line breaks and white space. After you read it, turn and talk about how and why the poet used line breaks and white space.

▶ After students read and discuss the poem in pairs, ask a few students to share their thinking with the class.

## Summarize and Apply

Summarize the learning and remind students to pay attention to line breaks and white space when they read poetry.

Why do poets use line breaks?

Why do poets use white space?

▶ Record students' responses on chart paper, making the lines on the chart look like the lines and stanzas of a poem. Write the principle at the top of the chart.

If you read poetry today during independent reading, pay attention to how the poet uses line breaks and white space. Bring one poem that you would like to share when we come back together.

## Share

Following independent reading time, gather students together in the meeting area to talk about poetry.

Who would like to share a poem that you read today? What did you notice about the poem?

## Extend the Lesson (Optional)

After assessing students' understanding, you might decide to extend the learning.

▶ Have students recite poems to the class to give them practice in observing line breaks and white space.

▶ Encourage students to think about how to use line breaks and white space effectively when they write their own poems.

**Poets use line breaks and white space to show you how to read the poem.**

Line breaks . . .                    line break

   group certain words together

   tell you to pause slightly

   make the poem sound a certain way

                 white space

White space . . .

   separates different parts of the poem

   tells you to pause a little longer

**Section 2: Literary Analysis**

# RML4
## LA.U6.RML4

**Reading Minilesson Principle**
## Poets use imagery to make you see, hear, and feel things.

**Studying Poetry**

### You Will Need

- two or three familiar poems that contain imagery, such as the following from Text Set: Genre Study: Poetry:
  - "The Caribbean Flamingo" from *On the Wing* by David Elliott
  - "Fan" and "Crescent" from *Shape Me a Rhyme* by Jane Yolen
- document camera (optional)
- chart paper and markers
- sticky notes

### Academic Language / Important Vocabulary

- poet
- poem
- poetry
- imagery

### Continuum Connection

- Notice and understand some elements of poetry: e.g., figurative language, rhyme, repetition, onomatopoeia, layout/line breaks (shape), imagery, alliteration, assonance (p. 58)

- Notice and understand some elements of poetry when they appear in nonfiction: e.g., figurative language, rhyme, repetition, onomatopoeia, layout/ line breaks (shape), imagery, alliteration, assonance (p. 62)

## Goal

Notice and understand how poets use imagery to appeal to the senses.

## Rationale

When you teach students to recognize imagery in poetry, they are better able to understand the poem's meaning and appreciate the poet's craft.

## Assess Learning

Observe students when they read and talk about poetry and notice if there is evidence of new learning based on the goal of this minilesson.

- ▶ Do students notice imagery in poems?
- ▶ Do they talk about how imagery impacts the meaning of the poem?
- ▶ Do they use vocabulary such as *poet, poem, poetry,* and *imagery*?

# Minilesson

To help students think about the minilesson principle, use familiar poems to engage them in a discussion about imagery in poetry. Here is an example.

> I'm going to read a part of a poem to you. As I read, I want you to close your eyes, listen carefully, and use the words to make a picture in your mind.

▶ Read the poem "The Caribbean Flamingo" from *On the Wing*. Explain the meaning of unfamiliar words as necessary.

> What did you see in your mind while I read from this poem?
>
> What did you imagine you could feel?

▶ Display the poem so all students can see it, using a document camera if possible.

> How did the poet help you create sounds and images in your mind and feel a certain way?

▶ Record responses on chart paper.

> Now close your eyes again and listen carefully as I read another poem.

▶ Read "Fan" from *Shape Me a Rhyme*.

> What did you imagine seeing or hearing while I read this poem?

▶ Display the poem.

> How did the poet help you imagine sights and sounds?

▶ Record responses on the chart.

## Have a Try

Invite the students to talk with a partner about the imagery in "Crescent."

▶ Display "Crescent" from *Shape Me a Rhyme* and read it aloud.

> What did the poet do to create images in your mind? Turn and talk to your partner about that.

▶ After students turn and talk, ask a few students to share. Record responses on the chart.

## Summarize and Apply

Summarize the learning and remind students to notice and think about imagery in poetry.

> You noticed that poets use certain words and phrases that help you see, hear, and feel things in your mind. This is called imagery. The language appeals to your senses. Why do you think poets often use imagery?

▶ Write the principle at the top of the chart.

> If you read poetry today, notice if the poet uses imagery to help you see, hear, or feel things in your mind. If you find an example of imagery, mark it with a sticky note and bring your book to share when we come back together.

| Poets use imagery to make you see, hear, and feel things. | | |
|---|---|---|
| Poem | Imagery | What the Poet Did to Create Imagery |
| "The Caribbean Flamingo" | • Sights: a red spark; huge flames  • Feeling: heat | • Used the word ember  • Used the word conflagration |
| "Fan" | • Sights: shells on the sand  • Sounds: Jingling of the shells | • Described shells fanned out on the sand  • Used musical words—single, Jingle, dingle |
| "Crescent" | • Sights: a thin sliver of the moon | • Compared the moon to the side of a penny (copper cent) |

## Share

Following independent reading time, gather students together in the meeting area to share examples of imagery.

> Who found an example of imagery in a poem today?

> Please read aloud the example you found. What did you imagine while you read the poem? How did the imagery help you better understand or enjoy the poem?

## Extend the Lesson (Optional)

After assessing students' understanding, you might decide to extend the learning.

▶ Show an image (e.g., a sunset) or play a sound (e.g., a thunderstorm). Have students write phrases to help readers imagine the image or sound.

▶ **Writing About Reading** Have students write in a reader's notebook about the imagery in a poem.

**Reading Minilesson Principle**
## Poets use rhythm so you can enjoy the language.

### You Will Need

- two familiar poems that have an obvious, consistent rhythm, such as the following:
  - "Circle" and "Triangle" from *Shape Me a Rhyme* by Jane Yolen, from Text Set: Genre Study: Poetry
- document camera (optional)
- chart paper and markers

### Academic Language / Important Vocabulary

- poem
- poet
- poetry
- rhythm

### Continuum Connection

- Notice how aspects of a text like rhyme, rhythm, and repetition affect appreciation or enjoyment (p. 140)

### Goal

Notice and understand a poet's use of rhythm.

### Rationale

Rhythm makes poetry enjoyable to read aloud and easy to remember. When you teach students to notice rhythm in poetry, they are better able to understand and appreciate the language and meaning of poetry. They also think about the decisions poets make when writing poetry, which helps them when writing their own poems.

### Assess Learning

Observe students when they read and discuss poetry and notice if there is evidence of new learning based on the goal of this minilesson.

- Do students notice when a poem has a consistent rhythm?
- Do they use vocabulary such as *poem, poet, poetry,* and *rhythm*?

## Minilesson

To help students think about the minilesson principle, use familiar poems to engage them in noticing rhythm in poetry. Here is an example.

- Display "Circle" from *Shape Me a Rhyme* so all students can see it, using a document camera if possible.

  As I read this poem aloud, listen carefully to how the poem sounds.

- Read the poem aloud, emphasizing its very regular, sing-song rhythm. Prompt discussion about the poem's rhythm.

  What did you notice about how this poem sounds?

  What makes this poem fun to read aloud?

  This poem has a rhythm. That means that the sounds of the words in the poem follow a pattern. This pattern of sounds makes the poem fun to read aloud and easy to remember. The rhythm of a poem is similar to the beat of a song. We can clap along to a poem just like we can clap along to a song.

- To help students notice the rhythm of the poem, reread the first verse while you clap along with the rhythm.

  What do you notice about how the poet created the rhythm of this poem? What did she do to give it a rhythm?

  How would you describe the rhythm? Is it always the same or does it change? Why do you think the poet gave this poem about a circle the same rhythm for every line?

- Record students' responses on chart paper.

## Have a Try

Invite the students to talk with a partner about "Triangle."

▶ Display the poem "Triangle" from *Shape Me a Rhyme* and read it aloud, emphasizing its rhythm.

Turn and talk to your partner about what you notice about the rhythm of this poem. What gives this poem its rhythm?

▶ After students turn and talk, invite several pairs to share their thinking. Record their responses on the chart.

## Summarize and Apply

Summarize the learning and remind students to notice rhythm when they read poetry.

What did you notice about the poems we read aloud today?

You noticed that the poems we read have a rhythm. Rhythm is a repeated pattern of beats. Why do you think poets use rhythm?

▶ Write the principle at the top of the chart.

If you read poetry today during independent reading, think about how the poems would sound if you read them aloud. If you read a poem that has an interesting rhythm, bring it to share when we come back together.

## Share

Following independent reading time, gather students together in the meeting area to talk about rhythm in poetry.

Who read a poem with an interesting rhythm today?

Read aloud the poem, or at least a part that shows the rhythm.

Read it aloud again, and this time we will clap the beats while you read.

## Extend the Lesson (Optional)

After assessing students' understanding, you might decide to extend the learning.

▶ Find poems with obvious rhythms to use for choral reading with the class. Clap out the beats to emphasize the rhythm.

---

**Poets use rhythm so you can enjoy the language.**

| | |
|---|---|
| "Circle" by Jane Yolen | • Repetition of a pattern ("Round as ___") |
| | • Regular rhythm, like something rolling along or something that keeps going and doesn't end |
| "Triangle" by Jane Yolen | • Repeated rhythm (two short lines, one longer line; two short lines, one longer line) |
| | • Rhyming (the two short lines rhyme; the two longer lines rhyme) |

# RML 6
## LA.U6.RML6

**Reading Minilesson Principle**
## Poets repeat words with the same sounds.

## Studying Poetry

### You Will Need

- three or four familiar poems that contain alliteration and/or assonance, such as the following from Text Set: Genre Study: Poetry:
  - "European Paper Wasp" from *A Place to Start a Family* by David L. Harrison
  - "The Bowerbird" and "The Dippers" from *On the Wing* by David Elliott
  - "Crescent" from *Shape Me a Rhyme* by Jane Yolen
- document camera (optional)
- chart paper and markers

### Academic Language / Important Vocabulary

- repetition
- vowel
- consonant
- alliteration
- assonance

### Continuum Connection

- Notice and understand some elements of poetry: e.g., figurative language, rhyme, repetition, onomatopoeia, layout/line breaks (shape), imagery, alliteration, assonance (p. 58)
- Notice and understand some elements of poetry when they appear in nonfiction: e.g., figurative language, rhyme, repetition, onomatopoeia, layout/ line breaks (shape), imagery, alliteration, assonance (p. 62)
- Notice how aspects of a text like rhyme, rhythm, and repetition affect appreciation or enjoyment (p. 140)

### Goal

Notice when poets use alliteration and assonance.

### Rationale

Alliteration and assonance lend coherence to poems and make them enjoyable for the reader or listener. Teaching students to notice alliteration and assonance is likely to deepen their appreciation of poetry. It also encourages them to think about the decisions poets make when writing poetry, which helps them when writing their own poems.

### Assess Learning

Observe students when they read and talk about poetry and notice if there is evidence of new learning based on the goal of this minilesson.

- Do students notice alliteration and assonance in poetry?
- Can they define alliteration and assonance?
- Do they use vocabulary such as *repetition, vowel, consonant, alliteration,* and *assonance*?

## Minilesson

To help students think about the minilesson principle, use familiar poems to help them notice alliteration and assonance in poetry. Here is an example.

- Display "European Paper Wasp" from *A Place to Start a Family* so all students can see it. Read the first two lines of the poem.

  What do you notice about the words in the first two lines of this poem?

  The first four words all start with the letter *w*. This is called alliteration. Alliteration is when two or more words close together start with the same consonant sound.

- Display "The Bowerbird" from *On the Wing*. Read it aloud.

  Who can find an example of alliteration in this poem?

- Write the definition of alliteration and examples of alliteration from these poems on chart paper.

- Display "The Dippers" from *On the Wing*. Read the third line.

  What do you notice about the words *skip, little,* and *dippers*?

  These words have a short *i* sound. When a vowel sound is repeated in words close together, it's called assonance.

- Write the definition of assonance and the examples on the chart.

## Have a Try

Invite the students to talk with a partner about alliteration and assonance in a poem.

▶ Display "Crescent" from *Shape Me a Rhyme* and read it aloud.

> With your partner, see if you can find any examples of repeated sounds in this poem. If you find any, talk about whether they are alliteration or assonance.

▶ After students turn and talk, invite a few pairs to share their thinking. Record examples on the chart.

## Summarize and Apply

Summarize the learning and remind students to notice alliteration and assonance when they read poetry.

> What did you notice about the poems we read today?

> You noticed that the poets repeated certain sounds in different words. You learned that this is called alliteration and assonance. What's the difference between alliteration and assonance?

> Why do you think poets sometimes use alliteration and assonance?

▶ Write the principle at the top of the chart.

> If you read poetry today, notice if the poet uses alliteration or assonance. If you find any examples, bring them to share when we come back together.

## Share

Following independent reading time, gather students together in the meeting area to share examples of alliteration and assonance.

> Did anyone find any examples of alliteration or assonance in poetry today?

> Please share the examples you found.

## Extend the Lesson (Optional)

After assessing students' understanding, you might decide to extend the learning.

▶ Encourage students to write or find poems with alliteration or assonance to share with the class.

**Poets repeat words with the same sounds.**

| | Definition | Examples |
|---|---|---|
| Alliteration | The repetition of consonant sounds at the beginning of words | winged, warriors warn, with<br><br>fancy, feathers<br><br>side, cent |
| Assonance | The repetition of vowel sounds | skip, little, dippers, moon, new |

Section 2: Literary Analysis

## Assessment

After you have taught the minilessons in this umbrella, observe students as they talk and write about their reading across instructional contexts: interactive read-aloud, independent reading, guided reading, shared reading, and book club, as well as their poetry writing in writers' workshop. Use *The Literacy Continuum* (Fountas and Pinnell 2017) to guide the observation of students' reading and writing behaviors.

▶ What evidence do you have of new understandings related to the characteristics of poetry?

- Can students identify the characteristics of poetry?

- Do they pay attention to line breaks and white space in poetry?

- Do they notice and understand imagery in poetry?

- Do they notice and enjoy the rhythm of certain poems?

- Do they notice when poets use alliteration and assonance?

- Do they use academic language, such as *poetry, poet, poem, line break, white space, imagery, rhythm, alliteration,* and *assonance*?

▶ In what other ways, beyond the scope of this umbrella, are students talking about genre?

- Are students noticing different types of fiction and nonfiction books?

Use your observations to determine the next umbrella you will teach. You may also consult Minilessons Across the Year (pp. 59–61) for guidance.

## Read and Revise

After completing the steps in the genre study process, help students read and revise their definition of the genre based on their new understandings.

▶ **Before:** Poetry is a kind of writing that uses few words to describe an idea in an imaginative or artistic way. The poet uses line breaks and white space.

▶ **After:** Poetry is an imaginative, artistic kind of writing that uses few words. Poems can describe an idea or emotion, tell a story, or give information about a topic. The poet uses line breaks and white space and often uses imagery, rhythm, and repetition.

## Reader's Notebook

When this umbrella is complete, provide a copy of the minilesson principles (see resources.fountasandpinnell.com) for students to glue in the reader's notebook (in the Minilessons section if using *Reader's Notebook: Intermediate* [Fountas and Pinnell 2011]), so they can refer to the information as needed.

## Minilessons in This Umbrella

**RML1**  A lyrical poem is a songlike poem that has rhythm and sometimes rhyme.

**RML2**  A free verse poem doesn't have to rhyme or have rhythm.

**RML3**  A limerick is a rhyming poem that is usually surprising, funny, and nonsensical.

**RML4**  Haiku is an ancient Japanese form of non-rhyming poetry that creates a picture and often conveys emotion.

**RML5**  A concrete poem is shaped to show what the poem is about.

## Before Teaching Umbrella 7 Minilessons

"Poetry is compact writing characterized by imagination and artistry and imbued with intense meaning" (Fountas and Pinnell 2012c, 19). Studying poetry helps students understand the role poetry plays in their lives as readers. Looking closely at and discussing the characteristics of different kinds of poems prepares students to understand the range of emotions poetry can make one feel.

Select poems that represent the characteristics of different kinds of poetry (lyrical, free verse, haiku, limerick, concrete). Choose some poems that have rhythm, rhyme, and descriptive or figurative language and that create a shape that shows what the poem is about. Be sure students enjoy each poem and think and talk about the meaning. After reading many poems they will be able to notice and generalize the characteristics of different kinds of poetry. Use the following books from the *Fountas & Pinnell Classroom™ Interactive Read-Aloud Collection* text sets, or choose poetry texts from your own library to support students in studying poetry.

**Poetry**

*Shape Me a Rhyme*
by Jane Yolen

**Douglas Florian**

**Floyd Cooper**

**Patricia McKissack**

**Genre Study: Poetry**

> *The Barefoot Book of Earth Poems*
> compiled by Judith Nicholls

> *A Place to Start a Family: Poems About Creatures That Build*
> by David L. Harrison

> *What Are You Glad About? What Are You Mad About?*
> by Judith Viorst

> *Shape Me a Rhyme: Nature's Forms in Poetry* by Jane Yolen

**Author/Illustrator Study: Douglas Florian**

> *Lizards, Frogs, and Polliwogs*

> *Mammalabilia*

**Illustrator Study: Floyd Cooper**

> *Meet Danitra Brown* by Nikki Grimes

**Author Study: Patricia McKissack**

> *Stitchin' and Pullin': A Gee's Bend Quilt*

As you read aloud and enjoy these texts together, help students

- think and talk about the meaning of each poem, and
- notice and generalize the characteristics of poetry.

**Reading Minilesson Principle**

# A lyrical poem is a songlike poem that has rhythm and sometimes rhyme.

## Exploring Different Kinds of Poetry

### You Will Need

- several familiar lyrical poems, such as the following:
  - "Horse of the Sea" from *The Barefoot Book of Earth Poems* compiled by Judith Nicholls and "Red Ovenbird" from *A Place to Start a Family* by David L. Harrison, from Text Set: Genre Study: Poetry
  - "Jump Rope Rhyme" from *Meet Danitra Brown* by Nikki Grimes, from Text Set: Illustrator Study: Floyd Cooper
- chart paper and markers
- document camera to project poems, or the poems written in advance on chart paper
- two sticky notes, one that says *Rhythm* and one that says *Rhyme*
- sticky notes
- basket of poetry books or poems

### Academic Language / Important Vocabulary

- lyrical
- rhythm
- rhyme

### Continuum Connection

- Recognize and understand some specific types of poetry: e.g., lyrical poetry, free verse, limerick, haiku, narrative poetry, ballad, epic/saga, concrete poetry [pp. 58, 62]
- Notice and understand some elements of poetry: e.g., figurative language, rhyme, repetition, onomatopoeia, layout/line breaks [shape], imagery, alliteration, assonance [pp. 58, 62]

## Goal

Recognize and understand the characteristics of a lyrical poem.

## Rationale

When you help students understand the characteristics of lyrical poems they know what to expect when reading a lyrical poem and will understand the poem more deeply.

## Assess Learning

Observe students when they read and discuss poetry. Notice if there is evidence of new learning based on the goal of this minilesson.

- ▶ Can students recognize a lyrical poem?
- ▶ Are they able to describe the characteristics of a lyrical poem?
- ▶ Do they use the words *lyrical, rhythm,* and *rhyme*?

## Minilesson

To help students think about the minilesson principle, engage them in noticing the characteristics of lyrical poems. Here is an example.

- ▶ Project or display "Horse of the Sea" from *The Barefoot Book of Earth Poems.* Read it aloud once and then again, emphasizing the rhythmic qualities.

  What is the poet trying to say?

  What do you notice about how the lines of this poem sound?

  What do they make you feel like doing?

- ▶ Record responses on chart paper.

  A word for that is *rhythm*.

- ▶ Have a student place the sticky note for *Rhythm* on the chart.
- ▶ Project or display "Jump Rope Rhyme" from *Meet Danitra Brown.* Read it aloud once and then again, emphasizing the rhyme.

  What is this poet trying to say?

  What do you notice about how some of the words in this poem sound?

- ▶ Record rhyming words that students name on the chart. Have a student place the sticky note for *Rhyme* on the chart.

  Poems like the ones you just heard could easily be set to music. They have songlike qualities. The name for this type of poem is *lyrical*.

## Have a Try

Invite the students to talk with a partner about "Red Ovenbird" from *A Place to Start a Family.*

▸ Ask a student to read the poem aloud twice.

　Turn and talk to your partner about what the poet is trying to say. What do you notice about the lines and words in this poem?

▸ Record responses on the chart.

## Summarize and Apply

Summarize the learning and remind students to notice rhythm and rhyme in lyrical poems.

　Today you heard some lyrical poems. How can you describe a lyrical poem?

▸ Invite responses and write the principle at the top of the chart.

　Today when you read, choose a book of poetry from this basket. Notice if the poem you read has rhythm or rhyme. If it does, mark it with a sticky note and bring it to share when we meet.

## Share

Following independent reading time, gather students together in groups of three or four to discuss the poems they read.

　Is the poem you read today a lyrical poem? How can you tell that it is or isn't?

## Extend the Lesson (Optional)

After assessing students' understanding, you might decide to extend the learning.

▸ Encourage students to continue reading poetry. Add titles of lyrical poems to the chart.

▸ Encourage students to write and illustrate poems that have rhythm and rhyme.

▸ **Writing About Reading** Have students write in a reader's notebook their thoughts about a poem they have read. They can comment on the rhythm, rhyme, topic, or some other aspect of the poem.

---

**A lyrical poem is a songlike poem that has rhythm and sometimes rhyme.**

**Rhythm**
- feels like I want to clap along
- feels like a song
- feels like the poem has a beat

**Rhyme**
- name/same
- spin/in
- hide/inside
- round/ground
- sing/ring

*Section 2: Literary Analysis*

# RML2
## LA.U7.RML2

**Reading Minilesson Principle**
# A free verse poem doesn't have to rhyme or have rhythm.

## Exploring Different Kinds of Poetry

### You Will Need

- several familiar free verse poems from texts, such as the following:
  - "Stories to Tell" from *Meet Danitra Brown* by Nikki Grimes, from Text Set: Illustrator Study: Floyd Cooper
  - "Where to Start" and "Remembering" from *Stitchin' and Pullin'* by Patricia C. McKissack, from Text Set: Author Study: Patricia McKissack
- chart paper prepared to make a word web (center oval in center, spokes)
- markers
- sticky notes
- basket of poetry books, including free verse poems

### Academic Language / Important Vocabulary

- free verse
- rhythm
- rhyme
- characteristic

### Continuum Connection

- Recognize and understand some specific types of poetry: e.g., lyrical poetry, free verse, limerick, haiku, narrative poetry, ballad, epic/saga, concrete poetry (pp. 58, 62)

## Goal

Recognize and understand the characteristics of free verse poetry.

## Rationale

Free verse poetry is unbound by rhythm and rhyme, although some elements of poetry (e.g., figurative language, alliteration, assonance) may be present. Helping students understand that not all poetry is bound by certain characteristics allows them to expand their definition of poetry when both reading and writing poems.

## Assess Learning

Observe students when they read and discuss poetry. Notice if there is evidence of new learning based on the goal of this minilesson.

- ❯ Can students describe what they notice about the poems they read?
- ❯ Do they talk about free verse poems not needing to have rhythm or rhyme?
- ❯ Do they use the words *free verse*, *rhythm*, *rhyme*, and *characteristic*?

## Minilesson

To help students think about the minilesson principle, engage them in noticing the characteristics of free verse poems using familiar examples. Here is an example.

- ❯ Read "Stories to Tell" from *Meet Danitra Brown*.

    What is the writer trying to say?

    What do you notice about the way she wrote this poem? Is it similar to or different from other poems you have read?

    How is it the same or different?

- ❯ Record responses around the center oval on the chart.
- ❯ Repeat this process with "Where to Start" from *Stitchin' and Pullin'*.

    What are you noticing about these poems, especially as compared with many other poems you have read?

    These poems don't have to have the "usual" characteristics of poetry, such as rhythm and rhyme, though they might have some characteristics of poetry. These poems are free of any poetic "have to's," so they are called free verse.

## Have a Try

Invite the students to talk with a partner about "Remembering" from *Stitchin' and Pullin'*.

❱ Ask two students to read the poems aloud.

> Turn and talk to your partner. Are these free verse poems or another type of poetry? How do you know?

❱ Record responses on the chart.

## Summarize and Apply

Summarize the learning and remind students to notice the characteristics of free verse.

> Look at the chart we made today. What can you say about free verse poems?

❱ Write the principle at the top of the chart.

> Today when you read, choose a book of poetry from this basket. Decide if the poem you read is free verse. If it is, mark it with a sticky note and bring it to share when we meet.

## Share

Following independent reading time, gather students together in groups of three or four to discuss the poems they read.

> Did you read a free verse poem today? Why do you think that? Did you notice anything about your poem that we should add to the chart?

## Extend the Lesson (Optional)

After assessing students' understanding, you might decide to extend the learning.

❱ Encourage students to continue reading poetry. Add titles of free verse poems to the chart.

❱ Encourage students to write and illustrate free verse poems.

❱ **Writing About Reading** Ask students to write in a reader's notebook their opinion of a free verse poem they have read.

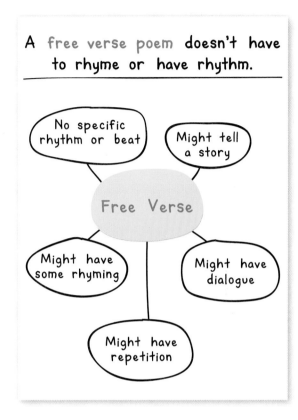

A free verse poem doesn't have to rhyme or have rhythm.

- No specific rhythm or beat
- Might tell a story
- Free Verse
- Might have some rhyming
- Might have dialogue
- Might have repetition

**Reading Minilesson Principle**

# A limerick is a rhyming poem that is usually surprising, funny, and nonsensical.

## Exploring Different Kinds of Poetry

### You Will Need

- several familiar limericks, such as "Shivery Winter Song" and "What Terry Told Me While We Were Eating Our Ice Cream," from *What Are You Glad About? What Are You Mad About?* by Judith Viorst, from Text Set: Genre Study: Poetry

- chart paper prepared with a limerick

- markers

- basket of poetry books, including limericks

### Academic Language / Important Vocabulary

- limerick

- rhyming

- nonsensical

### Continuum Connection

- Recognize and understand some specific types of poetry: e.g., lyrical poetry, free verse, limerick, haiku, narrative poetry, ballad, epic/saga, concrete poetry (pp. 58, 62)

- Notice and understand some elements of poetry: e.g., figurative language, rhyme, repetition, onomatopoeia, layout/line breaks (shape), imagery, alliteration, assonance (pp. 58, 62)

## Goal

Recognize and understand the characteristics of limericks.

## Rationale

When students study limericks and discuss their observations, they know what to expect when reading limericks.

## Assess Learning

Observe students when they read and discuss poetry. Notice if there is evidence of new learning based on the goal of this minilesson.

- ▶ Can students recognize a limerick?

- ▶ Are they able to explain why a particular poem is a limerick?

- ▶ Do they use the words *limerick, rhyming,* and *nonsensical*?

# Minilesson

To help students think about the minilesson principle, use familiar limericks to engage students in noticing the characteristics. Here is an example.

- ▶ Read "Shivery Winter Song" from *What Are You Glad About? What Are You Mad About?* and "Lemonade."

    What do you notice about these poems?

- ▶ If necessary, prompt students to notice the rhyme and rhythm patterns of lines 1, 2, and 5 and of lines 3 and 4 in each stanza.

    How are these poems similar to and different from other poems you have read?

- ▶ List responses on chart paper.

    These poems are limericks. They have a pattern of rhyme and rhythm that is easy to recognize and very different from other poems. How can you describe what the poems are about?

## Have a Try

Invite the students to talk with a partner about "What Terry Told Me While We Were Eating Our Ice Cream" from *What Are You Glad About? What Are You Mad About?*

▶ Read the limerick.

Turn and talk to your partner. Is this poem a limerick? How can you tell?

## Summarize and Apply

Summarize the learning and remind students to notice the characteristics of limericks.

Today you learned about a kind of poem called a limerick.

▶ Write the principle at the top of the chart.

Today when you read, choose a book of poetry from this basket. Think about the meaning and the characteristics of the poems you read. You might notice a lyrical poem, a free verse poem, or a limerick. If you read a limerick, mark it with a sticky note and bring it to share when we meet.

## Share

Following independent reading time, gather students together in groups of three or four to discuss the poems they read.

Did anyone read a limerick today? If so, how do you know it is a limerick? If no one in your group read a limerick, talk about the characteristics of the poem you did read.

## Extend the Lesson (Optional)

After assessing students' understanding, you might decide to extend the learning.

▶ Encourage students to continue reading poetry. Add titles of limericks to the chart.

▶ Encourage students to write and illustrate limericks. Have them read them aloud.

▶ **Writing About Reading** Ask students to respond in a reader's notebook to a limerick or other poem.

A limerick is a rhyming poem that is usually surprising, funny, and nonsensical.

**Lemonade**
by Ella G.
Lemonade, lemonade is so sweet,
Stomp those lemons with your feet.
  Sweet and sour—very good,
  Make it for the neighborhood.
Cheers together for this yummy treat!

- Has rhyming words
- Has 5 lines
- Lines 1, 2, and 5 rhyme
- Lines 1, 2, and 5 have the same rhythm
- Lines 3 and 4 have the same rhythm
- Funny
- Doesn't always make sense

**Reading Minilesson Principle**

# Haiku is an ancient Japanese form of non-rhyming poetry that creates a picture and often conveys emotion.

## Exploring Different Kinds of Poetry

### You Will Need

- select haiku from a variety of sources, such as "Arch: A Haiku" from *Shape Me a Rhyme* by Jane Yolen, from Text Set: Genre Study: Poetry

- document camera to project poems, or the poems written in advance on chart paper

- chart paper and markers

- basket of poetry books and poems, including haiku

### Academic Language / Important Vocabulary

- haiku
- non-rhyming
- emotions

### Continuum Connection

- Recognize and understand some specific types of poetry: e.g., lyrical poetry, free verse, limerick, haiku, narrative poetry, ballad, epic/saga, concrete poetry (pp. 58, 62)

- Notice and understand some elements of poetry: e.g., figurative language, rhyme, repetition, onomatopoeia, layout/line breaks (shape), imagery, alliteration, assonance (pp. 58, 62)

## Goal

Recognize and understand the characteristics of haiku.

## Rationale

When you study haiku with students, it broadens their understanding of different kinds of poems, teaches them to create a picture in the mind when reading poems, and gives them the opportunity to discuss the emotions conveyed by haiku, all of which supports them in understanding more about reading poetry.

## Assess Learning

Observe students when they read and discuss poetry. Notice if there is evidence of new learning based on the goal of this minilesson.

- ❯ Can students recognize haiku?
- ❯ Are they able to describe the characteristics of haiku?
- ❯ Do they use the words *haiku, non-rhyming,* and *emotions*?

## Minilesson

To help students think about the minilesson principle, engage them in listening to and noticing the characteristics of haiku. Here is an example.

- ❯ Read several haiku, such as "Arch: A Haiku" from *Shape Me a Rhyme*.

  What do you notice is the same about these poems?

  What do you notice about the topics of these poems?

  Think about the syllables in each line. What do you notice?

  What do you think the author is trying to get you to think about?

- ❯ Record responses on the chart paper.

  These poems are an ancient Japanese form of poetry called haiku.

## Have a Try

Invite the students to talk with a partner about another haiku.

▶ Read another haiku aloud.

Turn and talk to your partner. Is this a haiku? How do you know?

## Summarize and Apply

Summarize the learning and remind students to notice the characteristics of haiku.

Today you learned about a form of poetry called haiku.

▶ Write the principle at the top of the chart.

Today when you read, choose a poetry book or poem from this basket. Think about whether the poem is a haiku or another type of poetry. Be prepared to talk about the poem when we meet.

## Share

Following independent reading time, gather students together in the meeting area to talk about their reading.

Did anyone read a haiku? Read it aloud for us.

How did you know it was a haiku?

If you didn't read a haiku, tell us about the poem you did read.

## Extend the Lesson (Optional)

After assessing students' understanding, you might decide to extend the learning.

▶ Encourage students to continue reading, writing, and illustrating haiku. Often the use of watercolors is a good medium for conveying the meaning and tone. Create a wall display of their haiku and art.

▶ Teach minilessons on several different kinds of poems. For descriptions of several poetic structures, visit resources.fountasandpinnell.com.

▶ **Writing About Reading** Ask students to write a response to a haiku in a reader's notebook.

---

**Haiku** is an ancient Japanese form of non-rhyming poetry that creates a picture and often conveys emotion.

- Short

- No rhyme or rhythm

- About something in nature

- Creates a picture in your mind

- 5 syllables in the first and last lines

- 7 syllables in the middle line

 Haiku

**Reading Minilesson Principle**

# A concrete poem is shaped to show what the poem is about.

## Exploring Different Kinds of Poetry

### You Will Need

- several familiar concrete poems, such as the following:
  - "The Python" from *Lizards, Frogs, and Polliwogs* by Douglas Florian, from Text Set: Author/Illustrator Study: Douglas Florian
  - "The Bactrian Camel" and "The Porcupine" from *Mammalabilia* by Douglas Florian, from Text Set: Author/Illustrator Study: Douglas Florian
  - "Wave" from *Shape Me a Rhyme* by Jane Yolen, from Text Set: Genre Study: Poetry
- chart paper and markers
- document camera (optional)
- collection of poetry books and concrete poems
- sticky notes

### Academic Language / Important Vocabulary

- concrete

### Continuum Connection

- Recognize and understand some specific types of poetry: e.g., lyrical poetry, free verse, limerick, haiku, narrative poetry, ballad, epic/saga, concrete poetry (pp. 58, 62)
- Notice and understand some elements of poetry: e.g., figurative language, rhyme, repetition, onomatopoeia, layout/line breaks (shape), imagery, alliteration, assonance (pp. 58, 62)

## Goal

Recognize and understand the characteristics of concrete poetry.

## Rationale

When you teach students to notice the shape of a poem as it is laid out in print, they learn to use the layout to help them understand what a poem is about.

## Assess Learning

Observe students when they read and discuss poetry. Notice if there is evidence of new learning based on the goal of this minilesson.

- Do students notice when a poem has a unique shape?
- Can they discuss how the shape of a poem reflects what the poem is about?
- Do they use the word *concrete* when talking about poetry?

# Minilesson

To help students think about the minilesson principle, use poems that create shapes to help them think about the poet's rationale. Project the poems with a document camera, if available. Here is an example.

- Show "The Python" from *Lizards, Frogs, and Polliwogs* to all the students.

  As I read this poem, think about how the poet placed the words on the page.

  What shape did the poet use? Why do you think he chose that shape? What does the shape help you to understand?

- Record responses on the chart paper.
- Repeat this process with "The Bactrian Camel" and "The Porcupine" from *Mammalabilia*.
- What do all these poems have in common?

  The way the poet arranged the words of these poems makes a shape. These are called concrete poems.

  What do you notice about each shape?

## Have a Try

Invite the students to talk with a partner about "Wave" from *Shape Me a Rhyme*.

▶ Show the poem and read it aloud.

Turn and talk to your partner. How does the shape of the poem tell you what the poem is about?

▶ Record responses on the chart.

## Summarize and Apply

Summarize the learning and remind students to notice the shape of a poem.

Today you learned about concrete poems.

▶ Invite responses and write the principle at the top of the chart.

Today when you read, choose a book of poetry or a poem from this basket. Notice if the poem you read has a shape—is a concrete poem—and think about how that reflects the meaning of the poem. Mark it with a sticky note and bring it to share when we meet.

## Share

Following independent reading time, gather students together in the meeting area to talk about their reading.

Did anyone read a concrete poem today? How did the shape help you understand what the poem was about?

If you didn't read a concrete poem, tell us about the poem you did read.

## Extend the Lesson (Optional)

After assessing students' understanding, you might decide to extend the learning.

▶ Provide the opportunity for students to write and illustrate their own poems. Encourage them to think about how creating a shape with the words could help the reader understand what the poem is about.

▶ **Writing About Reading** Ask students to respond to a concrete poem in a reader's notebook, including what they noticed about the shape and how that helped them understand the poem's meaning.

A **concrete poem** is shaped to show what the poem is about.

A poem about a snake in the shape of a snake is a concrete poem.

| | How does the shape of the poem help you? |
|---|---|
| | "The Python"<br>• Picture the python squeezing its prey |
| | "The Bactrian Camel"<br>• Picture humps of a camel<br>• Have fun with the poem |
| | "The Porcupine"<br>• Picture the quills on a porcupine<br>• See how they "sprout out"<br>• Hear the rhyming words |
| | "Wave"<br>• Picture things in nature that are the shape of a wave<br>• Know when to pause<br>• Helps you hear the rhyme |

**Section 2: Literary Analysis**

## Assessment

After you have taught the minilessons in this umbrella, observe students as they talk and write about their reading across instructional contexts: interactive read-aloud, independent reading, guided reading, shared reading, and book club. Use *The Literacy Continuum* (Fountas and Pinnell 2017) to guide the observation of students' reading and writing behaviors.

◗ What evidence do you have of new understandings related to different kinds of poetry?

- Do students understand and discuss the different kinds of poetry—lyrical, free verse, limerick, haiku, and concrete?
- Can they talk about the characteristics of each kind of poetry?
- Do they notice how a poem's shape reflects its meaning?
- Do they use academic language, such as *rhythm, rhyme, free verse, limerick, haiku,* and *concrete*?

◗ In what other ways, beyond the scope of this umbrella, are students talking about the poetry they read?

- Are students discussing why a poet chose certain words?
- Can they compare and contrast two poems written about the same topic?
- Are they able to compare and contrast two different types of poems?

Use your observations to determine the next umbrella you will teach. You may also consult Minilessons Across the Year (pp. 59–61) for guidance.

## Link to Writing

After teaching the minilessons in this umbrella, help students link the new learning to their own writing:

◗ When students write their own poetry, encourage them to try out different forms. Suggest that they try writing two poems about the same topic, using a different form of poetry for each.

## Reader's Notebook

When this umbrella is complete, provide a copy of the minilesson principles (see resources.fountasandpinnell.com) for students to glue in the reader's notebook (in the Minilessons section if using *Reader's Notebook: Intermediate* [Fountas and Pinnell 2011]), so they can refer to the information as needed.

## Minilessons in This Umbrella

**RML1**  The author has a purpose for writing a book.

**RML2**  The author gives a message in a fiction book.

**RML3**  The author gives a message in a nonfiction book.

**RML4**  Several authors can give the same message.

**RML5**  Think about what the author's message means to you, to society, or to the world.

## Before Teaching Umbrella 8 Minilessons

The minilessons in this umbrella are designed to help students think about and discuss the author's purpose and message in both fiction and nonfiction.

It is important to note the difference between message and theme. Theme is the big, universal idea or larger aspect of human existence explored in a literary work (e.g., courage, kindness). The message is a specific aspect of the theme. In a book that explores the theme of courage, the message might be "You can conquer fears." If the theme is kindness, the message might be "Treat others as you would like to be treated." After teaching this umbrella, you may want to follow it with Umbrella 9: Thinking About Themes to help your students broaden their thinking about messages and consider the more general or universal idea of the book.

To prepare for these minilessons, read and discuss a variety of engaging fiction and nonfiction books with clear messages and a variety of purposes. Use the following texts from the *Fountas & Pinnell Classroom™ Interactive Read-Aloud Collection* text sets or choose books from your classroom library.

### Friendship

*The Other Side* by Jacqueline Woodson

*The Dunderheads* by Paul Fleischman

### Figuring Out Who You Are

*The Junkyard Wonders* by Patricia Polacco

### Empathy

*The Boy and The Whale* by Mordicai Gerstein

*A Symphony of Whales* by Steve Schuch

### Taking Action, Making Change

*One Hen* by Katie Smith Milway

### Innovative Thinking and Creative Problem Solving

*Parrots Over Puerto Rico* by Susan L. Roth and Cindy Trumbore

*Hands Around the Library* by Susan L. Roth and Karen Leggett Abouraya

*One Plastic Bag* by Miranda Paul

As you read aloud and enjoy these texts together, help students

- infer and discuss the author's purpose and message(s), and
- make connections between two or more texts that have similar messages.

**Friendship**

**Figuring Out Who You Are**

**Empathy**

**Taking Action, Making Change**

**Innovative Thinking and Creative Problem Solving**

Section 2: Literary Analysis

# RML1
### LA.U8.RML1

**Reading Minilesson Principle**
## The author has a purpose for writing a book.

**Thinking About the Author's Purpose and Message**

### You Will Need

- three familiar fiction and nonfiction books with different authors' purposes (e.g., to persuade, inform, or entertain), such as the following:
  - *Parrots Over Puerto Rico* by Susan L. Roth and Cindy Trumbore, from Text Set: Innovative Thinking and Creative Problem Solving
  - *One Hen* by Katie Smith Milway, from Text Set: Taking Action, Making Change
  - *The Dunderheads* by Paul Fleischman, from Text Set: Friendship
- chart paper and markers

### Academic Language / Important Vocabulary

- author
- purpose
- persuade
- information
- entertain

### Continuum Connection

- Infer a writer's purpose in writing a fiction text (p. 58)
- Infer a writer's purpose in a nonfiction text (p. 63)

## Goal

Infer the author's purpose in writing a text.

## Rationale

When you teach students to infer the author's purpose in writing a text, they are better able to recognize and understand how authors use different writing techniques to achieve their goals, such as giving information or conveying a message. They can also use their understanding of these craft techniques to write their own texts for different purposes.

## Assess Learning

Observe students when they read and talk about books and notice if there is evidence of new learning based on the goal of this minilesson.

- Can students infer an author's purpose for writing a text?
- Do they understand that an author can have more than one purpose?
- Do they use academic vocabulary, such as *author, purpose, persuade, information,* and *entertain*?

## Minilesson

To help students think about the minilesson principle, use familiar nonfiction and fiction texts to help them identify the author's purpose. Here is an example.

- Show the cover of *Parrots Over Puerto Rico* and read the title.

  What is this book about?

  Why do you think the authors wrote this book?

- Record responses on chart paper.

  The reason an author writes a book is called the author's purpose. The authors of this book wrote it to give information about the history of Puerto Rican parrots. Sometimes authors have more than one reason for writing a book. Can anyone think of another reason why the authors of this book may have wanted to write about Puerto Rican parrots?

- Show the cover of *One Hen* and read the title.

  What did you learn about from this book?

  Why did the author write a book about Kojo and his loan?

  Does anyone have any other ideas about why the author might have written this book?

- Record all reasonable responses on the chart.

## Have a Try

Invite the students to talk with a partner about the author's purpose for writing *The Dunderheads*.

▶ Show the cover of *The Dunderheads* and read the title. Briefly review some pages to remind students of the story.

> Turn and talk to your partner about the author's purpose for writing this book. Why do you think the author wrote it?

▶ After students turn and talk, invite a few students to share their thinking. Record all reasonable responses on the chart.

## Summarize and Apply

Summarize the learning and remind students to think about the author's purpose when they read.

> Today you thought about author's purpose. An author's purpose is the reason for writing a book. Sometimes authors have more than one reason for writing. What are some of the reasons authors write books?

▶ Write the principle at the top of the chart.

> When you read today, think about the purpose the author might have had in mind. Be ready to share your thinking when we come back together.

## Share

Following independent reading time, gather students together in the meeting area to talk about their reading.

> Turn and talk to your partner about the book you read today. What do you think was the author's purpose for writing the book?

## Extend the Lesson (Optional)

After assessing students' understanding, you might decide to extend the learning.

▶ During interactive read-aloud, pause to point out and discuss specific techniques authors use to inform, entertain, and persuade readers.

▶ **Writing About Reading** Have students write in a reader's notebook about the author's purpose for writing a particular book. They should support their ideas with specific evidence from the text.

### The author has a purpose for writing a book.

- to give information about the history of Puerto Rican parrots
- to teach people about the importance of protecting wild animals

- to give information about how loans help people
- to persuade people to give loans to those in need
- to teach people that a little bit of help can make a big difference

- to entertain people
- to make people laugh

Section 2: Literary Analysis

**Reading Minilesson Principle**
# The author gives a message in a fiction book.

## Thinking About the Author's Purpose and Message

### You Will Need

- three familiar fiction books with clear messages, such as the following:
  - *The Other Side* by Jacqueline Woodson, from Text Set: Friendship
  - *The Boy and The Whale* by Mordicai Gerstein, from Text Set: Empathy
  - *The Junkyard Wonders* by Patricia Polacco, from Text Set: Figuring Out Who You Are
- chart paper and markers

### Academic Language / Important Vocabulary

- author
- message
- fiction
- story

### Continuum Connection

- Infer the messages in a work of fiction (p. 58)
- Understand that there can be different interpretations of the meaning of a fiction text (p. 59)

## Goal

Infer messages in a work of fiction.

## Rationale

Authors often write stories to convey one or more messages to their readers. When students think about what the author is really trying to say, they are able to think more deeply about the story's meaning and to learn from the story.

## Assess Learning

Observe students when they talk about stories and notice if there is evidence of new learning based on the goal of this minilesson.

- ▶ Can students infer the author's message(s) in a story?
- ▶ Do they understand that a story can have more than one message?
- ▶ Do they use vocabulary such as *author, message, fiction,* and *story*?

## Minilesson

To help students think about the minilesson principle, use familiar stories to engage students in a discussion about author's message. Here is an example.

- ▶ Show the cover of *The Other Side* and read the title. Briefly review some pages to remind students of the story.

  What happens in this story?

  What do you think the author wants you to learn, or understand, from reading this story?

  Talk about how you know that.

- ▶ Record students' responses on chart paper.

  What the author wants you to learn or understand from the book is called the author's message. Different readers may have different opinions about what the author's message is; they may take different meanings from a book. Does anyone have any other ideas about what the author's message in this story is?

- ▶ Show the cover of *The Boy and the Whale* and show some of the pages.

  How did the boy help the whale in this story?

  What do you think the author wants you to learn from this story? What is his message?

- ▶ Record students' responses on the chart.

## Have a Try

Invite the students to talk with a partner about the author's message in *The Junkyard Wonders*.

▶ Show the cover of *The Junkyard Wonders* and review some pages.

> Turn and talk to your partner about what you think is the author's message in this story.

▶ After time for discussion, invite a few students to share their thinking. Record responses on the chart.

## Summarize and Apply

Summarize the learning and remind students to think about the author's message when they read.

> What did you notice about the fiction books we talked about today?

> You noticed that in each of these books the author has a message. The author's message is something that the author wants you to learn from reading the book. A book can have more than one message, and different readers can have different opinions about what the message is.

▶ Write the principle at the top of the chart.

> If you read a fiction book today, think about the author's message. Be ready to share your thinking when we come back together.

## Share

Following independent reading time, gather students together in the meeting area to talk about their reading.

> Raise your hand if you read a fiction book today.

> What do you think is the author's message in the book you read? Why do you think that?

## Extend the Lesson (Optional)

After assessing students' understanding, you might decide to extend the learning.

▶ **Writing About Reading** Have students write about and reflect on an author's message in a reader's notebook. Encourage them to make connections to their own lives and/or to other books.

Section 2: Literary Analysis

**The author gives a message in a fiction book.**

| | |
|---|---|
| **The Other Side** | • Don't be afraid to make friends with people who look different from you.<br>• The color of someone's skin does not matter.<br>• Change happens little by little, one person at a time. |
| **The Boy and the Whale** | • It is important to help animals that are in danger.<br>• Sometimes what seems to be impossible is possible if you try.<br>• Listen to your heart and do what you think is right. |
| **The Junkyard Wonders** | • It's okay to be different.<br>• Everyone has special talents.<br>• All people are geniuses in their own ways. |

## RML3
### LA.U8.RML3

**Reading Minilesson Principle**
## The author gives a message in a nonfiction book.

### Thinking About the Author's Purpose and Message

**You Will Need**

- three familiar nonfiction books with clear messages, such as the following:
  - *Parrots Over Puerto Rico* by Susan L. Roth and Cindy Trumbore and *Hands Around the Library* by Susan L. Roth and Karen Leggett Abouraya, from Text Set: Innovative Thinking and Creative Problem Solving
  - *One Hen* by Katie Smith Milway, from Text Set: Taking Action, Making Change
- chart from RML1 (optional)
- chart paper and markers

**Academic Language / Important Vocabulary**

- nonfiction
- author
- message
- big idea

**Continuum Connection**

- Infer the larger ideas and messages in a nonfiction text (p. 63)

### Goal

Infer messages in a work of nonfiction.

### Rationale

When you teach students to think about the message in a nonfiction book, you help them think not only about the information the author wants the reader to learn and understand but also about why the writer chose to share the information.

### Assess Learning

Observe students when they talk about nonfiction books and notice if there is evidence of new learning based on the goal of this minilesson.

- Can students infer the author's message(s) in a nonfiction book?
- Do they understand that a nonfiction book can have more than one message?
- Do they use vocabulary such as *nonfiction, author, message,* and *big idea*?

## Minilesson

To help students think about the minilesson principle, use familiar nonfiction texts to engage students in a discussion about author's message. Here is an example.

- Display the cover of *Parrots Over Puerto Rico* and read the title. (If you taught RML1 and made the chart, you might want to review it here.)

  Why do you think the authors wrote this book?

  In addition to giving you facts about a topic, nonfiction authors also try to communicate a message, or big idea, that they want you to understand. What big idea do you think the authors of this book want you to understand?

- Record responses on chart paper.

  Remember that a book can have more than one message and that different readers may have different opinions about what the message is. What other messages might the authors be giving in this book?

- Show the cover of *Hands Around the Library* and read the title.

  Why did the people in this book hold hands around their library?

  What is the authors' message?

  What makes you think that?

- Record responses on the chart.

## Have a Try

Invite the students to talk with a partner about the author's message in *One Hen*.

▷ Show the cover of *One Hen* and briefly review some pages to remind students of the book. (You might refer again to the chart from RML1 if you have it.)

> Turn and talk to your partner about what the author's message is in this book and why you think that.

▷ After students turn and talk, invite a few of them to share their thinking. Record responses on the chart.

## Summarize and Apply

Summarize the learning and remind students to think about the author's message when they read.

> What did you notice about the nonfiction books we discussed today?

> You noticed that each of these authors gave a message or more than one message. The author's message is something that the author wants you to understand from reading the book. It's a big idea—not just a fact.

▷ Write the principle at the top of the chart.

> When you read today, think about the author's message. Be ready to share your thinking when we come back together.

## Share

Following independent reading time, gather students together in the meeting area to talk about their reading.

> Raise your hand if you read a nonfiction book today.

> What is the author's message in the book you read? Tell what makes you think that.

## Extend the Lesson (Optional)

After assessing students' understanding, you might decide to extend the learning.

▷ **Writing About Reading** Have students write about the message of a nonfiction book in a reader's notebook. Encourage them to give their own opinion about the author's message (e.g., what it is and why it is important), supporting it with details from the book, their background knowledge, and/or their personal experiences.

### The author gives a message in a nonfiction book.

| | |
|---|---|
|  | • Some animals are endangered because of the actions of humans. <br> • Humans can work together to save endangered animals. |
|  Hands Around the Library: Protecting Egypt's Treasured Books | • People can work together to create change. <br> • Books and libraries are worth saving. <br> • The love of books can unite people. |
|  One Hen | • Change happens one person at a time. <br> • A little help can make a big difference. <br> • Do what you can to help others. |

# RML4
### LA.U8.RML4

**Reading Minilesson Principle**
# Several authors can give the same message.

## You Will Need

- two sets of two books that share a similar message, such as the following:
  - *The Boy and The Whale* by Mordicai Gerstein and *A Symphony of Whales* by Steve Schuch, from Text Set: Empathy
  - *One Hen* by Katie Smith Milway, from Text Set: Taking Action, Making Change and *One Plastic Bag* by Miranda Paul, from Text Set: Innovative Thinking and Creative Problem Solving
- chart paper and markers

## Academic Language / Important Vocabulary

- message
- author

### Continuum Connection

- Think across texts to derive larger messages, themes, or ideas [p. 59]
- Infer the larger ideas and messages in a nonfiction text [p. 63]

## Goal

Think across works of fiction and nonfiction to derive larger messages.

## Rationale

When you teach students that sometimes different authors give the same or very similar messages in their books, they build an understanding of universal ideas and the recognition that people are connected by common ideas.

## Assess Learning

Observe students when they talk about author's message and notice if there is evidence of new learning based on the goal of this minilesson.

- ◗ Do students notice when two or more books have the same or a very similar message?
- ◗ Do they use the terms *message* and *author*?

## Minilesson

To help students think about the minilesson principle, use familiar fiction and nonfiction texts to help students identify the author's message. Here is an example.

- ◗ Show the cover of *The Boy and the Whale.*

    When we discussed *The Boy and the Whale*, you noticed that one of the author's messages is "It is important to help animals that are in danger."

- ◗ Write the message on chart paper.

    Now let's think about the author's message in another book you have read.

- ◗ Show the cover of *A Symphony of Whales* and read the title. Briefly review some of the pages to remind students of the story.

    What happens in this story?

    What do you think the author wants you to learn or understand from this story? What is his message?

- ◗ Record students' responses on the chart.

    What do you notice about the author's message in both these books?

    Sometimes more than one author gives the same message or very similar messages in their books.

## Have a Try

Invite the students to talk with a partner about the author's message in *One Plastic Bag*.

> ▶ Show the cover of *One Hen* and read the title.
>
>> You noticed that one of the author's messages in this book is "One person can make change happen."
>
> ▶ Write the author's message on the chart. Then show the cover of *One Plastic Bag*. Briefly review some pages.
>
>> Turn and talk to your partner about the author's message in *One Plastic Bag*. What big idea does the author want you to understand?
>
> ▶ Invite a few students to share their thinking, and record students' responses on the chart.
>
>> What do you notice about the author's message in both these books?

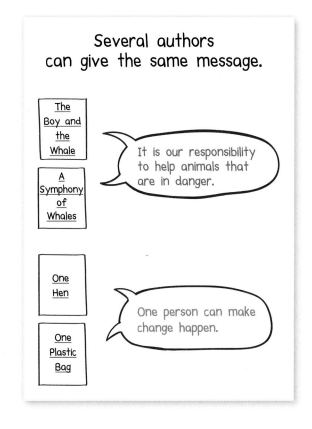

Several authors can give the same message.

The Boy and the Whale / A Symphony of Whales — It is our responsibility to help animals that are in danger.

One Hen / One Plastic Bag — One person can make change happen.

## Summarize and Apply

Summarize the learning and remind students to think about the author's message when they read.

> What did you notice about the authors' messages in the books we discussed today?

> ▶ Write the principle at the top of the chart.
>
>> When you read today, think about the author's message and be ready to share it when we come back together. We'll see if any of your books have the same message.

## Share

Following independent reading time, gather students together in the meeting area to talk about their reading.

> Who would like to share the author's message in the book you read today?

> Did anyone else read a book with the same or a similar message?

## Extend the Lesson (Optional)

After assessing students' understanding, you might decide to extend the learning.

> ▶ As students read books and discover the same or similar messages among them, keep a list or organize baskets of books that have the same or similar messages.

> ▶ Discuss how two authors teach the same message in similar or different ways.

**Reading Minilesson Principle**
# Think about what the author's message means to you, to society, or to the world.

## Thinking About the Author's Purpose and Message

### You Will Need

- two familiar fiction and nonfiction books with clear messages, such as the following:
  - *The Other Side* by Jacqueline Woodson, from Text Set: Friendship
  - *Hands Around the Library* by Susan L. Roth and Karen Leggett Abouraya, from Text Set: Innovative Thinking and Creative Problem Solving
- chart paper and markers

### Academic Language / Important Vocabulary

- author
- message
- society

### Continuum Connection

- Understand that the messages or big ideas in fiction texts can be applied to their own lives or to other people and society [p. 58]
- Infer the significance of nonfiction content to their own lives [p. 63]

## Goal

Understand that the messages or big ideas can be applied to students' own lives or to other people and society.

## Rationale

When you teach students to think about how an author's message can be applied in real life, they think about why an author's message is important. Students are more likely to understand the importance of the message and become active, engaged, and compassionate members of society.

## Assess Learning

Observe students when they talk about books and notice if there is evidence of new learning based on the goal of this minilesson.

- Can students identify the author's message in fiction and nonfiction books?
- Can they explain how an author's message can be applied to their own life, to society, or to the world?
- Do they use the terms *author, message,* and *society*?

## Minilesson

To help students think about the minilesson principle, use familiar fiction and nonfiction texts to engage them in a discussion about the author's message. Here is an example.

- Show the cover of *The Other Side*. (You might also use the chart from RML1 if you have it.)

  Even though this story takes place quite a long time ago, when our country was different in a lot of ways, you can still learn important ideas from it and use them in your own life. You noticed that two of the author's messages are "Don't be afraid to make friends with people who look different from you" and "The color of someone's skin does not matter." What do these messages mean to you, as a fourth grader in the twenty-first century?

  How could you learn from these messages and apply them to your own life? You can also think about what an author's message means to society. A society is a group of people who live together in a community. For example, all the people in our town, state, country, and the world are members of a society. How could our society use the messages taught in this book?

  What could members of our society do differently?

- Record students' responses on chart paper.

## Have a Try

Invite the students to talk with a partner about the author's message in another book.

▶ Show the cover of *Hands Around the Library*.

You noticed that one of the authors' messages is "People can work together to create change." Turn and talk about how you could use this message.

▶ Invite a few students to share, and record their responses on the chart.

Turn and talk to your partner about some ways societies could use this message.

▶ Record responses on the chart.

## Summarize and Apply

Summarize the learning and remind students to think about the author's message when they read.

Today you thought about the author's message in a couple of books. You thought about how the message could be applied to your own life, to society, or to the world.

▶ Write the principle at the top of the chart.

When you read today, think about the author's message. Then think about what this message means to you and how you could use it in your own life or how society could use it. Be ready to share your thinking when we come back together.

## Share

Following independent reading time, gather students together in the meeting area to talk about their reading.

Who would like to share the author's message in the book you read today?

How could this message be applied to your own life, to society, or to the world?

## Extend the Lesson (Optional)

After assessing students' understanding, you might decide to extend the learning.

▶ Continue to discuss the author's message as you read more books aloud. Discuss specific ways that students can apply each message and help them do so when feasible.

▶ **Writing About Reading** Have students write in a reader's notebook about how the author's message in a book could be applied to their own lives, society, or the world.

Think about what the author's message means to you, to society, or to the world.

"Don't be afraid to make friends with people who look different from you."

"The color of someone's skin does not matter."

- At recess, I can talk to someone whom I've never talked to before, especially if the person seems lonely.
- Societies should not separate people by the color of their skin.
- Societies should not build walls that separate people.

"People can work together to create change."

- Our class could work together to clean up a park in our town.
- People can start organizations that help create change (for example, an organization that helps libraries).
- Leaders of countries can sign an agreement to work together on a big issue (for example, the environment).

## Assessment

After you have taught the minilessons in this umbrella, observe students as they talk and write about their reading across instructional contexts: interactive read-aloud, independent reading, guided reading, shared reading, and book club. Use *The Literacy Continuum* (Fountas and Pinnell 2017) to guide the observation of students' reading and writing behaviors.

▶ What evidence do you have of new understandings related to the author's purpose and message?

- Can the students infer the author's purpose and message in both fiction and nonfiction books?
- Do they understand that a book can have more than one purpose and message?
- Do they notice when two or more books have the same or a very similar message?
- Do they talk about ways to apply an author's message to real life?
- Do they use academic vocabulary, such as *purpose* and *message*?

▶ In what other ways, beyond the scope of this umbrella, are students talking about fiction and nonfiction books?

- Are they talking about the theme of books?
- Are they noticing and talking about illustrations?
- Are they noticing different genres of fiction and nonfiction?

Use your observations to determine the next umbrella you will teach. You may also consult Minilessons Across the Year (pp. 59–61) for guidance.

## Link to Writing

After teaching the minilessons in this umbrella, help students link the new learning to their own writing:

▶ When students write both fiction and nonfiction texts, remind them to think about their purpose for writing, the message they want to convey to readers, and how they want to convey it.

## Reader's Notebook

When this umbrella is complete, provide a copy of the minilesson principles (see resources.fountasandpinnell.com) for students to glue in the reader's notebook (in the Minilessons section if using *Reader's Notebook: Intermediate* [Fountas and Pinnell 2011]), so they can refer to the information as needed.

## Minilessons in This Umbrella

**RML1**    The theme of a fiction book is what the book is really about.

**RML2**    The theme of a nonfiction book is more than the topic of the book.

**RML3**    Books often have themes that address human challenges and social issues.

**RML4**    Different books can have the same theme.

## Before Teaching Umbrella 9 Minilessons

It is important to understand the difference between message and theme. Theme is the big, universal idea or larger aspect of human existence explored in a literary work (e.g., courage, kindness). The message is a specific aspect of the theme—a directive or special understanding for the reader. The message in a book that explores the theme of courage might be "You can conquer fears." If the theme is kindness, the message might be "Treat others as you would like to be treated." We strongly recommend that you teach Umbrella 8: Thinking About the Author's Purpose and Message before teaching this umbrella.

To prepare for these minilessons, read and discuss a variety of engaging fiction and nonfiction books with clear themes, such as these from the *Fountas & Pinnell Classroom™ Interactive Read-Aloud Collection.*

**Empathy**

*A Symphony of Whales*
    by Steve Schuch

*The Boy and the Whale*
    by Mordicai Gerstein

**Innovative Thinking and Creative Problem Solving**

*Hands Around the Library: Protecting Egypt's Treasured Books* by Susan L. Roth and Karen Leggett Abouraya

*Ivan: The Remarkable True Story of the Shopping Mall Gorilla* by Katherine Applegate

*One Plastic Bag: Isatou Ceesay and the Recycling Women of the Gambia* by Miranda Paul

**Perseverance**

*Barbed Wire Baseball*
    by Marissa Moss

*Strong to the Hoop* by John Coy

**The Idea of Home**

*The Lotus Seed* by Sherry Garland

**What It Means to Be a Family**

*In Our Mothers' House*
    by Patricia Polacco

**Author Study: Patricia McKissack**

*Goin' Someplace Special*

As you read aloud and enjoy these texts together, help students

* think about the big ideas explored in each book and across books, and

* discuss the authors' treatment of human challenges and social issues.

**Empathy**

*The Boy and the Whale* by Mordicai Gerstein

**Innovative Thinking**

**Perseverance**

**Home**

**Family**

**Patricia McKissack**

Section 2: Literary Analysis

**Reading Minilesson Principle**

# The theme of a fiction book is what the book is really about.

## Thinking About Themes

### You Will Need

- two or three familiar fiction books with clear themes, such as the following:
  - *The Lotus Seed* by Sherry Garland, from Text Set: The Idea of Home
  - *The Boy and the Whale* by Mordicai Gerstein, from Text Set: Empathy
  - *Strong to the Hoop* by John Coy, from Text Set: Perseverance
- chart paper and markers

### Academic Language / Important Vocabulary

- theme
- message
- author
- fiction

### Continuum Connection

- Understand that there can be different interpretations of the meaning of a fiction text (p. 59)
- Think across texts to derive larger messages, themes, or ideas (p. 59)

### Goal

Infer the major themes of a fiction book.

### Rationale

A theme is a big, universal idea or concept explored in a book or other artistic work. Thinking about the themes in a story helps students relate to the story on a personal level, keeping them engaged.

### Assess Learning

Observe students when they read and talk about fiction books and notice if there is evidence of new learning based on the goal of this minilesson.

- Can students infer the theme(s) of a story?
- Do they use academic language, such as *theme, message, author,* and *fiction*?

## Minilesson

To help students think about the minilesson principle, use familiar fiction books to help them analyze the theme. Here is an example.

- Show the cover of *The Lotus Seed* and read the title.

  Remember, this story is about a Vietnamese woman who carries a special seed with her all her life. But that's not *all* that it's about.

- Read aloud from the second paragraph of page 21 ("It is the flower of life and hope") through page 23.

  What big idea does the author want you to think about?

  The theme of a story is what it is really about. It is the big idea. Some of the themes, or big ideas, of this story are hope, family, and memory.

- Record students' responses on chart paper. If students offer multiple themes, record all reasonable responses. Explain that a book can have more than one theme and that different readers can have different ideas about what the theme is.

- Explain the difference between theme and message.

  An author's message is a specific lesson that the author wants you to learn. A theme is more general. It's not about the specific characters and events in the story. It's a really big idea. The theme of a book can usually be expressed in one word or just a few words.

- Show the cover of *The Boy and the Whale* and read the title.

  What is the theme of this story? What are the big ideas?

- Record responses on the chart.

## Have a Try

Invite the students to talk with a partner about the theme of *Strong to the Hoop*.

▶ Show the cover of *Strong to the Hoop* and briefly review the story.

> Turn and talk to your partner about what you think is the theme of this story. What is the big idea that it is *really* about?

▶ After students turn and talk, invite several students to share their thinking. Record responses on the chart.

## Summarize and Apply

Summarize the learning and remind students to think about theme when they read fiction.

> Today you thought about the theme of a few fiction books. Why do you think fiction authors write stories with themes? Why are themes important?

▶ Write the principle at the top of the chart.

> If you read a fiction book today, think about the theme of your book. Be ready to share your thinking when we come back together.

## Share

Following independent reading time, gather students together in the meeting area to talk about their reading.

> Who read a fiction book today? What do you think is the theme or themes of the story you read?

## Extend the Lesson (Optional)

After assessing students' understanding, you might decide to extend the learning.

▶ **Writing About Reading** Have students write about the theme of a fiction book in a reader's notebook. They should state the theme and provide evidence from the text that supports their interpretation.

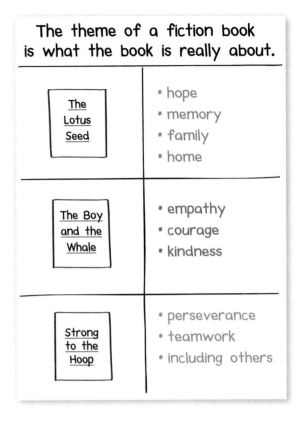

The theme of a fiction book is what the book is really about.

| The Lotus Seed | • hope<br>• memory<br>• family<br>• home |
| The Boy and the Whale | • empathy<br>• courage<br>• kindness |
| Strong to the Hoop | • perseverance<br>• teamwork<br>• including others |

Section 2: Literary Analysis

# RML2
## LA.U9.RML2

**Reading Minilesson Principle**
# The theme of a nonfiction book is more than the topic of the book.

## Thinking About Themes

### You Will Need

- two or three familiar nonfiction books with clear themes, such as the following from Text Set: Innovative Thinking and Creative Problem Solving:
  - *Hands Around the Library* by Susan L. Roth and Karen Leggett Abouraya
  - *Ivan* by Katherine Applegate
  - *One Plastic Bag* by Miranda Paul
- chart paper and markers

### Academic Language / Important Vocabulary

- theme
- topic
- author
- nonfiction

### Continuum Connection

- Understand that there can be different interpretations of the meanings of a text (p. 63)
- Infer the larger ideas and messages in nonfiction text (p. 63)

### Goal

Infer the major themes of a nonfiction book.

### Rationale

Thinking about themes in nonfiction books helps students understand that a nonfiction book is more than just a collection of facts. They develop an understanding of the big ideas that nonfiction authors explore in their work.

### Assess Learning

Observe students when they read and talk about nonfiction books and notice if there is evidence of new learning based on the goal of this minilesson.

- Can students infer the theme(s) of a nonfiction book?
- Can they differentiate between the theme and the topic of a nonfiction book?
- Do they understand that a nonfiction book can have more than one theme and that different readers may interpret the theme(s) differently?
- Do they use academic language, such as *theme, topic, author,* and *nonfiction?*

## Minilesson

To help students think about the minilesson principle, use familiar nonfiction books to help them infer the themes. Here is an example.

- Show the cover of *Hands Around the Library* and read the title.

  What is the topic of this book?

- Record responses on chart paper.

  This book is about how people in Egypt protected their library, but that's not all that it's about. What do you think is the theme, or big idea, of the book? What makes you think that?

- Record all reasonable responses on the chart, emphasizing that a nonfiction book can have more than one theme and that different readers can have different interpretations of the theme.

  The theme of a nonfiction book is more than the topic of the book. The theme is what the book is *really* about.

- Show the cover of *Ivan* and read the title.

  What is the topic of this book?

- Record responses on the chart.

  What do you think is the theme of the book?

- Record responses.

## Have a Try

Invite the students to talk with a partner about the theme of *One Plastic Bag*.

▶ Show the cover of *One Plastic Bag* and read the title.

Do you remember this book about how Isatou Ceesay found a way to recycle plastic bags in the Gambia? Turn and talk to your partner about what you think is the theme of this book. What big ideas does the author want you to think about?

▶ After students turn and talk, invite a few students to share their thinking. Record all reasonable responses on the chart.

## Summarize and Apply

Summarize the learning and remind students to think about theme when they read nonfiction.

Today you thought about the topic and theme of a few nonfiction books you've read. How are the topic and the theme of a book different?

▶ Write the principle at the top of the chart.

If you read a nonfiction book today, be sure to think about the theme or themes of your book. Be ready to share your thinking when we meet after reading time.

## Share

Following independent reading time, gather students together in the meeting area to talk about their reading.

Did you read a nonfiction book today?

What do you think is the theme of the book you read?

## Extend the Lesson (Optional)

After assessing students' understanding, you might decide to extend the learning.

▶ Help students notice when the title of a nonfiction book reveals clues about the theme.

▶ **Writing About Reading** Have students write about the theme of a nonfiction book in a reader's notebook.

Section 2: Literary Analysis

**The theme of a nonfiction book is more than the topic of the book.**

| Nonfiction Book | Topic | Theme: BIG Idea |
|---|---|---|
| *Hands Around the Library* | • how people in Egypt protected the Alexandria Library | • working together<br>• the importance of books and the ideas in them<br>• preserving culture |
| *IVAN* | • Ivan, the shopping mall gorilla | • animal welfare<br>• creating change |
| *One Plastic Bag* | • how Isatou Ceesay found a way to recycle plastic bags | • making a difference in people's lives<br>• protecting the environment |

**Reading Minilesson Principle**

# Books often have themes that address human challenges and social issues.

## Thinking About Themes

### You Will Need

- two or three familiar fiction books that explore human challenges or social issues, such as the following:
  - *Goin' Someplace Special* by Patricia C. McKissack, from Text Set: Author Study: Patricia McKissack
  - *In Our Mothers' House* by Patricia Polacco, from Text Set: What It Means to Be a Family
- chart paper and markers

### Academic Language / Important Vocabulary

- theme
- human challenge
- social issue
- prejudice
- discrimination
- fiction

### Continuum Connection

- Notice and understand themes reflecting important human challenges and social issues: e.g., self and self-esteem, popularity, bullying, sportsmanship, transition to adolescence, life cycles, survival, interconnectedness of humans and the environment, social justice, social awareness and responsibility (p. 59)
- Understand themes and ideas that are mature issues and require experience to interpret (p. 59)

## Goal

Notice and understand themes reflecting important human challenges and social issues.

## Rationale

When students notice and think about themes reflecting human challenges and social issues, they learn about important ideas and values (e.g., equality, compassion, justice) and think about how to apply them to their lives. They are more likely to become engaged, active, and compassionate members of society.

## Assess Learning

Observe students when they read and talk about fiction books and notice if there is evidence of new learning based on the goal of this minilesson.

- Do students notice and discuss themes that address human challenges and social issues?
- Do they understand vocabulary such as *theme, human challenge, social issue, prejudice, discrimination,* and *fiction*?

## Minilesson

To help students think about the minilesson principle, use familiar fiction books to engage them in reflecting on the themes. Here is an example.

- Show the cover of *Goin' Someplace Special* and read the title.

  What problem does 'Tricia Ann have?

  In the story, 'Tricia Ann's grandmother tells her "You are somebody, a human being—no better, no worse than anybody else in this world." This gives us a hint about the story's theme, or what it's *really* about. What do you think is the theme of this story?

- Record all reasonable responses on chart paper.

## Have a Try

Invite the students to talk with a partner about the theme of *In Our Mothers' House*.

▶ Show the cover of *In Our Mothers' House* and read the title.

> What do you think is the theme of this book? What is it really about? Turn and talk to your partner about what you think.

▶ After students turn and talk, invite several students to share their thinking. Record responses on the chart.

## Summarize and Apply

Summarize the learning and remind students to notice themes addressing human challenges and social issues.

> Some books have themes that address human challenges and social issues. Human challenges and social issues are problems or challenges that affect people, particularly problems having to do with living together in a society. Prejudice or discrimination against a particular group of people is an example of this. Both of these books have themes, like acceptance and equality, that address this issue.

▶ Write the principle at the top of the chart.

> If you read a fiction book today, think about the theme or themes of your book. If your book has themes addressing human challenges or social issues, bring it to share when we come back together.

## Share

Following independent reading time, gather students together in the meeting area to talk about their reading.

> Is anyone reading a fiction book with themes addressing human challenges or social issues? What challenge or social issue do the characters face?

> What do you think is the theme of your book?

## Extend the Lesson (Optional)

After assessing students' understanding, you might decide to extend the learning.

▶ **Writing About Reading** Have students write in a reader's notebook about a book with themes addressing human challenges or social issues.

---

**Books often have themes that address human challenges and social issues.**

| *Goin' Someplace Special* | • equality<br>• acceptance |
|---|---|
| *In Our Mothers' House* | • acceptance<br>• being different<br>• equality<br>• love<br>• family |

# RML 4
## LA.U9.RML4

# Different books can have the same theme.

## Thinking About Themes

### You Will Need

- two sets of two familiar fiction books that share the same theme, such as the following:
  - *A Symphony of Whales* by Steve Schuch and *The Boy and the Whale* by Mordicai Gerstein, from Text Set: Empathy
  - *Barbed Wire Baseball* by Marissa Moss and *Strong to the Hoop* by John Coy, from Text Set: Perseverance
- chart paper and markers

### Academic Language / Important Vocabulary

- theme
- fiction
- empathy
- perseverance

### Continuum Connection

- Connect texts by a range of categories: e.g., content, theme, message, genre, author/illustrator, character, setting, special forms, text structure, or organization (p. 58)
- Make connections (similarities and differences) among texts that have the same author/illustrator, setting, characters, or theme (p. 58)

## Goal

Make connections among texts that have the same theme.

## Rationale

When students notice the same theme in different books, they build an understanding of universal ideas and values. They can compare and contrast how different authors handle the same theme. They learn that certain big ideas are important across time and space yet are treated differently by different cultures and individuals.

## Assess Learning

Observe students when they read and talk about fiction books and notice if there is evidence of new learning based on the goal of this minilesson.

- Can students infer the theme(s) of a book?
- Do they notice when two or more books have the same theme?
- Do they understand and use the terms *theme, fiction, empathy,* and *perseverance*?

## Minilesson

To help students think about the minilesson principle, use familiar fiction books to engage them in identifying themes across texts. Here is an example.

- Show the cover of *A Symphony of Whales*.

  What do you think is the theme of this story? What is it *really* about?

- Record all reasonable responses on chart paper.

  One of the themes of this story is empathy. Can you think of any other books we've read that have the theme of empathy—understanding and even feeling the feelings of others?

- If necessary, show the covers of a few books whose themes you have already discussed, including *The Boy and the Whale*.

  Do any of these books have the theme of empathy?

  When we talked about *The Boy and the Whale*, some of you noticed that it has the theme of empathy. Do these two books have any other themes in common?

- Record responses on the chart.
- Show the cover of *Barbed Wire Baseball*.

  What do you think is the theme of this story? What big idea does the author want you think about?

- Record all reasonable responses on the chart.

## Have a Try

Invite the students to talk with a partner about stories with the theme of perseverance.

▶ Display some of the books whose themes you have already discussed, such as *Strong to the Hoop*.

One of the themes of *Barbed Wire Baseball* is perseverance. What other stories have we read that have the theme of perseverance? Turn and talk to your partner about what you think.

▶ After students turn and talk, invite several students to share their thinking, and record responses on the chart.

## Summarize and Apply

Summarize the learning and remind students to notice when different books have the same theme.

Authors write books about big ideas—like hope, memory, perseverance, empathy, and family—because they are important to a lot of people all around the world.

▶ Write the principle at the top of the chart.

If you read a fiction book today, think about the theme of your book. When we come back together, we'll see if anyone else read a different book that has the same theme.

## Share

Following independent reading time, gather students together in the meeting area to talk about their reading.

Did you read a fiction book today? What is the theme of the book you read?

Did anyone else read a different book that has the same theme?

## Extend the Lesson (Optional)

After assessing students' understanding, you might decide to extend the learning.

▶ Write some common themes (e.g., family, hope, home, perseverance) on chart paper. Prompt students to add book titles to the list as appropriate.

▶ **Writing About Reading** Have students compare and contrast two books with the same theme in a reader's notebook. You might have them use a Venn diagram or two-column chart to plan their writing.

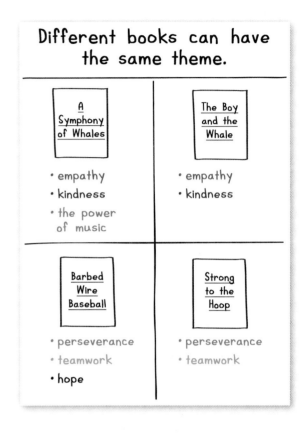

Different books can have the same theme.

**A Symphony of Whales**
• empathy
• kindness
• the power of music

**The Boy and the Whale**
• empathy
• kindness

**Barbed Wire Baseball**
• perseverance
• teamwork
• hope

**Strong to the Hoop**
• perseverance
• teamwork

## Assessment

After you have taught the minilessons in this umbrella, observe students as they talk and write about their reading across instructional contexts: interactive read-aloud, independent reading, guided reading, shared reading, and book club. Use *The Literacy Continuum* (Fountas and Pinnell 2017) to guide the observation of students' reading and writing behaviors.

▶ What evidence do you have of new understandings related to thinking about themes?

- Can students infer the theme(s) of both fiction and nonfiction books?
- How well do they notice and discuss themes related to human challenges and social issues?
- Do they notice when two or more books share similar themes?
- Do they use academic language, such as *theme*, *message*, and *topic*?

▶ In what other ways, beyond the scope of this umbrella, are students talking about books?

- Are students noticing different genres of fiction and nonfiction books?
- Are they thinking about the elements of plot?
- Are they discussing illustrations and graphics?

Use your observations to determine the next umbrella you will teach. You may also consult Minilessons Across the Year (pp. 59–61) for guidance.

## Link to Writing

After teaching the minilessons in this umbrella, help students link the new learning to their own writing:

▶ When students write their own fiction and nonfiction books, remind them to think about the theme(s) they want to explore in their work.

▶ Have students choose a theme represented in two or more of the books they have read and write about how they see that theme in their own lives.

## Reader's Notebook

When this umbrella is complete, provide a copy of the minilesson principles (see resources.fountasandpinnell.com) for students to glue in the reader's notebook (in the Minilessons section if using *Reader's Notebook: Intermediate* [Fountas and Pinnell 2011]), so they can refer to the information as needed.

## Minilessons in This Umbrella

**RML1**  Writers choose precise words to create a mood.

**RML2**  Writers use punctuation to make their writing interesting.

**RML3**  Writers use different techniques to create humor.

**RML4**  Writers use similes and metaphors to compare one thing to another.

**RML5**  Writers use words from languages other than English to add authenticity.

**RML6**  Writers use unconventional grammar for effect.

**RML7**  Writers use personification to describe something in a clear and interesting way.

**RML8**  Writers use repetition in interesting ways.

## Before Teaching Umbrella 10 Minilessons

The lessons in this umbrella are related to a writer's craft decisions. They do not need to be taught consecutively but can be taught when you observe a need. Once students have enjoyed the texts as readers, have them look at them as writers, noting elements of writer's craft. Use the following books from the *Fountas & Pinnell Classroom™ Interactive Read-Aloud Collection* or choose other texts that will engage your class.

**Perseverance**

*Barbed Wire Baseball*
  by Marissa Moss

*Razia's Ray of Hope*
  by Elizabeth Suneby

*Rescue & Jessica* by Jessica Kensky
  and Patrick Downes

*Strong to the Hoop* by John Coy

*King for a Day* by Rukhsana Khan

**Genre Study: Poetry**

*On the Wing* by David Elliott

**Author/Illustrator Study:
Douglas Florian**

*In the Swim*

*Insectlopedia*

**Telling a Story with Photos**

*A Little Book* of Sloth
  by Lucy Cooke

**Biography: Artists**

*Me, Frida* by Amy Novesky

**Illustrator Study: Floyd Cooper**

*A Dance Like Starlight*
  by Kristy Dempsey

*Meet Danitra Brown*
  by Nikki Grimes

**Exploring Identity**

*Be Water, My Friend*
  by Ken Mochizuki

As you read aloud and enjoy books together, help students notice the craft moves that authors make.

**Perseverance**

**Poetry**

**Douglas Florian**

**Telling a Story with Photos**

**Biography: Artists**

**Floyd Cooper**

**Exploring Identity**

**Reading Minilesson Principle**
# Writers choose precise words to create a mood.

Reading Like a Writer:
Analyzing the Writer's Craft

### You Will Need

- three or four familiar fiction books, such as the following from Text Set: Perseverance:
  - *Barbed Wire Baseball* by Marissa Moss
  - *Razia's Ray of Hope* by Elizabeth Suneby
  - *Rescue & Jessica* by Jessica Kensky and Patrick Downes
- chart paper and markers
- document camera (optional)
- sticky notes

### Academic Language / Important Vocabulary

- mood
- feeling
- precise

### Continuum Connection

- Notice and think critically about a writer's word choice (pp. 60, 64)
- Notice language that conveys an emotional atmosphere (mood) in a text, affecting how the reader feels (e.g., tension, sadness, joy) (pp. 60, 64)

## Goal

Notice language that conveys an emotional atmosphere (mood) in a text, affecting how the reader feels (e.g., tension, sadness, whimsicality, joy).

## Rationale

Writers choose words to create a mood or feeling in their writing, which helps readers connect to the characters and the plot. When you support students in noticing these language choices, you engage them in their reading and make books more enjoyable. You also help them think about how to learn from the writer's decisions to support their own writing decisions.

## Assess Learning

Observe students when they talk about the writer's craft. Notice if there is evidence of new learning based on the goal of this minilesson.

- Can students identify when an author uses language to help the reader experience a feeling?

- Do they point out a writer's use of language during individual reading conferences, book clubs, or small-group guided reading?

- Do they understand how the words *mood, feeling,* and *precise* are used in this lesson?

## Minilesson

To help students think about the minilesson principle, help them notice the author's use of language. If a document camera is available, consider projecting the pages to provide visual support. Here is an example.

- From *Barbed Wire Baseball* show and read page 9.

  What do these sentences tell you about where the boys live?

  How does that make you feel?

  What are some of the words that make you feel that way?

- Record words on the chart paper.

  Writers choose words carefully when they write. They choose the precise, or exact, words that create the moods they want the readers to feel.

- Repeat this process with page 29 of *Barbed Wire Baseball*.

  How does the writer's language make you feel?

  Which words help create that mood?

- If time allows, repeat this process with page 2 of *Razia's Ray of Hope*.

## Have a Try

Invite the students to talk with a partner about the language writers choose to create a mood.

▶ Show *Rescue & Jessica* and read page 2.

Turn and talk to your partner. What mood did the writers create? How did they do it?

▶ Ask a couple of students to share. Record the language that creates the mood.

## Summarize and Apply

Summarize the learning and remind students to notice how writers use language to create a mood.

How do writers create a mood in their writing?

▶ Write the principle at the top of the chart.

As you read today, be on the lookout for words the author uses to create a mood. Use a sticky note to mark the pages. Bring your book when we come back together so you can share.

## Share

Following independent reading time, gather students together in small groups to talk about their reading.

If you marked a page that helped you notice the mood of a story, share the writer's language with your group. What mood did the author's words create?

▶ Choose a few students to share with the class.

## Extend the Lesson (Optional)

After assessing students' understanding, you might decide to extend the learning.

▶ Many of the words authors use to create a mood describe the setting. During interactive read-aloud, talk with students about how the setting impacts the mood of a story.

▶ **Writing About Reading** Encourage students to collect in a reader's notebook language authors used to create a certain mood in their writing.

| \multicolumn{3}{c}{Writers choose precise words to create a mood.} | | |
|---|---|---|
| Title | Author's Words | How do the words make you feel? |
|  | • "bleak and gray and dusty"<br>• "stark barracks"<br>• "a dull, coppery sky"<br>• "he felt as if he were shrinking into a tiny hard ball" | • depressed<br>• sad<br>• miserable<br>• gloomy<br>• alone |
|  | • "new grass"<br>• "the sun bathed everything in a gentle warmth"<br>• "a perfect day" | • hopeful<br>• content<br>• excited about getting ready to play |
| Razia's Ray of Hope | • "ribbons brightened the dry earth"<br>• "chocolates wrapped in shiny papers" | • excited<br>• eager |
| Rescue & Jessica | • "How will I do things on my own?"<br>• "When will I be able to walk again?" | • afraid<br>• worried |

# RML 2
## LA.U10.RML2

**Reading Minilesson Principle**
## Writers use punctuation to make their writing interesting.

### Reading Like a Writer: Analyzing the Writer's Craft

#### You Will Need

- three or four familiar books or poems with interesting use of punctuation, such as the following:
  - "The Australian Pelican" from *On the Wing* by David Elliott, from Text Set: Poetry
  - *Me, Frida* by Amy Novesky, from Text Set: Biography: Artists
  - "The Sea Horse" from *In the Swim* by Douglas Florian, from Text Set: Author/Illustrator Study: Douglas Florian
  - *Meet Danitra Brown* by Nikki Grimes, from Text Set: Illustrator Study: Floyd Cooper
- document camera (optional)
- chart paper and markers
- sticky notes

#### Academic Language / Important Vocabulary

- punctuation
- parentheses
- dash
- emphasis
- clarify

#### Continuum Connection

- Recognize and reflect punctuation with the voice: e.g., period, question mark, exclamation point, dash, comma, ellipses, when reading in chorus or individually (p. 139)

### Goal

Notice how writers use punctuation in interesting ways to communicate meaning.

### Rationale

Typically, writers use punctuation to clarify their writing. Sometimes, however, they use it in an interesting way to communicate additional meaning or perhaps to add voice to the writing. Readers need to pay attention to punctuation especially when they are reading aloud [see SAS.U4.RML1]. When you encourage students to notice punctuation that is used interestingly, you help them appreciate the writer's craft and gain a better understanding of the text. They also learn possibilities for their own writing.

### Assess Learning

Observe students when they talk about the writer's craft. Notice if there is evidence of new learning based on the goal of this minilesson.

- Do students notice punctuation that adds interest to an author's writing?
- Can they discuss an author's decisions about punctuation?
- Can they use the terms *punctuation, parentheses,* and *dash*? Do they understand the terms *emphasis* and *clarify*?

## Minilesson

To help students think about the minilesson principle, use enlarged texts that they can view easily, like big books or shared reading texts. You might also project the pages with a document camera, if available. Here is an example.

- Show *On the Wing* and read the poem "The Australian Pelican." Make sure students can see the print.

  Why do you think the author chose to use a dash here?

- Briefly discuss how a reader pauses at a dash and thinks about why the writer chose to put emphasis in that place. Record responses on a chart.

- Repeat the process with the second page of text from *Me, Frida,* where the author uses a dash to set off the explanation of Frida's painting. Again, make sure students can see the print.

## Have a Try

Invite the students to notice with a partner how writers use punctuation.

▶ Read "The Sea Horse" from *In the Swim*.

   Turn and talk to your partner. Why did the writer choose to use parentheses here?

▶ Ask a couple of students to share. Record responses.

▶ Repeat this process, reading the beginning of the poem "Coke-bottle Brown" from *Meet Danitra Brown*.

## Summarize and Apply

Summarize the learning and remind students to notice how writers use punctuation.

   What did you learn about how writers use punctuation marks?

▶ Write the principle at the top of the chart.

   Parentheses and dashes are types of punctuation, just like periods, exclamation points, commas, and question marks. When you read today, notice how the writer uses punctuation in the book. Mark a page with a sticky note where the writer uses punctuation in an interesting way. Think about how this helps you understand what you are reading. Bring the book when we come back together so you can share.

## Share

Following independent reading time, gather students together in the meeting area to talk about their reading.

   Who found an interesting example of punctuation in their reading today? Why do you think the author chose to do that?

## Extend the Lesson (Optional)

After assessing students' understanding, you might decide to extend the learning.

▶ Explore how authors use periods in interesting ways by reading "The Whale" from *In the Swim*. Add examples to the chart.

▶ Explore other ways authors use dashes by reading the poem "The Tick" from *Insectlopedia*. Add examples to the chart.

| Writers use punctuation to make their writing interesting. | | |
|---|---|---|
| Poem | Dash<br>—<br>• Pause<br>• Give extra emphasis | Parentheses<br>( )<br>• Clarify<br>• Add more information |
| "The Australian Pelican" | Emphasizes the size of the fish and the bird's bill | |
| Me, Frida | Adds a pause before the description of Frida's painting | |
| "The Sea Horse" | | Explains why a sea horse can't race |
| "Coke-bottle Brown" | | The narrator doesn't want to make a big deal out of the bifocals. |

**Reading Minilesson Principle**
## Writers use different techniques to create humor.

**Reading Like a Writer:**
**Analyzing the Writer's Craft**

### You Will Need

- two or three familiar fiction texts or poems with clear examples of humor, such as the following:
  - *A Little Book of Sloth* by Lucy Cooke, from Text Set: Telling a Story with Photos
  - "The Clam" from *In the Swim* by Douglas Florian, from Text Set: Author/Illustrator Study: Douglas Florian
  - "Black Widow" from *Insectlopedia* by Douglas Florian, from Text Set: Author/Illustrator Study: Douglas Florian
- chart paper and markers
- sticky notes

### Academic Language / Important Vocabulary

- humor
- humorous
- techniques

### Continuum Connection

- Recognize how a writer creates humor (p. 60)

### Goal

Recognize how a writer creates humor.

### Rationale

Humorous stories may feel abstract to students; determining what makes a story humorous can be challenging because humor is personal. When you teach students to notice how writers create humor, stories become more enjoyable. They also learn to create humor in their own stories.

### Assess Learning

Observe students when they talk about the writer's craft. Notice if there is evidence of new learning based on the goal of this minilesson.

- ▶ Can students identify places in a story that they found funny?
- ▶ Can they talk about how an author made a story humorous?
- ▶ Do they understand and use the words *humor, humorous,* and *techniques*?

## Minilesson

To help students think about the minilesson principle, use familiar books that bring in an element of humor that is tangible and concrete. Here is an example.

- ▶ Show *A Little Book of Sloth* and read page 33.

    What do you think about this page?

    What is humorous, or funny, here?

    What did the writer do to create humor, or make you laugh?

    The writer says that sloths are like laundry hanging on a clothesline to dry. Clothespins keep laundry from falling off the clothesline, but because sloths wrap their paws around branches to stay on, no clothespins are needed. Would you really hang a sloth on a clothesline? Of course not!

- ▶ Record responses on a chart.
- ▶ Repeat the process again by reading and showing the illustration of the poem "The Clam" from *In the Swim*.

## Have a Try

Invite the students to notice with a partner how writers create humor.

- Read the poem "Black Widow" from *Insectlopedia*, and show the illustration.

  Turn and talk to your partner. What does the author do to make this part humorous?

- Ask a couple of students to share. Record responses. If necessary, explain that widows traditionally wear black.

## Summarize and Apply

Summarize the learning and remind students to notice when they read humorous books how writers create humor.

  The chart shows different ways authors create humor, or techniques they use.

- Write the principle at the top of the chart.

  When you read today, notice places in your book that you find humorous and mark them with a sticky note. Bring the book when we meet so you can share.

## Share

Following independent reading time, gather students together in the meeting area to talk about their reading.

  Who read something humorous today? What did the writer do to create humor?

## Extend the Lesson (Optional)

After assessing students' understanding, you might decide to extend the learning.

- Take time during interactive read-aloud to talk about why an author has included humor and how successful students think the humor is.

- **Writing About Reading** Students may start a page or a section in a reader's notebook to jot down ways writers make their stories funny or examples of humorous texts.

- **Writing About Reading** Encourage students to share in their weekly letters about reading (see Umbrella 3: Writing Letters to Share Thinking About Books, found in Section Four: Writing About Reading) humorous parts of their reading and why they think those parts are humorous.

**Writers use different techniques to create humor.**

| Book | Humorous Part | What makes it humorous? |
|---|---|---|
| little book of sloth | "When their beauty treatment finishes, the baby sloths are hung out to dry. Of course, with sloths there's no need for clothespins." | Silly ideas |
| in the swim — Douglas Florian | Illustration shows a person being crammed inside. | Silly illustrations |
| INSECTLOPEDIA | Illustration shows black clothing hanging on the spider web. The spider is a widow, so she doesn't wear blue denim. | Silly illustrations<br><br>Funny concept— wearing black not blue because she's a widow spider |

**Section 2: Literary Analysis**

# RML4
### LA.U10.RML4

### Reading Minilesson Principle
# Writers use similes and metaphors to compare one thing to another.

## Reading Like a Writer: Analyzing the Writer's Craft

### You Will Need

- three or four familiar texts or poems with similes and metaphors, such as the following:
  - *Strong to the Hoop* by John Coy, from Text Set: Perseverance
  - "The Flounders" from *In the Swim* by Douglas Florian, from Text Set: Author/Illustrator Study: Douglas Florian
  - *A Little Book of Sloth* by Lucy Cooke, from Text Set: Telling a Story with Photos
- chart paper and markers
- document camera (optional)
- three sticky notes labeled *simile*, one sticky note labeled *metaphor*
- sticky notes for students to use
- a basket of familiar texts containing metaphors or similes

### Academic Language / Important Vocabulary

- simile
- metaphor
- compare
- comparison

### Continuum Connection

- Notice and understand how the author uses idioms and literary language, including metaphor, simile, symbolism, and personification (p. 60)

## Goal

Notice and understand how the author uses similes and metaphors.

## Rationale

Writers use metaphors and similes to make abstract ideas more concrete and to prompt readers to use their imagination to create lasting images. Students can think about how they might use figurative language in their own writing.

## Assess Learning

Observe students when they talk about the writer's craft. Notice if there is evidence of new learning based on the goal of this minilesson.

- Do students notice similes and metaphors in books they hear read aloud or read independently?
- Can they describe what the simile or metaphor means?
- Do they use the terms *simile, metaphor, compare,* and *comparison*?

# Minilesson

To help students think about the minilesson principle, use familiar texts with similes and/or metaphors to help your students understand the writer's craft. If a document camera is available, consider projecting the pages to provide visual support. Here is an example.

- Hold up *Strong to the Hoop* and read page 16.

  What would it be like to run into a rock?

  What does the author mean by "It's like running into a rock"?

- Record responses on the chart. Then repeat the process with page 26.

  Who is ferocious like a lion?

  Why does the author say that?

  The author could have written many different words to describe how the character moved. Instead, he compared his movements to something you know—a ferocious lion. When an author compares two things using the words *like* or *as*, it is called a simile.

- Have a volunteer underline the word *like* in each example. Have another volunteer add a sticky note labeled *simile* next to each example.

  When you read the words *like* or *as*, think about the simile, or what the author is comparing.

- Repeat this process using "The Flounders" on page 25 of *In the Swim*.

## Have a Try

Invite the students to talk about how writers sometimes compare one thing to another.

▶ Hold up *A Little Book of Sloth*, and read pages 11 and 17.

How does the author describe sloths?

When a writer makes a direct comparison by saying that something *is* something else, it is called a metaphor.

▶ Record responses on the chart and have a volunteer place the sticky note labeled *metaphor*.

## Summarize and Apply

Summarize the learning and remind students to think about how writers use similes and metaphors.

How do writers use similes and metaphors?

▶ Write the principle at the top of the chart.

You may choose a book from this basket to read today. As you read, notice whether the author uses metaphors or similes. Mark the page with a sticky note, and bring the book when we meet so you can share.

## Share

Following independent reading time, gather students together in the meeting area to talk about their reading.

Tell us about a simile or metaphor you found in your reading. What did it help you to understand?

## Extend the Lesson (Optional)

After assessing students' understanding, you might decide to extend the learning.

▶ Have students help you collect examples of metaphors and similes on a large poster to display so that they can be inspired to use language in creative and evocative ways when they do their own writing.

▶ **Writing About Reading** When students write letters about books they have read in a reader's notebook, encourage them to share similes and metaphors they have found and describe how the comparisons helped them understand the writer's craft.

**Writers use similes and metaphors to compare one thing to another.**

| Book | Comparison | Purpose/Meaning |
|------|------------|-----------------|
| STRONG to the HOOP | "It's <u>like</u> running into a rock." *simile*<br><br>"ferocious <u>like</u> a lion." *simile* | • Helps you feel how hard it is to move past Marcus<br><br>• Describes the character<br>• He is very strong and powerful. |
| in the swim | "Flat <u>as a</u>—." *simile* | • Describes the flounder<br>• You can imagine how flat the fish is. |
| little hooky sloth | Sloths are— "the absolute masters of mellow"<br><br>"Jedi masters of the hug" *metaphor* | • Describes the sloths<br>• Sloths are so relaxed.<br>• Sloths are really good at hugging. |

**Reading Minilesson Principle**
# Writers use words from languages other than English to add authenticity.

## Reading Like a Writer: Analyzing the Writer's Craft

### You Will Need

- several familiar texts with words written in a language other than English, such as:
  - *Me, Frida* by Amy Novesky, from Text Set: Biography: Artists
  - *King for a Day* by Rukhsana Khan and *Razia's Ray of Hope* by Elizabeth Suneby, from Text Set: Perseverance
- prepared chart with *Book* and *Words Used* columns completed, as in the example
- markers
- three sticky notes labeled *Spanish, Arabic,* and *Dari*
- sticky notes
- document camera (optional)

### Academic Language / Important Vocabulary

- authenticity

### Continuum Connection

- Notice and think critically about a writer's word choice (pp. 60, 64)
- Notice a writer's use of some words from languages other than English (p. 60)

## Goal

Notice and understand how the author uses words from languages other than English to create a feeling of authenticity.

## Rationale

Having a word or words written in the native language of a character, or the language of the setting of a story, helps give the narrative a more authentic feel. If a student speaks another language, they can think about how to use that in their own writing.

## Assess Learning

Observe students when they talk about the writer's craft. Notice if there is evidence of new learning based on the goal of this minilesson.

- Do students notice the use of words from languages other than English?
- Can they explain why an author would choose to use words from languages other than English?
- Can students use a glossary to find the meaning of the words?
- Do they use the term *authenticity*?

## Minilesson

To help students think about the minilesson principle, use familiar texts with words from a language other than English to help students think about the writer's decisions. If a document camera is available, consider projecting the pages to provide visual support. Here is an example.

- Hold up *Me, Frida*. Read the page beginning "They lived at."

  What is different about some of the words the author chose to use?

  Does anyone know what language these words are from, or what the words mean?

  Why do you think the writer decided to use some Spanish words?

- Discuss with students how the author's use of words from Frida's native language makes the book feel more authentic, or real.
- Record responses and have a student place the Spanish sticky note on the prepared chart.
- Repeat this process with *King for a Day*, reading the first two pages of text. Then show the copyright page.

  In this book, the writer lists the words not from the English language and provides the definitions.

## Have a Try

Invite the students to talk with a partner about a writer's choice of words to enhance authenticity.

▶ Read three pages from *Razia's Ray of Hope*, beginning with "One night."

> Turn and talk to your partner. Which words stand out to you? What was the author's purpose in choosing to use these words?

▶ Ask a few students to share. Add responses to the chart.

## Summarize and Apply

Summarize the learning and remind students to notice the words an author chooses.

> Take a look at the chart. What can you say about what some writers do when crafting a story?

▶ Ask a few students to share, and write the principle at the top of the chart.

> As you read today, notice if the author chooses to use words from a language other than English. Mark the page with a sticky note, and bring the book when we meet so you can share.

## Share

Following independent reading time, gather students together in the meeting area to talk about interesting words authors use.

> Did anyone read a story today with words in it from a language other than English? Share an example and talk about why the author chose to use those specific words.

> Did anyone find examples of other interesting words that the author chose to use?

## Extend the Lesson (Optional)

After assessing students' understanding, you might decide to extend the learning.

▶ **Writing About Reading** Have students write in a reader's notebook about the effect of an author's use of words from a language other than English. Is it helpful for the author use words from other languages? Does it make reading the book harder or easier? What would the experience be like if the author didn't do that?

**Writers use words from languages other than English to add authenticity.**

| Book | Words Used | Meaning of the Words | Purpose |
|---|---|---|---|
| Spanish | • cafe con leche<br>• corridos<br>• querida | • A drink<br>• Mexican folk songs<br>• My dear or my love | • Authenticity: Frida and her husband are from Mexico |
| Arabic | • Basant<br>• Insha Allah | • The spring kite festival<br>• If God wills | • Gives the feeling of being in Pakistan, hearing children talking |
| Dari | • Baba<br>• Baba gi<br>• burqas | • Father<br>• Grandfather<br>• Wraps some Muslim women wear in public to cover themselves from head to toe | • Gives the feeling of being in Afghanistan<br>• Hints of Muslim culture make the story feel more authentic |

# RML 6
## LA.U10.RML6

**Reading Minilesson Principle**
# Writers use unconventional grammar for effect.

## Reading Like a Writer: Analyzing the Writer's Craft

### You Will Need

- familiar texts that use unconventional grammar, such as the following:
  - *A Dance Like Starlight* by Kristy Dempsey and *Meet Danitra Brown* by Nikki Grimes, from Text Set: Illustrator Study: Floyd Cooper
  - *Be Water, My Friend* by Ken Mochizuki, from Text Set: Exploring Identity
- chart paper prepared with example text (see next page)
- markers

### Academic Language / Important Vocabulary

- unconventional
- grammar

### Continuum Connection

- Notice a writer's intentional use of language that violates conventional grammar to provide authentic dialogue to achieve the writer's voice (p. 60)

## Goal

Notice a writer's intentional use of language that violates conventional grammar to provide authentic dialogue or to achieve the writer's voice.

## Rationale

Conventional grammar rules help you communicate clearly in speech and in writing. However, a writer may use unconventional grammar to get a particular meaning across or to make the story sound a certain way, especially in a character's dialogue. Noticing this helps the reader understand the story more deeply.

## Assess Learning

Observe students when they talk about the writer's craft. Notice if there is evidence of new learning based on the goal of this minilesson.

- ❱ Do students notice when writers use unconventional grammar?
- ❱ Do they understand why a writer might break the rules of grammar?
- ❱ Do they understand the terms *unconventional* and *grammar*?

## Minilesson

To help students think about the minilesson principle, use familiar texts to help them notice unconventional grammar. Here is an example.

- ❱ Show *A Dance Like Starlight* and read from the page that begins "I turned away."

  > The Ballet Master said to Janet, "Brava, ma petite. Brava."

- ❱ Point to the text on the chart.

  > What do you notice about the sentences that the Ballet Master speaks?

  > They are not complete sentences, are they? Why did the author use incomplete sentences in the Ballet Master's dialogue?

- ❱ Record responses on the chart paper.

- ❱ Now show *Meet Danitra Brown*. Read the first page of print and then point to the phrase on the chart.

  > Is *'cause* a word? Why did the writer use it instead of *because*?

  > These two writers made choices about how they wrote their words and sentences to achieve a certain effect.

## Have a Try

Invite the students to talk with a partner about how writers use unconventional grammar.

▶ Show *Be Water, My Friend*. Read from the page that begins "Suddenly Bruce's arms flew out, wrapping up."

> Turn and talk to your partner about the words I wrote on the chart. What did the author do here? Why?

▶ Record responses on the chart.

## Summarize and Apply

Summarize the learning and remind students to notice a writer's choices.

> Take a look at the chart. What does it show you?

▶ Ask a few students to share ideas, summarizing them as necessary, and then write the principle at the top of the chart.

> Today when you read, look for ways that the author chose to use unconventional grammar. Place a sticky note on the page so you can share when we come back together.

## Share

Following independent reading time, gather students together in the meeting area to share. Use a document camera, if available.

> Did anyone notice that an author used unconventional grammar? Why do you think the writer wrote it that way?

## Extend the Lesson (Optional)

After assessing students' understanding, you might decide to extend the learning.

▶ During interactive read-aloud, help students notice and discuss why an author made the decision to use unconventional grammar.

| Writers use unconventional grammar for effect. | | |
|---|---|---|
|  | "Brava, ma petite." "Brava." | • One-word sentence<br><br>• Sounds like natural dialogue |
|  | "'cause she sticks out" | • <u>Because</u> is abbreviated.<br><br>• Fits the rhythm and language of the poem |
| | "Contact! Quick! Sticking hands again!" | • Short and one-word sentences<br><br>• Gives a feeling of action |

**Reading Minilesson Principle**

# Writers use personification to describe something in a clear and interesting way.

## You Will Need

- several familiar texts with personification, such as the following:

  - "The Caterpillar" and "The Inchworm" from *Insectlopedia* by Douglas Florian, from Text Set: Author/Illustrator Study: Douglas Florian

  - *Rescue & Jessica* by Jessica Kensky and Patrick Downes, from Text Set: Perseverance

  - *A Little Book of Sloth* by Lucy Cooke, from Text Set: Telling a Story with Photos

- chart paper and markers

- sticky notes

## Academic Language / Important Vocabulary

- personification

### Continuum Connection

- Notice and understand how the author uses idioms and literary language, including metaphor, simile, symbolism, and personification (p. 60)

## Goal

Notice and understand how the author uses personification.

## Rationale

Personification brings nonhuman things to life and helps a reader connect with an object. This creates a clear image in readers' minds, which allows them to have a deeper understanding of their reading. Students may then try to use personification in their own writing.

## Assess Learning

Observe students when they discuss writer's craft. Notice if there is evidence of new learning based on the goal of this minilesson.

- ▶ Do students recognize personification in their reading?

- ▶ Can students describe what is being personified and how?

- ▶ Do they understand and use the word *personification*?

## Minilesson

To help students think about the minilesson principle, use familiar texts with at least one example of personification. Here is an example.

- ▶ Hold up *Insectlopedia* and read "The Caterpillar" and "The Inchworm."

  What do you notice about the caterpillar's and the inchworm's behavior? What do they do in these poems?

- ▶ Record the actions of the caterpillar and inchworm on chart paper.

- ▶ Read pages 2, 9, 15, and 16 from *Rescue & Jessica*.

  What do you notice about Rescue's behavior?

- ▶ Record what Rescue does and then draw attention to the chart.

  Are these the actions of real caterpillars, inchworms, and dogs?

  When an author writes about an animal or an object that does something that only a human would do, it is called personification. Notice that the word *person* is in *personification*.

## Have a Try

Invite the students to talk with a partner about why writers use personification.

▶ Read page 26 of *A Little Book of Sloth*.

Turn and talk to your partner. Where does the author use personification? How does this help you understand the story?

▶ Invite a few students to share. Record responses on the chart.

## Summarize and Apply

Summarize the learning and remind students to notice how writers use personification.

What does the chart show you?

▶ Write the principle at the top of the chart.

Writers use personification to make their writing interesting and to help readers understand the story even more by creating an image. Today when you read, be on the lookout for personification. If you find an example, mark it with a sticky note and bring the book back when we meet so you can share.

## Share

Following independent reading time, gather students together in the meeting area to talk about personification.

Who marked a page in their reading where the writer decided to use personification?

What is the human action the author uses? How does it help you understand that part of the story?

## Extend the Lesson (Optional)

After assessing students' understanding, you might decide to extend the learning.

▶ Gather books or short stories with examples of personification. Offer these to students to read during independent reading.

▶ Continue adding examples of personification to the class chart.

▶ **Writing About Reading** When students write letters about their reading, encourage them to share examples of personification.

**Writers use personification to describe something in a clear and interesting way.**

| Book | Human Quality | Effect |
|---|---|---|
| INSECTLOPEDIA | "The Caterpillar" · Rents a room and checks out of the room "The Inchworm" · Never gets a speeding ticket | · Helps you understand their actions |
| Rescue & Jessica | · Rescue wonders and worries. · Rescue has thoughts. He thinks Jessica is amazing. | · Makes the story even more real · Creates a partner story with Jessica |
| little book of SLOTH | · Ubu, the sloth, could win a gold medal. · Mateo, the sloth, dreams. | · Helps you understand the sloths' behaviors · Makes the story interesting |

**Section 2: Literary Analysis**

**Reading Minilesson Principle**
## Writers use repetition in interesting ways.

**Reading Like a Writer:
Analyzing the Writer's Craft**

### You Will Need

- two or three familiar texts with examples of repetition, such as the following:
  - *Meet Danitra Brown* by Nikki Grimes, from Text Set: Illustrator Study: Floyd Cooper
  - *Barbed Wire Baseball* by Marissa Moss and *Strong to the Hoop* by John Coy, from Text Set: Perseverance
- chart paper prepared with words and sentences from *Meet Danitra Brown, Barbed Wire Baseball,* and *Strong to the Hoop* [see next page]
- markers
- sticky notes

### Academic Language / Important Vocabulary

- repetition
- characters
- plot
- emphasis

### Continuum Connection

- Notice a writer's use of poetic language and sound devices: e.g., rhythm, rhyme, repetition, refrain, onomatopoeia, alliteration, assonance (p. 60)

### Goal

Notice and understand how the author uses repetition.

### Rationale

Writers use repetition to provide clues about characters and plot, create rhythm, and place emphasis on important details. When you teach students to notice repetition, you teach them to be aware of how a writer directs a reader's attention.

### Assess Learning

Observe students when they discuss writer's craft. Notice if there is evidence of new learning based on the goal of this minilesson.

- ▶ Do students notice different kinds of repetition in writing?
- ▶ Can they describe what the repetition helps them to understand?
- ▶ Do they use the academic language *repetition, characters, plot,* and *emphasis*?

## Minilesson

To help students think about the minilesson principle, use familiar texts with examples of repetition. Here is an example.

- ▶ Show and read "Purple" from *Meet Danitra Brown*.

  What do you hear in the writing on this page?

  Why do you think the writer decided to repeat the word *purple*?

- ▶ Record responses on the prepared chart.
- ▶ From *Barbed Wire Baseball*, read the parts of the pages that show repetition of the word *now* (pp. 16, 21, 26).

  What word do you hear repeated in these parts of the story?

- ▶ Record responses on sticky notes and add them to the chart. Guide the students as necessary if they don't talk about repetition.

  Why do writers decide to repeat words?

  When a writer repeats words, it is called repetition.

## Have a Try

Invite the students to talk with a partner about why and how writers use repetition.

▶ From *Strong to the Hoop*, read the first page.

Turn and talk to your partner. What repetition do you notice? How did the author use the repetition?

▶ Invite a few students to share, and add to the chart.

## Summarize and Apply

Summarize the learning and remind students to notice repetition.

Take a look at the chart. What do you notice writers sometimes do?

▶ Write the principle at the top of the chart.

As you read today, look for examples of repetition. Place a sticky note on the pages and be prepared to share why you think the author repeated words when we come back together.

## Share

Following independent reading time, gather students together in the meeting area to share in groups of three or four.

Did anyone find an example of repetition? Why did the author choose to do that?

## Extend the Lesson (Optional)

After assessing students' understanding, you might decide to extend the learning.

▶ Gather a variety of books in which the writer decided to use repetition. Ask students to read in pairs, noticing the repeated words and discussing why the author might have used repetition.

▶ **Writing About Reading** As students find more examples of repetition, encourage them to write about why they think the writer made the decision to use repetition in a reader's notebook.

### Writers use repetition in interesting ways.

| Book | The Author's Words | Purpose/ Meaning |
|------|--------------------|------------------|
| | Repeats <u>purple</u> throughout the poem. | Emphasizes that Danitra wears a lot of purple. |
| | Repeats <u>now</u> in different sentences across several pages | Shows how the characters feel<br><br>Shows time passing; it takes time to make a ballpark |
| | Repeats <u>wump</u> three times | Imitates the sound of a basketball bouncing |

## Assessment

After you have taught the minilessons in this umbrella, observe students as they talk and write about their reading across instructional contexts: interactive read-aloud, independent reading, guided reading, shared reading, and book club. Use *The Literacy Continuum* (Fountas and Pinnell 2017) to guide the observation of students' reading and writing behaviors.

▶ What evidence do you have of new understandings related to analyzing the writer's craft?

- Do students recognize how a writer uses words to create a mood?

- Can they share examples of punctuation used in interesting ways?

- Are they able to talk about different ways writers use humor?

- Do they notice a writer's use of figurative language?

- Do they notice and discuss when writers use a language other than English?

- Can they identify unconventional grammar?

- Are they able to discuss why a writer might repeat phrases or words within a piece of writing?

▶ In what other ways, beyond the scope of this umbrella, are students talking about writer's craft?

- Can students compare and contrast the work of two writers?

Use your observations to determine the next umbrella you will teach. You may also consult Minilessons Across the Year (pp. 59–61) for guidance.

## Link to Writing

After teaching the minilessons in this umbrella, help students link the new learning to their own writing:

▶ Encourage students to apply some of the techniques of writer's craft to their own writing.

## Reader's Notebook

When this umbrella is complete, provide a copy of the minilesson principles (see resources.fountasandpinnell.com) for students to glue in the reader's notebook (in the Minilessons section if using *Reader's Notebook: Intermediate* [Fountas and Pinnell 2011]), so they can refer to the information as needed.

## Minilessons in This Umbrella

**RML1**  Study illustrators to learn about their craft.

**RML2**  Illustrators create art to add to the meaning of the text.

**RML3**  Illustrators create art to show the mood.

**RML4**  Illustrators use perspective in their art to communicate an idea or a feeling.

**RML5**  Illustrators use specific details to make something appear real.

**RML6**  Illustrators use short scenes for different purposes.

**RML7**  Illustrators show time passing in the pictures to help you understand the story.

## Before Teaching Umbrella 11 Minilessons

Read and discuss books that have strong illustration support and that engage students' intellectual curiosity and emotions. The minilessons in this umbrella use the following books from the *Fountas & Pinnell Classroom™ Interactive Read-Aloud Collection* text sets; however, you can use books that have strong illustration support and are based on the experiences and interests of the students.

**Illustrator Study: Floyd Cooper**

*Ruth and the Green Book*
   by Calvin Alexander Ramsey

*Ma Dear's Aprons* by Patricia C. McKissack

*Meet Danitra Brown* by Nikki Grimes

*These Hands* by Margaret Mason

*A Dance Like Starlight: One Ballerina's Dream*
   by Kristy Dempsey

**Author/Illustrator Study: Allen Say**

*Tea with Milk*

*The Bicycle Man*

**Genre Study: Memoir**

*Twelve Kinds of Ice*
   by Ellen Bryan Obed

**Friendship**

*The Other Side*
   by Jacqueline Woodson

**Illustration Study: Craft**

*Gecko* by Raymond Huber

*Eye to Eye: How Animals See the World* by Steve Jenkins

*Giant Squid* by Candace Fleming

**Genre Study: Historical Fiction**

*Dad, Jackie, and Me*
   by Myron Uhlberg

As you read aloud and enjoy these texts together, help students look closely at the illustrations so that they can understand and appreciate the many decisions an illustrator makes about how to support the text.

**Floyd Cooper**

**Allen Say**

**Memoir**

**Friendship**

**Craft**

**Historical Fiction**

Section 2: Literary Analysis

**Reading Minilesson Principle**
## Study illustrators to learn about their craft.

Studying Illustrators and Analyzing an Illustrator's Craft

### You Will Need

- a variety of books by the same illustrator, such as from Text Set: Illustrator Study: Floyd Cooper
- chart paper and markers
- sticky notes
- document camera (optional)

### Academic Language / Important Vocabulary

- illustrator
- perspective
- distance
- angle
- craft
- authentic

### Continuum Connection

- Make connections (similarities and differences) among texts that have the same author/illustrator, setting, characters, or theme (p. 58)
- Connect text by a range of categories: e.g., content, theme, message, genre, author/illustrator, character, setting, special forms, text structure, or organization (pp. 58, 62)

### Goal

Understand that an illustrator might illustrate several books and that there are often recognizable characteristics across the books.

### Rationale

When students recognize the characteristics of an illustrator's work, they begin to appreciate that illustrating books is a process of decision making and that artistry is involved. Students become aware of the illustrator's craft and how it contributes to the full meaning of the book. Note that this lesson format can be used to study an author, illustrator, or author/illustrator (see p. 42).

### Assess Learning

Observe students when they talk about an illustrator's craft and notice if there is evidence of new learning based on the goal of this minilesson.

- Do students recognize an illustrator's work across books?
- Can they describe how understanding an illustrator's work gives greater understanding of the books drawn by that illustrator?
- Do they understand the terms *illustrator, perspective, distance, angle, craft,* and *authentic*?

## Minilesson

To help students think about the minilesson principle, provide an interactive lesson to study an illustrator's craft. Here is an example.

- Show covers of several books illustrated by Floyd Cooper.

    You have read several books illustrated by Floyd Cooper. Let's look at a few illustrations by Floyd Cooper and talk about them. What do you notice about his illustrations?

- Show a few illustrations from several books, such as *Dance Like Starlight, Ruth and the Green Book,* and *These Hands.*

    Think about what things you *always* notice in Floyd Cooper's illustrations and what things you *often* notice in his illustrations.

- The following prompts can be used to support the conversation:
    - *Talk about how the illustrations add to the meaning of the story.*
    - *What does the perspective of the illustration help you understand?*
    - *How do the illustrations make the characters and backgrounds seem real?*
- On chart paper, create a noticings chart with a column title for *Always* and a column for *Often.* Add student responses to the chart.

## Have a Try

Invite the students to talk in groups about an illustrator.

❱ Provide each group with a book by Floyd Cooper.

Talk about what you notice about Floyd Cooper's illustrations. How do they help you understand more about the story?

❱ After time for discussion, ask students to share. Add to chart.

## Summarize and Apply

Summarize the learning and remind students to think about an illustrator's craft.

Today you learned that when you read many books that are illustrated by the same person, you begin to notice decisions the illustrator makes. When an illustrator chooses how to draw, that is part of the illustrator's craft.

During independent reading time today, you can select a book illustrated by Floyd Cooper or by another illustrator you enjoy. As you read, think about the illustrator's craft. Mark any pages you want to remember with a sticky note. Bring the book when we meet so you can share.

## Share

Following independent reading time, gather students in the meeting area.

Who would like to share what you noticed about an illustrator's craft? Share any illustrations that show what you are thinking.

## Extend the Lesson (Optional)

After assessing students' understanding, you might decide to extend the learning.

❱ Ask students to compare and contrast the illustrations of two illustrators. Talk about how each illustrator helps the reader understand the story.

❱ **Writing About Reading** Have students glue into a reader's notebook an illustrator chart (available at resources.fountasandpinnell.com) that they can use to think and write about illustrators.

---

**Floyd Cooper: Illustrator**

**Noticings:**

| Always | Often |
|---|---|
| • Includes details to make the characters and the settings seem realistic or authentic | • Uses color to change the mood, like from ordinary to hopeful |
| • Provides new information in the illustrations to help the reader understand the story | • Uses specific details to make something appear real |
| • Adds details to make the story more historically accurate | • Illustrates from different angles to help readers focus on something important |

Section 2: Literary Analysis

**Reading Minilesson Principle**
# Illustrators create art to add to the meaning of the text.

Studying Illustrators and Analyzing an Illustrator's Craft

## You Will Need

- several familiar fiction books with easily identifiable character interactions, such as the following:
  - *These Hands* by Margaret Mason, from Text Set: Illustrator Study: Floyd Cooper
  - *Tea with Milk* by Allen Say, from Text Set: Author/Illustrator Study: Allen Say
  - *The Other Side* by Jacqueline Woodson, from Text Set: Friendship
- chart paper and markers
- sticky notes
- document camera (optional)

## Academic Language / Important Vocabulary

- illustrations
- details
- meaning

### Continuum Connection

- Notice how illustrations and graphics help to communicate the writer's message (pp. 61, 65)

## Goal

Gain new information from the illustrations in fiction books and understand that illustrations can be interpreted in different ways.

## Rationale

When you teach students to notice that authors and illustrators use words and illustrations together in fiction books to create meaning, students develop a deeper understanding of an illustrator's craft. Teaching students that illustrations can be interpreted in different ways increases students' understandings of stories and enhances the conversations they have about books.

## Assess Learning

Observe students when they discuss illustrations and notice if there is evidence of new learning based on the goal of this minilesson.

- ▶ Do students notice information in illustrations that helps them understand the story?
- ▶ Are they able to discuss different interpretations of the same illustration?
- ▶ Do they use the terms *illustrations, details,* and *meaning*?

## Minilesson

To help students think about the minilesson principle, provide an interactive lesson about how illustrations enhance the meaning of a story. Here is an example.

- ▶ Show the cover of *These Hands.*

    Think about the illustrations as I read and show a few pages from *These Hands.*

- ▶ Read and show the illustrations on the page that begins "Well, these" and the five pages that follow.

    What do you notice about the way the illustrations add to the meaning of the story?

- ▶ As students provide ideas, create a chart that shows what the illustrations help a reader understand. Ask students to provide specific text examples.

- ▶ Show the cover of *Tea with Milk.*

    Now think about the illustrations in *Tea with Milk* as I read and show a few pages.

- ▶ Read pages 8 and 12 and show the corresponding illustrations.

    What other meanings do the illustrations add?

- ▶ Add students' ideas to chart.

## Have a Try

Invite the students to talk with a partner about illustrations.

▶ Show and read an example from *The Other Side*, such as the pages on which you can see the two girls in town, but only parts of the moms.

> Turn and talk about how the illustrations on these pages help you understand the story.

▶ After time for discussion, ask students to share. Add to chart.

## Summarize and Apply

Summarize the learning and remind students to think about how illustrations add meaning when they read fiction stories.

> Take a look at the chart. What are you thinking about illustrations?

▶ Add the principle to the chart.

> As you read today, you can choose a book with illustrations and think about how they add to the meaning of the story. Add a sticky note on any pages you would like to share. Bring the book when we meet.

## Share

Following independent reading time, gather students in the meeting area. Ask several volunteers to share.

> Who noticed illustrations that added to the meaning of the book? Talk about what you noticed and share any pages.

## Extend the Lesson (Optional)

After assessing students' understanding, you might decide to extend the learning.

▶ **Writing About Reading** Encourage students to write about illustrations they notice and how the illustrations add to the meaning of a book.

| Illustrators create art to add to the meaning of the text. | | |
|---|---|---|
| **Title** | **What the Illustrations Help You Understand** | |
| THESE HANDS | • a character's actions | Example: The illustrations show that people march together to change unfair laws. |
| TEA with MILK | • a character's feelings | Examples: Large empty space around May shows loneliness. The stiffness of the two characters shows shyness and discomfort. |
| The Other Side | • what is not in the words | Examples: The words say "everyone ... seemed far away" but the illustration shows that the girls don't want to be far away from each other. |

**Reading Minilesson Principle**
## Illustrators create art to show the mood.

### Studying Illustrators and Analyzing an Illustrator's Craft

### You Will Need

- several familiar fiction books that show clear of examples of illustrations adding meaning to the story, such as the following:
  - *Giant Squid* by Candace Fleming, from Text Set: Illustration Study: Craft
  - *Ruth and the Green Book* by Calvin Alexander Ramsey and *A Dance Like Starlight* by Kristy Dempsey, from Text Set: Illustrator Study: Floyd Cooper
- chart paper and markers
- sticky notes
- document camera (optional)

### Academic Language / Important Vocabulary

- illustrations
- physical space
- texture
- mood

### Continuum Connection

- Notice and infer how illustrations contribute to mood in a fiction text (p. 61)
- Notice how illustrations and graphics help to communicate the writer's message (p. 65)

### Goal

Understand that illustrators create and change the mood of the story using different techniques.

### Rationale

Illustrators use color, size, and physical space to create and change the mood of the story. When students notice these techniques, they can better understand the mood that the author and illustrator want to convey.

### Assess Learning

Observe students when they talk about illustrations and notice if there is evidence of new learning based on the goal of this minilesson.

- ❱ Are students able to identify examples of an illustrator's use of color, size, and physical space to create and change the mood of the story?
- ❱ Do they use the terms *illustrations, physical space, texture,* and *mood*?

## Minilesson

To help students think about the minilesson principle, provide an interactive lesson about the impact an illustrator has on mood. Here is an example.

- ❱ Prior to this lesson, ensure that your students understand what is meant by the term *mood*.

  Think about the illustrations on a few pages from *Giant Squid*.

- ❱ Show the first three pages before the title page and the center two-page spread that shows the dark ink surrounding the squid.

  How does the illustrator want you to feel? What is the mood of these illustrations?

- ❱ Record students' responses about the illustration and mood on chart paper.

  Now think about a few illustrations from *Ruth and the Green Book*.

- ❱ Show and read the two-page spread where the family stops to use the restroom at the gas station.

  What mood does the illustrator create here?

- ❱ Record responses.

## Have a Try

Invite the students to talk with a partner about how illustrations create mood.

▶ Show and read the page from *A Dance Like Starlight* on which the ballet master is holding the girl's face. Then read and show the following page.

  Turn and talk about how these illustrations create or change mood.

▶ As needed, prompt student conversations to notice the change in color and the impact it has on mood.

▶ After time for discussion, ask a few students to share. Add to chart.

## Summarize and Apply

Summarize the learning and remind students to think about mood in illustrations when they read fiction stories.

  Look back at the chart. What are you thinking about the role of the illustrator in creating mood?

▶ Add the principle to the chart.

  When you read today, notice if any illustrations create or change the mood for you as a reader. You might find examples beyond color and size. Place a sticky note on those pages. Bring the book when we meet so you can share.

## Share

Following independent reading time, gather students in small groups.

  With your group, talk about any illustrations you found that created or changed the mood.

▶ After time for discussion, ask a few students to share. If you have access to a projector, you can project the illustrations that students share.

## Extend the Lesson (Optional)

After assessing students' understanding, you might decide to extend the learning.

▶ Have students look for examples of an illustrator's use of physical space (empty space, proximity) and texture (sharp and rounded edges). Talk about how these techniques affect mood.

▶ **Writing About Reading** Encourage students to use a reader's notebook to write about examples they find of illustrators creating or changing the mood.

| Title | Illustration | Mood |
|---|---|---|
| GIANT SQUID | • dark background<br>• squid tentacles slowly becoming visible | • mystery<br>• feeling of the unknown |
| | • bluish-black ink on the entire page | • alarming or uncomfortable feeling of not being able to see |
| Ruth and the Green Book | • large gas station and small illustration of the family<br>• Daddy is crouched down next to Ruth. | • feeling of being small and unimportant |
| | • brownish background changing to pink | • change from wishing to hoping<br>• change from dreaming to working hard |

### Illustrators create art to show the mood.

**Reading Minilesson Principle**

## Illustrators use perspective in their art to communicate an idea or a feeling.

**Studying Illustrators and Analyzing an Illustrator's Craft**

### You Will Need

- several familiar fiction books, such as the following:
  - *Eye to Eye: How Animals See the World* by Steve Jenkins, from Text Set: Illustration Study: Craft
  - *These Hands* by Margaret Mason, from Text Set: Illustrator Study: Floyd Cooper
  - *Dad, Jackie, and Me* by Myron Uhlberg, from Text Set: Genre Study: Historical Fiction
- chart paper and markers
- sticky notes
- document camera (optional)

### Academic Language / Important Vocabulary

- perspective
- illustrations

### Continuum Connection

- Notice how illustrators create perspective in their pictures (using images close up, far away, creating distance in between, etc.) (p. 61)

### Goal

Understand that illustrators use perspective to communicate an idea or feeling.

### Rationale

Helping students notice perspective in illustrations teaches them to consider what an illustrator might be bringing to their attention at that point in the story. Illustrators might zoom in on a central image to bring it closer to the reader or place an image in the distance to create a feeling of space.

### Assess Learning

Observe students when they talk about perspective in illustrations and notice if there is evidence of new learning based on the goal of this minilesson.

- Are students able to identify when an illustrator uses perspective to communicate an idea or a feeling (e.g., illustrations that are zoomed in, far away, or have distance between them)?
- Do they use academic language, such as *perspective* and *illustrations*?

## Minilesson

To help students think about the minilesson principle, provide an interactive lesson to think about perspective in illustrations. Here is an example.

- Show any page from *Eye to Eye*.

  Notice how Steve Jenkins drew the illustrations from this perspective. I wonder why he decided to illustrate the animals close up and even to exaggerate the size of some animals. What do you think about that?

- On chart paper, record student responses in two columns, one for the illustration perspective example and one for the idea or feeling it supports.

  Now think about an illustration in *These Hands*.

- Show the page on which the grandfather is telling the grandson about the time when he was not allowed to make bread.

  What do you notice about this illustration?

- As needed, provide a prompt such as this: *Why does the illustrator choose to draw from this perspective?*

- Record students' responses on the chart.

- Show the last two-page spread in *These Hands*.

  What do you notice about this illustration?

- Record responses on the chart.

## Have a Try

Invite the students to talk in a group of three about perspective in illustrations.

▶ Show and read the page from *Dad, Jackie, and Me* that has the illustration of Jackie being spiked by the opposing player.

> Turn and talk about the feeling or idea that the illustrator creates. How does the illustrator do that?

▶ Prompt the conversation so students discuss perspective. After time for discussion, record students' responses.

## Summarize and Apply

Summarize the learning and remind students to think about perspective in illustrations when they read fiction stories.

> Look back at the chart. What can you say about illustrators?

▶ Add the principle to the chart.

> When you read today, notice if the illustrator uses perspective in the illustrations to communicate a feeling or idea. Mark any pages that you would like to share with a sticky note. Bring the book when we meet.

## Share

Following independent reading time, gather students in a meeting area.

> Did anyone notice an example of an illustrator's use of perspective to show a feeling or an idea? Share what you noticed.

▶ As a few volunteers share, you might choose to project the illustrations so students can see the details.

## Extend the Lesson (Optional)

After assessing students' understanding, you might decide to extend the learning.

▶ Have students look for other examples of perspective in illustrations to add to the chart.

▶ **Writing About Reading** Encourage students to use a reader's notebook to write about the idea or feeling they get when looking at illustrations. Ask them to think about the perspective from which the illustration is created and write about that.

Illustrators use perspective in their art to communicate an idea or a feeling.

| Title | Perspective of the Illustration | Idea or Feeling |
|---|---|---|
| EYE TO EYE STEVE JENKINS | large, close-up picture of two pairs of eyes on the jumping spider | importance fear |
| THESE HANDS | grandfather with broom looking through the window where a white man makes bread | inferiority inadequacy being an outsider |
| THESE HANDS | grandfather and grandson looking up to the wide open sky | endless possibilities |
| DAD JACKIE AND ME | Jackie's calm face and a large image of the player spiking Jackie | calmness in the face of prejudice |

# RML5

LA.U11.RML5

## Reading Minilesson Principle
# Illustrators use specific details to make something appear real.

### Studying Illustrators and Analyzing an Illustrator's Craft

**You Will Need**

- several familiar fiction books, such as the following:
  - *Eye to Eye: How Animals See the World* by Steve Jenkins and *Giant Squid* by Candace Fleming, from Text Set: Illustration Study: Craft
  - *Dad, Jackie, and Me* by Myron Uhlberg, from Text Set: Genre Study: Historical Fiction
- chart paper and markers
- sticky notes
- document camera [optional]

**Academic Language / Important Vocabulary**

- illustrations
- authentic
- textures

**Continuum Connection**

- Notice how illustrations and graphics go together with the text in a meaningful way [p. 61]
- Notice how illustrations and graphics help to communicate the writer's message [p. 65]

## Goal

Understand that illustrators use specific details to make something look authentic.

## Rationale

When students are taught to look for details that provide authenticity in illustrations, they learn to look critically at them and to understand that the illustrator makes thoughtful decisions about what to show and how to show it.

## Assess Learning

Observe students when they talk about details in illustrations and notice if there is evidence of new learning based on the goal of this minilesson.

- ◗ Do students recognize and discuss the authentic details in illustrations?
- ◗ Do they use details in the illustrations to help them understand the story?
- ◗ Do they understand the terms *illustrations*, *authentic*, and *textures*?

## Minilesson

To help students think about the minilesson principle, provide an interactive lesson to help them think about how details in illustrations add to the story or topic. Here is an example.

- ◗ Show the illustration from *Eye to Eye* of the Atlantic bay scallop and the jumping spider.

    Look at how the illustrator created these illustrations.

    What do you notice that the illustrator did to make these illustrations look authentic or real?

- ◗ As needed, prompt the conversation by asking students to notice the way the illustrator used torn and cut paper to give the illustrations texture.
- ◗ On chart paper, record students' responses.

    Now think about the illustrations in another book, *Giant Squid*.

- ◗ Show a few illustrations that display the squid's details.

    Talk about what the illustrator did to make these illustrations look authentic or real.

- ◗ Record students' responses.

    Why do you think an illustrator might decide to make the illustrations look authentic, or real?

    For what kind of books would an illustrator decide to make the illustrations look authentic?

## Have a Try

Invite the students to talk with a partner about details in illustrations.

‣ Show the two-page spread of the neighborhood in *Jackie, Dad, and Me*.

Turn and talk about how the illustrator made this illustration seem real and why he might have decided to draw it that way.

‣ After time for discussion, ask students to share. Record responses.

## Summarize and Apply

Summarize the learning and remind students to think about details in illustrations.

What did you notice about how illustrators make illustrations seem real? What do they do?

‣ As needed, prompt the conversation to help students discuss the way illustrators use specific details, textures, and colors. Add the principle to the chart.

When you read today, choose a book with illustrations. Notice details that the illustrator uses to make the illustrations seem authentic. Place a sticky note on any pages you want to remember. Bring the book when we meet so you can share.

## Share

Following independent reading time, gather students in small groups.

Who would like to share the details you noticed in an illustration?

‣ Ask a few volunteers to share. You may want to project the illustrations to help students notice details.

## Extend the Lesson (Optional)

After assessing students' understanding, you might decide to extend the learning.

‣ During interactive read-aloud, discuss the possible reasons for illustrators' decisions about how to make their illustrations and what to show in them.

‣ **Writing About Reading** Encourage students to use a reader's notebook to write about illustrations they find that have specific details that make the illustrations seem authentic.

### Illustrators use specific details to make something appear real.

| Title | Illustration | What makes the illustration look real? |
|---|---|---|
| EYE TO EYE | Atlantic bay scallop: • Detailed, multi-color shell • Cilia, or hairs, that help it eat — Jumping spider: • Hairs on the leg • Stripes on the spider | Torn and cut paper give the illustrations texture. |
| GIANT SQUID | • Curve of squid's beak • Length • Color of the tentacles | Shades of color and shadows make it seem real. |
| JACKIE, DAD, AND ME | • 1947 neighborhood | Cars, fire truck, and clothes match the time period. Child on his tricycle seems real. |

Section 2: Literary Analysis

# RML 6
LA.U11.RML6

Reading Minilesson Principle
## Illustrators use short scenes for different purposes.

## Studying Illustrators and Analyzing an Illustrator's Craft

### You Will Need

- several familiar fiction books that include illustrations with short scenes, such as the following:
  - *Gecko* by Raymond Huber, from Text Set: Illustration Study: Craft
  - *The Bicycle Man* by Allen Say and *Twelve Kinds of Ice* by Allen Say, from Text Set: Author/Illustrator Study: Allen Say
- chart paper and markers
- sticky notes
- document camera (optional)

### Academic Language / Important Vocabulary

- illustrations
- scenes
- actions
- character traits

### Continuum Connection

- Notice how illustrations and graphics help to communicate the writer's message (pp. 61, 65)

## Goal

Understand how and why illustrators use short scenes for different purposes.

## Rationale

Illustrators use short scenes as a way of showing the same action at different times or to capture the passage of time. When students look for short scenes within illustrations and discuss the meaning of those scenes, they have a greater understanding of the action in a book.

## Assess Learning

Observe students when they talk about how illustrators use scenes in illustrations and notice if there is evidence of new learning based on the goal of this minilesson.

- ❯ Do students notice and describe the reason for short scenes within some illustrations?
- ❯ Do they understand the terms *illustrations, scenes, actions,* and *character traits*?

## Minilesson

To help students think about the minilesson principle, provide an interactive lesson to think about how illustrators use scenes for different purposes. Here is an example.

- ❯ Show and read the two-page spread of the gecko shedding its skin in *Gecko*.

  Turn and talk about these illustrations in *Gecko*. What do you notice?

- ❯ Ask a few volunteers to respond.

  What do you notice about the way these three short scenes have been placed together?

- ❯ As students share their thinking, record responses on chart paper.

  Now think about the short scenes created by the illustrator of *The Bicycle Man*.

- ❯ Show the two-page spread with the children doing chores and then the other that shows the children and adults playing games.

  What do you think the illustrator's purpose was in making these illustrations they way they are?

- ❯ Record responses on the chart.

## Have a Try

Invite the students to talk in a small group about the way illustrators sometimes use short scenes for different purposes.

▶ Show and read parts of pages 33–35 from *Twelve Kinds of Ice*.

> Why do you think the illustrator included these illustrations in *Twelve Kinds of Ice*? Turn and talk to your group about that.

▶ After time for discussion, prompt students.

> What do these short scenes help you understand?

▶ Record responses.

## Summarize and Apply

Summarize the learning and remind students to think about short scenes that illustrators create when they read fiction stories.

> Look at the chart. What did you learn about why illustrators sometimes decide to include short scenes within a story?

▶ Add principle to chart.

> When you read today, look for examples of illustrators creating small scenes. Think about why the illustrator might have done that. Place a sticky note on the page. Bring the book when we meet so you can share.

## Share

Following independent reading time, gather students in the meeting area.

> Who would like to share an example of a short scene in an illustration?

▶ If no one found an example of a short scene, prompt a discussion about what students did notice in the illustrations. Ask a few volunteers to share. You may want to project the illustrations so students can notice details together.

## Extend the Lesson (Optional)

After assessing students' understanding, you might decide to extend the learning.

▶ **Writing About Reading** Have students use a reader's notebook to write about a small scene they noticed in a book they are reading. Encourage them to write about the illustrator's purpose in creating the scene.

### Illustrators use short scenes for different purposes.

| Title | Illustration | Purpose |
|---|---|---|
| Gecko | • gecko beginning to lose skin<br>• gecko's skin almost gone<br>• gecko eating dead skin | • shows the different actions<br>• shows time passing |
| THE BICYCLE MAN by Allen Say | • children doing different chores<br>• children playing tug-of-war, piggyback races, adults doing the two-legged race | • shows the characters' different actions |
| TWELVE KINDS of ICE | • Dad skating with broom<br>• Dad in a snowbank<br>• Dad skating off ice by accident<br>• Dad standing under the hose | • shows the character's different actions<br>• shows a character's trait |

# RML7
## LA.U11.RML7

**Illustrators show time passing in the pictures to help you understand the story.**

### Studying Illustrators and Analyzing an Illustrator's Craft

**You Will Need**

- several familiar fiction books, such as the following:
  - *Tea with Milk* by Allen Say, from Text Set: Author/Illustrator Study: Allen Say
  - *Ruth and the Green Book* by Calvin Alexander Ramsey, from Text Set: Illustrator Study: Floyd Cooper
  - *Twelve Kinds of Ice* by Ellen Bryan Obed, from Text Set: Genre Study: Memoir
- chart paper and markers
- sticky notes
- document camera (optional)

**Academic Language / Important Vocabulary**

- illustrations
- passage of time

### Continuum Connection

- Notice how illustrations and graphics help to communicate the writer's message (pp. 61, 65)

## Goal

Notice how an illustrator shows the passage of time through illustrations (e.g., changes in light or weather).

## Rationale

Illustrators may show the passage of time through details within the illustrations. Helping students notice these details supports them in better understanding how much time passes between parts of the story.

## Assess Learning

Observe students when they talk about the passage of time in illustrations and notice if there is evidence of new learning based on the goal of this minilesson.

- ▶ Are students able to describe how an illustrator shows the passage of time?
- ▶ Can they describe how noticing the passage of time helps a reader's understanding of the story?
- ▶ Do they understand the terms *illustrations* and *passage of time*?

## Minilesson

To help students think about the minilesson principle, provide an interactive lesson to think about the way illustrators show the passage of time. Here is an example.

- ▶ Show the first two illustrations in *Tea with Milk*.

  What do you notice about the way the illustrator has shown the passage of time in these illustrations from *Tea with Milk*?

- ▶ Write students' responses on chart paper. Include the example and use an arrow to show the connection between illustrations that shows the passage of time.

  Now think about the illustrations in *Ruth and the Green Book*. What do you notice about the passage of time?

- ▶ Show the first two-page spread and then the one that follows.

  What do you notice?

- ▶ Record students' responses.

## Have a Try

Invite the students to talk with a partner about the passage of time in illustrations.

▶ Show the illustrations on pages 9, 13, and 25 from *Twelve Kinds of Ice*.

Turn and talk about how the illustrations in *Twelve Kinds of Ice* help you notice the passage of time.

▶ After time for discussion, ask a few students to share their thinking. Add to the chart.

## Summarize and Apply

Summarize the learning and remind students to think about the way illustrators show the passage of time when they read fiction stories.

Today you talked about how illustrations help you understand the passage of time in a story.

▶ Add the principle to the chart.

When you read today, see if you notice illustrations that show the passage of time. Place a sticky note on the pages and bring the book when we meet so you can share.

## Share

Following independent reading time, gather students in the meeting area.

Who would like to share illustrations that show the passage of time? Tell about them.

▶ If no one found an example of time passing, prompt a discussion about what students did notice in the illustrations. You may want to project the illustrations so students can study them together.

## Extend the Lesson (Optional)

After assessing students' understanding, you might decide to extend the learning.

▶ During interactive read-aloud, help students notice and discuss illustrations that show the passage of time.

▶ Encourage students to add illustrations that show the passage of time to their own writing.

▶ **Writing About Reading** Have students use a reader's notebook to write about illustrations that show the passage of time.

| | Illustrators show time passing in the pictures to help you understand the story. | | |
|---|---|---|---|
| **Title** | **Illustrations Show** | **Example** | |
| TEA with MILK | years passing | black and white illustration of a young child ↓ color illustration of the same person as a young woman | |
| Ruth and the Green Book | time passing while driving | car in the city ↓ car driving along a country road | |
| TWELVE KINDS of ICE | weather changing | children's clothing: • long-sleeved shirts ↓ • sweaters and some hats ↓ • coats, hats, scarves | |

## Assessment

After you have taught the minilessons in this umbrella, observe students as they talk and write about illustrations across instructional contexts: interactive read-aloud, independent reading, guided reading, shared reading, and book club. Use *The Literacy Continuum* (Fountas and Pinnell 2017) to guide the observation of students' reading and writing behaviors.

▶ What evidence do you have of new understandings related to illustrations?

- Do students notice and discuss characteristics of an illustrator after reading several books by that illustrator?

- Can they discuss how illustrations add to the meaning of the text?

- Do they understand how and why illustrators create and change the mood, show perspective, and use realistic details?

- Do they understand why illustrators use short scenes?

- Can they discuss the ways that illustrators show the passage of time?

- Do they use vocabulary such as *illustrations, perspective, details, meaning,* and *mood*?

▶ In what other ways, beyond the scope of this umbrella, are students demonstrating an understanding of illustrations?

- Do students use other graphics and text features to gain knowledge?

Use your observations to determine the next umbrella you will teach. You may also consult Minilessons Across the Year (pp. 59–61) for guidance.

## Link to Writing

After teaching the minilessons in this umbrella, help students link the new learning to their own writing:

▶ When students illustrate their own stories, encourage them to experiment with some of the illustration techniques they have learned about (e.g., create and change mood, use perspective, show specific details to make something appear real, use short scenes, and show the passage of time).

## Reader's Notebook

When this umbrella is complete, provide a copy of the minilesson principles (see resources.fountasandpinnell.com) for students to glue in the reader's notebook (in the Minilessons section if using *Reader's Notebook: Intermediate* [Fountas and Pinnell 2011]), so they can refer to the information as needed.

## Minilessons in This Umbrella

**RML1**  Authors honor/thank people and give information about themselves in parts outside the main text.

**RML2**  An author's note or an afterword often provides additional information about the book.

**RML3**  Authors provide resources outside the main text to help you find information or understand more about the story or topic.

**RML4**  The design (book jacket, cover, title page, endpapers) often adds to or enhances the meaning or appeal of the book.

## Before Teaching Umbrella 12 Minilessons

The minilessons in this umbrella help students understand the peritext—the text resources outside the body of the text. Read and discuss engaging fiction and nonfiction books that have peritext resources, such as a dedication, an acknowledgments page, or an author's note, from the following *Fountas & Pinnell Classroom™ Interactive Read-Aloud Collection* text sets or from your classroom library.

**Friendship**

*Mangoes, Mischief, and Tales of Friendship: Stories from India* by Chitra Soundar

**Perseverance**

*Barbed Wire Baseball: How One Man Brought Hope to the Japanese Internment Camps of WWII* by Marissa Moss

**Genre Study: Biography (Individuals Making a Difference)**

*Six Dots: A Story of Young Louis Braille* by Jen Bryant

**Taking Action, Making Change**

*Follow the Moon Home: A Tale of One Idea, Twenty Kids, and a Hundred Sea Turtles* by Philippe Cousteau and Deborah Hopkinson

**Innovative Thinking and Creative Problem Solving**

*Hands Around the Library: Protecting Egypt's Treasured Books* by Susan L. Roth and Karen Leggett Abouraya

*Parrots Over Puerto Rico* by Susan L. Roth and Cindy Trumbore

*One Plastic Bag: Isatou Ceesay and the Recycling Women of the Gambia* by Miranda Paul

As you read aloud and enjoy these texts together, help students notice and discuss peritext resources, such as dedications, acknowledgments, author's notes, endpapers, glossaries, and tables of contents.

**Friendship**

**Perseverance**

**Biography**

**Taking Action**

**Innovative Thinking**

Section 2: Literary Analysis

**Reading Minilesson Principle**

# Authors honor/thank people and give information about themselves in parts outside the main text.

## Noticing Book and Print Features

### You Will Need

▸ at least three familiar books that contain a dedication, acknowledgments, and/or author information, such as the following:

- *Follow the Moon Home* by Philippe Cousteau and Deborah Hopkinson, from Text Set: Taking Action, Making Change

- *Parrots Over Puerto Rico* by Susan L. Roth and Cindy Trumbore and *Hands Around the Library* by Susan L. Roth and Karen Leggett Abouraya, from Text Set: Innovative Thinking and Creative Problem Solving

▸ chart paper and markers

### Academic Language / Important Vocabulary

▸ author

▸ dedication

▸ acknowledgments

▸ author page

### Continuum Connection

▸ Notice and use and understand the purpose of some text resources outside the body (peritext): e.g., dedication, acknowledgments, author's note, illustrator's note, endpapers (pp. 61, 65)

## Goal

Notice, use, and understand the purpose of the dedication, acknowledgments, and author page.

## Rationale

When you teach students to notice and read peritext resources, such as the dedication, acknowledgments, and author page, they understand that behind every book is a real person who was helped, inspired, and influenced by many others. Depending on the specific resource, they may gain insight into the author's creative process, who or what inspired the author to write the book, and/or who helped the author write the book.

## Assess Learning

Observe students when they read and talk about books and notice if there is evidence of new learning based on the goal of this minilesson.

▸ Do students notice, read, and understand the purpose of peritext resources, such as the dedication, acknowledgments, and author page?

▸ Do they use academic vocabulary, such as *author, dedication, acknowledgments,* and *author page*?

## Minilesson

To help students think about the minilesson principle, engage students in noticing and understanding the purpose of peritext resources. Here is an example.

▸ Show the cover of *Follow the Moon Home* and read the title. Turn to the copyright page and point to the dedications. Read each aloud.

> What do you notice about this part of the book?

> Does anyone know what this part of the book is called?

> This part of the book is called the dedication. In this book, there are three dedications. Why do you think there are three?

▸ Point out that the initials after the three dedications correspond with the names of the two authors and the illustrator.

> Why do you think Deborah Hopkinson dedicated the book to someone who helped sea turtles?

▸ Read the dedications in one or two other books. Ask students what they noticed about the dedications and then ask them to help you come up with a definition of a dedication. Record the definition and students' noticings on chart paper.

▸ Continue in a similar manner with the acknowledgments page in *Parrots Over Puerto Rico*. Record students' noticings on the chart.

## Have a Try

Invite the students to talk with a partner about the author information in *Hands Around the Library*.

▶ Turn to the back flap of *Hands Around the Library* and read the information about the authors.

> Turn and talk to your partner about this part of the book. What do you notice? What kind of information did the authors give in this part?

▶ After students turn and talk, ask a few pairs to share their thinking. Help students come up with a definition of the author page and record the definition and students' noticings on the chart.

## Summarize and Apply

Summarize the learning and remind students to notice and read dedications, acknowledgments, and author pages.

> Today we looked at some parts of books that are outside the main body of the text. What did you notice about these parts?

▶ Write the principle at the top of the chart.

> When you read today, notice if your book has a dedication, acknowledgments, or an author page. If so, be sure to read them. Be ready to share what you learned from these parts of your book when we come back together.

## Share

Following independent reading time, gather students together in the meeting area to discuss their reading.

> Turn and talk to your partner about what you noticed or learned from the dedication, acknowledgments, or author page in the book you read today.

## Extend the Lesson (Optional)

After assessing students' understanding, you might decide to extend the learning.

▶ When students write their own books, encourage them to include a dedication, an acknowledgment, and/or an author page.

---

**Authors honor/thank people and give information about themselves in parts outside the main text.**

### Dedication

I dedicate this book to . . .

- Shows they care about someone in their family
- Honors someone who inspired them to write the book

### Acknowledgments

Thank you to . . .

- Thanks people who helped the author do research
- Thanks people who provided photographs
- Thanks people who read the author's first draft

### Author Page

The author lives in . . .

- Says where the author lives
- Says what else the author does besides writing books
- Says what inspired the author to write the book

---

Section 2: Literary Analysis

# RML2

**LA.U12.RML2**

**Reading Minilesson Principle**

# An author's note or an afterword often provides additional information about the book.

## Noticing Book and Print Features

### You Will Need

- two or three familiar books that contain an author's and/or illustrator's note or an afterword, such as the following:
  - *Hands Around the Library* by Susan L. Roth and Karen Leggett Abouraya, from Text Set: Innovative Thinking and Creative Problem Solving
  - *Barbed Wire Baseball* by Marissa Moss, from Text Set: Perseverance
  - *Parrots Over Puerto Rico* by Susan L. Roth and Cindy Trumbore, from Text Set: Innovative Thinking and Creative Problem Solving
- chart paper and markers

### Academic Language / Important Vocabulary

- author's note
- illustrator's note
- afterword

### Continuum Connection

- Notice, use, and understand the purpose of some text resources outside the body (peritext): e.g., dedication, acknowledgments, author's note, illustrator's note, endpapers (pp. 61, 65)

## Goal

Notice and understand that an author's/illustrator's note or an afterword can provide more information about the book.

## Rationale

An author's or illustrator's note may reveal the inspiration for writing or illustrating the book or offer important contextual information. An afterword, usually written by someone other than the author, might give further information about the topic. When students read and think about the author's or illustrator's note or an afterword, they gain a deeper understanding of the book and of the process and purpose behind the creation of the book.

## Assess Learning

Observe students when they read and talk about books and notice if there is evidence of new learning based on the goal of this minilesson.

- Do students understand the purpose of an author's/illustrator's note and an afterword?
- Do they use academic language, such as *author's note, illustrator's note,* and *afterword*?

## Minilesson

To help students think about the minilesson principle, use familiar books to help them notice the purpose of author's/illustrator's notes and afterwords. Here is an example.

- Show the cover of *Hands Around the Library* and read the title.

  What did you learn from this book?

  One of the authors of this book wrote a special page at the end of the book that I'd like to share with you.

- Turn to the author's note (A Note from Susan L. Roth) and read the first two paragraphs aloud.

  What do you notice about the author's note?

- Record students' responses on chart paper.

- Show the cover of *Barbed Wire Baseball* and read the title. Turn to page 39 and read the author's note and the illustrator's note.

  Why are there two notes on this page?

  What did you learn from the two notes?

- Record students' responses on the chart.

## Have a Try

Invite the students to talk with a partner about the afterword in *Parrots Over Puerto Rico*.

▶ Show the cover of *Parrots Over Puerto Rico* and read the title. Turn to the afterword.

> At the end of this book is a special section called an afterword. Why do you think it has that name?

▶ Read the first two paragraphs of the afterword aloud.

> Turn and talk to your partner about what you noticed and learned from the afterword.

▶ After students turn and talk, ask a few pairs to share their thinking. Record their responses on the chart.

## Summarize and Apply

Summarize the learning and remind students to read author's and illustrator's notes.

> What did you learn about today?

> An afterword is similar to an author's note. Often, an afterword is written by someone other than the author.

▶ Record the principle at the top of the chart.

> When you read today, notice if your book has an author's note, illustrator's note, or afterword. If so, be sure to read it. Be ready to share what you learned from it when we come back together.

## Share

Following independent reading time, gather students together in the meeting area to discuss their reading.

> Who read an author's note, an illustrator's note, or an afterword today?

> What did you learn from it?

## Extend the Lesson (Optional)

After assessing students' understanding, you might decide to extend the learning.

▶ Encourage students to include an author's note or ask someone to write an afterword when they write their own books.

An author's note or an afterword often provides additional information about the book.

| | |
|---|---|
| Author's Note | • What inspired the author/illustrator to write/illustrate the book |
| | • Why the topic of the book is important |
| Illustrator's Note | • How the illustrator made the illustrations |
| Afterword | • More information about the topic of the book |

Section 2: Literary Analysis

**Reading Minilesson Principle**
## Authors provide resources outside the main text to help you find information or understand more about the story or topic.

### Noticing Book and Print Features

**You Will Need**

- two or three familiar books that contain a glossary, table of contents, and/or pronunciation guide, such as the following:
  - *Mangoes, Mischief, and Tales of Friendship* by Chitra Soundar, from Text Set: Friendship
  - *One Plastic Bag* by Miranda Paul and *Hands Around the Library* by Susan L. Roth and Karen Leggett Abouraya, from Text Set: Innovative Thinking and Creative Problem Solving
- chart paper and markers
- document camera (optional)

**Academic Language / Important Vocabulary**

- table of contents
- glossary
- pronunciation guide

### Continuum Connection

- Notice, use, and understand the purpose of some organizational tools: e.g., title, table of contents, chapter title [p. 61]
- Notice, use, and understand the purpose of some other text resources: e.g., glossary (pp. 61, 65)

## Goal

Notice, use, and understand the purpose of a glossary, table of contents, and pronunciation guide.

## Rationale

When students know how to use a table of contents, they are able to find out what topics or chapters are included in a book and where each is located. When they know how to use a glossary and pronunciation guide, they are better equipped to determine the meaning and pronunciation of unfamiliar words while reading.

## Assess Learning

Observe students when they read and talk about books and notice if there is evidence of new learning based on the goal of this minilesson.

- Are students able to use and explain the purpose of a table of contents, a glossary, and a pronunciation guide?
- Do they use academic language, such as *table of contents*, *glossary*, and *pronunciation guide*?

## Minilesson

To help students think about the minilesson principle, discuss the use of a table of contents, glossary, and pronunciation guide. Here is an example.

- Open to and display the table of contents (if possible, project with a document camera) of *Mangoes, Mischief, and Tales of Friendship*.

  What is on this page of the book?

  What is a table of contents?

  How do you use a table of contents?

- Show the table of contents in a familiar nonfiction book. Ask students how the table of contents differs in fiction and nonfiction books. Summarize students' noticings about tables of contents on chart paper.

- Turn to the Wolof Glossary and Pronunciation Guide near the back of *One Plastic Bag*. Read the heading and the first few entries.

  What kind of information does this page give you?

  This page has a glossary. What does the glossary tell you?

  This page also includes a pronunciation guide. What is a pronunciation guide?

- Record students' noticings about the glossary and pronunciation guide on the chart.

## Have a Try

Invite the students to talk about the glossary and pronunciation guide in *Hands Around the Library*.

▶ Show the cover of *Hands Around the Library* and read the title. Open to the part in the back called A Few Words from the Protest Signs. Read aloud the heading and the first few entries.

> What do you notice about this part of the book? What information does it give you?

▶ Invite a few students to share their thinking.

## Summarize and Apply

Summarize the learning and remind students to use peritext resources.

> Today we looked at the table of contents, glossary, and pronunciation guide in a few books. Why are these resources important?

▶ Write the principle at the top of the chart.

> When you read today, notice if your book has a table of contents, glossary, or pronunciation guide. If so, think about how it helps you. Bring your book to share when we come back together.

| Authors provide resources outside the main text to help you find information or understand more about the story or topic. | |
| --- | --- |
| **Table of Contents**<br><br>Contents<br>Book One    vii<br>Book Two    87 | • Tells what each chapter is called in a fiction book<br>• Tells what topics are in a nonfiction book<br>• Tells what page each chapter or topic begins on |
| **Glossary**<br><br>omo   soap<br>waaw   yes | • Gives the definition of important or difficult words in the book<br>• May contain words from another language |
| **Pronunciation Guide**<br><br>ho-RAY-ah | • Tells how to pronounce, or say aloud, challenging words<br>• May contain words from another language |

## Share

Following independent reading time, gather students together in the meeting area to share examples of peritext resources.

> Who read a book today that has a table of contents, glossary, or pronunciation guide? Tell us about that.

## Extend the Lesson (Optional)

After assessing students' understanding, you might decide to extend the learning.

▶ **Writing About Reading** Have students create a table of contents, glossary, and/or pronunciation guide for a book that does not already have one.

## Reading Minilesson Principle

# The design (book jacket, cover, title page, endpapers) often adds to or enhances the meaning or appeal of the book.

## Noticing Book and Print Features

### You Will Need

- two or three familiar books that have a book jacket, cover, title page, and/or endpapers that add to or enhance the meaning of the book, such as the following:

  - *Six Dots* by Jen Bryant, from Text Set: Genre Study: Biography (Individuals Making a Difference)

  - *Barbed Wire Baseball* by Marissa Moss, from Text Set: Perseverance

  - *Hands Around the Library* by Susan L. Roth and Karen Leggett Abouraya, from Text Set: Innovative Thinking and Creative Problem Solving

- chart paper and markers

### Academic Language / Important Vocabulary

- design
- book jacket
- cover
- title page
- endpapers

### Continuum Connection

- Infer the cultural or symbolic significance of the peritext (for example, design features) (p. 61)

- Appreciate artistry in text design: e.g., book jacket, cover, end pages, title page (peritext) (pp. 61, 65)

- Notice and understand other features of the peritext that have symbolic and cultural significance, add to aesthetic enjoyment, or add meaning (p. 65)

## Goal

Understand and appreciate that the design of the peritext often adds to the meaning of the text and sometimes has cultural or symbolic significance.

## Rationale

The book jacket, cover, title pages, and endpapers are part of the art of the book and add to or enhance its meaning. When you encourage students to notice the design of these features and to think about how they relate to the meaning of the book, they develop an appreciation for the thought and care that went into creating the book.

## Assess Learning

Observe students when they read and talk about books and notice if there is evidence of new learning based on the goal of this minilesson.

- ❯ Can students explain how the design of the book jacket, cover, title pages, and/or endpapers add to or enhance the meaning of a book?

- ❯ Can they infer the cultural or symbolic significance of certain design features in the peritext?

- ❯ Do they use academic language, such as *design, book jacket, cover, title page,* and *endpapers*?

## Minilesson

To help students think about the minilesson principle, use familiar books to make them aware of the design of the peritext. Here is an example.

- ❯ Show the cover of *Six Dots* and read the title.

  What do you find interesting about the cover of this book?

  Why are there dots under all the words? What do the dots mean?

  How do the braille words relate to the rest of the book?

- ❯ Record students' responses on chart paper.

- ❯ Show the cover of *Barbed Wire Baseball* and read the title.

  What did you learn from this book?

- ❯ Turn to the title page.

  Look at the title page. What do you notice about this page?

  What do you notice about how the title page is designed?

  What does the design of the title page have to do with the meaning of the book?

- ❯ Record students' responses on the chart.

## Have a Try

Invite the students to talk with a partner about the endpapers and book jacket of *Hands Around the Library*.

▶ Show the cover of *Hands Around the Library*. Turn to the endpapers and back flap of the book jacket.

> Look at the endpapers and the book jacket of this book. What do you notice about the design? How do they relate to the meaning of the book? Turn and talk to your partner about what you think.

▶ After students turn and talk, invite a few pairs to share their ideas. Record their responses on the chart.

## Summarize and Apply

Summarize the learning and remind students to notice the design of the peritext when they read.

> Today you looked at the cover, the title page, the endpapers, and the book jacket of a few books.

▶ Write the principle at the top of the chart.

> When you read today, take a few minutes to look at the design of parts of your book outside the main text, such as the cover, title page, endpapers, and book jacket. Think about how the design of these pages adds to the meaning of your book. Bring your book to share when we come back together.

## Share

Following independent reading time, gather students together in the meeting area to share what they noticed about the design of the peritext in their book.

> Turn and talk to your partner about how the design of the book jacket, cover, title pages, or endpapers add to or relate to the meaning of your book.

## Extend the Lesson (Optional)

After assessing students' understanding, you might decide to extend the learning.

▶ During interactive read-aloud, point out how authors use different fonts throughout a book. Discuss the purpose and effect of the fonts.

▶ When students create their own books, encourage them to think about how to enhance the meaning of their book through the design of the cover, title page, endpapers, and/or book jacket.

The design (book jacket, cover, title pages, endpapers) often adds to or enhances the meaning or appeal of the book.

| | Cover | • shows the title, author's name, and Illustrator's name written in braille<br>∗ important because the book is about how braille was invented |
|---|---|---|
| | Title page | • words are designed to look like a baseball ticket<br>• a barbed wire fence in the background<br>∗ important because the book is about people who played baseball in internment camps |
| | Endpapers<br><br>Book Jacket | • show Egyptian people holding hands<br>• show traditional Egyptian patterns and writing<br>∗ important because the book is about how people held hands to protect a place that is important to the culture of Egypt |

**Section 2: Literary Analysis**

### Assessment

After you have taught the minilessons in this umbrella, observe students as they talk and write about their reading across instructional contexts: interactive read-aloud, independent reading, guided reading, shared reading, and book club. Use *The Literacy Continuum* (Fountas and Pinnell 2017) to guide the observation of students' reading and writing behaviors.

▶ What evidence do you have of new understandings related to book and print features?

- Do students read and understand the purpose of peritext resources such as the dedication, the acknowledgments, and the author's note?

- Do they notice the design of the book jacket, the cover, the title page, and/or the endpapers? Can they explain how they add to the meaning of the book?

- Do they use peritext resources, such as the table of contents and glossary?

- Do they use academic language related to text resources, such as *dedication, acknowledgments, author's note,* and *table of contents?*

▶ In what other ways, beyond the scope of this umbrella, are students talking about books?

- Are students noticing and using text features, such as headings, sidebars, and indexes?

- Are they noticing the different ways nonfiction books are organized?

Use your observations to determine the next umbrella you will teach. You may also consult Minilessons Across the Year (pp. 59–61) for guidance.

### Link to Writing

After teaching the minilessons in this umbrella, help students link the new learning to their own writing:

▶ Encourage students to create text resources when they write their own books.

### Reader's Notebook

When this umbrella is complete, provide a copy of the minilesson principles (see resources.fountasandpinnell.com) for students to glue in the reader's notebook (in the Minilessons section if using *Reader's Notebook: Intermediate* [Fountas and Pinnell 2011]), so they can refer to the information as needed.

**Genre Study: Memoir**

## Minilessons in This Umbrella

| | |
|---|---|
| **RML1** | Memoirs are alike in many ways. |
| **RML2** | The definition of memoir is what is always true about it. |
| **RML3** | Writers tell about a memory of a time, place, person, or event in their lives and why it was important to them. |
| **RML4** | Most memoirs are written in the first person. |
| **RML5** | A memoir often has a turning point, or a point when an important decision is made. |
| **RML6** | The writer usually expresses new insight or a larger message. |

## Before Teaching Umbrella 13 Minilessons

When students study a genre, they learn what to expect when reading a text, expand important comprehension skills, examine the distinguishing characteristics of a genre, and develop the tools they need to navigate a variety of types of written documents. There are six broad steps in the process of a genre study, which are described on pages 39–41.

Prior to beginning a genre study of memoir, select a variety of clear examples of memoir for students to read and enjoy. Before guiding students to look for genre characteristics, be sure that they first become immersed in the books, thinking and talking about the meaning of each text and enjoying the stories. These shared literary experiences will provide a backdrop of examples. Choose texts that focus on an important time, place, person, or event and have a reflective element in which the writer learns something about himself and the reader learns a larger message.

Use the following books from the *Fountas & Pinnell Classroom™ Interactive Read-Aloud Collection* text sets or use memoirs that you have on hand.

**Genre Study: Memoir**

*Play Ball!* by Jorge Posada

*The Upside Down Boy* by Juan Felipe Herrera

*The Scraps Book: Notes from a Colorful Life* by Lois Ehlert

As you read aloud and enjoy memoirs together, help students

- notice similarities between them,

- notice what is always true and often true,

- identify what the writers learned about themselves,

- notice if the story is told in first person,

- identify the turning point and its effect on the writer, and

- recognize the larger message.

**Reading Minilesson Principle**
# Memoirs are alike in many ways.

## You Will Need

- basket of familiar memoirs
- chart paper with *Noticings* written near the top and two columns headed *Always* and *Often*
- markers

## Academic Language / Important Vocabulary

- characteristics
- memoir
- genre
- point of view

### Continuum Connection

- Connect texts by a range of categories: e.g., content, message, genre, author/illustrator special form, text structure, or organization [p. 62]
- Notice and understand the characteristics of some specific nonfiction genres: e.g., expository, narrative, procedural and persuasive texts, biography, autobiography, memoir, hybrid text [p. 62]

## Goal

Notice and understand the characteristics of memoir as a genre.

## Rationale

When students study memoir, they develop a deeper understanding of the genre and individual stories.

## Assess Learning

Observe students when they read and compare memoirs. Notice if there is evidence of new learning based on the goal of this minilesson.

- Are students able to discuss the characteristics found in all memoirs?
- Can they describe characteristics that are found in some, but not all, memoirs?
- Do they understand the academic language *characteristics, memoir, genre,* and *point of view*?

# Minilesson

Once students have immersed themselves in reading memoirs, you can have them look across the books to find commonalities. Here is an example.

- Display several examples of memoirs that students have read or heard read aloud.

    You know all of these books. What kind, or genre, are they?

    They are called memoir. Think about what these memoirs have in common. What can you say about all of the memoirs? Some characteristics are *always* true about memoirs. Other characteristics are *often* true. Turn to a partner and talk about what is true about all memoirs.

    Now talk about what is often true.

- After time for discussion, ask students to share with the whole group what is always or often true about memoirs. If necessary, prompt them using the following questions:

    - *Why might a writer write a memoir?*
    - *What do you notice about how a memoir is written? What word do you see a lot?*
    - *What does the writer write about?*

- Record noticings in the *Always* and *Often* columns on the premade chart.

## Have a Try

Invite the students to talk with a partner about a book they are reading.

> Are you currently reading a memoir? How do you know it is a memoir? Use the chart to help you decide.

▶ After time to turn and talk, ask a few students to share.

## Summarize and Apply

Summarize the learning and remind students of the characteristics of memoir.

> Today you noticed how memoirs are alike.

▶ Add the title *Memoir* to the chart and review the noticings.

> When you read today, think about your current book. Is it a memoir? If so, bring it with you to share.

## Share

Following independent reading time, gather students in the meeting area as a whole group.

> Did anyone read a memoir today? How could you tell?

> How many descriptions from the chart did you find in the memoir?

> Is there anything you want to add to the chart?

## Extend the Lesson (Optional)

After assessing students' understanding, you might decide to extend the learning.

▶ Continue to add noticings to the chart as students read and experience additional memoirs.

▶ Introduce your students the Genre Thinkmark for memoir. A Genre Thinkmark is a tool that guides readers to note certain elements of a genre as they read. Students can quickly note the page numbers of parts of the book where they see evidence of the characteristics of memoir and share it with others. To download a Genre Thinkmark, visit resources.fountaspinnell.com.

▶ **Writing About Reading** Have students write brief book recommendations for memoirs they read and post them in or near the classroom library so other students can find books to enjoy reading.

### Memoir

**Noticings:**

| Always | Often |
|---|---|
| • Tells the story (or a memory) of an important time, place, person, or event in the writer's life | • Uses quotes |
| | • Uses a lot of description |
| • Tells why that was important to the writer | • Has photographs |
| | • Includes the setting or cultural influences from the author's life |
| • Gives factual information about the writer's own life | • Has a turning point or a point when an important decision is made |
| | • Has a larger message |
| | • Written in the first person. |

**Reading Minilesson Principle**
# The definition of memoir is what is always true about it.

## Studying Memoir

### You Will Need

- noticings chart from RML1
- chart paper and markers
- a memoir with which students are familiar, such as *The Upside Down Boy* by Juan Felipe Herrera, from Text Set: Genre Study: Memoir
- a basket of memoirs

### Academic Language / Important Vocabulary

- memoir
- definition

### Continuum Connection

- Understand that a memoir is an account of a memory or set of memories written by the person who experienced it (p. 62)

## Goal

Construct a working definition of memoir.

## Rationale

When students engage in co-constructing a definition for memoir, they are better able to articulate the characteristics of memoir and understand what to expect of the genre. They learn to revise their understandings as they gain additional experience with stories written about people's lives.

## Assess Learning

Observe students when they read and discuss memoir. Notice if there is evidence of new learning based on the goal of this minilesson.

- ▶ Can students clearly and concisely articulate what memoir is and is not?
- ▶ Do they know which books are memoirs and which are not, and why?
- ▶ Are they using the terms *memoir* and *definition*?

## Minilesson

To help students think about the definition of memoir, engage students in noticing its characteristics. Here is an example.

- ▶ Show the memoir noticings chart from RML1 and review the characteristics.

  What did you notice about memoir?

  The definition of memoir tells what is always true about it.

- ▶ On chart paper, write the words *Memoir is*, leaving space for constructing a working definition.

  To finish this sentence with a definition that tells what memoir is, what would you write? Turn and talk about that, thinking about the noticings chart.

- ▶ After time for discussion, ask students to share ideas. Use the ideas to construct a working definition with the class and write it on the chart paper. Ask a student to read the definition.

## Have a Try

Invite the students to talk with a partner about how *The Upside Down Boy* fits the definition of memoir.

▶ Review the definition.

> With a partner, talk about whether *The Upside Down Boy* fits the definition of memoir. What makes you think that?

▶ After students turn and talk, invite a few to share their thinking.

## Summarize and Apply

Summarize the learning and remind students to think about the definition of memoir.

▶ Ask a student to reread the definition.

> Is there anything else you would like to add?

> When you read today, you might like to choose a memoir from the basket and think about how the book fits the definition. Bring the book when we meet so you can share.

## Share

Following independent reading tme, gather the students in the meeting area to talk about memoir.

> Did anyone read a memoir? How does it fit our definition?

## Extend the Lesson (Optional)

After assessing students' understanding, you might decide to extend the learning.

▶ Keep the definition posted so that it can be revised as students become aware of further characteristics of memoir (see p. 292).

▶ If students write their own memoirs, remind them to think about the definition of memoir to make sure their writing includes the characteristics of the genre.

▶ **Writing About Reading** Have students write about how the books they are reading independently fit or do not fit the definition of memoir.

## Memoir

Memoir is a true story that a writer tells about an important time in his or her life.

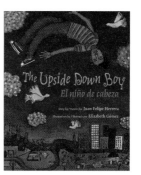

**Reading Minilesson Principle**
## Writers tell about a memory of a time, place, person, or event in their lives and why it was important to them.

### You Will Need

- familiar memoirs, such as the following from Text Set: Genre Study: Memoir:
  - *Play Ball!* by Jorge Posada
  - *The Scraps Book* by Lois Ehlert
  - *The Upside Down Boy* by Juan Felipe Herrera
- chart paper and makers
- a basket of memoirs

### Academic Language / Important Vocabulary

- perspective

### Continuum Connection

- Understand that a memoir is an account of a memory or set of memories written by the person who experienced it (p. 62)
- Understand memoir or personal narrative as a brief, often intense, memory of or reflection on a person, time, or event (p. 275)

## Goal

Understand that memoir writers tell about a memory of a time, place, person, or event in their lives and why it is important to them.

## Rationale

When students think about the personal topics that authors choose to write about in a memoir, they consider the choices an author makes as well as discern why the topic is important to the author.

## Assess Learning

Observe students when they read and discuss memoir. Notice if there is evidence of new learning based on the goal of this minilesson.

- ▶ Can students understand why the time, event, place, or person is important to the writer?
- ▶ Do they discuss how the writer makes the story relatable to the reader?
- ▶ Do they understand the academic term *perspective* when talking about memoir?

## Minilesson

To help students think about the minilesson principle, help them consider how the event, time, place, or person in a memoir is important to the writer. Here is an example.

- ▶ Show the cover of *Play Ball!* and invite students to turn and discuss the book.

  What part of his life does Jorge Posada focus on in this book?

  Why was this an important time for him? What makes you think that?

  How does this help you know Jorge Posada better?

- ▶ Invite a few students to respond. Add responses to a chart.
- ▶ Repeat this process for *The Scraps Book*.

## Have a Try

Invite the students to repeat the lesson with a partner using *The Upside Down Boy*.

▶ After time for discussion, ask a few students to share. Add a row to the chart.

## Summarize and Apply

Summarize the learning and remind students to think about why the focus of a memoir is important to its author.

> What did you learn about a memoir today?

▶ Review the chart and write the principle at the top.

> When you read today, you might want to choose a memoir from this basket. If you read a memoir, think about why the writer wrote about a particular time, place, person, or event. How does that help you to understand the writer better? Bring the book when we meet so you can share.

## Share

Following independent reading time, gather students in pairs to talk about their reading.

> Turn and talk with your partner about the memoir you read today. What part of the writer's life was it about?

> Why was that important to the writer? How do you know that?

## Extend the Lesson (Optional)

After assessing students' understanding, you might decide to extend the learning.

▶ When you read a memoir during interactive read-aloud, take time for students to share their thinking about why the writer decided to focus on a particular time, place, person, or event.

▶ As students write their own memoirs, encourage them to think about what is important to them and how they can make that clear to the reader.

▶ **Writing About Reading** Encourage students to write about why the writer of a memoir wrote about a particular time, place, person, or event. Students can do this in a weekly letter or use a grid to build a chart like the one you created together (see resources.fountasandpinnell.com). Students can glue the grid into a reader's notebook and enter new information whenever they read a memoir.

---

**Writers tell about a memory of a time, place, person, or event in their lives and why it was important to them.**

| Title | Memory | Why the Memory Is Important to the Writer |
|---|---|---|
| PLAY BALL! | When he was a child and learned to be a switch hitter | • The moment he decided he was going to work hard and put in extra effort to play professional baseball |
| SCRAPS | Her journey as an artist and a children's book author | • She followed her dream of becoming an artist and an author.<br>• She learned to look for art in unexpected places. |
| The Upside Down Boy | His move to a new house and community | • He adjusted and settled into his new community.<br>• He developed interests and talents in writing, music, and poetry at his new school. |

# RML4

**LA.U13.RML4**

Reading Minilesson Principle
## Most memoirs are written in the first person.

## Studying Memoir

### You Will Need

- familiar memoirs, such as *The Upside Down Boy* by Juan Felipe Herrera and *The Scraps Book* by Lois Ehlert, from Text Set: Genre Study: Memoir
- chart paper and markers

### Academic Language / Important Vocabulary

- narrator
- point of view
- first person

### Continuum Connection

- Understand that a memoir is an account of a memory or set of memories written by the person who experienced it (p. 62)

### Goal

Understand that a memoir often is written from the author's point of view or perspective.

### Rationale

When students think about who is telling a story, they can anticipate the kind of information the writer can reveal, such as internal thoughts, feelings, and motivations told from the author's perspective. They also begin to use context clues to infer the writer's point of view.

### Assess Learning

Observe students when they discuss memoir. Notice if there is evidence of new learning based on the goal of this minilesson.

- Can students identify from whose point of view a story is being told?
- Can they recognize when a book is written in first-person point of view?
- Can they use the academic language *narrator, point of view,* and *first person*?

## Minilesson

To help students understand how first-person point of view provides important information to the reader, engage them in noticing the voice in familiar texts. Here is an example.

- Hold up *The Upside Down Boy* and read a page clearly written in the first person, such as page 18.

  Turn and talk to a partner. Who is telling the story? Who is the narrator?

  How do you know that?

- After they turn and talk, ask a few students to share. Chart responses. If necessary, revise the responses throughout the lesson to make them more generative.

  Turn and talk to your partner again. What are some things you learn about Juan *because* it is told from Juan's point of view?

- After they turn and talk, ask a few students to share. Chart responses.

  Memoirs are usually told from the writer's point of view. The writer is telling the story. This is called first-person point of view.

  When a story is told from the writer's point of view, how do you learn what other people in the story are thinking and feeling?

- Record the responses.

## Have a Try

Invite the students to repeat the lesson in small groups using *The Scraps Book*.

▶ Read a page clearly written in the first person, such as the page beginning "I created lots of art."

## Summarize and Apply

Summarize the learning and remind students to think about first-person point of view.

> What did you learn today?

▶ Review the chart and write the minilesson principle at the top.

> You might want to read a memoir today. If you do, think about who is telling the story. Is it first-person point of view? What do you learn about the writer?

## Share

Following independent reading time, gather students together in the meeting area to talk in small groups.

> Talk to your group about the book you read today. Who is telling the story? How do you know? What did you learn about the writer?

## Extend the Lesson (Optional)

After assessing students' understanding, you might decide to extend the learning.

▶ Some fiction books are written in the first person. If you read such a book during interactive read-aloud, help students notice that all of the story's action is seen through the narrator's eyes. Help them to notice when a fiction story is written in the style of a memoir.

▶ Discuss with students how a memoir can help them learn about and develop empathy for someone who may be different from them.

▶ **Writing About Reading** Encourage students to write in a reader's notebook about how first-person point of view impacts a story they read.

Most memoirs are written in the first person.

| | |
|---|---|
| Writer uses words such as | The narrator tells the story from his/her point of view. |
| • I | |
| • me | |
| • my | |
| • we | |
| • us | |
| to tell the story | |
| Reader has to look for clues to understand other people's thoughts, feelings, and actions. | Reader knows what the narrator is thinking and feeling. |

**Reading Minilesson Principle**

# A memoir often has a turning point, or a point when an important decision is made.

## Studying Memoir

### You Will Need

- familiar memoirs that teach a larger message, such as the following from Text Set: Genre Study: Memoir:
  - *Play Ball!* by Jorge Posada
  - *The Upside Down Boy* by Juan Felipe Herrera
- chart paper and markers
- basket of memoirs
- sticky notes

### Academic Language / Important Vocabulary

- turning point

### Continuum Connection

- Notice and understand the characteristics of some specific nonfiction genres: e.g., expository, narrative, procedural and persuasive texts, biography, autobiography, memoir, hybrid text (p. 62)
- Understand that a narrative nonfiction text includes selected important events and turning points (p. 276)

## Goal

Understand that memoir texts often have a turning point, or a point when an important decision is made.

## Rationale

When students think about the turning point in a memoir, the moment when a decision is made, they can better understand why the story is important to and how it shaped the writer's life.

## Assess Learning

Observe students when they read and discuss memoir. Notice if there is evidence of new learning based on the goal of this minilesson.

- ⦿ Do students recognize the turning point in a memoir?
- ⦿ Can they discuss the turning point's impact on the writer?
- ⦿ Do they understand the academic term *turning point* when talking about memoir?

## Minilesson

To help students think about the minilesson principle, engage them in a discussion about the significance of a turning point in a memoir. Here is an example.

- ⦿ Hold up *Play Ball!*

    Turn and talk to the person next to you. When in the story did Jorge Posada decide he was going to work extra hard to be the best baseball player he could be—perhaps even a professional player?

    This was a big moment in Jorge's life because it signaled change. This is called the turning point.

- ⦿ Record responses on chart paper.

    How did this decision change Jorge Posada's life?

- ⦿ Record responses.

## Have a Try

Invite the students to talk with a partner about the turning point in a memoir.

▶ Show the cover of *The Upside Down Boy*.

Turn and talk to your partner. What is the turning point in this memoir? How did that moment influence the writer's life?

▶ After students turn and talk, ask a few pairs to share their thinking.

## Summarize and Apply

Summarize the learning and remind students to notice the turning point as they read memoir.

What did you learn about memoirs today?

▶ Review the chart and write the principle at the top.

Choose a memoir from the basket to read today if you are not already reading one. Think about the turning point in the book. It might be a point at which the writer learned or understood something that could change his life. How did the turning point affect the writer? Write it on a sticky note and bring it with you to share.

A memoir often has a turning point, or a point when an important decision is made.

| Book | Turning Point | Change to Writer's Life |
|------|---------------|-------------------------|
| PLAY BALL! | Jorge had a conversation with friends, followed by a trip to Yankee Stadium. | • Jorge was inspired to put in the extra effort to be a switch hitter.<br>• He began dreaming of playing professional baseball. |
| The Upside Down Boy | Juanito was asked to sing in class. | • Juanito starts to feel confident and finds his place in his new school.<br>• He discovers that he enjoys music and is passionate about it. |

## Share

Following independent reading time, gather students to talk about their reading in small groups.

Turn and talk to your partners about the turning point in the memoir you read today. How did that moment change the writer?

## Extend the Lesson (Optional)

After assessing students' understanding, you might decide to extend the learning.

▶ Continue to read memoirs and ask students to notice whether there is a turning point or an important decision. Discuss the writer's decision to include or omit a turning point.

▶ Have students map out the events in a memoir using a timeline. They can make their own or fill in a graphic organizer (visit resources.fountasandpinnell.com to download a timeline). Ask students to indicate the turning point on the timeline.

▶ **Writing About Reading** As students demonstrate they can talk about the turning point in a memoir, suggest they begin to include examples in their reading letters.

Section 2: Literary Analysis

# The writer usually expresses new insight or a larger message.

## Studying Memoir

### You Will Need

- familiar memoirs that teach a larger message, such as the following from Text Set: Genre Study: Memoir:
  - *The Scraps Book* by Lois Ehlert
  - *The Upside Down Boy* by Juan Felipe Herrera
  - *Play Ball!* by Jorge Posada
- chart paper and markers

### Academic Language / Important Vocabulary

- reflection
- message
- insight

### Continuum Connection

- Infer the larger ideas and messages in a nonfiction text (p. 63)

### Goal

Understand that memoir writers usually have a larger message that they are communicating through their story.

### Rationale

When students notice a writer's larger message in a memoir, they gain a deeper understanding of the writer, the significance of the story, and life in general.

### Assess Learning

Observe students when they read and discuss memoir. Notice if there is evidence of new learning based on the goal of this minilesson.

- Can students recognize a writer's personal insight about an event, time, or person they have written about?
- Do they discuss the larger message or reflection of a memoir in whole- or small-group discussion?
- Do they use the terms *reflection, message,* or *insight* in conversation or in writing?

## Minilesson

Engage students in a discussion of the larger meaning of familiar memoirs to help them think about the minilesson principle. Here is an example.

> When a writer chooses to write a memoir, she often does so because she has reflected on a moment in her life and realizes that she learned something about herself in that moment that she wants to share. This is called insight.

- Hold up *The Scraps Book*.

  Turn and talk to the person next to you. What did Lois Ehlert learn about herself in this book?

- Record responses on a chart.

  What can you learn from Lois Ehlert? Why is she telling her story? What do you think she wants you to know?

- Chart responses.
- Repeat this process with *The Upside Down Boy*.

## Have a Try

Invite the students to talk with a partner about a familiar memoir.

▶ Show the cover of *Play Ball!*

> Turn and talk to your partner. What did Jorge Posada learn about himself in this memoir? What is a larger message he wants to share?

▶ After students turn and talk, ask a few pairs to share their thinking.

## Summarize and Apply

Summarize the learning and remind students to think about the larger message of a memoir.

> Today you noticed how writers express new insights or a larger message in a memoir.

▶ Review the chart and write the principle at the top.

> If you read a memoir today, think about what the writer learned about himself and how that helps you think about the larger message.

## Share

Following independent reading time, gather students to talk about their reading in small groups.

> If you read a memoir today, talk to your partner about what you think the writer learned about herself and how that helps you think about the larger message.

▶ Ask a few students to share.

## Extend the Lesson (Optional)

After assessing students' understanding, you might decide to extend the learning.

▶ Take time during interactive read aloud to talk about the larger message of the story.

▶ **Writing About Reading** As students demonstrate they can talk about the larger message in a memoir, you may suggest they fill in a graphic organizer, similar to the chart in this lesson, with information from the memoirs they have read in their genre study (visit resources.fountasandpinnell.com to download a graphic organizer).

▶ **Writing About Reading** As students talk and write about memoirs they are reading, encourage them to write about larger messages and what the writer learned.

### The writer usually expresses new insight or a larger message.

| Title | What Writer Has Learned | Larger Message of the Memoir |
|---|---|---|
| *The Scraps Book* | • Dreams can take years to come true.<br>• If she continued working on her art, she would one day achieve her dream. | • Art is all around, if you take the time to look.<br>• Inspiration is all around us. |
| *The Upside Down Boy / El niño de cabeza* | • His voice is important and beautiful.<br>• He could share his gift with his community, and later the world. | • Don't be afraid to share your gifts with the world. |
| *Play Ball!* | • Being a switch hitter is hard, but it opens up opportunities. | • Hard work and determination lead to success. |

## Assessment

After you have taught the minilessons in this umbrella, observe students as they talk and write about their reading across instructional contexts: interactive read-aloud, independent reading, guided reading, shared reading, and book club. Use *The Literacy Continuum* (Fountas and Pinnell 2017) to guide the observation of students' reading and writing behaviors across instructional contexts.

▶ What evidence do you have of new understandings related to the study of memoir?

- Do students notice how memoirs are alike?
- Can they identify why the event, time, place, or person is important to the writer?
- Do they notice from what point of view the story is told?
- Can they understand and articulate the larger message?
- Do they notice a turning point in the story, and how it affects the writer?
- Do they use language such as *genre, memoir, point of view, perspective, reflection, message, turning point,* and *insight*?

▶ In what other ways, beyond the scope of this umbrella, are students talking about nonfiction texts?

- Have students expressed an interest in reading biographies or historical fiction?

Use your observations to determine the next umbrella you will teach. You may also consult Minilessons Across the Year (pp. 59–61) for guidance.

## Read and Revise

After completing the steps in the genre study process, help students read and revise their definition of the genre based on their new understandings.

▶ **Before:** Memoir is a true story that a writer tells about an important time in his or her life.

▶ **After:** Memoir is a true story that a writer tells about an important moment, series of events, person, or place in his or her life and has an important message for the reader.

## Reader's Notebook

When this umbrella is complete, provide a copy of the minilesson principles (see resources.fountasandpinnell.com) for students to glue in the reader's notebook (in the Minilessons section if using *Reader's Notebook: Intermediate* [Fountas and Pinnell 2011]), so they can refer to the information as needed.

## Minilessons in This Umbrella

| RML1 | Biographies are alike in many ways. |
|---|---|
| RML2 | The definition of biography is what is always true about it. |
| RML3 | Biographers choose their subjects for a variety of reasons. |
| RML4 | Biographers decide when to start and stop telling the story of the subject's life. |
| RML5 | Biographers include details about the society and culture of the time in which the subject lived. |
| RML6 | Biographers usually include the people who influenced the subject's life. |
| RML7 | Biographers choose to include facts that reveal something important about the subject's personality traits and motivations. |
| RML8 | Sometimes biographers include some imagined scenes but base them on facts. |
| RML9 | Sometimes biographers include quotes by the subject. |
| RML10 | Think about how the subject's accomplishments have influenced life today. |

## Before Teaching Umbrella 14 Minilessons

During a genre study (pp. 39–41), students learn what to expect when reading the genre, expand comprehension skills, notice distinguishing characteristics, and develop tools to navigate a variety of texts. Before beginning this genre study, students must read many biographies.

Select books that are clear examples of biography, such as the following books from the *Fountas & Pinnell Classroom™ Interactive Read-Aloud Collection.*

**Biography: Artists**

*Action Jackson* by Jan Greenberg and Sandra Jordan

*The East-West House* by Christy Hale

*Radiant Child: The Story of Young Artist Jean-Michel Basquiat* by Javaka Steptoe

*Mary Cassatt: Extraordinary Impressionist Painter* by Barbara Herkert

*Me, Frida* by Amy Novesky

**Genre Study: Biography (Individuals Making a Difference)**

*Six Dots: A Story of Young Louis Braille* by Jen Bryant

*The Secret Kingdom* by Barb Rosenstock

*Farmer Will Allen and the Growing Table* by Jacqueline Briggs Martin

*Fly High! The Story of Bessie Coleman* by Louise Borden and Mary Kay Kroeger

As you read aloud and enjoy these texts together, help students

• notice things that are *always* and *often* true about biographies, and

• understand the choices a biographer makes when writing a biography.

**Biography: Artists**

*Radiant Child* by Javaka Steptoe

**Genre Study: Biography**

*Farmer Will Allen and the Growing Table* by Jacqueline Briggs Martin

**Section 2: Literary Analysis**

### Studying Biography

**You Will Need**

- a variety of familiar biographies
- chart paper and markers
- basket of biographies
- sticky notes

**Academic Language / Important Vocabulary**

- biography
- genre
- characteristics

**Continuum Connection**

- Notice and understand the characteristics of some specific nonfiction genres: e.g., expository, narrative, procedural and persuasive texts, biography, autobiography, memoir, hybrid text (p. 62)

### Goal

Notice and understand the characteristics of biography as a genre.

### Rationale

When you teach students the characteristics of biography, they will know what to expect when reading a book written by one person about another person's life.

### Assess Learning

Observe students when they talk about biographies and notice if there is evidence of new learning based on the goal of this minilesson.

- Are students able to discuss the ways biographies are alike?
- Can they articulate the characteristics of biography?
- Do they understand that characteristics either always or often occur across various biographies?
- Do they use the terms *biography, genre,* and *characteristics*?

## Minilesson

To help students think about the minilesson principle, engage them in noticing common characteristics of biography. Here is an example.

- Show the covers of multiple biographies that students are familiar with.

  Think about these biographies. In what ways are they alike?

- As students share ideas, record their responses. For each suggestion, prompt the students to think about whether the ways they are alike occur always or often. Create separate places on the chart for each category.

- Select a few of the biographies to discuss in greater detail by revisiting a few pages of text and illustrations.

  What other things do you notice?

  Where should we add that information to the chart?

- Continue recording responses. The following prompts may be used as needed:

  - *What do you notice about the person's life?*
  - *What do you notice about the types of things the author chooses to write about?*
  - *Why do you think the author chose this person to write about?*

## Have a Try

Invite the students to talk in groups about the characteristics of biography.

▶ Provide each group with a biography.

Think about what is written on the chart as you look through this book with your group. See how many things from the chart can be found in the book. Look for anything new to add to the chart.

▶ After time for discussion, ask if students found anything new that can be added to the chart.

## Summarize and Apply

Summarize the learning and remind students to think about what *always* or *often* occurs in biographies.

▶ Write the title *Biography* and revisit the chart.

Today choose a biography from the basket unless you are already reading one. As you read, look back at the chart to see which things you can find in the biography you are reading. If you notice something you want to remember, add a sticky note to the page. Bring the book when we meet so you can share.

## Share

Following independent reading time, gather students in the meeting area.

What did you notice about the biography you read today?

## Extend the Lesson (Optional)

After assessing students' understanding, you might decide to extend the learning.

▶ Have students use a reader's notebook to make a list of the biographies they read.

▶ **Writing About Reading** Introduce students to the Genre Thinkmark for biography (to download this resource, see resources.fountasandpinnell.com). A Genre Thinkmark is a tool that guides students to note certain elements of a genre in their reading. On it, they can quickly note page numbers on which they see evidence of the characteristics of biographies so that they can share information with their classmates.

---

# Biography

## Noticings:

| Always: | Often: |
|---|---|
| • The author tells the story of another person's life or a part of it. | • The author tells about the person's life in the order it happened. |
| • The author chooses facts to include about the person's life. | • The author includes some imagined scenes, but they are based on facts. |
| • The author tells about the important things a person did or why the person is interesting. | • The author includes quotes by the person. |
| • The author includes the setting and people who influenced the person's life. | • The author includes additional information at the end of the book (e.g., timelines). |
| | • The author includes photographs and illustrations. |
| | • Biographies are told like a story. |

**Reading Minilesson Principle**
## The definition of biography is what is always true about it.

### Studying Biography

#### You Will Need

- several familiar biographies, such as the following:
  - *The East-West House* by Christy Hale, from Text Set: Biography: Artists
  - *Fly High!* by Louise Borden and Mary Kay Kroeger, from Text Set: Genre Study: Biography [Individuals Making a Difference]
- chart paper and markers
- basket of biographies
- sticky notes

#### Academic Language / Important Vocabulary

- biography
- definition
- subject

#### Continuum Connection

- Understand that a biography is the story of a person's life written by someone else (p. 62)

### Goal

Create a working definition for biography.

### Rationale

When you teach students to construct a working definition of biography, they learn what to expect from the genre. They will be able to revise and expand their understandings as they read more biographies.

### Assess Learning

Observe students when they discuss biographies and notice if there is evidence of new learning based on the goal of this minilesson.

- ❱ Do students cooperate to create a working definition of biography?
- ❱ Do they understand that a definition of biography tells what is true of all biographies?
- ❱ Do they use the terms *biography, definition,* and *subject*?

## Minilesson

To help students think about the minilesson principle, engage them in creating a working definition of the biography genre. Here is an example.

- ❱ Show the biography noticings chart and discuss the characteristics of a biography.

  Think about biographies you have read. A biography is about a person, who is called the subject. What else do you know about biography?

  The definition of biography tells what is always true about books in this genre.

- ❱ On chart paper, write the words *A biography is*, leaving space for constructing a working definition.

  How could this sentence be finished in a way that describes what all biographies are like? Think about the noticings chart. Turn and talk about that.

- ❱ After time for discussion, ask students to share. Use the ideas to create a working definition and add it to the chart. Ask a volunteer to read the definition.

- ❱ Show the cover and a few pages of *The East-West House*.

  Think about *The East-West House*. Does it fit the definition of biography?

- ❱ As students share, ask for text examples to show that it fits the definition.

## Have a Try

Invite the students to talk with a partner about the definition of biography.

> ▶ Show the cover of *Fly High!* and revisit a few pages.
>
>   Turn and talk about whether *Fly High!* fits the definition of biography.
>
> ▶ Ask a few volunteers to share their thinking. Have them point out examples from the book to show that it fits the definition.

## Summarize and Apply

Summarize the learning and remind students to think about what is always true about biographies.

>   Remember that the definition of biography tells what is always true about it.
>
> ▶ Add the principle to the top of chart.
>
>   When you read today, choose a biography if you are not already reading one. Think about whether it fits the definition and mark pages in the book that show what makes it a biography. Bring the book when we meet so you can share.

## Share

Following independent reading time, gather students in the meeting area.

>   Who read a biography today? Share the pages you marked to show that the book fits the definition.

## Extend the Lesson (Optional)

After assessing students' understanding, you might decide to extend the learning.

> ▶ Have students create a collection of biographies to display in the classroom library. They can make notecards that describe how each book fits the definition.

---

> The definition of biography is what is always true about it.
>
> A biography is the story of a person's life written by someone else.

**Reading Minilesson Principle**
# Biographers choose their subjects for a variety of reasons.

## Studying Biography

### You Will Need

- several familiar biographies, such as the following:
  - *Six Dots* by Jen Bryant and *Fly High* by Louise Borden and Mary Kay Kroeger, from Text Set: Genre Study: Biography (Individuals Making a Difference)
  - *Me, Frida* by Amy Novesky, from Text Set: Biography: Artists
  - *The Secret Kingdom* by Barb Rosenstock, from Text Set: Genre Study: Biography (Individuals Making a Difference)
- chart paper and markers
- basket of biographies
- sticky notes

### Academic Language / Important Vocabulary

- biography
- biographer
- subject
- accomplished
- obstacles
- message

### Continuum Connection

- Infer the importance of a subject's accomplishments (biography) (p. 62)
- Understand that a biography is the story of a person's life written by someone else (p. 62)
- Infer a writer's purpose in a nonfiction text (p. 63)

## Goal

Understand that biographers choose their subjects for a variety of reasons.

## Rationale

When students understand that an author chooses the subject of a biography, they understand that the life of the subject is an important consideration in deciding whom to write about, and they begin to think about the biographer's craft.

## Assess Learning

Observe students when they talk about biographies and notice if there is evidence of new learning based on the goal of this minilesson.

- Do students understand that a biographer chooses the subject to write about?
- Are they discussing the reasons biographers choose a particular subject to write about?
- Do they use the terms *biography, biographer, subject, accomplished, obstacles,* and *message*?

## Minilesson

To help students think about the minilesson principle, engage them in a discussion about why a biographer chooses a subject. Here is an example.

- Revisit pages 27–28 of *Six Dots*.

  Think about the subject of this biography, Louis Braille. What can you say about Louis Braille?

  Why do you think the biographer decided to write about Louis Braille?

- On chart paper, create one column for title and subject. Create another column and make a generalization based on the student's response, listing one reason the biographer might have decided to write about the subject.

- The chart created in your class may look different from the sample chart because it will be based on your students' noticings. The important thing is that students are thinking about why a biographer chooses a subject.

  Now think about the biography of Bessie Coleman, *Fly High*.

- Show the cover and read the first paragraph of the author's note.

  Think about what Bessie Coleman did and why the biographers might have chosen to write about her.

- Add responses to the chart.

- Repeat the activity with *Me, Frida*.

## Have a Try

Invite the students to talk with a partner about why a biographer chooses a particular subject.

▶ Show the cover of *The Secret Kingdom*.

> Think about Nek Chand and the beautiful rock garden he created. Why was his life important enough for the biographer to write about?

▶ After time for discussion, ask a few volunteers to share. Summarize their thinking on the chart.

## Summarize and Apply

Summarize the learning and remind students to think about the reasons why biographers choose a subject.

> What does the chart say about why biographers choose their subjects?

▶ Add the principle to the chart.

> If you are not already reading a biography, choose one from the basket. As you read, think about the subject's life and why the biographer decided to write about that person. Mark any pages with sticky notes that give a clue. Bring the book when we meet so you can share.

## Share

Following independent reading time, gather students in small groups. Make sure at least one person in each group read a biography today.

> If you read a biography today, share with your group the reasons why you think the biographer chose that subject to write about.

## Extend the Lesson (Optional)

After assessing students' understanding, you might decide to extend the learning.

▶ **Writing About Reading** Encourage students to use a reader's notebook to make a list of the reasons they might choose the subject of a biography. They can include ideas from the chart and add new ideas as they read other biographies and think about why the authors wrote them.

| Biographers choose their subjects for a variety of reasons. | |
| --- | --- |
| Title and Subject | The author might have chosen this subject because . . . |
| SIX DOTS Louis Braille | . . . he accomplished something important that really helped blind people. |
| Fly High! Bessie Coleman | . . . she overcame obstacles and fulfilled her dream. |
| Frida Kahlo | . . . she is interesting to read about and made interesting art. |
| The Secret Kingdom Nek Chand | . . . his life sends a message. |

# Biographers decide when to start and stop telling the story of the subject's life.

## Studying Biography

### You Will Need

- several familiar biographies, such as these from Text Set: Biography: Artists:
  - *Mary Cassatt* by Barbara Herkert
  - *Action Jackson* by Jan Greenberg and Sandra Jordan
  - *The East-West House* by Christy Hale
- chart paper and markers
- basket of biographies

### Academic Language / Important Vocabulary

- biography
- biographer
- subject
- decisions

### Continuum Connection

- Understand that a biography is the story of a person's life written by someone else (p. 62)

## Goal

Analyze the craft decisions the biographer makes in writing a biography.

## Rationale

When you teach students to think critically about the way a biographer begins and ends a biography, they think about the decisions made by a biographer and deepen their thinking about an author's craft.

## Assess Learning

Observe students when they talk about a biographer's decisions and notice if there is evidence of new learning based on the goal of this minilesson.

- ▶ Can students identify the different times in a subject's life with which a biography can begin and end?
- ▶ Are they aware that a biographer makes choices when writing a biography?
- ▶ Do they understand the terms *biography, biographer, subject,* and *decisions*?

## Minilesson

To help students think about the minilesson principle, engage them in noticing the decisions an author makes when writing a biography. Here is an example.

- ▶ Display a familiar biography, such as *Mary Cassatt*. Show the illustrations from the beginning and the end and read enough words from the text to show the points in Mary's life at which the biographer begins and ends the book.

  At what points in Mary's life did the biographer decide to begin and end this story about her?

- ▶ As students share, create a chart to show where the story begins and ends. Add student responses to the chart.
- ▶ Revisit the beginning and ending of *Action Jackson*.

  What do you notice about the biographers' decision about which period of time in Jackson's life to write about?

- ▶ Add responses to the chart.

  Do the biographers we just talked about tell the same part of their subjects' lives?

  Why do you think biographers choose different parts of people's lives to write about?

## Have a Try

Invite the students to talk with a partner about a biographer's decisions.

▶ Show the cover of *The East-West House* and revisit the beginning and the ending.

> Think about *The East-West House*. What decision did the biographer make about when to begin and end the story of Isamu Noguchi's life? Turn and talk about that.

▶ After time for discussion, ask several volunteers to share their thinking. Add to chart.

## Summarize and Apply

Summarize the learning and remind students to think about the biographer's decisions when they read biographies.

> What does the chart show you about biographies?

▶ Add the principle to the top of the chart.

> If you are not already reading a biography, choose one from the basket. As you read, notice the period of a subject's life that the biographer decided to write about. Bring the book when we meet so you can share.

## Share

Following independent reading time, gather students in the meeting area.

> Who read a biography today? Share some of the decisions the biographer made to tell the story of someone's life.

## Extend the Lesson (Optional)

After assessing students' understanding, you might decide to extend the learning.

▶ The next time you read a biography during interactive read-aloud, talk about the decisions that the biographer made to present the story of the subject's life.

▶ Make a Venn diagram to illustrate how a biography and a realistic fiction story are alike (e.g., a person figures prominently in each, events are often told in chronological order, there is a beginning and an ending) and different (e.g., biography is true/nonfiction, a realistic fiction story seems like it could be true but it isn't).

**Biographers decide when to start and stop telling the story of the subject's life.**

| Title | Begin | End |
|---|---|---|
| Mary Cassatt | When Mary Cassatt is a young girl | When she is a successful artist |
| Action Jackson | One afternoon when Jackson is an adult | Two months later |
| the east-west house | When Isamu Noguchi is a baby | When he is an older boy |

# RML 5

LA.U14.RML5

**Reading Minilesson Principle**

# Biographers include details about the society and culture of the time in which the subject lived.

## Studying Biography

### You Will Need

- several familiar biographies that have details about the time in which the subject lived, such as the following:
  - *The Secret Kingdom* by Barb Rosenstock and *Fly High* by Louise Borden and Mary Kay Kroeger, from Text Set: Genre Study: Biography (Individuals Making a Difference)
  - *Mary Cassatt* by Barbara Herkert, from Text Set: Biography: Artists
- chart paper and markers
- basket of biographies
- sticky notes

### Academic Language / Important Vocabulary

- biography
- biographer
- subject
- time period
- society
- culture

### Continuum Connection

- Understand that biographies are often set in the past (p. 62)
- Notice how the writer reveals the setting in a biographical or historical text (p. 64)

## Goal

Understand why biographers include details about the society and culture of the time in which the subject lived.

## Rationale

When students learn to think about the details that a biographer chooses to include about the time period, they learn to consider how culture and society affected the subject and prompted the subject's accomplishments.

## Assess Learning

Observe students when they talk about the time period in a biography and notice if there is evidence of new learning based on the goal of this minilesson.

- ▶ Are students talking about the significance of the details about the time period that the biographer chooses to include?
- ▶ Do they use the terms *biography, biographer, subject, time period, society,* and *culture*?

## Minilesson

To help students think about the minilesson principle, help them notice the effect of the time period's society and culture on the subject. Here is an example.

- ▶ Begin to build students' awareness of how the time period influenced the subject of a biography. Hold up *The Secret Kingdom*.

  How does the biographer let you know when Nek Chand lived?

  What do you know about that time period?

  Why do you think the author includes information about Nek's time period?

- ▶ As students offer suggestions, record their thinking on chart paper. Make a column for the title and subject, the time period, and the significance of the time period.

  Now think about the biography about Bessie Coleman. Think about the facts that the authors include about the time period.

- ▶ Show the illustrations on pages 18 and 21 of *Fly High*. Read the first three lines of text on page 23 and the author's note.

  What information do the illustrations and words give you about the time period in which Bessie lived?

  Why is it important that you know about the society and culture at that time to understand Bessie Coleman's accomplishments?

- ▶ Record students' responses.

## Have a Try

Invite the students to talk with a partner about the significance of time-period details in a biography.

▶ Read and show pages 1–2 and the author's note of *Mary Cassatt*.

 Think about the details that the author includes about the time Mary Cassatt lived. Turn and talk about why these details are important in a book about Mary Cassatt's life.

▶ After time for discussion, ask students to share. Add to the chart.

## Summarize and Apply

Summarize the learning and remind students to think about the facts about time period in biographies.

 Today you talked about why a biographer includes facts about the time period in a biography.

▶ Add the principle to the chart.

 If you are not already reading a biography, choose one from the basket, As you read, think about facts that the biographer included and why they are important. Mark any pages with sticky notes that give a clue. Bring the book when we meet so you can share.

## Share

Following independent reading time, gather students in small groups. Make sure at least one person in each group read a biography.

 If you read a biography today, share with your group the reasons you think the author included facts about the time period and why those facts are important.

## Extend the Lesson (Optional)

After assessing students' understanding, you might decide to extend the learning.

▶ **Writing About Reading** Suggest that students write in a reader's notebook about what might have happened if the subject of a biography lived in a different time period. For example, would Nek Chand have built his garden if he lived fifty years earlier or later? Would Louise Borden and Mary Kay Kroeger write about Bessie Coleman if Bessie became a pilot today?

| Biographers include details about the society and culture of the time in which the subject lived. | | |
|---|---|---|
| **Title and Subject** | **Time Period** | **Why is it important that the author included facts about when the subject lived?** |
| Nek Chand | 1947 and after | • In 1947, Pakistan and India were divided, so Nek had to leave his home. <br> • His memories of home inspired him to make the rock garden. |
| Bessie Coleman | early 1900s | • Women and African Americans did not fly planes in those days. <br> • Bessie was the first African American to get a pilot's license. |
| Mary Cassatt | 1860s | • Women did not become artists at that time. <br> • Mary had to work very hard to become an artist because it was not considered proper for women. |

Section 2: Literary Analysis

**Reading Minilesson Principle**

## Biographers usually include the people who influenced the subject's life.

### Studying Biography

#### You Will Need

- several familiar biographies that include facts about people who influenced the lives of the subjects, such as the following from Text Set: Biography: Artists:
  - *Radiant Child* by Javaka Steptoe
  - *Mary Cassatt* by Barbara Herkert
  - *Me, Frida* by Amy Novesky
- chart paper and markers
- basket of biographies
- sticky notes

#### Academic Language / Important Vocabulary

- biography
- biographer
- subject
- influenced
- inspiration

#### Continuum Connection

- Infer the importance of a subject's accomplishments (biography) (p. 62)

### Goal

Understand and infer the influence of the subject's relationships.

### Rationale

When students understand that people act in certain ways due to the influence of other people, they learn that the subject of a biography is a product of multiple factors (see also LA.U14.RML5). They may also learn to understand the influence that the people in their own lives might have upon them.

### Assess Learning

Observe students when they talk about biographies and notice if there is evidence of new learning based on the goal of this minilesson.

- ▶ Do students notice facts about people who influenced a biography subject's life?
- ▶ Are they talking about the facts that a biographer chooses to include about a subject's inspiration?
- ▶ Do they understand the terms *biography, biographer, subject, influenced,* and *inspiration*?

## Minilesson

To help students think about the minilesson principle, engage them in noticing how people and their accomplishments are influenced by people in their lives. Here is an example.

- ▶ Revisit pages 7–12 ("His art comes from his mother" through "what it means to be a famous artist") of *Radiant Child*.

  What do you learn about Jean-Michel on these pages?

  Why do you think Javaka Steptoe included this information?

  Do you think Jean-Michel would have become an artist without his mother's influence and the inspiration from the museum visit? Tell what makes you think that.

- ▶ Explain the meanings of *influence* and *inspiration* as needed. On a chart, list the title, subject, and person who influenced the subject. Record student responses on the chart.

  Now think about another biography you know, one about Mary Cassatt.

- ▶ Revisit pages 9–10, 15–16, and 26.

  What do you learn about Mary on these pages?

  Why do you think the author included this information?

- ▶ Add responses to the chart.

## Have a Try

Invite the students to talk with a partner about why a biographer includes facts about people who influenced the subject.

▶ Revisit pages 23–26 of *Me, Frida*.

Turn and talk about who influenced Frida's art and how.

▶ After time for discussion, ask a few volunteers to share. Add to the chart.

## Summarize and Apply

Summarize the learning and remind students to think about the reasons biographers include facts about who influenced the subject.

What does the chart show about what a biographer usually includes in a biography?

▶ Add the principle to the chart.

If you are not already reading a biography, choose one from the basket. As you read, notice how the subject was influenced by another person or by other people. Mark any pages with sticky notes that give a clue. Bring the book when we meet so you can share.

## Share

Following independent reading time, gather students in the meeting area.

Who read a biography today? Was the subject influenced by anyone? How? Share what you noticed.

## Extend the Lesson (Optional)

After assessing students' understanding, you might decide to extend the learning.

▶ As students listen to and read more biographies, encourage them to talk about the facts a biographer includes about who influenced the subject.

▶ **Writing About Reading** Have students write in a reader's notebook about the influences that inspired the subject of a biography.

**Biographers usually include the people who influenced the subject's life.**

| Title and Subject | Who influenced the subject? | How was the subject influenced? |
|---|---|---|
| Radiant Child — Jean-Michel Basquiat | Jean-Michel's mom | His mother was artistic. She took him to museums to learn about art and artists. |
| Mary Cassatt — Mary Cassatt | The famous painter, Edgar Degas | He invited her to join a group of painters that painted the way they wanted to. She liked the way they painted. |
| Me, Frida — Frida Kahlo | Frida's husband, Diego Rivera, who is also a famous painter | He took her to San Francisco, which was a new experience for Frida. He encouraged her to paint in her own style. |

Section 2: Literary Analysis

**Reading Minilesson Principle**

# Biographers choose to include facts that reveal something important about the subject's personality traits and motivations.

### You Will Need

- several familiar biographies, such as the following:
  - *Action Jackson* by Jan Greenberg and Sandra Jordan, from Text Set: Biography: Artists
  - *The Secret Kingdom* by Barb Rosenstock, from Text Set: Genre Study: Biography (Individuals Making a Difference)
- chart paper and markers
- basket of biographies
- sticky notes

### Academic Language / Important Vocabulary

- biography
- biographer
- subject
- reveal
- personality traits
- motivations

### Continuum Connection

- Infer the importance of a subject's accomplishments (biography) (p. 62)
- Understand that a biography is the story of a person's life written by someone else (p. 62)

## Goal

Infer a subject's personality traits and motivations from the facts and details the biographer includes about the subject's life.

## Rationale

When you teach students to think about what the facts in a biography reveal about a subject, they begin to think about the decisions a biographer makes about how to reveal what the subject is like.

## Assess Learning

Observe students when they talk about what the facts in a biography reveal and notice if there is evidence of new learning based on the goal of this minilesson.

- Can students identify facts in a biography that reveal something about the subject?
- Are they talking about the decisions a biographer makes about which facts to include about the subject?
- Do they understand the terms *biography*, *biographer*, *subject*, *reveal*, *personality traits*, and *motivations*?

## Minilesson

To help students think about the minilesson principle, engage them in noticing what the facts reveal about the subjects in biographies. Here is an example.

- Show the cover of *Action Jackson* and revisit the first two paragraphs on page 8.

  How would you describe Jackson Pollock, based on the information on this page?

  How do the biographers show you what Jackson was like?

- As students share their thinking, record their responses along with examples from the book. Then read pages 14–16 (top).

  What do you learn about Jackson Pollock's personality traits and motivations from these pages?

  What did the biographers do to show you what Jackson was like?

- Explain the meanings of *personality traits* and *motivations* as needed. Add responses to the chart.

## Have a Try

Invite the students to talk with a partner about how a biographer shows the personality traits and motivations of a subject.

▶ Show the cover of *The Secret Kingdom*.

Think about what the biographer reveals about Nek's personality traits and motivations as I read.

▶ Revisit pages 14, 18, and 24.

Turn and talk about what the facts reveal about Nek's personality traits and motivations.

▶ After time for discussion, ask students to share their thinking. Add responses to the chart.

## Summarize and Apply

Summarize the learning and remind students to think about what the facts in a biography show about the subject's personality traits and motivations.

What does the chart show about the information biographers choose to include in their biographies?

▶ Add the principle to the chart.

If you are not already reading a biography, choose one from the basket. As you read, think about facts that the biographer included and what the facts show about the subject. Mark any pages with sticky notes that you want to remember. Bring the book when we meet so you can share.

## Share

Following independent reading time, gather students in the meeting area.

Did anyone read a biography today? Share any facts you noticed that show something about the subject's personality traits and motivations.

## Extend the Lesson (Optional)

After assessing students' understanding, you might decide to extend the learning.

▶ **Writing About Reading** Encourage students to write in a reader's notebook their thoughts about the facts that a biographer included in a biography and what those facts show about the subject.

| Biographers choose to include facts that reveal something important about the subject's personality traits and motivations. | | |
| --- | --- | --- |
| **Title and Subject** | **What the Subject Is Like** | **How the Biographer Shows What the Subject Is Like** |
| ACTION JACKSON / Jackson Pollock | • different from other painters, unique <br><br> • inspired by nature | • wrote how Jackson did the opposite of most painters (painted no base coat, used regular house paint) <br> • told about Jackson walking on the beach <br> • included a quote |
| The Secret Kingdom / Nek Chand | • a thinker and dreamer <br> • careful of the environment <br> • private, quiet | • wrote about his thoughts and dreams <br> • told how he picked things up from the roadside <br> • told how Nek kept the garden secret for a long time |

Section 2: Literary Analysis

**Reading Minilesson Principle**
# Sometimes biographers include some imagined scenes but base them on facts.

## You Will Need

- several familiar biographies, such as the following from Text Set: Biography: Artists:
  - *Action Jackson* by Jan Greenberg and Sandra Jordan
  - *Me, Frida* by Amy Novesky
- chart paper prepared ahead of time with four headings: *Title and Subject, Imagined Scene, Importance*, and *Does it feel authentic*?
- markers
- basket of biographies
- sticky notes

## Academic Language / Important Vocabulary

- biography
- biographer
- subject
- decisions
- imagined
- facts

### Continuum Connection

- Understand that a biography is the story of a person's life written by someone else (p. 62)

## Goal

Analyze the craft decisions the biographer makes in writing a biography.

## Rationale

It is important for students to understand that biographers sometimes present imagined scenes in a biography so that the students realize which parts of a biography are true and which are based on facts but not necessarily true. When students understand the choices the biographer makes and the reasons for them, they deepen their thinking about an author's craft.

## Assess Learning

Observe students when they talk about a biographer's decisions to include imagined scenes and notice if there is evidence of new learning based on the goal of this minilesson.

- Can students identify scenes that are imagined?
- Are students aware that a biographer makes decisions about what to include when writing a biography?
- Do they understand the terms *biography, biographer, subject, decisions, imagined,* and *facts*?

# Minilesson

To help students think about the minilesson principle, engage them in noticing characteristics of the imagined scenes a biographer includes. Here is an example.

- Hold up a familiar biography, such as *Action Jackson*. Show and read page 21.

  Do you think the biographers know for sure that Jackson climbed the ladder at this time? Why or why not?

- As students share their thinking, begin filling in the prepared chart.

  How do you know this is authentic, or that this is something that Jackson might have really done?

- Continue adding to the chart.

  Why do you think the biographers made the decision to include this scene?

  Why is it important to the story?

- Add to the chart. If students need more support, continue the conversation with a few more scenes from the book.

- Show students the pages of notes and sources in the back of the book. Emphasize that although biographers might make up a scene, they do it based on facts.

## Have a Try

Invite the students to talk with a partner about biographers' decisions.

▶ Read and show page 14 of *Me, Frida*.

Turn and talk about this scene. Have a conversation about whether this is exactly what Frida experienced on that day or if the biographer imagined it. Think about whether it feels authentic and why it is important to the biography.

▶ After time for discussion, ask several volunteers to share their thinking. Add to chart.

## Summarize and Apply

Summarize the learning and remind students to think as they read about the decisions a biographer makes when writing a biography.

What does the chart show you about biographies?

What are some choices you noticed that a biographer can make in the way he or she chooses to tell a story?

▶ Add the principle to the top of the chart.

If you are not already reading a biography, choose one from the basket. As you read, think about the scenes that the biographer included. Place a sticky note on any pages you want to remember. Bring the book when we meet so you can share.

## Share

Following independent reading time, gather students in the meeting area.

Did anyone notice the decisions the biographer made in a biography you read today? Share what you noticed.

## Extend the Lesson (Optional)

After assessing students' understanding, you might decide to extend the learning.

▶ The next time you read a biography during interactive read-aloud, highlight a scene in the book and lead a discussion about its purpose. Why did the biographer include it? What does it tell about the subject?

▶ Have students do some research on the subject of a biography they have read and notice which details match up with what the biographer wrote in the biography.

| Sometimes biographers include some imagined scenes but base them on facts. | | | |
|---|---|---|---|
| Title and Subject | Imagined Scene | Importance | Does it feel authentic? |
| ACTION JACKSON — Jackson Pollock | Jackson stopped painting and climbed a ladder to look at his art. | Jackson spent time thinking about his art. | Yes. This seems like something Jackson would really do because we know that he reflected a lot on his art. |
| Me, Frida — Frida Kahlo | Frida touched birds in cages. Chinatown smelled of incense, fish, and fog. | These details make it seem like the reader is walking with Frida. The reader feels empathy for Frida. | Yes. This seems like what Frida would really come across in Chinatown in San Francisco at that time. |

Section 2: Literary Analysis

**RML 9**

LA.U14.RML9

**Reading Minilesson Principle**
## Sometimes biographers include quotes by the subject.

### Studying Biography

**You Will Need**

- several familiar biographies, such as the following from Text Set: Biography: Artists:
  - *Action Jackson* by Jan Greenberg and Sandra Jordan
  - *Radiant Child* by Javaka Steptoe
  - *Mary Cassatt* by Barbara Herkert
- prepared chart with four columns: *Title and Subject, Quote, Importance,* and *Does it feel authentic?*
- markers
- basket of biographies
- sticky notes

**Academic Language / Important Vocabulary**

- biography
- biographer
- subject
- decisions
- quotes
- authentic

**Continuum Connection**

- Understand that a biography is the story of a person written by someone else (p. 62)

## Goal

Analyze the craft decisions the biographer makes in writing a biography.

## Rationale

When you teach students to think critically about the quotes a biographer includes in a biography, they understand the choices the biographer makes and deepen their thinking about an author's craft.

## Assess Learning

Observe students when they talk about a biographer's decisions and notice if there is evidence of new learning based on the goal of this minilesson.

- ▹ Can students explain why biographers sometimes include quotes by the subject?
- ▹ Do they understand the terms *biography, biographer, subject, decisions, quotes,* and *authentic*?

## Minilesson

To help students think about the minilesson principle, engage them in a discussion about a biographer's use of quotes. Here is an example.

- ▹ Display the cover of *Action Jackson*. Show and read the quote on page 20. Prompt students to think critically about it and evaluate whether it feels authentic.

    Why do you think the biographers include this quote?

- ▹ As students share their thinking, begin filling in the prepared chart with their ideas.

    Does the quote feel authentic? In other words, does it seem like something Jackson really said? Why or why not?

- ▹ Read the endnote on page 31 indicating that the quote is real.

    In the book, the authors give you information at the end to let you know this is a real quote. How can you think about whether a quote is real if a biographer doesn't give you this information? Think about that as I share another quote.

- ▹ Show and read the quote from *Radiant Child*, page 21. After reading, prompt the conversation to help students think critically about the quote.

    Why do you think the biographer includes this quote?

    Does it feel authentic, or like something Jean-Michel might say? Why?

- ▹ As students respond, add to the chart.

## Have a Try

Invite the students to talk with a partner about the quotes a biographer decides to include.

▶ Read the quote on page 10 of *Mary Cassatt*.

Think about this quote. Why is it important to the story? Turn and talk about whether it seems authentic. Do you think it is an actual quote?

▶ After time for discussion, ask several volunteers to share their thinking. Add to chart.

## Summarize and Apply

Summarize the learning and remind students to think about a biographer's decisions when they read biographies.

What does the chart show you about some decisions a biographer makes?

▶ Add the principle to the top of the chart.

Today when you read, choose a biography from the basket unless you are already reading one from our library. As you read, notice whether the biographer includes quotes. Think about why they are important. Do they seem authentic? Mark the pages with a sticky note and bring the book when we meet so you can share.

## Share

Following independent reading time, gather students in the meeting area.

Did anyone notice quotes in a biography you read today? Share what you noticed.

▶ Add new ideas to the chart.

## Extend the Lesson (Optional)

After assessing students' understanding, you might decide to extend the learning.

▶ Talk with students about how biographers find quotations to use in their biographies. Lead them to understand that biographers do a lot of research so that they can write accurately about someone else's life.

---

### Sometimes biographers include quotes by the subject.

| Title and Subject | Quote | Importance | Does it feel authentic? |
|---|---|---|---|
| **Action Jackson** — Jackson Pollock | "The painting has a life of its own." (p. 20) | This helps us understand how Jackson Pollock thought about and viewed art. | Yes. The endnote says Jackson Pollock really said this. |
| **Radiant Child** — Jean-Michel Basquiat | "Papa, I will be very, very famous one day." (p. 21) | This makes the story more interesting. It feels like we are there listening to how Jean-Michel talked to his dad. | Yes. This is probably made-up. Jean-Michel wanted to be famous, so he might say something like this. |
| **Mary Cassatt** — Mary Cassatt | "I saw art then as I wanted to see it." (p. 10) | This makes us feel empathy because we can understand how she felt about art. | Yes. Mary probably said this when she was older and thinking about her early days as an artist. |

**Reading Minilesson Principle**

## Think about how the subject's accomplishments have influenced life today.

### You Will Need

- several familiar biographies, such as the following:
  - *Farmer Will Allen and the Growing Table* by Jacqueline Briggs Martin, from Text Set: Genre Study: Biography (Individuals Making a Difference)
  - *Mary Cassatt* by Barbara Herkert, from Text Set: Biography: Artists
  - *Six Dots* by Jen Bryant, from Text Set: Genre Study: Biography (Individuals Making a Difference)
- chart paper and markers
- basket of biographies
- sticky notes

### Academic Language / Important Vocabulary

- biography
- biographer
- subject
- accomplishments
- influenced

### Continuum Connection

- Infer the significance of nonfiction content to their own lives (p. 63)

### Goal

Infer ways the subject's accomplishments have influenced life today.

### Rationale

When students learn to infer the influence that a biographical subject has had on life today, they think about how biographers choose their subjects and consider why biographies are written about certain people.

### Assess Learning

Observe students when they talk about a subject's accomplishments and notice if there is evidence of new learning based on the goal of this minilesson.

- Can students identify the accomplishments of the subject of a biography?
- Are they able to infer the way that a subject's accomplishments have influenced life today?
- Do they understand the terms *biography, biographer, subject, accomplishments,* and *influenced*?

## Minilesson

To help students think about the minilesson principle, engage them in analyzing the subject's influence on life today. Here is an example.

- Show the cover of *Farmer Will Allen and the Growing Table.*

  Think about this biography of Farmer Will Allen. Why do you think the biographer decided to write about him?

- Revisit a few parts of the book that show the impact he has had on life today. As needed, talk about the meanings of the words *accomplishments* and *influenced*. Use the words in the conversation.

  What are Will Allen's accomplishments?

  How has Farmer Will Allen influenced, changed, or improved life today?

- As students respond, add their ideas to a chart.

- Show the cover of *Mary Cassatt.*

  Now think about the biography about Mary Cassatt. Why do you think the biographer wrote a book about her?

- Revisit a few parts of the book that show Cassatt's influence.

  What are Mary Cassatt's accomplishments?

  How have her accomplishments influenced life today?

- Add students' responses to the chart.

## Have a Try

Invite the students to talk with a partner about how the subject of a biography has influenced life today.

▶ Show the cover of *Six Dots*.

> Think about Louis Braille and how he has influenced life today. Turn and talk about that.

▶ After time for discussion, ask a few volunteers to share. Summarize their thinking on the chart.

## Summarize and Apply

Summarize the learning and remind students to think about the influence that the subjects of biographies have on life today.

> Today you talked about biographies. What did you learn?

▶ Add the principle to the chart.

> If you are not already reading a biography, choose one from the basket. As you read, think about how the subject of the biography has influenced life today. Mark any pages with sticky notes that you want to remember. Bring the book when we meet so you can share.

| Think about how the subject's accomplishments have influenced life today. | |
|---|---|
| **Title and Subject** | **How the subject's accomplishments have influenced life today** |
| Farmer Will Allen and the Growing Table <br><br> Will Allen | He completely changed urban farming. He helped people who live in cities learn how to grow good food. |
| Mary Cassatt <br><br> Mary Cassatt | She was a role model for future female artists. She painted everyday moments, especially of children, and made them beautiful. |
| Six Dots <br><br> Louis Braille | He invented an alphabet for people who are blind. He made it possible for people who are blind to read independently. a b c |

## Share

Following independent reading time, gather students in small groups.

> If you read a biography today, talk with your group about the ways that the subject of the biography has influenced life today.

## Extend the Lesson (Optional)

After assessing students' understanding, you might decide to extend the learning.

▶ **Writing About Reading** Have students write about how life today might be different without the accomplishments of the person in a biography.

## Assessment

After you have taught the minilessons in this umbrella, observe students as they talk and write about biographies across instructional contexts: interactive read-aloud, independent reading, guided reading, and book club. Use *The Literacy Continuum* (Fountas and Pinnell 2017) to guide the observation of students' reading and writing behaviors.

▶ What evidence do you have of new understandings related to biographies?

- Can students articulate the ways biographies are alike and create a definition of biography?

- Are they talking about the reasons a biographer chooses a subject to write about?

- Can they discuss the influence of people and the time period on a subject?

- Are they talking about the decisions an author makes in writing a biography (e.g., which facts to include, whether to use quotes, where to begin and end the story)?

- Can they identify the ways that a subject's accomplishments have influenced life today?

- Do they use vocabulary such as *biography, biographer, subject, decisions,* and *authentic*?

▶ In what other ways, beyond the scope of this umbrella, are students demonstrating an understanding of genre?

- Are students reading historical fiction or types of nonfiction?

Use your observations to determine the next umbrella you will teach. You may also consult Minilessons Across the Year (pp. 59–61) for guidance.

## Read and Revise

After completing the steps in the genre study process, help students read and revise their definition of the genre based on their new understandings.

▶ **Before:** A biography is the story of a person's life written by someone else.

▶ **After:** A biography is the story of all or part of a real person's life written by someone else. The subject of the biography can be someone who is living or dead.

## Reader's Notebook

When this umbrella is complete, provide a copy of the minilesson principles (see resources.fountasandpinnell.com) for students to glue in the reader's notebook (in the Minilessons section if using *Reader's Notebook: Intermediate* [Fountas and Pinnell 2011]), so they can refer to the information as needed.

## Minilessons in This Umbrella

**RML1**   Authors write to persuade you to believe or do something.

**RML2**   Notice the ways the author tries to persuade you.

**RML3**   Consider an author's qualifications and sources when you read a persuasive text.

## Before Teaching Umbrella 15 Minilessons

Students should be familiar with recognizing an author's opinion or message before you begin this umbrella. Read and discuss high-quality, engaging nonfiction books that present a variety of topics and viewpoints. Explore and discuss the notes and resources found at the end of nonfiction books. Focus on persuasive texts, most of which are nonfiction. Consider collecting and reading shorter persuasive texts, such as news articles and essays. Use the following books from the *Fountas & Pinnell Classroom™ Interactive Read-Aloud Collection* and *Independent Reading Collection* or choose books from your classroom library.

### Interactive Read-Aloud Collection

**Perseverance**

*Razia's Ray of Hope: One Girl's Dream of an Education* by Elizabeth Suneby

**Taking Action, Making Change**

*Follow the Moon Home: A Tale of One Idea, Twenty Kids, and a Hundred Sea Turtles* by Philippe Cousteau and Deborah Hopkinson

### Independent Reading Collection

*Attack of the Bullfrogs* by Therese Shea

*How Can We Reduce Household Waste?* by Mary K. Pratt

As you read aloud and enjoy these texts together, help students

- think about the author's opinion or message,

- notice if the text is a persuasive text,

- identify what the author is persuading them to believe or do,

- notice the author's style and technique for presenting information in the book, and

- understand the author's qualifications to write on the topic.

*Interactive Read-Aloud*
**Perseverance**

**Taking Action, Making Change**

*Independent Reading*

**Section 2: Literary Analysis**

# RML1
## LA.U15.RML1

### Reading Minilesson Principle
## Authors write to persuade you to believe or do something.

## Exploring Persuasive Texts

### You Will Need

- a collection of familiar persuasive texts, such as the following:
  - *Attack of the Bullfrogs* by Therese Shea, from *Independent Reading Collection*
  - *How Can We Reduce Household Waste?* by Mary K. Pratt, from *Independent Reading Collection*
- chart paper and markers

### Academic Language / Important Vocabulary

- nonfiction
- persuade
- persuasive text

### Continuum Connection

- Notice and understand the characteristics of some specific nonfiction genres: e.g., expository, narrative, procedural and persuasive texts, biography, autobiography, memoir, hybrid text (p. 62)
- Infer a writer's purpose in a nonfiction text (p. 63)

### Goal

Understand that sometimes authors write books or articles to persuade you to believe or do something.

### Rationale

When students learn to notice an author's intent in a persuasive text (book or article), they can draw conclusions about the author's purpose and consider their own new beliefs or actions. Students should have an understanding of author's purpose for this minilesson (see LA.U8.RML1).

### Assess Learning

Observe students when they read and discuss persuasive texts. Notice if there is evidence of new learning based on the goal of this minilesson.

- Can students identify persuasive texts?
- Are they able to identify what an author is trying to persuade readers to believe or do?
- Do they understand and use the terms *nonfiction, persuade,* and *persuasive text*?

## Minilesson

To help students think about the minilesson principle, use familiar persuasive texts to engage them in noticing how authors persuade the reader. Here is an example:

- Show and review the information on pages 12 and 14 of *Attack of the Bullfrogs*.

  What do you think the author wants you to think about bullfrogs?

  On these pages, the author describes some problems that bullfrogs cause when they start living in places where they don't belong.

- Now show and review the information on pages 20 and 21.

  Why are these pages here?

- Record responses on the chart.

  The author gave you information about how bullfrogs can be harmful to the environment when they are in places where they don't belong so that you would understand the problem. Then the author gave information about some actions that people can take to reach the goal of stopping the frogs from spreading so that you will do something about the problem.

## Have a Try

Invite the students to talk with a partner about what the author tries to persuade them to believe or do in *How Can We Reduce Household Waste?*

▶ Review in general the information the author gives in this book.

> Turn and talk to your partner. What does the author want you to think about household waste? What does the author want you to believe or do?

▶ Invite a few students to share with the class. Record responses on the chart.

## Summarize and Apply

Summarize the learning and remind students to think about what authors persuade readers to do or believe.

> Look at the chart. Why do authors write books like the two we looked at today?

▶ Review the chart and write the principle at the top.

> Choose a nonfiction book to read today. Notice whether or not it is a persuasive text. If it is, when we come back together, be ready to share what you think the author is persuading you to believe or do.

## Share

Following independent reading time, gather students together in the meeting area to talk about persuasive texts.

> Who read a persuasive book today? What did the author try to persuade you to believe or do?

## Extend the Lesson (Optional)

After assessing students' understanding, you might decide to extend the learning.

▶ Introduce your students to Genre Thinkmarks for persuasive texts (visit resources.fountasandpinnell.com to download this resource). A Genre Thinkmark is a tool that guides readers to note certain elements of a genre in their reading. Once students can identify persuasive texts, they can use this resource to note points the author is arguing as well as supporting details.

▶ **Writing About Reading** After reading a persuasive text, have students write in a reader's notebook about what the author was persuading them to believe or do.

| Authors write to persuade you to believe or do something. | |
|---|---|
| **Book** | **What the Author Wants You to Believe or Do** |
| *ATTACK OF THE BULLFROGS* | Bullfrogs cause problems in parts of the world, so you should help stop the spread of bullfrogs in places they don't belong. |
| *How Can We Reduce Household Waste?* | Too much waste hurts the environment, so you should find ways to reduce, reuse, and recycle. |

**Reading Minilesson Principle**
# Notice the ways the author tries to persuade you.

## Exploring Persuasive Texts

### You Will Need

- several familiar persuasive texts, such as the following:
  - *Follow the Moon Home* by Philippe Cousteau and Deborah Hopkinson, from Text Set: Taking Action, Making Change
  - *Razia's Ray of Hope* by Elizabeth Suneby, from Text Set: Perseverance
  - *How Can We Reduce Household Waste?* by Mary K. Pratt, from *Independent Reading Collection*
- chart paper and markers
- basket of familiar persuasive texts, letters, speeches, or simple newspaper editorials
- sticky notes

### Academic Language / Important Vocabulary

- persuasive text
- persuasive language
- statistics

### Continuum Connection

- Notice and think critically about an author's word choice (p. 64)
- Recognize a writer's use of the techniques for persuasion in a persuasive text (p. 64)

## Goal

Recognize a writer's use of the techniques for persuasion.

## Rationale

When students use critical thinking as they read, they notice the techniques authors use in a persuasive text, learn about the craft of writing, and may apply those techniques to their own persuasive writing.

## Assess Learning

Observe students when they read and discuss persuasive texts. Notice if there is evidence of new learning based on the goal of this minilesson.

- Can students identify techniques an author uses to persuade?
- Do they understand terms such as *persuasive text, persuasive language,* and *statistics*?

## Minilesson

To help students think about the minilesson principle, use familiar persuasive texts to help them notice techniques the author uses to persuade. Here is an example:

- Show Letter to Young Activists from *Follow the Moon Home* and read the second paragraph.

  Why did the authors include Letter to Young Activists in this book?

  The authors want to persuade you to find a way to make a positive change in the world. How do the authors try to do that?

- Record responses on a chart.
- Read the fifth paragraph and the first sentences of the next five paragraphs.

  What do the authors do here to try to persuade you?

- Record responses on the chart.
- Read the last sentence.

  What do you notice about the language the authors use to persuade you?

- Record responses on the chart.
- Show and read Education for Everyone from *Razia's Ray of Hope*.
- What does the author want you to think?

  The author wants you to believe that everyone should have access to education. How does the author try to persuade you of that?

- Record responses on the chart.

## Have a Try

Invite the students to talk with a partner about how the author tries to persuade readers in *How Can We Reduce Household Waste?*

▷ Read the subheadings from chapters two and three.

> Turn and talk to your partner. How does the author try to persuade you to protect the environment from household waste?

▷ Ask a few students to share with the class. Record responses on the chart.

## Summarize and Apply

Summarize the learning and remind students to notice how authors try to persuade readers.

> What did you learn about persuasive writing?

▷ Review the chart and write the principle at the top.

> You can choose a persuasive text from this basket to read today. When you notice a way the author is trying to persuade you, mark it with a sticky note so you can share when we come back together.

## Share

Following independent reading time, gather students in the meeting area to talk about persuasive texts.

> Who would like to share about the persuasive text you read today? What was the author trying to persuade you to do or believe?

> How did the author try to do that?

## Extend the Lesson (Optional)

After assessing students' understanding, you might decide to extend the learning.

▷ Discuss the realistic fiction stories *Razia's Ray of Hope* and *Follow the Moon Home*, which precede the persuasive texts at the back of the books. Talk about how the authors used the stories as tools to help persuade readers to believe or do something.

▷ Gather two or three examples of suitable opinion columns or articles from newspapers or online sources. Examine them with students to discover how the writers use language to persuade the audience to believe or do something.

---

### Notice the ways the author tries to persuade you.

- Tells about his/her own life

- Provides steps for you to follow

- Speaks directly to you

- Includes important facts and statistics

- Describes a problem and the solution

- Uses persuasive language that inspires you to do something

**Reading Minilesson Principle**

# Consider an author's qualifications and sources when you read a persuasive text.

## Exploring Persuasive Texts

### You Will Need

- several familiar persuasive texts, such as the following:
  - *Follow the Moon Home* by Philippe Cousteau and Deborah Hopkinson, from Text Set: Taking Action, Making Change
  - *Razia's Ray of Hope* by Elizabeth Suneby, from Text Set: Perseverance
  - *How Can We Reduce Household Waste?* by Mary K. Pratt, from *Independent Reading Collection*
- chart paper and markers

### Academic Language / Important Vocabulary

- biography
- persuade
- qualified
- evaluate
- believable
- sources

### Continuum Connection

- Critically examine the quality or accuracy of the text, citing evidence for opinions (p. 64)

## Goal

Evaluate an author's qualifications and sources when you read a persuasive text.

## Rationale

When students apply critical thinking and research skills to their reading, they can evaluate a writer's claims and begin to draw their own conclusions from persuasive texts.

## Assess Learning

Observe students when they talk about persuasive texts. Notice if there is evidence of new learning based on the goal of this minilesson.

- Are students able to identify ways to check an author's qualifications and sources?
- Can they explain why evaluation of qualifications and sources is important?
- Do they use language such as *biography, persuade, qualified, evaluate, believable,* and *sources*?

# Minilesson

To help students understand how to evaluate an author's qualifications and sources when reading a persuasive text, use familiar texts in which the author tries to persuade the readers. Here is an example.

- Read Philippe Cousteau's biography from the book jacket of *Follow the Moon Home* and show Letter to Young Activists.

  Philippe Cousteau, the author, tries to persuade you to take action to solve problems in your community. Why do you think the author is able—or qualified—to tell you this? How does the author's biography help you to know this?

- Record responses on a chart.
- Read the third and fourth paragraphs of The Real Razia Jan from *Razia's Ray of Hope* and show Education for Everyone.

  The author tries to persuade you that everyone should have access to education. What do you learn from this note that helps you judge—or evaluate—whether or not the author is qualified to persuade you of that idea?

- Record responses on the chart.

## Have a Try

Invite the students to consider with a partner how to evaluate an author's qualifications and sources.

▶ Read a few titles of books and websites from Learn More About Household Waste from *How Can We Reduce Household Waste?*

How could these other sources of information help you to decide if the author is qualified to persuade you of that? Turn and talk to your partner.

▶ Ask a few students to share. Add to the chart.

## Summarize and Apply

Summarize the learning and remind students to think about how readers consider an author's qualifications and sources.

Look at the chart. How did you learn about an author's qualifications and sources?

▶ Review the chart and write the principle at the top.

Choose a nonfiction book to read today. As you read, notice if the author is trying to persuade you to believe or do something. If so, think about whether or not the author is qualified to try to persuade you, and why. Be ready to share your thoughts with the class.

## Share

Following independent reading time, gather students in the meeting area to talk about persuasive texts.

Who would like to share about the persuasive text you read today? Is the author qualified to talk to you about the topic? How do you know that?

## Extend the Lesson (Optional)

After assessing students' understanding, you might decide to extend the learning.

▶ Have students work with a partner to conduct research in a library or on the internet based on the notes or resources they find in a persuasive text. Encourage them to discuss what they find as they conduct their research and draw conclusions about whether an author is qualified on the topic.

| Consider an author's qualifications and sources when you read a persuasive text. ||
| Where to Look for an Author's Qualifications and Sources | How You Know an Author Is Qualified to Persuade You |
| --- | --- |
| Biographical Information | Author's experience and background gives him knowledge and makes him believable. |
| Afterword Author's Notes | Shares more information about why the topic is important to the author. Additional facts support what the author wrote. |
| Other Resources/Sources:<br>• Other nonfiction books<br>• Websites<br>• Interviews | You can read more to check if the author is correct. |

**Section 2: Literary Analysis**

## Assessment

After you have taught the minilessons in this umbrella, observe students as they talk and write about their reading across instructional contexts: interactive read-aloud, independent reading, guided reading, shared reading, and book club. Use *The Literacy Continuum* (Fountas and Pinnell 2017) to guide the observation of students' reading and writing behaviors.

▶ What evidence do you have of new understandings related to persuasive texts?

- Can students identify what the author is trying to persuade them believe or do?

- Can they identify the writing techniques an author uses to persuade?

- Are they evaluating an author's qualifications and sources?

- Do they use academic vocabulary, such as *nonfiction, persuade, persuasive text, evaluate,* and *sources*?

▶ In what other ways, beyond the scope of this umbrella, are students talking about nonfiction?

- Do students discuss the themes in nonfiction books?

Use your observations to determine the next umbrella you will teach. You may also consult Minilessons Across the Year (pp. 59–61) for guidance.

## Link to Writing

After teaching the minilessons in this umbrella, help students link the new learning to their own writing:

▶ Ask students to think about a topic on which they feel strongly. Invite them to write a persuasive story on the topic. Remind them that they should try to convince the reader to believe or do something. Encourage students to think about their sources and how they will present the information to be persuasive. Students may use Analyzing Persuasive Writing to create an outline for their writing (visit resources.fountasandpinnell.com to download this resource).

## Reader's Notebook

When this umbrella is complete, provide a copy of the minilesson principles (see resources.fountasandpinnell.com) for students to glue in the reader's notebook (in the Minilessons section if using *Reader's Notebook: Intermediate* [Fountas and Pinnell 2011]), so they can refer to the information as needed.

## Minilessons in This Umbrella

**RML1** Nonfiction authors tell information in time order like a story.

**RML2** Nonfiction authors organize information into categories and subcategories.

**RML3** Nonfiction authors organize information by comparing and contrasting two things.

**RML4** Nonfiction authors organize information using cause and effect.

**RML5** Nonfiction authors organize information by explaining the problem and solution.

**RML6** Nonfiction authors organize information in several ways within the same book.

## Before Teaching Umbrella 16 Minilessons

Read and discuss a variety of high-quality, engaging nonfiction books that are organized in different ways. Use the following texts from the *Fountas & Pinnell Classroom™ Interactive Read-Aloud Collection* and *Independent Reading Collection* or choose nonfiction books whose information is organized in different ways from your classroom library.

### Interactive Read-Aloud Collection

**Innovative Thinking and Creative Problem Solving**

*Ivan: The Remarkable True Story of the Shopping Mall Gorilla* by Katherine Applegate

*Parrots Over Puerto Rico* by Susan L. Roth and Cindy Trumbore

*One Plastic Bag: Isatou Ceesay and the Recycling Women of the Gambia* by Miranda Paul

**Illustration Study: Craft**

*Eye to Eye: How Animals See the World* by Steve Jenkins

*Magnificent Birds* by Narisa Togo

**Telling a Story with Photos**

*Face to Face with Whales* by Flip and Linda Nicklin

*A Bear's Life* by Nicholas Read

### Independent Reading Collection

*How Can We Reduce Household Waste?* by Mary K. Pratt

As you read aloud and enjoy these texts together, help students notice the different ways that authors organize information.

**Reading Minilesson Principle**
# Nonfiction authors tell information in time order like a story.

## You Will Need

- two or three familiar narrative nonfiction books, such as the following from Text Set: Innovative Thinking and Creative Problem Solving:
  - *Ivan* by Katherine Applegate
  - *One Plastic Bag* by Miranda Paul
  - *Parrots Over Puerto Rico* by Susan L. Roth and Cindy Trumbore
- chart paper and markers

## Academic Language / Important Vocabulary

- nonfiction
- author
- organize
- information
- time order
- story

### Continuum Connection

- Notice a nonfiction writer's use of narrative text structure in biography and narrative nonfiction (p. 63)
- Understand when a writer is telling information in a sequence (chronological order) (p. 63)

## Goal

Notice when an author uses a narrative text structure and tells information in chronological order.

## Rationale

When you teach students that some nonfiction books have a narrative text structure, they understand that, though such a book may be told like a story, it is still nonfiction because it provides true information. They also learn that nonfiction authors must make decisions about how best to convey information.

## Assess Learning

Observe students when they read and talk about nonfiction books and notice if there is evidence of new learning based on the goal of this minilesson.

- ◗ Do students notice when a nonfiction book has a narrative text structure?
- ◗ Can they identify the sequence of events in a narrative nonfiction book?
- ◗ Do they use academic language, such as *nonfiction, author, organize, information, time order,* and *story*?

# Minilesson

To help students think about the minilesson principle, use familiar nonfiction books to help them notice narrative text structures. Here is an example.

- ◗ Show the cover of *Ivan* and read the title. Read pages 1–4.

    What happens at the beginning of this book?

    What happens next? Then what happens?

    How does the book end?

- ◗ Record students' responses on chart paper.

    What do you notice about how the author organized the information about Ivan's life? In what order did she put the information?

- ◗ Show the cover of *One Plastic Bag* and briefly go through the pages to remind students of the book.

    What happened at the beginning, the middle, and the end of this book?

- ◗ Record students' responses on the chart.

    How do you think the author decided what to tell at the beginning, what to tell about the events in the middle, and what to tell at the end of the book? Talk about the way the writer organized the information.

## Have a Try

Invite the students to talk with a partner about *Parrots Over Puerto Rico*.

▶ Show the cover of *Parrots Over Puerto Rico* and read the title. Briefly go through the pages of the book.

Turn and talk to your partner about how the authors organized the information in this book.

▶ After students turn and talk, invite a few students to share their thinking. Record responses on the chart.

## Summarize and Apply

Summarize the learning and remind students to notice the organization of nonfiction books.

Sometimes nonfiction authors tell information in the order that events happened, like a story. This is called narrative nonfiction.

▶ Write the principle at the top of the chart.

If you read a nonfiction book today, think about how the author organized the information. If the information in your book is in time order like a story, bring it to share when we come back together.

## Share

Following independent reading time, gather students together in the meeting area to talk about their reading.

Who read a nonfiction book that was organized like a story?

What happened at the beginning, middle, and end of your book?

## Extend the Lesson (Optional)

After assessing students' understanding, you might decide to extend the learning.

▶ Have students look for words and phrases that signal chronological order, such as *first*, *next*, *finally*, *previously*, *after*, and *three years later (earlier)*. You might wish to make an anchor chart of examples of time-order words for students to refer to when they write. For a list of words that show chronological order, visit resources.fountasandpinnell.com.

▶ **Writing About Reading** Have students make a timeline of the events in a narrative nonfiction book. Students can make their own timelines or fill in a graphic organizer (visit resources.fountasandpinnell.com).

**Section 2: Literary Analysis**

**Reading Minilesson Principle**

# Nonfiction authors organize information into categories and subcategories.

## Noticing How Nonfiction Authors Choose to Organize Information

### You Will Need

- two familiar nonfiction books that have information organized into categories and, optimally, subcategories, such as the following from Text Set: Illustration Study: Craft:
  - *Eye to Eye* by Steve Jenkins
  - *Magnificent Birds* by Narisa Togo
- chart paper and markers

### Academic Language / Important Vocabulary

- nonfiction
- author
- organize
- information
- category
- subcategory

### Continuum Connection

- Notice a nonfiction writer's use of categories and subcategories to organize an informational text [p. 63]

### Goal

Notice when nonfiction authors organize information into categories and subcategories.

### Rationale

When students notice the organization of information into categories and subcategories, they are able to recognize relationships and make connections between different details. They are also better able to find information in nonfiction books and organize their own nonfiction texts.

### Assess Learning

Observe students when they read and talk about nonfiction books and notice if there is evidence of new learning based on the goal of this minilesson.

- Do students notice when the information in a nonfiction book is organized into categories and subcategories?
- Do they use academic language, such as *nonfiction, author, organize, information, category,* and *subcategory*?

## Minilesson

To help students think about the minilesson principle, use familiar nonfiction books to help students notice categories and subcategories of information. Here is an example.

- Show the cover of *Eye to Eye* and read the title. Open to pages 3–4. Read aloud the first paragraph of the section titled "The first eyes."

  What is the topic of this whole book?

  What kind of information is in this part of the book?

- Read aloud the section titled "Four kinds of eye."

  What kind of information is on the bottom half of these pages?

  How did the author organize the information on these two pages?

  The author organized the information on these pages in two big categories. The first category is about the first eyes and the second category is about different kinds of eyes. How did the author organize the information about different kinds of eyes?

  The author organized the information about different kinds of eyes in four smaller categories, each about a different kind of eye. When a category is split up into smaller categories, each of the smaller categories is called a subcategory.

- Make a chart showing how the information on these pages is divided into categories and subcategories.

## Have a Try

Invite the students to talk with a partner about the organization of the information in *Magnificent Birds*.

▶ Show the cover of *Magnificent Birds* and read the title. Display a few pages of the book.

> Turn and talk to your partner about how the author of this book organized the information about birds.

▶ After students turn and talk, invite a few students to share their thinking. If needed, guide students to understand that the author organized the information into categories—each page is about a different kind of bird.

## Summarize and Apply

Summarize the learning and remind students to notice the organization of nonfiction books.

> What did you notice about how the authors of the nonfiction books organized their information?

▶ Write the principle at the top of the chart.

> If you read a nonfiction book today, think about how the author organized the information. If the information in your book is organized into categories and subcategories, bring it to share when we come back together.

## Share

Following independent reading time, gather students together in the meeting area to talk about their reading.

> Did anyone read a nonfiction book that is organized by category?

> What categories of information did you read about?

> Were any of those categories divided into subcategories?

## Extend the Lesson (Optional)

After assessing students' understanding, you might decide to extend the learning.

▶ Have students write their own nonfiction texts that are organized into categories and subcategories. Show them how to use graphic organizers to plan their writing.

▶ **Writing About Reading** Have students write about a nonfiction book in which the information is organized into categories and subcategories. They should explain why this helped them to better understand the content.

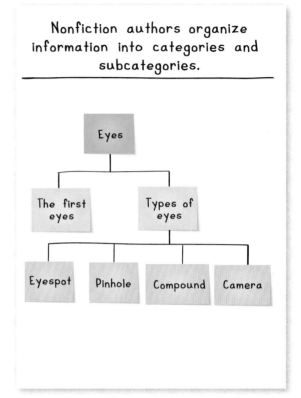

Nonfiction authors organize information into categories and subcategories.

Eyes
- The first eyes
- Types of eyes
  - Eyespot
  - Pinhole
  - Compound
  - Camera

**Reading Minilesson Principle**

# Nonfiction authors organize information by comparing and contrasting two things.

## Noticing How Nonfiction Authors Choose to Organize Information

### You Will Need

- two familiar nonfiction books that contain examples of compare-and-contrast text structure, such as the following from Text Set: Telling a Story with Photos:
  - *Face to Face with Whales* by Flip and Linda Nicklin
  - *A Bear's Life* by Nicholas Read
- chart paper and markers

### Academic Language / Important Vocabulary

- nonfiction
- author
- organize
- information
- compare
- contrast

### Continuum Connection

- Recognize and understand a writer's use of underlying text structures: e.g., categorical, description, sequence (chronological, temporal), compare and contrast, cause and effect, problem and solution, question and answer, combination (p. 63)

## Goal

Notice when nonfiction authors organize information using a compare-and-contrast structure.

## Rationale

When you teach students to recognize compare-and-contrast text structures, they are better able to acquire and understand information about how two things are alike or different. They also understand that nonfiction writers must make decisions about how best to present information.

## Assess Learning

Observe students when they read and talk about nonfiction books and notice if there is evidence of new learning based on the goal of this minilesson.

- Do students notice compare-and-contrast structures in nonfiction books?
- Do they use academic language, such as *nonfiction, author, organize, information, compare,* and *contrast*?

## Minilesson

To help students think about the minilesson principle, use familiar nonfiction books to help them notice compare-and-contrast text structures. Here is an example.

- Show the cover of *Face to Face with Whales* and read the title. Read aloud pages 18–21.

  What do you notice about how the author organized information in this part of the book?

- Record students' responses on chart paper.

  The author wrote about two main types of whales and explained how they are different. When writers write about how two things are the same or different, they compare and contrast them. What are the two types of whales, and how are they different?

- Use students' responses to make a chart contrasting types of whales.

## Have a Try

Invite the students to talk with a partner about the organization of the information in *A Bear's Life*.

▶ Show the cover of *A Bear's Life* and read the title. Read pages 4–7.

> Turn and talk to your partner about what you notice about how the author organized information in this part of the book.

▶ After students turn and talk, invite a few students to share their thinking.

## Summarize and Apply

Summarize the learning and remind students to notice how nonfiction books are organized.

> What did you notice today about how some nonfiction authors sometimes organize information?

▶ Write the principle at the top of the chart.

> If you read a nonfiction book today, think about how the writer organized the information in your book. If you find a page or a section in your book that the writer organized by comparing and contrasting two things, bring it to share when we come back together.

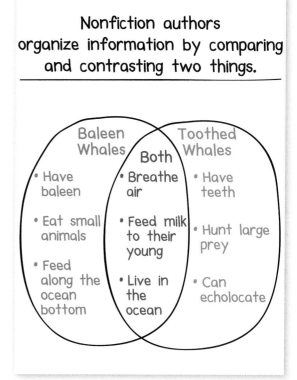

## Share

Following independent reading time, gather students together in the meeting area to talk about their reading.

> Who found an example of compare-and-contrast organization in your book?

> How did the comparison (or contrast) help you understand what the author wanted you to learn?

## Extend the Lesson (Optional)

After assessing students' understanding, you might decide to extend the learning.

▶ Point out words and phrases that indicate items are being compared or contrasted, such as *same as, similar to, like, different (or differs) from, opposite of,* and *unlike.* For a list of words that signal comparison and contrast, see resources.fountasandpinnell.com. You might have students make a poster of these words to refer to when they write.

Section 2: Literary Analysis

# RML4
## LA.U16.RML4

**Reading Minilesson Principle**
## Nonfiction authors organize information using cause and effect.

### Noticing How Nonfiction Authors Choose to Organize Information

**You Will Need**

- two familiar nonfiction books that contain examples of cause-and-effect text structure, such as the following:
  - *How Can We Reduce Household Waste?* by Mary K. Pratt, from *Independent Reading Collection*
  - *Parrots Over Puerto Rico* by Susan L. Roth and Cindy Trumbore, from Text Set: Innovative Thinking and Creative Problem Solving
- chart paper and markers

**Academic Language / Important Vocabulary**

- nonfiction
- author
- organize
- information
- cause
- effect

**Continuum Connection**

- Recognize and understand a writer's use of underlying text structures: e.g., categorical, description, sequence (chronological, temporal), compare and contrast, cause and effect, problem and solution, question and answer, combination (p. 63)

## Goal

Notice when nonfiction authors organize information using cause and effect.

## Rationale

When you teach students to recognize cause-and-effect text structures, they are better able to understand causal relationships. They also understand that nonfiction writers must make decisions about how best to present information.

## Assess Learning

Observe students when they read and talk about nonfiction books and notice if there is evidence of new learning based on the goal of this minilesson.

- ▶ Do students notice cause-and-effect structures in nonfiction books?
- ▶ Do they use academic language, such as *nonfiction, author, organize, information, cause,* and *effect*?

## Minilesson

To help students think about the minilesson principle, use familiar nonfiction books to help them notice cause-and-effect text structures. Here is an example.

▶ Show the cover of *How Can We Reduce Household Waste?* and read the title. Read pages 25–26.

Let's think about how the author organized information on these pages. What is page 26 about?

Page 26 is about the effects of pollution from cleaning products. What are the effects?

What causes these effects?

▶ Record students' responses on chart paper.

On page 25, the author tells about the cause of these effects: people use soaps and shampoos, and then the chemicals get washed down the drain and build up in the environment. What could you say about how the author organized information on these pages?

The author organized information using cause and effect. She tells about the cause on page 25 and the effects on page 26. A cause is something that makes something else happen, and an effect is something that happens because of a cause.

## Have a Try

Invite the students to talk with a partner about the how the information is organized in *Parrots Over Puerto Rico*.

▶ Show the cover of *Parrots Over Puerto Rico* and read the title. Read page 28.

> Think about how the authors organized the information on this page. What was the cause and what were the effects? Turn and talk to share your thinking with your partner.

▶ After time for discussion, invite a few students to share. Record their responses on the chart.

## Summarize and Apply

Summarize the learning and remind students to notice how nonfiction books are organized.

> What did you notice today about how nonfiction authors sometimes organize information?

▶ Write the principle at the top of the chart.

> If you read a nonfiction book today, think about how the information in your book is organized. If you find a page or a section in your book that is organized using cause and effect, bring it to share when we come back together.

## Share

Following independent reading time, gather students together in the meeting area to talk about their reading.

> Did anyone notice information the writer organized by cause and effect?

> In the book you read, what is the cause and what is the effect?

## Extend the Lesson (Optional)

After assessing students' understanding, you might decide to extend the learning.

▶ Help students understand that something can be both a cause and an effect (if *X* causes *Y*, which then causes *Z*, then *Y* is both a cause and an effect).

▶ Teach students that one effect can have more than one cause and that one cause can lead to more than one effect.

▶ Point out words and phrases that show cause and effect, such as *because, so, if . . . then, as a result of, due to,* and *as a consequence of.* You might have students make a poster to refer to when they write.

---

> Nonfiction authors organize information using cause and effect.

| CAUSE | EFFECT |
|---|---|
| (Something that makes something else happen) | (Something that happens because of a cause) |
| Cleaning products get washed down the drain.  | Animals and people have health problems. |
| Hurricane Hugo  | Buildings, homes, and trees destroyed |

### Reading Minilesson Principle
# Nonfiction authors organize information by explaining the problem and solution.

## Noticing How Nonfiction Authors Choose to Organize Information

### You Will Need

- two familiar nonfiction books that contain examples of problem-and-solution text structure, such as the following:
  - *How Can We Reduce Household Waste?* by Mary K. Pratt, from *Independent Reading Collection*
  - *Parrots Over Puerto Rico* by Susan L. Roth and Cindy Trumbore, from Text Set: Innovative Thinking and Creative Problem Solving
- chart paper and markers

### Academic Language / Important Vocabulary

- nonfiction
- author
- organize
- information
- problem
- solution

### Continuum Connection

- Recognize and understand a writer's use of underlying text structures: e.g., categorical, description, sequence (chronological, temporal), compare and contrast, cause and effect, problem and solution, question and answer, combination (p. 63)

## Goal

Notice when nonfiction authors organize information by explaining the problem and solution.

## Rationale

When you teach students to recognize problem-and-solution text structures, they are better able to acquire and understand information pertaining to problems and solutions. They also understand that nonfiction writers must make decisions about how best to present information.

## Assess Learning

Observe students when they read and talk about nonfiction books and notice if there is evidence of new learning based on the goal of this minilesson.

- Do students notice problem-and-solution structures in nonfiction books?
- Do they use academic language, such as *nonfiction, author, organize, information, problem,* and *solution*?

## Minilesson

To help students think about the minilesson principle, use familiar nonfiction books to help students notice problem-and-solution structures. Here is an example.

- Show the cover of *How Can We Reduce Household Waste?* and read the title. Read pages 26–27.

  The author told about the problems caused by cleaning products on page 26. What is page 27 about?

  Page 27 is about the solution to these problems. What solution did the author suggest?

- Write the problem and the solution on chart paper.

  How did the author organize information on these pages?

  The author organized information by explaining the problem and then explaining the solution.

## Have a Try

Invite the students to talk with a partner about how the information is organized in *Parrots Over Puerto Rico*.

▸ Show the cover of *Parrots Over Puerto Rico* and read the title. Read page 24.

> Think about how the authors organized information on this page by explaining the problem and the solution. What was the problem and what was the solution? Turn and talk to your partner about what you think.

▸ After students turn and talk, invite a few students to share their thinking. Record responses on the chart.

## Summarize and Apply

Summarize the learning and remind students to notice how nonfiction books are organized.

> What did you notice today about how nonfiction authors sometimes organize information?

▸ Write the principle at the top of the chart.

> If you read a nonfiction book today, think about how the author organized the information in your book. If you find a page or a section in your book that the author organized by explaining the problem and solution, bring it to share when we come back together.

## Share

Following independent reading, gather students together in the meeting area to talk about their reading.

> Did anyone read a book in which the author organized information by explaining the problem and the solution?

> What was the problem and what was the solution?

## Extend the Lesson (Optional)

After assessing students' understanding, you might decide to extend the learning.

▸ Point out words and phrases that show cause and effect, such as *problem, solution, to solve the problem, one reason is that, this led to that, so that, therefore,* and *nevertheless.* You might have students make a poster to refer to when they write.

---

Nonfiction authors organize information by explaining the problem and solution.

| PROBLEM | SOLUTION |
|---|---|
| Pollution from cleaning products | Use cleaning products that have few harmful chemicals. |
| Only 13 parrots were left in the rain forest. | Scientists built nesting boxes. |

Section 2: Literary Analysis

**Reading Minilesson Principle**

# Nonfiction authors organize information in several ways within the same book.

## Noticing How Nonfiction Authors Choose to Organize Information

### You Will Need

- two familiar nonfiction books that contain multiple text structures, such as the following:
  - *Parrots Over Puerto Rico* by Susan L. Roth and Cindy Trumbore, from Text Set: Innovative Thinking and Creative Problem Solving
  - *How Can We Reduce Household Waste?* by Mary K. Pratt, from *Independent Reading Collection*
- chart paper and markers

### Academic Language / Important Vocabulary

- nonfiction
- author
- organize
- information

### Continuum Connection

- Recognize and understand a writer's use of underlying text structures: e.g., categorical, description, sequence (chronological, temporal), compare and contrast, cause and effect, problem and solution, question and answer, combination (p. 63)

## Goal

Understand that sometimes nonfiction authors use several different organizational structures within the same book.

## Rationale

When students notice that nonfiction authors sometimes use several different organizational structures within the same book, they understand that nonfiction writers are constantly making decisions about how best to organize information and that different types of information are suited to different structures.

## Assess Learning

Observe students when they read and talk about nonfiction books and notice if there is evidence of new learning based on the goal of this minilesson.

- Can students identify multiple organizational structures within a single nonfiction book?
- Do they use academic language, such as *nonfiction, author, organize,* and *information*?

## Minilesson

To help students think about the minilesson principle, use familiar nonfiction books to help students notice the variety of organizational structures writers use in books. Here is an example.

- Show the cover of *Parrots Over Puerto Rico.*

  We have been talking about different ways that authors organize information in nonfiction books. What did you notice about how the authors of *Parrots Over Puerto Rico* organized the information?

- Record students' responses on chart paper. If necessary, revisit the specific pages from the book that you discussed during previous minilessons (problem and solution: p. 24; cause and effect: p. 28) and ask:

  What did you notice about how the authors organized information on this page?

  You noticed that the authors of this book organized information in several different ways.

- Show the cover of *How Can We Reduce Household Waste?*

  What did you notice about how the author of this book organized information?

- Record students' responses on the chart. Revisit pages 25–27 if necessary.

## Have a Try

Invite the students to talk with a partner about how the information is organized in *How Can We Reduce Household Waste?*

❱ Display the table of contents of *How Can We Reduce Household Waste?*

What's another way that the author of *How Can We Reduce Household Waste?* organized information? The table of contents gives a clue. Turn and talk to your partner about that.

❱ After students turn and talk, invite a few students to share their thinking. If needed, help students understand that the author also organized information using categories. Add responses to the chart.

## Summarize and Apply

Summarize the learning and remind students to notice how nonfiction books are organized.

What did you notice today about how writers organize information in some nonfiction books?

❱ Write the principle at the top of the chart.

If you read a nonfiction book today, think about all the different ways the information in your book is organized. Be ready to share when we meet again after independent reading.

## Share

Following independent reading time, gather students together in the meeting area to talk about their reading.

Who read a nonfiction book today?

In what ways is the information in your book organized?

## Extend the Lesson (Optional)

After assessing students' understanding, you might decide to extend the learning.

❱ **Writing About Reading** Have students make a list in a reader's notebook of all the different organizational structures they found in a particular nonfiction book and provide evidence of each. Have them make note of the signal words the writer used.

---

### Nonfiction authors organize information in several ways within the same book.

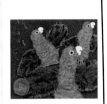

- Time order
- Cause and effect
- Problem and solution

- Cause and effect
- Problem and solution
- Categories

## Assessment

After you have taught the minilessons in this umbrella, observe students as they talk and write about their reading across instructional contexts: interactive read-aloud, independent reading, guided reading, shared reading, and book club. Use *The Literacy Continuum* (Fountas and Pinnell 2017) to guide the observation of students' reading and writing behaviors.

- ❱ What evidence do you have of new understandings related to organizational structures in nonfiction?
  - Are students able to identify organizational structures (e.g., narrative, categories and subcategories, compare and contrast, cause and effect, problem and solution)?
  - Do students understand that writers can organize information in multiple ways within the same text?
  - Do they use academic language, such as *nonfiction, author, organize, information, category, compare, contrast, cause,* and *effect*?
- ❱ In what other ways, beyond the scope of this umbrella, are students talking about nonfiction?
  - Have they noticed that there are different genres of nonfiction?
  - Have they started to read nonfiction with a critical eye?
  - Are they thinking about illustrations and graphics?
  - Are they using text features to gain information?

Use your observations to determine the next umbrella you will teach. You may also consult Minilessons Across the Year (pp. 59–61) for guidance.

## Link to Writing

After teaching the minilessons in this umbrella, help students link the new learning to their own writing:

- ❱ Give students various opportunities to write their own nonfiction texts throughout the school year. Remind them of the different ways to organize nonfiction and discuss how to choose the most appropriate organizational structure for the topic.

## Reader's Notebook

When this umbrella is complete, provide a copy of the minilesson principles (see resources.fountasandpinnell.com) for students to glue in the reader's notebook (in the Minilessons section if using *Reader's Notebook: Intermediate* [Fountas and Pinnell 2011]), so they can refer to the information as needed.

## Minilessons in This Umbrella

**RML1**  Notice how the author feels about the topic.

**RML2**  Notice the difference between fact and opinion.

**RML3**  Read multiple sources of information about a topic.

**RML4**  Use multiple sources to answer a bigger question.

**RML5**  Think about the accuracy and quality of the nonfiction books you read.

## Before Teaching Umbrella 17 Minilessons

When students read informational text like a scientist, they approach each informational text with a critical eye. They consider how the author's point of view influences his or her approach to the topic, and they are able to differentiate between fact and opinion. They evaluate the quality and accuracy of the texts they read, and they synthesize information from multiple sources to arrive at a deeper understanding of a topic or an idea.

Before teaching the minilessons in this umbrella, read and discuss engaging informational texts about a variety of high-interest topics. Use the following texts from the *Fountas & Pinnell Classroom™ Interactive Read-Aloud Collection* and *Guided Reading Collection* or choose nonfiction books from your classroom library.

### Interactive Read-Aloud Collection

**Telling a Story with Photos**

*Face to Face with Whales* by Flip and Linda Nicklin

*A Little Book of Sloth* by Lucy Cooke

**Genre Study: Biography (Individuals Making a Difference)**

*Six Dots* by Jen Bryant

**Innovative Thinking and Creative Problem Solving**

*Hands Around the Library* by Susan L. Roth and Karen Leggett Abouraya

*Ivan* by Katherine Applegate

### Guided Reading Collection

*The Sloth: Living with Less* by Kirsten W. Larson

*Temple Grandin's Squeeze Machine* by Alice B. McGinty

*Daniel Kish: A Different Way to See* by Julius Smitherson

As you read aloud and enjoy these texts together, help students

- infer the author's attitude toward the topic,
- identify facts and opinions, and
- express opinions about books.

*Interactive Read-Aloud*
**Photos**

*Face to Face with Whales* by Flip and Linda Nicklin

**Biography**

**Innovative Thinking**

**Guided Reading**

**Section 2: Literary Analysis**

# RML1
## LA.U17.RML1

### Reading Minilesson Principle
## Notice how the author feels about the topic.

## Reading Informational Text Like a Scientist

### You Will Need

- two or three familiar nonfiction books that reveal clues about how the author feels about the topic, such as the following:
  - *Face to Face with Whales* by Flip and Linda Nicklin, from Text Set: Telling a Story with Photos
  - *Ivan* by Katherine Applegate, from Text Set: Innovative Thinking and Creative Problem Solving
  - *A Little Book of Sloth* by Lucy Cooke, from Text Set: Telling a Story with Photos
- chart paper and markers

### Academic Language / Important Vocabulary

- author
- nonfiction
- point of view
- topic

### Continuum Connection

- Infer the writer's attitude toward a topic (p. 63)
- Infer the importance of a topic of a nonfiction text (p. 63)

## Goal

Infer the writer's attitude or point of view toward the topic of a nonfiction book.

## Rationale

When you teach students to infer a nonfiction writer's attitude or point of view toward the topic of the book, they begin to understand that the author's feelings about the topic influence how the book is written. Eventually they will come to the understanding that, although nonfiction books are based in fact, they are not completely objective.

## Assess Learning

Observe students when they read and talk about nonfiction books and notice if there is evidence of new learning based on the goal of this minilesson.

- Do students make inferences about the author's point of view?
- Can they explain why it is important to consider the author's attitude?
- Do they use academic vocabulary, such as *author, nonfiction, point of view,* and *topic*?

## Minilesson

To help students think about the minilesson principle, use familiar nonfiction books to engage them in analyzing the author's attitude toward a topic. Here is an example.

- Show the cover of *Face to Face with Whales* and read the title.

  As I read a couple of pages from this book, think about how the authors feel about whales.

- Read pages 5–7.

  How do the authors feel about whales? How do you know?

- Record students' responses on chart paper.

  Every nonfiction author has an attitude or point of view toward the topic they are writing about. Someone's point of view is how that person looks at or thinks about a topic or issue.

- Show the cover of *Ivan* and read the title. Read pages 7–10.

  What do you think is the author's point of view toward the people who took Ivan out of the forest? How does she feel about them?

  How do you know?

- Record students' responses on the chart.

  How might this book be different if the people who took Ivan from the forest wrote the book?

## Have a Try

Invite the students to talk with a partner about *A Little Book of Sloth*.

▶ Show the cover of *A Little Book of Sloth* and then read page 2.

> Turn and talk to your partner about how the author feels about sloths. What is her point of view toward sloths? Be sure to explain how you know.

▶ After students turn and talk, invite a few students to share their thinking. Record their responses on the chart.

> How might the book be different if the author didn't like sloths at all?

## Summarize and Apply

Summarize the learning and remind students to think about the author's point of view when they read nonfiction.

> Today you thought about the author's attitude, or point of view, toward the topic in a few nonfiction books. Why might it be important to think about how the author feels about a topic?

▶ Write the principle at the top of the chart.

> Today you will read a nonfiction book. Think about the author's point of view, or how the author feels about the topic.

## Share

Following independent reading time, gather students together in the meeting area to talk about their reading.

> What is the author's point of view toward the topic of the book you read today? How do you know?

## Extend the Lesson (Optional)

After assessing students' understanding, you might decide to extend the learning.

▶ Help students understand that authors sometimes reveal their point of view directly (as in *Face to Face with Whales* and *A Little Book of Sloth*) and sometimes indirectly (as in *Ivan*). Discuss how an author's choice of words can indirectly reveal his or her point of view (e.g., the word *stole* instead of *took*).

### Notice how the author feels about the topic.

| Book | Author's Point of View | Evidence |
|------|------------------------|----------|
| Face to Face with Whales | He is excited about and fascinated by whales. | "I tried to quiet my excited breathing" <br><br> "It was thrilling . . ." |
| Ivan | She thinks it was wrong to capture Ivan and take him to America. | "cruel hands" <br><br> "stole the little gorilla" |
| A Little Book of Sloth | She loves sloths. | "I love sloths" <br><br> "I love their sweet smiles, slow-mo lifestyle, and innate hugability". |

Section 2: Literary Analysis

## RML2
### LA.U17.RML2

**Reading Minilesson Principle**
# Notice the difference between fact and opinion.

## Reading Informational Text Like a Scientist

### You Will Need

- two familiar nonfiction books that contain clear examples of both facts and opinions, such as the following:
  - *A Little Book of Sloth* by Lucy Cooke, from Text Set: Telling a Story with Photos
  - *Hands Around the Library* by Susan L. Roth and Karen Leggett Abouraya, from Text Set: Innovative Thinking and Creative Problem Solving
- chart paper prepared with a fact sentence and an opinion sentence from *A Little Book of Sloth* [see next page]
- markers
- sticky notes

### Academic Language / Important Vocabulary

- nonfiction
- author
- fact
- opinion

### Continuum Connection

- Distinguish fact from opinion [p. 63]

## Goal

Distinguish fact from opinion.

## Rationale

When you teach students how to distinguish fact from opinion, they are better able to read nonfiction with a critical eye. They are better able to assess the quality and accuracy of the books they read. They also learn when to use facts and when to use opinions, both orally and in writing.

## Assess Learning

Observe students when they read and talk about nonfiction books and notice if there is evidence of new learning based on the goal of this minilesson.

- ▶ Can students identify both facts and opinions in nonfiction books?
- ▶ Can they explain the difference between a fact and an opinion?
- ▶ Do they use academic vocabulary, such as *nonfiction, author, fact,* and *opinion*?

# Minilesson

To help students think about the minilesson principle, use familiar nonfiction books to engage them in distinguishing between facts and opinions. Here is an example.

- ▶ Show the cover of *A Little Book of Sloth*. Read the two sentences on the chart aloud.

   > What do you notice about these sentences from the book?

- ▶ If necessary, prompt students to notice how they are different from each other.

   > One of these sentences contains facts, and one of them contains opinions. Which one contains facts? What makes you think that?

   > This sentence sounds like a fact because it gives specific, detailed information about sloths' bodies. If I want to make sure that the sentence contains facts, or true information, I can check by looking in other resources for information about sloths.

   > How can you tell that the other sentences contain opinions?

   > These are opinions because they cannot be proven true or false. Which words give you a clue that the author is giving her opinion?

   > Sometimes authors will use words like *love, think,* or *believe* when they are telling their opinions.

- ▶ Discuss the definition of *fact* and *opinion* and write the agreed-upon definitions in the definition column on the chart.

## Have a Try

Invite the students to talk with a partner about *Hands Around the Library*.

▶ Read aloud page 5 of *Hands Around the Library*.

Is this a fact or an opinion: "They had set fire to cars and to a police station"? Turn and talk to your partner about that.

▶ After students turn and talk, invite a few of them to share their thinking. Add the sentence to the chart.

▶ Read page 7.

Think about the sentence "Alexandria Library . . . is the most beautiful modern building in all of Egypt." Turn and talk to your partner about whether this is a fact or an opinion.

▶ After time for discussion, ask volunteers to explain their reasoning. Add the sentence to the chart.

### Notice the difference between fact and opinion.

|  | Definition | Examples |
|---|---|---|
| FACT | Information that can be proven to be true | "Three-fingered sloths are the only mammal on the planet with extra neck vertebrae and can turn their heads up to 270 degrees."<br><br>"They had set fire to cars and to a police station." |
| OPINION | An idea that somebody thinks or believes. It cannot be proven true or false. | "I love sloths. I love their sweet smiles, slo-mo lifestyle, and innate hugability."<br><br>"Alexandria Library . . . is the most beautiful modern building in all of Egypt." |

## Summarize and Apply

Summarize the learning and remind students to remember the difference between fact and opinion when they read nonfiction.

Should nonfiction books have more facts or more opinions? Why?

▶ Write the principle at the top of the chart.

When you finish the book you are reading, read a nonfiction book. Use sticky notes to mark an example of a fact and an example of an opinion, and bring your examples to share when we come back together.

## Share

Following independent reading time, gather students together in the meeting area to talk about their reading.

Who would like to share an example of a fact from the book you read today?

Who would like to share an example of an opinion?

## Extend the Lesson (Optional)

After assessing students' understanding, you might decide to extend the learning.

▶ Help students understand that, although they cannot be proven true or false, opinions can be either well supported or poorly supported by evidence.

Section 2: Literary Analysis

# RML 3
## LA.U17.RML3

Reading Minilesson Principle
# Read multiple sources of information about a topic.

### Reading Informational Text Like a Scientist

## You Will Need

- three sources of information about a single topic, such as the following:
  - *A Little Book of Sloth* by Lucy Cooke, from Text Set: Telling a Story with Photos
  - *The Sloth: Living with Less* by Kirsten W. Larson, from *Guided Reading Collection*
  - an internet resource about why sloths are inactive (e.g., "Why are sloths so slow?" by Cristen Conger, HowStuffWorks.com)
- chart paper and markers

## Academic Language / Important Vocabulary

- information
- multiple
- source
- topic
- nonfiction

## Continuum Connection

- Think across nonfiction texts to construct knowledge of a topic (p. 63)

## Goal

Think across nonfiction texts to construct knowledge of a topic and confirm accuracy of content.

## Rationale

When you teach students to read multiple sources of information about a topic, they learn more about the topic and develop their ability to synthesize information and judge its accuracy across sources. They learn that every resource is incomplete because the writer has selected information, and they begin to read nonfiction with a more critical eye.

## Assess Learning

Observe students when they read and talk about nonfiction books and notice if there is evidence of new learning based on the goal of this minilesson.

- Can students explain why it is important to read multiple sources of information?
- Can they explain how each source adds to their learning about the topic?
- Do they use academic vocabulary, such as *information, multiple, source, topic,* and *nonfiction*?

# Minilesson

To help students think about the minilesson principle, use familiar nonfiction books to provide an inquiry-based lesson about reading multiple sources of information. Here is an example.

- Show the cover of *A Little Book of Sloth*. Read page 12 aloud.

  What did you learn about sloths from this page?

- Record students' responses on chart paper.

  Listen carefully as I read a page from another book about sloths. Notice if there is any new information.

- Show the cover of *The Sloth: Living with Less*. Read page 4.

  What did you learn from this page about why sloths move as little as possible?

- Record responses on the chart.

  How did reading another source about sloths add to your learning? What did it help you understand?

  The first source taught you that sloths don't move very much, but it doesn't really explain why. The second source explains that sloths stay still in order to stay safe. It also gives more details about how slow sloths are and how much time they spend resting.

## Have a Try

Invite the students to talk with a partner about how a third source adds to or contradicts their knowledge.

▶ Show students the internet resource about sloths. Read or paraphrase a short portion (for example, paragraph 4 of "Why are sloths so slow?").

Turn and talk to your partner about how this source adds to your learning about sloths. What does it help you understand about sloths?

▶ After students turn and talk, invite a few students to share their thinking. Record their responses.

## Summarize and Apply

Summarize the learning and remind students to read multiple sources of information.

Today we read three sources of information about sloths. Why is it important to read multiple sources of information about a topic?

When you read like a scientist, you read multiple sources of information so you can be sure you are gaining an accurate and more complete understanding of the topic.

▶ Write the principle at the top of the chart.

If you read a nonfiction book today, think whether you'd like to learn more about the topic or confirm the information by reading additional sources. If so, look for another source of information about the topic, and ask me for help if you need it.

## Share

Following independent reading time, gather students together in the meeting area to talk about their reading.

Who found multiple sources of information about a topic today?

How did reading multiple sources add to your learning?

## Extend the Lesson (Optional)

After assessing students' understanding, you might decide to extend the learning.

▶ Help students compare and contrast two sources of information about a topic. Discuss why the authors may have made different choices about what information to include or how to present it.

| Read multiple sources of information about a topic. | |
|---|---|
| Source 1: A Little Book of Sloth | • Sloths spend their whole lives hanging about in trees. |
| Source 2: The Sloth: Living with Less | • Sloths spend about 15 hours a day hanging from branches.<br>• Staying still helps sloths stay safe. |
| Source 3: "Why are sloths so slow?" (website) | • Sloths are slow because they have little energy.<br>• They have little energy because they eat nothing but leaves, fruits, flowers, and branches. |

Section 2: Literary Analysis

## Reading Informational Text Like a Scientist

### You Will Need

- three nonfiction sources centered around a single topic or theme, such as the following:
  - *Six Dots* by Jen Bryant, from Text Set: Genre Study: Biography (Individuals Making a Difference)
  - *Daniel Kish: A Different Way to See* by Julius Smitherson and *Temple Grandin's Squeeze Machine* by Alice B. McGinty, from *Guided Reading Collection*
- a research question about the sources listed above
- several other research questions and basket of relevant sources for each one (see Summarize and Apply)
- chart paper and markers

### Academic Language / Important Vocabulary

- source
- nonfiction

### Continuum Connection

- Think across nonfiction texts to compare and expand understanding of content and ideas from academic disciplines: e.g., social responsibility, environment, climate, history, social and geological history, cultural groups (p. 63)

### Goal

Use multiple sources of information to answer a research question.

### Rationale

When you teach students to use multiple sources to answer a bigger question, they gain the ability to read nonfiction purposefully. They also develop the understanding that different nonfiction writers may approach the same theme or topic from different angles and that reading multiple sources allows them to gain a more complete understanding of the topic.

### Assess Learning

Observe students when they read and talk about nonfiction books and notice if there is evidence of new learning based on the goal of this minilesson.

- Do students read multiple sources when they are trying to answer a research question?
- Can they explain how each source helps them answer the question?
- Do they use academic vocabulary, such as *source* and *nonfiction*?

## Minilesson

To help students think about the minilesson principle, use familiar nonfiction books to engage them in thinking about how to use multiple sources to answer a bigger question. Here is an example.

- Write the research question that you prepared before class on chart paper (for example, "How do people with disabilities overcome challenges?").

  Sometimes when you read multiple sources about a theme or topic, you may have a big question that you want to answer. Think about this question as I reread a couple of pages from *Six Dots*.

- Show the cover of *Six Dots* and reread the last two pages.

  How does this book help you answer our question? What does it teach you about how people with disabilities overcome challenges?

- Record students' responses on chart paper.

- Show the cover of *Daniel Kish: A Different Way to See*. Read pages 6–7.

  What does this book help you understand about how people with disabilities overcome challenges?

- Record responses on the chart.

## Have a Try

Invite the students to talk with a partner about *Temple Grandin's Squeeze Machine*.

▶ Show the cover of *Temple Grandin's Squeeze Machine* and then reread page 12.

> Turn and talk to your partner about how this source helps you answer our big question.

▶ After students turn and talk, invite a few students to share their thinking. Record responses on the chart.

> What can we conclude about how people with disabilities overcome challenges?

▶ After time for discussion, invite several students to share their thinking. Combine their responses to create an agreed-upon class answer. Record it on the chart.

## Summarize and Apply

Summarize the learning for students.

> How can using multiple sources help you answer a bigger question?

▶ Display a sheet of chart paper that lists several bigger questions. For example: *How can people work together to create change? How can one person make a difference? Why is it important to learn about vanishing cultures? How should people treat wild animals?* Provide a basket of resources centered around each question.

> When you read today, think about one of these questions and read multiple sources to help you answer it. You can also come up with your own question and find your own sources in our classroom library.

## Share

Following independent reading time, gather students together to talk about their reading.

> What question did you think about? How did multiple sources help you answer it?

## Extend the Lesson (Optional)

After assessing students' understanding, you might decide to extend the learning.

▶ Have students write a research paper or information article. Have them define a research question. Then walk them through finding relevant sources, reading the sources and taking notes, organizing their information, and writing and editing.

---

**Use multiple sources to answer a bigger question.**

Big Question: How do people with disabilities overcome challenges?

| | |
|---|---|
|  | Louis Braille invented a way to read with his fingers since he couldn't read with his eyes. |
|  | Daniel Kish came up with a way to "see" with his ears since he can't see with his eyes. |
|  | Temple Grandin invented a machine that helped her get used to being touched. |

Answer: People with disabilities often use other abilities to find ways to do things that would otherwise be difficult or impossible for them.

Section 2: Literary Analysis

# RML5
## LA.U17.RML5

**Reading Minilesson Principle**
# Think about the accuracy and quality of the nonfiction books you read.

## Reading Informational Text Like a Scientist

### You Will Need

- two familiar nonfiction books, such as the following:
  - *A Little Book of Sloth* by Lucy Cooke, from Text Set: Telling a Story with Photos
  - *Ivan* by Katherine Applegate, from Text Set: Innovative Thinking and Creative Problem Solving
- another reliable source of information (book or website) about the topic of the first book you are using
- chart paper and markers

### Academic Language / Important Vocabulary

- nonfiction
- quality
- accuracy
- opinion
- information

### Continuum Connection

- Critically examine the quality or accuracy of the text, citing evidence for opinions (p. 64)

## Goal

Examine the quality or accuracy of the text, citing evidence for opinions.

## Rationale

Evaluating the quality and accuracy of nonfiction books is an essential component of reading with a critical eye—or "reading like a scientist." When students learn how to do so, they begin to understand that although nonfiction books are based in fact they are not necessarily perfect sources of information. This underlines the importance of reading multiple sources of information to learn about a topic.

## Assess Learning

Observe students when they read and talk about nonfiction books and notice if there is evidence of new learning based on the goal of this minilesson.

- Do students understand that some nonfiction books may contain inaccurate information?
- Do they understand and use the terms *nonfiction, quality, accuracy, opinion,* and *information*?

## Minilesson

To help students think about the minilesson principle, model examining the quality and accuracy of a familiar nonfiction book. Here is an example.

- Show the cover of *A Little Book of Sloth* and then reread page 31.

  I wonder if it's true that three-fingered sloths can turn their heads up to 270 degrees.

- Display another reliable source of information about three-fingered sloths.

  This website also says that three-fingered sloths can turn their heads up to 270 degrees. Two sources state the fact. That makes me think that the information in this nonfiction book is probably accurate. What did you notice about what I just did?

  When you think about the accuracy of the information in a nonfiction book, you think about whether it's true or correct.

  Some sources we looked at provided more detailed information than other sources. For example, this book contains the fact that sloths stay still most of the time but doesn't provide a reason why. This book doesn't always give a lot of specific details and facts. However, I still think it's a high-quality book. The author's writing is funny and playful, which made me want to read and learn more about sloths. Quality is how well done something is. How did I give my opinion about the quality of this book?

## Have a Try

Invite the students to talk with a partner about another book.

▸ Show the cover of *Ivan* and read the title.

Turn and talk to your partner about how you could check the accuracy of the information in this book.

▸ Ask a few students to share. Record responses on chart paper.

Now turn and talk to give your opinion about the quality of this book. Be sure to explain your reasons for your opinion.

▸ After time for discussion, invite a few students to share their opinions, and make a general list of the kinds of things they talk about.

## Summarize and Apply

Summarize the learning and remind students to think about the quality and accuracy of the nonfiction books they read.

Today you thought about the quality and accuracy of some nonfiction books. Why is it important to think about the quality and accuracy of the books you read?

▸ Write the principle at the top of the chart.

If you read a nonfiction book today, be sure to think about the quality and accuracy of the book. You can look for other sources if you want to check that the information in your book is accurate.

## Share

Following independent reading time, gather students together in the meeting area to talk about their reading.

Raise your hand if you read a nonfiction book today.

What is your opinion about the quality and accuracy of the book you read?

## Extend the Lesson (Optional)

After assessing students' understanding, you might decide to extend the learning.

▸ Discuss how to determine if a website is a reliable source of information. Explain that web addresses that end in .edu or .gov are usually good sources.

---

**Think about the accuracy and quality of the nonfiction books you read.**

| Accuracy | Quality |
|---|---|
| • Check the credentials of the author. | • What do I think of the author's writing style? |
| • Check the research the author has done on the topic. | • Is the book interesting and enjoyable? |
| • Read other books or websites about the topic. | • Did the book make me want to learn more about the topic? |
| • Compare the information in the book to the information in other sources. | • Are there high-quality photographs, illustrations or other helpful graphics? |

Section 2: Literary Analysis

## Assessment

After you have taught the minilessons in this umbrella, observe students as they talk and write about their reading across instructional contexts: interactive read-aloud, independent reading, guided reading, shared reading, and book club. Use *The Literacy Continuum* (Fountas and Pinnell 2017) to guide the observation of students' reading and writing behaviors.

▶ What evidence do you have of new understandings related to reading informational text like a scientist?

- Can students infer the author's point of view toward the topic?

- Can they distinguish fact from opinion?

- Can they demonstrate reading multiple sources to answer a bigger question?

- Can they evaluate the quality and accuracy of nonfiction books?

- Do they use academic vocabulary, such as *point of view, fact, opinion, source, information, quality, accuracy,* and *nonfiction*?

▶ In what other ways, beyond the scope of this umbrella, are students talking about nonfiction books?

- Are they noticing different organizational structures in nonfiction?

- Are they using text features to gain information?

Use your observations to determine the next umbrella you will teach. You may also consult Minilessons Across the Year (pp. 59–61) for guidance.

## Link to Writing

After teaching the minilessons in this umbrella, help students link the new learning to their own writing:

▶ Remind students to read and write like a scientist when they are researching and writing their own informational texts. Encourage them to use multiple sources of information, to evaluate the quality and accuracy of each one, and to synthesize information across sources. Remind them that informational texts include mostly facts, not opinions, and that all the information they include must be supported by evidence.

## Reader's Notebook

When this umbrella is complete, provide a copy of the minilesson principles (see resources.fountasandpinnell.com) for students to glue in the reader's notebook (in the Minilessons section if using *Reader's Notebook: Intermediate* [Fountas and Pinnell 2011]), so they can refer to the information as needed.

## Minilessons in This Umbrella

**RML1**   Authors use a variety of illustrations and graphics to provide information.

**RML2**   Authors use graphics to help you understand bigger ideas.

**RML3**   Authors use infographics to show several kinds of information in a clear and interesting way.

## Before Teaching Umbrella 18 Minilessons

Read and discuss high-quality, engaging nonfiction picture books that include illustrations and a variety of graphics, such as photographs, maps, diagrams, and infographics. Use the following books from the *Fountas & Pinnell Classroom™ Interactive Read-Aloud Collection* and *Guided Reading Collection* or choose nonfiction books with clear illustrations and graphics from your classroom library.

### Interactive Read-Aloud Collection

**Illustration Study: Craft**

*Eye to Eye: How Animals See the World* by Steve Jenkins

**Genre Study: Memoir**

*The Scraps Book: Notes from a Colorful Life* by Lois Ehlert

**Telling a Story with Photos**

*Face to Face with Whales* by Flip and Linda Nicklin

### Guided Reading Collection

*The Great Pacific Garbage Patch* by Laura Johnson

As you read aloud and enjoy these texts together, help students

- notice and discuss illustrations and graphics, and
- understand information and ideas conveyed through graphics.

*Interactive Read-Aloud*
**Illustration Study: Craft**

**Genre Study: Memoir**

**Telling a Story with Photos**

**Guided Reading**

Section 2: Literary Analysis

**Reading Minilesson Principle**
# Authors use a variety of illustrations and graphics to provide information.

## You Will Need

- a selection of familiar nonfiction books that contain a variety of types of illustrations and graphics
- chart paper and markers

## Academic Language / Important Vocabulary

- nonfiction
- author
- information
- illustration
- graphic

### Continuum Connection

- Understand that graphics provide important information [p. 65]
- Notice how illustrations and graphics help to communicate the writer's message [p. 65]

## Goal

Understand that authors provide information using a variety of illustrations and graphics.

## Rationale

When students notice and think about illustrations and graphics in nonfiction books, they acquire information and better understand the topic of the book. They also understand that there are many different ways to communicate information and that authors must make decisions about how best to do so.

## Assess Learning

Observe students when they read and talk about nonfiction books and notice if there is evidence of new learning based on the goal of this minilesson.

- Do students notice and think about illustrations and graphics in nonfiction books?
- Can they explain what they learned from an illustration or graphic?
- Can they identify different types of graphics (photographs, maps, diagrams, etc.)?
- Do they use academic language, such as *nonfiction, author, information, illustration,* and *graphic*?

## Minilesson

To help students think about the minilesson principle, use familiar nonfiction texts to engage them in noticing information in illustrations and graphics. Here is an example.

- Divide students into groups of three or four. Give each group at least one nonfiction book.

    Look through the nonfiction book I've given you and talk about the images. Images are pictures, photographs, or graphics such as maps, diagrams, or charts that give information. What kinds of images are there in your book? Are there illustrations, photographs, or other kinds of graphics?

- After students have had a few minutes to look through their books, invite them to share the images they found. Ask them to name and show an example of each kind of image (e.g., illustration, map, diagram) they found. Make a list of their responses on chart paper.

## Have a Try

Invite the students to talk with their groups about a specific illustration or graphic.

> With your group, choose one illustration or graphic in your book and talk about what information it gives you. What did you learn from the illustration or graphic? Why did the author include this illustration or graphic in the book?

❱ After time for discussion, invite several groups to share their thinking.

## Summarize and Apply

Summarize the learning and remind students to notice illustrations and graphics when they read nonfiction books.

> Why do nonfiction authors include illustrations and graphics in their books?

❱ Write the principle at the top of the chart.

> If you read a nonfiction book today, be sure to look at the illustrations and graphics. Notice what kinds of illustrations and graphics are in your book and think about what you are learning from them. Be ready to share when we come back together.

## Share

Following independent reading time, gather students together in the meeting area to talk about their reading.

> Who read a nonfiction book today?

> What kinds of illustrations or graphics did you see in your book? What did you learn from them?

## Extend the Lesson (Optional)

After assessing students' understanding, you might decide to extend the learning.

❱ When students write their own nonfiction books, encourage them to think about what kinds of illustrations and graphics to include.

❱ **Writing About Reading** Have students write in a reader's notebook about how a specific illustration or graphic communicates important information.

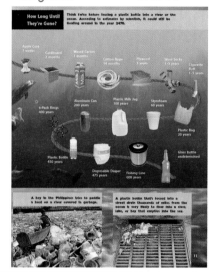

Authors use a variety of illustrations and graphics to provide information.

- illustrations
- photographs
- diagrams
- maps
- infographics
- charts

**Reading Minilesson Principle**

# Authors use graphics to help you understand bigger ideas.

## Learning Information from Illustrations/Graphics

### You Will Need

- two or three familiar nonfiction books that contain graphics that help communicate bigger ideas and messages, such as the following:
  - *Eye to Eye* by Steve Jenkins, from Text Set: Illustration Study: Craft
  - *The Scraps Book* by Lois Ehlert, from Text Set: Genre Study: Memoir
  - *Face to Face with Whales* by Flip and Linda Nicklin, from Text Set: Telling a Story with Photos
- chart paper and markers

### Academic Language / Important Vocabulary

- graphic
- diagram
- map
- big idea
- nonfiction
- author

### Continuum Connection

- Notice how illustrations and graphics help to communicate the writer's message (p. 65)

## Goal

Understand that authors use graphics to help you understand bigger ideas and messages.

## Rationale

Authors use graphics such as diagrams, charts, and maps to convey information visually. These graphics enhance the information in the text and often help to communicate a big idea. When students understand how to acquire information from graphics in nonfiction books, they are better able to understand the author's big ideas or central messages.

## Assess Learning

Observe students when they read and talk about nonfiction books and notice if there is evidence of new learning based on the goal of this minilesson.

- Can students explain how a graphic helps to communicate a bigger idea?
- Do they use academic language, such as *graphic, diagram, map, big idea, nonfiction,* and *author*?

## Minilesson

To help students think about the minilesson principle, use familiar nonfiction texts to engage students in noticing information in graphics. Here is an example.

- Show the cover of *Eye to Eye* and read the title. Turn to page 29. Read the page aloud, pointing to each text element as you read it.

  What do you notice about the graphics, or images, on this page?

  These graphics are called diagrams. A diagram shows the parts of something or how something works. What do these diagrams show?

- Record students' responses on chart paper.

  These diagrams show the different parts of different types of eyes. What big idea about the eye do these diagrams help you understand?

- Record students' responses on the chart.

- Show the cover of *The Scraps Book* and read the title. Turn to pages 21–22. Read the text. Point to the thumbnail sketches for *Feathers for Lunch*.

  What does this diagram show?

  This diagram shows Lois Ehlert's rough sketches of all the pages in one of her books. Why do you think she included this diagram in her book? What big idea does she want you to understand?

- Record students' responses on the chart.

## Have a Try

Invite the students to talk with a partner about *Face to Face with Whales*.

▶ Show page 29 of *Face to Face with Whales*. Point out the map and read the caption and map key.

Turn and talk to your partner about the map on this page. Talk about what the map shows about the big ideas it helps you understand.

▶ After time for discussion, invite a few students to share their thinking. Record responses on the chart.

## Summarize and Apply

Summarize the learning and remind students to notice graphics in nonfiction books.

Today you thought about graphics, such as diagrams and maps, in nonfiction books. What did you notice about why authors include graphics in nonfiction books?

Nonfiction authors often use graphics to help you understand bigger ideas.

▶ Write the principle at the top of the chart.

If you read a nonfiction book today, remember to notice, read, and think about the graphics. If you find an example of a graphic that helps you understand a bigger idea, bring your book to share when we come back together.

## Share

Following independent reading time, gather students together in the meeting area to talk about their reading.

Did anyone find an example of a graphic that helped you understand a bigger idea?

What bigger idea does the graphic help you understand?

## Extend the Lesson (Optional)

After assessing students' understanding, you might decide to extend the learning.

▶ When you read a nonfiction book with an interesting graphic during interactive read-aloud, discuss how it illustrates the author's big idea.

**Authors use graphics to help you understand bigger ideas.**

| Book | Type of Graphic | What does it show? | Big Idea |
|---|---|---|---|
| Eye to Eye | Diagram | The parts of different kinds of eyes | How the eye has evolved over time |
| The Scraps Book | Diagram | Rough sketches of all the pages in a book | Writing and illustrating a book takes a lot of planning. |
| Face to Face with Whales | Map | The migration routes of different whales | Whales live in all the world's oceans. Some migrate long distances. |

**Reading Minilesson Principle**

# Authors use infographics to show several kinds of information in a clear and interesting way.

## Learning Information from Illustrations/Graphics

### You Will Need

- two examples of infographics from a familiar nonfiction book, such as *The Great Pacific Garbage Patch* by Laura Johnson, from *Guided Reading Collection*
- chart paper and markers
- document camera (optional)

### Academic Language / Important Vocabulary

- infographic
- information
- nonfiction
- graphic
- author

### Continuum Connection

- Recognize and use information in a variety of graphics: e.g., photo and/or drawing with label or caption, diagram, cutaway, map with legend and scale, infographic (p. 65)
- Notice how illustrations and graphics help to communicate the writer's message (p. 65)

## Goal

Understand that authors use infographics to show several kinds of information in a clear and eye-catching way.

## Rationale

In today's digital age, infographics are used more and more frequently to convey complex information in a clear and eye-catching way, both online and in print publications. When you teach students how to read infographics, they are better prepared to acquire information from the many infographics that they will inevitably encounter.

## Assess Learning

Observe students when they read and talk about infographics and notice if there is evidence of new learning based on the goal of this minilesson.

- Do students notice and read infographics?
- Can they explain what they learned from an infographic?
- Do they use academic vocabulary, such as *infographic, information, nonfiction, graphic,* and *author*?

## Minilesson

To help students think about the minilesson principle, use a familiar nonfiction text to engage them in thinking about how to read infographics. Here is an example.

- Display the infographic from page 13 of *The Great Pacific Garbage Patch*.

    What do you notice about this graphic?

- Read the text aloud, pointing to each text element as you read it.

    What did you notice about how I read this graphic? Where did I start?

    I started by reading the title, and then I read each of the numbered items in order from one to ten. What did you learn from this graphic?

    This is a special kind of graphic called an infographic. Why do you think it's called that?

    How do the parts of the word *infographic* help us know what it means? Let's look at the first part, *info*. What does *info* mean?

    Now let's look at the second part, *graphic*. What does *graphic* mean?

- With students' input, label the different parts of the infographic.

## Have a Try

Invite the students to talk with a partner about another infographic.

▸ Display the infographic from page 11 of *The Great Pacific Garbage Patch* (see chart in RML1).

Think about this infographic with your partner. Turn and talk about what you notice about this infographic and what you learned from it.

▸ After time for discussion, invite several students to share their thinking. Ask how they read the infographic, what they noticed about how the infographic displays information, and what they learned from it.

## Summarize and Apply

Summarize the learning and remind students to read and think about infographics.

What did you learn about infographics today?

Why do you think authors use infographics? Why are they helpful?

▸ Write the principle at the top of the chart.

If you read a nonfiction book today, notice if it has any infographics. If it does, be sure to look closely at them and think about all of the information they provide. If you find an example of an infographic, bring it to share when we come back together.

## Share

Following independent reading time, gather students in small groups in the meeting area to talk about infographics. Make sure at least one student in each group found an infographic.

How did the infographic help you learn more about the topic of the book?

## Extend the Lesson (Optional)

After assessing students' understanding, you might decide to extend the learning.

▸ Infographics are easily found on the internet. Find infographics that are engaging and appropriate for your class and use them as models for students to use in their nonfiction writing.

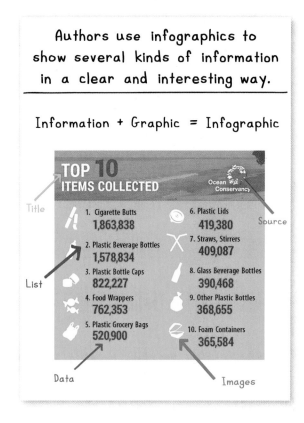

Authors use infographics to show several kinds of information in a clear and interesting way.

Information + Graphic = Infographic

TOP **10** ITEMS COLLECTED — Ocean Conservancy

Title

1. Cigarette Butts 1,863,838
2. Plastic Beverage Bottles 1,578,834
3. Plastic Bottle Caps 822,227
4. Food Wrappers 762,353
5. Plastic Grocery Bags 520,900
6. Plastic Lids 419,380
7. Straws, Stirrers 409,087
8. Glass Beverage Bottles 390,468
9. Other Plastic Bottles 368,655
10. Foam Containers 365,584

List

Source

Data

Images

## Assessment

After you have taught the minilessons in this umbrella, observe students as they talk and write about their reading across instructional contexts: interactive read-aloud, independent reading, guided reading, shared reading, and book club. Use *The Literacy Continuum* (Fountas and Pinnell 2017) to guide observation of students' reading and writing behaviors.

▶ What evidence do you have of new understandings related to learning information from illustrations and graphics?

- Do students talk about what they learn from illustrations and other graphics in nonfiction books?

- Can they explain how a particular graphic helps communicate a bigger idea?

- Do they know how to read infographics?

- Do they use academic language, such as *illustration, photograph, graphic, author, illustrator, map, diagram,* and *infographic*?

▶ In what other ways, beyond the scope of this umbrella, are students talking about nonfiction?

- Have they noticed that there are different genres of nonfiction?

- Have they started to read nonfiction with a critical eye?

- Are they noticing different ways that nonfiction authors organize information?

- Are they using text features to gain information?

Use your observations to determine the next umbrella you will teach. You may also consult Minilessons Across the Year (pp. 59–61) for guidance.

## Link to Writing

After teaching the minilessons in this umbrella, help students link the new learning to their own writing:

▶ Give students numerous opportunities to write their own nonfiction books. Let them decide whether to include illustrations, photographs, infographics, or other types of graphics, and help them find or create relevant images.

## Reader's Notebook

When this umbrella is complete, provide a copy of the minilesson principles (see resources.fountasandpinnell.com) for students to glue in the reader's notebook (in the Minilessons section if using *Reader's Notebook: Intermediate* [Fountas and Pinnell 2011]), so they can refer to the information as needed.

## Minilessons in This Umbrella

**RML1**   Authors use headings and subheadings to indicate the category of information that will follow.

**RML2**   Authors and illustrators use sidebars to emphasize or give additional information about the topic.

**RML3**   Authors use timelines to show when important things happened.

**RML4**   Authors include an index at the end of the book to help you find information quickly.

**RML5**   Authors include a bibliography show the resources used to find information for the book.

## Before Teaching Umbrella 19 Minilessons

Before teaching this umbrella, you might find it helpful to teach Umbrella 16: Noticing How Nonfiction Authors Choose to Organize Information. Additionally, be sure to read and discuss a number of engaging, high-quality nonfiction books that include a variety of text and organizational features, such as headings and subheadings, sidebars, timelines, indexes, and bibliographies. Use the following texts from the *Fountas & Pinnell Classroom™ Interactive Read-Aloud Collection* and *Independent Reading Collection* or choose books from your classroom library that have text and organizational features.

### Interactive Read-Aloud Collection

**Telling a Story with Photos**

*Face to Face with Whales* by Flip and Linda Nicklin

**Perseverance**

*Barbed Wire Baseball: How One Man Brought Hope to the Japanese Internment Camps of WWII* by Marissa Moss

**Genre Study: Biography (Individuals Making a Difference)**

*The Secret Kingdom* by Barb Rosenstock

*Fly High! The Story of Bessie Coleman* by Louise Borden and Mary Kay Kroeger

**Innovative Thinking and Creative Problem Solving**

*Parrots Over Puerto Rico* by Susan L. Roth and Cindy Trumbore

*One Plastic Bag: Isatou Ceesay and the Recycling Women of the Gambia* by Miranda Paul

### Independent Reading Collection

*I Wonder Why Stars Twinkle and Other Questions About Space* by Carole Stott

As you read aloud and enjoy these texts together, help students discuss the main idea of each page or section and notice text features and organizational tools.

*Interactive Read-Aloud*
**Photos**

**Perseverance**

**Biography**

**Innovative Thinking**

**Independent Reading**

**Section 2: Literary Analysis**

**Reading Minilesson Principle**

# Authors use headings and subheadings to indicate the category of information that will follow.

Using Text Features to Gain Information

## You Will Need

- two familiar nonfiction books that have headings, including at least one that has subheadings, such as the following:
  - *Face to Face with Whales* by Flip and Linda Nicklin, from Text Set: Telling a Story with Photos
  - *Fly High! The Story of Bessie Coleman* by Louise Borden and Mary Kay Kroeger, from Text Set: Biography (Individuals Making a Difference)
- document camera (optional)
- chart paper and markers

## Academic Language / Important Vocabulary

- nonfiction
- heading
- subheading
- category
- subcategory
- information

### Continuum Connection

- Notice a nonfiction writer's use of organizational tools: e.g., title, table of contents, heading, subheading, sidebar (p. 63)
- Notice and use and understand the purpose of some organizational tools: e.g., title, table of contents, chapter title, heading, subheading (p. 65)

## Goal

Notice, use, and understand the purpose of headings and subheadings.

## Rationale

When students notice and read headings and subheadings, they know what the upcoming section will be about and are better prepared for the information they will encounter. Using the headings and subheadings may help them consider what they already know about the topic and gain a better understanding of how the author has organized the information.

## Assess Learning

Observe students when they read and talk about nonfiction books and notice if there is evidence of new learning based on the goal of this minilesson.

- Do students understand the purpose of headings and subheadings?
- Can they use headings and subheadings to predict what a page or section will be about?
- Do they use academic language, such as *nonfiction, heading, subheading, category, subcategory,* and *information*?

## Minilesson

To help students think about the minilesson principle, use familiar nonfiction texts to engage students in noticing headings and subheadings. Here is an example.

- Show the cover of *Face to Face with Whales* and read the title. Turn to page 23 and point to the heading (if possible, project the text so all students can see it).

  What do you notice about this print? How is it different from the rest of the print on the page?

  The large print near the top of the page is called the heading.

- Read the heading aloud and then the first paragraph.

  Why did the authors use a heading?

- Point to the subheadings on pages 28–29.

  What do you notice about this print?

  The medium-sized words are called subheadings.

- Read the subheading that says Food and the paragraph beneath it.

  Why did the authors use a subheading?

  How are the subheadings different from the heading?

## Have a Try

Invite the students to talk with a partner about the headings in *Fly High! The Story of Bessie Coleman*.

▶ Show the cover of *Fly High!* and read the title. Then display pages 1–2 (use a document camera, if possible).

Turn and talk to your partner about what you think the information in this part of the book will be about and how you know.

▶ After students turn and talk, ask a few pairs to share their thinking.

## Summarize and Apply

Summarize the learning and remind students to read headings and subheadings.

Today you learned to recognize headings and subheadings and you talked about why authors use them.

▶ Use students' responses to make a chart summarizing their noticings about headings and subheadings. Write the principle at the top of the chart.

If you read a nonfiction book today, notice if it has headings and subheadings. If so, remember to read them and think about the category of information you'll find on the page or in the section you're about to read.

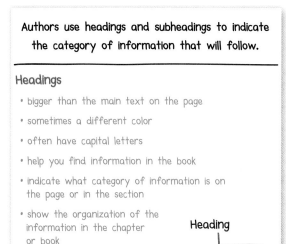

Authors use headings and subheadings to indicate the category of information that will follow.

**Headings**

• bigger than the main text on the page
• sometimes a different color
• often have capital letters
• help you find information in the book
• indicate what category of information is on the page or in the section
• show the organization of the information in the chapter or book

**Subheadings**

• smaller than headings
• give more details about the category
• show the organization of the information under the heading

Heading → Facts at a Glance
Subheading → Lifespans
→ Food

## Share

Following independent reading time, gather students together in the meeting area to talk about their reading.

Who read a nonfiction book with headings and subheadings today?

How did the headings and subheadings help you while you read?

## Extend the Lesson (Optional)

After assessing students' understanding, you might decide to extend the learning.

▶ **Writing About Reading** Display a page from a nonfiction book that does not have headings. Have students work with a partner to write headings and subheadings for the page.

**Reading Minilesson Principle**

# Authors and illustrators use sidebars to emphasize or give additional information about the topic.

## Using Text Features to Gain Information

### You Will Need

- two familiar nonfiction books that have sidebars, such as the following:
  - *Face to Face with Whales* by Flip and Linda Nicklin, from Text Set: Telling a Story with Photos
  - *I Wonder Why Stars Twinkle and Other Questions About Space* by Carole Stott, from Independent Reading
- chart paper and markers

### Academic Language / Important Vocabulary

- author
- illustrator
- nonfiction
- sidebar
- information

### Continuum Connection

- Gain new understandings from searching for and using information found in text body, sidebars, and graphics (p. 65)

## Goal

Gain new information about the topic from the sidebar and understand how it is related to the information in the body of the text.

## Rationale

When students know how to look for, read, and think about the additional information provided in sidebars, they gain a fuller understanding of the topic of the book.

## Assess Learning

Observe students when they read and talk about nonfiction books and notice if there is evidence of new learning based on the goal of this minilesson.

- ▶ Do students read and understand the purpose of sidebars?
- ▶ Can they explain how the information in a sidebar relates to the information in the text body?
- ▶ Do they use the academic vocabulary *author, illustrator, nonfiction, sidebar,* and *information*?

## Minilesson

To help students think about the minilesson principle, use familiar nonfiction books to illustrate the role of the sidebars. Here is an example.

- ▶ Show the cover of *Face to Face with Whales* and read the title. Then display and read aloud pages 5–6. Point to the sidebar and read it aloud.

  What do you notice about this part of the page?

  How does it look different from the rest of the page?

  Do you know what this text feature is called? It is called a sidebar. What do you notice about the information in the sidebar? How does it relate to the information on the rest of the page? How is it different?

  On this page, the authors use a sidebar to talk about how whales are like sea monsters. This information doesn't quite fit in with the rest of the page, but it is extra, interesting information about whales. A writer may also use a sidebar to emphasize information or give additional information that is on the page.

- ▶ Turn to page 17. Invite a volunteer to identify the sidebar on this page. Then read aloud the text body followed by the sidebar.

  What do you notice about this sidebar?

  What does the information in the sidebar have to do with the information on the rest of the page?

## Have a Try

Invite the students to talk with a partner about *I Wonder Why Stars Twinkle and Other Questions About Space.*

▶ Display page 16 from *I Wonder Why Stars Twinkle and Other Questions About Space.* Read the text body followed by the sidebar.

> What does the information in the sidebar have to do with the information on the rest of the page? Why do you think the author put this information in a sidebar instead of in the body of the text? Turn and talk to your partner about what you think.

▶ After time for discussion, invite a few students to share their thinking.

## Summarize and Apply

Summarize the learning and remind students to read sidebars.

> What did you notice about sidebars today?

> Why do some nonfiction authors use sidebars in their books?

▶ Record students' responses on chart paper. Write the principle at the top of the chart.

> When you read today, remember to read every part of the page. If your book has sidebars, be sure to read them. Think about what the information in the sidebar has to do with the information in the rest of the book and how it helps you learn more about the topic. Bring your book to share when we come back together.

## Share

Following independent reading time, gather students together in the meeting area to talk about their reading.

> Who found a sidebar in the book you read today?

> What did you learn from the sidebars in your book? What did the sidebars have to do with the rest of the book?

## Extend the Lesson (Optional)

After assessing students' understanding, you might decide to extend the learning.

▶ Encourage students to include sidebars when they write their own nonfiction books.

---

**Authors and illustrators use sidebars to emphasize or give additional information about the topic.**

Authors use sidebars to . . .

- give extra information about the topic

- give "fun facts" about the topic

- give more details about something discussed on the page

- emphasize important information about the topic

Sidebar ⟶

**Fun Fact**

side + bar = sidebar!

**Section 2: Literary Analysis**

**Reading Minilesson Principle**

# Authors use timelines to show when important things happened.

## Using Text Features to Gain Information

### You Will Need

- two familiar nonfiction books that contain timelines, such as the following from Text Set: Innovative Thinking and Creative Problem Solving:
  - *One Plastic Bag* by Miranda Paul
  - *Parrots Over Puerto Rico* by Susan L. Roth and Cindy Trumbore
- chart paper and markers
- document camera (optional)

### Academic Language / Important Vocabulary

- nonfiction
- author
- timeline

### Continuum Connection

- Understand that graphics provide important information (p. 65)
- Recognize and use information in a variety of graphics: e.g., photo and/or drawing with label or caption, diagram, cutaway, map with legend and scale, infographic (p. 65)

## Goal

Notice and understand why authors include timelines in nonfiction.

## Rationale

When students notice and read timelines, they are better able to understand and remember the dates of important events as well as understand patterns and relationships between events.

## Assess Learning

Observe students when they read and talk about nonfiction books and notice if there is evidence of new learning based on the goal of this minilesson.

- ▶ Do students notice and read timelines?
- ▶ Can they explain the purpose of a timeline and how it helps them when they read nonfiction?
- ▶ Do they use academic vocabulary, such as *nonfiction, author,* and *timeline?*

## Minilesson

To help students think about the minilesson principle, use familiar nonfiction texts to engage students in noticing the characteristics of timelines. Here is an example.

- ▶ Show the cover of *One Plastic Bag* and read the title. Open to and display the timeline near the end of the book. Read the heading and the first few entries.
- ▶ Use questions such as the following to prompt discussion:
  - *What do you notice about this page?*
  - *What is a timeline?*
  - *Why do you think the author included a timeline at the end of her book?*
  - *How do timelines help you learn more when you read nonfiction books?*
- ▶ Record students' responses on chart paper.

## Have a Try

Invite the students to talk with a partner about the timeline in *Parrots Over Puerto Rico*.

▶ Show the cover of *Parrots Over Puerto Rico* and read the title. Turn to the timeline near the end of the book.

> Take a look at this timeline. What do you notice about it? What does this timeline help you understand? Why do you think the authors included it? Turn and talk to your partner about what you think.

▶ After students turn and talk, ask a few students to share their thinking. Record any new insights about timelines on the chart.

## Summarize and Apply

Summarize the learning and remind students to notice and read timelines.

> What did you notice about timelines today?

> Why do authors sometimes include timelines in nonfiction books?

▶ Write the principle at the top of the chart.

> If the book you read today has a timeline, be sure to read it and think about the information in it. Bring your book to share when we come back together.

## Share

Following independent reading time, gather students together in the meeting area to talk about their reading.

> Who found a timeline in the book you read today?

> Show us the timeline. What did you learn from it? How did it help you understand more about the book's topic?

## Extend the Lesson (Optional)

After assessing students' understanding, you might decide to extend the learning.

▶ Encourage students to include timelines when they write their own nonfiction texts, as appropriate.

▶ **Writing About Reading** Have students make a timeline showing the important events from a nonfiction book.

---

> **Authors use timelines to show when important things happened.**
>
> Timelines . . .
>
> • show when important things happened
>
> • give more information about the topic
>
> • help you keep track of events
>
> • help you understand the order of events
>
> • explain what happened over a long period of time using few words
>
> • remind you of and help you remember the important events in a book

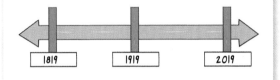

1819    1919    2019

*Section 2: Literary Analysis*

RML4

LA.U19.RML4

**Reading Minilesson Principle**

## Authors include an index at the end of the book to help you find information quickly.

**Using Text Features to Gain Information**

**You Will Need**

- two familiar nonfiction books that have an index, such as the following:
  - *Barbed Wire Baseball* by Marissa Moss, from Text Set: Perseverance
  - *Face to Face with Whales* by Flip and Linda Nicklin, from Text Set: Telling a Story with Photos
- chart paper and markers
- document camera (optional)

**Academic Language / Important Vocabulary**

- nonfiction
- topic
- subtopic
- information
- index
- alphabetical

**Continuum Connection**

- Notice and use and understand the purpose of some other text resources: e.g., glossary, index (p. 65)

## Goal

Notice, use, and understand the purpose of the index.

## Rationale

When students know how to use an index, they are able to find information about a specific topic or subtopic in a nonfiction book.

## Assess Learning

Observe students when they read and talk about nonfiction books and notice if there is evidence of new learning based on the goal of this minilesson.

- ▶ Do students know how to use an index?
- ▶ Can they use an index to find information?
- ▶ Do they understand that the entries in an index are arranged in alphabetical order?
- ▶ Do they use academic language, such as *nonfiction, topic, subtopic, information, index,* and *alphabetical*?

## Minilesson

To help students think about the minilesson principle, use familiar nonfiction texts to engage them in learning about the characteristics of indexes. Here is an example.

- ▶ Show the cover of *Barbed Wire Baseball* and read the title. Then show the index.

  What is the purpose of this part of the book?

  Why is the number *26* next to the words *Fresno, California*? What does this mean?

  What do you notice about the words underneath *Fresno, California*? What do they have to do with Fresno?

  This index lists both topics and subtopics. Fresno, California, is a topic. This topic is divided into smaller subtopics, like baseball teams in Fresno and building a ballpark in Fresno. The index tells you where to find information about all these topics and subtopics.

  What do you notice about the order of the topics and subtopics in the index?

  The topics are listed in alphabetical, or ABC, order. The subtopics under each topic are also in alphabetical order.

## Have a Try

Invite the students to talk with a partner about the index in *Face to Face with Whales*.

▶ Show the cover of *Face to Face with Whales* and read the title. Then display the index.

> What do you notice about the index in this book? How is it the same as the index in *Barbed Wire Baseball*? How is it different? Turn and talk to your partner about what you notice.

▶ After students turn and talk, invite a few pairs to share their thinking. If nobody mentions it, point out the boldface page numbers that indicate illustrations.

## Summarize and Apply

Summarize the learning and remind students to use the index to find specific information in nonfiction books.

> How does an index help you when you read a nonfiction book?

▶ Make a chart to remind students of what they learned about indexes. Write the principle at the top.

> If you read a nonfiction book today, check to see if it has an index. If so, use it to find information about a specific topic or subtopic. Be ready to share how you used the index when we come back together.

## Share

Following independent reading time, gather students together in the meeting area to talk about their reading.

> Who read a nonfiction book with an index today?

> How did you use the index? How did it help you?

## Extend the Lesson (Optional)

After assessing students' understanding, you might decide to extend the learning.

▶ Discuss the similarities and differences between a table of contents and an index.

▶ Encourage students to include an index when they write their own nonfiction books.

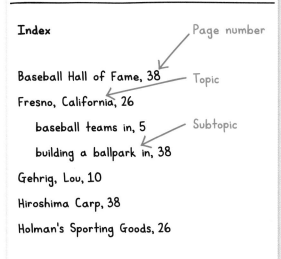

Authors include an index at the end of the book to help you find information quickly.

Index — Page number

Baseball Hall of Fame, 38 — Topic
Fresno, California, 26
    baseball teams in, 5 — Subtopic
    building a ballpark in, 38
Gehrig, Lou, 10
Hiroshima Carp, 38
Holman's Sporting Goods, 26

# RML 5
## LA.U19.RML5

**Reading Minilesson Principle**
## Authors include a bibliography to show the resources used to find information for the book.

## Using Text Features to Gain Information

### You Will Need

- two familiar nonfiction books that have a bibliography, such as the following:
  - *The Secret Kingdom* by Barb Rosenstock, from Text Set: Genre Study: Biography (Individuals Making a Difference)
  - *Parrots Over Puerto Rico* by Susan L. Roth and Cindy Trumbore, from Text Set: Innovative Thinking and Creative Problem Solving
- chart paper and markers
- document camera (optional)

### Academic Language / Important Vocabulary

- author
- nonfiction
- resource
- information
- bibliography

### Continuum Connection

- Notice and use and understand the purpose of some other text resources: e.g., glossary, index (p. 65)

### Goal

Notice and understand the purpose of the bibliography.

### Rationale

When students understand the purpose of the bibliography, they begin to understand the enormous amount of research that goes into writing a nonfiction book. They realize that the information in nonfiction books must be supported by other sources. They can also use the bibliography to verify information in a nonfiction book or do further reading about the topic.

### Assess Learning

Observe students when they read and talk about nonfiction books and notice if there is evidence of new learning based on the goal of this minilesson.

- Can students explain the purpose of a bibliography?
- Do they use the academic vocabulary *author, nonfiction, resource, information,* and *bibliography*?

## Minilesson

To help students think about the minilesson principle, use familiar nonfiction texts to help them notice the details in bibliographies. Here is an example.

- Show the cover of *The Secret Kingdom* and read the title. Then show the bibliography.

    What do you notice about this page in the book?

    What do you think this page is for?

- Record students' responses on chart paper.

    A bibliography is a list of the resources the author used to find information about the topic of the book. Let's take a closer look at some of the resources this author used.

- Point to a few different entries in the bibliography and read them aloud. Ask students what they notice about the kinds of resources the author used.

    This author used books, websites, newspapers, and videos. She did a lot of research to write this book. What kind of information does the author give about each resource?

- Record students' responses on the chart.

## Have a Try

Invite the students to talk with a partner about the bibliography in *Parrots Over Puerto Rico*.

▶ Show the cover of *Parrots Over Puerto Rico* and read the title. Then display the bibliography.

Turn and talk to your partner about what you notice about the bibliography in this book. What kinds of resources did the authors use?

▶ After students turn and talk, invite a few students to share their thinking.

## Summarize and Apply

Summarize the learning and remind students to notice bibliographies in nonfiction books.

What did you learn about a bibliography today?

Authors include a bibliography to show where they got the information to write the book. All the information in a nonfiction book must be accurate, so it's important that an author can show that it is true by giving the information sources. You can use the resources in the bibliography to check if the information in a book is accurate or to learn more about the topic of the book.

▶ Write the principle at the top of the chart.

If you read a nonfiction book today, notice if your book includes a bibliography. If it does, notice what resources the author used and think about how you might use the bibliography.

## Share

Following independent reading time, gather students together in the meeting area to talk about their reading.

Who read a book that included a bibliography?

What did you notice about the bibliography in your book?

## Extend the Lesson (Optional)

After assessing students' understanding, you might decide to extend the learning.

▶ Demonstrate how to use a resource listed in a bibliography to verify information in a nonfiction book.

---

**Authors include a bibliography to show the resources used to find information for the book**

- A bibliography is a list of the resources the author used.

- A bibliography lists different kinds of resources (books, websites, newspaper articles, etc.).

- The author gives the title, author, date, and other important information about each resource.

> Rosenstock, Barb. 2018. The Secret Kingdom. Somerville, MA: Candlewick Press.

- You can read the resources in the bibliography to check if the information in the book is true.

- You can read the resources in the bibliography to learn more about the topic.

Section 2: Literary Analysis

## Assessment

After you have taught the minilessons in this umbrella, observe students as they talk and write about their reading across instructional contexts: interactive read-aloud, independent reading, guided reading, shared reading, and book club. Use *The Literacy Continuum* (Fountas and Pinnell 2017) to guide observation of students' reading and writing behaviors.

> What evidence do you have of new understandings related to using text features to gain information?
> > • Do students understand the purpose of headings and subheadings?
> >
> > • Can they explain how headings and subheadings relate to the content that follows them?
> >
> > • Do they read and discuss information found in sidebars and timelines?
> >
> > • Can they explain how information in a sidebar relates to the information in the body of the text?
> >
> > • Are they able to use an index to find information quickly?
> >
> > • Do they understand the purpose of a bibliography?
> >
> > • Do they use academic language, such as *nonfiction, heading, subheading, information, sidebar, timeline, index,* and *bibliography*?
>
> In what other ways, beyond the scope of this umbrella, are students talking about nonfiction books?
> > • Have they noticed that there are different types of nonfiction books (e.g., biography, memoir)?

Use your observations to determine the next umbrella you will teach. You may also consult Minilessons Across the Year (pp. 59–61) for guidance.

## Link to Writing

After teaching the minilessons in this umbrella, help students link the new learning to their own writing:

> When students write their own nonfiction texts, encourage them to include some of the text features from this umbrella.

## Reader's Notebook

When this umbrella is complete, provide a copy of the minilesson principles (see resources.fountasandpinnell.com) for students to glue in the reader's notebook (in the Minilessons section if using *Reader's Notebook: Intermediate* [Fountas and Pinnell 2011]), so they can refer to the information as needed.

## Minilessons in This Umbrella

**RML1**   Realistic fiction stories could happen in real life.

**RML2**   Realistic fiction stories can help you understand people and your world.

**RML3**   Evaluate whether the plot of a realistic fiction book is believable.

## Before Teaching Umbrella 20 Minilessons

Before teaching the minilessons in this umbrella, students should be familiar with realistic fiction as a genre and be able to recognize texts as realistic fiction and name some characteristics of the genre.

Use the following books from the *Fountas & Pinnell Classroom™ Interactive Read-Aloud Collection* text sets or choose other realistic fiction texts with which your students are familiar.

**Figuring Out Who You Are**

*The Junkyard Wonders* by Patricia Polacco

*La Mariposa* by Francisco Jiménez

**Perseverance**

*Strong to the Hoop* by John Coy

*King for a Day* by Rukhsana Khan

**Friendship**

*Better Than You* by Trudy Ludwig

As you read aloud and enjoy these texts together, help students

* identify what makes them realistic fiction,

* think about what makes the characters, setting, and plot realistic,

* identify the author's message and think about how to apply lessons learned to their own lives, and

* consider whether or not everything that happens in a realistic fiction story is believable.

**Figuring Out Who You Are**

**Perseverance**

**Friendship**

# RML1
## LA.U20.RML1

**Reading Minilesson Principle**
# Realistic fiction stories could happen in real life.

## Understanding Realistic Fiction

### You Will Need

- two or three familiar realistic fiction texts, such as the following:
  - *The Junkyard Wonders* by Patricia Polacco, from Text Set: Figuring Out Who You Are
  - *Strong to the Hoop* by John Coy, from Text Set: Perseverance
  - *La Mariposa* by Francisco Jiménez, from Text Set: Figuring Out Who You Are
- chart paper and markers

### Academic Language / Important Vocabulary

- realistic fiction
- character
- plot
- setting

### Continuum Connection

- Understand when a story could happen in real life (realistic fiction) and when it could not happen in real life (traditional literature, fantasy) (p. 58)

## Goal

Understand that one of the characteristics of realistic fiction is that the characters, plot, and setting could exist in real life.

## Rationale

When students understand that the characters, plot, and setting in realistic fiction books seem real, they can engage with and make authentic personal connections to their reading.

## Assess Learning

Observe students when they read and talk about realistic fiction. Notice if there is evidence of new learning based on the goal of this minilesson.

- Can students identify realistic fiction by evaluating the characters, setting, and plot?
- Are they using academic language, such as *realistic fiction, character, plot,* and *setting*?

# Minilesson

To help students think about the minilesson principle, use familiar texts to engage students in thinking about how the characters, setting, and plot in realistic fiction could exist in real life.

- Show *The Junkyard Wonders* and revisit a few pages to remind students of the story.

  This book is realistic fiction. What makes this story realistic?

- Help students to notice that realistic settings and characters are imagined by the author but could be real. As necessary, support the conversation with these prompts:
  - *Could the characters exist in real life?*
  - *Could the setting in the story be a real place?*
  - *What happens in the story that could happen in real life?*
- Record responses on a chart. Then repeat this process with *Strong to the Hoop*.

## Have a Try

Invite the students to talk with a partner about whether *La Mariposa* is realistic fiction.

> Turn and talk to a partner about the characters, setting, and plot of this book. How do you know this is realistic fiction?

▶ After students turn and talk, ask a few students to share, and record their responses on the chart.

## Summarize and Apply

Summarize the learning and remind students to think about whether the characters, setting, and plot in a book seem real.

> What did you notice today about realistic fiction books?

▶ Review the chart and write the principle at the top.

> Choose a realistic fiction book to read today, or continue reading one you have already started. Think about what makes it seem real to you. Be prepared to share when we come back together.

## Share

Following independent reading time, gather students together to share as a group.

> Did you read a realistic fiction book today?

> How do you know your book is realistic fiction?

## Extend the Lesson (Optional)

After assessing students' understanding, you might decide to extend the learning.

▶ Introduce your students to Genre Thinkmarks for realistic fiction. A Genre Thinkmark is a tool that guides readers to note certain elements of a genre in their reading. They can quickly note the page numbers of parts of the book where they see evidence of the characteristics of realistic fiction and share it with others. To download this resource, visit resources.fountasinnell.com.

▶ **Writing About Reading** Encourage students to write a letter about reading in which they explain how they know a book is realistic fiction.

### Realistic fiction stories could happen in real life.

| Book | Character | Plot | Setting |
|------|-----------|------|---------|
| The Junkyard Wonders — Patricia Polacco | The main character goes to school. She is good at drawing. | Trisha feels like she doesn't fit in. She doesn't like her class at first, but learns they each have special talents. | You can go to Michigan. |
| STRONG to the HOOP | The main character plays basketball and practices. | The other kids don't think James can play on their team because he is so young. | You can go to a basketball court. |
| La Mariposa — Francisco Jiménez | Francisco speaks Spanish and tries hard to understand English at his new school. | Francisco does not understand English yet and has a hard time at school. | You can go to tent cities and schools. |

## Reading Minilesson Principle
# Realistic fiction stories can help you understand people and your world.

### Understanding Realistic Fiction

**You Will Need**

- two or three realistic fiction texts that have a clear message, such as the following:
  - *Strong to the Hoop* by John Coy, from Text Set: Perseverance
  - *The Junkyard Wonders* by Patricia Polacco, from Text Set: Figuring Out Who You Are
  - *Better Than You* by Trudy Ludwig, from Text Set: Friendship
- chart paper and markers

**Academic Language / Important Vocabulary**

- realistic fiction
- author's message
- perseverance

### Continuum Connection

- Understand that the message or big ideas in fiction texts can be applied to their own lives or to other people and society (p. 58)
- Learn from vicarious experiences with characters in stories (p. 59)

### Goal

Relate texts to their own lives and think about the author's message.

### Rationale

When students recognize that a realistic fiction text can help them understand more about people and the world, they think more deeply about the author's message and how it can be applied to their own lives. You my want to teach LA.U8.RML2 before this lesson to be sure students know how to notice the author's message.

### Assess Learning

Observe students when they talk about realistic fiction. Notice if there is evidence of new learning based on the goal of this minilesson.

- ▶ Can students infer the author's message?
- ▶ Do they discuss how an author's message applies to their own lives?
- ▶ Do they understand and use the terms *realistic fiction, author's message,* and *perseverance*?

## Minilesson

To help students think about the minilesson principle, use familiar realistic fiction texts to help them think about how stories help them understand people and their world. Here is an example.

- ▶ Show *Strong to the Hoop*. Read the pages with illustrations of James going for a lay-up and then the two pages before the last page of text.

  Does James learn a lesson in this story? What is it?

  The author wrote the story so that the main character, James, learns a lesson. What can you learn from James's lesson?

- ▶ Record responses on chart paper.

  Have any of you ever had an experience like James's from which you learned a similar lesson? What was the lesson you learned?

- ▶ Show *The Junkyard Wonders*. Read the two pages with an illustration of Mrs. Peterson leading her class to a junkyard and then the following page.

  What does Trisha realize about herself and her class?

  What can you learn from reading this story?

- ▶ Record responses on the chart.

  Have any of you ever learned a lesson similar to Trisha's? What was the lesson you learned? Turn and talk to a partner about that.

## Have a Try

Invite the students to talk with a partner about the message in *Better Than You*.

▶ Read the last four pages of text.

> Turn and talk to your partner. What does the author want you to learn from this story? Why do you think that?

▶ After students turn and talk, ask a few students to share their ideas. Record their responses on the chart.

## Summarize and Apply

Summarize the learning and remind students to think about how they can apply the lessons in a realistic fiction text to their own lives.

> Realistic fiction stories are like real life, so you can understand people and your world better.

▶ Write the principle at the top of the chart.

> When you read today, choose a realistic fiction story to read. As you read, think about what the author is saying about people and the world. Be ready to share your thinking when we come back together.

## Share

Following independent reading time, gather students together in the meeting area to talk about their reading.

> Who read a realistic fiction book today that teaches an important lesson about people or the world?

> What lesson is the author trying to teach? How will it help you in your life?

## Extend the Lesson (Optional)

After assessing students' understanding, you might decide to extend the learning.

▶ Encourage students to recommend books that offer important messages about life and the world (see MGT.U3.RML3 for a minilesson on how to give book talks to recommend books and WAR.U5.RML5 for a minilesson on writing recommendations).

▶ **Writing About Reading** Have students write about how a realistic fiction book helps them understand something about people or the world.

---

**Realistic fiction stories can help you understand people and your world.**

Understandings About People and the World

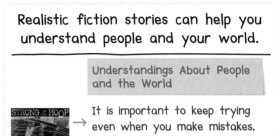

→ It is important to keep trying even when you make mistakes.

↘ Hard work and perseverance can help you reach your goals.

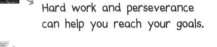

→ Every person has special gifts and talents.

↘ It is important to encourage and find the good in one another.

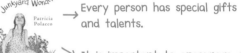

→ People who brag can end up pushing friends away.

↘ Choose friends who are kind and respectful.

*Section 2: Literary Analysis*

**Reading Minilesson Principle**
# Evaluate whether the plot of a realistic fiction book is believable.

### You Will Need

- two or three realistic fiction texts, such as the following:
  - *King for a Day* by Rukhsana Khan, from Text Set: Perseverance
  - *La Mariposa* by Francisco Jiménez, from Text Set: Figuring Out Who You Are
- chart paper and markers

### Academic Language / Important Vocabulary

- realistic fiction
- believable
- plot
- evaluate

### Continuum Connection

- Evaluate the logic and believability of the plot and its resolution (p. 59)

## Goal

Evaluate the believability of a realistic fiction text.

## Rationale

A key characteristic of realistic fiction is that, even though parts are imagined by the author, it has to be believable. When you teach students to read realistic fiction with this awareness, looking to see that each part of the story seems real, you are teaching them to read critically.

## Assess Learning

Observe students when they talk about realistic fiction. Notice if there is evidence of new learning based on the goal of this minilesson.

- ▶ Can students decide whether the elements of a realistic fiction story are believable or not?
- ▶ Are they thinking critically about realistic fiction stories?
- ▶ Can they use important language, such as *realistic fiction, believable, plot,* and *evaluate*?

## Minilesson

To help students think about the minilesson principle, use familiar realistic fiction texts to help students consider the believability of the plot. Here is an example.

- ▶ Show *King for a Day*. Read the two pages of text starting with "The bully picks up his other kite."

  This book is realistic fiction. What happens in the story that you think could happen in real life?

- ▶ Record responses on a chart.

  Are there also parts of the plot that you don't believe could actually happen in real life? Why do you think that?

- ▶ Record responses on the chart.

## Have a Try

Invite the students to talk with a partner about *La Mariposa*.

> What happens in *La Mariposa* that is believable? Is there a part that is hard to believe? Talk about that.

▶ After they turn and talk, ask a few students to share. Record responses on the chart.

## Summarize and Apply

Summarize the learning and remind students to evaluate the believability of the plot in a realistic fiction text.

> What did you learn about the plots of realistic fiction stories?

> A realistic fiction story has characters, a setting, and a plot that could be real, but you may not always find the elements believable. You can think about—or evaluate—whether you think the story is believable.

▶ Write the principle at the top of the chart.

> Choose a realistic fiction book to read today. As you read, think about whether you think the plot is believable. Be ready to share when we come back together.

## Share

Following independent reading time, gather students together in the meeting area to talk about realistic fiction.

> Was the plot in the realistic fiction book you read today believable? Why or why not?

## Extend the Lesson (Optional)

After assessing students' understanding, you might decide to extend the learning.

▶ If a plot seems hard to believe, encourage students to look for notes or resources in the book that support the believability of the plot.

▶ Have students discuss why an author might include an event or a character in a realistic fiction story that doesn't seem realistic.

▶ **Writing About Reading** Students could write about the believability of a realistic fiction story in their weekly letters (see Umbrella 3: Writing Letters to Share Thinking About Books in the Writing About Reading section).

**Evaluate whether the plot of a realistic fiction book is believable.**

| Book | What seems believable? | What seems unbelievable? |
|---|---|---|
| King for a Day | Malik had to deal with a bully. This is something you might have to do in real life. | Kite-fighting against a bully from the top of a building seems too dangerous to do in real life. |
| La Mariposa | Francisco didn't speak English, so he had trouble in school. Francisco was good at drawing. | So many good things happened at the end. Usually things don't work out that well in real life. |

## Assessment

After you have taught the minilessons in this umbrella, observe students as they talk and write about their reading across instructional contexts: interactive read-aloud, independent reading, guided reading, shared reading, and book club. Use *The Literacy Continuum* (Fountas and Pinnell 2017) to guide the observation of students' reading and writing behaviors.

▶ What evidence do you have of new understandings related to realistic fiction?

- Are students able to identify realistic fiction texts?
- Can they explain how the characters, setting, and plot are realistic?
- Do they understand that they can learn about people and the world from realistic fiction stories?
- Do they make connections between the text and their own lives?
- Can they make connections between the text and the people and world around them?
- Do they identify parts of the story that may not be as believable as other parts of the story, and can they explain their thinking?
- Do they use academic language, such as *realistic fiction, character, setting, plot,* and *author's message*?

▶ In what other ways, beyond the scope of this umbrella, are students talking about realistic fiction?

- Do students notice that there are other types of fiction texts?

Use your observations to determine the next umbrella you will teach. You may also consult Minilessons Across the Year (pp. 59–61) for guidance.

## Link to Writing

After teaching the minilessons in this umbrella, help students link the new learning to their own writing:

▶ When students write a realistic fiction story, remind them that the characters, plot, and setting must seem like they could exist in real life. Ask them to consider what the message is for the reader, and how the details they provide support this message.

## Reader's Notebook

When this umbrella is complete, provide a copy of the minilesson principles (see resources.fountasandpinnell.com) for students to glue in the reader's notebook (in the Minilessons section if using *Reader's Notebook: Intermediate* [Fountas and Pinnell 2011]), so they can refer to the information as needed.

## Minilessons in This Umbrella

| | |
|---|---|
| **RML1** | Fantasy stories are alike in many ways. |
| **RML2** | The definition of fantasy is what is always true about it. |
| **RML3** | Fantasy stories cannot happen in the real world. |
| **RML4** | Fantasy stories can be set in the real world or in a completely imagined world. |
| **RML5** | Human and animal characters and normal objects are often magical. |
| **RML6** | Fantasy stories are often about good versus evil. |
| **RML7** | Fantasy stories often reveal a lesson or something true about the world. |

## Before Teaching Umbrella 21 Minilessons

When students study a genre, they learn what to expect when reading a text, expand important comprehension skills, understand the distinguishing characteristics of a genre, and develop the tools they need to navigate a variety of texts. There are six broad steps in a genre study, which are described on pages 39–41.

Prior to teaching this series of minilessons, read and discuss a variety of fantasy books, including both modern fantasy and traditional literature. Modern fantasy includes animal fantasy, low fantasy, high fantasy, and science fiction. Traditional literature includes folktales, fairy tales, fables, legends, epics, ballads, and myths. This umbrella uses examples of modern fantasy. Use the following books from the *Fountas & Pinnell Classroom™ Interactive Read-Aloud Collection* or choose fantasy stories from the classroom library.

**Genre Study: Fantasy**

*The Wolves in the Walls* by Neil Gaiman

*Weslandia* by Paul Fleischman

*Night of the Gargoyles* by Eve Bunting

*Tuck Everlasting* by Natalie Babbitt

*The Field Guide (The Spiderwick Chronicles, Book 1)*
   by Tony DiTerlizzi and Holly Black

As you read aloud and enjoy these texts together, help students

- notice similarities between them,

- become aware of the characteristics of fantasy stories, and

- understand that fantasy stories often reveal a truth about the world.

**Genre Study: Fantasy**

**Section 2: Literary Analysis**

# RML1

## LA.U21.RML1

**Reading Minilesson Principle**
# Fantasy stories are alike in many ways.

## Studying Fantasy

### You Will Need

- a variety of familiar fantasy stories
- chart paper and markers
- basket of fantasy books
- sticky notes

### Academic Language / Important Vocabulary

- fantasy
- genre
- characteristics
- magical
- imagined

### Continuum Connection

- Notice and understand the characteristics of some specific genres: e.g., realistic fiction, historical fiction, folktale, fairy tale, fractured fairy tale, fable, myth, legend, epic, ballad, fantasy including science fiction, hybrid text [p. 58]

### Goal

Notice and understand the characteristics of fantasy as a genre.

### Rationale

When you teach students the characteristics of the fantasy genre, they will recognize that fantasy stories could not happen in real life and often have magic, good versus evil, and life lessons, and they will know what to expect when reading fantasy stories. Note that the examples used here are considered modern fantasy.

### Assess Learning

Observe students when they read and discuss fantasy stories and notice if there is evidence of new learning based on the goal of this minilesson.

- Can students discuss the ways fantasy stories are alike?
- Do they talk about the characteristics of fantasies?
- Do they understand that characteristics *always* occur, *often* occur, or *sometimes* occur in fantasy stories?
- Do they use the terms *fantasy, genre, characteristics, magical,* and *imagined*?

## Minilesson

To help students think about the minilesson principle, engage the students in noticing the characteristics of the fantasy genre across several stories. Here is an example.

- Show the covers of multiple fantasy books that are familiar to students.

   Turn and talk about some ways that all these fantasy stories are alike. As you talk about each statement, think about whether it is true *always, often,* or *sometimes* in fantasy stories.

- After time for discussion, ask students to share ideas. Record responses on chart paper in three separate sections: *Always, Often,* and *Sometimes.*
- Select several fantasy books to discuss in greater detail.

   What other things do you notice about these books in the fantasy genre?

- Continue recording responses. The following prompts may be helpful to continue the conversation:
  - *What do you notice about the characters?*
  - *What do you notice about the settings?*
  - *What do you notice about the lessons that the stories reveal?*
  - *What do you notice about magic, technology, or science?*

## Have a Try

Invite the students to talk with a small group about a fantasy story.

▶ Provide each group with a fantasy book.

> Look through the book with your group. What noticings from the chart are true about your book?

## Summarize and Apply

Summarize the learning and remind students to think about the characteristics of fantasy books.

▶ Add the title *Fantasy Books* to the chart and revisit the noticings.

> Today choose a fantasy book from the basket if you are ready to start a new book. Look for the characteristics on the chart and mark where you see them with a sticky note. Bring the book when we meet so you can share.

## Share

Following independent reading time, gather students in small groups. Make sure each group has at least one student who read a fantasy book.

> Tell your group which noticings from the chart you found. Point out what you noticed on the pages you marked with a sticky note.

## Extend the Lesson (Optional)

After assessing students' understanding, you might decide to extend the learning.

▶ Have students record the fantasy stories they read in a reader's notebook.

▶ Visit resources.fountasandpinnell.com to download Genre Thinkmarks. Have students use a Genre Thinkmark to note elements of the fantasy genre. They can add page numbers to remember where they saw evidence of characteristics of fantasy books and share with classmates.

---

### Fantasy Books

**Noticings:**

| Always | Often |
|---|---|
| • Cannot happen in the real world | • Have magical objects |
| | • Are about good vs. evil |
| | • Characters have magic powers or use magical objects |
| | • Reveal a lesson or something true about the world |

**Sometimes**

• Set in the real world

• Set in a completely imagined world

• Involve technology and scientific advances that may not be possible (science fiction)

**Reading Minilesson Principle**
# The definition of fantasy is what is always true about it.

## Studying Fantasy

### You Will Need

- several familiar fantasy books, such as the following from Text Set: Genre Study: Fantasy:
  - *Weslandia* by Paul Fleischman
  - *Night of the Gargoyles* by Eve Bunting
- noticings chart from RML1
- chart paper and markers
- basket of fantasy books
- sticky notes

### Academic Language / Important Vocabulary

- fantasy
- genre
- definition
- elements

### Continuum Connection

- Notice and understand the characteristics of some specific fiction genres; e.g., realistic fiction, historical fiction, folktale, fairy tale, fractured fairy tale, fable, myth, legend, epic, ballad, fantasy including science fiction, hybrid text [p. 58]

## Goal

Create a working definition of a fantasy.

## Rationale

When you teach students to construct a working definition of fantasy stories, they can form their understandings so they will know what to expect from the genre. They will learn to revise their understandings as they gain additional experience with the fantasy genre.

## Assess Learning

Observe students when they read and discuss fantasy stories and notice if there is evidence of new learning based on the goal of this minilesson.

- Do students work together to create a working definition of a fantasy story?
- Do they understand the definition of a fantasy story and can they tell what is always true about it?
- Do they use the terms *fantasy*, *genre*, *definition*, and *elements*?

## Minilesson

To help students think about the minilesson principle, engage them in constructing a definition of fantasy. Here is an example.

- Show the fantasy noticings chart and discuss the characteristics.

    What would you say is true about a fantasy? Think about the characters, the setting, and what happens in the story.

- On chart paper, write the words *A fantasy is*, leaving space for constructing a working definition.

    What would you write to finish this sentence? The sentence should describe what fantasy stories are like. Look back at the noticings chart for ideas.

- Using students' ideas, create a working definition on chart paper. Ask a volunteer to read the definition.

    The definition of a fantasy story describes what is always true about books in this genre.

- Show the cover of *Weslandia*.

    Think about *Weslandia*. Does it fit the definition of a fantasy story?

- Refer students to the definition and ask for a text example to show that *Weslandia* fits the definition. As needed, revise the definition based on new understandings.

## Have a Try

Invite the students to talk with a partner about whether *Night of the Gargoyles* is a fantasy story.

▶ Show the cover of *Night of the Gargoyles*.

Turn and talk about whether *Night of the Gargoyles* fits the definition of a fantasy story. What makes you think that?

▶ Ask a few students to share. Encourage them to give text examples to support their thinking. Revise the definition as needed.

## Summarize and Apply

Summarize the learning and remind students to think about the definition of a fantasy story.

Today we created a definition of a fantasy story. Choose a fantasy book from the basket to read today if you are ready to start a new book. Think about how the book fits the definition. Add sticky notes to pages that show examples. Bring the book when we meet so you can share.

## Share

Following independent reading time, gather students in small groups to talk about fantasy books.

Talk about the fantasy story you read today or one you read recently. Share how it fits the definition and show any pages with sticky notes to support your thinking.

## Extend the Lesson (Optional)

After assessing students' understanding, you might decide to extend the learning.

▶ Have students create a collection of fantasy books to display in the classroom library. Encourage them to think and talk about how each book fits the definition of fantasy.

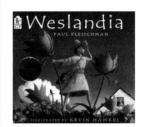

Fantasy

A fantasy is a made-up, magical story.

**Reading Minilesson Principle**
# Fantasy stories cannot happen in the real world.

### You Will Need

- several familiar fantasy stories, such as the following from Text Set: Genre Study: Fantasy:
  - *Tuck Everlasting* by Natalie Babbitt
  - *Night of the Gargoyles* by Eve Bunting
  - *Weslandia* by Paul Fleischman
- chart paper prepared with three columns, headings, and book titles (see next page)
- three sticky notes, each labeled *No*
- markers
- basket of fantasy books
- sticky notes

### Academic Language / Important Vocabulary

- fantasy
- real world
- elements

### Continuum Connection

- Notice when a story could happen in real life (realistic fiction) and when it could not happen in real life (traditional literature, fantasy) (p. 58)

## Goal

Notice and understand that a defining characteristic of fantasy is that the story could never happen in the real world.

## Rationale

When you teach students that fantasy stories have aspects that cannot happen in real life, they begin to talk about the imaginative elements in fantasy stories and learn what to expect when they read books in this genre.

## Assess Learning

Observe students when they read and discuss fantasy stories and notice if there is evidence of new learning based on the goal of this minilesson.

- Do students understand that fantasy stories have elements that could not happen in real life?
- Are they able to identify which characters, settings, objects, or events could not happen in real life?
- Do they use the terms *fantasy, real world,* and *elements*?

## Minilesson

To help students think about the minilesson principle, engage them in noticing the real or imagined characteristics of fantasy stories. Here is an example.

- Display the prepared three-column chart and the cover of *Tuck Everlasting*.

  Think about the spring Winnie finds and about what happens to people when they drink from it. Turn and talk about whether this could happen in the real world.

- After time for discussion, ask students to share their thinking.

  Are there elements in this book that could not happen in the real world?

  Why couldn't this story happen in the real world?

- Write *No* on a sticky note and ask a volunteer to place it in the middle column of the chart. Then ask for and record an example of an element from *Tuck Everlasting* that could not happen in the real world. Discuss the fact that some parts of fantasy books might be possible in the real world but that all modern fantasy books have one or more imagined elements.

  Think about another fantasy story, *Night of the Gargoyles*. Could this story happen in the real world? Why or why not?

- Ask a volunteer to add another sticky note to the chart.

## Have a Try

Invite the students to talk with a partner about the fantasy genre.

> Think about the fantasy book *Weslandia*. Talk about whether the story could happen in the real world and why or why not.

▶ After time for discussion, add responses to the chart.

## Summarize and Apply

Summarize the learning and remind students to think about the elements in fantasy books that could not happen in the real world.

> What does the chart show you about fantasy stories?

▶ Write the minilesson principle at the top of the chart paper.

> When you read today, select a fantasy book from the basket, unless you are already reading one. Think about which elements could not happen in the real world. Use sticky notes to mark pages with examples. Bring the book when we meet so you can share.

## Share

Following independent reading time, gather students in small groups.

> With your group, talk about the fantasy story you read today. Show examples from the book that could not happen in the real world.

## Extend the Lesson (Optional)

After assessing students' understanding, you might decide to extend the learning.

▶ **Writing About Reading** Although a fantasy story cannot happen in real life, the story has to be believable within the context of the fantasy world that the author created. Have students write a few sentences in a reader's notebook about which of the three books discussed in this minilesson they thought was the most believable and why.

**Fantasy stories cannot happen in the real world.**

| Title | Could this happen in the real world? | Why? |
|---|---|---|
| *Tuck Everlasting* | No | Water can't keep people from growing older. |
| *Night of the Gargoyles* | No | Statues can't come to life. |
| *Weslandia* | No | Magic seeds can't fly in and plant themselves. |

Section 2: Literary Analysis

# Fantasy stories can be set in the real world or in a completely imagined world.

## Studying Fantasy

### You Will Need

- several fantasy stories with unusual settings or settings in both real and imagined worlds, such as the following from Text Set: Genre Study: Fantasy:
  - *The Field Guide* by Tony DiTerlizzi and Holly Black
  - *The Wolves in the Walls* by Neil Gaiman
  - *Weslandia* by Paul Fleischman
- chart paper prepared with four columns, headings, and book titles (see next page)
- markers
- basket of fantasy books
- sticky notes

### Academic Language / Important Vocabulary

- fantasy
- genre
- setting
- real world
- imagined world

### Continuum Connection

- Infer the importance of the setting to the plot of the story in realistic and historical fiction and fantasy (p. 59)

## Goal

Notice and understand that the setting of a fantasy story can be in the real world or in an imagined world and is often important to the plot of the story.

## Rationale

When you teach students that the setting could be real or imagined in a fantasy story, you make them aware that in some fantasy stories realistic elements exist alongside fantastical elements. You also make them aware that the setting can affect the plot of the story. Having this information will help students comprehend and engage with fantasy stories more fully.

## Assess Learning

Observe students when they read and discuss fantasy stories and notice if there is evidence of new learning based on the goal of this minilesson.

- ▶ Can students tell whether the places in a story are real or imagined?
- ▶ Do they use the terms *fantasy, genre, setting, real world,* and *imagined world*?

## Minilesson

To help students think about the minilesson principle, engage them in noticing the unusual settings of familiar fantasy stories. Here is an example.

- ▶ Show the cover of *The Field Guide*.

  Where does *The Field Guide* take place?

- ▶ Prompt the conversation as needed so students realize that part of the setting could be real and part could never exist in the real world. Add student responses to the chart.

  How is the setting important to the story? Turn and talk about that.

- ▶ After time for discussion, add students' ideas to the chart. Show the cover of *The Wolves in the Walls*.

  Think about the setting in *The Wolves in the Walls*. What do you notice?

- ▶ Show a few illustrations of the house and the walls inside the house from *The Wolves in the Walls*.

  Could the places be real?

  How is the setting important to this story?

- ▶ Add responses to the chart.

## Have a Try

Invite the students to talk with a partner about the setting in a fantasy story.

▶ Show the cover of *Weslandia*.

Think about the setting in *Weslandia*. Remember that some places could be real and some might be imagined and could never be real. Turn and talk about the setting in *Weslandia*.

▶ After time for discussion, ask students to share. Add to the chart.

## Summarize and Apply

Summarize the learning and remind students to think about the unusual settings in fantasy stories.

What did you notice about the setting in fantasy stories?

▶ Write the minilesson principle at the top of the chart paper.

When you read today, choose a fantasy book from the basket or continue one you have already started. Notice if all or part of the setting is unusual and whether it could exist in the real world or if it is imagined. Place a sticky note on pages that you would like to share. Bring the book when we meet.

## Share

Following independent reading time, gather students in small groups.

With your group, share the fantasy story you read today and talk about the setting. Was the setting real or imagined? Were some places real and some places imagined?

## Extend the Lesson (Optional)

After assessing students' understanding, you might decide to extend the learning.

▶ During interactive read-aloud, discuss the ways that setting is important to the plot and how the story would be different if the setting were to change.

▶ **Writing About Reading** Have students choose a setting from a fantasy story and write in a reader's notebook how it was important to the story.

**Fantasy stories can be set in the real world or in a completely imagined world.**

| Title | Real/Could Be Real | Imagined/Could Never Be Real | How is setting important to the story? |
|---|---|---|---|
| Spiderwick | The Grace family's house | The secret rooms of the faeries | The house is a regular old house, but strange things happen inside it. |
| Wolves in the Walls | Lucy's house | The walls in Lucy's house | The story is about what lives inside the walls. |
| Weslandia | Wesley's house | Wesley's magic garden | The magic garden helps Wesley solve his problem. |

# RML5
## LA.U21.RML5

# Human and animal characters and normal objects are often magical.

## Studying Fantasy

### You Will Need

- several familiar fantasy stories, such as the following from Text Set: Genre Study: Fantasy:
  - *Weslandia* by Paul Fleischman
  - *Tuck Everlasting* by Natalie Babbitt
  - *Night of the Gargoyles* by Eve Bunting
- chart paper prepared with three columns, headings, and book titles (see next page)
- markers
- basket of fantasy stories

### Academic Language / Important Vocabulary

- fantasy
- genre
- magical
- objects

### Continuum Connection

- Notice recurring themes or motifs in traditional literature and fantasy: e.g., struggle between good and evil, the hero's quest (p. 59)
- Identify elements of traditional literature and modern fantasy: e.g., the supernatural; imaginary otherworldly creatures; gods and goddesses; talking animals, toys, and dolls; heroic characters; technology or scientific advances; time travel; aliens or outer space (p. 58)

## Goal

Understand that a common motif in fantasy is that normal objects and things can be magical.

## Rationale

When students understand that objects and things can be magical in fantasy stories, they know what to expect from reading books in this genre and are able to recognize stories as fantasies.

## Assess Learning

Observe students when they read and discuss fantasy stories and notice if there is evidence of new learning based on the goal of this minilesson.

- Can students identify the magic in fantasies?
- Can they discuss the characteristics of magical objects?
- Are they able to connect the relevance of the magic to the overall story?
- Do they use the terms *fantasy, genre, magical,* and *objects*?

## Minilesson

To help students think about the minilesson principle, help them notice the magic in familiar fantasy stories. Here is an example.

- Show the cover of *Weslandia*.

  Think about the garden in *Weslandia*. Turn and talk about what happens after the seeds arrive.

  What is unusual about the garden?

- After time for discussion, ask students to share ideas. As needed, prompt two or three students to talk about why the garden is unusual and to use the word *magical*. Draw or ask a volunteer to draw a picture of the plants on the chart.

  Turn and talk about how the garden is important to the story.

- After time for discussion, ask students to share a few ideas. Add to chart.
- Show the cover of *Tuck Everlasting*.

  Now think about another story, *Tuck Everlasting*. What is unusual about the spring that Winnie finds?

  What is unusual about Jesse Tuck?

- Add a drawing of the spring to the chart. Ask students to discuss how the spring is magical and important to the story. Add to chart.

## Have a Try

Invite the students to talk with a partner about the magic in fantasy stories.

▶ Show the cover of *Night of the Gargoyles*.

   Think about *Night of the Gargoyles*. Turn and talk about the magical objects and how magic is important to the story.

▶ After time for discussion, ask students to share. Add responses to the chart.

## Summarize and Apply

Summarize the learning and remind students to think about the magical characters or objects in fantasy books.

   Today you noticed magical characters or objects in fantasy stories and talked about why the magic is important in the story.

▶ Write the minilesson principle at the top of the chart.

   When you read today, choose a fantasy book from the basket if you are not already reading one. Notice if there is magic in the story and think about why it is important. Bring the book when we meet so you can share.

## Share

Following independent reading time, gather students in a circle to talk about fantasy books.

   Who read a fantasy book today that had a magical character or object? Talk about the magic and how it is important to the story.

## Extend the Lesson (Optional)

After assessing students' understanding, you might decide to extend the learning.

▶ If students have seen the movie version of *Tuck Everlasting*, have them offer their opinions of how the book and movie compare. Was the magic more convincing in the book or in the movie?

| Title | Magical Character or Object | How is magic important to the story? |
|---|---|---|
| Weslandia | | The flowers that bloom in the garden lead to the creation of Weslandia. |
| natalie BABBITT TUCK EVERLASTING | | The book centers around whether drinking the water and living forever is good or bad, and what choice Winnie will make. |
| NIGHT OF THE GARGOYLES | | The gargoyles are unhappy during the day but they come alive and have fun at night. |

**Human and animal characters and normal objects are often magical.**

# RML6
## LA.U21.RML6

Reading Minilesson Principle
# Fantasy stories are often about good versus evil.

## Studying Fantasy

### You Will Need

- several familiar fantasy books that emphasize good and bad characters, such as the following from Text Set: Genre Study: Fantasy:
  - *Weslandia* by Paul Fleischman
  - *The Wolves in the Walls* by Neil Gaiman
  - *The Field Guide* by Tony DiTerlizzi and Holly Black
- chart paper and markers
- sticky notes

### Academic Language / Important Vocabulary

- fantasy
- genre
- struggle
- good
- evil

### Continuum Connection

- Notice recurring themes or motifs in traditional literature and fantasy: e.g., struggle between good and evil, the hero's quest (p. 59)

## Goal

Notice and understand that an important theme in fantasy stories is good versus evil.

## Rationale

When you teach students to notice the struggle of good versus evil in fantasy stories, they begin to recognize characteristics of the genre and think deeply about character traits and behavior in fantasy.

## Assess Learning

Observe students when they read and discuss fantasy stories and notice if there is evidence of new learning based on the goal of this minilesson.

- ▶ Are students able to identify good and evil in fantasy stories?
- ▶ Do they discuss the struggle between good and evil that often occurs in fantasy books?
- ▶ Do they use the terms *fantasy, genre, struggle, good,* and *evil*?

# Minilesson

To help students think about the minilesson principle, engage them in thinking about the struggle between good and evil in fantasy stories. Here is an example.

- ▶ Show the cover of *Weslandia*.

    **Think about Wesley and the struggle he has with other characters in the story. Turn and talk about that.**

- ▶ After time for discussion, have students share their thinking. Prompt the conversation as needed so students talk about the struggle between good and evil in the story. Write or have a student write responses on the chart. If you use *vs.* on the chart, explain that it is an abbreviation for *versus*, which means "against."

- ▶ Show the cover of *The Wolves in the Walls*.

    **How about *The Wolves in the Walls*? Think about the good characters and the bad characters. What issues do they have with each other?**

- ▶ Have a conversation about the struggle between good and evil in the story. Then ask a volunteer to add to the chart.

## Have a Try

Invite the students to talk with a partner about the struggle of good versus evil in fantasy stories.

- Show the cover of *The Field Guide*.

  Think about *The Field Guide*. Turn and talk about the struggle between good and evil in this story.

- After time for discussion, ask students to share ideas. Add responses to the chart.

## Summarize and Apply

Summarize the learning and remind students to think about good and evil in fantasy books.

  What did you notice about fantasy stories today?

- Write the minilesson principle at the top of the chart paper.

  Today, choose a fantasy book from the basket or continue reading one you have started. Look for good and evil and the struggle between them. Bring the book when we meet so you can share.

## Share

Following independent reading time, gather students in a circle.

  Did anyone notice a struggle between good and evil in a fantasy story you read today? Share what you noticed.

## Extend the Lesson (Optional)

After assessing students' understanding, you might decide to extend the learning.

- Encourage students to think more deeply about good and evil. Have them consider that good characters might have some bad traits and evil characters might have good traits or be misunderstood.

- **Writing About Reading** Ask students to write in a reader's notebook about the good versus evil struggle in a fantasy story.

### Fantasy stories are often about good versus evil.

| Title | Good | vs. | Evil |
|---|---|---|---|
| Weslandia | Wesley | vs. | The bullying behavior of the other kids |
| The Wolves in the Walls | Lucy | vs. | The wolves when they take over Lucy's house and scare her family |
| Spiderwick | The Grace children | vs. | The boggart when he does mean things to the children |

**Section 2: Literary Analysis**

## RML 7
### LA.U21.RML7

**Reading Minilesson Principle**
# Fantasy stories often reveal a lesson or something true about the world.

### You Will Need

- several familiar fantasy books that include a life lesson or universal truth, such as the following from Text Set: Genre Study: Fantasy:
  - *Weslandia* by Paul Fleischman
  - *Tuck Everlasting* by Natalie Babbitt
  - *The Wolves in the Walls* by Neil Gaiman
- chart paper prepared with columns, headings, and book titles (see next page)
- markers
- sticky notes

### Academic Language / Important Vocabulary

- fantasy
- genre
- lesson
- universal truth
- reveal

### Continuum Connection

- Understand that the messages or big ideas in fiction texts can be applied to their own lives or to other people and society (p. 58)

## Goal

Understand that the messages or big ideas in fantasy stories can be applied to their own lives or to other people and society.

## Rationale

When you teach students that fantasy stories often have a lesson or universal truth, they begin to see connections and apply lessons learned from reading fantasy stories to their own lives.

## Assess Learning

Observe students when they read and discuss fantasy stories and notice if there is evidence of new learning based on the goal of this minilesson.

- Do students recognize that fantasy stories often reveal a lesson or universal truth?
- Can they apply a lesson or universal truth from a fantasy story to their own lives?
- Do they use the terms *fantasy, genre, lesson, universal truth,* and *reveal?*

## Minilesson

To help students think about the minilesson principle, engage them in thinking about the universal truths in fantasy stories. Here is an example.

- Show the last illustration in *Weslandia*.

  Think about Wesley's journey throughout this book. What did you learn from his journey? Turn and talk about his experience.

- After time for discussion, ask students to share. Prompt the conversation so that students discuss the lesson or universal truth that is revealed by the story.

  If we want to write down the lesson or universal truth that this story reveals, what might that be?

- Write student ideas on the chart.

  In what way could you apply the lesson from *Weslandia* to your own life?

- Ask students for ideas and then add one or more to the chart.

- Show the cover of *Tuck Everlasting*.

  What lesson or universal truth does this story reveal?

  How could you apply it to your own life?

- Ask students for ideas and then add one or more to the chart.

## Have a Try

Invite the students to talk with a partner about the lessons or universal truths in *The Wolves in the Walls*.

▸ Show the cover of *The Wolves in the Walls*.

> Think about another fantasy story, *The Wolves in the Walls*. Are there any lessons or universal truths revealed in this story? Talk about that with a partner. Tell your partner how any lessons could be applied to your own life.

## Summarize and Apply

Summarize the learning and remind students to think about lessons or universal truths in fantasy stories.

> Today you talked about the lessons and universal truths in fantasy stories.

▸ Write the minilesson principle at the top of the chart paper.

> When you read today, select a fantasy book from the basket or continue reading one you have started. Look for a lesson or a universal truth and how you could use the lesson in your own life. Bring the book when we meet so you can share.

## Share

Following independent reading time, gather students in a circle.

> Who noticed a lesson or universal truth in a fantasy story? Talk about that and how you could apply the lesson or universal truth to your own life.

## Extend the Lesson (Optional)

After assessing students' understanding, you might decide to extend the learning.

▸ **Writing About Reading** Encourage students to write in a reader's notebook about the lesson or universal truth revealed in a fantasy story. Have them make connections to their own life in their writing.

**Fantasy stories often reveal a lesson or something true about the world.**

| Title | Lesson or Universal Truth | Connection to My Life |
|---|---|---|
| Weslandia | Sometimes you can make friends by doing things your own way. | I can do things I like, and others might like those things, too. |
| natalie babbitt TUCK EVERLASTING | Sometimes in life, difficult choices must be made. | When I have a hard choice to make, I can think carefully about the consequences of each choice before deciding. |
| THE WOLVES IN THE WALLS | Some problems require facing your fears. | I can be brave and believe in myself when I face a challenge. |

## Assessment

After you have taught the minilessons in this umbrella, observe students as they talk and write about their reading across instructional contexts: interactive read-aloud, independent reading, guided reading, shared reading, and book club. Use *The Literacy Continuum* (Fountas and Pinnell 2017) to guide the observation of students' reading and writing behaviors.

▶ What evidence do you have of new understandings related to fantasy books?

- Can students describe ways that fantasy stories are alike?
- Are they aware that fantasy stories cannot happen in the real world but that the setting can be in the real world or an imagined world?
- Do they notice that characters and objects are often magical?
- Do they discuss ways that fantasy stories often involve good and evil?
- Can they recognize the lesson in a fantasy story?
- Do they use terms such as *fantasy, genre, magical, imagined, elements,* and *setting*?

▶ In what other ways, beyond the scope of this umbrella, are students talking about fiction books?

- Are students reading and talking about fairy tales?
- Do they notice elements of an author's craft?

Use your observations to determine the next umbrella you will teach. You may also consult Minilessons Across the Year (pp. 59-61) for guidance.

## Read and Revise

After completing the steps in the genre study process, help students read and revise their definition of the genre based on their new understandings.

▶ **Before:** A fantasy is a made-up, magical story.

▶ **After:** A fantasy is a made-up story that has some elements that could not be true or could not happen in the real world, such as magical objects. The stories often are about good versus evil and include a lesson.

## Reader's Notebook

When this umbrella is complete, provide a copy of the minilesson principles (see resources.fountasandpinnell.com) for students to glue in the reader's notebook (in the Minilessons section if using *Reader's Notebook: Intermediate* [Fountas and Pinnell 2011]), so they can refer to the information as needed.

## Minilessons in This Umbrella

**RML1**  Fairy tales are alike in many ways.

**RML2**  The definition of a fairy tale is what is always true about it.

**RML3**  Fairy tales always include magic or the supernatural.

**RML4**  The same types of fairy tales exist in many cultures but are told in different ways.

**RML5**  The lesson or outcome reflects what the culture might value.

**RML6**  The characters often keep the same traits and seldom change.

**RML7**  Good triumphs over evil in fairy tales.

**RML8**  Fairy tales often have romance and adventure.

**RML9**  Fairy tales often begin and end in similar ways.

## Before Teaching Umbrella 22 Minilessons

When students study a genre, they examine its distinguishing characteristics. There are six broad steps in a genre study, which are described on pages 39–41.

Before beginning this genre study, select a variety of clear examples of fairy tales. Read and enjoy them with students. Fairy tales are a type of traditional literature along with fables, folktales, legends/epics/ballads, and myths. Use the following books from the *Fountas & Pinnell Classroom™ Interactive Read-Aloud Collection* text sets or use fairy tales that you have on hand.

**Genre Study: Fairy Tales**

*Rumpelstiltskin* by Paul O. Zelinsky

*Beauty and the Beast* by Jan Brett

*The Dragon Prince: A Chinese Beauty and the Beast Tale* by Laurence Yep

*Brave Red, Smart Frog: A New Book of Old Tales* by Emily Jenkins

**Cinderella Stories**

*Yeh-Shen: A Cinderella Story from China* by Louie Ai-Ling

*Sootface: An Ojibwa Cinderella Story* by Robert D. San Souci

*The Persian Cinderella* by Shirley Climo

*Domítila: A Cinderella Tale from the Mexican Tradition* by Jewell Reinhart Coburn

*The Rough-Face Girl* by Rafe Martin

As you read aloud and enjoy these texts together, help students notice common elements of fairy tales.

**Fairy Tales**

**Cinderella Stories**

Section 2: Literary Analysis

**Reading Minilesson Principle**
# Fairy tales are alike in many ways.

### You Will Need

- basket of fairy tales with which students are familiar
- chart paper and markers
- sticky notes

### Academic Language / Important Vocabulary

- fairy tale
- gender
- characteristics
- traditional literature (optional)

### Continuum Connection

- Notice and understand the characteristics of some specific fiction genres: e.g., realistic fiction, historical fiction, folktale, fairy tale, fractured fairy tale, fable, myth, legend, epic, ballad, fantasy including science fiction, hybrid texts (p. 58)

## Goal

Notice and understand the characteristics of fairy tales as a genre.

## Rationale

When you teach students the ways that fairy tales are alike, they will know what to expect when reading them and understand the characteristics of this kind of traditional literature. Traditional literature provides a foundation for understanding and enjoying fantasy.

## Assess Learning

Observe students when they read and talk about fairy tales. Notice if there is evidence of new learning based on the goal of this minilesson.

- ▶ Are students able to talk about the ways that fairy tales are alike?
- ▶ Do they understand that some characteristics always occur and some characteristics often occur in fairy tales?
- ▶ Do they use the terms *fairy tale, gender, characteristics,* and *traditional literature*?

## Minilesson

To help students think about the minilesson principle, help them analyze the characteristics of fairy tales across several examples. Here is one example.

- ▶ Ask students to sit in small groups. Show the covers of multiple fairy tales with which students are familiar.

  Think about these fairy tales and the different ways they are all alike. As you share your ideas think about whether each is *always* or *often* true in a fairy tale.

- ▶ After time for discussion, ask students to share noticings. Create an *Always* section and an *Often* section on chart paper. As students share, record responses.

  What other things do you remember about these fairy tales?

- ▶ Continue to record responses. Consider providing one or more of the following prompts:

  - *What did you notice about the characters and events?*
  - *What did you notice about the endings?*
  - *What did you notice about how the characters behave?*
  - *How do the characters solve their problems?*

## Have a Try

Invite the students to examine more fairy tales in a small group.

▶ Provide each group with one of the fairy tales.

Talk with each other about the characteristics listed on the chart. How many can you find in the story? Do you notice anything we did not mention yet?

▶ After they turn and talk, add noticings to the chart.

## Summarize and Apply

Summarize the learning and remind students to notice the characteristics of fairy tales.

Today we talked about fairy tales.

▶ Add the title *Fairy Tales* to the chart and review the noticings.

When you read today, choose a fairy tale from the basket. As you read, see if you notice characteristics from the chart and add a sticky note to that page. Bring the book when we meet so you can share.

## Share

Following independent reading time, gather students in small groups. Make sure at least one person in each group read a fairy tale.

Tell your group which characteristics from our chart you found in the book. Show any pages that you marked with sticky notes and point out what you noticed on that page.

## Extend the Lesson (Optional)

After assessing students' understanding, you might decide to extend the learning.

▶ Using a reader's notebook, students can keep track of the number of fairy tales they read in two ways: first, by marking *Traditional Literature* on their reading lists, and second, by tallying how many fairy tales they have read on the reading requirements page (see Umbrella 1: Introducing a Reader's Notebook, found in Section Four: Writing About Reading).

▶ Introduce your students to Genre Thinkmarks for fairy tales. A Genre Thinkmark is a tool that guides readers to note certain elements of a genre in their reading. To download this resource, visit resources.fountasandpinnell.com.

---

### Fairy Tales

**Noticings:**

| Always | Often |
|---|---|
| • Come from all different cultures | • Good wins over evil. |
| • Characters and events can't exist in real life. | • Goodness rewarded and evil punished |
| • Same types of characters appear. | • Characters simple—either good or bad |
| • Magic or the supernatural in the stories. | • Happy ending |
| | • Romance and adventure |
| | • Lesson or outcome reflects the values of the culture. |
| | • Repetition |
| | • Similar language, such as "once upon a time" or "long ago" |

---

# RML2
## LA.U22.RML2

Reading Minilesson Principle
# The definition of a fairy tale is what is always true about it.

## Studying Fairy Tales

### You Will Need

- a fairy tale with which students are familiar, such as:
  - *Rumpelstiltskin* by Paul O. Zelinsky, from Text Set: Genre Study: Fairy Tales
  - *The Rough-Face Girl* by Rafe Martin, from Text Set: Cinderella Stories
- fairy tale noticings chart from RML1
- chart paper and markers
- basket of fairy tales
- sticky notes

### Academic Language / Important Vocabulary

- fairy tale
- genre
- definition
- traditional literature (optional)

### Continuum Connection

- Notice and understand the characteristics of some specific fiction genres: e.g., realistic fiction, historical fiction, folktale, fairy tale, fractured fairy tale, fable, myth, legend, epic, ballad, fantasy including science fiction, hybrid texts (p. 58)

## Goal

Create a working definition of fairy tales.

## Rationale

When you teach students to construct a working definition of fairy tales, they are able to form their own understandings so they will know what to expect of the genre, as well as learn to revise their understandings as they gain additional experiences with traditional literature. Understanding the elements of a fairy tale provides a base for comprehending fantasy.

## Assess Learning

Observe students when they read and talk about fairy tales. Notice if there is evidence of new learning based on the goal of this minilesson.

- Do students participate in creating a working definition of a fairy tale?
- Do they understand that a working definition of fairy tales is what is always true about them?
- Can they use the vocabulary *fairy tale, genre, definition*, and *traditional literature*?

## Minilesson

To help students think about a definition of fairy tales, engage them in summarizing the characteristics from the Always list (RML1). Here is an example.

- Show the fairy tale noticings chart and review the characteristics.

  What are some things you know about fairy tales?

  The definition of fairy tales tells what is always true about them.

- On chart paper, write the words *Fairy tales are*, leaving space for constructing a working definition.

  What would you write to finish this sentence with a definition that tells what fairy tales are? Turn and talk about that. Use the noticings chart to help you.

- After time for discussion, ask students to share ideas. Use the ideas to create a working definition for the class and write it on the chart paper. Ask a volunteer to read the definition.

- If appropriate you might want to discuss the term *traditional literature*.

  A fairy tale is a story that emphasizes magic and the supernatural. It is a kind of traditional literature that was passed down orally from one group to another over a long time.

## Have a Try

Invite the students to talk with a partner about how *Rumpelstiltskin* or *The Rough-Face Girl* fit the definition of a fairy tale.

> Does the book fit the definition of a fairy tale? What makes you think that?

▶ Ask a few students to share. Add to the definition as new ideas emerge from the conversation.

## Summarize and Apply

Summarize the learning and remind students to think about the definition of a fairy tale.

▶ Read the definition aloud with students and ask whether there is anything else that should be added.

> When you read today, choose a fairy tale from the basket and think about how the book fits the definition. Add a sticky note to any pages that make you think about the definition of a fairy tale. Bring the book when we meet so you can share.

## Share

Following independent reading time, gather students in the meeting area to talk about their reading.

> Who would like to share how the fairy tale you read fits the definition and what examples from the fairy tale helped you know that? Show any pages with sticky notes and talk about what you noticed on those pages.

## Extend the Lesson (Optional)

After assessing students' understanding, you might decide to extend the learning.

▶ Have students create a display of fairy tales in your classroom or school library. Include book reviews or posters in the display.

▶ If students have been giving book talks, have two or three students recommend fairy tales (see MGT.U3.RML2).

---

## Fairy Tales

Fairy tales are imagined stories that include magic. The characters and events couldn't exist in real life.

**Reading Minilesson Principle**
# Fairy tales always include magic or the supernatural.

## You Will Need

- several familiar fairy tales that include the element of magic or the supernatural, such as:
  - *Sootface* by Robert D. San Souci, from Text Set: Cinderella Stories
  - *The Dragon Prince* by Laurence Yep and *Brave Red, Smart Frog* by Emily Jenkins, from Text Set: Genre Studies: Fairy Tales
- chart paper and markers
- basket of fairy tales
- sticky notes

## Academic Language / Important Vocabulary

- fairy tale
- traditional tale
- supernatural

### Continuum Connection

- Identify elements of traditional literature and modern fantasy: e.g., the supernatural; imaginary and otherworldly creatures; gods and goddesses; talking animals, toys, and dolls; heroic characters; technology or scientific advances; time travel; aliens or outer space (p. 58)

## Goal

Understand that the use of magic and the presence of the supernatural are important elements of fairy tales.

## Rationale

When students understand that magic and the presence of the supernatural are elements of fairy tales it helps them to identify and gain a deeper understanding of this type of traditional tale. These understandings become a base for comprehending complex fantasy.

## Assess Learning

Observe students when they read and talk about fairy tales. Notice if there is evidence of new learning based on the goal of this minilesson.

- Do students recognize and discuss the magical or supernatural elements of fairy tales?
- Do they use the vocabulary *fairy tale, traditional tale,* and *supernatural*?

## Minilesson

To help students think about the minilesson principle, engage them in a discussion about magic or the supernatural as an element of fairy tales. Here is an example:

- Show the cover of *Sootface*. Read a few pages that demonstrate magical or supernatural elements, such as the magic comb or Sootface's scars washing away.

  What happened to Sootface in this part of the fairy tale?

- Record responses on a chart.
- Repeat this process with *The Dragon Prince*, reading the pages where the serpent turned into a dragon (p. 3) and the dragon turned into a man (p. 13).

## Have a Try

Invite the students to talk in small groups about magic or supernatural elements in another fairy tale.

- ◗ Show the title page of "Snow White" from *Brave Red, Smart Frog*. Read the page on which the mirror answers the stepmother (p. 5) and the page on which Snow White is alive but not breathing or moving (p. 15).

  What happened in these parts of this fairy tale?

- ◗ After time for discussion, ask a few groups to share. Record responses.

## Summarize and Apply

Summarize the learning and remind students that fairy tales always include magic or the supernatural.

  Look at the chart. What do you notice about what happens in all of these stories?

- ◗ Gather ideas and clarify, writing the principle at the top of the chart.

  If you have finished the book you are reading, choose a fairy tale from this basket. When you find a magical or supernatural part, place a sticky note on it so you can share it when we come back together.

## Share

Following independent reading time, gather students in small groups to talk about fairy tales.

  With your group, talk about the fairy tale you read today. Share the pages you marked with a sticky note and talk about the magical or supernatural elements.

## Extend the Lesson (Optional)

After assessing students' understanding, you might decide to extend the learning.

- ◗ Encourage students to record the genre of the book they read as traditional literature (TL) in a reader's notebook.

- ◗ **Writing About Reading** Invite students to write in a reader's notebook about a magical or supernatural element in a fairy tale they have read. They could write about how the element was important to the story or about who had those special powers.

### Fairy tales always include magic or the supernatural.

| Book | Magical or Supernatural Part |
|---|---|
| SOOTFACE | • A magic comb made Sootface's hair long and thick.<br>• Water washed away her hurt and sadness. |
| | • The serpent turned into a dragon.<br>• The dragon turned into a man. |
| BRAVE RED SMART FROG | • The queen's mirror spoke to her.<br>• Snow White seemed lifeless, but was not. She awoke with a kiss from a prince. |

Section 2: Literary Analysis

# RML 4
## LA.U22.RML4

**Reading Minilesson Principle**
## The same types of fairy tales exist in many cultures but are told in different ways.

## Studying Fairy Tales

### You Will Need

- several versions of a familiar fairy tale from various cultures from Text Set: Cinderella Stories, such as:
  - *The Persian Cinderella* by Shirley Climo
  - *Yeh-Shen* by Louie Ai-Ling
  - *The Rough-Face Girl* by Rafe Martin
- chart paper and markers
- basket of fairy tales from different cultures
- sticky notes

### Academic Language / Important Vocabulary

- fairy tale
- culture

### Continuum Connection

- Notice and understand the characteristics of some specific fiction genres: e.g., realistic fiction, historical fiction, folktale, fairy tale, fractured fairy tale, fable, myth, legend, epic, ballad, fantasy including science fiction, hybrid texts [p. 58]

## Goal

Understand that the same fairy tales exist in many cultures but are told in ways that reflect the culture of the place of origin.

## Rationale

Students can compare and contrast the same fairy tale from different cultures to enhance their understanding of the tale and their appreciation of diverse cultures.

## Assess Learning

Observe students when they read similar fairy tales from different cultures. Notice if there is evidence of new learning based on the goal of this minilesson.

- ▶ Can students describe the different ways fairy tales from other cultures are told?
- ▶ Are they using the academic language *fairy tale* and *culture*?

## Minilesson

To help students think about the minilesson principle, engage them in a discussion of similar fairy tales from different cultures. Here is an example:

- ▶ Gather *The Persian Cinderella* and *The Rough-Face Girl*.

  What do you notice about these two stories? What do they have in common?

- ▶ Read a few pages from each to support the conversation, or consider using these prompts:
  - *What is the setting in each version?*
  - *What do you notice about the characters of these different versions?*
  - *What is similar/different in terms of the plot of these versions?*
- ▶ Record responses on a chart.

## Have a Try

Invite the students to talk with a small group about another version of Cinderella.

> Talk about how you would fill in the chart for *Yeh-Shen*.

❱ After time for discussion, ask a few groups to share. Record responses on the chart.

## Summarize and Apply

Summarize the learning and remind students that the same types of fairy tales exist in other cultures.

> What does the chart show about fairy tales?

❱ To emphasize the similarities, highlight the common words and write the principle at the top.

> If you have finished the book you are reading, choose a fairy tale to read. Bring the book with you to share when we come back together.

## Share

Following independent reading time, gather students together in the meeting area to talk about their reading.

> If you read a fairy tale today, talk about whether there is a similar version of it from another country.

## Extend the Lesson (Optional)

After assessing students' understanding, you might decide to extend the learning.

❱ Ask students to list the details in each version that give the story its cultural feel.

❱ **Writing About Reading** When students write about a fairy tale, ask them to link it to a similar tale when appropriate.

❱ **Writing About Reading** Have students write in a reader's notebook about how different versions of fairy tales exist in many cultures but are told in different ways. An alternative is to have them fill in a grid similar to the chart in this minilesson (visit resources.fountasandpinnell.com to download a grid that students can fill in and then glue into a reader's notebook).

### The same types of fairy tales exist in many cultures but are told in different ways.

| The PERSIAN CINDERELLA | The Rough-Face Girl | Yeh-Shen |
|---|---|---|
| Takes place in Persia | Takes place on shores of Lake Ontario | Takes place in Southern China |
| Treated cruelly by stepmother and stepsisters | Treated cruelly by older sisters | Treated cruelly by stepmother |
| Got clothes for No Ruz from magic jug | Made clothes from birch bark | Got clothes for spring celebration from magic fish bones |
| Went to No Ruz and lost an anklet | | Went to spring celebration and lost a golden slipper |
| Married the prince | Married the Invisible Being | Married the king |

**Reading Minilesson Principle**
# The lesson or outcome reflects what the culture might value.

## You Will Need

- fairy tales reflecting cultural values from Text Set: Cinderella Stories, such as:
  - *Domítila* by Jewell Reinhart Coburn
  - *The Rough-Face Girl* by Rafe Martin
  - *The Persian Cinderella* by Shirley Climo
- chart paper and markers

## Academic Language / Important Vocabulary

- lesson
- outcome
- theme
- compassion
- culture
- value

### Continuum Connection

- Infer and understand the moral lesson or cultural teaching in traditional literature (p. 58)

## Goal

Infer the moral or lesson and understand that the story outcome or lesson reflects the values of the culture of the place of origin.

## Rationale

When students understand that the moral or lesson of a fairy tale reflects the values of the culture of origin, they can think more deeply about the theme of that version of the tale and the culture.

## Assess Learning

Observe students when they discuss the moral or lesson of fairy tales. Notice if there is evidence of new learning based on the goal of this minilesson.

- Can students describe what values the fairy tale reflects?
- Do they use the vocabulary *lesson*, *outcome*, *theme*, *compassion*, *culture*, and *value*?

## Minilesson

To help students think about the minilesson principle, engage them in a discussion of the lesson or outcome of a fairy tale. Here is an example.

- From *Domítila*, read the paragraph in the second column of the first page of print.

  What lesson does this writer want you to think about?

  What do you think the people who retold this story might value? What makes you think that?

- Record responses on chart paper.
- Choose a few proverbs from the book to read.

  Why do you think the author included these?

- Record responses on the chart.
- Repeat this process with *The Rough-Face Girl*, reading a few parts of the book that show the importance of nature and inner beauty.

## Have a Try

Invite the students to talk with a partner about *The Persian Cinderella*.

> The author's note tells that the prince's name, *Mehrdad*, means "one who shows compassion." That means he is concerned with the suffering of others. Why do you think the author chose that name? What do you notice in the story that makes you think that? Does the name relate to the lesson of the tale? Turn and talk to a partner.

▶ Ask a few partners to share. Record responses.

## Summarize and Apply

Summarize the learning and remind students to notice how the lesson or outcome reflects what the culture might value.

> Today you talked about the lessons learned in fairy tales. What do the lessons tell you about the culture from which the story comes?

▶ Review the chart and write the principle at the top.

> Today choose a fairy tale to read. Think about what values are important in the story and be ready to share when we come back together.

## Share

Following independent reading time, gather students together to talk about their reading.

> Today you read fairy tales from a variety of cultures. What do you think the culture of each fairy tale might value? Why do you think that?

## Extend the Lesson (Optional)

After assessing students' understanding, you might decide to extend the learning.

▶ Continue reading more fairy tales from different cultures and discuss what the culture might value.

▶ **Writing About Reading** Have students write in a reader's notebook about what the values of a particular culture might be, using evidence from a fairy tale.

### The lesson or outcome reflects what the culture might value.

| | Place of Origin | Lesson/ Outcome of the Tale | How do you know? |
|---|---|---|---|
| Domitila | Mexico | • Work, help, and love are important. | • The author includes some proverbs. |
| The Rough-Face Girl | An Algonquin Indian Cinderella | • Nature is important. <br> • Inner beauty is more important than outer beauty. | • Shows the great beauty of the earth and skies <br> • The wise woman could see all the way down to your heart. |
| The Persian Cinderella | Persia | • Be patient, caring, and compassionate. | • Mehrdad's name means compassion. <br> • Settareh gives an old woman coins for clothes. <br> • The prince patiently cares for the injured turtle dove. |

*Section 2: Literary Analysis*

## RML 6
LA.U22.RML6

**Reading Minilesson Principle**
## The characters often keep the same traits and seldom change.

## Studying Fairy Tales

### You Will Need

- familiar fairy tales with characters that exemplify static traits, such as:
  - *Brave Red, Smart Frog* by Emily Jenkins, from Text Set: Genre Study: Fairy Tales
  - *Yeh-Shen* by Louie Ai-Ling, from Text Set: Cinderella Stories
- chart paper and markers
- basket of fairy tales
- sticky notes

### Academic Language / Important Vocabulary

- fairy tale
- character traits
- seldom

### Continuum Connection

- Notice predictable or static characters (characters that do not change) as typical in traditional literature (p. 59)

### Goal

Understand that the characters in fairy tales are usually flat (i.e., either good or bad) and static.

### Rationale

When students notice that characters in fairy tales often keep the same traits from the beginning of the story to the end, they will recognize clear examples of these traits in their own lives and gain a deeper understanding of fairy tales. They begin to understand the opposition of good and evil in traditional literature and fantasy.

### Assess Learning

Observe students when they discuss characters from fairy tales. Notice if there is evidence of new learning based on the goal of this minilesson.

- Do students notice that characters in fairy tales seldom change (or change very little)?
- Can they use that information to predict how characters might act?
- Are students able to use the terms *fairy tale, character traits,* and *seldom*?

## Minilesson

To help students think about the minilesson principle, engage them in an interactive discussion about how characters in fairy tales remain static. Here is an example.

- Display the cover of *Brave Red, Smart Frog* and then turn to "Snow White."

  Think about the main characters in "Snow White." Turn and talk about the words you would use to describe Snow White and the Queen, or tell what they are like.

  When you describe what they are like, you identify their character traits.

- Read a few pages that demonstrate the characters' traits if students need a reminder. After time for discussion, create a chart. Ask students to share ideas about the characters and add observations to the chart.

  You have identified what these characters are like. Are you thinking about how they are at the beginning of the story, at the end, or in the whole story?

- Repeat this process for *Yeh-Shen*.

## Have a Try

Invite the students to talk with a partner about the characters in fairy tales.

> Take a look at the character traits we listed for these fairy tale characters. Think about the beginning, middle, and end of each fairy tale. Are the characters the same in each part of the story, or do they change? Talk about that with your partner.

▶ As each character is discussed, ask a volunteer to write *Yes* or *No* on a sticky note and place it on the chart.

## Summarize and Apply

Summarize the learning and ask students what they notice about fairy tales.

> What does the chart show about fairy tale characters?

▶ Write the principle at the top of the chart.

> When you read today, you may choose a fairy tale from this basket. Place sticky notes when you notice a character trait of a main character. As you read, think about whether these characters change. Bring the book back when we meet so you can share.

## Share

Following independent reading time, gather students in small groups to talk about their reading. Make sure at least one person in each group read a fairy tale.

> Talk about the main characters in the fairy tale you read today. What are they like? Did they change?

> If you read another kind of fiction story, did you notice if the main character changed?

## Extend the Lesson (Optional)

After assessing students' understanding, you might decide to extend the learning.

▶ Gather other fairy tales or different versions of fairy tales. Read aloud or have students read independently and then discuss the characters in those fairy tales.

▶ **Writing About Reading** Have students write in a reader's notebook about a character in a fairy tale.

**The characters often keep the same traits and seldom change.**

| Book | Character | Traits | Does the character change? |
|---|---|---|---|
| BRAVE RED SMART FROG | • Snow White | • hardworking, gentle, warm, bright, kind | No |
| | • New Queen, January | • cold, evil, selfish, jealous | No |
| Yeh-Shen | • Yeh-Shen | • Hardworking, lonely, generous | No |
| | • Stepmother | • Evil, selfish, jealous | No |

Section 2: Literary Analysis

**Reading Minilesson Principle**
# Good triumphs over evil in fairy tales.

## You Will Need

- fairy tales with good triumphing over evil from Text Set: Genre Study: Fairy Tales, such as:
  - *Brave Red, Smart Frog* by Emily Jenkins
  - *Rumpelstiltskin* by Paul O. Zelinsky
  - *The Dragon Prince* by Laurence Yep
- chart paper and markers
- basket of fairy tales
- sticky notes

## Academic Language / Important Vocabulary

- fairy tale
- characters
- message/theme
- triumph

## Continuum Connection

- Notice reoccurring themes or motifs in traditional literature and fantasy: e.g., struggle between good and evil, the hero's quest (p. 59)

## Goal

Understand that a reoccurring theme in fairy tales is that good triumphs over evil.

## Rationale

When students understand that good triumphs over evil in fairy tales, they can turn their focus to the characters, plot, and other themes. This understanding builds a foundation for understanding complex fantasy.

## Assess Learning

Observe students when they read and talk about fairy tales. Notice if there is evidence of new learning based on the goal of this minilesson.

- ◗ Do students understand that in most fairy tales good wins over evil?
- ◗ Do they use the vocabulary *fairy tale*, *characters*, *message/theme*, and *triumph*?

# Minilesson

To help students think about the minilesson principle, engage them in noticing a commonality among fairy tales: good triumphs over evil. Here is an example.

- ◗ Remind students of the story "Hansel and Gretel" from *Brave Red, Smart Frog*.

  > What happens at the end of this story?

  > Who ends up triumphing at the end?

  > Who doesn't end up well?

- ◗ Record responses on chart.
- ◗ Repeat these questions with *Rumpelstiltskin*. Record responses on the chart.

## Have a Try

Invite the students to talk with a small group about what happens to the characters at the end of *The Dragon Prince*.

▶ Read a few pages of *The Dragon Prince*.

Talk about what happens to the characters at the end.

▶ Ask two groups to share with the whole group. Record responses on the chart.

## Summarize and Apply

Summarize the learning and remind students to notice what happens to the characters at the end of a fairy tale.

What does the chart show about characters at the end of a fairy tale?

▶ Support students' thinking about how good triumphs over evil in these tales. Write the principle on the chart.

If you have finished the book you are reading, choose a fairy tale to read. As you read, notice how the book ends. Jot down on a sticky note an example of how good triumphs over evil. Bring the book and the sticky note when we meet so you can share.

## Share

Following independent reading time, gather students in the meeting area to talk about their reading.

If you read a fairy tale, what did you notice about how good triumphs over evil?

▶ Ask two or three students to share what they wrote on their sticky notes and add the sticky notes to the chart.

## Extend the Lesson (Optional)

After assessing students' understanding, you might decide to extend the learning.

▶ Continue adding to the chart as students notice other examples of good triumphing over evil.

▶ Talk about other themes represented in fairy tales, such as inner beauty being more important than outer beauty.

▶ **Writing About Reading** Have students write in a reader's notebook about the characters in a fairy tale and how good characters triumph over evil characters.

| Good triumphs over evil in fairy tales. | |
|---|---|
| **Book** | **What Happens at the End of the Story** |
| BRAVE RED SMART FROG A NEW BOOK OF OLD TALES  EMILY JENKINS | • Hansel, Gretel, and their father go home and are a family again.<br>• Old Mother and Stepmother die. |
| Rumpelstiltskin | • The queen keeps her son.<br>• Rumpelstiltskin is never heard from again. |
| | • Seven lives a long happy life with the prince.<br>• Three is sent back home to her family. |

**Reading Minilesson Principle**
# Fairy tales often have romance and adventure.

## Studying Fairy Tales

### You Will Need

- fairy tales with romance and/or adventure, such as:
  - *Brave Red, Smart Frog* by Emily Jenkins and *The Dragon Prince* by Laurence Yep, from Text Set: Genre Study: Fairy Tales
  - *The Persian Cinderella* by Shirley Climo, from Text Set: Cinderella Stories
- chart paper, with the principle written at the top
- markers
- basket of fairy tales

### Academic Language / Important Vocabulary

- fairy tale
- romance
- adventure

### Continuum Connection

- Identify elements of traditional literature and modern fantasy: e.g., the supernatural; imaginary and otherworldly creatures; gods and goddesses; talking animals, toys, and dolls; heroic characters; technology or scientific advances; time travel; aliens or outer space (p. 58)

- Notice reoccurring themes or motifs in traditional literature and fantasy: e.g., struggle between good and evil, the hero's quest (p. 59)

## Goal

Understand that fairy tales often have an element of romance and/or adventure.

## Rationale

When students understand that most fairy tales have romance and/or adventure they can focus their attention on other important parts of the tale.

## Assess Learning

Observe students when they discuss fairy tales. Notice if there is evidence of new learning based on the goal of this minilesson.

- ❭ Are students able to describe the romance and adventure found in most fairy tales?
- ❭ Do they use the vocabulary *fairy tale, romance,* and *adventure*?

## Minilesson

To help students think about the minilesson principle, engage them in a discussion of specific examples of romance and adventure in fairy tales. Here is an example.

> When we created the noticings chart about fairy tales you said that many fairy tales have romance and adventure.
>
> What happened in "The Frog Prince" that you think is romance or adventure?

- ❭ Prompt students by reading romantic or adventurous parts of "The Frog Prince" from *Brave Red, Smart Frog*, if necessary. Record responses on a chart.
- ❭ Repeat this process with *The Dragon Prince*.

## Have a Try

Invite the students to talk with a partner about romance and adventure in *The Persian Cinderella*.

> Turn and talk about the romance and adventure you notice in this book.

▶ After time for discussion, ask students to share how romance and adventure occurred and add to the chart.

## Summarize and Apply

Summarize the learning and remind students to notice romance or adventure in fairy tales.

> What did you notice about fairy tales today?

▶ Review the chart.

> If you have finished the book you are reading, choose a fairy tale from this basket. Notice the romance and adventure. Bring the book when we meet so you can share.

## Share

Following independent reading time, gather students in the meeting area to talk about fairy tales in small groups. Make sure at least one student in each group read a fairy tale.

> If you read a fairy tale today, talk to your group about the examples of romance and/or adventure you noticed.

## Extend the Lesson (Optional)

After assessing students' understanding, you might decide to extend the learning.

▶ Add more examples of romance and adventure to the chart as students read more fairy tales.

▶ **Writing About Reading** Have students compare and contrast in writing the romance and adventure in two different fairy tales. For example, *Beauty and the Beast* and *The Dragon Prince* or *Beauty and the Beast* and "The Frog Prince."

| Fairy tales often have romance and adventure. | | |
|---|---|---|
| **Book** | **Romance** | **Adventure** |
| BRAVE RED SMART FROG | • A true love's kiss turned the frog into a human again. | • The frog and the princess talked about adventures they had. |
| | • The Dragon Prince and Seven get married.<br>• The prince's heart told him that Three was impersonating Seven. | • The dragon takes Seven on a flight around parts of the world and then down under the water. |
| The PERSIAN CINDERELLA | • Prince Mehrdad wanted to marry Settareh. | • Settareh went to the marketplace and saw many treasures, helped a woman, and bought the broken blue jug. |

Section 2: Literary Analysis

Umbrella 22: Studying Fairy Tales ▪ 409

**Reading Minilesson Principle**
# Fairy tales often begin and end in similar ways.

## You Will Need

- fairy tales that begin and end with traditional literary language patterns, such as:
  - *Beauty and the Beast* by Jan Brett, from Text Set: Genre Study: Fairy Tales
  - *The Persian Cinderella* by Shirley Climo, from Text Set: Cinderella Stories
  - *The Dragon Prince* by Laurence Yep, from Text Set: Genre Study: Fairy Tales
- a chart prepared with the beginning and ending quotes from the three books with the ending sentences covered
- markers
- sticky notes
- highlighters
- basket of fairy tales

## Academic Language / Important Vocabulary

- beginning
- ending
- fairy tale

## Continuum Connection

- Notice and remember literary language patterns that are characteristic of traditional literature: e.g., *once upon a time, long ago and far away, therefore, finally, at long last, happily ever after* [p. 60]

## Goal

Notice and remember literary language patterns that are characteristic of the beginning and ending of fairy tales.

## Rationale

When students recognize the familiar way many fairy tales begin and end (usually happily), they free themselves to focus their attention on other aspects of the fairy tales, such as characters' traits, setting, plot, and theme.

## Assess Learning

Observe students when they talk about fairy tales. Notice if there is evidence of new learning based on the goal of this minilesson.

- Can students describe how fairy tales often begin and end?
- Do they use the terms *beginning, ending,* and *fairy tale*?

## Minilesson

To help students think about how fairy tales begin and end, engage them in listening to examples of beginnings and endings.

- Hold up *Beauty and the Beast, The Persian Cinderella,* and *The Dragon Prince*.

  Here are three fairy tales that you know. Look at the sentences I've written on the chart from the beginning of each book. What do you notice about them?

- Guide students to notice the similarity in the way each fairy tale begins. Invite a student to highlight the similar words on the chart.

## Have a Try

Invite the students to talk as a group about endings of fairy tales.

▶ Reveal the ending sentences and repeat the minilesson process.

What do you notice about how these fairy tales end?

## Summarize and Apply

Summarize the learning and remind students to notice that fairy tales often begin and end in similar ways.

▶ Review the chart.

What do you notice about the beginnings and endings of these fairy tales?

▶ Write the principle at the top of the chart.

If you have finished the book you are reading, read a fairy tale today and pay attention to how the tale begins and ends. Does it end happily?

Mark with a sticky note the page that makes you think so. Bring the book when we come back together so you can share what you noticed.

## Share

Following independent reading time, gather students together in small groups.

If you read a fairy tale today, discuss with your group what you noticed about the beginning and ending of the tale. Did it end happily for the good characters?

## Extend the Lesson (Optional)

After assessing students' understanding, you might decide to extend the learning.

▶ Add language to the chart that is used to begin and end other fairy tales.

▶ **Writing About Reading** Encourage students to collect examples in a reader's notebook of the way fairy tales begin and end. They may share those with other readers.

### Fairy tales often begin and end in similar ways.

| Book | Beginning | Ending |
|---|---|---|
| | "Once upon a time, there lived..." | "They were married the very next day, and went on to live happily ever after." |
| | "Long ago, when Persia was a land of princes and poets, there lived a maiden..." | "But it was just the beginning of happiness for Settareh." |
| | "Once there was a poor old farmer with seven daughters..." | "And then Seven and the Prince and the old woman settled down to a long happy life together." |

**Section 2: Literary Analysis**

## Assessment

After you have taught the minilessons in this umbrella, observe students as they talk and write about their reading across instructional contexts: interactive read-aloud, independent reading, guided reading, shared reading, and book club. Use *The Literacy Continuum* (Fountas and Pinnell 2017) to guide the observation of students' reading and writing behaviors.

> What evidence do you have of new understandings related to fairy tales?
>
> - Do students notice the ways that fairy tales are alike?
> - Can they describe the magical or supernatural elements of fairy tales?
> - What do they notice about fairy tales from different cultures?
> - Are they aware that characters in fairy tales are either good or bad?
> - Do they notice that in most fairy tales good triumphs over evil and there is usually a happy ending?
> - Do they use vocabulary such as *fairy tale*, *characteristics*, *traditional literature*, and *culture*?
>
> In what other ways, beyond the scope of this umbrella, are students talking about traditional literature?
>
> - Do students show interest in reading other types of traditional literature?

Use your observations to determine the next umbrella you will teach. You may also consult Minilessons Across the Year (pp. 59–61) for guidance.

## Read and Revise

After completing the steps in the genre study process, help students read and revise their definition of the genre based on their new understandings.

> **Before:** Fairy tales are imagined stories that include magic. The characters and events couldn't exist in real life.

> **After:** Fairy tales are traditional tales that include magic. The characters and events couldn't exist in real life. The characters often have similar traits and rarely change. Fairy tales often include romance and adventure and good usually triumphs over evil.

## Reader's Notebook

When this umbrella is complete, provide a copy of the minilesson principles (see resources.fountasandpinnell.com) for students to glue in the reader's notebook (in the Minilessons section if using *Reader's Notebook: Intermediate* [Fountas and Pinnell 2011]), so they can refer to the information as needed.

**Genre Study:
Historical Fiction**

## Minilessons in This Umbrella

**RML1**    Historical fiction stories are alike in many ways.

**RML2**    The definition of historical fiction is what is always true about it.

**RML3**    The setting is important to the story in historical fiction.

**RML4**    Historical fiction is always imagined but may be based on real people, places, or events.

**RML5**    Historical fiction writers often use the language of the times in the dialogue.

**RML6**    Historical fiction writers use the past to give a message that can be applied today.

## Before Teaching Umbrella 23 Minilessons

Genre study supports students in knowing what to expect when beginning to read a text in a genre. It helps students develop an understanding of the distinguishing characteristics of a genre and gives students the tools they need to navigate a variety of texts. There are six broad steps in the genre study process, and they are described on pages 39–41. Before engaging in genre study, students must read and discuss multiple examples of the genre.

Prior to teaching this series of minilessons, read and discuss a variety of historical fiction stories that include diverse people, cultures, time periods, and circumstances. For this umbrella, it is important to select books that are clear examples of historical fiction. Find examples in the following books from the *Fountas & Pinnell Classroom™ Interactive Read-Aloud Collection* text sets or choose historical fiction books from your own library.

**Author/Illustrator
Study: Allen Say**

### Genre Study: Historical Fiction

*Uncle Jed's Barbershop* by Margaret King Mitchell

*The Buffalo Storm* by Katherine Applegate

*The Glorious Flight: Across the Channel with Louis Blériot* by Alice and Martin Provensen

*The Houdini Box* by Brian Selznick

*Dad, Jackie, and Me* by Myron Uhlberg

### Author/Illustrator Study: Allen Say

*Tea with Milk*

As you read aloud and enjoy these texts together, help students

- notice similarities across them,

- think about whether the stories are are based on real past events, and

- make connections to their own lives.

# RML1

## LA.U23.RML1

**Reading Minilesson Principle**
# Historical fiction stories are alike in many ways.

## Studying Historical Fiction

### You Will Need

- collection of familiar historical fiction books
- chart paper with the headings *Historical Fiction* and *Noticings* and sections for *Always* and *Often*
- markers

### Academic Language / Important Vocabulary

- historical fiction
- narrative structure
- characteristics

### Continuum Connection

- Notice and understand the characteristics of some specific fiction genres: e.g., realistic fiction, historical fiction, folktale, fairy tale, fractured fairy tale, fable, myth, legend, fantasy including science fiction and hybrid (p. 58)

## Goal

Notice and understand the characteristics of historical fiction.

## Rationale

When students study the historical fiction genre through inquiry, they gain a deeper understanding both of individual stories and the genre as a whole. When they develop an understanding of historical fiction, they will know what to expect when they encounter books of that genre (see pages 39–41). In addition, historical fiction can make past times come alive for students.

## Assess Learning

Observe students when they read and talk about historical fiction and notice if there is evidence of new learning based on the goal of this minilesson.

- Can students notice similarities across several historical fiction stories?
- Do they use academic language, such as *historical fiction, narrative structure,* and *characteristics*?

# Minilesson

To help students think about the minilesson principle, engage the students in noticing the characteristics across texts. Here is an example.

- Have students sit in small groups and provide each group with several examples of familiar historical fiction books. As needed, groups can rotate the books so they have an opportunity to compare several examples.

  We have read many historical fiction books in class, and you may have read others on your own. Talk with your group about how the historical fiction books you know are alike.

  What did you notice about how they are alike?

- As students share, have a conversation to get them thinking about the ways that historical fiction books are *always* alike and *often* alike. The following prompts may be helpful:

  - *What have you noticed about historical fiction stories?*
  - *What have you noticed about the characters, setting, and plot, or narrative structure?*
  - *When do the stories take place?*
  - *What type of dialogue do you notice?*
  - *Does that always or often occur in historical fiction?*

- Record students' noticings on the prepared chart paper.

## Have a Try

Invite the students to talk with a partner about historical fiction.

> Think about a book you are reading or that we have recently read in class. Turn and talk about whether the book is historical fiction. Why do you think that? Look back to the chart and talk about each of the categories as they relate to the book.

## Summarize and Apply

Summarize the learning and remind students to think about the characteristics of historical fiction.

> Today you created a list of the characteristics of historical fiction. You decided which characteristics *always* occur in historical fiction and which characteristics *often* occur.

> When you read today, think about whether the book you are reading is historical fiction. If it is, bring it when we meet so you can share.

## Share

Following independent reading time, gather students in the meeting area to talk about historical fiction.

> Who read a historical fiction book today?

> Tell us how you know the book is historical fiction.

## Extend the Lesson (Optional)

After assessing students' understanding, you might decide to extend the learning.

▶ Continue to add to the noticings chart as students read more historical fiction stories and notice more about the genre.

▶ Introduce students to Genre Thinkmarks for historical fiction (visit resources.fountasandpinnell.com to download this resource). A Genre Thinkmark is a tool that guides readers to note certain elements of a genre in their reading. They can quickly note the page numbers or parts of the book where they see evidence of the characteristics of historical fiction and share it with others.

---

### Historical Fiction

**Noticings:**

| Always | Often |
|---|---|
| • Stories are imagined but take place in the real world. | • The characters, plot, and setting are usually believable. |
| • They have characters, plot, and setting (narrative structure). | • The stories are often based on real people or events from the past. |
| • The stories focus on problems and issues of life in the past. | • The stories are often connected to the author's own personal experiences. |
| | • Authors often use the language of the time in the dialogue. |

Section 2: Literary Analysis

<table>
<tr><td>

## RML2
**LA.U23.RML2**

</td><td>

**Reading Minilesson Principle**
# The definition of historical fiction is what is always true about it.

</td></tr>
</table>

## Studying Historical Fiction

### You Will Need

- a familiar historical fiction story, such as *The Houdini Box* by Brian Selznick, from Text Set: Genre Study: Historical Fiction
- the historical fiction noticings chart from RML1
- chart paper and markers

### Academic Language / Important Vocabulary

- historical fiction
- genre
- definition

### Continuum Connection

- Notice and understand the characteristics of some specific fiction genres: e.g., realistic fiction, historical fiction, folktale, fairy tale, fractured fairy tale, fable, myth, legend, fantasy including science fiction and hybrid (p. 58)

## Goal

Construct a working definition of historical fiction.

## Rationale

When you help students construct a working definition of historical fiction, you help them summarize the most important characteristics of the genre. Over time, the definition can be revised as students experience additional examples of historical fiction.

## Assess Learning

Observe students when they think and talk about the characteristics of historical fiction and notice if there is evidence of new learning based on the goal of this minilesson.

- Can students describe the characteristics of historical fiction?
- Can they determine whether a particular book fits the definition of historical fiction?
- Do they use academic language, such as *historical fiction, genre,* and *definition*?

## Minilesson

Guide students in constructing a definition of historical fiction from the noticings chart in RML1. Here is an example.

- Review the noticings chart created during the previous minilesson.

    You created a list of the ways that historical fiction stories are alike.

- Ask one or more volunteers to read the noticings.

    Look at the ways that historical fiction stories are *always* alike and think about a definition for historical fiction. What is always true about historical fiction?

- Write *Historical fiction stories are* on chart paper.

    Think about how you could finish this sentence to create a definition for all books in the historical fiction genre. Turn and talk about that.

- After time for discussion, ask students to share.

- Help students add to the ideas of classmates to assist them in collaborating to construct a definition. Using students' ideas, create a definition of historical fiction and write it on the chart.

## Have a Try

Invite the students to talk with a partner about a familiar historical fiction book and whether it fits the definition.

▶ Show the cover of a familiar historical fiction book, such as *The Houdini Box*. Revisit a few pages as needed.

> Turn and talk about whether *The Houdini Box* fits the definition of historical fiction. Explain your thinking.

▶ After time for discussion, ask several students to share their thinking. Encourage them to refer back to the chart as they offer their explanations.

## Summarize and Apply

Summarize the learning and remind students to think about the definition of historical fiction as they read.

> Today you helped write a definition that describes historical fiction.

> Choose a fiction book to read today and think about whether it fits the definition of historical fiction. If it does, bring the book to share when we meet.

## Share

Following independent reading time, gather students in the meeting area to talk about their reading.

> Who read a book today that fits the definition of historical fiction? Tell us a little bit about the book and why you think it is historical fiction.

## Extend the Lesson (Optional)

After assessing students' understanding, you might decide to extend the learning.

▶ Lead a discussion about similarities and differences between historical fiction and realistic fiction.

▶ Historical fiction writers do a lot of research to write about something that took place during a specific time period. When you read a historical fiction book during interactive read-aloud, take time to talk about what the author needed to know to write the book and how the author might have found that information.

### Historical Fiction

Historical fiction stories are made-up stories that take place in the past and tell about something in history.

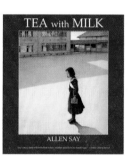

# RML3
## LA.U23.RML3

### Reading Minilesson Principle
## The setting is important to the story in historical fiction.

## Studying Historical Fiction

### You Will Need

▶ several familiar historical fiction books, such as the following:

- *The Buffalo Storm* by Katherine Applegate, from Text Set: Genre Study: Historical Fiction

- *Tea with Milk* by Allen Say, from Text Set: Author/Illustrator Study: Allen Say

- *Uncle Jed's Barbershop* by Margaret King Mitchell, from Text Set: Genre Study: Historical Fiction

▶ chart paper prepared with maps of the United States and Japan

▶ markers

### Academic Language / Important Vocabulary

▶ historical fiction
▶ setting
▶ impact
▶ consistent

### Continuum Connection

▶ Infer the importance of the setting to the plot of the story in realistic and historical fiction and fantasy (p. 59)

## Goal

Infer the importance of the setting to the plot of the story in historical fiction.

## Rationale

When students understand the importance of setting in historical fiction stories, they begin to think about the ways that writers create a sense of authenticity and the ways that setting drives characters and plot, developing their understanding of an author's craft.

## Assess Learning

Observe students when they read and talk about historical fiction books and notice if there is evidence of new learning based on the goal of this minilesson.

▶ Do students understand that setting is important in historical fiction books?

▶ Are students able to analyze the link between setting, characters, and plot?

▶ Do they use the terms *historical fiction, setting, impact,* and *consistent*?

## Minilesson

To help students think about the minilesson principle, use familiar historical fiction books to help students analyze the setting. Here is an example.

▶ Show pages 9–10 of *The Buffalo Storm*.

What can you say about the setting in *The Buffalo Storm*?

Why is it important that this story takes place on the Oregon Trail during the 1800s?

▶ As students share ideas, engage them in a conversation about the importance of setting in historical fiction. The following prompts may be helpful:

- *What impact does the setting have on the story, or how does the setting drive the story?*

- *Would the events in this story be as likely to occur in a different time and place? Why not?*

▶ Show pages 5 and 15 from *Tea with Milk*.

Now think about the setting in another historical fiction book you know, *Tea with Milk*. What do you know about the setting?

How is the setting important to the story?

▶ Add responses to the chart.

## Have a Try

Invite the students to talk with a partner about the setting in historical fiction books.

▶ Show pages 11–12 of *Uncle Jed's Barbershop*.

Think about the setting in *Uncle Jed's Barbershop*. When and where does it take place? How does the setting impact the story? Turn and talk about that.

▶ After time for discussion, ask students to share. Add to the chart.

## Summarize and Apply

Summarize the learning and remind students to think about how the setting impacts the story in historical fiction.

Today you learned that the setting is important in historical fiction stories. The author has to write about the characters and events in a way that fits with the historical time and place.

▶ Add the principle to the chart.

As you read historical fiction, think about the setting and why it is important to the story. If you read historical fiction today, bring your book when we meet so you can share.

## Share

Following independent reading time, gather students in the meeting area to talk about the importance of setting in historical fiction.

Did you read a historical fiction book today? Tell us about the setting and why it is important to the story.

## Extend the Lesson (Optional)

After assessing students' understanding, you might decide to extend the learning.

▶ When you read aloud historical fiction set in places outside the United States, mark the locations on a world map.

▶ **Writing About Reading** Have the students use a reader's notebook to do a short write about a setting they have read about in a historical fiction book and how the setting impacts the characters and plot.

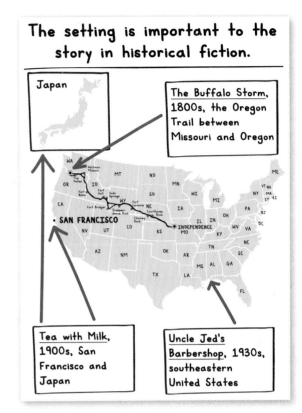

The setting is important to the story in historical fiction.

Japan

The Buffalo Storm, 1800s, the Oregon Trail between Missouri and Oregon

SAN FRANCISCO

Tea with Milk, 1900s, San Francisco and Japan

Uncle Jed's Barbershop, 1930s, southeastern United States

**Reading Minilesson Principle**

# Historical fiction is always imagined but may be based on real people, places, or events.

## You Will Need

- several familiar historical fiction books, such as the following from Text Set: Genre Study: Historical Fiction:
  - *The Glorious Flight* by Alice and Martin Provensen
  - *The Houdini Box* by Brian Selznick
  - *Dad, Jackie, and Me* by Myron Uhlberg
- chart paper and markers
- basket of historical fiction books

## Academic Language / Important Vocabulary

- historical fiction
- imagined
- real people
- real events

## Continuum Connection

- Notice and understand the characteristics of some specific fiction genres: e.g., realistic fiction, historical fiction, folktale, fairy tale, fractured fairy tale, fable, myth, legend, fantasy including science fiction and hybrid (p. 58)

## Goal

Understand that historical fiction is always imagined but may be based on real people, places, and events.

## Rationale

When students recognize that historical fiction stories are always imagined but that they may be based on real people, places, and events, they are better able to connect to the characters and events and evaluate the authenticity of historical fiction books they read.

## Assess Learning

Observe students when they read and talk about historical fiction books and notice if there is evidence of new learning based on the goal of this minilesson.

▷ Do students recognize that historical fiction stories are imagined but may be based on real people or events?

▷ Do they use the terms *historical fiction, imagined, real people,* and *real events*?

# Minilesson

To help students think about the minilesson principle, use familiar historical fiction books to help them notice what is imagined and what is real. Here is an example.

▷ Show the cover of *The Glorious Flight*.

> In this historical fiction book, *The Glorious Flight,* what do you know about the main character, setting, and events?

▷ Read the information located at the top of the copyright page about Louis Blériot and his flight across the English Channel.

> Which parts are imagined and which parts are based on real people or real events? What is real about the setting?

▷ As students respond, create a chart with headings for *Title, Real Person, Real Event,* and *Real Place.* Add the details for this book to the chart using student responses.

> Think about another historical fiction book, *The Houdini Box.*

▷ Read all or part of An Interesting Note at the end of the book, which explains which details are facts and which are fiction.

> Which characters and events are imagined, and which are based on real people or real events?

▷ Add responses to the chart.

## Have a Try

Invite the students to talk with a partner about whether a historical fiction book is based on real people or events.

▸ Show the cover of *Dad, Jackie, and Me*.

Turn and talk about whether this historical fiction book is based on real people, places, or events.

▸ After time for discussion, share the newspaper clippings and photos from the inside covers. Ask students to share their thinking and add to chart.

## Summarize and Apply

Summarize the learning and remind students to think about whether a historical fiction book they read is based on real people, places, or events.

What does the chart show you about historical fiction?

▸ Add the principle to the chart.

As you read historical fiction, think about whether the book is based on real people or events. Notice if the setting is a real place. If you read historical fiction today, bring the book when we meet so you can share.

## Share

Following independent reading time, gather students in the meeting area to talk about historical fiction.

Who read a historical fiction book today? Talk about whether it was based on real people or real events.

## Extend the Lesson (Optional)

After assessing students' understanding, you might decide to extend the learning.

▸ Have students do some research on one of the characters or events that they have read about and then analyze the way the author blended fact with fiction in the story.

▸ Have students fill in a Historical Fiction Evidence from Text chart (visit resources.fountasandpinnell.com to download this resource) to record page numbers and historical evidence in books they read. Once they fill in the chart, they can glue it into a reader's notebook.

| Historical fiction is always imagined but may be based on real people, places, or events. | | | |
|---|---|---|---|
| Title | Real Person | Real Event | Real Place |
| | Louis Blériot | the first flight across the English Channel | France, England |
| | Houdini the magician | Houdini's death on Halloween | New York |
| | Jackie Robinson | Brooklyn Dodgers and the 1947 baseball season | Brooklyn |

Section 2: Literary Analysis

**Reading Minilesson Principle**

# Historical fiction writers often use the language of the times in the dialogue.

## Studying Historical Fiction

### You Will Need

- several familiar historical fiction books, such as the following from Text Set: Genre Study: Historical Fiction:
  - *Dad, Jackie, and Me* by Myron Uhlberg
  - *The Buffalo Storm* by Katherine Applegate
  - *The Glorious Flight* by Alice and Martin Provensen
- chart paper and markers

### Academic Language / Important Vocabulary

- historical fiction
- language
- dialogue
- authentic

### Continuum Connection

- Notice and think critically about an author's word choice (p. 60)

## Goal

Understand that historical fiction writers often use the language of the times in the dialogue to make the text feel authentic.

## Rationale

When you teach students to recognize and analyze dialogue and language in historical fiction stories, they are able to evaluate the authenticity of a writer's voice and think about how word choice helps create the setting.

## Assess Learning

Observe students when they read and talk about historical fiction stories and notice if there is evidence of new learning based on the goal of this minilesson.

- Do students understand why an author uses dialogue and language that differs from the way we speak today?
- Are they using the terms *historical fiction*, *language*, *dialogue*, and *authentic*?

## Minilesson

To help students think about the minilesson principle, use familiar historical fiction books to help students notice the dialogue and language. Here is an example.

- Show the cover of *Dad, Jackie, and Me* and read the print in the middle of the back cover.

  Imagine you are at a baseball game in 1947. What kinds of things would you hear?

  Would people be saying the same exact things at a baseball game today?

- Show page 13 and point out the peanut salesman in the illustration. Read the first line, emphasizing the way that the peanut salesman would speak.

  What does the author do to make this dialogue feel authentic, or real, as if you were at that game in 1947?

- Create a chart that lists the title, the time period, the language used, and how the language shows the time period.

- Show the cover of *The Buffalo Storm* and read the two lines that begin with "You'll see buffalo."

  What do you notice?

  How does this dialogue show the time period?

- Add responses to the chart.

## Have a Try

Invite the students to talk with a partner about dialogue in historical fiction books.

▶ Show the cover of *The Glorious Flight* and read page 8.

> Turn and talk about what you notice about the dialogue on this page.

▶ After time for discussion, ask students to share. Add to chart.

## Summarize and Apply

Summarize the learning and remind students to think about how an author uses dialogue to make a historical fiction story feel authentic.

> What did you learn about how writers of historical fiction make their writing sound authentic?

▶ Add the principle to the chart.

> As you read historical fiction, notice if the author uses dialogue and language in a way that is authentic for the time period. If you read historical fiction today, bring the book when we meet so you can share.

## Share

Following independent reading time, gather students in the meeting area to talk about the writer's choice of language.

> Did anyone notice authentic dialogue or language in a historical fiction book today? Share what you noticed.

## Extend the Lesson (Optional)

After assessing students' understanding, you might decide to extend the learning.

▶ Discuss with students the kind of language that a future author might use to give a flavor of the present time in a historical fiction story.

▶ **Writing About Reading** Have students use the dialogue in a historical fiction book to create a readers' theater script.

| Historical fiction writers often use the language of the times in the dialogue. | | | |
|---|---|---|---|
| Title | Time Period | Dialogue | How does language show the time period? |
| | 1947 | "Hey, peanuts! Hey, hot dogs! Get 'em while they're hot!" | • He says '<u>em</u> instead of <u>them</u>. The way he speaks is an old-fashioned way to talk. |
| | 1800s | "You'll see buffalo, child, too many to count. What a gift to hear the earth rumble as they run!" | • Calling a girl <u>child</u> is not common now. <br> • A grandma today wouldn't be telling her granddaughter to watch out for buffalo as she travels west. |
| | 1901 | "Hark!" | • This is not something people say anymore. |

# RML6
## LA.U23.RML6

# Historical fiction writers use the past to give a message that can be applied today.

## You Will Need

- several familiar historical fiction books, such as the following from Text Set: Genre Study: Historical Fiction:
  - *The Glorious Flight* by Alice and Martin Provensen
  - *Uncle Jed's Barbershop* by Margaret King Mitchell
  - *The Buffalo Storm* by Katherine Applegate
- chart paper and markers

## Academic Language / Important Vocabulary

- historical fiction
- message
- apply

### Continuum Connection

- Understand that the messages or big ideas in fiction texts can be applied to their own lives or to other people and society (p. 58)

## Goal

Understand that the messages in historical fiction can be applied to their own lives, to other people's lives, or to society today.

## Rationale

When you teach students to notice and think about the message in a historical fiction book, they understand that events that happened in the past affect how we live our lives in the present. You may want to teach LA.U8.RML2 before this lesson to be sure that students understand how to notice the author's message.

## Assess Learning

Observe students when they read and talk about historical fiction and notice if there is evidence of new learning based on the goal of this minilesson.

- ▶ Can students identify the message(s) in historical fiction stories?
- ▶ Are they able to describe how the message in a historical fiction story applies to their own lives?
- ▶ Do they use the terms *historical fiction, message,* and *apply*?

## Minilesson

To help students think about the minilesson principle, use familiar historical fiction books to help students think about how the message applies to life today. Here is an example.

- ▶ Show the cover of *The Glorious Flight*.

   Think about the messages that the authors want you to take away from this book. Turn and talk about that.

- ▶ After time for discussion, ask students to share one or two messages. Write them on chart paper beside the title.

   Are these messages that apply only to the time period of the story, or could these messages apply to your own life today?

- ▶ Have one or two students share an example of how they could be persistent, could keep trying, to reach a goal. Write or have students write how the message could apply to their lives.

- ▶ Show the cover of *Uncle Jed's Barbershop*.

   Now think about the message in another historical fiction book, *Uncle Jed's Barbershop*. What is the message?

- ▶ Add responses to the chart. Ask one or two students to share how they could follow a dream. Write or have students write the responses on the chart.

## Have a Try

Invite the students to talk with a partner about how the messages in historical fiction stories can be applied to their own lives.

▶ Show the cover of *The Buffalo Storm*.

> Think about the messages in *The Buffalo Storm*. Turn and talk about the messages and then talk about how the messages could be applied to your own life.

▶ After time for discussion, ask students to share ideas. Add a few ideas to the chart.

## Summarize and Apply

Summarize the learning and remind students to think about how the message in a historical fiction book might be applied to their own lives.

> What does the chart show about historical fiction?

▶ Add the principle to the chart.

> As you read historical fiction, think about the message and how it applies to your own life. If you read historical fiction today, bring the book when we meet so you can share.

## Share

Following independent reading time, gather students in the meeting area to talk about the messages in historical fiction stories.

> Who read a historical fiction book today? Did you notice the message and think about how it applies to your own life? Tell us about that.

## Extend the Lesson (Optional)

After assessing students' understanding, you might decide to extend the learning.

▶ If you read historical fiction stories during interactive read-aloud, ask students to identify the message and think about how it applies to their own lives.

▶ Have students think beyond themselves to how the messages learned from historical fiction books can be applied to other people or to modern society.

▶ **Writing About Reading** Have students use a reader's notebook to write about how a message from a historical fiction book applies to their own lives.

| Historical fiction writers use the past to give a message that can be applied today. | | |
|---|---|---|
| **Title** | **Message(s)** | **How It Applies Today** |
| THE GLORIOUS FLIGHT | Be persistent to reach your goals.<br><br>Keep trying, even when things go wrong. | "work hard in school to be an astronaut" —Joaquin<br><br>"keep practicing adding fractions even when I get the wrong answer" —Jayna |
| | Don't give up on your dreams. | "to be in a Broadway musical, even if it takes a long time" —Sydney<br><br>"keep practicing soccer so I can play on the high school team" —Mano |
| The Buffalo Storm | It is okay to be afraid sometimes.<br><br>Older people have wisdom. | "I can hike with my family even though I'm afraid of snakes." —Angel<br><br>"I can listen to my grandma when she gives advice." —Tawny |

## Assessment

After you have taught the minilessons in this umbrella, observe students as they talk and write about their reading across instructional contexts: interactive read-aloud, independent reading, guided reading, shared reading, and book club. Use *The Literacy Continuum* (Fountas and Pinnell 2017) to guide observation of students' reading and writing behaviors.

▶ What evidence do you have of new understandings related to historical fiction?

- Do students recognize historical fiction stories and notice how they are alike?
- Do they understand that historical fiction is always imagined but that it can be based on real characters, settings, and events?
- Do they recognize when writers use language of the times in dialogue?
- Can students identify messages in historical fiction stories that can be applied today?
- Do they use academic vocabulary, such as *historical fiction*, *narrative structure*, *setting*, *characteristics*, *genre*, *dialogue*, and *message*?

▶ In what other ways, beyond the scope of this umbrella, are students talking about books?

- Do they show interest in reading other kinds of books that take place in the past, such as biographies?

Use your observations to determine the next umbrella you will teach. You may also consult Minilessons Across the Year (pp. 59–61) for guidance.

## Read and Revise

After completing the steps in the genre study process, help students read and revise their definition of the genre based on their new understandings.

▶ **Before:** Historical fiction stories are made-up stories that take place in the past and tell about something in history.

▶ **After:** Historical fiction stories are made up by the author but have characters, events, and settings that could be real. They take place in the past.

## Reader's Notebook

When this umbrella is complete, provide a copy of the minilesson principles (see resources.fountasandpinnell.com) for students to glue in the reader's notebook (in the Minilessons section if using *Reader's Notebook: Intermediate* [Fountas and Pinnell 2011]), so they can refer to the information as needed.

## Minilessons in This Umbrella

**RML1**  Writers use poetic or descriptive language to help you understand the setting.

**RML2**  The setting can be a real or an imagined place in this time or in the past.

**RML3**  The setting is often important to the story.

## Before Teaching Umbrella 24 Minilessons

Read aloud and discuss engaging realistic fiction and fantasy books that take place in a variety of locations and time periods. Include books that take place in both real and imagined places. As much as possible, choose books in which the setting is central to the story. Read aloud books in which the setting is richly described with poetic or descriptive language. Use the following books from the *Fountas & Pinnell Classroom™ Interactive Read-Aloud Collection* text sets or choose books from your classroom library that feature the setting prominently.

### Friendship

*Snook Alone* by Marilyn Nelson

*Better Than You* by Trudy Ludwig

*The Other Side* by Jacqueline Woodson

### Empathy

*The Crane Wife* by Odds Bodkin

*A Symphony of Whales* by Steve Schuch

As you read aloud and enjoy these texts together, help students

- talk about when and where the story takes place,

- notice whether the setting is real or imagined,

- notice and discuss poetic or descriptive language that describes the setting, and

- discuss the importance of the setting to the plot.

**Friendship**

**Empathy**

Section 2: Literary Analysis

**Reading Minilesson Principle**

# Writers use poetic or descriptive language to help you understand the setting.

## Thinking About the Setting in Fiction Books

### You Will Need

- two or three familiar fiction books that contain poetic or descriptive language about the setting, such as the following:
  - *Snook Alone* by Marilyn Nelson, from Text Set: Friendship
  - *A Symphony of Whales* by Steve Schuch and *The Crane Wife* by Odds Bodkin, from Text Set: Empathy
- chart paper and markers

### Academic Language / Important Vocabulary

- author
- setting
- fiction
- poetic
- descriptive
- language

### Continuum Connection

- Notice and understand long stretches of descriptive language important to understanding setting and characters [p. 60]
- Notice when a fiction writer uses poetic or descriptive language to show the setting, appeal to the five senses, or to convey human feelings such as loss, relief or anger [p. 60]

## Goal

Notice and understand the poetic or descriptive language used to show the setting.

## Rationale

Poetic and descriptive language helps readers visualize and understand settings. When you guide students to think about how authors use such language, they develop an appreciation for and understanding of how writers construct believable settings. They can also use this knowledge in their own fiction writing.

## Assess Learning

Observe students when they read and talk about fiction and notice if there is evidence of new learning based on the goal of this minilesson.

- Do students notice poetic and descriptive language about settings?
- Can they describe what such language reveals about the story's setting?
- Do they use the terms *author*, *setting*, *fiction*, *poetic*, *descriptive*, and *language*?

## Minilesson

To help students think about the minilesson principle, use familiar fiction books to help them notice an author's use of poetic and descriptive language to describe the setting. Here is an example.

- Show the cover of *Snook Alone* and read the title. Turn to page 10. Read from the second paragraph on page 10 ("Like the other islands . . .") through the first paragraph on page 11.

    **Which words help you imagine and understand the setting?**

    **What does the author want you to picture in your mind?**

- Record examples of poetic and descriptive language and students' responses on chart paper.
- Show the cover of *A Symphony of Whales* and read the title. Turn to page 7 and read the first three paragraphs.

    **What do you notice about how the author describes the bay?**

    **What does the author want you to feel, see, hear, and know about this place?**

- Record examples of poetic and descriptive language and students' responses on the chart.

## Have a Try

Invite the students to talk with a partner about the setting of *The Crane Wife*.

▶ Show the cover of *The Crane Wife* and read the title. Read the first three sentences on page 1.

> Turn and talk to your partner about how the author shows the setting.

▶ After students turn and talk, invite a few students to share their thinking. Record responses on the chart.

## Summarize and Apply

Summarize the learning and remind students to notice poetic and descriptive language.

> What did you notice about the language authors use to describe a story's setting?

> Poetic and descriptive language helps you imagine the setting and feel, see, hear, and understand certain things.

▶ Write the principle at the top of the chart.

> If you read a fiction book today, notice if the writer uses poetic or descriptive language to help you understand the setting. If so, put a sticky note on a good example and bring your book to share when we come back together.

| Writers use poetic or descriptive language to help you understand the setting. | | |
|---|---|---|
| | **The Writer's Words** | **What the Words Show** |
| *Snook Alone* | "mile-long crescent of beach"<br><br>"salt-resistant bushes, papaya and casuarina trees" | • what the island looks like |
| | "a black line thickened on the horizon" | • that a storm is coming |
| *A Symphony of Whales* | "great bay of open water, surrounded on all sides by ice and snow" | • how cold and icy the setting is |
| | "the water seemed to be heaving and boiling, choked with white whales" | • how many whales are stuck |
| *The Crane Wife* | "high above the sea, on a hilltop" | • that the setting is wild and isolated |
| | "green salt marsh below, dotted with white cranes" | |

## Share

Following independent reading time, gather students together in the meeting area to talk about their reading.

> Who found an example of poetic or descriptive language that describes a setting today? Explain how it helped you understand the setting.

## Extend the Lesson (Optional)

After assessing students' understanding, you might decide to extend the learning.

▶ Use shared writing to model how to use poetic and descriptive language when writing about a setting. Have students describe a setting they know very well—for example, the classroom, the playground, or a spot in the community—in as much detail as possible. Or show them a photograph or painting of a setting and encourage them to describe it using poetic and descriptive language.

Section 2: Literary Analysis

# RML2
**LA.U24.RML2**

# The setting can be a real or an imagined place in this time or in the past.

## Thinking About the Setting in Fiction Books

### You Will Need

- a selection of familiar fiction books from *Interactive Read-Aloud Collection* or your classroom library
- chart paper and markers

### Academic Language / Important Vocabulary

- setting
- fiction

### Continuum Connection

- Notice and understand settings that are distant in time and place from a students' own experiences (p. 59)
- Recognize and understand that fiction texts may have settings that reflect a wide range of places, language, and cultures, and that characters' behaviors may reflect those settings (p. 59)

## Goal

Notice and understand that settings can be familiar or distant in time and place from readers' own experiences.

## Rationale

When students notice that settings can be real or imagined places in this time or the past, they think about how an author chooses a setting and realize that there are no limits to what fiction writers can write about.

## Assess Learning

Observe students when they read and talk about fiction and notice if there is evidence of new learning based on the goal of this minilesson.

- Can students identify whether a story is set in a real or an imagined place in modern or historical times?
- Do they use the terms *setting* and *fiction*?

## Minilesson

To help students think about the minilesson principle, use familiar fiction books to engage them in a discussion about setting. Here is an example.

- Create a chart with four sections labeled *Real Place, Imagined Place, Now,* and *In the Past*. Write *Setting* at the top.
- Divide students into four or five small groups and give each group a familiar fiction book.

  With your group, talk about whether the story takes place in a real place or an imagined place and whether it takes place in the present or the past. An imagined place is described by the author, but sometimes it doesn't have a name. Instead, you might determine that it is a small town or a large city, but not one that exists in the real world.

- After time for discussion, invite each group to share their thinking. Prompt discussion with questions such as the following:
  - *Where does _____ take place? Is that a real or an imagined place? How do you know?*
  - *When does _____ take place? What details in the story helped you figure that out?*
- List each book discussed in the appropriate section(s) of the chart, along with a few words about its setting.

## Have a Try

Invite the students to talk with a partner about the setting of other books they have read.

> Think of a fiction story you have read recently. When and where did It take place? Did it take place in a real or imagined place, now or in the past? Turn and talk to your partner about what you remember.

▶ After students turn and talk, invite several students to offer ideas. Add their suggestions to the appropriate lists.

## Summarize and Apply

Summarize the learning and remind students to notice settings when they read fiction.

> What did you notice about the settings in fiction books today?

▶ Add the principle to the top of the chart.

> If you read a fiction book today, think about the setting of the story. Notice if the story takes place in a real or an imagined place, in this time or in the past. Be ready to share when we come back together.

## Share

Following independent reading time, gather students together in the meeting area to talk about their reading.

> Who read a fiction book today?

> What is the setting of the book you read? Is it a real or an imagined place, in this time or in the past?

## Extend the Lesson (Optional)

After assessing students' understanding, you might decide to extend the learning.

▶ Discuss how the illustrations in fiction books contribute to the development of the setting.

▶ **Writing About Reading** Have students write in a reader's notebook about the setting in a fiction book. They should identify the time and place of the setting and support their remarks with specific details from the story.

**The setting can be a real or an imagined place in this time or in the past.**

| | Setting | |
|---|---|---|
| | **Real Place** | **Imagined Place** |
| **WHERE** | A Symphony of Whales (Siberia) | Better Than You (a town) |
| | Snook Alone (Avocaire Island) | The Other Side (a small, rural town) |
| | The Crane Wife (Japan) | |
| | **Now** | **In the Past** |
| **WHEN** | Better Than You (a town) | A Symphony of Whales (1980s) |
| | | The Crane Wife (ancient times) |
| | | The Other Side (mid-1900s?) |

Section 2: Literary Analysis

# RML 3
## LA.U24.RML3

**Reading Minilesson Principle**
# The setting is often important to the story.

## Thinking About the Setting in Fiction Books

### You Will Need

- two or three familiar fiction books, such as the following:
  - *The Other Side* by Jacqueline Woodson and *Better Than You* by Trudy Ludwig, from Text Set: Friendship
  - *The Crane Wife* by Odds Bodkin, from Text Set: Empathy
- chart paper and markers

### Academic Language / Important Vocabulary

- setting
- plot
- fiction

### Continuum Connection

- Infer the importance of the setting to the plot of the story in realistic and historical fiction and fantasy [p. 59]

## Goal

Infer the importance of the setting to the plot of the story.

## Rationale

When you teach students to think about the importance of the setting to the plot of a story, they understand that the setting is not an arbitrarily chosen time and place because it has to make sense with the story. They think about how people's behavior and values are influenced by their environment and culture, and they begin to understand what it means to be a member of a society. They develop an understanding of universal ideas and ideas that are heavily shaped by time and place.

## Assess Learning

Observe students when they read and talk about fiction and notice if there is evidence of new learning based on the goal of this minilesson.

- ▶ Can students explain how the setting of a story is important to the plot?
- ▶ Do they use the terms *setting, plot,* and *fiction*?

## Minilesson

To help students think about the minilesson principle, use familiar fiction books to engage them in thinking about the importance of setting. Here is an example.

- ▶ Show the cover of *The Other Side* and read the title.

  What is the setting of this story? When and where does it take place?

  Why is it important that this story takes place in a town where a fence separates the areas where people live? How does this affect the plot, or what happens in the story?

  This story takes place a long time ago, perhaps in the 1950s. Why is it important that the story takes place at this time? How might the story be different if it took place today?

- ▶ Record students' responses on chart paper.
- ▶ Show the cover of *Better Than You* and read the title.

  Is the setting a real, specific place with a name or an imagined place?

  The author doesn't say where the story takes place. Why do you think she decided to set the story somewhere that isn't any particular place?

- ▶ Record students' responses on the chart.

  Sometimes authors set their stories in a place that could be almost anywhere. This lets readers in a lot of different places relate to the situation in the story and learn from the story's lessons.

## Have a Try

Invite the students to talk with a partner about the setting in *The Crane Wife*.

▶ Show the cover of *The Crane Wife* and read the title.

Turn and talk to your partner about the setting of this story. When and where does the story take place, and why is the setting important to the story?

▶ Invite a few students to share their thinking. Record responses on the chart.

## Summarize and Apply

Summarize the learning and remind students to think about why the setting is important when they read fiction.

You noticed that the setting of a story is often important to the plot, or what happens in the story. Often, the events in a story would not happen if the story was set in a different place or a different time.

▶ Write the principle at the top of the chart.

If you read a fiction book today, think about the setting of the story and why it is important. Be ready to share your thinking when we meet after independent reading.

## Share

Following independent reading time, gather students together in the meeting area to talk about their reading.

Who read a fiction book that has a setting that's important to the story?

What is the setting of the story you read? Why is it important?

How might the story be different if it were set in a different place or time?

## Extend the Lesson [Optional]

After assessing students' understanding, you might decide to extend the learning.

▶ See LA.U23.RML3 for a minilesson that focuses specifically on the importance of the setting in historical fiction.

▶ Read aloud modern retellings of traditional stories or various versions of the same folktale from different cultures (e.g., Cinderella stories). Discuss how changing the story's setting affects the story.

**The setting is often important to the story.**

| Title | Setting | Why It's Important |
|---|---|---|
| The Other Side | • a town that has a fence separating the areas where white people and black people live <br> • around the 1950s <br> • could be anywhere in southern U.S. | • A white girl and a black girl become friends despite the fence that separates them. <br> • The story takes place during a time when there was segregation. It would have been a big deal for the two girls to be friends with each other. |
| BETTER THAN YOU | • an ordinary town that could be anywhere <br> • in recent times | • Readers anywhere can relate to the story and learn from it. |
| The Crane Wife | • Japan, on a hilltop near the sea <br> • in ancient times | • The main character makes sails with his wife. They probably wouldn't make sails if they didn't live near the sea. |

Section 2: Literary Analysis

## Assessment

After you have taught the minilessons in this umbrella, observe students as they talk and write about their reading across instructional contexts: interactive read-aloud, independent reading, guided reading, shared reading, and book club. Use *The Literacy Continuum* (Fountas and Pinnell 2017) to guide the observation of students' reading and writing behaviors.

- ▶ What evidence do you have of new understandings related to setting?
  - Can students identify and talk about when and where a story takes place?
  - Can they explain how poetic or descriptive language helps them understand the setting?
  - Do they understand whether a story's setting is real or imagined and modern or historical?
  - How well can they explain the importance of a story's setting to the plot?
  - Do they use academic language, such as *setting, plot,* and *fiction*?
- ▶ In what other ways, beyond the scope of this umbrella, are students talking about fiction?
  - Do students notice the elements of plot?
  - Are they talking about how authors develop characters?
  - Are they noticing different kinds of fiction stories?

Use your observations to determine the next umbrella you will teach. You may also consult Minilessons Across the Year (pp. 59–61) for guidance.

## Link to Writing

After teaching the minilessons in this umbrella, help students link the new learning to their own writing:

- ▶ Give students numerous opportunities throughout the school year to write their own stories. Encourage them to plan the setting before they start writing. Some students may benefit from drawing the setting before writing about it. Remind them to think about how the setting will influence the story's action. Teach them how to use poetic or descriptive language to describe settings.

## Reader's Notebook

When this umbrella is complete, provide a copy of the minilesson principles (see resources.fountasandpinnell.com) for students to glue in the reader's notebook (in the Minilessons section if using *Reader's Notebook: Intermediate* [Fountas and Pinnell 2011]), so they can refer to the information as needed.

## Minilessons in This Umbrella

**RML1**   The plot is what happens in a story.

**RML2**   Stories can have more than one problem.

**RML3**   The high point of a story is the exciting part.

**RML4**   Stories usually have a beginning, a series of events, a high point, and an ending.

**RML5**   Writers use flashbacks or a story-within-a-story.

**RML6**   Use what you know to predict what will happen next or at the end of the story.

## Before Teaching Umbrella 25 Minilessons

Read and discuss a variety of high-quality fiction books with events that readers can follow, a clearly defined problem (or problems), a high point, and a solution. The minilessons in this umbrella use the following books from the *Fountas and Pinnell Classroom™ Interactive Read-Aloud Collection* text sets; however, you can use books that are based on the experiences and interests of the students in your class and have the characteristics listed above.

**Figuring Out Who You Are**

*The Gold-Threaded Dress* by Carolyn Marsden

**Friendship**

*The Dunderheads* by Paul Fleischman

*Snook Alone* by Marilyn Nelson

*The Other Side* by Jacqueline Woodson

**Author/Illustrator Study: Allen Say**

*The Lost Lake*

*Kamishibai Man*

**Illustrator Study: Floyd Cooper**

*A Dance Like Starlight: One Ballerina's Dream* by Kristy Dempsey

*These Hands* by Margaret H. Mason

As you read aloud and enjoy these texts together, help students

• think about the problem(s) and solution(s) in the story,

• notice the story's structure, including the series of events and the high point that lead to the solution, and

• summarize the story, including the problem, events, high point, and solution.

**Figuring Out Who You Are**

**Friendship**

**Author/Illustrator Study: Allen Say**

**Illustrator Study: Floyd Cooper**

**Reading Minilesson Principle**
# The plot is what happens in a story.

## You Will Need

- several familiar fiction books, such as the following:
  - *The Other Side* by Jacqueline Woodson and *The Dunderheads* by Paul Fleischman, from Text Set: Friendship
  - *A Dance Like Starlight* by Kristy Dempsey, from Text Set: Illustrator Study: Floyd Cooper
- chart paper prepared with book titles and columns as shown
- markers

## Academic Language / Important Vocabulary

- plot
- events
- problem
- solution
- narrative text structure

### Continuum Connection

- Recognize and discuss aspects of narrative structure: e.g., beginning, series of events, high point of the story, problem resolution, ending (p. 59)

## Goal

Notice and understand that the plot is the sequence of events in a story, including the problem and solution.

## Rationale

When students learn that a plot is what happens in a story, they can follow the events, think about cause and effect, and understand how the story works as a whole.

## Assess Learning

Observe students when they talk about plot and notice if there is evidence of new learning based on the goal of this minilesson.

- Do students understand that the plot is what happens in a story?
- Can they identify the events, problem, and solution?
- Do they understand and use academic language, such as *plot, events, problem, solution,* and *narrative text structure*?

## Minilesson

To help students think about the minilesson principle, engage students in thinking about the characteristics of the plot in stories. Here is an example.

- Show the cover of *The Other Side*.

    Think about *The Other Side*. What happens in this story?

    What is the problem in the story?

    How is the problem solved?

- As students respond, next to the title succinctly write the problem, the main event(s) that led to the solution, and the solution on the prepared chart.

    In a narrative, or story, there is a text structure that we can expect. We know how the story goes. Let's think about the narrative text structure in another book, *The Dunderheads*.

- Show the cover of *The Dunderheads*.

    What events happen in this story?

    What is the problem? The solution?

- As students provide the problem, events, and solution, add them to the chart.

## Have a Try

Invite the students to talk with a partner about plot.

▶ Show the cover of *A Dance Like Starlight*.

> Think about the plot in this story you know, *A Dance Like Starlight*. Turn and talk about what happens in the story. Include the events and the main problem and solution in your conversation.

▶ After time for discussion, ask students to share the plot of the story. Add to chart.

## Summarize and Apply

Summarize the learning and remind students to think about the plot when they read fiction stories.

> Today you talked about the plot, or what happens in a story.

▶ Add the principle to top of chart.

> During independent reading time today, if you finish a book, select a fiction book. As you read, think about what happens in the story, or the plot. Remember that the plot includes the problem, the events, and the solution. Bring the book when we meet so you can share.

## Share

Following independent reading time, gather students in groups of three. Make sure at least one student in each group read a fiction book.

> Who read a fiction book today?

> Share the problem and tell how it was solved.

## Extend the Lesson (Optional)

After assessing students' understanding, you might decide to extend the learning.

▶ As students talk about ideas for writing their own fiction stories, have them talk about what the main problem and solution will be, as well as the events that will happen.

▶ **Writing About Reading** Have students fill in a graphic organizer about problem and solution (see resources.fountasandpinnell.com). When it is complete, they can glue it into a reader's notebook.

| The plot is what happens in a story. | | | |
| --- | --- | --- | --- |
| **Title** | **Plot: What Happens?** | | |
| | **Problem** | **Events** | **Solution** |
| *The Other Side* | The girls play on different sides of the fence. | Two girls decide to play together. | The fence is no longer a barrier. |
| *The Dunderheads* | Miss Breakbone takes Junkyard's cat statue. | The kids work together to get the cat back. | Junkyard gives the statue to his mom for her birthday. |
| *Dance Like Starlight* | A young girl wants to be a ballerina. The girl only sees white ballerinas on the stage. | The Ballet Master gives the girl a chance to dance. The girl goes to watch an African American ballerina on stage. | The girl will follow her dreams. |

# RML2
## LA.U25.RML2

### Reading Minilesson Principle
## Stories can have more than one problem.

## Understanding Plot

### You Will Need

- several familiar fiction books, such as the following:
  - *The Lost Lake* by Allen Say, from Text Set: Author/Illustrator Study: Allen Say
  - *The Other Side* by Jacqueline Woodson and *The Dunderheads* by Paul Fleischman from Text Set: Friendship
- chart paper and markers
- sticky notes

### Academic Language / Important Vocabulary

- plot
- problem
- narrative text structure

### Continuum Connection

- Follow a complex plot with multiple events, episodes, or problems (p. 59)

## Goal

Understand that stories can have more than one problem.

## Rationale

When students understand that some stories have more than one problem, they learn how to follow the plot in more complex works of fiction and understand the connection between each problem and the overall story and solution.

## Assess Learning

Observe students when they discuss the problems in a story and notice if there is evidence of new learning based on the goal of this minilesson.

- ▶ Can students recognize multiple problems in a story?
- ▶ Are they able to talk about how the problems are connected across the events of the story?
- ▶ Do they use academic language, such as *plot, problem,* and *narrative text structure*?

## Minilesson

To help students think about the minilesson principle, engage them in noticing multiple problems in a story. Here is an example.

> Think about *The Lost Lake* and the different problems the boy and his dad face. What problems do they have?

- ▶ As students share ideas, encourage them to talk about the main problem and the other problems. Use these prompts as needed to support the conversation:
  - *What is the main problem of the story?*
  - *It might help to think about the ending of the story and what is solved.*
  - *What are some of the other problems faced by the characters?*
- ▶ Write students' ideas on chart paper next to the title.

  > Think about another book, *The Other Side*. What is the main problem in the story?

  > What is another problem in the story?

- ▶ Add responses to the chart.

## Have a Try

Invite the students to talk with a partner about a story with multiple problems.

▶ Show the cover of *The Dunderheads*.

Think about *The Dunderheads*. Turn and talk about the main problem that is solved at the end. Think about any other problems the characters face and talk about those, too.

▶ After time for discussion, ask students to share. Add responses to the chart.

## Summarize and Apply

Summarize the learning and remind students to think about multiple problems in stories.

What do you know about problems in stories?

▶ Write the minilesson principle at the top of the chart.

During independent reading time today, if you finish a book, select a fiction book from the basket. As you read, think about whether there is more than one problem in the story. Use sticky notes to mark pages with examples. Bring the book when we meet so you can share.

## Share

Following independent reading time, gather students in a circle.

Did anyone read a story today that has more than one problem? Share what you noticed.

## Extend the Lesson (Optional)

After assessing students' understanding, you might decide to extend the learning.

▶ **Writing About Reading** Encourage students to write in a reader's notebook about stories they read in which a character faces more than one problem.

| Stories can have more than one problem. | |
|---|---|
| **Title** | **Problems** |
| THE LOST LAKE<br>ALLEN SAY | • The boy wants Dad's attention.<br>• Dad is too busy.<br>• The Lost Lake is too crowded.<br>• Dad wants to camp in a quiet place. |
| The Other Side | • The new girl doesn't have friends.<br>• A fence separates people by race. |
| The Dunderheads<br>PAUL FLEISCHMAN ... DAVID ROBERTS | • The cat statue is taken away.<br>• The teacher is mean.<br>• Junkyard's mom needs a birthday gift.<br>• The house is hard to get into. |

## RML3
LA.U25.RML3

### Reading Minilesson Principle
# The high point of a story is the exciting part.

## Understanding Plot

### You Will Need

- several familiar fiction books, such as the following:
  - *Kamishibai Man* and *The Lost Lake* by Allen Say, from Text Set: Author/Illustrator Study: Allen Say
  - *The Dunderheads* by Paul Fleischman, from Text Set: Friendship
- chart paper and markers
- sticky notes

### Academic Language / Important Vocabulary

- plot
- high point
- climax

### Continuum Connection

- Recognize and discuss aspects of narrative structure: e.g., beginning, series of events, high point of the story, problem resolution, ending (p. 59)

### Goal

Understand how a story leads up to and changes after the climax.

### Rationale

When students learn that the problem in a story reaches a high point, they begin to think about the author's craft and more deeply comprehend the plot.

### Assess Learning

Observe students when they talk about the high point of a story and notice if there is evidence of new learning based on the goal of this minilesson.

- Are students able to identify the high point of a story?
- Can they explain why a certain event is the high point of a story?
- Do they use academic language, such as *plot, high point,* and *climax*?

## Minilesson

To help students think about the minilesson principle, engage them in an interactive lesson about the high point in a story. Here is an example.

- Show page 5 of *Kamishibai Man*.

  Do you remember in *Kamishibai Man* when the old man thinks about his younger days? He told stories and sold candy to the children in town in those days.

- Turn to page 25.

  He thinks about those times as he travels through town, and he remembers the last day he did that.

  Do you remember what happens next?

- Turn the page and ask students to confirm what happens next.

  How do you think the man feels at this point in the story?

  This point is called the high point. It is the most exciting part of the story and it leads to the solution. It is sometimes called the climax.

  How would you describe the high point in this story?

- Write responses on chart paper.

- Repeat the activity with another story, such as *The Lost Lake*. After discussion, add responses to the chart.

## Have a Try

Invite the students to talk with a partner about the high point in another story.

▶ Show the cover of *The Dunderheads*.

Think about the different events in *The Dunderheads*. Which event is the most exciting and leads to the problem being solved? Turn and talk about that.

▶ After time for discussion, ask students to share. Add to chart.

## Summarize and Apply

Summarize the learning and remind students to notice the high point of a story they are reading.

What do you know about the high point of a story?

▶ Write the minilesson principle at the top of the chart paper.

If you are not already reading a fiction book, choose one to read today. As you read, notice if you come to the high point of the story. Put a sticky note on the page. Bring the book when we meet so you can share.

## Share

Following independent reading time, gather students in a circle.

Did anyone notice the high point of a story you read today? Share what you noticed. If you marked a page in the book, share that also.

## Extend the Lesson (Optional)

After assessing students' understanding, you might decide to extend the learning.

▶ **Writing About Reading** Encourage students to write in a reader's notebook about the high point in a fiction story. Have them write about how the high point leads to the solution of the main character's problem.

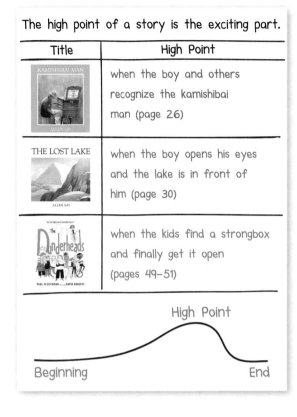

The high point of a story is the exciting part.

| Title | High Point |
|---|---|
| KAMISHIBAI MAN | when the boy and others recognize the kamishibai man (page 26) |
| THE LOST LAKE | when the boy opens his eyes and the lake is in front of him (page 30) |
| The Dunderheads | when the kids find a strongbox and finally get it open (pages 49–51) |

High Point

Beginning                                    End

**Reading Minilesson Principle**

# Stories usually have a beginning, a series of events, a high point, and an ending.

## Understanding Plot

### You Will Need

- several familiar fiction books, such as the following:
  - *Snook Alone* by Marilyn Nelson, from Text Set: Friendship
  - *A Dance Like Starlight* by Kristy Dempsey, from Text Set: Illustrator Study: Floyd Cooper
- chart paper prepared with a simple graph that includes labels for beginning, several events, high point, and ending
- markers
- sticky notes

### Academic Language / Important Vocabulary

- plot
- beginning
- series of events
- high point
- ending
- narrative text structure

### Continuum Connection

- Recognize and discuss aspects of narrative structure: e.g., beginning, series of events, high point of the story, problem resolution, ending (p. 59)

## Goal

Recognize and discuss aspects of narrative structure: beginning, series of events, high point of the story, problem resolution, and ending.

## Rationale

When students learn to identify the parts of a story, they learn to expect that stories have a beginning, events, high point, and ending and can look for these parts as they read and think deeply about them.

## Assess Learning

Observe students when they talk about narrative text structure and notice if there is evidence of new learning based on the goal of this minilesson.

- Are students able to identify the beginning, events, high point, and ending?
- Do they use the terms *plot, beginning, series of events, high point, ending,* and *narrative text structure*?

## Minilesson

To help students think about the minilesson principle, invite them to talk about elements of narrative structure. Here is an example.

- Show the prepared chart paper.

  **What do you notice about what I have written?**

- As needed, talk about the aspects of narrative text structure that you have written on the chart.

- Show the cover of *Snook Alone.*

  **Think about *Snook Alone*. What happens at the beginning of the story?**

- Write a student's response on a sticky note. Place the sticky note next to the word *Beginning* on the chart.

  **What is the first major event that happens?**

  **What happens after that?**

- As needed, review a few pages or illustrations from the story. Add students' responses to the chart.

  **What do you notice about the parts that are added to the chart?**

  **What do you notice about the order that the sticky notes are being placed on the chart?**

- Continue in this way with the remaining events, high point, and ending to *Snook Alone.*

## Have a Try

Invite the students to talk with a partner about narrative text structure for another book.

▶ Show the cover of *A Dance Like Starlight*.

> Turn and tell your partner about *A Dance Like Starlight*. Include the parts that are labeled on the chart: the beginning, events, the high point, and the ending.

▶ After time for discussion, ask a few students to share. Add responses on sticky notes and place on the chart.

## Summarize and Apply

Summarize the learning and remind students to think about the parts of a story when they read.

> What do you know about the plot?

▶ Write the minilesson principle at the top of the chart paper.

> If you are not already reading a fiction book, choose one to read today. As you read, think about the plot of the story. Bring the book when we meet so you can share.

## Share

Following independent reading time, gather students in small groups.

> Share with your group which parts of the story you noticed when you read today. Look back at the chart and include any of the parts that are labeled, which are the *beginning, events, high point,* and *ending.*

## Extend the Lesson (Optional)

After assessing students' understanding, you might decide to extend the learning.

▶ **Writing About Reading** Have students write in a reader's notebook about the different parts of the plot in a book they are reading.

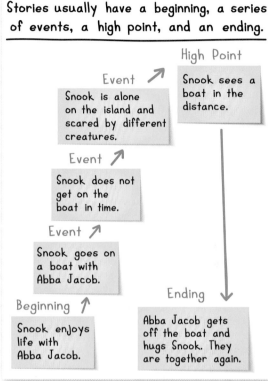

Stories usually have a beginning, a series of events, a high point, and an ending.

**High Point**
Snook sees a boat in the distance.

**Event** ↗
Snook is alone on the island and scared by different creatures.

**Event** ↗
Snook does not get on the boat in time.

**Event** ↗
Snook goes on a boat with Abba Jacob.

**Beginning** ↗
Snook enjoys life with Abba Jacob.

**Ending** ↓
Abba Jacob gets off the boat and hugs Snook. They are together again.

Section 2: Literary Analysis

**Reading Minilesson Principle**
# Writers use flashbacks or a story-within-a-story.

## Understanding Plot

### You Will Need

- several familiar fiction books, such as the following:
  - *These Hands* by Margaret Mason, from Text Set: Illustrator Study: Floyd Cooper
  - *The Gold-Threaded Dress* by Carolyn Marsden, from Text Set: Figuring Out Who You Are
  - *Kamishibai Man* by Allen Say, from Text Set: Author/Illustrator Study: Allen Say
- chart paper and markers
- sticky notes

### Academic Language / Important Vocabulary

- plot
- present day
- flashback
- story-within-a-story

### Continuum Connection

- Recognize the text structure when the writer uses literary devices: e.g., flashback, story-within-a-story (p. 59)

## Goal

Recognize when writers use literary devices such as flashbacks or a story-within-a-story.

## Rationale

When students recognize that authors sometimes use flashbacks, a story within the main story about something that happened in the past, they are better able to follow the plot in more complex and longer texts.

## Assess Learning

Observe students when they talk about flashbacks and notice if there is evidence of new learning based on the goal of this minilesson.

- Do students understand that sometimes authors use flashbacks, or tell a story-within-a-story?
- Can they differentiate between the main story and flashbacks or stories-within-stories?
- Do they use the terms *plot, present day, flashback,* and *story-within-a-story*?

## Minilesson

To help students think about the minilesson principle, engage them in noticing the characteristics of flashbacks. Here is an example.

- Show pages 1–2 of *These Hands*.

  What is happening between the boy and his grandpa in this story?

- Turn to pages 9–10.

  What do you notice about these illustrations?

  What do you notice going on in this part of the story?

- As needed, talk about what is happening in the present time and about how to recognize a flashback. As students respond, create a chart with two headings, one that identifies events occurring in the main story, and another for events occurring in a flashback, or a separate story at a previous time. Add responses to the correct column.

  Now think about another book, *The Gold-Threaded Dress*.

  What events from *The Gold-Threaded Dress* could be added to the chart?

- Guide the conversation so students identify what happens in the present time and what happens in flashbacks. As students respond, add to the chart.

  Why do you think authors sometimes include flashbacks in their stories?

## Have a Try

Invite the students to talk with a partner about flashbacks.

▶ Show the cover of *Kamishibai Man*.

Think about *Kamishibai Man*. Are there parts of the story that could be added to both columns of the chart? Turn and talk about that.

▶ After time for discussion, ask students to share. Add to chart.

## Summarize and Apply

Summarize the learning and remind students to notice a flashback or a story-within-a-story as they read.

Today you noticed that sometimes authors use flashbacks.

▶ Write the minilesson principle at the top of the chart paper.

If you aren't already reading a fiction book, choose one to read today. Notice if the author uses any flashbacks or tells a story-within-a-story. Add a sticky note on any pages you want to remember. Bring the book when we meet so you can share.

## Share

Following independent reading time, gather students in a circle.

Did anyone find that an author used a flashback or story-within-a-story in a book you read? Share what you noticed.

## Extend the Lesson (Optional)

After assessing students' understanding, you might decide to extend the learning.

▶ Talk more about why authors use flashbacks as students read more books that have them. Suggested books include *Journey* by Patricia MacLachlan, *Stitchin' and Pullin': A Gee's Bend Quilt* by Patricia C. McKissack, and *A Million Fish . . . More or Less* also by Patricia C. McKissack.

▶ **Writing About Reading** Have students fill in a graphic organizer about flashbacks (see resources.fountasandpinnell.com). They can glue the chart in a reader's notebook and then use it to think and write about flashbacks in stories they read.

### Writers use flashbacks or a story-within-a-story.

| Title | Present Day | Flashback |
|---|---|---|
| THESE HANDS | Joseph and his grandpa spend time together. | Joseph's grandpa tells Joseph about the things he did with his hands when he was younger. |
| Gold Threaded Dress | Oy lives in America. | Oy thinks about stories of life in Thailand before Oy's family came to America. |
| KAMISHIBAI MAN | The man is very old and lives with his wife. | The man thinks about the days when he was younger and told stories and sold candy to young children. |

**Reading Minilesson Principle**
## Use what you know to predict what will happen next or at the end of the story.

### Understanding Plot

### You Will Need

- independent reading books that students have selected
- chart paper and markers

### Academic Language / Important Vocabulary

- predict
- evidence
- outcome

### Continuum Connection

- Predict what will happen next in a story and outcomes of the plot [p. 59]

### Goal

Predict what will happen next in a story and the outcomes of the plot.

### Rationale

When students learn to assess what they know about a character to make predictions about what will happen next in a story, they begin to understand motivation, which can be applied to their own lives.

### Assess Learning

Observe students when they make predictions and notice if there is evidence of new learning based on the goal of this minilesson.

- ❱ Do students apply what they know so far when making predictions?
- ❱ Are they using evidence from the text to support their predictions?
- ❱ Do they use the terms *predict, evidence,* and *outcome*?

## Minilesson

To help students think about the minilesson principle, engage them in using what they know to make predictions. Here is an example.

- ❱ Ask each student to bring a familiar fiction book that she is reading independently but has not yet finished.

    Think about the book you are reading right now. What do you know about the main character so far?

- ❱ Ask one volunteer to share. Then continue the conversation with that same student.

    Based on what you know so far, what do you predict will happen next?

    What evidence from the book makes you think that?

- ❱ As the student shares, generalize her thinking to begin creating a list of general actions for making predictions.

    Who else would like to share a prediction about what will happen next in the story you are reading? Remember to give examples from the story to support your prediction.

- ❱ Have one or two more students share their predictions. Continue adding to the list of general actions for making predictions.

## Have a Try

Invite the students to talk in a small group about predictions.

> In your group, share a prediction. Talk about the evidence from the book that helps you make that prediction.

▶ After time for discussion, ask several more students to share. Continue adding to the chart.

## Summarize and Apply

Summarize the learning and remind students to think about what might happen next in a story.

> What did you learn about making predictions?

▶ Write the minilesson principle at the top of the chart paper.

> If you aren't already reading a fiction book, choose one to read today. Notice if any of your predictions are correct. You can also make a new prediction based on information you get from reading. Bring the book when we meet so you can share.

## Share

Following independent reading time, gather students in a circle.

> Did anyone find out the outcome of a prediction you made? Did you make any new predictions? Talk about that.

▶ Based on students' responses, add any new actions for making predictions to the chart.

## Extend the Lesson (Optional)

After assessing students' understanding, you might decide to extend the learning.

▶ During interactive read-aloud, stop to ask students to make predictions. Ask them to support predictions with evidence from the text.

▶ **Writing About Reading** Have students use a reader's notebook to write predictions as they read and then revisit their predictions and write about whether the prediction came true or not.

---

**Use what you know to predict what will happen next or at the end of the story.**

Look at the front and back cover for clues.

What has the character said so far?

What has the character done so far?

What have you learned about the character?

What have others said about the character?

What has happened in the story that gives a hint?

---

## Assessment

After you have taught the minilessons in this umbrella, observe students as they talk and write about plot across instructional contexts: interactive read-aloud, independent reading, guided reading, shared reading, and book club. Use *The Literacy Continuum* (Fountas and Pinnell 2017) to guide the observation of students' reading and writing behaviors.

▶ What evidence do you have of new understandings related to understanding plot?

- Do students understand that plot is defined as what happens in the story?

- Are they aware that sometimes stories have more than one problem?

- Can they discuss aspects of narrative text structure, such as the beginning, the series of events, the high point, and the ending?

- Do they recognize that sometimes writers use flashbacks or a story-within-a-story?

- Are they able to use what they know to predict what will happen next in a story?

- Do they use vocabulary such as *plot, events, problem, solution,* and *predict*?

▶ In what other ways, beyond the scope of this umbrella, are students talking about plot?

- Are students talking about other story elements, such as characters and setting?

Use your observations to determine the next umbrella you will teach. You may also consult Minilessons Across the Year (pp. 59–61) for guidance.

## Link to Writing

After teaching the minilessons in this umbrella, help students link the new learning to their own writing:

▶ As students write their own fiction stories, encourage them to include narrative text structural elements, such as a beginning, a series of events, a high point, and an ending.

## Reader's Notebook

When this umbrella is complete, provide a copy of the minilesson principles (see resources.fountasandpinnell.com) for students to glue in the reader's notebook (in the Minilessons section if using *Reader's Notebook: Intermediate* [Fountas and Pinnell 2011]), so they can refer to the information as needed.

## Minilessons in This Umbrella

**RML1**    Notice what the characters think, say, and do to understand how they are feeling.

**RML2**    Notice what the characters say and do to understand their relationships.

**RML3**    Notice how one character might see things differently from another character.

**RML4**    Think about what characters really want.

**RML5**    Evaluate whether the characters behave in ways consistent with the time in which they live.

**RML6**    Think critically about whether a character is believable and authentic.

## Before Teaching Umbrella 26 Minilessons

Read and discuss books with characters whose feelings can be observed through their words and the illustrations, as well as books with diverse time periods, locations, and characters. Students should be reading fiction books during independent reading, or fictions books should be available. The minilessons in this umbrella use the following books from the *Fountas and Pinnell Classroom™ Interactive Read-Aloud Collection* text sets; however, you can use other books from your classroom that have characters whose feelings are easily observed.

**Figuring Out Who You Are**

*Heroes* by Ken Mochizuki

*The Junkyard Wonders* by Patricia Polacco

*La Mariposa* by Francisco Jiménez

**Friendship**

*Better Than You* by Trudy Ludwig

**Author/Illustrator Study: Allen Say**

*The Bicycle Man*

*The Lost Lake*

**Illustrator Study: Floyd Cooper**

*Ma Dear's Aprons* by Patricia C. McKissack

*Ruth and the Green Book* by Calvin Alexander Ramsey

As you read aloud and enjoy these texts together, help students

- notice characters' thoughts, words, and actions that are both explicit and implicit,

- consider how characters' thoughts, words, and actions show how they feel about themselves and others,

- think about what motivates characters,

- make inferences about characters,

- make predictions based on what they know about a character, and

- notice details about different time periods and places and think about how that impacts the characters.

**Figuring Out Who You Are**

**Friendship**

**Author/Illustrator Study: Allen Say**

**Illustrator Study: Floyd Cooper**

**Reading Minilesson Principle**
## Notice what the characters think, say, and do to understand how they are feeling.

### Understanding Characters' Feelings, Motivations, and Intentions

#### You Will Need

- several familiar fiction books that have characters with clear feelings, such as the following:
  - *La Mariposa* by Francisco Jiménez, from Text Set: Figuring Out Who You Are
  - *Better Than You* by Trudy Ludwig, from Text Set: Friendship
- chart paper and markers
- sticky notes

#### Academic Language / Important Vocabulary

- feelings
- motivations
- intentions
- infer

#### Continuum Connection

- Infer character's intentions, feelings, and motivations as revealed through thought, dialogue, behavior, and what others say or think about them (p. 59)

### Goal

Infer characters' feelings as revealed through thought, dialogue, and behavior.

### Rationale

When students learn to infer characters' feelings, motivations, and intentions, they learn to relate to characters and deepen their comprehension of the text.

### Assess Learning

Observe students when they talk about characters' feelings and notice if there is evidence of new learning based on the goal of this minilesson.

- ▷ Do students connect a character's thoughts, words, and actions with that character's feelings?
- ▷ Are they using evidence from the text to make inferences about a character's feelings?
- ▷ Do they use the terms *feelings, motivations, intentions,* and *infer*?

## Minilesson

To help students think about the minilesson principle, engage them in thinking about the ways authors show how characters feel. Here is an example.

> Think about Francisco as I read part of *La Mariposa*.

- ▷ Read the first paragraph from page 9.

  > What do you notice about how he is feeling?

- ▷ As needed, prompt the conversation so students recognize that Francisco turns away when people look at him because he is feeling self-conscious about not being able to speak English.

- ▷ As students identify the way Francisco feels and how the author shows Francisco's feelings, begin a chart with students' responses.

  > Think about how Francisco might be feeling as I read another part of the story.

- ▷ Read the last two paragraphs on page 25.

  > How is Francisco feeling? How do you know?

- ▷ Add responses to the chart.

- ▷ Read the last page of the book. Repeat the discussion and add responses to chart.

## Have a Try

Invite the students to talk with a partner about a character's feelings.

> Think about how Tyler might be feeling as I read a few parts from *Better Than You.*

▶ Read page 6 and then read page 24.

> Turn and talk about how Tyler might be feeling and how the author shows you Tyler's feelings.

▶ After time for discussion, ask students to share. Add responses to the chart.

## Summarize and Apply

Summarize the learning and remind students to think about characters' feelings when they read fiction stories.

> You talked about how characters might be feeling. What did you notice?

▶ Add the principle to the top of the chart.

> If you read a fiction book during independent reading today, think about how a character might be feeling and notice how the author shows you that. Mark any pages you want to remember with a sticky note. Bring the book when we meet so you can share.

## Share

Following independent reading time, gather students in small groups. Make sure at least one student in each group read a fiction book today.

> Did you notice how a character might be feeling and how the author showed you how a character feels? Talk to your group about that.

## Extend the Lesson (Optional)

After assessing students' understanding, you might decide to extend the learning.

▶ **Writing About Reading** Encourage students to write in a reader's notebook about how a character might be feeling. Ask them to use evidence from the text to support their thinking.

| Notice what the characters think, say, and do to understand how they are feeling. | | |
|---|---|---|
| Title | How is the character feeling? | How do you know? |
| *La Mariposa* | self-conscious | **Actions** Francisco turns away when people look at him because he is uncomfortable about not speaking English. |
| | sad | **Thoughts** Francisco could not imagine flying over the fields to Papá. |
| | proud confident | **Words** Francisco says "It's yours" when Curtis admires Francisco's butterfly drawing. |
| *Better Than You* | like he is not good enough | **Thoughts** Tyler thinks of all the places he would rather be than with Jake. |
| | confident supportive | **Words** Tyler tells Jake, "I'm going to stay here with Niko." |

**Section 2: Literary Analysis**

**Reading Minilesson Principle**

# Notice what the characters say and do to understand their relationships.

## Understanding Characters' Feelings, Motivations, and Intentions

### You Will Need

- several familiar fiction books with easily identifiable character interactions, such as the following:
  - *Ruth and the Green Book* by Calvin Alexander Ramsey and *Ma Dear's Aprons* by Patricia C. McKissack, from Text Set: Illustrator Study: Floyd Cooper
  - *Better Than You* by Trudy Ludwig, from Text Set: Friendship
- chart paper and markers
- sticky notes

### Academic Language / Important Vocabulary

- character
- relationships
- dialogue
- behavior
- inference

### Continuum Connection

- Infer relationships between characters as revealed through dialogue and behavior (p. 60)

## Goal

Infer relationships between characters as revealed through dialogue and behavior.

## Rationale

When students learn to make inferences about how characters feel about others from what they say and do, they deepen comprehension of the text and build empathy.

## Assess Learning

Observe students when they discuss characters' feelings and notice if there is evidence of new learning based on the goal of this minilesson.

- ▶ Are students talking about characters' relationships?
- ▶ Do they use evidence from the text to support inferences about how characters' words and actions show how they feel about other characters?
- ▶ Do they understand the terms *character, relationships, dialogue, behavior,* and *inference*?

## Minilesson

To help students think about the minilesson principle, engage them in noticing how characters feel about each other. Here is an example.

> Listen and notice the words and illustrations as I read these pages from *Ruth and the Green Book*.

- ▶ Read pages 7–8 and show the illustrations.

  > What do you notice about the choices the author and illustrator made on these pages when they wrote about and drew the characters?

  > How did they show how the characters feel about each other?

- ▶ As students respond, create a chart with a column for the title, a column for students' inferences about character relationships, and a column for evidence from the text. Add students' ideas to the chart.

  > Now think about character relationships in another book, *Ma Dear's Aprons*.

- ▶ Read and show pages 23–24.

  > What choices did the author and illustrator make about the characters?

  > What clues do they give about how the characters are feeling?

## Have a Try

Invite the students to talk with a partner about how characters feel about each other.

> Think about the characters in *Better Than You*.

▶ Show and read page 25.

> Turn and talk about what clues the author and illustrator give about how the characters feel about each other.

▶ After time for discussion, ask students to share ideas. Add ideas to the chart.

## Summarize and Apply

Summarize the learning and remind students to think about character relationships when they read fiction stories.

> Today you talked about how characters might be feeling about each other. What did you learn?

▶ Add the principle to the top of the chart.

> If you read a fiction book today, think about character relationships and how you know the way characters might be feeling about one another. Mark any pages you want to remember with a sticky note. Bring the book when we meet so you can share.

## Share

Following independent reading time, gather students in a circle.

> Did anyone notice the way the author and illustrator give you clues to help you know how characters feel about each other? Talk about that and share any pages that would be helpful to explain your thinking.

## Extend the Lesson (Optional)

After assessing students' understanding, you might decide to extend the learning.

▶ **Writing About Reading** Have students fill in the Exploring Relationships Between Characters graphic organizer (available from resources.fountasandpinnell.com) and then glue the chart into a readers' notebook so that they can think and write more about character relationships.

| Notice what the characters say and do to understand their relationships. | | |
|---|---|---|
| Title | Relationships | How do you know? |
| Ruth and the Green Book | Daddy cares about his family and wants to take care of them. | He tries to get a hotel room and points to his family and smiles. He feels frustrated when he can't rent a room for his family. |
| Ma Dear's Aprons | Ma Dear and David Earl love and care about each other. | They laugh and say funny things to each other when it is bath time. |
| BETTER THAN YOU | Tyler and Niko like each other and want to be good friends. | They hang out, talk, and play guitar together. |

**Reading Minilesson Principle**

# Notice how one character might see things differently from another character.

**Understanding Characters' Feelings, Motivations, and Intentions**

## You Will Need

- several familiar fiction books that show characters with differing perspectives, such as the following:
  - *The Lost Lake* by Allen Say, from Text Set: Author/ Illustrator Study: Allen Say
  - *Ruth and the Green Book* by Calvin Alexander Ramsey, from Text Set: Illustrator Study: Floyd Cooper
  - *La Mariposa* by Francisco Jiménez, from Text Set: Figuring Out Who You Are
- chart paper and markers
- sticky notes

## Academic Language / Important Vocabulary

- main character
- secondary character
- perspective

### Continuum Connection

- Infer relationships between characters as revealed through dialogue and behavior (p. 60)

## Goal

Notice how main and secondary characters sometimes have a different point of view.

## Rationale

When students think about the perspective of two different characters, they understand that each character has a unique point of view. Multiple perspectives not only deepen readers' understanding of the story but also demonstrate that different people have different perspectives.

## Assess Learning

Observe students when they talk about the way different characters see a situation and notice if there is evidence of new learning based on the goal of this minilesson.

- Do students notice that different characters might see things differently?
- Do they understand the terms *main character, secondary character,* and *perspective*?

## Minilesson

To help students think about the minilesson principle, provide an interactive lesson to think about the different perspectives of characters. Here is an example.

- Show the illustration on page 5 and read the first sentence on page 4 from *The Lost Lake*.

  You know what a main character is, but there are other characters in a story, too. They are called secondary characters. In *The Lost Lake*, who is the main character and who is the secondary character? You have a clue by noticing who is telling the story.

- As students respond, create a chart. Use students' ideas to begin filling in the chart with the title and names of the main character and secondary character.

- Revisit the text and illustration on pages 6–7.

  Turn and talk about how the boy and his dad see this situation.

- After time for discussion, ask students to share ideas. Continue filling in the chart.

  Now think about Ruth and her mom in *Ruth and the Green Book*. Do they see things differently from each other, or have a different perspective?

- Revisit pages 5–6.

  Do Ruth and Mama see the situation in the same way, or in a different way?

- Add responses to the chart.

## Have a Try

Invite the students to talk with a partner about the way different characters sometimes see things differently.

▶ Revisit pages 19–20 from *La Mariposa*.

> Turn and talk about how Francisco and Curtis are feeling. How do they see things differently from each other?

▶ After time for discussion, ask students to share. Add ideas to the chart.

## Summarize and Apply

Summarize the learning and remind students to think about the way characters sometimes see things differently from each other.

> Today you talked about how characters see things differently. What did you notice?

▶ Add the principle to the top of the chart.

> As you read fiction, think about the main character and any secondary characters and how they view things that happen in the story. If you read fiction today, mark any pages you want to remember with a sticky note. Bring the book when we meet so you can share.

## Share

Following independent reading time, gather students in a circle.

> Did anyone read a fiction story that has characters who see things differently? Share what you noticed.

## Extend the Lesson (Optional)

After assessing students' understanding, you might decide to extend the learning.

▶ **Writing About Reading** Encourage students to use a reader's notebook to write about the viewpoints of a main character and a secondary character in a fiction book. Ask them to share their thinking about whether the characters see things the same or differently and why.

### Notice how one character might see things differently from another character.

| Title | Events | Main Character | Secondary Character |
|---|---|---|---|
| THE LOST LAKE | The boy puts magazine pictures of mountains, rivers, and lakes on the wall in his room. | *the boy<br>The boy thinks that his dad is mad at him for cutting up his magazines. | *the dad<br>The dad is thinking how nice it would be to take a trip to find the Lost Lake, like he used to do with his own father. |
| Ruth and the Green Book | The family stops at a gas station, but the attendant will not give them keys to the restroom because they are African American. | *Ruth<br>Ruth feels embarrassed because she feels like she is doing something wrong, and she has not experienced this type of direct racism. | *Mama<br>Mama is angry because she understands that the attendant is behaving in a racist way. She knows that it is not acceptable when they are treated differently because of their skin color. |
| La Mariposa | Francisco and Curtis fight over a jacket. | *Francisco<br>Francisco was given the jacket by the principal, so he thinks it is his. He wants to protect his jacket. | *Curtis<br>The jacket belongs to Curtis, and he thinks that Francisco took it. When he yells at Francisco to return his jacket, Francisco does not listen. |

Section 2: Literary Analysis

# RML4
## LA.U26.RML4

**Reading Minilesson Principle**
## Think about what characters really want.

### Understanding Characters' Feelings, Motivations, and Intentions

### You Will Need

- several familiar fiction books, such as the following:
  - *Heroes* by Ken Mochizuki, from Text Set: Figuring Out Who You Are
  - *Ruth and the Green Book* by Calvin Alexander Ramsey, from Text Set: Illustrator Study: Floyd Cooper
  - *The Junkyard Wonders* by Patricia Polacco, from Text Set: Figuring Out Who You Are
- chart paper and markers
- sticky notes

### Academic Language / Important Vocabulary

- character
- motivations
- dialogue
- behavior

### Continuum Connection

- Infer characters' intentions, feelings, and motivations as revealed through thought, dialogue, behavior, and what others say or think about them (p. 59)

### Goal

Infer characters' motivations as revealed through dialogue, behavior, and what others say or think about them.

### Rationale

Understanding what a character wants reveals the character's motivation behind his words and actions. Often what the character wants is the root of the story's problem and provides the grist for the plot.

### Assess Learning

Observe students when they talk about characters' motivations and notice if there is evidence of new learning based on the goal of this minilesson.

- Are students discussing the ways that characters' words and actions indicate what they want?
- Do they use evidence from the text to support opinions about characters' motivations?
- Do they understand the terms *character, motivations, dialogue,* and *behavior*?

## Minilesson

To help students think about the minilesson principle, engage them in thinking about a character's motivation. Here is an example.

- Revisit the text and illustrations on pages 1–5 of *Heroes*.

  Think about the things Donnie and the other characters say, do, or think. What do their words, actions, and thoughts tell you about what Donnie really wants?

- As students offer suggestions, prompt them to provide examples from the story that show Donnie's motivations. Create a chart that includes a column for text examples and a column for what a character wants. Add student ideas to the chart.

  Now think about Daddy in *Ruth and the Green Book*. As I revisit a few pages, notice what the other characters say or do that helps you know what Daddy really wants.

- Revisit pages 7, 8, and 11.

  What did you notice?

- Add student ideas to the chart.

  When you notice what a character really wants, you have probably identified the main problem in the story. The rest of the story will be about how the character tries to get what she wants.

## Have a Try

Invite the students to talk with a partner about a character's motivation.

▶ Revisit the text and illustrations on pages 7–10 in *The Junkyard Wonders*.

> Turn and talk about how Patricia Polacco shows you what Trisha really wants.

▶ After time for discussion, ask students to share. Add ideas to the chart.

## Summarize and Apply

Summarize the learning and remind students to think about what characters really want.

> You talked about what characters really want. When you think about what the character wants it helps you understand the story.

▶ Add the principle to the top of the chart.

> As you read fiction, think about what a character really wants and how the author shows you that. If you read fiction today, mark any pages you want to remember with a sticky note. Bring the book when we meet so you can share.

## Share

Following independent reading time, gather students in a circle.

> Did anyone notice what a character really wants when you read today? Share what you noticed.

## Extend the Lesson (Optional)

After assessing students' understanding, you might decide to extend the learning.

▶ Talk about how what a character really wants usually leads to the main problem in a story. The character's efforts to solve the problem make up most of the plot.

▶ **Writing About Reading** Encourage students to use a reader's notebook to write about how what a character really wants leads to the problem in the story. Ask them to support their thinking with evidence from the text.

### Think about what characters really want.

| Title | What Characters Do and Say | What the Character Wants |
|---|---|---|
| HEROES | Donnie asks his dad to drop him off down the street from school. Zach says Donnie must be the enemy because he looks like the enemy. Donnie says that his dad and uncle were soldiers for the U.S. army in the war. | Donnie does not want to be treated differently because of his race. |
| Ruth and the Green Book | The man at the hotel will not rent a room to Daddy. Eddy plays music with Daddy and Alice cooks food and gives them a place to sleep. | Daddy wants to be treated fairly and kindly by others. He wants his family to have a warm place to sleep. |
| The Junkyard Wonders Patricia Polacco | Trisha talks to Thom and the other kids at recess and asks about her new class. Trisha cries and tells her Dad that her class is called the Junkyard. | Trisha wants to be treated fairly and not teased or judged just because she is in a special class. |

**Reading Minilesson Principle**

# Evaluate whether the characters behave in ways consistent with the time in which they live.

## Understanding Characters' Feelings, Motivations, and Intentions

### You Will Need

- several familiar fiction books with characters who live in different time periods, such as the following:
  - *Ruth and the Green Book* by Calvin Alexander Ramsey, from Text Set: Illustrator Study: Floyd Cooper
  - *Heroes* by Ken Mochizuki, from Text Set: Figuring Out Who You Are
  - *Ma Dear's Aprons* by Patricia C. McKissack, from Text Set: Illustrator Study: Floyd Cooper
- chart paper and markers
- sticky notes

### Academic Language / Important Vocabulary

- character
- behave
- consistent
- time period

### Continuum Connection

- Evaluate the consistency of characters' actions within a particular setting (p. 61)

## Goal

Evaluate the consistency of characters' actions within a particular setting.

## Rationale

When students evaluate whether characters are behaving in ways that are consistent with the time period in which they live, they are thinking deeply about the author's craft and developing critical thinking skills.

## Assess Learning

Observe students when they talk about the words and actions of characters and notice if there is evidence of new learning based on the goal of this minilesson.

- ▶ Are students able to identify the time period in which characters live?
- ▶ Can they think critically about the setting by discussing whether characters speak and behave in ways that are consistent with the time period in which they live?
- ▶ Do they use the terms *character, behave, consistent,* and *time period*?

## Minilesson

To help students think about the minilesson principle, engage students in thinking about whether characters speak and behave in a way that is consistent with the time in which they live. Here is an example.

- ▶ Revisit the text and illustrations from a few pages of *Ruth and the Green Book* that show the time period, such as the cover and pages 1–6.

  What do you notice about the time period in which this family lives?

  Do you think this family talks and acts like a family that lives at this time would? What makes you think that?

- ▶ Share other pages as needed to help identify examples showing that the time period is the 1950s, prior to the civil rights movement.

- ▶ As students share ideas, create a chart with their noticings. Have a volunteer add a sticky note with *yes* or *no* in one column to show if the character talks and behaves like a person from that time. Ask volunteers to share examples from the text to support their thinking and write their ideas in another column.

  Think about another book, *Heroes*. What do you know about the time period?

  Do Donnie and the other characters act in a way that you think people would act at that time? Talk about that.

- ▶ Ask a volunteer to write *Yes* or *No* on a sticky note and add it to the chart. Ask students to share examples from the text and add to the chart.

## Have a Try

Invite the students to talk with a partner about characters' behaviors in a particular time period.

▶ Show the cover of *Ma Dear's Aprons* and revisit a few pages of text and illustrations that show the time period.

> Turn and talk about the time period of *Ma Dear's Aprons*. Do you think people living at that time would talk and act like these characters? Talk about why you think that.

▶ After time for discussion, ask students to share ideas. Add to chart.

## Summarize and Apply

Summarize the learning and remind students to think about the time in which characters live and how characters talk and behave when they read fiction stories.

> Today you talked about whether characters talk and act like people would during the time in which the story takes place. Why is that important?

▶ Add the principle to the top of the chart.

> As you read fiction, think about the time period in which the story takes place and whether the characters act and talk in a way that people would at that time. If you read fiction today, mark any pages you want to remember with a sticky note. Bring the book when we meet so you can share.

## Share

Following independent reading time, gather students in a circle to talk about their reading.

> Did anyone read a story that takes place in a different time period? What did you notice about the characters? Share what you noticed.

## Extend the Lesson (Optional)

After assessing students' understanding, you might decide to extend the learning.

▶ **Writing About Reading** Encourage students to use a reader's notebook to make a list of the different time periods they read about and how the characters behave and speak. Ask them to write about whether they think the characters act and speak in a way that is consistent with people who would have lived during that time period.

| Title | Time Period | Do characters talk and act like people would during that time period? | Why or why not? |
|---|---|---|---|
| *Ruth and the Green Book* | 1950s | Yes | The family experiences racism in some places because this was before civil rights. They need to behave differently sometimes to stay safe. |
| *Heroes* | after the Korean War | Yes | The boys play war games and talk about the war that just happened in Korea. |
| *Ma Dear's Aprons* | early 1900s | Yes | The boy helps his mom with household chores that were normal at that time. They say things that would have been said at that time. |

*Evaluate whether characters behave in ways consistent with the time in which they live.*

# RML 6

**LA.U26.RML6**

## Reading Minilesson Principle
## Think critically about whether a character is believable and authentic.

**Understanding Characters' Feelings, Motivations, and Intentions**

### You Will Need

- several familiar fiction books, such as the following:
  - *The Junkyard Wonders* by Patricia Polacco, from Text Set: Figuring Out Who You Are
  - *The Bicycle Man* by Allen Say, from Text Set: Author/ Illustrator Study: Allen Say
  - *Heroes* by Ken Mochizuki, from Text Set: Figuring Out Who You Are
- chart paper and markers
- sticky notes

### Academic Language / Important Vocabulary

- character
- believable
- authentic
- critically

### Continuum Connection

- Think critically about the authenticity and believability of characters and their behavior, dialogue, and development (p. 60)

## Goal

Think critically about the authenticity and believability of characters and their behavior and dialogue.

## Rationale

When students think about the authenticity of characters, they develop critical thinking skills and begin to evaluate the way authors develop characters.

## Assess Learning

Observe students when they talk about character authenticity and notice if there is evidence of new learning based on the goal of this minilesson.

- ▶ Do students discuss whether a character's behavior is believable?
- ▶ Are they able to analyze whether dialogue seems real?
- ▶ Do they use the terms *character, believable, authentic,* and *critically*?

## Minilesson

To help students think about the minilesson principle, engage them in thinking about the authenticity of characters. Here is an example.

- ▶ Revisit pages 7–10 of *The Junkyard Wonders*.

  What do you notice about the things Trisha says and how she acts?

  Do you know anyone who might act like she did in the same situation?

- ▶ As students share ideas, introduce the terms *believable* and *authentic*. Use these words in the conversation as students talk about Trisha.

- ▶ Create a chart with one column to show whether a character is believable and authentic and another column for evidence from the text. Ask a volunteer to talk about whether Trisha is authentic. Then, have the volunteer write *yes* or *no* on a sticky note and add it to the chart. In the other column, write examples from the story.

  Now think about another story you know, *The Bicycle Man*. As I read a few pages, think about whether the characters are authentic and believable.

- ▶ Revisit pages 11–18.

  What did you notice about whether the author makes the characters authentic and believable?

- ▶ Ask a volunteer to write *Yes* or *No* on a sticky note and add it to the chart. Ask other students to give examples from the text to support their thinking. As they do, write their responses on the chart.

## Have a Try

Invite the students to talk with a partner about whether a character is believable.

> Think about the characters in *Heroes*.

> ▸ As needed, revisit a few pages to show the ways the characters talk and act.

> > Turn and talk about whether the characters in *Heroes* are authentic and believable.

> ▸ After time for discussion, ask a volunteer to add a sticky note to the chart. Ask others to share text examples and write their examples on the chart.

## Summarize and Apply

Summarize the learning and remind students to think about character authenticity when they read fiction stories.

> > Today you talked about whether characters are authentic and believable. What did you notice?

> ▸ Add the principle to the top of the chart.

> > If you read a fiction book during independent reading time, think about whether the characters are authentic and believable and how the author shows you that. Mark any pages you want to remember with a sticky note. Bring the book when we meet so you can share.

## Share

Following independent reading time, gather students in small groups. Make sure that each group has at least one student who read a fiction book.

> > With your group, talk about what you noticed about characters when you read today. Were they authentic and believable? Share any pages that will be helpful to the conversation.

## Extend the Lesson (Optional)

After assessing students' understanding, you might decide to extend the learning.

> ▸ **Writing About Reading** Have students think critically about the authenticity of characters they read about by using a reader's notebook to write about their noticings. Ask them to provide text examples to support their thinking.

**Think critically about whether a character is believable and authentic.**

| Title | Is the character believable and authentic? | Why or why not? |
|---|---|---|
| The Junkyard Wonders — Patricia Polacco | Yes | • When Trisha talks to the other kids, the way they talk seems real.<br>• The worries that Trisha has about school seem like how a real girl would feel. |
| THE BICYCLE MAN — by Allen Say | Yes | • The things the kids say to each other about the soldiers seem like what kids would say when seeing someone from a different race for the first time.<br>• The games they play and things they eat seem like what kids in Japan would do and eat at that time. |
| HEROES | Yes | • The way the kids and adults talk seems real.<br>• The things the boys do and how Donnie feels seem like that could be how kids could have acted after the Korean War. |

Section 2: Literary Analysis

## Assessment

After you have taught the minilessons in this umbrella, observe students as they talk and write about characters across instructional contexts: interactive read-aloud, independent reading, guided reading, shared reading, and book club. Use *The Literacy Continuum* (Fountas and Pinnell 2017) to guide the observation of students' reading and writing behaviors.

▶ What evidence do you have of new understandings related to characters' feelings, motivations, and intentions?

- Are students able to determine how a character is feeling from what the character thinks, says, and does?
- Can they infer how characters feel about each other?
- Are they able to identify a character's motivations?
- How well do they understand that different characters see things differently?
- Do they analyze whether a character's behavior is consistent with the time in which the character lives?
- Are they talking about whether a character is authentic?
- Do they understand vocabulary such as *feelings, motivations, intentions, infer,* and *behavior*?

▶ In what other ways, beyond the scope of this umbrella, are students demonstrating an understanding of characters?

- Do students think and talk about character traits when they read fiction stories?

Use your observations to determine the next umbrella you will teach. You may also consult Minilessons Across the Year (pp. 59–61) for guidance.

## Link to Writing

After teaching the minilessons in this umbrella, help students link the new learning to their own writing:

▶ Suggest that students write a play using dialogue that gives clues about the characters' feelings, motivations, and/or intentions.

## Reader's Notebook

When this umbrella is complete, provide a copy of the minilesson principles (see resources.fountasandpinnell.com) for students to glue in the reader's notebook (in the Minilessons section if using *Reader's Notebook: Intermediate* [Fountas and Pinnell 2011]), so they can refer to the information as needed.

## Minilessons in This Umbrella

**RML1**   Behaviors, thoughts, and dialogue show a character's traits.

**RML2**   Characters can be complex individuals.

**RML3**   Characters change because of the things that happen to them.

**RML4**   Evaluate whether the writer makes you feel empathy for the character.

## Before Teaching Umbrella 27 Minilessons

Read and discuss books with characters whose traits are clearly observable through behavior, dialogue, thoughts, and story events, as well as characters who do and do not make mistakes, change, and learn lessons. Students should be reading fiction books during independent reading, and plenty of fiction books should be available in the classroom library. The minilessons in this umbrella use the following books from the *Fountas & Pinnell Classroom™ Interactive Read-Aloud Collection* text sets; however, you can use different books that feature characters with clearly observable traits.

**Exploring Identity**

### Genre Study: Historical Fiction

*The Glorious Flight: Across the Channel with Louis Blériot* by Alice and
   Martin Provensen

*The Buffalo Storm* by Katherine Applegate

*Dad, Jackie, and Me* by Myron Uhlberg

**Perseverance**

### Exploring Identity

*The Royal Bee* by Frances Park and Ginger Park

### Perseverance

*Strong to the Hoop* by John Coy

*Razia's Ray of Hope: One Girl's Dream of an Education* by Elizabeth Suneby

*Rescue & Jessica: A Life-Changing Friendship* by Jessica Kensky and
   Patrick Downes

As you read aloud and enjoy these texts together, help students

• determine a character's traits from the story,

• notice that sometimes good characters make mistakes,

• identify the ways that a character changes due to things that happen to the character, and

• talk about the ways a writer causes a reader to feel empathy toward a character.

**Section 2: Literary Analysis**

# RML1
## LA.U27.RML1

### Reading Minilesson Principle
# Behaviors, thoughts, and dialogue show a character's traits.

## Understanding a Character's Traits and Development

### You Will Need

- several familiar fiction books that have character traits that are identifiable by behavior, thoughts, and dialogue, such as the following:
  - *The Royal Bee* by Frances Park and Ginger Park, from Text Set: Exploring Identity
  - *The Glorious Flight* by Alice and Martin Provensen, from Text Set: Genre Study: Historical Fiction
  - *Strong to the Hoop* by John Coy, from Text Set: Perseverance
- chart paper and markers
- sticky notes

### Academic Language / Important Vocabulary

- character
- behavior
- thoughts
- dialogue
- traits

### Continuum Connection

- Infer characters' traits as revealed through thought, dialogue, behavior, and what others say or think about them, and use evidence from the text to describe them (p. 59)

### Goal

Infer characters' traits as revealed through their behavior, dialogue, and inner thoughts.

### Rationale

When students think about what thoughts, dialogue, and behavior show about a character's traits, they have a deeper comprehension of the story and develop empathy for the characters.

### Assess Learning

Observe students when they talk about character traits and notice if there is evidence of new learning based on the goal of this minilesson.

- ◗ Do students notice the thoughts, behavior, and dialogue of characters?
- ◗ Do they think about what is revealed about a character by analyzing thoughts, behavior, and dialogue?
- ◗ Do they use the terms *character, behavior, thoughts, dialogue,* and *traits*?

## Minilesson

To help students think about the minilesson principle, use familiar fiction stories to engage them in noticing how writers reveal character traits. Here is an example.

- ◗ Show and revisit a few pages of *The Royal Bee* that show Song-Ho's character traits. For example, you might choose when Song-Ho listens outside the school door to learn, when he says he will give a gift to his mom if he wins, when he is told to go home by Master Min, and when the students choose Song-Ho to represent them at the Royal Bee.

  > Think about Song-Ho's personality, or character traits. What words could you use to describe Song-Ho?

  > How do you know what Song-Ho is like?

- ◗ As students have a conversation, create a chart with the title and character's name. Add the students' character trait words and the examples from the story that support their thinking. Encourage them to think about the behavior, thoughts, and dialogue of the character, as well as what other characters do and say that show the character's personality.

- ◗ Repeat the activity with another familiar book, such as *The Glorious Flight*. As students provide character trait words and examples from the story to support their thinking, add them to the chart.

## Have a Try

Invite the students to talk with a partner about character traits.

- Revisit a few pages in *Strong to the Hoop*, such as when James keeps practicing basketball and the part when he is told he is too small.

  Turn and talk about what James is like and how you know.

- After time for discussion, ask students to share. Add to chart.

## Summarize and Apply

Summarize the learning and remind students to think about character traits when they read fiction stories.

  You talked about how authors show you about a character's traits. What did you notice?

- Add the principle to the top of the chart.

  When you read today, you might select a fiction book. As you read, think about the behavior, thoughts, and dialogue that help you know about a character's traits. Use a sticky note to mark any pages you want to remember. Bring the book when we meet so you can share.

## Share

Following independent reading time, gather students in small groups. Make sure each group has at least one person who read a fiction book during independent reading.

  Did you notice a character's traits and how the author showed you those traits through behavior, thoughts, or dialogue? Talk to your group about that.

## Extend the Lesson (Optional)

After assessing students' understanding, you might decide to extend the learning.

- Teach students that a character's traits are often the same in each book in a series. The *Fountas & Pinnell Classroom™ Independent Reading Collection* has several characters that could be used for this lesson, such as Anna Wang in *Year of the Book* and *Year of the Fortune Cookie*, or Mrs. Jewls from the Wayside School stories.

- **Writing About Reading** Have students fill in a character trait analysis graphic organizer (see resources.fountasandpinnell.com) and then glue it into a reader's notebook so that they can use it to think and write about a character's traits.

**Behaviors, thoughts, and dialogue show a character's traits.**

| Title and Character | Behavior, Thoughts, Dialogue | Character Traits |
|---|---|---|
| Song-Ho | Song-Ho's behavior: Song-Ho listens outside the school door to learn. Song-Ho's thoughts: Song-Ho has dreams of reading and writing. He thinks that he would give his mother a gift if he won. | determined committed goal-oriented generous |
| Papa | Papa's behavior: Papa keeps trying to make a flying machine, even when many things go wrong. | persistent creative |
| James | James's thoughts: James wishes he could play, but practices instead. He imagines he is a basketball star. Another characters' words: Another player tells James "You can't guard me" and "You're too small," but he plays hard anyway. | determined fearless competitive |

Section 2: Literary Analysis

## Understanding a Character's Traits and Development

### You Will Need

- several familiar fiction books that have complex characters, such as the following:
  - *Razia's Ray of Hope* by Elizabeth Suneby, from Text Set: Perseverance
  - *The Royal Bee* by Frances Park and Ginger Park, from Text Set: Exploring Identity
  - *Strong to the Hoop* by John Coy, from Text Set: Perseverance
- chart paper and markers
- sticky notes

### Academic Language / Important Vocabulary

- character
- complex
- mistake

### Continuum Connection

- Recognize that characters can have multiple dimensions; e.g., can be good but make mistakes, can change [p. 59]

## Goal

Recognize that characters can have multiple dimensions.

## Rationale

When students recognize that characters can be complex and that good characters can make mistakes, they learn to connect the lives of characters to their own lives and understand that good people can make mistakes sometimes.

## Assess Learning

Observe students when they discuss characters and notice if there is evidence of new learning based on the goal of this minilesson.

- ▶ Are students able to talk about different aspects of a character's personality?
- ▶ Are they aware that an author can decide to make a character complex?
- ▶ Do they understand the terms *character, complex,* and *mistake*?

## Minilesson

To help students think about the minilesson principle, engage students in a discussion about what makes characters complex. Here is an example.

- ▶ Revisit the pages in *Razia's Ray of Hope* when Razia takes too much candy and when she goes to school even though her family tells her not to.

  Think about Razia, who is strong and has courage. What do you think about the way Razia acts during these parts of the story?

- ▶ On chart paper, make columns for title and character, examples that show that the character is complex, and what this shows about the character. Fill in the details based on students' suggestions.

  Does doing something she is not supposed to mean that Razia is a bad person? Why or why not?

- ▶ Add responses to the chart.
- ▶ Revisit the pages from another book that show a character making a mistake or doing something he is not supposed to. For example, share the part in *The Royal Bee* when Song-Ho sneaks around the school when he was told to leave.

  What do you think about Song-Ho's behavior during this part of the story? What does this show about Song-Ho?

- ▶ Add responses to the chart. Then talk about how authors make their characters complex personalities to make them seem more like real people.

## Have a Try

Invite the students to talk with a partner about how characters can be complex or make mistakes.

▶ Show and read the part in *Strong to the Hoop* when James rips Marcus's shirt and when James says "good game" to Marcus at the end.

  Turn and talk about what this shows about James.

▶ After time for discussion, ask students to share ideas. Add ideas to the chart.

## Summarize and Apply

Summarize the learning and remind students to think about the complexity of characters when they read fiction stories.

  You talked about how good characters sometimes do things wrong or make mistakes. What did you learn?

▶ Add the principle to the top of the chart.

  If you are reading a fiction book, think about whether a good character does something wrong or makes a mistake. Mark any pages you want to remember with a sticky note. Bring the book when we meet so you can share.

## Share

Following independent reading time, gather students in a circle.

  Did anyone notice a good character who does something wrong or makes a mistake? Talk about that and share any pages that would be helpful to explain your thinking.

## Extend the Lesson (Optional)

After assessing students' understanding, you might decide to extend the learning.

▶ **Writing About Reading** Have students fill in the Characters: Noticing Characters Across a Text graphic organizer (see resources.fountasandpinnell.com) and then glue it into a reader's notebook so that they can use it to think and write about different aspects of a character's personality.

| Characters can be complex individuals. | | |
|---|---|---|
| Title and Character | How the Character Is Complex | What This Shows About the Character |
| Razia | • Razia takes too much candy.<br><br>• Razia goes to school when her family told her not to. | Razia can be strong and have courage, but sometimes she does things she is not supposed to do. |
| Song-Ho | • Song-Ho sneaks around the school when he is told to leave. | Song-Ho is persistent and goes after his goals, but sometimes he does things that he is told not to do. |
| James | • James keeps playing even after he misses a shot, gets teased, and hurts his knee.<br>• James rips Marcus's shirt.<br>• James says "good game" to Marcus, even though Marcus had said mean things and elbowed him. | James is determined, persistent, and works hard to meet his goals, but he loses his temper sometimes.<br><br>James can be forgiving. |

## RML 3
**LA.U27.RML3**

### Reading Minilesson Principle
## Characters change because of the things that happen to them.

**Understanding a Character's Traits and Development**

### You Will Need

- several familiar fiction books in which characters change because of story events, such as the following:

  - *Rescue & Jessica* by Jessica Kensky and Patrick Downes, from Text Set: Perseverance

  - *Dad, Jackie, and Me* by Myron Uhlberg and *The Glorious Flight* by Alice and Martin Provensen, from Text Set: Genre Study: Historical Fiction

- chart paper and markers

- sticky notes

### Academic Language / Important Vocabulary

- character change

- event

- traits

### Continuum Connection

- Notice character change and infer reasons from events of the plot [p. 59]

- Notice how an author creates characters that are complex and change over many events of a plot [p. 60]

### Goal

Notice character change and infer reasons from events of the plot.

### Rationale

When students think about the way events cause a character to change, they deepen their understanding of both the character and the plot of the story.

### Assess Learning

Observe students when they talk about character change and notice if there is evidence of new learning based on the goal of this minilesson.

- ◗ Are students able to identify the events that cause a character to change?
- ◗ Do they infer why a character changes?
- ◗ Do they use the terms *character change*, *event*, and *traits*?

## Minilesson

To help students think about the minilesson principle, engage them in a discussion about why and how characters change. Here is an example.

- ◗ Revisit several parts of *Rescue & Jessica* that show the time before and after Jessica gets a rescue dog.

  > You noticed that Jessica was sad and frustrated when she was trying to learn to walk after her accident, but then her feelings changed.

  > Why did her feelings change?

- ◗ On chart paper, make columns for title and character, what happened, and how the character changed. Ask for students' suggestions to fill in the chart. Encourage them to talk about the events leading to the change, the change itself, and how the character is different.

  > Think about the dad and the son in *Dad, Jackie, and Me*. What event caused a change in both the dad and the son?

- ◗ Revisit pages as needed to show Dad receiving a ticket to the Brooklyn Dodgers game and pages that show the ways that the characters changed.

  > What did you notice?

- ◗ Add student ideas to the chart.

## Have a Try

Invite the students to talk with a partner about why and how characters change.

▶ Revisit the text and illustrations of *The Glorious Flight* that show Papa seeing a flying machine and then the ways that Papa changed.

> Turn and talk about the event that caused Papa to change and the ways that he changed.

▶ After time for discussion, ask students to share. Add ideas to the chart.

## Summarize and Apply

Summarize the learning and remind students to think about the events that caused a character to change and the ways that the character changed because of those events.

> You talked about events that caused characters to change and the ways those characters changed.

▶ Add the principle to the top of the chart.

> If you are reading a fiction book, think about whether a character changed. Use a sticky note to mark any pages you want to remember. Bring the book when we meet so you can share.

## Share

Following independent reading time, gather students in small groups to talk about how and why a character changed.

> Talk with your group about a character that changed in the book you read today. Share how the character changed and what you think caused the character to change.

## Extend the Lesson (Optional)

After assessing students' understanding, you might decide to extend the learning.

▶ During interactive read-aloud, talk about characters who change in some way from the beginning of the story to the end of the story. Talk about how that change is important to the story.

▶ **Writing About Reading** Have students write in a reader's notebook about why and how a character changed in a story. Suggest that they include how the character's change is important to the story.

### Characters change because of the things that happen to them.

| Title and Character | What Happened | How the Character Changed |
|---|---|---|
| *Rescue & Jessica* — Jessica | Jessica got Rescue for a service dog. | • became independent • felt happy |
| Dad / Son | Dad got tickets to a Brooklyn Dodgers game. | • supported someone else who suffered prejudice • became a baseball fan • learned to play baseball, which he couldn't do when he was young because he was deaf • appreciated what his dad did to communicate and prove himself • understood about discrimination |
| Papa | Papa saw a machine flying in the sky. | • built many machines until one worked • learned to be a pilot • flew across the English Channel |

Section 2: Literary Analysis

## Understanding a Character's Traits and Development

### You Will Need

- several familiar fiction books that invoke empathy, such as the following:
  - *The Buffalo Storm* by Katherine Applegate, from Text Set: Genre Study: Historical Fiction
  - *Rescue & Jessica* by Jessica Kensky and Patrick Downes and *Razia's Ray of Hope* by Elizabeth Suneby, from Text Set: Perseverance
- chart paper and markers
- sticky notes

### Academic Language / Important Vocabulary

- character
- empathy

### Continuum Connection

- Assess the extent to which a writer makes readers feel empathy or identify with characters (p. 60)

## Goal

Assess the extent to which a writer makes readers feel empathy for or identify with characters.

## Rationale

When students recognize that an author can use techniques to cause a reader to feel empathy toward a character, they think more deeply about the author's craft and how ideas gained from reading can be applied to their own lives. Feeling empathy causes students to engage more deeply with the story, think about their own feelings, and learn from the characters and situations.

## Assess Learning

Observe students when they talk about whether they feel empathy for characters and if there is evidence of new learning based on the goal of this minilesson.

- ⟩ Are students able to recognize when they feel empathy for a character?
- ⟩ Do they understand and use the terms *character* and *empathy*?

## Minilesson

To help students think about the minilesson principle, help them think about whether an author encourages a reader to feel empathy for a character. Here is an example.

- ⟩ Revisit a few pages from *The Buffalo Storm* to show how Hallie is feeling or what she is facing, such as when she rides the horse at the beginning and when she says goodbye to her grandma.

  > Do you think the author is successful in getting you to know what it would be like to feel the same way Hallie felt? Turn and talk about that.

- ⟩ Allow students time for discussion and then add the title and main character's name to the chart.

  > When you share the same feelings as someone else, you have empathy for that person. Did the author make you feel empathy for Hallie?

- ⟩ Have a student share her thinking and place a sticky note (labeled *Yes* or *No*) on the chart. Add examples from the story, along with her thoughts on why the author did or did not create a feeling of empathy.

- ⟩ Ask a second student to add a sticky note and share his thinking.

  > Now think about whether the authors of *Rescue & Jessica* caused you to feel empathy for Jessica as I revisit a few pages.

- ⟩ Revisit the pages where Jessica feels frustrated about having to learn to walk again, as well as the end matter. Add the title and Jessica's name to the chart. Then ask a few students to add sticky notes and share thinking as before.

## Have a Try

Invite the students to talk with a partner about whether the author causes them to feel empathy for a character.

▶ Revisit a few pages from *Razia's Ray of Hope*, such as when Razia dreams of going to school, when her brother tells her she cannot attend school, and then when he changes his mind.

> Turn and talk about whether the author of *Razia's Ray of Hope* makes you feel empathy for Razia.

▶ After time for discussion, ask students to share ideas. Add responses to the chart.

## Summarize and Apply

Summarize the learning and remind students to think about whether they feel empathy for characters in fiction stories.

> You thought critically about some stories to evaluate whether the authors were able to cause you to feel empathy toward the characters.

▶ Add the principle to the top of the chart.

> If you are reading a fiction book, think about whether the author made you feel empathy for any of the characters. Bring the book when we meet so you can share.

## Share

Following independent reading time, gather students in a circle to talk about feeling empathy for a character.

> Did anyone read about a character for whom you felt empathy? Tell what the author did to try to make the reader feel empathy for the character.

## Extend the Lesson (Optional)

After assessing students' understanding, you might decide to extend the learning.

▶ During interactive read-aloud, ask students about characters for whom they feel empathy and why.

▶ **Writing About Reading** Have students fill in the Recording Feeling: Relating to Writing organizer (see resources.fountasandpinnell.com) and then glue it into a reader's notebook so they can use it to think and write more about the way an author causes a reader to feel empathy).

**Evaluate whether the writer makes you feel empathy for the character.**

| Title and Character | Do you feel empathy? | Examples | Why or why not? |
|---|---|---|---|
| Hallie | No | "I was not afraid of anything (except maybe storms)." | "I could not imagine myself feeling like Hallie by reading this book." —Bella |
| | Yes | "When a storm starts, wrap this round you and think of me." | "When Hallie talked about her grandma, it made me miss my grandma. I knew how she felt." —Minh |
| Jessica | Yes | Jessica feels frustrated.  Description of the new things Jessica has to learn | "I can imagine how hard it would be for me to do what Jessica did." —Akisha |
| | Yes | Author's note and acknowledgments at end | "The author's writing makes me think how I'd feel if it was me." —Sean |
| Razia | No | Razia dreams about going to school like her brothers. | "I did not feel like the author had enough description about how Razia feels." —Jana |
| | Yes | Aziz first says that Razia can't go to school. Later, he changes his mind. | "When Razia was disappointed, I felt disappointed. When Razia was excited, I was excited." —Jorge |

## Assessment

After you have taught the minilessons in this umbrella, observe students as they talk and write about characters across instructional contexts: interactive read-aloud, independent reading and literacy work, guided reading, and book club. Use *The Literacy Continuum* (Fountas and Pinnell 2017) to observe students' reading and writing behaviors.

▶ What evidence do you have of new understandings related to characters' traits and development?

- Can students identify the ways authors reveal a character's traits?

- Do they talk about the ways that authors sometimes create complex characters?

- Do they notice why characters change?

- Do they understand that authors write in a particular way to cause a reader to feel empathy for a character?

- Do they use academic language, such as *character, behavior, dialogue, traits,* and *empathy*?

▶ In what other ways, beyond the scope of this umbrella, are students demonstrating an understanding of characters?

- Are students thinking about the author's craft?

- Are they writing about characters in a reader's notebook?

Use your observations to determine the next umbrella you will teach. You may also consult Minilessons Across the Year (pp. 59–61) for guidance.

## Link to Writing

After teaching the minilessons in this umbrella, help students link the new learning to their own writing:

▶ Encourage students to plan a fiction story by thinking about how they can develop a character's traits by writing about the character's behavior, using dialogue, and showing a character's thoughts.

## Reader's Notebook

When this umbrella is complete, provide a copy of the minilesson principles (see resources.fountasandpinnell.com) for students to glue in the reader's notebook (in the Minilessons section if using *Reader's Notebook: Intermediate* [Fountas and Pinnell 2011]), so they can refer to the information as needed.

## Minilessons in This Umbrella

**RML1**    Writers end stories in different ways.

**RML2**    Sometimes writers use symbolism to represent a big idea.

**RML3**    Writers choose the narrator and the perspective of the story.

**RML4**    Evaluate whether a narrator's voice is likable and believable.

## Before Teaching Umbrella 28 Minilessons

Read and discuss fiction picture books that exemplify the choices authors make when they write their books: stories that end in different ways, include symbolism, and have different narrators and perspectives. Support students by including books that relate to historical periods, events, and places. Though fiction, the books you choose might have characters, settings, and events that could exist in contemporary life or in another historical period.

    Choose books that engage students' intellectual curiosity and emotions. Use the following books from the *Fountas & Pinnell Classroom™ Interactive Read-Aloud Collection* text sets or choose fiction from your classroom library.

**Coping with Loss**

*Dad's Camera* by Ross Watkins

*Eight Days: A Story of Haiti* by Edwidge Danticat

**Author Study: Patricia McKissack**

*Goin' Someplace Special*

*The Honest-to-Goodness Truth*

*Stitchin' and Pullin': A Gee's Bend Quilt*

**Innovative Thinking and Creative Problem Solving**

*One Plastic Bag: Isatou Ceesay and the Recycling Women of the Gambia* by Miranda Paul

**Friendship**

*The Other Side* by Jacqueline Woodson

**What It Means to Be a Family**

*Jalapeño Bagels* by Natasha Wing

*Buffalo Bird Girl: A Hidatsa Story* by S. D. Nelson

**Perseverance**

*Rescue & Jessica: A Life-Changing Friendship* by Jessica Kensky and Patrick Downes

As you read aloud and enjoy these texts together, help students

- notice how writers craft endings,
- think about how writers use symbolism,
- think about the narrator and the perspective of the story, and
- evaluate the authenticity and appeal of the narrator's voice.

**Coping with Loss**

**Patricia McKissack**

**Innovative Thinking and Creative Problem Solving**

**Friendship**

**What It Means to Be a Family**

**Perseverance**

*Section 2: Literary Analysis*

# RML1
## LA.U28.RML1

## Writers end stories in different ways.

### Analyzing the Writer's Craft in Fiction Books

#### You Will Need

- three or four familiar fiction books with different types of endings, such as the following:
  - *Dad's Camera* by Ross Watkins, from Text Set: Coping with Loss
  - *Goin' Someplace Special* and *The Honest-to-Goodness Truth* by Patricia C. McKissack, from Text Set: Author Study: Patricia McKissack
  - *One Plastic Bag* by Miranda Paul, from Text Set: Innovative Thinking and Creative Problem Solving
- chart paper and markers
- a basket of familiar fiction texts

#### Academic Language / Important Vocabulary

- unexpected

#### Continuum Connection

- Analyze texts to determine aspects of a writer's style: e.g., use of language, choice of setting, plot, characters, themes and ideas (p. 60)

### Goal

Notice the different ways writers craft endings to their stories.

### Rationale

Writers craft story endings to give readers satisfaction and a lasting impression (e.g., surprise, hope, a lesson). Teaching this aspect of writer's craft helps students better understand texts. It also helps them think of possibilities for their own stories. Before teaching this lesson, familiarize students with Umbrella 8: Thinking About the Author's Purpose and Message.

### Assess Learning

Observe students when they talk about the writer's craft. Notice if there is evidence of new learning based on the goal of this minilesson.

- Can students describe how the writer ends a story?
- Can they discuss why a writer might have ended a story in a particular way?
- Do they understand and use the term *unexpected*?

## Minilesson

To help students think about the minilesson principle, use familiar fiction texts to help them notice a variety of endings. Here is an example.

- Show *Dad's Camera* and read the last two pages.

  How would you describe this ending?

  What would you call this kind of ending?

  You can also describe a surprise ending as an unexpected ending.

- Record responses on a chart. Show *Goin' Someplace Special* and read the last two pages.

  What does the ending of this book make you think about?

  Why do you think the writer chose to end the book this way?

  This ending teaches you a message, or a big idea: that everyone should be made to feel welcome.

- Record responses on the chart. If time allows, repeat this process with *The Honest-to-Goodness Truth*, reading the last two lines on the second to last page and then the last page.

  Writers decide how to end their stories based on how they want you, the reader, to feel at the end of the story.

## Have a Try

Invite the students to talk with a partner about the ending of a story.

▌ Show *One Plastic Bag* and read the last two pages.

What are you thinking about the ending of this book? What might you call this type of ending? Turn and talk to your partner about that.

▌ Ask a couple of students to share. Record responses.

## Summarize and Apply

Summarize the learning and remind students to think about how a writer chooses to end a story.

Take a look at the chart. What might you say about endings of fiction books?

▌ Write the principle at the top of the chart.

When you read today, choose a book you have read before from this basket. Think about how the author decided to end the book. Why do you think the author chose to end it that way? Bring your book when we meet so you can share.

## Share

Following independent reading time, gather students together in the meeting area to talk about their reading with a partner.

What did you notice about the ending of your book? Why did the author choose to end it that way?

▌ Have a few students share with the class. Add rows to the chart.

## Extend the Lesson (Optional)

After assessing students' understanding, you might decide to extend the learning.

▌ As you read books aloud, discuss how the writer crafted the ending. Ask students their opinions of whether the ending was satisfying and why.

▌ **Writing About Reading** Have students write in a reader's notebook about the ending of a book they liked. They should explain what it is about the ending that caused them to like it.

| Writers end stories in different ways. | |
|---|---|
| **Book** | **The ending** |
| DAD'S CAMERA | Unexpected |
| Goin' Someplace Special | Teaches a lesson or has a message |
| the HONEST-to-GOODNESS TRUTH | Teaches a lesson or has a message |
| ONE PLASTIC BAG | Hopeful |

**Reading Minilesson Principle**
# Sometimes writers use symbolism to represent a big idea.

## You Will Need

- several familiar fiction texts with clear examples of symbolism, such as the following:

  - *The Other Side* by Jacqueline Woodson, from Text Set: Friendship

  - *Stitchin' and Pullin'* by Patricia C. McKissack, from Text Set: Author Study: Patricia McKissack

  - *One Plastic Bag* by Miranda Paul, from Text Set: Innovative Thinking and Creative Problem Solving

- chart paper and makers

## Academic Language / Important Vocabulary

- symbolism

### Continuum Connection

- Notice and understand how the author uses idioms and literary language, including metaphor, simile, symbolism, and personification (p. 60)

## Goal

Notice and understand how a writer uses symbolism.

## Rationale

When you teach students that writers use symbolism to represent ideas and feelings, you support their noticing symbolism while reading, and in understanding in a deeper way.

## Assess Learning

Observe students when they read and discuss fiction. Notice if there is evidence of new learning based on the goal of this minilesson.

- ▶ Are students able to identify and discuss objects or ideas in stories that are symbolic?
- ▶ Can they discuss how symbolism is important to understanding a story?
- ▶ Do they understand and use the term *symbolism*?

# Minilesson

To help students think about the minilesson principle, lead them in an inquiry-based lesson emphasizing the writer's use of symbolism. Here is an example.

▶ Show *The Other Side*.

> What object is important in this book?

> What makes you think that?

> Sometimes, authors use an object to represent a big idea. In this book, the author uses an actual fence to stand for the idea of separation. Even the title refers to a fence—the other side of a fence.

> Listen as I read the last page. What do you think the author means?

▶ Record responses on a chart.

▶ Repeat this process with *Stitchin' and Pullin'*, reading aloud the last page of the book.

> What do you think about the choice of a quilt as a symbol? Is there something else the author could have used as a symbol?

## Have a Try

Invite the students to talk with a partner about the symbolism in *One Plastic Bag*.

▶ Show *One Plastic Bag*. Read the page that begins "She chooses a purse" and the last two pages of the book.

> Turn and talk to your partner. What symbol is important in this book? What does it mean?

▶ Have a few students share. Record responses on the chart.

## Summarize and Apply

Summarize the learning and remind students to think about symbolism when they read.

> Take a look at the chart. What do you notice about all of these fiction books?

> When a writer uses an object to represent something else, like segregation, memories, or hope, it is called symbolism.

▶ Write the principle at the top of the chart.

> Today when you read, notice if there is an object in the book that is an important symbol and think about why it is important. Bring the book with you when we meet so you can share your thinking.

## Share

Following independent reading time, gather students together as a group.

> Did anyone read a book today in which the writer used symbolism? Tell us about that.

## Extend the Lesson (Optional)

After assessing students' understanding, you might decide to extend the learning.

▶ Continue to add to the chart as students find other examples of symbolism.

▶ Invite students to choose a book from a basket of books, poems, or short stories with examples of symbolism. Ask them to share examples of symbolism with partners or the whole class.

▶ **Writing About Reading** Have students write in a reader's notebook about an example of symbolism from their reading. Be sure they include the object from the book, what it represents, and how it helped them understand the book better.

**Sometimes writers use symbolism to represent a big idea.**

| Book | Symbol | What the Symbol Stands For |
|---|---|---|
| *The Other Side* | [fence] | • Segregation |
| *Stitchin' and Pullin'* | [quilt] | • A person's life and memories |
| *One Plastic Bag* | [purse] | • Hope for the future |

Section 2: Literary Analysis

**Reading Minilesson Principle**

# Writers choose the narrator and the perspective of the story.

### You Will Need

- several familiar fiction texts with examples of different kinds of narration, such as the following:
  - *Jalapeño Bagels* by Natasha Wing, from Text Set: What It Means to Be a Family
  - *Dad's Camera* by Ross Watkins, from Text Set: Coping with Loss
  - *Rescue & Jessica* by Jessica Kensky and Patrick Downes, from Text Set: Perseverance
- chart paper and markers

### Academic Language / Important Vocabulary

- narrator
- perspective
- first-person narration
- third-person narration

### Continuum Connection

- Notice the narrator of a text and notice a change in narrator and perspective (p. 60)

## Goal

Notice the narrator and the perspective of a story.

## Rationale

Authors usually tell their stories in first-person narration or third-person narration. Once students identify the narrator, they know from whose perspective the story is told. They understand that what they learn about the events in the story is influenced by what the characters think and how they feel.

## Assess Learning

Observe students when they read and talk about fiction texts. Notice if there is evidence of new learning based on the goal of this minilesson.

- ❿ Are students able to identify the narrator of a story?
- ❿ Can they describe the character's perspective?
- ❿ Do they understand the academic language *narrator*, *perspective*, *first-person narration*, and *third-person narration*?

## Minilesson

Use fiction texts with a clearly identifiable narrator to help students identify the writer's choice of narrator and perspective. Here is an example.

- ❿ Show *Jalapeño Bagels*.

  Listen as I read a few pages.

  Who is the narrator? Who is telling the story?

  How do you know?

- ❿ Record responses on the chart.

  Pablo tells the story, so he is the narrator. You can tell because he uses the words *I, we,* and *me*. This is called first-person narration. We, the readers, see the story unfold as Pablo sees it and we know only what the narrator knows. The story is told from Pablo's perspective.

- ❿ Have a volunteer underline the words that show the narration is first person.

- ❿ Repeat this process with *Dad's Camera*, asking students to identify who the narrator is (the boy) and how they know (words such as *I* and *me*).

## Have a Try

Invite the students to talk with a partner about the narrator of a story.

▶ Read four pages from *Rescue & Jessica*, starting on the page that begins with "Back in the country."

> Talk to your partner. Who is narrating the story? From whose perspective is the story told?

▶ Record responses.

> When an author uses the words *he, she,* and *they,* this is called third-person narration. The narrator (point of view) in this story stayed the same, but the perspective changed: sometimes Rescue's perspective, sometimes Jessica's perspective, and sometimes both Jessica's and Rescue's perspective.

## Summarize and Apply

Summarize the learning and remind students to think about narrator and perspective in a story.

> Take a look at the chart. What do you notice?

▶ Write the principle on the chart.

> If you read fiction today, think about who the writer chose to be the narrator, and from whose perspective, or through whose eyes, the story is told. Bring your book when we come back together so you can share.

## Share

Following independent reading time, gather students together to share with a partner.

> Did anyone read fiction today? What choices did the author make about the narrator and perspective?

## Extend the Lesson (Optional)

After assessing students' understanding, you might decide to extend the learning.

▶ Talk about how *Dad's Camera* would be different if the author had chosen Dad to be the narrator. It would still be first person, but the perspective would be very different.

▶ **Writing About Reading** Have students write about the narrator and perspective in a reader's notebook, or provide them with a graphic organizer similar to the chart in this lesson to fill in and glue into a reader's notebook (visit resources.fountasandpinnell.com).

| Writers choose the narrator and the perspective of the story. | | | |
|---|---|---|---|
| Book | Narrator | How do you know? | Whose perspective? |
| | • Pablo<br>• First-person narration | • We walk<br>• I help my mother | • Pablo's |
| DAD'S CAMERA | • The boy<br>• First-person narration | • Mom explained to me<br>• I remembered | • The boy's |
| Rescue & Jessica | • Unnamed character<br>• Third-person narration | • Jessica was learning<br>• She was<br>• Rescue was learning<br>• He wore | • Sometimes Jessica's<br>• Sometimes Rescue's |

Section 2: Literary Analysis

# RML4
## LA.U28.RML4

**Reading Minilesson Principle**
# Evaluate whether a narrator's voice is likable and believable.

## Analyzing the Writer's Craft in Fiction Books

### You Will Need

- several familiar fiction texts with an obvious narrator, such as the following:
  - *Eight Days* by Edwidge Danticat, from Text Set: Coping with Loss
  - *The Honest-to-Goodness Truth* by Patricia C. McKissack, from Text Set: Author Study: Patricia McKissack
  - *Buffalo Bird Girl: A Hidatsa Story* by S. D. Nelson, from Text Set: What It Means to Be a Family
- chart paper and markers

### Academic Language / Important Vocabulary

- narrator
- voice
- evaluate

### Continuum Connection

- Think critically about the authenticity and appeal of a narrator's voice (p. 60)

## Goal

Think critically about the authenticity and appeal of the narrator's voice.

## Rationale

When we teach students to evaluate whether a narrator's voice is likable and believable, we support students in thinking critically about the author's decisions.

## Assess Learning

Observe students when they read and discuss fiction. Notice if there is evidence of new learning based on the goal of this minilesson.

- Are students able to evaluate the narrator's voice as likable and believable?
- Do they understand the words *narrator, voice,* and *evaluate*?

## Minilesson

To help students think about the minilessons principle, use familiar books to help them evaluate the narrator's voice. Here is an example.

- Show *Eight Days* and read aloud the first and last pages.

  Who is telling this story?

  What do you think about the boy's voice as he narrates the story? Is his voice believable? Why do you think that?

- Record responses on a chart.
- Repeat this process with *The Honest-to-Goodness Truth*, reading aloud the page beginning "All the children" and the page beginning "Don't say those."

## Have a Try

Invite the students to talk with a partner about narrator's voice.

▶ Read a few pages from *Buffalo Bird Girl*.

Turn and talk to your partner. Who is the narrator? Is her voice believable and likable?

▶ Have a few students share. Record responses.

## Summarize and Apply

Summarize the learning and remind students to evaluate a narrator's voice.

Take a look at the chart we created. What are you thinking about a narrator's voice?

▶ Write the principle at the top of the chart.

When you decide if a narrator's voice is likable and believable you are evaluating the narrator's voice. Today as you read, evaluate the writer's choice for the narrator's voice. Is the voice likable and believable? Be prepared to share when we come back together.

## Share

Following independent reading time, gather students together in the meeting area to talk about their reading with a partner.

If you read a fiction book today, talk to your partner about the writer's choice of a narrator. Was the narrator's voice likable and believable? Why?

## Extend the Lesson (Optional)

After assessing students' understanding, you might decide to extend the learning.

▶ Add to the chart as you read other interactive read-aloud books or as students read independently.

▶ **Writing About Reading** Encourage students to write in a reader's notebook their thoughts about narrator's voice.

### Evaluate whether a narrator's voice is likable and believable.

| Book | Who is the narrator? | Is the narrator's voice likable and believable? | Why? |
|---|---|---|---|
| *Eight Days: A Story of Haiti* | The boy | Yes | • Feels like the boy is talking to me.<br>• Feels like I am in the story with the boy. |
| *The Honest-to-Goodness Truth* | An unnamed character | Yes | • You can understand the feelings and actions of the different characters.<br>• You want the characters to be happy. |
| *Buffalo Bird Girl* | Buffalo Bird Woman | Yes | • You feel like she is teaching you about her real life a long time ago. |

## Assessment

After you have taught the minilessons in this umbrella, observe students as they talk and write about their reading across instructional contexts: interactive read-aloud, independent reading, guided reading, shared reading, and book club. Use *The Literacy Continuum* (Fountas and Pinnell 2017) to guide the observation of students' reading and writing behaviors.

▶ What evidence do you have of new understandings related to analyzing writer's craft in fiction books?

- Can students describe how the writer crafts the ending of a story?
- Are they noticing and discussing how the writer uses symbolism?
- Are they able to discuss the narrator and the perspective of a story?
- Can they think critically about the authenticity and appeal of the narrator's voice?
- Are they using language such as *unexpected*, *symbolism*, *perspective*, *narrator*, *evaluate*, and *voice*?

▶ In what other ways, beyond the scope of this umbrella, are students talking about writer's craft?

- Do students discuss the writer's purpose for writing a fiction text?
- Can they make connections between different fiction texts written by the same author?

Use your observations to determine the next umbrella you will teach. You may also consult Minilessons Across the Year (pp. 59–61) for guidance.

## Link to Writing

After teaching the minilessons in this umbrella, help students link the new learning to their own writing:

▶ Encourage students to think about who the narrator should be when they write a story and why they would choose first-person narration or third-person narration.

▶ Have students rewrite a short portion of a first-person text with third-person narration (or vice versa). Then talk about how that changes the story.

## Reader's Notebook

When this umbrella is complete, provide a copy of the minilesson principles (see resources.fountasandpinnell.com) for students to glue in the reader's notebook (in the Minilessons section if using *Reader's Notebook: Intermediate* [Fountas and Pinnell 2011]), so they can refer to the information as needed.

**Strategies and Skills**

The Strategies and Skills minilessons are designed to bring a few important strategic actions to temporary, conscious attention so that students can apply them in their independent reading. By the time students participate in these minilessons, they should have engaged these strategic actions successfully in guided reading lessons as they continue to strengthen in-the-head literacy processing systems. These lessons reinforce effective and efficient reading behaviors.

# 3 Strategies and Skills

## Minilessons in This Umbrella

**RML1**   Break a multisyllable word between consonants but keep consonant digraphs together.

**RML2**   Break a multisyllable word after the vowel if the syllable has a long vowel sound and after the consonant if the syllable has a short vowel sound.

**RML3**   Break a multisyllable word between vowels.

**RML4**   Break a multisyllable word before the consonant and *le*.

**RML5**   Remove the prefix or suffix to take apart a word.

**RML6**   Look for a part of the word that can help.

## Before Teaching Umbrella 1 Minilessons

Most of the word work you do with your students will take place during small-group guided reading or a separate word study lesson. However, there are minilessons that may serve as reminders and be helpful to the whole class. They can be taught any time you see a need among your students. Before teaching these minilessons, make sure students know terms such as *syllable*, *multisyllable*, *word part*, *consonant*, and *vowel*. Students must also be able to recognize consonant digraphs, prefixes, and suffixes. Use the examples that are provided in these minilessons or choose multisyllable words from texts your students are reading. Use two- and three-syllable words and unknown words as examples of each principle.

Section 3: Strategies and Skills

## Reading Minilesson Principle
# Break a multisyllable word between consonants but keep consonant digraphs together.

### Solving Multisyllable Words

**You Will Need**

▸ word cards: *tunnel, compute, brother, sentence, fashion, kingdom, practice, frantic, blossom, gather, entire, feather, thirty, distant, graphic*

▸ chart paper prepared with a strip of colored paper for the principle attached to the top

▸ markers

**Academic Language / Important Vocabulary**

▸ consonant

▸ consonant digraph

▸ syllable

**Continuum Connection**

▸ Recognize and use syllables in words with the VCCV pattern (syllable juncture); e.g., *ber/ry, both/er, dis/may, hel/met* (p. 380)

### Goal

Learn to take apart multisyllable words between consonants, keeping consonant diagraphs together.

### Rationale

Students need to know how to break multisyllable words apart to read new words more efficiently, to write words accurately, and to know where to break words at the end of a line when they are writing by hand. Two-syllable words with medial consonants are broken between the consonants, while words with digraphs are broken after the digraph.

### Assess Learning

Observe students when they solve unknown words. Notice if there is evidence of new learning based on the goal of this minilesson.

▸ Do students know to break apart unknown words into syllables to read them?

▸ Do they understand the terms *consonant, consonant digraph,* and *syllable*?

## Minilesson

To help students practice solving unknown words by breaking them apart, use examples of words that have medial consonants and medial consonant digraphs. Here is an example.

▸ Show the word card for *tunnel*. Have students tap the syllables in the word and tell where to break it. Write the word on the left side of the chart and draw a slash between the two syllables (*tun/nel*).

▸ Repeat with the word *compute*.

   **What do you notice about where each word is broken?**

   **Break the word between the two consonants in the middle.**

▸ Show the word card for *brother*. Have students tap the word to note the number of syllables. Start a column on the right side of the chart. Write the word and draw a slash between the two syllables (*broth/er*).

▸ Continue showing the word cards, having students tap the syllables in each word, and writing the words in the correct column on the chart: *sentence, fashion, kingdom, practice, frantic, blossom, gather,* and *entire*.

   **What do you notice about the words in the left-hand column? Where are they broken?**

   **What do you notice about the words in the right-hand column? What do you notice about how to break them?**

## Have a Try

Invite the students to break apart words with medial consonants and consonant digraphs.

- Show the word card for *thirty*.

    Turn and talk to your partner about where you would break this word.

- Write (or have volunteers write) the word on the chart and draw a slash between the syllables. Repeat with *feather*, *distant* and *graphic*.

## Summarize and Apply

Summarize the learning and remind students to break words apart between two consonants but keep consonant digraphs together.

    Look at the chart. What do you notice about where to break apart words when they have consonants in the middle?

- Write the principle on the colored strip at the top of the chart.

    If you come to a new word when you read today, break it apart to read it. Be prepared to share what you did when we come back together.

## Share

Following independent reading time, gather students together in the meeting area to talk about how they solved unknown words.

    Did anyone come to a new word while reading? What did you do?

## Extend the Lesson (Optional)

After assessing students' understanding, you might decide to extend the learning.

- Challenge students to break apart words that have a consonant and a consonant digraph in the middle, e.g., *dolphin*, *quickly*, and *neighbor*.

- During shared writing, model how to write multisyllable words by saying them and listening for the parts.

**Break a multisyllable word between consonants but keep consonant digraphs together.**

| | |
|---|---|
| tun/nel | broth/er |
| com/pute | fash/ion |
| sen/tence | king/dom |
| prac/tice | gath/er |
| fran/tic | feath/er |
| blos/som | graph/ic |
| en/tire | |
| thir/ty | |
| dis/tant | |

Section 3: Strategies and Skills

# RML 2
## SAS.U1.RML2

**Reading Minilesson Principle**

## Break a multisyllable word after the vowel if the syllable has a long vowel sound and after the consonant if the syllable has a short vowel sound.

### Solving Multisyllable Words

### You Will Need

- word cards: *frozen, music, shadow, student, river, beside, travel, visit, local, famous, vanish, demand, novel, silence, honest, station*
- chart paper prepared with a strip of colored paper attached to the top
- markers

### Academic Language / Important Vocabulary

- long vowel sound
- short vowel sound
- multisyllable
- syllable

### Continuum Connection

- Recognize and use open syllables—syllables that end with a single vowel, which usually represents a long vowel sound: e.g., *o/pen, pi/lot, ti/ger* (p. 380)
- Recognize and use closed syllables—syllables that end with a consonant and usually have a short vowel sound: e.g., *can/dle, fif/teen, mod/ern* (p. 380)

## Goal

Learn to take apart words with long vowel sounds and words with short vowel sounds.

## Rationale

Students learn to take words apart and write multisyllable words accurately by listening for syllable breaks. Two-syllable words are generally broken after the vowel if the first syllable has a long vowel sound (open syllable) and after the consonant if the first syllable has a short vowel sound (closed syllable).

## Assess Learning

Observe students when they solve unknown words. Notice if there is evidence of new learning based on the goal of this minilesson.

- Do students listen for the vowel sound in the first syllable so they know where to break a word apart?
- Do they use the language *long vowel sound, short vowel sound, multisyllable,* and *syllable*?

## Minilesson

To help students practice solving unknown words by breaking them apart, engage them in breaking apart multisyllable words that you think will be meaningful to them. Here is an example.

- Show the word card for *frozen*. Have students tap the syllables in the word and tell where to break it. Write the word on the left side of the chart and draw a slash between the two syllables (*fro/zen*).
- Repeat with the word *music* (*mu/sic*).

  What do you notice about where each word is broken? What vowel sound do you hear?

  Break the word after the vowel.

- Show the word card for *shadow*. Have students tap the syllables in the word and tell where to break it. Start a new column on the right. Write the word and draw a slash between the two syllables (*shad/ow*).

- Continue showing the word cards, having students tap the syllables, and telling where to break it. Write the words in the correct column on the chart: *student, river, beside, travel, visit, local, famous, vanish, demand, novel, silence.*

  What do you notice about the words in the left-hand column? Where are the words broken?

  What do you notice about the words in the right-hand column? How are they different from the words on the left?

## Have a Try

Invite the students to break apart the words *honest* and *station* with a partner.

▶ Show the word card for *honest*.

> Where would you break this word?

▶ Write the word on the chart and draw a slash between the syllables. Repeat the process with *station*.

## Summarize and Apply

Summarize the learning and remind students to break a word after the vowel if the syllable has a long vowel sound and after the consonant if the syllable has a short vowel sound.

> Look at the chart. What do you notice about where the words are broken?

▶ Guide students to notice that when the first syllable has a long vowel sound, the syllable ends with the vowel. When the first syllable has a short vowel sound, the syllable ends with the consonant. Write the principle at the top of the chart.

> When you read today, if you get to a new word, you may need to break the word in a couple of different places and try each vowel sound to find out which is correct. Be prepared to share what you did when we come back together.

Break a multisyllable word after the vowel if the syllable has a long vowel sound and after the consonant if the syllable has a short vowel sound.

| | |
|---|---|
| fro/zen | shad/ow |
| mu/sic | riv/er |
| stu/dent | trav/el |
| be/side | vis/it |
| lo/cal | van/ish |
| fa/mous | nov/el |
| de/mand | hon/est |
| si/lence | |
| sta/tion | |

## Share

Following independent reading time, gather students together in the meeting area to talk about how they solved unknown words.

> Did anyone come to a word you didn't know? What did you do?

## Extend the Lesson (Optional)

After assessing students' understanding, you might decide to extend the learning.

▶ During shared writing, model how to write multisyllable words by saying them, listening for the parts, and writing one part at a time.

Section 3: Strategies and Skills

**Reading Minilesson Principle**
# Break a multisyllable word between vowels.

### You Will Need

- word cards: *science, ruin, create, diet, giant, duet, react, radio, diagram, experience*
- chart paper and markers

### Academic Language / Important Vocabulary

- vowel
- syllable

### Continuum Connection

- Recognize and use syllables in words with the VV pattern: e.g., *gi/ant, ru/in* (p. 380)

### Goal

Learn to take apart a word between vowels.

### Rationale

When you remind students that they may need to try more than once to find where to break apart a word and read it correctly, they are prepared to recognize that in some words vowels are broken to form syllables.

### Assess Learning

Observe students when they solve unknown words. Notice if there is evidence of new learning based on the goal of this minilesson.

- ⟩ Do students break unknown words into parts?
- ⟩ Do they break multisyllable words into parts between two vowel sounds if the first syllable is an open syllable (long vowel sound)?
- ⟩ Are they using the terms *vowel* and *syllable*?

## Minilesson

To help students think about the minilesson principle, engage them in a demonstration of breaking apart words between vowels. Here is an example.

- ⟩ Show the word card for *science*. Have students tap the syllables in the word and tell where to break it. Write the word on the chart and draw a slash between the syllables (*sci/ence*).
- ⟩ Repeat with the word *ruin*.

  What do you notice about where each word is broken?

- ⟩ Prompt the students to say that you broke the word apart between the two vowels and that the sound of each vowel could be heard.
- ⟩ Repeat this process with the words *create, diet, giant, duet, react, radio*, and *diagram*.

  When you get to a word you don't know, break it between the two vowels and say the short or long vowel sound of each. If that doesn't work, the two vowels make one sound together and make a one-syllable word (for example, *rain, boat, house*).

## Have a Try

Invite the students to break apart the word *experience* with a partner.

> Turn and talk to your partner. Where do you break the word *experience*?

❭ Ask a student to write the syllable breaks on the chart.

## Summarize and Apply

Summarize the learning and remind students to break new multisyllable words apart between vowels.

> Look at the chart. What do you notice about where the words are broken?

❭ Write the principle at the top of the chart.

> When you read today, if you come to a new multisyllable word, you may need to break the word between the vowels. Be ready to share when we come back together.

## Share

Following independent reading time, gather students together in the meeting area to talk about word solving.

> Did anyone come to a word you didn't know? What did you do?

## Extend the Lesson (Optional)

After assessing students' understanding, you might decide to extend the learning.

❭ During shared writing, model how to write multisyllable words by saying them slowly, listening for the parts, and writing one part at a time.

---

**Break a multisyllable word between vowels.**

| | |
|---|---|
| sci/ence | du/et |
| ru/in | re/act |
| cre/ate | ra/di/o |
| di/et | di/a/gram |
| gi/ant | ex/per/i/ence |

**Section 3: Strategies and Skills**

**Reading Minilesson Principle**
## Break a multisyllable word before the consonant and *le*.

### Solving Multisyllable Words

### You Will Need

- word cards: *table, middle, cattle, miracle, scribble, idle, article, scramble, example, vehicle*
- chart paper and markers

### Academic Language / Important Vocabulary

- consonant
- syllable

### Continuum Connection

- Recognize and use consonant + *le* syllables—syllables that contain a consonant followed by the letters *le*: e.g., *a/ble, ea/gle, scram/ble, tem/ple* (p. 380)

### Goal

Learn to take apart words before the consonant and *le*.

### Rationale

Students learn to take words apart and write multisyllable words accurately by listening for the syllable breaks. Students learn that in most words that end with *le*, the syllable is broken before the consonant and *le*.

### Assess Learning

Observe students when they take apart unknown words ending with a consonant and *le*. Notice if there is evidence of new learning based on the goal of this minilesson.

- Do students break unknown words into parts when word solving?
- Do they know to break multisyllable words before the consonant and *le*?
- Are they using the terms *consonant* and *syllable*?

## Minilesson

To help students think about the minilesson principle, engage them in a demonstration of breaking apart words ending with a consonant and *le*. Here is an example.

- Show the word card for *table*. Have students tap the syllables in the word and tell where to break it. Write the word on the chart and draw a slash between the syllables (*ta/ble*).
- Repeat the process with *middle*.

  What do you notice about where each word is broken?

  Break the word before the consonant and *le*.

- Repeat this process with the words *cattle, miracle, scribble, idle, article, scramble*, and *example*.

  When you get to a word you don't know, break it before the consonant and *le* to help you read the word.

## Have a Try

Invite the students to break apart the word *vehicle* with a partner.

> Turn and talk to your partner. Where should you break the word *vehicle*?

▶ Ask a student to show the syllable breaks on the chart.

## Summarize and Apply

Summarize the learning and remind students to break new words apart before the consonant and *le*.

> Look at the chart. What do you notice about where the words are broken?

▶ Review the chart and write the principle at the top.

> When you read today, if you come to a new word, break it apart to help you read it. Be ready to share when we come back together.

## Share

Following independent reading time, gather students together in the meeting area to talk about word solving.

> Did anyone come to a word you didn't know? What did you do?

## Extend the Lesson (Optional)

After assessing students' understanding, you might decide to extend the learning.

▶ During shared writing, model how to write multisyllable words by saying them slowly, listening for the parts, and writing one part at a time.

---

**Break a multisyllable word before the consonant and le.**

| | |
|---|---|
| ta/ble | i/dle |
| mid/dle | ar/ti/cle |
| cat/tle | scram/ble |
| mir/a/cle | ex/am/ple |
| scrib/ble | ve/hi/cle |

Section 3: Strategies and Skills

# RML5

**SAS.U1.RML5**

**Reading Minilesson Principle**
# Remove the prefix or suffix to take apart a word.

## Solving Multisyllable Words

### You Will Need

- chart paper prepared with the first column filled in: *misbehave, placement, misplace, agreeable, childish, tasteful, comfortable, nonfiction*
- sticky notes or index card (optional)
- markers

### Academic Language / Important Vocabulary

- prefix
- suffix
- base word

### Continuum Connection

- Recognize and use word parts to solve an unknown word and understand its meaning: e.g., conference—prefix *con-* ("with" or "together"), Latin root *fer* ("to bring" or "to carry"), suffix *-ence* ("state of" or "quality of") (p. 382)

## Goal

Learn to take off the prefix or suffix to solve words.

## Rationale

When you teach students to take multisyllable words apart by removing the prefix or suffix and reading the base word, they can solve words more efficiently and keep their attention on meaning.

## Assess Learning

Observe students when they take apart unknown words with a prefix or suffix. Notice if there is evidence of new learning based on the goal of this minilesson.

- Do students break apart words between the base word and the prefix or suffix?
- Are they using the terms *prefix, suffix,* and *base word*?

# Minilesson

To help students think about the minilesson principle, engage them in a demonstration of removing a prefix or suffix to identify the base word. Here is an example.

- Display the prepared chart and read the first word. Use a sticky note or an index card to cover the prefix (*mis-*). Take apart the base word (*behave*) and then reveal the prefix. Reread the whole word to make sure it sounds right and looks right.

  > What did you notice that I did to read the word *misbehave*? Where did I break the word?

- Prompt the students to say that you removed the prefix, read the base word, and then added the prefix back onto the word and reread the whole word. You may want to point out that a prefix or suffix can have more than one syllable. Write on the chart how you broke apart the word.

- Repeat this process with the word *placement*.

  > You can remove the suffix so you can read the base word and then the whole word.

- Have students tell you where to break apart these words: *misplace, agreeable, childish,* and *tasteful*.

## Have a Try

Invite the students to break apart the words *comfortable* and *nonfiction* with a partner by removing the prefix or suffix.

> Turn and talk to your partner. How would you break these words apart? Remember to reread the whole word to make sure it looks right and sounds right.

▶ Ask a student to show the breaks.

## Summarize and Apply

Summarize the learning and remind students to solve new words by removing the prefix or suffix.

> Look at the chart. What do you notice about how the words were broken?

▶ Review the chart and write the principle at the top.

> When you read today, if you come to a new word, break it into parts to help you read it. Be ready to share when we come back together.

## Share

Following independent reading time, gather students together in the meeting area to talk about word solving.

> Did anyone come to a word you didn't know? What did you do?

## Extend the Lesson (Optional)

After assessing students' understanding, you might decide to extend the learning.

▶ During shared writing, model how to write multisyllable words by saying them slowly, listening for the parts, and writing one part at a time.

---

**Remove the prefix or suffix to take apart a word.**

| | |
|---|---|
| misbehave | mis / behave |
| placement | place / ment |
| misplace | mis/place |
| agreeable | agree/able |
| childish | child/ish |
| tasteful | taste/ful |
| comfortable | comfort / able |
| nonfiction | non / fiction |

# RML 6

## SAS.U1.RML6

### Reading Minilesson Principle
# Look for a part of the word that can help.

## Solving Multisyllable Words

### You Will Need

- From the books your students are reading, choose examples of multisyllable words that have parts that are familiar, or use the examples in this lesson. In advance of the lesson, write the words on chart paper.
- sticky notes
- index card (optional)
- markers
- highlighter

### Academic Language / Important Vocabulary

- word
- word part

### Continuum Connection

- Use known word parts (some are words) to solve unknown larger words: e.g., _in_/_into_, _can_/_canvas_, _us_/_crust_ (p. 382)

### Goal

Search for and use familiar parts of a word to help solve the word.

### Rationale

When you teach students to notice parts of a word they already know, you increase their efficiency in reading unknown words in continuous text, allowing them to improve fluency and focus on meaning.

### Assess Learning

Observe students when they take apart unknown words. Notice if there is evidence of new learning based on the goal of this minilesson.

- Do students use known word parts to solve words?
- Are they using the terms _word_ and _word part_?

## Minilesson

To help students think about the minilesson principle, engage them in a demonstration of using known word parts to read a new word. Here is an example.

- Display the prepared chart. Read the first word, _trapezoid_.

    I'm not sure what this word is, but I see part of the word that I know how to say.

- Use a sticky note or an index card to cover _ezoid_. Say the known part of the word (_trap_) and highlight it on the chart. Reveal the rest of the word, sound it out, and then say the whole word to make sure it looks right and sounds right.

    What did I do to read the word _trapezoid_?

    When you come to a word you don't know, look for a part or parts of the word you do know how to say.

- Repeat this process with the words _consistent_ and _particle_.

## Have a Try

Invite the students to break apart the words *diagram* and *canvas* with a partner by looking for a part they know.

> Turn and talk to your partner. What could these words be?

▶ Ask a student to highlight the parts of the words they know on the chart.

## Summarize and Apply

Summarize the learning and remind students to look for a part of the word that can help.

> Look at the chart. How can you read a word you don't know?

▶ Write the principle at the top.

> When you read today, if you come to a word you aren't sure of, look to see if there is a part that can help.

## Share

Following independent reading time, gather students together in the meeting area to talk about word solving.

> Did anyone come to a word you didn't know? Was there a part you did know that helped?

> How else can you figure out what a word is?

## Extend the Lesson (Optional)

After assessing students' understanding, you might decide to extend the learning.

▶ During guided and independent reading, remind students of the ways they can read new words.

| Look for a part of the word that can help. | |
|---|---|
| trapezoid | trap / ezoid |
| consistent | consis / tent |
| particle | part / icle |
| diagram | dia / gram |
| canvas | can / vas |

## Assessment

After you have taught the minilessons in this umbrella, observe students as they talk and write about their reading across instructional contexts: interactive read-aloud, independent reading, guided reading, shared reading, and book club. Use *The Literacy Continuum* (Fountas and Pinnell 2017) to guide the observation of students' reading and writing behaviors.

▸ What evidence do you have of new understandings related to solving multisyllable words?

- Are students flexible about applying ways to take apart words?
- Can they use known parts to solve words?
- Do they remove the prefix or suffix to find the base word to read an unfamiliar word?
- Are they using language such as *syllable*, *base word*, *prefix*, *suffix*, *consonant digraph*, and *vowel sound*?

▸ In what other ways, beyond the scope of this umbrella, are students talking about their reading?

- Do students need help navigating difficult texts?
- Do they read digital texts in a productive way?

Use your observations to determine the next umbrella you will teach. You may also consult Minilessons Across the Year (pp. 59–61) for guidance.

## Link to Writing

After teaching the minilessons in this umbrella, help students link the new learning to their own writing:

▸ When engaging in shared writing and independent writing, refer to resources you have in the room to make connections between known words and new words.

▸ When engaging in shared writing, demonstrate how slow articulation of unknown words while writing relates to reading unknown words.

## Reader's Notebook

When this umbrella is complete, provide a copy of the minilesson principles (see resources.fountasandpinnell.com) for students to glue in the reader's notebook (in the Minilessons section if using *Reader's Notebook: Intermediate* [Fountas and Pinnell 2011]), so they can refer to the information as needed.

## Minilessons in This Umbrella

**RML1**   A writer defines a word within the text to help you understand it.

**RML2**   A writer uses a word that is similar in meaning to help you understand a word you don't know.

**RML3**   A writer uses a word that is opposite or nearly opposite in meaning to help you understand a word you don't know.

**RML4**   A writer gives an example to help you understand what a word means.

**RML5**   Word parts help you understand what a word means.

**RML6**   Greek and Latin roots help you understand what a word means.

**Telling a Story with Photos**

*Face to Face with Whales* by Flip and Linda Nicklin

**Illustration Study: Craft**

## Before Teaching Umbrella 2 Minilessons

Although most of the teaching of problem solving while reading will happen during small-group instruction, there are some lessons that are worth presenting to the whole class. Once you teach these minilessons, you can follow them up in more detail when you meet with guided reading groups. For the minilessons in this umbrella, use books with strong examples of context-supported vocabulary. Look for language that defines unknown words within the sentence, the paragraph, or throughout the whole text; uses synonyms, antonyms, or examples to clarify meaning; and contains words with prefixes, suffixes, Greek roots, and Latin roots.

Use the following books from the *Fountas & Pinnell Classroom™ Interactive Read-Aloud Collection* text sets or choose other books that have strong contextual support for vocabulary.

**Telling a Story with Photos**

> *A Little Book of Sloth* by Lucy Cooke
>
> *Face to Face with Whales* by Flip and Linda Nicklin

**Illustration Study: Craft**

> *Eye to Eye: How Animals See the World* by Steve Jenkins
>
> *Gecko* by Raymond Huber

As you read aloud and enjoy these texts together, guide students to notice how the author helps the reader learn the meaning of new words through supportive context.

**Reading Minilesson Principle**

# A writer defines a word within the text to help you understand it.

## Using Context and Word Parts to Understand Vocabulary

### You Will Need

- two or three familiar texts that contain new or unfamiliar vocabulary, such as the following:
  - *Eye to Eye* by Steve Jenkins, from Text Set: Illustration Study: Craft
  - *A Little Book of Sloth* by Lucy Cooke, from Text Set: Telling a Story with Photos
- chart paper prepared with sentences from *A Little Book of Sloth* (p. 24) and *Eye to Eye* (pp. 20 and 10)
- markers and highlighters
- sticky notes

### Academic Language / Important Vocabulary

- define
- sentence
- paragraph

### Continuum Connection

- Derive the meaning of words from the context of a sentence, paragraph, or the whole story (p. 60)
- Derive the meaning of words from the context of a sentence, paragraph, or the whole text (p. 64)

## Goal

Understand that sometimes a writer tells the meaning of a word in the sentence, the paragraph, or elsewhere in the book.

## Rationale

When you teach students that the meaning of an unfamiliar word can sometimes be derived from the sentence or paragraph in which it appears or from the whole text, you give them a tool to solve problems independently.

## Assess Learning

Observe students when they use context to understand vocabulary. Notice if there is evidence of new learning based on the goal of this minilesson.

- Can students use context from the sentence, the paragraph, or elsewhere in the text to derive the meaning of an unfamiliar word?
- Are students using language such as *define, sentence,* and *paragraph?*

## Minilesson

To help students think about how to learn the meaning of new or unfamiliar words from the text, engage them in noticing how the writer gives information. Here is an example.

- Hold up *Eye to Eye*. Read the first sentence on the prepared chart paper. Underline the words *ultraviolet light*.

  How can you figure out what ultraviolet light is?

- Invite responses and then select a student to highlight clues to its meaning.

  Sometimes the author tells you the meaning of the term in the same sentence.

- Repeat this process with the next sentence, underlining the word *tapetum*.

  Notice that some information is in the same sentence as the word *tapetum*, and there is more information in the following sentence.

- Hold up *A Little Book of Sloth*. Read the sentences from the book on the chart. Underline the word *paraplegic*.

  How does the author help you understand what the word *paraplegic* means?

- Invite responses and then select a student to help highlight the clues to the meaning of the word.

  Sometimes an author tells you the meaning of a word not in the same sentence but in the same paragraph.

## Have a Try

Repeat the minilesson process, inviting the students to talk about using context to figure out the meaning of an unfamiliar word.

> If you picked up *A Little Book of Sloth* but didn't know what a sloth was, how could you figure it out? Turn and talk about that.

▶ After time for a brief discussion, ask a few students to share. Guide them to understand that the book itself provides clues in the photographs and in the text.

## Summarize and Apply

Summarize the learning and remind students to look for the meaning of a word in the sentence, the paragraph, or elsewhere in the text.

> What is one way you can learn the meaning of a new word?

▶ Write the principle at the top of the chart.

> If you come to a word you don't know or understand as you read today, use the information in the book to help you figure out what the word means. Mark the word with a sticky note, and bring the book when we come back together so you can share.

## Share

Following independent reading time, gather students together in the meeting area to discuss how they figured out the meaning of a new word.

> Did you come to an unfamiliar word meaning when you read today? What did you do?

## Extend the Lesson (Optional)

After assessing students' understanding, you might decide to extend the learning.

▶ During interactive read-aloud, model how to derive the meaning of a new word.

▶ During individual reading conferences, make sure students know that sometimes there are ways to figure out what a word means by using context.

---

> ### A writer defines a word within the text to help you understand it.
>
>
>
> "Its compound eyes are sensitive to <u>ultraviolet light</u>—high frequency light that is invisible to us."
>
> "At the back of the housecat's eye is a reflective layer called a <u>tapetum</u>. This layer bounces light back through the cat's retina, improving its eyesight in the dim light."
>
>
>
> "As a baby, Ubu lost his grip on his mother and fell. When he hit the ground he hurt his spine, and now his back legs don't work. But plenty of physical therapy has given this <u>paraplegic</u> baby sloth the upper body strength of a champion wrestler."

**Reading Minilesson Principle**

# A writer uses a word that is similar in meaning to help you understand a word you don't know.

## Using Context and Word Parts to Understand Vocabulary

### You Will Need

- two or three familiar texts that contain new or unfamiliar vocabulary, such as the following:
  - *Eye to Eye* by Steve Jenkins, from Text Set: Illustration Study: Craft
  - *Face to Face with Whales* by Flip and Linda Nicklin, from Text Set: Telling a Story with Photos
- chart paper prepared with sentences from *Eye to Eye* (p. 7) and *Face to Face with Whales* (pp. 11 and 20)
- markers and highlighters
- sticky notes

### Academic Language / Important Vocabulary

- similar
- synonym

### Continuum Connection

- Recognize and use synonyms (words that have almost the same meaning): e.g., *mistake/error, high/tall* (p. 379)
- Use connections between or among words that mean the same or almost the same to solve an unknown word: e.g., *damp, wet* (p. 382)

## Goal

Understand that writers sometimes use synonyms within a sentence to explain the meaning of a word.

## Rationale

When you teach students to search a sentence for clues to the meaning of an unfamiliar word—including for words that have the same or a similar meaning—it helps them learn new vocabulary independently.

## Assess Learning

Observe students when they use context to understand an unfamiliar word. Notice if there is evidence of new learning based on the goal of this minilesson.

- Can students use synonyms to help them understand the meaning of a word?
- Do they look for clues in the sentence to help them understand the meaning of an unfamiliar word?
- Do they understand the terms *similar* and *synonym*?

## Minilesson

To help students think about how to use synonyms to learn the meaning of new words, engage them in noticing how the writer gives information. Here is an example.

- Show page 7 from *Eye to Eye*.

  On this page, the writer shares information about how the pit viper sees.

- Read aloud the paragraph about the green pit viper. Point to the sentence on the prepared chart and underline the word *organs*.

  How does the writer help you understand what the word *organs* means?

- Invite responses and then select a student to help highlight the synonym.

  Sometimes an author uses a synonym—a word that means the same thing or something similar—to help explain what an unfamiliar word means. Can you highlight the synonym in the sentence that helps you knows what the word *organs* means?

- Ask a volunteer to highlight the synonym in the sentence that helps define *organs*.

- Repeat the process, underlining the word *migration* from page 11 of *Face to Face with Whales*.

  When you are reading, and you come to a word you don't understand, you look to see if the author put in one or more words that mean the same thing.

## Have a Try

Invite the students to use a synonym to figure out the meaning of a word with a partner.

▶ Read the sentence on the prepared chart from page 20 of *Face to Face with Whales*.

> Turn and talk to your partner. What does the word *fluke* mean? How do the authors help you understand the word?

▶ Invite a few students to share and highlight the synonym on the chart.

## Summarize and Apply

Summarize the learning and remind students to look for words that are similar in meaning to the word they don't know.

> What is one thing writers do to help you understand a word that might be unfamiliar? Look at the chart to help you remember.

▶ Write the principle at the top of the chart.

> If you come across a word you don't understand as you read today, look to see if the author put a word with a similar meaning—called a synonym—in the sentence to help you. Mark the word with a sticky note and bring the book with you when we come back together so you can share.

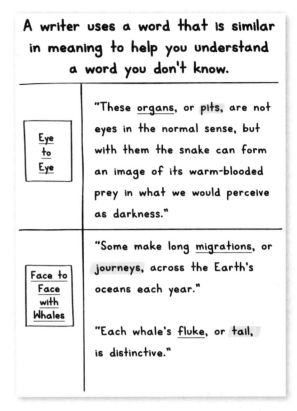

A writer uses a word that is similar in meaning to help you understand a word you don't know.

| | |
|---|---|
| Eye to Eye | "These organs, or pits, are not eyes in the normal sense, but with them the snake can form an image of its warm-blooded prey in what we would perceive as darkness." |
| Face to Face with Whales | "Some make long migrations, or journeys, across the Earth's oceans each year."<br><br>"Each whale's fluke, or tail, is distinctive." |

## Share

Following independent reading time, gather students together to talk about determining the meaning of new words.

> Did anyone come to a word you didn't know? What did you do?

## Extend the Lesson (Optional)

After assessing students' understanding, you might decide to extend the learning.

▶ During interactive read-aloud, model how to use a synonym to derive the meaning of a new word.

▶ During individual reading conferences, make sure students know that sometimes there are ways to figure out what a word means by using context.

**Reading Minilesson Principle**

# A writer uses a word that is opposite or nearly opposite in meaning to help you understand a word you don't know.

Using Context and Word Parts to Understand Vocabulary

## You Will Need

- two or three familiar texts that contain new or unfamiliar vocabulary, such as the following:
  - *A Little Book of Sloth* by Lucy Cooke and *Face to Face with Whales* by Flip and Linda Nicklin, from Text Set: Telling a Story with Photos
- chart paper prepared with sentences from *A Little Book of Sloth* [p. 21] and *Face to Face with Whales* [p. 23]
- markers and highlighters
- sticky notes

## Academic Language / Important Vocabulary

- contrast
- opposite
- antonym

### Continuum Connection

- Recognize and use antonyms [words that have opposite meanings]: e.g., *cold/hot*, *appear/vanish* [p. 379]
- Use connections between or among words that mean the opposite or almost the opposite to solve an unknown word: e.g., *stale, fresh* [p. 382]

## Goal

Understand that sometimes a writer uses a word that is opposite or nearly opposite in meaning to show the meaning of a word.

## Rationale

When you teach students to search sentences for information that will help them with the meaning of unfamiliar words—including for words that have the opposite meaning—it helps them develop a self-extending system for learning new vocabulary.

## Assess Learning

Observe students when they use context to understand an unfamiliar word. Notice if there is evidence of new learning based on the goal of this minilesson.

- ▶ Can students derive the meaning of new words through the use of antonyms?
- ▶ Do they understand the terms *contrast*, *opposite*, and *antonym*?

# Minilesson

To help students think about how antonyms can help them understand a new word, engage them in noticing how the writer gives information. Here is an example.

- ▶ Hold up page 21 of *A Little Book of Sloth*.

  On this page, the author gives information about how wild sloths and sanctuary sloths are a bit different from one another.

- ▶ Read the first sentence on the prepared chart paper. Underline the word *solitary* on the chart.

  Turn and talk with a partner about the underlined word. How does the author help you know what *solitary* means? What are some clues in the sentence?

- ▶ After time for discussion, invite responses. Select a student to highlight the clues to the meaning of the word.

  The author helps you know what *solitary* means by showing a contrast between how life for sloths in the sanctuary is different from life in the wild. The word *but* tells you that a contrast is coming. Someone who makes friends is not solitary.

## Have a Try

Invite the students to figure out the meaning of a word with a partner.

▸ Read the sentence on the prepared chart from page 23 of *Face to Face with Whales*.

> Turn and talk with your partner about the word *aggressive*. How do the authors help you understand the word? What are clues from the sentence that help you?

> *Aggressive* and *gentle* are antonyms. An antonym is a word that means the opposite, or nearly the opposite, of another word.

▸ Highlight the antonym on the chart.

## Summarize and Apply

Summarize the learning and remind students that sometimes writers use words that have the opposite or nearly opposite meaning to help you understand unfamiliar vocabulary.

> What did you learn about solving unfamiliar words today?

▸ Add the principle to the top of the chart.

> If you come across a word you don't understand as you read today, look to see if the author includes an antonym or a contrasting idea to help you. Mark the word with a sticky note and bring the book with you when we come back together so you can share.

## Share

Following independent reading time, gather students together to talk about determining the meaning of new words.

> Did anyone learn the meaning of an unfamiliar word today using an antonym?

## Extend the Lesson (Optional)

After assessing students' understanding, you might decide to extend the learning.

▸ Have students write one or more sentences to explain a word (e.g., a vocabulary word from math, science, or social studies) by using an antonym or a contrasting idea.

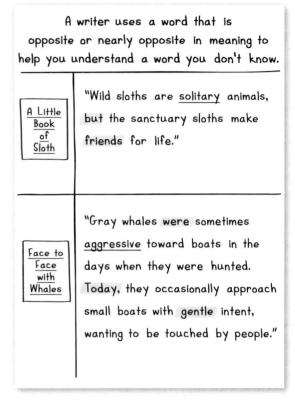

A writer uses a word that is opposite or nearly opposite in meaning to help you understand a word you don't know.

| A Little Book of Sloth | "Wild sloths are <u>solitary</u> animals, but the sanctuary sloths make friends for life." |
| Face to Face with Whales | "Gray whales were sometimes <u>aggressive</u> toward boats in the days when they were hunted. Today, they occasionally approach small boats with gentle intent, wanting to be touched by people." |

**Reading Minilesson Principle**

# A writer gives an example to help you understand what a word means.

## Using Context and Word Parts to Understand Vocabulary

### You Will Need

- two or three familiar texts that contain new or unfamiliar vocabulary, such as the following:
  - *Face to Face with Whales* by Flip and Linda Nicklin, from Text Set: Telling a Story with Photos
  - *Gecko* by Raymond Huber, from Text Set: Illustration Study: Craft
- chart paper prepared with sentences from *Face to Face with Whales* (p. 17) and *Gecko* (pp. 13 and 6)
- markers and highlighters
- sticky notes

### Academic Language / Important Vocabulary

- definition

### Continuum Connection

- Derive the meaning of words from the context of a sentence, paragraph, or the whole story (p. 60)
- Derive the meaning of words from the context of a sentence, paragraph, or the whole text (p. 64)

## Goal

Understand that sometimes writers use examples to show the meaning of a word.

## Rationale

When students learn multiple ways to solve unknown words, they are able to learn new vocabulary independently, read more fluently, and maintain comprehension of the text. Learning to look for examples in the text to help determine the meaning of an unfamiliar word is another tool students may use.

## Assess Learning

Observe students when they use context to understand an unfamiliar word. Notice if there is evidence of new learning based on the goal of this minilesson.

- ❯ Do students look for examples in the text to help them know the meaning of unfamiliar words?
- ❯ Do students understand the meaning of *definition*?

## Minilesson

To help students learn another way to use context to figure out an unfamiliar word, engage them in noticing how the writer gives information about a word. Here is an example.

- ❯ Hold up page 17 of *Face to Face with Whales*.

  On this page, the authors give us information about the different ways whales eat.

- ❯ Read the sidebar, which is also written on the prepared chart paper. Underline the word *baleen* on the chart.

  How do the authors help you understand what the word *baleen* means?

- ❯ Invite responses and then select a student to highlight the examples the authors use to illustrate the meaning of the word.

  Sometimes an author tells you the meaning of a word by giving an example. Can you highlight the examples in the sentence that help you to know the definition of the word *baleen*?

- ❯ Repeat the process with the word *camouflage* from *Gecko*.

## Have a Try

Invite the students to figure out the meaning of a word with a partner.

▶ Read the sentence about predators on the prepared chart.

> Turn and talk with your partner about the word *predator*. How does the author help you know what this word means?

▶ Invite a few students to share and highlight the examples on the chart.

## Summarize and Apply

Summarize the learning and remind students to look for examples when they encounter a word they don't know.

> How do some writers help you figure out the meaning of a new or unknown word?

▶ Invite responses and add the principle to the top of the chart.

> If you come to new vocabulary in your reading today, look to see if the author used examples to help you think about what the word might mean. Mark the word with a sticky note and bring the book with you when we come back together so you can share.

## Share

Following independent reading time, gather students together to talk with a partner about determining the meaning of unfamiliar words.

> Turn and talk about how you solved unknown words today. Did you find examples within the text to help you understand a new word?

## Extend the Lesson (Optional)

After assessing students' understanding, you might decide to extend the learning.

▶ Model how to derive the meaning of one or two unknown words during interactive read-aloud.

▶ When you meet with students for an individual conference, ask them to share how they figured out what an unfamiliar word meant.

---

**A writer gives an example to help you understand what a word means.**

| | |
|---|---|
| **Face to Face with Whales** | "Imagine taking a giant mouthful of cereal and milk. If you closed your teeth and squeezed the milk out, trapping the cereal inside, you would be eating like a baleen whale." |
| **Gecko** | "Gecko camouflage includes: dappled skin patterns and colours; turning lighter or darker; and skin folds that flatten out so that the body casts no shadow."<br><br>"They must take care when out in the open because they have many predators. Geckos are eaten by snakes, birds, cats, rats, scorpions, and large spiders." |

**Reading Minilesson Principle**
# Word parts help you understand what a word means.

Using Context and Word Parts to Understand Vocabulary

## You Will Need

- two or three familiar texts that contain words with prefixes and suffixes that are appropriate for your class, such as the following:
  - *Face to Face with Whales* by Flip and Linda Nicklin, from Text Set: Telling a Story with Photos
  - *Eye to Eye* by Steve Jenkins and *Gecko* by Raymond Huber, from Text Set: Illustration Study: Craft
- chart paper prepared with sentences from *Face to Face with Whales* (p. 6), *Eye to Eye* (p. 1), and *Gecko* (p. 13)
- markers and highlighters
- sticky notes

## Academic Language / Important Vocabulary

- prefix
- suffix
- base word

## Continuum Connection

- Understand and discuss the concept of prefixes and recognize their use in determining the meaning of some English words (p. 379)
- Understand and discuss the concept of suffixes and recognize their use in determining the meaning of some English words (p. 379)

## Goal

Understand that base words, suffixes, and prefixes can be used to figure out the meaning of a word.

## Rationale

When students know to look at the parts of a word (prefix, suffix, base word) to solve for meaning, they can problem solve more efficiently and keep their attention on the overall meaning of a text.

## Assess Learning

Observe students when they use word parts to solve unfamiliar words. Notice if there is evidence of new learning based on the goal of this minilesson.

- ▶ Do students look for known word parts when solving unfamiliar words?
- ▶ Can they identify the base word and its prefix and/or suffix?
- ▶ Are they using language such as *prefix*, *suffix*, and *base word*?

# Minilesson

To help students think about solving new or unfamiliar vocabulary words, engage them in using the meaning of word parts such as prefixes, suffixes, and base words. Here is an example.

- ▶ Read the first sentence on the chart from *Face to Face with Whales* and underline the word *motionless*.

  Turn and talk with a partner. What do you notice about the underlined word? What word parts do you see?

- ▶ Show how the word can be broken into the base word (*motion*) and the suffix (*less*).

  A suffix is a word part at the end of a word that changes the meaning of the word. What does the word *motionless* mean?

- ▶ Repeat this process to discuss prefixes with the word *invisible* from *Eye to Eye*.

## Have a Try

Read the sentence from *Gecko* and invite the students to talk with a partner about the word *disappear*.

> Turn and talk with a partner. What word parts do you see? How could you break apart the word *disappear*?

## Summarize and Apply

Summarize the learning and remind students to look for prefixes, suffixes, and base words to help them read and understand new words.

> What did you learn today about solving unfamiliar words?

▶ Review the chart and write the principle at the top.

> If you come to a word you don't know or understand while you are reading today, think about how you can try to solve it. If you solve it using what you know about prefixes, suffixes, and base words, mark the word with a sticky note and bring the book when we come back together so you can share.

## Share

Following independent reading time, gather students together in the meeting area to discuss in small groups how they solved unfamiliar words in their reading.

> Turn and talk with your group. Share how you solved unfamiliar words as you read today. Did you use prefixes or suffixes?

## Extend the Lesson (Optional)

After assessing students' understanding, you might decide to extend the learning.

▶ Support this behavior in guided or independent reading. Use prompts from *Prompting Guide Part 1* (Fountas and Pinnell 2009), such as the following:

- *Look at the prefix.*
- *Look at the suffix.*
- *Do you see a part that might help you?*

| Word parts help you understand what a word means. | |
|---|---|
| "It had stopped swimming and was hanging <u>motionless</u>, singing." | motion / less = without motion, not moving |
| "Some creatures can do no more than tell day from night, while others can see colors <u>invisible</u> to humans . . ." | in / visible = not visible, cannot be seen |
| "A hawk is hunting. Time to <u>disappear</u>." | dis / appear = not appear, go away |

# RML 6

SAS.U2.RML6

### Reading Minilesson Principle
## Greek and Latin roots help you understand what a word means.

## Using Context and Word Parts to Understand Vocabulary

### You Will Need

- two or three familiar texts that contain Greek or Latin roots, such as the following:
  - *Face to Face with Whales* by Flip and Linda Nicklin, from Text Set: Telling a Story with Photos
  - *Eye to Eye* by Steve Jenkins, from Text Set: Illustration Study: Craft
- sentence strips prepared with sentences from *Face to Face with Whales* (pp. 6 and 7) and *Eye to Eye* (p. 1)
- tape or glue stick
- markers and highlighters
- sticky notes

### Academic Language / Important Vocabulary

- roots

### Continuum Connection

- Understand and discuss the concept of Latin roots and recognize their use in determining the meanings of some English words (p. 379)
- Understand and discuss the concept of Greek roots and recognize their use in determining the meaning of some English words (p. 380)

## Goal

Understand that knowledge of Greek and Latin roots can be used to figure out what a word means.

## Rationale

Many words in the English language stem from Greek or Latin. Exposing students to and teaching them to look for a variety of Greek and Latin roots support students in independently solving unfamiliar vocabulary.

## Assess Learning

Observe students when they use Greek or Latin roots to understand unfamiliar words. Notice if there is evidence of new learning based on the goal of this minilesson.

- Do students look for known word parts in unfamiliar words?
- Are students using language such as *roots*?

## Minilesson

To help students think about learning new vocabulary while reading, engage them in using the meaning of Greek and Latin roots. Here is an example.

- Attach the first sentence from *Face to Face with Whales* to the chart and underline the word *photograph*.

  What do you notice about the underlined word? Is there a word part or parts you know?

- Prompt them as necessary to think about the word parts *photo* and *graph*.
  - *What other words do you know that have the word part* photo *or* graph?
  - *What do you think* photo *means?*
  - *What do you think* graph *means?*

  *Photo* is the Greek root for *light* and *graph* is the Greek root for *writing*.

- Write or have a student write the word *Greek* on a sticky note and add it to the chart. You may want to record other words with the Greek root *photo* or *graph* on the chart for reference.

  How does knowing these word parts help you to learn a new word?

- Repeat this process with the word *vision* from *Eye to Eye*.

  *Vis* is the Latin root for *to see, look at*, or *observe*.

## Have a Try

Attach the final sentence to the chart and invite the students to talk about the word *microphone* with a partner.

> Turn and talk with a partner about the word *microphone*. This word has two parts (roots). What word parts—or roots—do you see? What do you think these roots mean? How do they help you know the meaning of the word *microphone*?

▶ Invite responses and add them to the chart.

## Summarize and Apply

Summarize the learning and remind students to think about the Greek or Latin roots they know when they come to an unfamiliar word.

> What did you learn today about solving unknown words?

▶ Review the chart and write the principle at the top.

> If you come to a new vocabulary word as you read today, think about how you can try to solve it. If you solve it using what you know about Greek and Latin roots, mark the word with a sticky note and bring the book when we come back together so you can share.

## Share

Following independent reading time, gather students together in the meeting area to discuss with a partner how they solved unfamiliar words in their reading.

> Turn and talk with your partner. Share how you solved unfamiliar words as you read today. Did you use Greek or Latin roots, or did you use another way to figure out the meaning of an unfamiliar word?

## Extend the Lesson (Optional)

After assessing students' understanding, you might decide to extend the learning.

▶ Teach additional Greek and Latin roots (download a list from resources.fountasandpinnell.com) when you lead word study lessons.

---

**Greek and Latin roots help you understand what a word means.**

"It was thrilling to photograph a scientific breakthrough as it was happening."

photo = light      graph = writing    **GREEK**

- photographer, photogenic
- autograph, graphic, biography

"Most animals rely on their vision, more than any other sense, to find out what is going on around them."

vis = to see, look at, or observe    **LATIN**

- invisible, revision, television

"This humpback whale is singing into our underwater microphone."

micro = small      phone = sound    **GREEK**

- microscope, microwave
- telephone, symphony, xylophone

Section 3: Strategies and Skills

## Assessment

After you have taught the minilessons in this umbrella, observe students as they talk and write about their reading across instructional contexts: interactive read-aloud, independent reading, guided reading, shared reading, and book club. Use *The Literacy Continuum* (Fountas and Pinnell 2017) to guide the observation of students' reading and writing behaviors.

- What evidence do you have of new understandings related to solving unknown words?
  - Can students use context from a sentence, a paragraph, or elsewhere in a text to derive the meaning of unfamiliar words?
  - Can they use synonyms or antonyms to help them understand the meaning of unfamiliar words?
  - Do they use word parts (prefix, suffix, base word, Greek and Latin roots) to help them determine the meaning of unfamiliar words?
  - Are they using academic language, such as *synonym, antonym, prefix, suffix,* and *root*?

- In what other ways, beyond the scope of this umbrella, are students talking about solving unknown words?
  - Are students applying a variety of Greek and Latin roots in combination with prefixes and suffixes to determine the meaning of unfamiliar words?
  - Do they use known words to help them learn unknown words?
  - Can they use reference tools to solve and find information about unfamiliar words?

Use your observations to determine the next umbrella you will teach. You may also consult Minilessons Across the Year (pp. 59–61) for guidance.

## Link to Writing

After teaching the minilessons in this umbrella, help students link the new learning to their own writing:

- When students write independently, encourage them to think about how they can help their readers understand unfamiliar words.

## Reader's Notebook

When this umbrella is complete, provide a copy of the minilesson principles (see resources.fountasandpinnell.com) for students to glue in the reader's notebook (in the Minilessons section if using *Reader's Notebook: Intermediate* [Fountas and Pinnell 2011]), so they can refer to the information as needed.

## Minilessons in This Umbrella

**RML1**   Writers use connecting words to add on to an idea.

**RML2**   Writers use connecting words to show the passage of time or to sequence something.

**RML3**   Writers use connecting words to show cause and effect.

**RML4**   Writers use connecting words to show a different or opposite point of view.

## Before Teaching Umbrella 3 Minilessons

Connectives are words or phrases that help readers understand the relationship between and among ideas in a text. Easy texts have very simple connectives like *but*. As they read more complex texts, students will begin to encounter more sophisticated connectives, many of which are rare in everyday oral language, for example, *nevertheless*, *as a result*, or *consequently*. Overlooking connectives in a text can lead to a misunderstanding of the ideas the writer is presenting. A list of connecting words and phrases can be found in the appendix for grammar, usage, and mechanics in *The Literacy Continuum* (Fountas and Pinnell 2017, 642–644) and in the online resources for each lesson.

Read and discuss books with connecting words that indicate examples of adding on to an idea, cause and effect, the passage of time or sequence, or a different or opposite point of view. These minilessons use the following books from the *Fountas & Pinnell Classroom™ Interactive Read-Aloud Collection* text sets; however, you can choose books from your classroom library that have examples of connectives.

**Telling a Story with Photos**

*A Bear's Life* by Nicholas Read

*The Seal Garden* by Nicholas Read

*Wolf Island* by Nicholas Read

*Face to Face with Whales* by Flip and Linda Nicklin

**Genre Study: Memoir**

*Twelve Kinds of Ice* by Ellen Bryan Obed

**Innovative Thinking and Creative Problem Solving**

*Ivan: The Remarkable True Story of the Shopping Mall Gorilla* by Katherine Applegate

**Illustration Study: Craft**

*Eye to Eye: How Animals See the World* by Steve Jenkins

*Gecko* by Raymond Huber

**Biography: Artists**

*Mary Cassatt: Extraordinary Impressionist Painter* by Barbara Herkert

As you read aloud and enjoy these texts together, help students notice how the author has used connecting words to show the relationship between and among ideas.

**Telling a Story with Photos**

*A Bear's Life* by Nicholas Read

*The Seal Garden* by Nicholas Read

*Wolf Island* by Nicholas Read

*Face to Face with Whales* by Flip and Linda Nicklin

**Genre Study: Memoir**

**Innovative Thinking and Creative Problem Solving**

**Illustration Study: Craft**

**Biography: Artists**

*Section 3: Strategies and Skills*

## Understanding Connectives

### You Will Need

▸ two to three familiar texts that use connecting words, such as the following from Text Set: Telling a Story with Photos:
  • *The Seal Garden* by Nicholas Read
  • *A Bear's Life* by Nicholas Read
  • *Wolf Island* by Nicholas Read

▸ chart paper prepared with sentences from *The Seal Garden* (p. 11), *A Bear's Life* (p. 25), and *Wolf Island* (book jacket), with connectives highlighted

▸ markers

▸ sticky notes

### Academic Language / Important Vocabulary

▸ connecting words

### Continuum Connection

▸ Understand common (simple) connectives that link and clarify meaning and are frequently used in oral language when listening to a story (*and, but, so, because, before, after*) (p. 61)

▸ Understand the meaning of common (simple) connectives and some sophisticated connectives when listening to a nonfiction text (p. 64)

## Goal

Learn that connectives are words that link ideas together or clarify the relationships between ideas and information.

## Rationale

When students notice the connectives that writers use to expand on an idea, they can think about the relationship between the ideas to help them better understand the text.

## Assess Learning

Observe students when they talk about a text. Notice if there is evidence of new learning based on the goal of this minilesson.

▸ Can students identify when a writer uses connecting words to add on to an idea?

▸ Do they understand the purpose of connecting words?

▸ Are they using the term *connecting words*?

## Minilesson

To help students think about how connecting words clarify the meaning of a text, engage them in noticing how the connective signals that the writer is adding on to an idea. Here is an example.

▸ Display the prepared chart paper. Invite a student to read the first sentence.

   What does the author tell you about seals in this sentence?

   Notice that the author tells you that seals have a layer of blubber. Then he tells you that seals come in different colors. Both of these ideas are true. Which word connects those ideas?

▸ Highlight or have a student highlight *and*.

▸ Invite a student to read the next sentence on the chart.

   Why do bears eat masses of salmon?

   Which word connects the fact that bears eat masses of salmon and the reason? What relationship does it show?

▸ Highlight or have a volunteer highlight *because*.

   *And* and *because* are called connecting words. Connecting words signal that the author is adding information on to an idea or connecting ideas in one part of a sentence with ideas in another part of the sentence or a nearby sentence. These words show the relationship between the ideas.

## Have a Try

Invite the students to talk with a partner about how the writer used connecting words or phrases to add on to an idea.

▶ Invite a student to read the last sentence on the chart.

Turn and talk to your partner. What does the word *also* help you understand about the Great Bear Rainforest?

▶ Allow time to turn and talk.

*Also* is a connecting word. The author is adding information in the second sentence to the information in the first sentence.

## Summarize and Apply

Summarize the learning and remind students to think about how connecting words tell you the writer is adding more information.

What did you learn about connecting words today?

▶ Write the principle at the top of the chart.

As you read today, notice if the writer uses connecting words to relate or add information and mark it with a sticky note so you can share when we come back together.

## Share

Following independent reading time, gather students together in the meeting area to talk about their reading.

Did you notice connecting words? How did the author use connecting words to add onto an idea?

## Extend the Lesson (Optional)

After assessing students' understanding, you might decide to extend the learning.

▶ Teach students connectives, as appropriate, that they can use in their writing (download a list from resources.fountasandpinnell.com).

▶ Encourage students to use connecting words in their writing to make their ideas clearer.

---

### Writers use connecting words to add on to an idea.

| | |
|---|---|
| The Seal Garden | "They have a thick layer of blubber that keeps them warm in the cold Pacific waters, and they come in many different colors." |
| A Bear's Life | "Bears eat masses of salmon because they want to fatten themselves up for the long winter's sleep ahead." |
| Wolf Island | "The Great Bear Rainforest is a majestic place full of tall trees, huge bears, and endless schools of salmon. It's also the home of a lone wolf with a very big adventure ahead of him." |

**Reading Minilesson Principle**
# Writers use connecting words to show the passage of time or to sequence something.

## Understanding Connectives

### You Will Need

- two to three familiar texts that use connecting words, such as the following:
  - *Twelve Kinds of Ice* by Ellen Bryan Obed, from Text Set: Genre Study: Memoir
  - *Wolf Island* by Nicholas Read and *Face to Face with Whales* by Flip and Linda Nicklin, from Text Set: Telling a Story with Photos
- chart paper prepared with sentences from *Twelve Kinds of Ice* (pp. 40, 29), *Wolf Island* (p. 25), and *Face to Face with Whales* (p. 6), with connecting words highlighted
- markers
- sticky notes

### Academic Language / Important Vocabulary

- relationship
- sequence

### Continuum Connection

- Understand (when listening) some sophisticated connectives (words that link ideas and clarify meaning) that are used in written texts but do not appear often in everyday oral language: e.g., *although, however, meantime, meanwhile, moreover, otherwise, therefore, though, unless, until, whenever, yet* [p. 60]
- Understand the meaning of common (simple) connectives and some sophisticated connectives when listening to a nonfiction text [p. 64]

## Goal

Notice how writers use connectives to show the passage of time or sequence.

## Rationale

It is important for students to recognize that authors use connectives to link ideas and to clarify relationships. In this minilesson, students learn that connectives can be used to show the passage of time or a sequence.

## Assess Learning

Observe students when they discuss their reading. Notice if there is evidence of new learning based on the goal of this minilesson.

- ▶ Can students identify connecting words that show the passage of time or a sequence?
- ▶ Do they know how those words help them to understand the relationship between ideas?
- ▶ Do they understand and use the terms *relationship* and *sequence*?

## Minilesson

To help students think about connecting words, engage students in noticing how a writer used a connective to show the passage of time or a sequence. Here is an example.

- ▶ Display the prepared chart paper and invite a student to read the first sentence.

  Turn and talk with a partner. What do you notice about the highlighted words?

  What does the word *after* tell you? How does it help you understand the ideas better?

- ▶ Invite students to share their thinking about the purpose of the word *after* in this sentence.
- ▶ Repeat this process with the next sentence on the chart, discussing the connecting word *meanwhile*.
- ▶ Repeat this process with the third sentence on the chart, discussing the connecting phrase *in the meantime*.

  What do all the highlighted words have in common?

  They are words that the authors used to show the passing of time or a sequence (as in "after homework was done") or simultaneous events (as in "meanwhile, the girls were in the shed"). *Meanwhile* tells you that one thing is happening at the same time as something else.

## Have a Try

Invite the students to talk with a partner about connecting words that show the passage of time or a sequence.

▶ Invite a student to read the last sentence on the chart.

Turn and talk to a partner. What do you notice about the highlighted words in the sentence? What do you think they mean? How do they help you to understand the ideas better?

▶ Invite a few students to share.

## Summarize and Apply

Summarize the learning and remind students to notice connecting words that show the passage of time or to sequence something.

Today you learned about connecting words that help you understand when things happen.

▶ Write the principle at the top of the chart.

In your reading today, think about the words the writer uses to show the passage of time or to show a sequence. How does that help you understand what the author is writing about? Put a sticky note on an example and bring it back to share.

## Share

Following independent reading time, gather students together in the meeting area to talk about their reading.

Who noticed a connecting word in the book you read today? How did it help you to understand the relationship between the ideas the writer shared?

## Extend the Lesson (Optional)

After assessing students' understanding, you might decide to extend the learning.

▶ Teach students connectives, as appropriate, that they can use in their writing (download a list from resources.fountasandpinnell.com).

▶ Encourage students to use connecting words in their discussions and in their writing.

Writers use connecting words to show the passage of time or to sequence something.

| Twelve Kinds of Ice | "After homework was done, after Dad had flooded, after lights were out in neighbors' houses, my sister and I would sometimes go out for a skate."<br><br>"Meanwhile, the girls were in the shed, taking off their skates." |
| Wolf Island | In the meantime, they continued to enjoy the island for the bounty it had to offer. |
| Face to Face with Whales | "Until that day, we didn't know that we could get so close to singing whales and watch them while they sang. " |

# RML3
## SAS.U3.RML3

**Reading Minilesson Principle**
# Writers use connecting words to show cause and effect.

## Understanding Connectives

### You Will Need

- one or two familiar texts that use connecting words, such as the following:
  - *Gecko* by Raymond Huber, from Text Set: Illustration Study: Craft
  - *Wolf Island* by Nicholas Read, from Text Set: Telling a Story with Photos
- chart paper prepared with sentences from *Gecko* (pp. 6, 11) and *Wolf Island* (p. 2), with connective words highlighted
- markers
- sticky notes

### Academic Language / Important Vocabulary

- cause
- effect

### Continuum Connection

- Understand common (simple) connectives that link and clarify meaning and are frequently used in oral language when listening to a story (*and, but, so, because, before, after*) (p. 60)
- Understand the meaning of common (simple) connectives and some sophisticated connectives when listening to a nonfiction text (p. 64)

## Goal

Learn connectives that show cause and effect.

## Rationale

When students begin to recognize connecting words that show cause and effect in a text, it helps them to understand better the relationship between ideas in the text.

## Assess Learning

Observe students when they discuss their reading. Notice if there is evidence of new learning based on the goal of this minilesson.

- Can students identify connecting words that show cause and effect?
- Do they understand how connecting words that show cause and effect help them to understand the relationship between ideas?
- Do they understand and use the terms *cause* and *effect*?

## Minilesson

To help students think about the minilesson principle, help them notice connecting words that show cause and effect. Here is an example.

- Display the prepared chart and invite a student to read the first sentence.

  Turn and talk to a partner. What do you know about the word *because* in this sentence? What does it help you understand about geckos?

- Invite responses about the purpose of the word *because* in the sentence.

- Repeat this process with the next sentence on the chart, discussing what the word *so* helps them understand about geckos.

  Writers use connecting words, like *because* and *so*, to connect ideas. In the first sentence, *because* tells you that the reason geckos must take care when they are in the open is that they have so many predators. It links the cause (they have so many predators) with the effect (they must take care when out in the open).

## Have a Try

Invite the students to talk with a partner about connecting words.

▶ Invite a student to read the final sentence on the chart.

Turn and talk to a partner about the word *because*. How does this word connect the ideas in the sentence? Does it help you to understand the relationship between the two ideas: wolves are special and they can swim?

▶ Make sure students understand that the reason (cause) wolves are special is that they can swim.

## Summarize and Apply

Summarize the learning and remind students to notice how writers connect ideas in a text.

What did you learn today about how writers use connecting words?

▶ Write the principle at the top of the chart.

As you read today, notice if the writer connects ideas to show cause and effect or a "reason why." Mark a place in your book with a sticky note and bring it to share.

## Share

Following independent reading time, gather students together in the meeting area to discuss their ideas as a group.

Did anyone notice any connecting words that showed cause and effect? How did the connecting word help you understand this relationship?

## Extend the Lesson (Optional)

After assessing students' understanding, you might decide to extend the learning.

▶ Teach students connectives, as appropriate, that they can use in their writing (download a list from resources.fountasandpinnell.com).

▶ Encourage students to use connecting words in their writing to show the relationship between cause and effect.

Writers use connecting words to show cause and effect.

| Gecko | "They must take care when they are out in the open because they have many predators." "They eat the old skin so predators are not attracted by it." |
| Wolf Island | They're special because they can swim. |

## RML4

SAS.U3.RML4

**Reading Minilesson Principle**

# Writers use connecting words to show a different or opposite point of view.

### Understanding Connectives

**You Will Need**

- two or three familiar texts that use connecting words, such as:
  - *Ivan* by Katherine Applegate, from Text Set: Innovative Thinking and Creative Problem Solving
  - *Eye to Eye* by Steve Jenkins, from Text Set: Illustration Study: Craft
  - *Mary Cassatt* by Barbara Herkert, from Text Set: Biography: Artists
- chart paper prepared with sentences from *Ivan* (Author's Note), *Eye to Eye* (p. 9), and *Mary Cassatt* (Author's Note), with connective words highlighted
- markers
- sticky notes

**Academic Language / Important Vocabulary**

- opposite
- different
- point of view

### Continuum Connection

- Understand (when listening) some sophisticated connectives (words that link ideas and clarify meaning) that are used in written texts but do not appear often in everyday oral language: e.g., *although, however, meantime, meanwhile, moreover, otherwise, therefore, though, unless, until, whenever, yet* (p. 60)
- Understand the meaning of common (simple) and some sophisticated connectives when listening to a nonfiction text (p. 64)

## Goal

Learn connectives that show a different or opposite point of view.

## Rationale

As texts become more complex, it is important for students to notice connecting words that indicate a different or opposite point of view. This will help them have a better understanding of the relationship between and among the ideas in the texts they read.

## Assess Learning

Observe students when they discuss their reading. Notice if there is evidence of new learning based on the goal of this minilesson.

- ▷ Can students identify connecting words that indicate a different or opposite point of view?
- ▷ Do they use connecting words to show a different or opposite point of view in discussion or in writing?
- ▷ Can they discuss how connecting words that show a different or opposite point of view impact the meaning of a text?
- ▷ Are they using vocabulary such as *opposite, point of view,* and *different*?

## Minilesson

To help students think about the minilesson principle, engage them in noticing connecting words that show a different or opposite point of view. Here is an example.

- ▷ Display the chart and invite a student to read the first sentence.

  Turn and talk to a partner about the word *although*. What does it mean in this sentence? How does the word link the ideas in the sentence?

- ▷ Invite students to share responses.
- ▷ Repeat the process with the next sentence, discussing the word *however*.

  Writers use words such as *although* and *however* to let readers know that an opposite or different idea is coming up.

## Have a Try

Invite the students to talk with a partner about connecting words that show a different or opposite point of view.

▶ Invite a student to read the final sentence on the chart.

> Turn and talk to a partner. What does *instead* mean in this sentence? How does the word link the ideas in the sentence?

▶ Invite students to share their thinking.

## Summarize and Apply

Summarize the learning and remind students to notice and think about words that show a different or opposite point of view.

> What did you learn today about how authors use connecting words?

▶ Write the principle at the top of the chart.

> Today, reread a page or two of your book to notice if the author used a connecting word to show a different or opposite point of view. Mark that place with a sticky note and be prepared to share when we come back together.

## Share

Following independent reading time, gather students together in the meeting area to share as a group.

> Did you notice any connecting words today? Did they help you understand a different or opposite point of view?

> Did anyone find any other connecting words?

## Extend the Lesson (Optional)

After assessing students' understanding, you might decide to extend the learning.

▶ Teach students connectives, as appropriate, that they can use in their writing (download a list from resources.fountasandpinnell.com).

▶ Encourage students to begin using connecting words in their writing to show different or opposite points of view. Connecting words make writing more fluent and clear.

---

### Writers use connecting words to show a different or opposite point of view.

 "There was little for Ivan to do with his days, although he seemed to enjoy finger-painting, and often watched television."

 "The deep ocean waters where this squid lives are completely dark. Its huge eyes, however, can detect the faint glow of tiny bioluminescent creatures when they are disturbed by an approaching sperm whale, the squid's archenemy."

 "At that time, women were not admitted to the famous art school, the Ecole des Beaux Arts. Instead, she spent as much time as she could copying Old Masters at the Louvre Museum and took private art lessons."

Section 3: Strategies and Skills

## Assessment

After you have taught the minilessons in this umbrella, observe students as they talk and write about their reading across instructional contexts: interactive read-aloud, independent reading, guided reading, shared reading, and book club. Use *The Literacy Continuum* (Fountas and Pinnell 2017) to guide the observation of students' reading and writing behaviors.

- ❯ What evidence do you have of new understandings related to understanding connectives?
  - Do students notice the connecting words writers use to show relationships between and among ideas?
  - Can they talk about how authors use connecting words to add onto an idea?
  - Do they understand how writers use connecting words to indicate the passage of time, or a sequence, as well as cause and effect?
  - Can they discuss how authors use connecting words to write about a different or opposite point of view?
  - Are they using connecting words when they discuss their reading?
- ❯ In what other ways, beyond the scope of this umbrella, are students talking about connecting words?
  - Have students begun to use connecting words in their writing?
  - Are they noticing and understanding the meaning of more sophisticated connecting words from the texts they read?

Use your observations to determine the next umbrella you will teach. You may also consult Minilessons Across the Year (pp. 59–61) for guidance.

## Link to Writing

After teaching the minilessons in this umbrella, help students link the new learning to their own writing:

- ❯ Encourage students to use connecting words in their own writing. They may use connecting words to add on to an idea; show cause and effect, the passage of time, or a sequence, or to indicate a different or opposite point of view.

## Reader's Notebook

When this umbrella is complete, provide a copy of the minilesson principles (see resources.fountasandpinnell.com) for students to glue in the reader's notebook (in the Minilessons section if using *Reader's Notebook: Intermediate* [Fountas and Pinnell 2011]), so they can refer to the information as needed.

## Minilessons in This Umbrella

**RML1**   Notice how the author wants you to read the sentence.

**RML2**   Put your words together so it sounds like talking.

**RML3**   Make your reading sound smooth and interesting.

## Before Teaching Umbrella 4 Minilessons

Read aloud and discuss books with a variety of punctuation marks and print features, such as commas, italics, ellipses, dashes, and colons. Use a variety of large books, small books projected with a document camera, posters, and examples of poetry or shared writing—anything large enough for students to see the print. Make sure your primary focus is to support the meaning and enjoyment of the text. For this umbrella, use these suggested books from the *Fountas & Pinnell Classroom™ Interactive Read-Aloud Collection* text sets, or use books or student writing samples from your classroom. The minilessons in this umbrella can be taught together or individually throughout the year, depending on student needs.

**Genre Study: Memoir**

*Play Ball!* by Jorge Posada

**Illustration Study: Craft**

*Gecko* by Raymond Huber

*Giant Squid* by Candace Fleming

*Dingo* by Claire Saxby

**Telling a Story with Photos**

*Face to Face with Whales* by Flip and Linda Nicklin

**Figuring Out Who You Are**

*La Mariposa* by Francisco Jiménez

**Friendship**

*The Dunderheads* by Paul Fleischman

As you read aloud and enjoy these texts together, help students

• notice the punctuation marks and font styles in sentences,

• think about how to make their voices sound when they read aloud, and

• read fluently and expressively.

**Genre Study: Memoir**

**Illustration Study: Craft**

**Telling a Story with Photos**

*Face to Face with Whales* by Flip and Linda Nicklin

**Figuring Out Who You Are**

La Mariposa

**Friendship**

**Section 3: Strategies and Skills**

### Reading Minilesson Principle
## Notice how the author wants you to read the sentence.

### You Will Need

- several familiar books with a variety of punctuation marks and font styles, such as the following:
  - *Gecko* by Raymond Huber, from Text Set: Illustration Study: Craft
  - *Play Ball!* By Jorge Posada, from Text Set: Genre Study: Memoir
- chart paper and markers
- books students are reading independently or a basket of books
- document camera (optional)

### Academic Language / Important Vocabulary

- punctuation
- font
- dialogue
- ellipses
- dash
- italics

### Continuum Connection

- Recognize and reflect punctuation with the voice: e.g., period, question mark, exclamation point, dash, comma, ellipses, when reading in chorus or individually (p. 139)

- Recognize and reflect variations in print with the voice (e.g., italics, bold type, special treatments, font size) when reading in chorus or individually (p. 139)

### Goal

Understand how the voice changes to reflect the punctuation and font in a sentence.

### Rationale

When students adjust their voices for punctuation marks and font styles in order to read the way the writer intended, they gain confidence as readers and improve fluency.

### Assess Learning

Observe students when they read aloud. Notice if there is evidence of new learning based on the goal of this minilesson.

- Do students' voices reflect the punctuation marks and font styles in sentences they read aloud?
- Are they using the terms *punctuation, font, dialogue, ellipses, dash,* and *italics*?

## Minilesson

To help students think about the minilesson principle, engage them in noticing how to change the voice to reflect the writer's intention. Here is an example.

- Display page 14 from *Gecko*.

  > Notice the different punctuation and font styles on this page. Listen as I read the words aloud the way the author intended and notice what my voice does.

- Read the page, emphasizing voice changes for periods, question marks, exclamation marks, commas, boldface words, and words in all capital letters.

  > What did you notice about my voice?

- Write students' suggestions on chart paper, guiding the conversation so they notice what you did when coming to the different punctuation marks. Define any punctuation or font vocabulary that is new to students. Display the text at the bottom of page 13.

  > What punctuation marks do you notice in the long sentence at the bottom of the page?

- Read the sentence, emphasizing how your voice sounds when you come to the colon and semicolons. Ask students what they noticed and add to the chart.

- Display the sentence on page 10 in *Play Ball!* that includes dialogue, italics, and a dash. Model fluent reading for this sentence and then read the sentence with ellipses on page 18. Add responses to the chart.

  > What did you notice about my voice when I read the dialogue in quotation marks, words in italics, the dash, and the ellipses?

## Have a Try

Invite the students to practice fluency with a partner.

▶ Have students sit in pairs with independent reading books or have them choose books from a basket.

Choose a few sentences or pages to read to your partner. Think about the way the author wants you to read and make your voice change when you come to a punctuation mark or a font style.

▶ After a few minutes, ask several students to share what they noticed.

## Summarize and Apply

Summarize the learning and remind students to notice punctuation marks and font styles when they read.

What did you learn today about how you should read, especially when you read aloud?

▶ Add the principle to the chart.

Today when you read, practice how your voice should sound when you see different types of punctuation or font styles. Bring the book when we meet so you can share.

## Share

Following independent reading time, gather students in small groups to read aloud to one another.

In your group, read aloud one or more sentences the way you think the author wants you to read the sentence. Show how the author wants your voice to sound.

## Extend the Lesson (Optional)

After assessing students' understanding, you might decide to extend the learning.

▶ Provide examples of language with punctuation, including types that were not discussed in this lesson—for example, parentheses that are used to indicate that the author or character is speaking directly to the reader. Model how to read the print and then have students practice.

▶ Point out, as appropriate, that italics and boldface do not always mean that a word should be read with emphasis. For example, titles (e.g., book, movie) and foreign words are set in italics to set them apart from the surrounding text. Headings and glossary words are often in boldface.

**Notice how the author wants you to read the sentence.**

When you see ____, make your voice...

| | | | |
|---|---|---|---|
| . | go down and come to a full stop | *italics* | say the word a little louder |
| ? | go up | **bold** | make the word sound important |
| ! | show strong feeling | CAPITALS | say the word louder for emphasis |
| , | pause for a short breath | | |
| — | come to a full stop | underline | say the word a little louder |
| ... | drift away | | |
| : | pause to prepare for what comes next | ( ) | sound like speaking directly to reader |
| ; | pause to separate two parts of a sentence | font change | read a bit differently for emphasis |
| " " | sound like the character who is speaking | | |

**Reading Minilesson Principle**
## Put your words together so it sounds like talking.

### Maintaining Fluency

### You Will Need

- familiar books that have examples of different types of phrasing, such as the following:
  - *La Mariposa* by Francisco Jiménez, from Text Set: Figuring Out Who You Are
  - *Face to Face with Whales* by Flip and Linda Nicklin, from Text Set: Telling a Story with Photos
  - *Gecko* by Raymond Huber, From Text Set: Illustration Study: Craft
- chart paper and markers
- document camera (optional)

### Academic Language / Important Vocabulary

- fluency
- commas
- phrasing

### Continuum Connection

- Read orally with integration of all dimensions of fluency (e.g., pausing, phrasing, word stress, intonation, and rate) alone and while maintaining unison with others (p. 139)

## Goal

Read with phrasing.

## Rationale

When students read sentences with proper phrasing so that their reading sounds like talking, they can reflect on the author's meaning and increase their understanding of the text.

## Assess Learning

Observe students when they read aloud. Notice if there is evidence of new learning based on the goal of this minilesson.

- ▶ Do students put words together when they read aloud so it sounds like talking?
- ▶ Are they using the terms *fluency*, *commas*, and *phrasing?*

## Minilesson

To help students think about the minilesson principle, help them notice how to put their words together so it sounds like talking aloud. Here is an example.

- ▶ Display page 6 from *La Mariposa*. Read the page so that it sounds like fluent, natural speech. Then have students read the page with you.
- ▶ After reading with students, have a conversation about fluency. The following prompts may be helpful.
  - *What did you notice about how the words and sentences sounded?*
  - *What did you notice about the way I read the words between the commas? I put my words together. This is called phrasing.*
  - *In what ways did I try to make my voice sound like the character when reading dialogue?*
- ▶ As students provide ideas, make a list on chart paper of the benefits of putting words together when you read.

  Now let's look at another example. Think about the different uses of commas on this page and what my voice sounds like as I read.

- ▶ Display and read pages 5 and 15 from *Face to Face with Whales*. Depending on the needs of your students, you might talk about the different uses of commas and phrasing on these pages and how the author's intention affects the way the words are read (e.g., clauses, phrases, appositives, lists).

  What else can be added to the chart?

## Have a Try

Invite the students to practice phrasing with a partner.

▶ Show page 16 from *Gecko* by writing the sentences on chart paper.

> Take turns reading aloud this page from *Gecko* quietly to your partner. Think about how to read the sentences so it sounds like you are talking.

## Summarize and Apply

Summarize the learning and remind students to put words together when they read.

> Today you talked about putting words together in a natural way so that it sounds like talking when you read. That's called phrasing. Why is this important?

▶ Add the principle to the chart.

> When you read today, listen to how your reading sounds. Practice putting your words together so it sounds like talking. Bring your book when we meet so you can share.

## Share

Following independent reading time, gather students in pairs to read aloud to one another.

> Read one page from your book to your partner. As you do, practice putting your words together so it sounds like talking.

## Extend the Lesson (Optional)

After assessing students' understanding, you might decide to extend the learning.

▶ Have students talk to each other about a sample topic and then read a page from a book aloud. Have them think and talk about how they sound when they have a conversation and how they can make their reading sound similar to the way they sound when having a conversation.

▶ Continue to model fluent reading on a regular basis and from time to time ask students to reflect on the way fluent readers sound.

---

**Put your words together so it sounds like talking.**

- Your reading sounds smooth.

- You show that you understand what you read.

- People understand the meaning when you read aloud.

- You read like a character would say it.

Section 3: Strategies and Skills

**Reading Minilesson Principle**
## Make your reading sound smooth and interesting.

Maintaining Fluency

### You Will Need

- several familiar books with a variety of punctuation marks, font styles, and dialogue, such as the following:
  - *The Dunderheads* by Paul Fleischman, from Text Set: Friendship
  - *Dingo* by Claire Saxby, from Text Set: Illustration Study: Craft
  - *Giant Squid* by Candace Fleming, from Text Set: Illustration Study: Craft
- chart paper and markers
- document camera (optional)

### Academic Language / Important Vocabulary

- voice
- fluency
- phrasing
- smooth
- emphasis
- expression

### Continuum Connection

- Read orally with integration of all dimensions of fluency (e.g., pausing, phrasing, word stress, intonation, and rate) alone and while maintaining unison with others (p. 139)

### Goal

Learn how to integrate pausing, phrasing, stress, intonation, and rate to demonstrate fluent reading.

### Rationale

When students become aware of how to use rising and falling tones, pitch, and volume and to integrate all dimensions of fluency, their oral reading will sound smooth. This will also transfer to silent reading, resulting in better understanding and more enjoyment.

### Assess Learning

Observe students when they read aloud and notice if there is evidence of new learning based on the goal of this minilesson.

- Are students making their reading sound smooth and interesting?
- Do they understand the terms *voice, fluency, phrasing, smooth, emphasis,* and *expression*?

## Minilesson

To help students think about the minilesson principle, engage them in noticing the characteristics of fluent reading. Here is an example.

- Display page 14 from *The Dunderheads*.

  Listen to my voice and notice how it changes as I read this page.

- Read the page with appropriate rate, expression, pausing, and stress.

  What did you notice about how I made my reading sound smooth and interesting?

- As students respond, make a list on chart paper.

  Let's look at a few more pages in this book. I will read the page first. Then we will read it again together so you can make your voice sound the same.

- Show and read pages 11, 33, and 43. After reading each page, ask students to join in as you read a second time.

  What did you notice about what our voices did when we read these pages?

- If students need further practice, repeat the activity by reading pages 8, 16, 17, and 20 from *Dingo*.

- After reading, have students reflect on the way the voices sounded and add to chart.

## Have a Try

Invite the students to practice fluency with a partner.

▶ Display page 2 from *Giant Squid*.

Think about making your reading smooth and interesting as you take turns reading this page with a partner.

▶ Students can also practice reading dialogue with a partner, using page 29 from *The Dunderheads*.

## Summarize and Apply

Summarize the learning and remind students to make their reading sound smooth and interesting.

Today you noticed that when you read, you can change your voice in ways to make your reading sound smooth and interesting.

▶ Add the principle to the chart. Then, review the list on the chart.

When you read aloud, make your voice sound smooth and interesting. Think about that when you read today. Bring your book when we meet so you can share.

## Share

Following independent reading time, gather students in pairs to read aloud to one another.

Choose a page from the book you read today to read to your partner. Make your reading sound smooth and interesting.

## Extend the Lesson (Optional)

After assessing students' understanding, you might decide to extend the learning.

▶ Continue to model fluent reading and revisit the chart from time to time so students can reflect on the things they can do with their voices to make their reading sound smooth and interesting.

▶ Invite students to practice reading a picture book in preparation for reading it aloud to a younger class. This provides an authentic reason for making one's reading sound fluent, smooth, expressive, and interesting.

**Make your reading sound smooth and interesting.**

- make your voice volume louder or softer
  **louder** softer
- make your voice go up or down
- read with expression
- stress the words appropriately
- read with rhythm
- read like you are talking
- use the right speed
- sound smooth like you are talking
- read phrases together
- pause or stop the right amount of time
- sound like the character

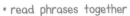

*Put together ... ...words that go together.*

Section 3: Strategies and Skills

## Assessment

After you have taught the minilessons in this umbrella, observe students as they talk and write about their reading across instructional contexts: interactive read-aloud, independent reading and literacy work, guided reading, shared reading, and book club. Use *The Literacy Continuum* (Fountas and Pinnell 2017) to guide the observation of students' reading and writing behaviors.

▶ What evidence do you have of new understandings related to fluency?

- Are students reading and responding appropriately to punctuation when they read aloud?

- Do they adjust their voices when reading aloud words in boldface, italics, or all capital letters?

- Do they integrate the various elements of fluency, such as pausing, phrasing, word stress, intonation, and rate when they read aloud?

- Do they notice dialogue and try to read the way the character would say it?

- Do they use terms such as *fluency, punctuation, font, italics,* and *dialogue*?

▶ In what other ways, beyond the scope of this umbrella, are students demonstrating fluency?

- Do students think about the author's voice and intentions when reading aloud?

- Are they using a confident and enthusiastic voice when they speak in front of others?

Use your observations to determine the next umbrella you will teach. You may also consult Minilessons Across the Year (pp. 59–61) for guidance.

## Link to Writing

After teaching the minilessons in this umbrella, help students link the new learning to their own writing:

▶ Encourage students to use a variety of types of punctuation in their own writing.

▶ Have students use dialogue in their own writing. Encourage them to think about how the character would say it and then write it that way.

## Reader's Notebook

When this umbrella is complete, provide a copy of the minilesson principles (see resources.fountasandpinnell.com) for students to glue in the reader's notebook (in the Minilessons section if using *Reader's Notebook: Intermediate* [Fountas and Pinnell 2011]), so they can refer to the information as needed.

## Minilessons in This Umbrella

**RML1** When you summarize a fiction story, tell the characters, setting, problem, important events, and solution in an organized way.

**RML2** When you summarize a biography, tell the important events in order.

**RML3** When you summarize an informational text, tell the most important information.

## Before Teaching Umbrella 5 Minilessons

The minilessons in this umbrella do not need to be taught consecutively; rather, you can teach them in conjunction with the relevant literary analysis minilessons. A summary of any text includes the most important details or information plus the message or lesson that the author is trying to convey.

Use the texts from the *Fountas & Pinnell Classroom™ Interactive Read-Aloud Collection* text sets listed below, or choose books from the classroom library to support students in their ability to summarize their reading. Read and discuss fiction texts with characters, settings, clear problems and solutions, and a message. Read and discuss informational texts with a variety of underlying text structures.

**Illustrator Study: Floyd Cooper**

*Ruth and the Green Book* by Calvin Alexander Ramsey

**Friendship**

*Better Than You* by Trudy Ludwig

**Genre Study: Biography (Individuals Making a Difference)**

*Six Dots: A Story of Young Louis Braille* by Jen Bryant

**Biography: Artists**

*Me, Frida* by Amy Novesky

**Illustration Study: Craft**

*Eye to Eye: How Animals See the World* by Steve Jenkins

*Gecko* by Raymond Huber

As you read aloud and enjoy these texts together, help students

- notice and discuss the events that shaped the life of a subject in a biography or a character in a fiction text,
- think about the message or lesson the author is trying to convey,
- understand what makes the subject of a biography notable, and
- notice the important information and the underlying text structures presented in an informational text.

**Illustrator Study: Floyd Cooper**

**Friendship**

**Genre Study: Biography (Individuals Making a Difference)**

**Biography: Artists**

**Illustration Study: Craft**

## RML1
### SAS.U5.RML1

**Reading Minilesson Principle**
# When you summarize a fiction story, tell the characters, setting, problem, important events, and solution in an organized way.

## Summarizing

### You Will Need

- two or three familiar fiction books with chronological sequence and clearly identified characters, setting, problem, and solution, such as the following:
  - *Ruth and the Green Book* by Calvin Alexander Ramsey, from Text Set: Illustrator Study: Floyd Cooper
  - *Better Than You* by Trudy Ludwig, from Text Set: Friendship
- chart paper prepared with a summary of *Ruth and the Green Book*
- chart paper and markers

### Academic Language / Important Vocabulary

- summary
- summarize
- chronological order
- characters
- setting
- problem
- solution
- message

### Continuum Connection

- Include the problem and its resolution in a summary of a text (p. 59)

## Goal

Tell the important events of a text in a sequence, including the characters, setting, problem, and solution.

## Rationale

When summarizing a fiction text, students must organize details about characters, setting, and plot in chronological order. This helps readers remember what they read as well as notice structural patterns, such as cause and effect and problem and solution. It is also important to include the author's message in a summary of a fiction story.

## Assess Learning

Observe students when they summarize fiction texts. Notice if there is evidence of new learning based on the goal of this minilesson.

- Can students give an organized book summary that includes characters, setting, main events in order, and the problem and solution?
- Do they distinguish between essential and nonessential information when they create a summary?
- Are they using language such as *summary, summarize, chronological order, characters, setting, problem, solution,* and *message*?

## Minilesson

To help students think about summarizing fiction books, engage them in noticing the characteristics of a summary that you have written on a chart. Here is an example.

- Read the written summary of *Ruth and the Green Book*.

    What did you notice about what I told you about this story?

    What parts of the story did I include?

    What kind of information is at the very end of the summary?

- Prompt as necessary to make the ideas generative, recording responses on the chart paper.

    When you tell the most important parts of a story, you summarize it, or give a summary. A summary is short but gives enough information so someone can understand the story. You need to organize the information so the summary makes sense.

## Have a Try

Invite the students to summarize *Better Than You* with a partner.

> One of you will give a summary of *Better Than You* to your partner. Your partner will listen for the characters, setting, important events, problem and solution, and author's message.

❱ If time allows, ask a student to share a summary.

## Summarize and Apply

Summarize the learning and remind students to think as they read about the parts of the story they will include in a short summary.

❱ Review the list of items to include in a summary. Write the principle on the chart.

> Choose a fiction book when you read today. As you read, think about how you would tell a summary of the story. Bring the book when we meet today so you can share.

## Share

Following independent reading time, gather students together in the meeting area to talk about their reading.

❱ Choose two or three students to share a summary of a fiction book with the class. Help all students notice the important information and organization.

## Extend the Lesson (Optional)

After assessing students' understanding, you might decide to extend the learning.

❱ During guided reading and individual conferences, ask students to give a book summary (or a summary of a section).

❱ **Writing About Reading** After students have demonstrated a strong oral summary, ask them to write a summary in a reader's notebook (see WAR.U5.RML4).

---

### Summary

The setting of <u>Ruth and the Green Book</u> by Calvin Alexander Ramsey is the 1950s. Ruth and her family traveled from Chicago to Alabama. They encountered many places with "White Only" signs. This worried them, but Daddy's friend, Eddy, told them to look for Esso stations, where people were helpful. At the first Esso station, Ruth and her family bought a Green Book, which listed places where they would be welcome. They used the Green Book to help them plan the rest of their drive to Grandma's house. This story shows how people survived in Jim Crow days.

---

When you summarize a fiction story, tell the characters, setting, problem, important events, and solution in an organized way.

**What to Include in a Story Summary**

• Characters

• Where the story takes place/setting

• The problem and solution

• Important events in chronological order

• The ending

• The writer's message

• Information that is organized

**Reading Minilesson Principle**

# When you summarize a biography, tell the important events in order.

## Summarizing

### You Will Need

- two or three familiar biographies, such as the following:
  - *Six Dots* by Jen Bryant, from Text Set: Genre Study: Biography (Individuals Making a Difference)
  - *Me, Frida* by Amy Novesky, from Text Set: Biography: Artists
- chart paper prepared with a summary of *Six Dots*
- chart paper and markers
- basket of biographies

### Academic Language / Important Vocabulary

- biography
- chronological order
- summary
- subject
- message

### Continuum Connection

- Tell a summary of a text after hearing it read [p. 62]

## Goal

Tell the important events in a biography in chronological order.

## Rationale

A biography often follows a chronological or narrative structure. Learning how to summarize a biography helps students learn to summarize other texts with a narrative structure. This lesson can also be used to help students summarize narrative nonfiction and memoir.

## Assess Learning

Observe students when they summarize a biography. Notice if there is evidence of new learning based on the goal of this minilesson.

- ▶ Can students give an organized summary of a biography?
- ▶ Do they distinguish between essential and nonessential details when summarizing?
- ▶ Are they using language such as *biography*, *chronological order*, *summary*, *subject*, and *message*?

## Minilesson

To help students think about the minilesson principle, engage them in noticing the important characteristics of a summary of a biography that you have written on a chart. Here is an example.

- ▶ Read the summary of *Six Dots*.

  What did you notice about the way I told you about this biography?

  What information did I include?

  What information is at the very end of the summary?

- ▶ Record responses on the chart, making them generative as necessary.

  Why is it important to tell about the events of a biography in order?

## Have a Try

Invite students to summarize *Me, Frida* with a partner.

> One of you will give a summary of *Me, Frida* to your partner. Your partner will listen for important information: whom the book is about, the setting, major events in Frida's life, challenges she had to overcome, and the author's message.

▷ If time allows, ask a student to share a summary with the class.

## Summarize and Apply

Summarize the learning and remind students to think about how to summarize a biography.

▷ Review the list of items to include in a summary. Write the principle at the top of the chart.

> Choose a biography from this basket when you read today. As you read, think about how you would tell a summary of the book. Bring the book when we meet today so you can share.

## Share

Following independent reading time, gather students together in the meeting area to share summaries.

▷ Choose two or three students to share a summary of a biography with the class.

## Extend the Lesson (Optional)

After assessing students' understanding, you might decide to extend the learning.

▷ Use this lesson as a model for teaching students to summarize narrative nonfiction and memoir.

▷ During guided reading and individual conferences, ask students to give a summary of a biography.

▷ **Writing About Reading** After students have demonstrated a strong oral summary of biography, ask them to write a summary in a reader's notebook (see WAR.U5.RML4).

### Summary

In <u>Six Dots</u>, Jen Bryant tells the story of Louis Braille. When Louis was a child, he suffered an accident that left him blind in both eyes. Many people helped him learn his way around his world, but he wanted to learn more. He was sent to a school for the blind in Paris. Although the school had books for blind people, they were difficult to read. Louis decided to make another way for blind people to read after he learned a code that was used by the military to send messages. After many years, he developed a system that made it possible for the blind to read and write quickly and easily. It is still used today. This story shows how a person can overcome disabilities and help others.

**When you summarize a biography, tell the important events in order.**

What to Include in the Summary of a Biography

• The subject of the book

• Why the subject is important

• Where and when the subject lived

• The important events in order

• The problem(s) the subject encountered and how they were solved

• The writer's message

Section 3: Strategies and Skills

**Reading Minilesson Principle**

# When you summarize an informational text, tell the most important information.

## Summarizing

### You Will Need

- two or three familiar biographies, such as the following from Text Set: Illustration Study: Craft:
  - *Eye to Eye* by Steve Jenkins
  - *Gecko* by Raymond Huber
- chart paper prepared with a summary of *Eye to Eye*
- chart paper and markers
- basket of informational books

### Academic Language / Important Vocabulary

- summary
- summarize
- message

### Continuum Connection

- Tell a summary of a text after hearing it read [p. 62]

## Goal

Tell the important information and ideas in an informational book.

## Rationale

When you teach students how to summarize informational books, you help them organize and clearly articulate the important information. This also helps them learn and notice a variety of informational text structures, such as categorical, descriptive, and compare and contrast.

## Assess Learning

Observe students when they summarize informational texts. Notice if there is evidence of new learning based on the goal of this minilesson.

- Can students distinguish between essential and nonessential information when summarizing?
- Do they notice the underlying text structure of an informational text?
- Are they using academic language, such as *summary, summarize,* and *message*?

# Minilesson

To help students think about the minilesson principle, engage them in noticing the most important information when summarizing informational texts. Here is an example.

- Read the summary of *Eye to Eye*.

  What did you notice about the information I shared?

  What did I include in the summary?

  What information is at the very end of the summary?

- Record responses on a chart. If students suggest subject matter, such as "Tells about the Eurasian buzzard's eyes," redirect them to something more generative ("example of the facts about the topic").

  A summary does not tell everything in a book, only enough important information to give someone an idea of what the book is about.

## Have a Try

Invite students to summarize *Gecko* with a partner.

> Take turns giving your partner a summary of *Gecko*. What should you include in your summary? Use the chart for ideas.

▶ If time allows, ask a couple of students to share.

## Summarize and Apply

Summarize the learning and remind students to think about including only important information when they tell about an informational book.

▶ Review the list of items to include in a summary. Write the principle at the top of the chart.

> If you are not already reading an informational book, choose one from this basket. As you read, think about how you would give a summary of the book. Bring the book when we meet today so you can share.

## Share

Following independent reading time, gather students in the meeting area to share summaries with a partner and then, if there's time, with the class.

> Share your summary with a partner. Think about the important information to include.

## Extend the Lesson (Optional)

After assessing students' understanding, you might decide to extend the learning.

▶ Teach students to include the underlying text structures in a summary of an informational text, e.g., "This book explains the causes and effects of . . . ," "tells about the problem and solution of . . . ," "describes . . . ."

▶ **Writing About Reading** After students have demonstrated a strong oral summary of an informational book, ask them to write a summary in a reader's notebook (see WAR.U5.RML4).

---

### Summary

In <u>Eye to Eye</u>, Steve Jenkins, the author, describes the different ways animals' eyes work and how they use their vision to survive. Some eyes are very simple, like a sea slug's, and can see only light. Some are very complex, like those of the Eurasian buzzard, which has the best eyesight of any animal. Animals' eyes are all so different and fascinating. This book shows the wonderful variety in nature.

---

**When you summarize an informational book, tell the most important information.**

What to Include in a Summary of an Informational Book

- The topic

- The most important facts or a couple of examples of the facts about the topic

- How the book is organized

- The author's feelings about the topic

- The main message or big idea

## Assessment

After you have taught the minilessons in this umbrella, observe students as they talk and write about their reading across instructional contexts: interactive read-aloud, independent reading, guided reading, shared reading, and book club. Use *The Literacy Continuum* (Fountas and Pinnell 2017) to guide the observation of students' reading and writing behaviors.

 ▶ What evidence do you have of new understandings related to summarizing reading?

 • Can students identify the characters, setting, problem, solution, and message in a fiction text?

 • Do they articulate a complete, well-organized summary of a fiction, nonfiction, or biographical text?

 • Are they able to distinguish between essential and nonessential information?

 • Do they use language such as *summary* and *summarize*?

 ▶ In what other ways, beyond the scope of this umbrella, are students talking about fiction and nonfiction books?

 • Have students begun to notice and discuss underlying text structures in nonfiction?

 • Do they notice and comment on text features in nonfiction books?

 • Are they noticing the author's craft in fiction books?

Use your observations to determine the next umbrella you will teach. You may also consult Minilessons Across the Year (pp. 59–61) for guidance.

## Link to Writing

After teaching the minilessons in this umbrella, help students link the new learning to their own writing:

 ▶ Have students write mini-summaries to attach to some books in the classroom library to help other students choose a book they will enjoy reading.

## Reader's Notebook

When this umbrella is complete, provide a copy of the minilesson principles (see resources.fountasandpinnell.com) for students to glue in the reader's notebook (in the Minilessons section if using *Reader's Notebook: Intermediate* [Fountas and Pinnell 2011]), so they can refer to the information as needed.

## Minilessons in This Umbrella

**RML1**  Prepare for reading by using the text features and resources.

**RML2**  Be persistent when you read a difficult text.

**RML3**  Notice when you don't understand what you're reading and take action.

**RML4**  Read short sections and stop to think about what the author is saying.

## Before Teaching Umbrella 6 Minilessons

The minilessons in this umbrella are intended to encourage students to use a variety of effective techniques when approaching texts that are difficult for them to read. You will not only address focus and persistence but also teach students to monitor their comprehension.

Unlike other minilessons in this book, these minilessons do not rely on previously read texts. Instead, provide real-world examples of texts that are likely difficult for your students, such as material from disciplinary reading. Expose students to reading materials that are beyond their instructional levels and that can be enlarged (written on chart paper or projected). Examples include practice testing booklets, online informational material and directions, scientific articles, textbooks, and primary source documents. The texts should be tailored to your group of students and what they find difficult, so readings will vary from class to class.

Introduce, read, and discuss a variety of texts that your students may find difficult. When you do,

- discuss what the text is about,

- demonstrate how to reread and check if a word makes sense, sounds right, and looks right,

- model how to keep track of who is speaking,

- think about the important information and details when you read,

- show how to stop and reread if something is confusing, and

- read short sections and then stop and think about what the author is trying to say.

# RML1
## SAS.U6.RML1

**Reading Minilesson Principle**
# Prepare for reading by using the text features and resources.

**Monitoring Comprehension of Difficult Texts**

## You Will Need

- prepared chart paper or projected documents with examples of text that may be difficult for your students and that includes at least some of these text features: titles, headings, an introduction, a summary, graphics, and keywords
- chart paper and markers
- document camera (optional)
- basket of texts (e.g., books, magazines, articles) that are challenging for students and that include a variety of text features

## Academic Language / Important Vocabulary

- difficult
- techniques
- text features
- resources

### Continuum Connection

- Notice, use, and understand the purpose of some organizational tools: e.g., title, table of contents, chapter title, heading, subheading (pp. 61, 65)

## Goal

Navigate a difficult text by previewing the title and headings, graphics, introduction, and summary.

## Rationale

Teach students to use text features and resources to preview a difficult text so that they have a way to begin to peel back the layers to find the meaning. They will benefit from knowing that navigating a difficult text usually requires more than one pass.

## Assess Learning

Observe students when they navigate difficult texts and notice if there is evidence of new learning based on the goal of this minilesson.

- Can students identify text features and resources to use in navigating difficult text?
- Do they understand the terms *difficult, techniques, text features,* and *resources*?

## Minilesson

To help students think about the minilesson principle, engage them in generating a list of text features and resources to use when navigating difficult texts. Here is an example.

- Display a text that has a variety of text features (e.g., title, headings, graphics) that can be used to determine what the text is about.

  If you to need to read a difficult text, what text features on the page can help you get information that will help you? What do you notice on this page that might help you understand what you will be reading about?

- Guide students to identify key features, such as the title, headings, and illustrations. As students name them, begin a list on chart paper.

  Some texts have an introduction or a summary that is short to read and gives you a general idea of what the text will be about.

- Continue showing examples of difficult texts that include a variety of text features, such as headings, an introduction, a summary, graphics, illustrations, and keywords. As students identify each, add to the list on the chart. The following prompts may be useful:

  - *What features of this text give you a clue about what you are reading?*
  - *What do you notice about the introduction?*
  - *How does the author identify keywords?*
  - *How could you get to know keywords that are unfamiliar?*
  - *How does a summary help you understand what you are reading?*

## Have a Try

Provide pairs of students with a nonfiction book or article.

> Talk with your partner about where you can look to find out what the book (or article) is about.

▶ After time for brief discussion, ask students to share what they found.

## Summarize and Apply

Summarize the learning and remind students to use text features and resources.

▶ Review the chart and write the principle at the top.

> When you read today, choose a text from the basket that may be difficult for you to read. Look for text features and resources that can help you. Bring the text when we meet so you can share.

## Share

Following independent reading time, gather students in small groups to talk about reading difficult texts.

> In your group, share what you read today and talk about text features that helped you understand what you read.

## Extend the Lesson (Optional)

After assessing students' understanding, you might decide to extend the learning.

▶ Continue to support techniques for approaching difficult texts during guided reading or independent reading. From *Prompting Guide, Part 2* (Fountas and Pinnell 2009), use prompts such as the following:

- *What does the (title, dust jacket, back cover, illustrations, chapter headings, dedication, opening page) tell you about the book?*
- *What print features does the book have (cartoons, speech bubbles, headings, special fonts)?*
- *What can you learn from these features?*
- *What kind of illustrations and graphics are included (photographs, drawings, diagrams, cross-sections, maps, sidebars)?*

---

**Prepare for reading by using the text features and resources.**

- Title

- Headings

- Introduction

- Graphics and illustrations

- Keywords

- Summary

---

*Section 3: Strategies and Skills*

**Reading Minilesson Principle**
# Be persistent when you read a difficult text.

### You Will Need

- chart paper or projected document that shows a text that is challenging for your students, prepared with highlighting and notes to assist with comprehension
- chart paper and markers
- sticky notes
- document camera (optional)
- basket of text that is difficult for students

### Academic Language / Important Vocabulary

- difficult
- techniques
- persistent
- focused

### Continuum Connection

- Notice and ask questions when meaning is lost or understanding is interrupted (pp. 58, 62)

## Goal

Use techniques to stay focused and persistent when reading.

## Rationale

When you teach students ways to access the content of a difficult text, you help them persist in reading that text. They learn it is normal to sometimes encounter texts that are difficult but that there are ways to unlock the meaning.

## Assess Learning

Observe students when they approach difficult texts and notice if there is evidence of new learning based on the goal of this minilesson.

- Are students able to generate a list of ways to approach difficult texts?
- Do they try more than one way to stay focused when reading a difficult text?
- Do they understand the terms *difficult, techniques, persistent,* and *focused?*

# Minilesson

To help students think about the minilesson principle, engage them in constructing a list of techniques to help them stay focused when navigating difficult texts. Here is an example.

- Ahead of time, find a text that is beyond the instructional level of most of your students and prepare an enlarged copy (or have a projector available). Annotate with highlighting, notes in the margins, and/or sticky notes.

  What does it feel like when you read something that is very difficult?

  One of the things I try to do before I read something that is really hard is to think about what I already know and might want to know about the topic. Let's look at this topic. What are some things you might want to learn or be interested in finding out about this topic?

- Show the prepared document and have a brief conversation about the topic.

  Here is something that is difficult to read. I have done some things to help me stay focused and persistent. What do you notice that I have done?

- As students provide ideas, make a list on chart paper. Continue the list with techniques that can be used while reading. Prompt the conversation as needed.

## Have a Try

Invite the students to talk with a partner about navigating difficult texts.

> What do you do when you read something difficult? Turn and talk about that.

▶ After time for discussion, ask students to share. Add new ideas to the chart.

## Summarize and Apply

Summarize the learning and remind students to stay focused and persistent when reading something that is difficult.

> When you read something difficult, it is important to stick with it and try different techniques. That means that you are focused and persistent.

▶ Add the principle to the chart.

> When you read today, choose something that may be very difficult for you to read. Try using one or more of the techniques we talked about before and during reading. Bring what you read when we meet so you can share.

## Share

Following independent reading time, gather students together to talk about their reading.

> Who would like to share what you read today and talk about what you did to help yourself understand it?

## Extend the Lesson (Optional)

After assessing students' understanding, you might decide to extend the learning.

▶ Continue to support techniques for approaching difficult texts during guided reading or independent reading. From *Prompting Guide, Part 2* (Fountas and Pinnell 2009), use prompts such as the following:

  - *What do you know about the genre that might help you?*
  - *What do you think the writer will teach you about _____?*
  - *How does that fit with what you know?*
  - *What questions do you still have?*
  - *What confused you?*

---

**Be persistent when you read a difficult text.**

**Before Reading**

- Think about what you know about the topic before reading.
- Think about what you want to learn or find out.
- Think about what you wonder. **?**

**While Reading**

- Use a highlighter to mark important words, phrases, or sentences.
- Write a note in the margin on the page.
- Add sticky notes.
- Reread a sentence or paragraph.
- Don't give up.

---

*Section 3: Strategies and Skills*

**Reading Minilesson Principle**

# Notice when you don't understand what you're reading and take action.

## Monitoring Comprehension of Difficult Texts

### You Will Need

- several samples of texts that are difficult for most students (e.g., challenging novel, science or technology article, medical journal)
- chart paper and markers
- document camera (optional)
- basket with examples of reading materials that are difficult for students

### Academic Language / Important Vocabulary

- techniques
- take action
- reread
- key vocabulary

### Continuum Connection

- Notice and ask questions when meaning is lost or understanding is interrupted (pp. 58, 62)

## Goal

Self-monitor and self-correct by rereading, finding the meaning of key vocabulary, and reading on to gain more information.

## Rationale

When you teach students to notice by self-monitoring when they do not understand what they are reading, they learn to self-correct by rereading, reading on, and/or looking up key vocabulary to gain meaning.

## Assess Learning

Observe students when they read challenging text and notice if there is evidence of new learning based on the goal of this minilesson.

- Do students notice when they do not understand what they are reading?
- Are they able to stop and take action when they do not comprehend a difficult text?
- Do they understand the terms *techniques*, *take action*, *reread*, and *key vocabulary*?

## Minilesson

To help students think about the minilesson principle, engage them in thinking about the actions that support comprehension. Here is an example.

> Sometimes you will come to a part of a book that doesn't make sense or that is difficult for you to understand.

- Show or project an example of difficult reading material. Read the first paragraph or a difficult section aloud with good momentum and no explanations.

> Did you understand what I read?

> I read that quickly. Sometimes you realize that the first time you read you are going too quickly to understand what the author is writing about. What can you do if that happens?

- As students provide ideas, make a list on chart paper.

> It's important to notice when you don't understand what you are reading. The first thing to do is stop. Then you can try some different actions to work out the meaning.

## Have a Try

Invite the students to talk with a partner about noticing when they don't understand what they are reading and taking action.

> We made a list of some things you can do when you don't understand what you are reading. Can you think of any others? Turn and talk about that.

▶ After time for brief discussion, ask if students have ideas to add to the chart.

## Summarize and Apply

Summarize the learning and remind students to notice when they don't understand what they are reading and to take action.

▶ Review the chart and write the principle at the top.

> When you read today, if you come to a part you don't understand, try one or more of the actions that are listed on the chart. Bring your reading when we meet so you can share.

Notice when you don't understand what you're reading and take action.

**TAKE ACTION**

- Slow down.
- Reread the part slowly.
- Read ahead to see if the meaning is clarified.
- Find key words in the glossary or other source.
- Think about what the whole book is about and how the information fits.

## Share

Following independent reading time, gather students in small groups to talk about reading difficult texts.

> In your group, share what you read today and talk about what you did to help you understand what you read.

## Extend the Lesson (Optional)

After assessing students' understanding, you might decide to extend the learning.

▶ Continue to support techniques for approaching difficult texts during guided reading or independent reading. From *Prompting Guide, Part 2* (Fountas and Pinnell 2009), use prompts such as the following:

- *Does that make sense?*
- *Were there parts where you wanted to slow down and think more?*
- *What do you think the author meant when she said _____?*
- *How do the illustrations enhance your understanding of the topic?*

**Reading Minilesson Principle**

# Read short sections and stop to think about what the author is saying.

## Monitoring Comprehension of Difficult Texts

### You Will Need

▸ prepared chart paper or projected text that may be difficult for your students

▸ chart paper and markers

▸ document camera (optional)

▸ basket of challenging reading materials

## Academic Language / Important Vocabulary

▸ actions

▸ section

▸ summarize

### Continuum Connection

▸ Tell a summary of a text after reading it (pp. 58, 62)

## Goal

Read short sections and think about what the author is saying.

## Rationale

When students reading difficult material learn to stop and think about what an author is saying, they begin to remember what they read, organize the information, and increase comprehension. In content-area studies and research, they will likely encounter difficult texts.

## Assess Learning

Observe students when they encounter difficult text and notice if there is evidence of new learning based on the goal of this minilesson.

▸ Do they read a short section and then think about what the author is trying to say?

▸ Do they understand the terms *actions, section,* and *summarize*?

# Minilesson

To help students think about the minilesson principle, engage them in a discussion about how to read a short section of a difficult text and then pause to think about what the author is trying to say.

▸ Show or project an example of text that is difficult for students.

> When you read something that is difficult to understand, there are different actions that you can take to be sure you understand what you are reading.

▸ Read a short section and then stop and ask the students what the author is trying to say. Briefly summarize the section with them.

▸ Read another short portion of the text. Then stop and repeat the process.

▸ Engage students in a discussion about what they noticed about the technique you used.

▸ Help students conclude that when they read a short section and pause to think about what they read, they can assure good understanding.

## Have a Try

Show or project another difficult text.

> With a partner, take turns reading a short section aloud and then think and talk about what the author is trying to say.

## Summarize and Apply

Summarize the learning and remind students to read a short section of a difficult text and think about what an author is trying to say.

> What can you do to help yourself when reading something that is difficult?

▶ Add the principle to the chart.

> When you read today, choose something that is very difficult for you. When you come to a part you don't understand, read a short section and then think about what the author is trying to say. Bring the text when we meet so you can share.

> ### Read short sections and stop to think about what the author is saying.
>
> | Mosquitoes are extremely resilient, and they are defeating our defenses. People in villages across Tanzania sleep under bed nets treated with insecticide, but lately the night-loving Anopheles mosquitoes are switching to daytime hours to get at the blood they crave. In many countries, the insects are becoming resistant to the insecticides used to eradicate them. | People are having a hard time getting rid of mosquitoes. |
> |---|---|
> | | The poison doesn't work to kill mosquitoes anymore. |

## Share

Following independent reading time, gather students in pairs to talk about their reading.

> With your partner, share what you read today and talk about any actions you took that helped you understand what you read.

## Extend the Lesson (Optional)

After assessing students' understanding, you might decide to extend the learning.

▶ Continue to support effective actions for monitoring comprehension during guided reading or independent reading. From *Prompting Guide, Part 2* (Fountas and Pinnell 2009), use prompts such as the following:

- *What is the author really trying to say?*
- *Why did the author say _____?*
- *What are some of the most important ideas?*
- *Did the writer compare (and contrast) anything?*
- *Why did the author decide to use italics (use a graphic text form, use free verse)?*
- *What does the author want you to know about?*
- *What kinds of words and language did the writer use?*

## Assessment

After you have taught the minilessons in this umbrella, observe students as they talk and write about their reading across instructional contexts: interactive read-aloud, independent reading, guided reading, shared reading, and book club. Use *The Literacy Continuum* (Fountas and Pinnell 2017) to guide the observation of students' reading and writing behaviors.

- ▶ What evidence do you have of new understandings related to monitoring comprehension of difficult texts?
  - Are students using text features and resources when reading?
  - Do they persist and stay focused when reading a difficult text?
  - Do students notice when they do not understand what they are reading and take action?
  - Do they stop and think about what an author is trying to say?
  - Do they understand the terms *difficult, techniques, persistent, focused, text features, resources, reread, take action,* and *summarize*?
- ▶ In what other ways, beyond the scope of this umbrella, are students talking about ways to monitor comprehension of difficult texts?
  - Are students engaging in conversations about difficult texts and providing support and ideas to classmates as they read text that is beyond their instructional level?

Use your observations to determine the next umbrella you will teach. You may also consult Minilessons Across the Year (pp. 59–61) for guidance.

## Reader's Notebook

When this umbrella is complete, provide a copy of the minilesson principles (see resources.fountasandpinnell.com) for students to glue in the reader's notebook (in the Minilessons section if using *Reader's Notebook: Intermediate* [Fountas and Pinnell 2011]), so they can refer to the information as needed.

## Minilessons in This Umbrella

**RML1**  Search efficiently and effectively for information on the internet.

**RML2**  Evaluate whether you have found the information you need.

**RML3**  Stay focused while reading on the internet.

**RML4**  Evaluate the credibility of the source of the information you read on the internet.

**RML5**  Evaluate whether a website presents one perspective or multiple perspectives.

## Before Teaching Umbrella 7 Minilessons

With the constant explosion of new technologies, children and teenagers spend more and more time reading in digital environments. A 2015 report by Common Sense Media (https://www.commonsensemedia.org/sites/default/files/uploads/research/census_researchreport.pdf, 21) found that eight- to twelve-year-old children spend an average of two and a half hours per day using digital media (e.g., computers, tablets, and smart phones) outside of school. Although the growth of digital technologies offers myriad benefits to children and adults alike, it also presents a number of challenges. Reading in digital environments requires a different set of skills than reading print publications. Students need teaching to show them how to effectively find the information they need, how to evaluate its relevance and credibility, and how to stay focused while doing so.

Before teaching the minilessons in this umbrella, determine how and when your students will have access to digital devices during the school day, and put structures in place for ensuring that they can use them safely. You might, for example, have students use a child-friendly search engine or give them lists of safe, trustworthy websites about different topics. Be sure to give your students numerous opportunities to use digital technology in different ways and for different purposes.

## Reading Minilesson Principle
# Search efficiently and effectively for information on the internet.

### You Will Need

- a computer or tablet with internet access (connected to a projector, if possible)
- chart paper and markers
- a list of possible questions for students to research on the internet (see Summarize and Apply)

### Academic Language / Important Vocabulary

- internet
- website
- information
- search engine
- keywords

### Continuum Connection

- Use different search strategies to increase the effectiveness of your searches including key words, search engine filters, and symbols (p. 353)
- Locate websites that fit one's needs and purpose (p. 353)

## Goal

Use different search techniques to increase the effectiveness of searches, including keywords, search engine filters, and symbols.

## Rationale

Many students understand the basics of searching for information on the internet but often find it challenging to find the information they actually need. When students are armed with a toolkit of effective searching techniques—for example, using filters and symbols, knowing how to phrase inquiries, knowing how to perform multistep searches—they are more likely to find the information they need (for resources, visit a website such as commonsense.org).

## Assess Learning

Observe students when they search for information on the internet and notice if there is evidence of new learning based on the goal of this minilesson.

- Do students know how to phrase search inquiries?
- When an initial search attempt fails to yield relevant results, are students able to revise their search strategy?
- Do they use and understand the terms *internet, website, information, search engine,* and *keywords*?

## Minilesson

Engage students in an interactive demonstration of how to search effectively for information on the internet. This lesson assumes the use of Google as a search engine.

- Display Google (or another search engine) on a projector or large screen.

    You will have many opportunities this year to search for and read information on the internet. The internet is a wonderful resource, but there is so much information that it can be hard to find exactly what you're looking for. What are some of the problems or challenges you've had?

- Make a list of students' responses on chart paper.
- Then discuss each problem one by one, inviting students to offer possible solutions. Add solutions to the chart in a second column. Offer your own search tips, as necessary.

    These are all great ideas. Now let's do a search together. I want to learn about sloths.

- Search for the word *sloths.*

    Uh oh . . . the search engine found 44 million websites about sloths! I need to think about what exactly I want to know about sloths. I recently read a great book about three-toed sloths, and I'd like to know what they eat. What should I search for?

▶ Search for *what three-toed sloths eat.*

> The first result gives me exactly the information I'm looking for. It says that three-toed sloths eat leaves, shoots, and fruit.

## Have a Try

Invite the students to talk with a partner about another search inquiry.

> Turn and talk to your partner about how to find out if more people live in Canada or Australia.

▶ If necessary, explain that some topics need to be broken down into multiple steps. Demonstrate searching for *population of Canada* (or *how many people live in Canada*) and then doing the same for Australia.

## Summarize and Apply

Summarize the learning and remind students to use these tips and techniques when searching for information on the internet.

▶ Ask students to summarize what they learned. Write the principle at the top of the chart.

▶ Have all students practice these search techniques (either individually or in pairs). Give students a list of topics/questions to search for. For example: *When and by whom was the first computer invented? What did three different kinds of dinosaurs eat? What famous people were born in the year 1990?*

## Share

Following independent reading time, gather students together in the meeting area.

> What information did you search for? What tips and tricks did you use to find the information you needed?

## Extend the Lesson (Optional)

After assessing students' understanding, you might decide to extend the learning.

▶ Share additional techniques for searching for information on the internet. For example, you might talk about Google image search, show students how to narrow down results by date, or show them how to search for results within a particular website.

### Search efficiently and effectively for information on the internet.

| Problem | Solution |
|---|---|
| I don't know what to write in the search box. | • Type only the most important keywords. |
| I can't find what I'm looking for. | • Is there another way to say what you're looking for? Use synonyms. <br> • Make your search terms more specific or less specific. |
| I don't know how to spell the thing I'm looking for. | • Don't worry about spelling. The search engine can often guess what word you mean, even if you spell it wrong! |
| I want to search for words in an exact order. | • Use quotation marks if you want to find websites that have your keywords in the same order. <br> "by the dawn's early light" |
| The results are about something completely different from what I'm looking for. | • Use a minus sign (−) in front of words you want to exclude. If you are looking for websites about Mars the planet, not the candy company, type this: <br> −candy mars |
| The websites are too hard to read—they're for adults. | • Type the word kids after your search terms to find websites that are for kids. <br> dinosaurs kids |

# RML2
### SAS.U7.RML2

**Reading Minilesson Principle**
# Evaluate whether you have found the information you need.

## Reading in Digital Environments

### You Will Need

- a computer or tablet with internet access (connected to a projector, if possible)
- chart paper and markers

### Academic Language / Important Vocabulary

- internet
- website
- information
- evaluate
- search engine

### Continuum Connection

- Locate websites that fit one's needs and purpose (p. 353)
- Identify the purpose of a website (p. 353)

## Goal

Evaluate whether you have found the appropriate information after doing a search.

## Rationale

When students are able to evaluate whether they have found the information they need after conducting an internet search, they spend more time reading relevant, interesting information and less time searching for information or going off task.

## Assess Learning

Observe students when they search for information on the internet and notice if there is evidence of new learning based on the goal of this minilesson.

- ▶ Can students choose a result that is very likely to be relevant?
- ▶ Once they have chosen a result, are they able to quickly skim the website to determine if it contains the information they need?
- ▶ Do they understand and use the terms *internet, website, information, evaluate,* and *search engine*?

## Minilesson

To help students think about the minilesson principle, engage them in a demonstration and discussion about how to evaluate search results. Here is an example.

- ▶ Display Google (or another search engine) on a projector or large screen.

   Today I'm going to search on the internet for information about dinosaurs. I want to know why dinosaurs died off, or became extinct.

- ▶ "Think aloud" choosing a result to click on. Here is an example, but note that your search results may differ.

   Google found a lot of results about this topic, and now I have to choose which one I want to click on first. I see an article about why dinosaurs became extinct. Below the title and the web address, Google shows a few sentences from the website. I really think this website will have the information I'm looking for. What did you notice about how I chose which search result to click on?

- ▶ Record students' responses on chart paper.
- ▶ Click on the search result you chose and "think aloud" to evaluate the source for relevancy.

   I want to make sure the page has the information I need, so I'm going to skim the website.

- ▶ Read aloud and point to any important words or phrases, subheadings, and text features.

This website has what I need, so I'm going to read the whole page closely. What did you notice about what I did after I chose a website to click on?

❯ Record responses on the chart.

## Have a Try

Invite the students to evaluate the relevancy of a website with a partner.

❯ Search for *turtle habitat*. Click on a search result that is *not* relevant (e.g., an online store that sells habitats for pet turtles).

Does this website have the information I need? Turn and talk to your partner.

This website clearly doesn't have the information I need, so I'm not going to waste my time reading it. I will choose another website from my search results.

## Summarize and Apply

Summarize the learning and remind students to evaluate the relevancy of search results.

What should you do if you determine that a website doesn't have what you need?

❯ Add any new insights to the chart and write the principle at the top.

If it's your turn to use the internet today, think about a topic that you would like to learn about or a question that you'd like to have answered. Evaluate whether you have found the information you need.

## Share

Following independent reading time, gather students together in the meeting area to talk about how they evaluated search results.

Who searched for information on the internet today?

How did you evaluate the websites you found?

## Extend the Lesson (Optional)

After assessing students' understanding, you might decide to extend the learning.

❯ Teach students how to recognize advertisements/sponsored links in search engine results and explain that they should generally be avoided.

---

**Evaluate whether you have found the information you need.**

**1. Decide which website to click on.**
- Check out the web address/source. (Is it a website that you've heard of before?)
- Read the titles.
- Read the short description, especially the words in bold.
- Click on the website that seems most likely to have the information you need.

**2. Evaluate whether the website you clicked on has the information you need.**
- Skim the website (look for titles, subheadings, text features, and key words and phrases).
- If it seems to have the information you need, read the website closely.
- If it doesn't, go back to your search results and choose another website.

Section 3: Strategies and Skills

# RML3

SAS.U7.RML3

**Reading Minilesson Principle**
## Stay focused while reading on the internet.

### Reading in Digital Environments

### You Will Need

▶ chart paper and markers

### Academic Language / Important Vocabulary

▶ internet
▶ website
▶ information
▶ link
▶ focused

### Continuum Connection

▶ Use a variety of digital resources such as websites, public and subscription-based databases, e-books, and apps to locate, evaluate, and analyze literary and informational content (p. 353)

## Goal

Stay focused on one thing at a time and be aware of hyperlinks that link to different content.

## Rationale

With practically an endless array of links, videos, advertisements, and other distractions, websites offer an optimal environment for distracted reading. When students are aware of this potential and know strategies for staying focused while reading on the internet, they are less likely to be easily distracted and will spend more time doing in-depth reading.

## Assess Learning

Observe students when they use the internet and notice if there is evidence of new learning based on the goal of this minilesson.

▶ Do students stay focused while reading on the internet?

▶ Can they explain what strategies they use to help them stay focused?

▶ Do they understand and use the terms *internet, website, information, link,* and *focused*?

# Minilesson

To help students think about the minilesson principle, engage them in a discussion about staying focused while reading on the internet.

▶ Use the following example to introduce the idea of distracted reading online or use your own example.

> You can learn a lot of interesting information by reading on the internet, but sometimes I and many people find it difficult to stay focused. The other day I was searching online to learn about gardening, but I ended up on a website about movies. Has something like this ever happened to any of you?
>
> One thing that helps me stay focused is to have a purpose for being on the internet. For example, one day my purpose might be to learn about whales. If I find myself getting tempted to click on a link, I'll ask myself, "Will this link help me learn more about whales?" If the answer is no, I won't click on it.
>
> What are some other techniques you might use to stay focused?

▶ Record students' responses on chart paper. Offer additional ideas of your own, as needed.

▶ Note: Some web browsers offer a "reader view" feature, which strips away all the clutter—images, advertisements, links, etc.—from a website, making it easier to focus on reading. If you have such a feature on your classroom devices, show students how to use it and add it to the chart.

## Have a Try

Invite the students to talk with a partner about how to stay focused while reading on the internet.

> Turn and talk to your partner about staying focused while reading on the internet. You might talk about problems you have had, which of these ideas you would like to try, or any other ideas you have for staying focused.

▶ After students turn and talk, invite several students to share their thinking. Add new ideas to the list.

## Summarize and Apply

Summarize the learning and remind students to stay focused while reading on the internet.

> What did you learn today about how to stay focused while reading on the internet?

▶ Write the principle at the top of the chart.

> If you read on the internet today, remember to stay focused on what you're reading. If you find it difficult to stay focused, review the chart we made and try some of these ideas.

## Share

Following independent reading time, gather students together in the meeting area to share how they stayed focused while reading on the internet.

> Who read on the internet today?

> How did you stay focused?

## Extend the Lesson (Optional)

After assessing students' understanding, you might decide to extend the learning.

▶ Display the chart in the technology area of your classroom. Revisit it from time to time and add new ideas that come up.

▶ Teach a minilesson about how to take notes while reading on the internet.

---

### Stay focused while reading on the internet.

- Always have a purpose, or reason, for using the internet. Don't click on links that won't help you with that purpose.

- Read or skim the whole website first before deciding what links to click on next.

- Use the "reader view" option on the web browser.

- Try to have only one tab open at a time.

- Take notes about what you are reading.

## RML 4
SAS.U7.RML4

**Reading Minilesson Principle**
# Evaluate the credibility of the source of the information you read on the internet.

## Reading in Digital Environments

### You Will Need

- a computer or tablet with internet access (connected to a projector, if possible)
- chart paper and markers

### Academic Language / Important Vocabulary

- internet
- website
- information
- credibility
- source

### Continuum Connection

- Determine when a website was last updated (p. 353)
- Be alert to an author's point of view, examine for bias, and validate the author's authority on the topic (p. 353)

## Goal

Evaluate the credibility of sources of the information read on the internet.

## Rationale

When you teach students how to evaluate the credibility of internet sources, they are more likely to access and acquire accurate information. Additionally, the ability to critically evaluate information will serve them in all aspects of their lives, whether they are reading print or digital publications or are engaged in discussions, and will help them develop into thoughtful and critical members of society.

## Assess Learning

Observe students when they read information on the internet and notice if there is evidence of new learning based on the goal of this minilesson.

- Do students evaluate the credibility of the websites they read on the internet?
- Can they explain how to evaluate the credibility of a website?
- Do they understand and use the terms *internet, website, information, credibility,* and *source*?

## Minilesson

To help students think about the minilesson principle, model evaluating the credibility of a website. Here is an example.

- Display Google (or another search engine). Search for *grizzly bears* (or another topic of your choice).

  I searched for grizzly bears on the internet, and I found these results. I want to make sure I choose a credible, or trustworthy, source that will give me good, accurate information about grizzly bears. Which of these results do you think are credible, or trustworthy? What makes you think that?

- If necessary, guide students to notice any results from well-known, credible publications. Click on one of them.

  What are some other things you would want to check to find out if this site is credible?

- Guide students to understand how to check the author's credentials, bibliography, and date website was last updated (if available).

## Have a Try

Invite the students to talk with a partner about how to evaluate the credibility of a website.

> What did we think about when we evaluated the credibility of a website? What are some of the questions we asked ourselves? Turn and talk to your partner.

▷ After students turn and talk, invite several pairs to share their thinking. Use their responses to make a chart.

## Summarize and Apply

Summarize the learning and remind students to evaluate the credibility of internet sources.

> What did you learn today about how to determine if a website is credible?

> Why is it important to think about whether a website is credible?

▷ Write the principle at the top of the chart.

> If it's your turn to use the internet today, think about what you would like to read about and search for information on the topic. Remember to evaluate the credibility of the websites you find.

## Share

Following independent reading time, gather students together in the meeting area to share how they evaluated the credibility of internet sources.

> Who read information on the internet today?

> How did you evaluate the credibility of the sources of information you found?

## Extend the Lesson (Optional)

After assessing students' understanding, you might decide to extend the learning.

▷ Involve students in creating and maintaining running lists of trusted internet sources about various topics. Display the lists in your classroom's technology area.

▷ Teach Umbrella 17: Reading Informational Text Like a Scientist in Section Two: Literary Analysis to further develop your students' ability to read and evaluate information with a critical eye.

---

**Evaluate the credibility of the source of the information you read on the internet.**

- Who created this website? Are they a trusted source (for example, a government agency, a university, or a major publication)? Web addresses that end in .gov or .edu are usually trustworthy.

- Who is the author? Is that person an expert on the topic?

- Does the author list the sources (a bibliography)?

- When was the website last updated? Is the information current?

---

Section 3: Strategies and Skills

**Reading Minilesson Principle**
# Evaluate whether a website presents one perspective or multiple perspectives.

## Reading in Digital Environments

### You Will Need

- a computer or tablet with internet access (connected to a projector, if possible)
- two student-friendly web articles about the same topic: one that presents a single perspective and one that presents multiple perspectives. For example, you might use an opinion piece about why zoos should be banned and another article that explains the pros and cons of zoos. Unless the articles are very short, choose in advance key sentences or paragraphs to read aloud.
- a web article about a different topic
- chart paper and markers

### Academic Language / Important Vocabulary

- internet
- website
- perspective
- evaluate

### Continuum Connection

- Determine whether a website presents one perspective or multiple perspectives (p. 353)

## Goal

Evaluate whether a website presents one perspective or multiple perspectives.

## Rationale

When students are able to evaluate whether a website presents one perspective or multiple perspectives, they are less likely to indiscriminately believe everything they read on the internet—or elsewhere. Understanding that authors' perspectives influence what information they choose to include in their writing, students begin to develop the ability to evaluate information analytically and forge their own perspectives.

## Assess Learning

Observe students when they read information on the internet and notice if there is evidence of new learning based on the goal of this minilesson.

- ▶ Can students evaluate whether a website presents one perspective or multiple perspectives?
- ▶ Can they explain how they evaluate the websites and why it is important to do so?
- ▶ Do they understand and use the terms *internet*, *website*, *perspective*, and *evaluate*?

## Minilesson

To help students think about the minilesson principle, engage them in a demonstration and discussion about how to evaluate whether a website presents one or more perspectives. Here is an example.

- ▶ Display the single-perspective web article.
- ▶ Read the title of the article and a few important passages from the article that clearly show the author's perspective on the topic.

    What is this website about?

    How an author feels about a topic is called perspective. What is the author's perspective on zoos? How can you tell?

    Does the author give any reasons why zoos might be a good thing?

    Does this website give one perspective or multiple perspectives about zoos?

- ▶ Display the multiple-perspective web article. Read the title and then a few select passages that discuss multiple perspectives.

    How do you think the author of this article feels about zoos?

    What reasons does the author give for why zoos are good?

    What reasons does he give for why zoos are bad?

    Does this website give one perspective or multiple perspectives about zoos?

## Have a Try

Invite the students to talk with a partner about another web article.

▶ Display the third web article. Read the title and a few important passages.

> Turn and talk to your partner about whether this website presents one perspective or multiple perspectives about the topic. Be sure to explain how you know.

▶ After students turn and talk, invite a few students to share their thinking.

## Summarize and Apply

Summarize the learning and remind students to evaluate whether websites present one or multiple perspectives.

> How can you tell if a website presents only one perspective on a topic or an issue?

> How can you tell if a website presents multiple perspectives?

▶ Use students' responses to make a chart. Write the principle at the top.

> If it's your turn to use the internet today, think about a topic or an issue that you would like to read about. Search for websites about that topic and remember to evaluate whether each website you read presents one or multiple perspectives.

## Share

Following independent reading time, gather students together in the meeting area to discuss how they evaluated websites.

> Who read on the internet today?

> How did you evaluate whether a website presented one perspective or multiple perspectives?

## Extend the Lesson (Optional)

After assessing students' understanding, you might decide to extend the learning.

▶ Explicitly discuss how an author's perspective on a topic influences how the author writes about it and what information she chooses to include and omit.

▶ Discuss why it is important to read multiple perspectives about a topic or an issue.

---

**Evaluate whether a website presents one perspective or multiple perspectives.**

| One Perspective | Multiple Perspectives |
|---|---|
| • It is obvious how the author feels about the topic. | • The title tells you what the website is about, but it doesn't tell you how the author feels. |
| • The author tells you that something is either GOOD or BAD. | • You don't necessarily know how the author personally feels about the topic. |
| • The author only gives reasons and evidence for ONE side of an issue. | • The author gives reasons and evidence for BOTH sides of an issue. |
| • The title tells you how the author feels. | |

Section 3: Strategies and Skills

## Assessment

After you have taught the minilessons in this umbrella, observe students as they use the internet. Use *The Literacy Continuum* (Fountas and Pinnell 2017) to guide the observation of students' reading and writing behaviors across instructional contexts.

▶ What evidence do you have of new understandings related to reading in digital environments?

- Are students able to use search engines effectively? If their initial search fails to yield relevant results, are they able to revise their search strategy?

- Are they able to evaluate whether they have found the information they need?

- Do they stay focused while reading on the internet?

- Do they evaluate the credibility of internet resources?

- Can they evaluate whether a website presents one perspective or multiple perspectives?

- Do they understand and use terms such as *internet, information, source, website, link, search engine, evaluate,* and *perspective*?

Use your observations to determine the next umbrella you will teach. You may also consult Minilessons Across the Year (pp. 59–61) for guidance.

## Link to Writing

After teaching the minilessons in this umbrella, help students link the new learning to their own writing:

▶ If you have your students conduct online research for writing projects, remind them to use the skills they learned from this umbrella. Teach them how to record the sources they use to avoid plagiarizing.

## Reader's Notebook

When this umbrella is complete, provide a copy of the minilesson principles (see resources.fountasandpinnell.com) for students to glue in the reader's notebook (in the Minilessons section if using *Reader's Notebook: Intermediate* [Fountas and Pinnell 2011]), so they can refer to the information as needed.

# Section 4 | Writing About Reading

Throughout the year, students will respond to what they read in a reader's notebook. These lessons help students use this important tool for independent literacy learning and make it possible for them to become aware of their own productivity, in the process building self-efficacy. All opportunities for writing about reading support the students in thinking about texts and articulating their understandings.

## Minilessons in This Umbrella

**RML1**   Collect your thinking in your reader's notebook.

**RML2**   Record each book you read on your reading list.

**RML3**   Keep a tally of the kinds of books you read.

**RML4**   Follow the guidelines to help you do your best reading and writing work.

## Before Teaching Umbrella 1 Minilessons

The minilessons in this umbrella are based on and intended to introduce *Reader's Notebook: Intermediate* (Fountas and Pinnell 2011); however, if you do not have it, a plain notebook can be used instead. The goal of a reader's notebook is for students to have a consistent place to collect their thinking about their reading (see pp. 50–51 for more on using a reader's notebook).

Students will do most of their writing about reading in a reader's notebook during independent reading. To establish routines for that time, teach the first minilesson in Umbrella 2: Getting Started with Independent Reading, found in Section One: Management. For this umbrella, use the following books from the *Fountas & Pinnell Classroom™ Independent Reading Collection* or any other books from your classroom library.

### Independent Reading Collection

*Chocolate Fever* by Robert Kimmel Smith

*Coyotes* by Tammy Gagne

**Independent Reading**

**Reader's Notebook**

Section 4: Writing About Reading

# RML1

**WAR.U1.RML1**

**Reading Minilesson Principle**
## Collect your thinking in your reader's notebook.

## Introducing a Reader's Notebook

### You Will Need

- a reader's notebook for each student (if using a plain notebook, set up tabbed sections for Reading List, Choosing Books, Minilessons, and Writing About Reading)
- chart paper prepared with a four-column chart
- markers

### Academic Language / Important Vocabulary

- reader's notebook
- reading list
- minilessons
- writing about reading

### Continuum Connection

- Form and express opinions about a text in writing and support those opinions with rationales and evidence (p. 194)
- Form and express opinions about a text and/or an author or illustrator in writing and support those opinions with rationales and evidence (p. 197)
- Compose notes, lists, letters, or statements to remember important information about a text (pp. 193, 196)

## Goal

Understand that a reader's notebook is a special place to collect thinking about books that have been read.

## Rationale

Students need numerous opportunities to respond to reading in different forms. A reader's notebook is a special place for them to keep a record of their reading lives and to share their thinking about books they have read.

## Assess Learning

Observe students when they use a reader's notebook and notice if there is evidence of new learning based on the goal of this minilesson.

- Do students understand the purpose of a reader's notebook and of each section?
- Do they understand the terms *reader's notebook*, *reading list*, *minilessons*, and *writing about reading*?

## Minilesson

Give each student a reader's notebook and provide a lesson that introduces students to the contents and purpose of the notebook. Here is an example.

> You each have your own reader's notebook, which you will use throughout the school year. Take a couple of minutes to look through it and see what you notice.
>
> What do you notice about your reader's notebook? What do you think you will do with it?

- Draw students' attention to the tabs at the top of the reader's notebook.

> What do you notice at the top of your reader's notebook?
>
> The reader's notebook has four sections, and you can use the tabs to find each section. Open your notebook to the yellow tab that says Reading List.
>
> What do you think you will write in this section?
>
> What information will you record about each book?

- Record students' responses in the first column of the chart, under the heading *Reading List*.

- Continue in a similar manner with the three remaining sections and headings (*Choosing Books*, *Minilessons*, and *Writing About Reading*). Explain that students will glue a copy of the minilesson principles in the Minilessons section so that they will have them to use as a reference.

▶ You might also wish to have students look at the different ways they will write about their reading on the Forms for Writing About Reading page and the Suggestions for Writing About Reading page in the Writing About Reading section.

## Have a Try

Invite the students to talk with a partner about the reader's notebook.

> Turn and talk to your partner about what you will do in your reader's notebook.

▶ After students turn and talk, invite a few students to share their thinking. Confirm their understanding of the reader's notebook and clear up any misconceptions that may have arisen.

## Summarize and Apply

Summarize the learning and remind students to collect their thinking about their reading in a reader's notebook.

> Today you got to know the different parts of your reader's notebook. Why do you think it's a good idea to have and use a reader's notebook?

▶ Write the principle at the top of the chart.

> After you read today, write a few sentences to share your thoughts about the book you read in the Writing About Reading section of your reader's notebook. Be ready to talk about what you wrote when we come back together.

## Share

Following independent reading time, gather students together in the meeting area to talk in pairs about what they wrote.

> Turn and talk to your partner about what you wrote in your reader's notebook today.

## Extend the Lesson (Optional)

After assessing students' understanding, you might decide to extend the learning.

▶ Encourage students to personalize the cover of their reader's notebook.

▶ Have students establish a place to store their reader's notebooks in their personal boxes (see MGT.U2.RML3).

### Collect your thinking in your reader's notebook.

| Reading List | Choosing Books | Minilessons | Writing About Reading |
|---|---|---|---|
| A list of books you have read (title, author, genre, etc.) | A list of books you want to read (title and author) | The minilesson principles | Your thinking about books you have read (letters, summaries, lists, etc.) |

**Reading Minilesson Principle**

## Record each book you read on your reading list.

### Introducing a Reader's Notebook

#### You Will Need

- two books, such as the following from *Independent Reading Collection*:
  - *Chocolate Fever* by Robert Kimmel Smith
  - *Coyotes* by Tammy Gagne
- chart paper prepared to look like the reading list in *Reader's Notebook: Intermediate* [Fountas and Pinnell 2011]
- markers
- document camera [optional]
- a reader's notebook for each student

#### Academic Language / Important Vocabulary

- reader's notebook
- reading list
- title
- author
- genre

#### Continuum Connection

- Record in Reader's Notebook the titles, authors, illustrators, genre of texts read, and the dates read [pp. 193, 196]

### Goal

Learn to record the book title, author, genre or form, the level of challenge the book provided, and the date it was completed in the reader's notebook.

### Rationale

Recording the books they have read on a reading list helps students remember which books they have read and enjoyed. It also helps them remember which books they found difficult or did not enjoy, and those examples help them make better reading choices and develop self-awareness as readers.

### Assess Learning

Observe students when they use a reader's notebook and notice if there is evidence of new learning based on the goal of this minilesson.

- Do students understand the purpose of the reading list and how to use it?
- Do they record the title, author, genre, date completed, and difficulty level of books they have read?
- Do they use the terms *reader's notebook*, *reading list*, *title*, *author*, and *genre*?

## Minilesson

To help students think about the minilesson principle, demonstrate how to fill in the reading list in a reader's notebook. Here is an example.

- Direct students to find the yellow tab that says Reading List. Then tell them to turn to the white page titled Reading List, and give them a couple of minutes to look over the page.

  What will you need to write on this page in your reader's notebook?

- Display the prepared chart or project the page. Hold up *Chocolate Fever*.

  If I was going to read this book today, how would I record it on my reading list?

  I will start by writing the title and author of the book in the columns that say *Title* and *Author*.

- Write the title and author. Then write the numeral *1* in the first column.

  Why do you think I wrote the number one here?

  What should I write on my list when I've finished reading it?

- Discuss the *Genre Code*, *Date Completed*, and *E, JR, D* columns on the chart and demonstrate filling them in. Direct students' attention to the Genres at a Glance page on the back of the yellow tab. Explain that poetry is a form of writing that may have the characteristics of any of the genres.

What do you notice about this page?

When you've finished reading your book, think about the genre of your book and try to find it on this list. Write the genre code on your reading list.

## Have a Try

Invite the students to talk with a partner about how to record books.

▶ Display the cover of *Coyotes*.

If I decided to read this book next, how would I list it on my reading list? Turn and talk to your partner about that.

▶ After students turn and talk, invite a few students to share their thinking. With students' input, write the title, author, and number on the chart.

## Summarize and Apply

Summarize the learning and remind students to list the books they read on the reading list.

Today you learned how to record each book you read on your reading list. Why do you think it's a good idea to keep a list of the books you read?

▶ Write the principle at the top of the chart.

When you read today, remember to write the title and author of the book you read on your reading list. When you finish reading it, fill in the rest of the information. Bring your reading list to share when we come back together.

## Share

Following independent reading time, gather students together in the meeting area to share their reading lists.

Turn and talk to your partner about the book you read today. Show what you wrote about the book on your reading list.

## Extend the Lesson (Optional)

After assessing students' understanding, you might decide to extend the learning.

▶ Invite students to look at their reading lists and notice whether they are reading all one type of book or whether they are reading a variety of genres.

### Record each book you read on your reading list.

| # | Title | Author | Genre Code | Date Completed | E, JR, D |
|---|-------|--------|-----------|----------------|----------|
| 1 | Chocolate Fever | Robert Kimmel Smith | F | 10/26 | JR |
| 2 | Coyotes | Tammy Gagne | | | |

**Reading Minilesson Principle**
# Keep a tally of the kinds of books you read.

## Introducing a Reader's Notebook

### You Will Need

▶ six fantasy books

▶ two poetry books

▶ chart paper prepared with the Reading Requirements page from *Reader's Notebook: Intermediate* (Fountas and Pinnell 2011), filled in with the specific reading requirements you have chosen for your students (the requirements given in this lesson are merely intended as examples)

▶ markers

▶ document camera (optional)

### Academic Language / Important Vocabulary

▶ reader's notebook

▶ genre

▶ requirement

▶ fantasy

▶ poetry

### Continuum Connection

▶ Record in Reader's Notebook the titles, authors, illustrators, genre of texts read, and the dates read. (p. 186, 189)

## Goal

Keep track of the number of books read in a particular genre or form (poetry).

## Rationale

When students read a certain number of books from each genre (and keep track of their progress), they become well-rounded readers. Reading books outside of their preferred genres allows students to step outside their comfort zone and expand their reading interests and literary knowledge.

## Assess Learning

Observe students when they use a reader's notebook and notice if there is evidence of new learning based on the goal of this minilesson.

▶ Do students keep a tally in their reader's notebook of the genres of the books they have read?

▶ Do they use the terms *reader's notebook, genre, requirement, fantasy,* and *poetry*?

## Minilesson

To help students think about the minilesson principle, demonstrate how to tally books on the *Reading Requirements* page of a reader's notebook (adjust to fit your specific reading requirements). Here is an example.

▶ Display the prepared chart or project the Reading Requirements page.

> The title of the chart is *Reading Requirements*. What is a requirement? A requirement is something that you're expected to do. Your reading requirement this year is to read at least forty books.

▶ Point to the numbers in the *Requirement* column. As you review the form, you may need to quickly define some of the genres.

> What do you think these numbers mean?

> You will be expected to read a certain number of books in each genre.

▶ Point to the *Tally* column.

> What do you think you'll write in this column?

> You will keep track of how many books you have read in each genre by keeping a tally. I'll show you how.

▶ Point to a pile of six fantasy books.

> Here are six fantasy books that I plan to read this year. After I read the first one, I will write one mark here.

❯ Demonstrate tallying the books on the chart, pausing after making the first four marks.

> After I read the fifth book, I'll make a mark that goes through the first four marks. After I read the sixth book, I will make a new mark that is separate from the first five. When I have read a lot of fantasy books, I will be able to count them easily by counting by fives.

## Have a Try

Invite the students to talk with a partner about how to tally books.

❯ Display two poetry books.

> Turn and talk to your partner about how to tally these books on the Reading Requirements page.

❯ After time for discussion, invite a volunteer to share his thinking. Add two tally marks to the Poetry row.

## Summarize and Apply

Summarize the learning and remind students to tally the kinds of books they read.

> This year you will read books from many different genres, but most of the books you read can be from any genre you like.

> During independent reading today, read any book you like. When you finish reading it, make a tally mark on the Reading Requirements page next to the genre of your book.

## Share

Following independent reading time, gather students together in the meeting area to share their Reading Requirements pages.

> Show your partner how you recorded the genre of the book you read.

## Extend the Lesson (Optional)

After assessing students' understanding, you might decide to extend the learning.

❯ You may want to talk with each student individually about their personal reading requirements.

❯ Review students' tallies regularly to make sure they are on track to meet the requirements and are reading a variety of books.

### Reading Requirements
### Total Books: 40

| Requirement | Genre or Type | Tally |
|---|---|---|
| 5 | (RF) Realistic Fiction | |
| | (HF) Historical Fiction | |
| 5 | (TL) Traditional Literature | |
| 5 | (F) Fantasy | ‖‖ / |
| | (SF) Science Fiction | |
| 3 | (B) Biography/Autobiography | |
| | (M) Memoir | |
| 5 | (I) Informational | |
| 1 | (H) Hybrid | |
| 1 | (P) Poetry | // |

Section 4: Writing About Reading

## Introducing a Reader's Notebook

### You Will Need

- chart paper prepared with the heading *Guidelines*
- markers

### Academic Language / Important Vocabulary

- reader's notebook
- guidelines

### Continuum Connection

- Listen with attention during instruction, and respond with statements and questions [p. 337]

## Goal

Learn and/or develop the guidelines for working together in the classroom.

## Rationale

When you teach students to follow guidelines, they are better equipped to do their best work. You might have students review the established guidelines in *Reader's Notebook: Intermediate* [Fountas and Pinnell 2011] or construct their own. When students play an active role in developing guidelines, they take ownership of them.

## Assess Learning

Observe students during literacy work and notice if there is evidence of new learning based on the goal of this minilesson.

- ▶ Do students follow the guidelines established during this minilesson?
- ▶ Do they use and understand the terms *reader's notebook* and *guidelines*?

## Minilesson

If you have *Reader's Notebook: Intermediate*, you can read and discuss the guidelines printed on the inside front cover, or you may choose to develop guidelines with your students, as demonstrated in the lesson below. You may simply add any additional guidelines to the printed ones. If you construct the guidelines with your students, provide a copy of the guidelines for them to glue into their reader's notebooks after the lesson.

▶ Divide students into small groups. Display the prepared chart.

> You have been learning about what to do during independent reading and how to use a reader's notebook. Today we're going to make a list of guidelines for that time. What do you think guidelines are?

> A guideline is a rule or suggestion about how something should be done. Talk with your group about what things you think you should all agree to do so that you all can do your best work.

▶ After time for discussion, invite each group to share their ideas. Record their responses on chart paper. If needed, prompt students with questions such as the following:

- *What should you do during independent reading?*
- *What voice level should you use during independent reading?*
- *What voice level should you use when you are working with a teacher?*
- *What should you do if you give a book a good chance but you're still not enjoying it?*
- *What should you do each time you start a new book?*

## Have a Try

Invite the students to talk with a partner about the guidelines.

> Turn and talk to your partner about anything else you think we should add to our guidelines.

▶ After students turn and talk, ask several students to share their thinking. Add any new guidelines to the list, if appropriate.

## Summarize and Apply

Summarize the learning and remind students to follow the guidelines for literacy work.

> Today we made a list of guidelines for reading and writing work. Why do you think it's important to follow these guidelines?

▶ Direct students to look at the guidelines inside the front cover of *Reader's Notebook: Intermediate* or provide copies for students to glue into a plain notebook.

> During independent reading, be sure to follow the guidelines we created together. If you think of anything else that you'd like to add to the guidelines, bring your ideas to share when we come back together.

## Share

Following independent reading time, gather students together in the meeting area to talk about the guidelines.

> How did the guidelines help you do your best work today?

> Does anyone have anything to add to our guidelines?

## Extend the Lesson (Optional)

After assessing students' understanding, you might decide to extend the learning.

▶ Revisit the list of guidelines with your students from time to time to see how they are working and to decide whether they need to be revised.

### Guidelines

1. Read a book or write down your thoughts about your reading.

2. Work silently so that you and your classmates can do your best work.

3. Use a level 1 voice when conferring with a teacher.

4. Select books that you think you'll enjoy.

5. Abandon books that you don't enjoy after you've given them a good chance.

6. Record each book you read on your reading list.

7. Always do your best work.

## Assessment

After you have taught the minilessons in this umbrella, observe students as they talk and write about their reading across instructional contexts: interactive read-aloud, independent reading, guided reading, shared reading, and book club. Use *The Literacy Continuum* (Fountas and Pinnell 2017) to guide the observation of students' reading and writing behaviors.

▶ What evidence do you have of new understandings related to using a reader's notebook?

- Do students understand the purpose of a reader's notebook?
- Do they understand the purpose of each section?
- Do they record the title, author, date completed, genre, and difficulty level of the books they read on their reading list?
- How well do they keep a tally of the kinds of books they have read?
- Do they follow the guidelines for working during independent reading?
- Do they use vocabulary such as *reader's notebook*, *genre*, and *guidelines*?

▶ What other parts of the reader's notebook might you have the students start using based on your observations?

Use your observations to determine the next umbrella you will teach. You may also consult Minilessons Across the Year (pp. 59–61) for guidance.

## Reader's Notebook

When this umbrella is complete, provide a copy of the minilesson principles (see resources.fountasandpinnell.com) for students to glue in the reader's notebook (in the Minilessons section if using *Reader's Notebook: Intermediate* [Fountas and Pinnell 2011]), so they can refer to the information as needed.

**Reader's Notebook**

## Minilessons in This Umbrella

**RML1**   Make a list of the books you want to read.

**RML2**   Keep a tally of the kinds of writing about reading that you use in your notebook.

**RML3**   Put your minilesson notes in your reader's notebook so you can refer to information you need.

## Before Teaching Umbrella 2 Minilessons

Before teaching the minilessons in this umbrella, teach the minilessons in Umbrella 1: Introducing a Reader's Notebook to introduce your students to the purpose and structure of *Reader's Notebook: Intermediate* (Fountas and Pinnell 2011). If you do not have it, a plain notebook can be used instead (see pp. 50–51 for more on using a reader's notebook). It would also be helpful to have taught the minilessons in Umbrella 3: Living a Reading Life in Section One: Management. The minilessons in this umbrella do not have to be taught consecutively; instead, each one be taught when it is relevant to the work students are doing in the classroom.

Before students begin to use a reader's notebook, they should have read and discussed a variety of high-quality books and participated in several writing lessons incorporating shared writing.

As you read aloud and discuss books together, help students

- talk about books they want to read and share their reasons for their choices, and

- write about their reading in different ways.

## Reading Minilesson Principle
# Make a list of the books you want to read.

## You Will Need

- a reader's notebook for each student (if using a plain reader's notebook, create copies of a Books to Read chart and a Tips for Choosing Books page)

- chart paper prepared to look like the Books to Read page from *Reader's Notebook: Intermediate* (Fountas and Pinnell 2011)

- a few books from your classroom library that your students might enjoy reading independently

- markers

## Academic Language / Important Vocabulary

- reader's notebook
- title
- author
- list

### Continuum Connection

- Record the titles, authors, and genres of books to recommend (p. 193)

## Goal

Create and maintain a list of books to read in the future.

## Rationale

When students keep a list of the books they would like to read, they are better able to make good book choices, and they develop an identity as a reader in a community of readers where books are recommended and shared.

## Assess Learning

Observe students when they talk and write about books they want to read and notice if there is evidence of new learning based on the goal of this minilesson.

- ▶ Do students add books to their Books to Read list?

- ▶ Do they use vocabulary such as *reader's notebook, title, author,* and *list*?

## Minilesson

To help students think about the minilesson principle, discuss ways to choose books and how to keep a list of books to read in a reader's notebook. Here is an example.

- ▶ Direct students to turn to the Tips for Choosing Books page, located on the front of the orange tab in *Reader's Notebook*. Have them read the page silently.

    What is this page about?

    Which of the things on this list do you already do?

    Which of these things would you like to try in the future?

- ▶ Tell students to turn to the Books to Read chart on the next page.

    What do you notice about this page? What do you think you'll write on it?

    You will make a list of books that you want to read on this page. Can anyone think of a book that you would like to read?

    You will be learning about many different ways to learn about great books to read.

- ▶ Invite a volunteer to name a book that he would like to read.

    _____ wants to read _____. How could he record this book on his Books to Read list? What should he write and where?

- ▶ Demonstrate writing the title and author on the prepared chart.

    What should he do when he has finished reading the book?

- ▶ Demonstrate adding a checkmark to the Check When Completed column.

## Have a Try

Invite the students to start their own Books to Read lists.

> I'm going to tell you about a few books from our classroom library. As you listen to my book talks, think about whether you would like to read each book.

▸ Give a brief book talk (see MGT.U3.RML2) about a few books from your classroom library. Allow time between talks for students to add the books to their Books to Read list, if they would like to.

> If there is a different book that you would like to read, feel free to add it to your list now.

## Summarize and Apply

Summarize the learning and remind students to add books they would like to read to their Books to Read list.

> Why is it a good idea to keep a list of books that you want to read?

> When you read today, you may want to start reading one of the books on your list. You can also add books to the list whenever you learn about one you would like to read. Bring your list to share when we come back together.

## Share

Following independent reading time, gather students together in the meeting area to discuss their Books to Read lists.

> Did anyone read one of the books on your Books to Read list or add a new book to your list?

> What book did you read or add to your list?

## Extend the Lesson (Optional)

After assessing students' understanding, you might decide to extend the learning.

▸ Refer to students' Books to Read lists during individual reading conferences to help them plan what to read next.

▸ Remind students of ways they can find out about good books to read (see MGT. U3.RML1).

### Books to Read

| Title | Author | Check When Completed |
|---|---|---|
| The Magic Half | Annie Barrows | ✓ |
| | | |
| | | |
| | | |

# Reading Minilesson Principle
# Keep a tally of the kinds of writing about reading that you use in your notebook.

## You Will Need

- chart paper resembling the Forms for Writing About Reading page in *Reader's Notebook: Intermediate* (Fountas and Pinnell 2011)
- markers
- document camera (optional)

## Academic Language / Important Vocabulary

- reader's notebook
- writing about reading
- tally

## Goal

Learn how to keep a tally of the different forms of writing about reading.

## Rationale

When you teach students to keep a tally of the kinds of writing they use, they are more likely to write about their reading in a wide variety of ways. It would be best to help students do this after each form of writing is introduced (see Section Four: Writing About Reading).

## Assess Learning

Observe students when they keep track of the kinds of writing they use and notice if there is evidence of new learning based on the goal of this minilesson.

- ▶ Do students keep a tally of the kinds of writing about reading they use?
- ▶ Do they understand how to make and count tally marks?
- ▶ Do they use and understand the terms *reader's notebook*, *writing about reading*, and *tally*?

## Minilesson

To help students think about the minilesson principle, demonstrate how to tally forms of writing in a reader's notebook. Discuss only the forms of writing that you have already introduced to your students. Here is an example.

- ▶ Display the prepared chart paper or project the Forms for Writing About Reading page from *Reader's Notebook: Intermediate*.

   What do you notice about this page in the reader's notebook? What do you think you will write on this page?

   This page lists some of the different ways that you can write about reading. Which of these kinds of writing have you used before?

- ▶ Based on students' responses, point to one kind of writing (e.g., book recommendation) on the list and read its definition.

   What do you notice about the third column in this chart? What does it tell you?

   This column gives the definition of each type of writing. The definition describes each type of writing.

- ▶ Point to the first column and read the heading, *Tally*.

   What do you think you will write in this column?

   In this column, keep a tally of the different kinds of writing you use. Who remembers how to keep a tally?

## Have a Try

Invite the students to enter tally marks for the kinds of writing they have used.

> If you have already used any of these types of writing about reading in your reader's notebook this year, add a tally mark on your list.

▶ Invite a volunteer to demonstrate how to add a tally mark next to one kind of writing about reading. Explain that after making four marks, students should draw a slash through the marks to make five.

## Summarize and Apply

Summarize the learning and remind students to keep track of the kinds of writing they use.

> What did you learn how to do today in your reader's notebook?

▶ Write the principle at the top of the chart.

> If you write about your reading today, remember to make a tally mark next to the kind of writing that you use.

## Share

Following independent reading time, gather students together in the meeting area to talk about their writing about reading.

> Who wrote about your reading today?
>
> What kind of writing did you use?
>
> How did you keep track of it in your reader's notebook?

## Extend the Lesson (Optional)

After assessing students' understanding, you might decide to extend the learning.

▶ You will need to decide which forms of writing about reading are appropriate for your students. After teaching each new form of writing, read aloud its definition on the Forms for Writing About Reading page and remind students to keep track of the kinds of writing they use.

### Forms for Writing About Reading

| Tally | Kind of Writing | Definition |
|---|---|---|
| | Letter to your teacher (or another reader) | a letter to share your thinking about your reading with another reader who writes back to you |
| | Short Write | an open-ended response or focused response to a specific prompt or question |
| | Notes | words, phrases, or a quick drawing to help you remember the book |
| | List | words, phrases, or sentences written one under the other |
| I | Book Recommendation | writing that gives another reader some information and advice on a book |

**Reading Minilesson Principle**

# Put your minilesson notes in your reader's notebook so you can refer to information you need.

Using a Reader's Notebook

## You Will Need

- a reader's notebook for each student and yourself
- chart paper prepared with principles from a previously taught minilesson plus added notes or a copy of the principles from the online resources plus added notes
- glue sticks
- markers
- To download the following from online resources, visit **resources.fountasandpinnell.com**: minilesson principles from a previously taught umbrella (a copy for each student)

## Academic Language / Important Vocabulary

- minilesson
- principle
- information

## Goal

Keep minilesson notes in a reader's notebook to refer to as needed.

## Rationale

*Reader's Notebook: Intermediate* (Fountas and Pinnell 2011) includes a section for information from minilessons. When students keep information from previous minilessons for reference, they are better able to remember what they learned and to use and build on that knowledge. At the end of each umbrella, download the principles list for students to glue in the Minilessons section. Alternatively, you may want to have students write the principles and a few examples themselves instead of gluing in copies. You could also provide small copies of charts instead of or in addition to the principles list. We recommend that you also display key reference charts on the walls of the classroom for student reference.

## Assess Learning

Observe students when they use the Minilessons section of the reader's notebook and notice if there is evidence of new learning based on the goal of this minilesson.

- Do students neatly glue or write minilesson principles into the Minilessons section of the reader's notebook?
- Do they understand the terms *minilesson*, *principle*, and *information*?

## Minilesson

Teach students how to glue or write minilesson principles into the reader's notebook and engage them in a discussion about how and when they might use them. Here is an example.

- Direct students to turn to the Minilessons section (blue tab) of the reader's notebook. Read the page aloud.

  When we have minilessons, we usually make a chart together. Often I write the minilesson principle at the top. The principle tells the important understanding you need to learn. To help you remember what you have learned, after several minilessons I will give you a copy of the minilesson principles to glue or write into your reader's notebook.

- Model how to glue (or write) the list of principles onto the first blank page of the Minilessons section in the reader's notebook.

  What do you notice about the notes I wrote about the minilesson principles?

  Because you will put all the principles in the same section, you will always know where to find them.

## Have a Try

Invite the students to talk with a partner about when and why they might use their notes from previous minilessons.

> The blue tab in the reader's notebook says, "You can look back at what you learned when you need to." When might you need to look back at the information from a minilesson? Turn and talk about when you might do this and why.

▶ After students turn and talk, invite several to share.

## Summarize and Apply

Summarize the learning and remind students to glue or write the minilesson principles in the Minilessons section.

> Let's make a chart to help you remember what you learned in this minilesson.

▶ After writing the chart with students' input, write the principle at the top.

▶ Provide each student with a copy of the principles discussed earlier in the lesson.

> Glue this list of principles into the Minilessons section of your reader's notebook during independent reading. Reread the principles and think about how they might help you when you're reading today. Then read a book!

## Share

Following independent reading time, gather students together in the meeting area to talk about the minilesson principles.

> Did anyone find the minilesson principles helpful today? How were they helpful?

## Extend the Lesson (Optional)

After assessing students' understanding, you might decide to extend the learning.

▶ A note at the end of each umbrella will remind you to download a copy of the principles for students to glue into the Minilessons section of the reader's notebook. At that time, you might want to review what students have learned about the concepts and ask them to make a few notes to remind them of what they have learned.

---

**Using a Reader's Notebook**

Make a list of the books you want to read.

Keep a tally of the kinds of writing about reading that you use in your notebook.

Look in my writing folder to check.

Put your minilesson notes in your reader's notebook so you can refer to information you need.

Make a few notes to remember what I learned.

---

**Put your minilesson notes in your reader's notebook so you can refer to information you need.**

- Glue or write the minilesson principles in the Minilessons section of your reader's notebook.

- If you want to, write some examples or notes to help you better remember the information.

- Reread the principles and notes when you need to.

## Assessment

After you have taught the minilessons in this umbrella, observe students as they talk and write about their reading across instructional contexts: interactive read-aloud, independent reading, guided reading, shared reading, and book club. Use *The Literacy Continuum* (Fountas and Pinnell 2017) to guide the observation of students' reading and writing behaviors.

▶ What evidence do you have of new understandings related to using the reader's notebook?

- Are students continuing to add to the list of books they want to read?
- Do they keep a tally of the forms of writing about reading they have done?
- Do they write or glue minilesson principles into their reader's notebooks and refer to them when appropriate?
- Do they use the terms *title, author, list, minilesson,* and *tally*?

▶ Based on your observations, what are other ways you might have your students write about reading in a reader's notebook?

Use your observations to determine the next umbrella you will teach. You may also consult Minilessons Across the Year (pp. 59–61) for guidance.

## Reader's Notebook

When this umbrella is complete, provide a copy of the minilesson principles (see resources.fountasandpinnell.com) for students to glue in the reader's notebook (in the Minilessons section if using *Reader's Notebook: Intermediate* [Fountas and Pinnell 2011]), so they can refer to the information as needed.

## Minilessons in This Umbrella

**RML1**  Share your thinking about your reading in a letter.

**RML2**  Provide evidence for your thinking in your letter.

**RML3**  Respond to the teacher's questions to you when you write your next letter.

**RML4**  Make your letter about reading interesting to read.

**RML5**  Know the qualities of a strong letter about your reading.

## Before Teaching Umbrella 3 Minilessons

Writing letters about reading is an authentic way for students to discuss texts with another reader. We suggest having each student write one letter about reading each week. We believe it is important that their writing is read by you and that you provide a response. You will need to develop a management system for receiving and responding to the letters. You might have all students turn in a reader's notebook on one day each week (e.g., Friday), or we suggest that you stagger the due dates for four or five students each day so you can provide regular responses to their thinking without being overwhelmed by a large stack. If responding every week is difficult, consider responding every other week (see pp. 51–53 for more about letters about reading and the reading-writing connection).

To teach the minilessons in this umbrella, we suggest having everyone write a letter so they can apply these understandings as the minilessons are taught. Sometimes students will start a new letter; other times they will revise a letter in progress.

To teach the minilessons in this umbrella, use letters that you have written as a model. For mentor texts, use the books from the *Fountas & Pinnell Classroom™ Interactive Read-Aloud Collection* text sets listed below or choose books from your own classroom library.

**Empathy**

*The Boy and the Whale*
  by Mordicai Gerstein

*A Symphony of Whales*
  by Steve Schuch

**Figuring Out Who You Are**

*A Boy and a Jaguar*
  by Alan Rabinowitz

**Friendship**

*The Dunderheads*
  by Paul Fleischman

*The Other Side*
  by Jacqueline Woodson

*Better Than You* by Trudy Ludwig

As you read aloud and enjoy these texts together, help students think, talk, and express opinions about texts.

**Empathy**

**Figuring Out
Who You Are**

**Friendship**

**Reader's Notebook**

Section 4: Writing About Reading

**Reading Minilesson Principle**
## Share your thinking about your reading in a letter.

## Writing Letters to Share Thinking About Books

### You Will Need

▸ chart paper prepared with a letter about a book that you recently read aloud to your students, such as one of the following:

- *The Boy and the Whale* by Mordicai Gerstein, from Text Set: Empathy

- *A Boy and a Jaguar* by Alan Rabinowitz, from Text Set: Figuring Out Who You Are

▸ chart paper and markers

▸ highlighters

▸ a reader's notebook for each student

### Academic Language / Important Vocabulary

▸ opinion

▸ genre

▸ summary

▸ message

### Continuum Connection

▸ Compose notes, lists, letters, or statements to remember important information about a text (pp. 193, 196)

▸ Provide details that are important to understanding the story problem, the setting, and the characters (p. 193)

### Goal

Understand some of the different ways to share thinking about books in a letter.

### Rationale

Students have been sharing their thinking about books verbally. In this minilesson, they will learn how to share their thoughts about their reading by writing a letter.

### Assess Learning

Assess students' letters. Notice if there is evidence of new learning based on the goal of this minilesson.

▸ Can students share their thinking about their reading in their letters?

▸ Do their letters contain evidence of various kinds of thinking about reading?

▸ Are they using vocabulary in their letters such as *opinion*, *genre*, *summary*, and *message*?

## Minilesson

To help students think about the minilesson principle, use a letter as a model to help students learn about the kind of thinking they can share in their letters. Here is an example.

▸ Display the prepared letter and read it aloud.

 **What do you notice about what I have written?**

▸ As needed, prompt students with questions, such as the following:

- *What form of writing is this?*

- *What is my letter mainly about?*

- *What types of things did I write about the book* The Boy and the Whale?

▸ Record students' responses on chart paper (generalizing them if they are overly specific). Highlight the relevant parts of the letter.

## Have a Try

Invite the students to talk with a partner about what they might include in a letter about their reading.

> Turn and talk about what you could write in a letter about *A Boy and a Jaguar*.

▶ Ask students to share ideas they talked about. Explain that what they talked about they can write about in their letters. Relate their ideas to the chart of writing ideas.

## Summarize and Apply

Summarize the learning and remind students to share their thinking about books in their letters.

> What is a way to share your thinking about reading?

▶ Write the principle at the top of the chart.

> Today, start writing a letter about *A Boy and a Jaguar* in your reader's notebook. You have already talked about the book with a partner, and we have a chart of ideas you might include in your writing. Use my letter as a model. Bring your reader's notebook when we come back together.

## Share

Following independent reading time, gather students together in the meeting area to talk about their letters.

> Who would like to read their letter about *A Boy and a Jaguar* aloud? It's okay if you are not finished writing. You will have a chance to work on your letter again later.

## Extend the Lesson (Optional)

After assessing students' understanding, you might decide to extend the learning.

▶ If your students need more support, use shared writing to compose a letter about a book with which all students are familiar.

▶ There is a list of starter ideas in the Writing About Reading section of *Reader's Notebook: Intermediate* (Fountas and Pinnell 2011) that students can refer to if they need help deciding what to write about.

---

November 14

Dear Class,

I enjoyed The Boy and the Whale by Mordicai Gerstein. In this story, the main character and his father found a whale tangled in their fishing net. The boy remembered the time he was caught like that, and he knew he had to save the whale. In the end the boy rescued the whale.

I love the illustrations. In one illustration, the boy looks out to an empty sea. There are no words on the page, but the illustration shows the mood: peaceful.

I admire the main character. He knew what to do. Have you ever had to make the right decision?

Your teacher,
Ms. Hsu

---

### Share your thinking about your reading in a letter.

- give a well-organized summary (characters, setting, problem, solution)
- tell about the illustrations
- tell what you learned about the characters and how they change
- give opinions about the book
- tell the author's message
- explain how the book reminds you of something in your own life, another book, or something happening in the world
- describe the setting and its importance
- give interesting examples of the writing
- pose questions or wonderings you have

## RML2
### WAR.U3.RML2

**Reading Minilesson Principle**
# Provide evidence for your thinking in your letter.

## Writing Letters to Share Thinking About Books

### You Will Need

- chart paper prepared with a letter about a book that you recently read aloud to your students (such as *A Symphony of Whales* by Steve Schuch, from Text Set: Empathy). Use the letter you used for RML1 or a different letter, as long as it contains evidence for your thinking.
- chart paper and markers
- highlighters
- a reader's notebook for each student

### Academic Language / Important Vocabulary

- evidence
- support

### Continuum Connection

- Provide evidence from the text or from personal experience to support written statements about a text (pp. 193, 196)
- Reference page numbers from a text in writing about important information (pp. 193, 196)

## Goal

Provide evidence from the text or personal experience to support written statements about a text.

## Rationale

When students support statements about a text with evidence from the text or personal experience, they read more closely and think critically about what they are reading. They learn that when they make a statement about their thinking, they should explain why.

## Assess Learning

Assess students' letters. Notice if there is evidence of new learning based on the goal of this minilesson.

- Do students support their ideas about a text with evidence from the text and/or personal experience?
- Do they understand the terms *evidence* and *support*?

## Minilesson

To help students think about the minilesson principle, use a sample letter to demonstrate how to provide evidence for one's thinking. Here is an example.

- Display the prepared letter. Read the first paragraph aloud.

  What is the main point that I made in the first paragraph?

  I wrote that it must be hard to live where Glashka lives. Do you believe my statement? Why?

  I provided evidence, or reasons, for what I wrote. When you provide evidence, you give specific details from the book or from your own life to show why you think something.

  What evidence did I give you to support my thinking?

- Highlight or have a student highlight the evidence.

  What do you notice about the punctuation for the evidence?

  If you copy the exact words from a book, use quotation marks. You should also put the page number that you got them from if the book has page numbers.

## Have a Try

Invite the students to talk with a partner about the evidence in the sample letter.

▷ Read aloud the rest of the letter.

   Turn and talk to your partner about what you notice about the thinking I shared and the evidence I gave.

▷ Ask a few students to respond. Highlight the evidence in the letter or ask a volunteer to do so.

## Summarize and Apply

Summarize the learning and remind students to provide evidence for their thinking in their letters.

   What did you notice about how I told about my thinking and also supported my thinking in my letter?

▷ Students can revise the letter they wrote in RML1, or they can start a new letter.

   Today, you will either add evidence to a letter that you are already working on or make sure to include evidence in a letter that you will start today about a book you are reading or just finished. Be ready to share your thinking when we come back together.

## Share

Following independent reading time, gather students together in the meeting area to talk with a partner about their reading, writing, and thinking.

   Turn and talk to your partner about evidence that you put in your letter about your reading.

## Extend the Lesson (Optional)

After assessing students' understanding, you might decide to extend the learning.

▷ If some students are struggling with providing evidence for their thinking, use shared writing to demonstrate the process.

▷ Have students highlight examples of evidence in their own letters.

▷ As you read a text aloud to your students, mark three or four places where you have some thoughts, feelings, predictions, or questions. Then, write a letter to the class, using the sticky notes to remind you of those parts you wanted to write about. Invite the students to do the same with their books.

---

November 15

Dear Class,

As I read A Symphony of Whales by Steve Schuch, I thought about how hard it must be to live in such a cold place. The author tells of the "long winter darkness" and how a blizzard lasted for three days. The illustrator drew bleak winter landscapes.

I also noticed how the author, Steve Schuch, not only helped me picture what was happening but also gave me a sense of the mood. "Everywhere Glashka looked, the water seemed to be heaving and boiling, choked with white whales." is a powerful sentence. The words "heaving" and "boiling" let me know the sea was choppy with nervous energy. When he used the word "choked" I knew that what was happening with the whales wasn't good.

What did you think about as we read this story?

Your teacher,
Ms. Hsu

---

**Reading Minilesson Principle**
# Respond to the teacher's questions to you when you write your next letter.

**Writing Letters to Share Thinking About Books**

## You Will Need

- chart paper prepared with a pair of letters between teacher and student about a book that you recently read (such as *The Dunderheads* by Paul Fleischman, from Text Set: Friendship)
- highlighters
- a reader's notebook for each student

## Academic Language / Important Vocabulary

- respond

## Continuum Connection

- Follow a topic and add to a discussion with comments on the same topic (p. 337)

## Goal

Understand that letters about reading are an ongoing conversation with the teacher.

## Rationale

When you teach students to respond to the questions you have asked them, they begin to understand that the purpose of the letters is to engage in an ongoing dialogue about books with another reader. Note: This minilesson should ideally be taught when students have already written at least two letters and have received two responses back from you. Make sure that you include at least one question in each of your responses.

## Assess Learning

Assess students' letters. Notice if there is evidence of new learning based on the goal of this minilesson.

- Do students write thoughtful responses to the questions you have asked them?
- Do they understand the term *respond*?

## Minilesson

To help students think about the minilesson principle, use a sample letter to demonstrate how to respond to your questions in their letters. Here is an example.

- Show the cover of *The Dunderheads*.

  We read and talked about *The Dunderheads* together recently. Roberto shared his thinking about the book in a letter. This is what I wrote back to him.

- Display and read aloud the first letter.

  What do you notice about this letter?

- Ask a volunteer to come up and highlight the questions in the letter.

  What do you think Roberto might write in his next letter?

- Help students understand that they should answer any questions that you pose in your letter. Then read the second letter.

  Every time you write a letter to me about your reading, I will write a letter back to you. Sometimes, I will ask you questions in my letter. It's important that you read my questions, think about them, and respond to them in your letter back to me. Our letters will be a dialogue, or conversation, about books.

## Have a Try

Invite the students to think about how they will respond to questions in the letters you write to them.

▶ Direct students to open their reader's notebooks to the most recent letter that you wrote to them.

> As you read my letter to you, look for questions and highlight them.

> Now turn and talk to your partner about one question that you found in my letter and how you might answer it.

## Summarize and Apply

Summarize the learning and remind students to respond to your questions in their letters.

> Today you will either work on a letter you have already started or begin writing a new letter. Check the last letter I wrote to you. Did I ask you a question? If so, be sure to answer it!

## Share

Following independent reading time, gather students together in the meeting area to talk about their letters.

> Who wrote a response to my questions?

## Extend the Lesson (Optional)

After assessing students' understanding, you might decide to extend the learning.

▶ Increase the complexity of your questions as students demonstrate the ability to respond thoughtfully to them. For example, in the beginning you might ask simple questions such as "What did you like about the book?" whereas later on you might ask questions like "Why do you think the main character did that?"

▶ Teach students to keep the conversation about books going by having them ask *you* questions when they write their letters.

---

November 19

Dear Roberto,

I also really enjoyed reading The Dunderheads by Paul Fleischman. Like you, I laughed a lot! I really liked how each character had a special and unusual talent—and that everyone in the class knew all about each other's talents and appreciated them. What do you think is the writer's message to readers?

In your letter you mentioned how much you liked the illustrations in this book. They are an important part in telling the story. Did you find one that was very interesting? What was it and why did it capture your interest?

Your teacher,

Ms. Hsu

---

November 24

Dear Ms. Hsu,

I just found out there is another book about the Dunderheads! I can't wait to read it. I think that the author wanted me to think about kids who might have a hard time fitting in. I think the author is trying to say that everyone has something they are good at and to appreciate everyone's special talents.

I really liked the illustrations on pages 22–23. Each little picture fit together like a puzzle. They showed me about Pencil's special talent. I learned a lot on these two pages.

From,

Roberto

---

Section 4: Writing About Reading

# RML 4
## WAR.U3.RML4

**Reading Minilesson Principle**
# Make your letter about reading interesting to read.

**Writing Letters to Share Thinking About Books**

## You Will Need

- chart paper prepared with a letter about a book that you recently read aloud (such as *The Other Side* by Jacqueline Woodson, from Text Set: Friendship)
- chart paper and markers
- highlighters
- a reader's notebook for each student

## Academic Language / Important Vocabulary

- voice
- personality

## Continuum Connection

- Write in a way that speaks directly to the reader (p. 280)
- Show enthusiasm and energy for the topic (p. 280)

## Goal

Write letters about reading with voice and interesting content.

## Rationale

Students need to understand that for a letter to be appealing to the reader it needs both an engaging writer's voice and interesting content. When you teach students to include genuine reactions and interesting thoughts in their letters, their writer's voice comes out and the letters become more enjoyable for the student to write and the reader to receive.

## Assess Learning

Assess students' letters. Notice if there is evidence of new learning based on the goal of this minilesson.

- Can you "hear the writer talking" when you read the students' letters?
- Do students understand the terms *voice* and *personality*?

## Minilesson

To help students think about the minilesson principle, use letters as models to help students learn how to include their voice in their letters. Here is an example.

- Display the prepared letter and read it aloud.

    **What do you notice about how the writing sounds?**

    **Does it give you an idea about what the writer is like? Turn and talk with your partner about that.**

- After a brief discussion, ask several students to share their thinking. Guide students to notice that they can hear the writer's voice. The letter sounds as if the student is talking to the reader and showing his personality.

- Highlight some parts that students thought sounded like talking. Then record students' ideas about why the letter sounds as if the student is talking.

    **Now turn and talk about what the writer wrote about. What makes it interesting or not interesting to you?**

- After a brief discussion, guide students to notice that a letter needs both an engaging writer's voice and interesting content.

## Have a Try

Invite the students to talk with a partner about the quality of the voice in their own reader's notebook letters.

> Find a letter you wrote that shows your writer's voice and is interesting to read. Turn and talk to your partner about the letter.

▶ When students have finished sharing with their partners, ask a few to share the interesting parts of their letters with the class. Add new ideas to the chart.

## Summarize and Apply

Summarize the learning and remind students to make their letters interesting.

▶ Write the principle at the top of the chart. Remind students when the next letter is due.

> Today, you will either work on making a letter you have already started more interesting to read, or you will start a new letter. Think about how to make your letter interesting. Be ready to share your thinking when we come back together.

## Share

Following independent reading time, gather students together in the meeting area to talk about their reading, thinking, and writing.

> Turn and talk to a partner. How do you think you can make your next letter interesting to read?

## Extend the Lesson (Optional)

After assessing students' understanding, you might decide to extend the learning.

▶ Create a bulletin board or chart of memorable sentences from student letters that show the readers' thoughtfulness. Invite students to notice good thinking in each other's letters and suggest sentences to add to the display.

▶ Using a text you have read aloud, model the writing of a paragraph, telling your students what you noticed about the book and your thoughts about it. Talk about ways to show your writer's voice and include interesting content.

---

November 21

Dear Mrs. Hsu,

I read <u>The Other Side</u> by Jacqueline Woodson. Wow, what a great book! Annie knew that segregation was wrong but wasn't sure what to do about it. This makes sense—she's a kid! Plus, I don't think a lot of grown-ups knew what to do about it either. When Annie played near the fence it made me think she was brave enough to get close to the line she wasn't supposed to cross. It showed Clover she wanted to be friends. Maybe this is the first chance Annie and Clover had to resist the ways things were in their town. What do you think?

From,
Lucy

---

**Make your letter about reading interesting to read.**

- Share the parts of the text you enjoyed or found interesting.

- Make your writing sound like talking.

- Support your thinking with evidence from the book or personal experience.

- Ask questions you have about the book.

Section 4: Writing About Reading

# RML 5
## WAR.U3.RML5

**Reading Minilesson Principle**
# Know the qualities of a strong letter about your reading.

## Writing Letters to Share Thinking About Books

### You Will Need

- chart paper prepared with a strong letter about a book that you recently read aloud (such as *Better Than You* by Trudy Ludwig, from Text Set: Friendship)
- chart paper and markers
- a reader's notebook for each student

### Academic Language / Important Vocabulary

- qualities
- evidence

### Continuum Connection

- Understand how to learn about writing notes, cards, invitations, emails, and friendly letters by noticing the characteristics of examples (p. 274)
- Hold the reader's attention with clear, focused content (p. 279)

## Goal

Identify the qualities of a strong letter including content and conventions.

## Rationale

When students can identify what makes a letter strong, and assess letters against those standards, they are able to think more deeply about the books they read and communicate their thinking clearly in their letters. Note: This minilesson should be taught after students have written at least three letters about their reading.

## Assess Learning

Assess students' letters. Notice if there is evidence of new learning based on the goal of this minilesson.

- ▶ Can students identify the qualities of a strong letter?
- ▶ Do they use these qualities when writing their own letters?
- ▶ Do they understand the terms *qualities* and *evidence*?

# Minilesson

To help students think about the minilesson principle, use a prepared letter example to engage students in a discussion about the qualities of a strong letter. Here is an example.

- ▶ Display the prepared letter and read it aloud.

  Here's a letter a student wrote that shows his best thinking. What makes it a strong letter?

- ▶ Invite student responses. If necessary, prompt students with questions such as these:

  - *How did he share thinking about the text?*
  - *What made this letter interesting to read?*
  - *Does his letter make sense?*
  - *How did he let you know what he was reading?*
  - *Did he respond to any questions that were asked?*
  - *Is his letter neat and easy to read?*

- ▶ Use the students' noticings to create a list of qualities of a strong letter on a chart. This will serve as a checklist for students to use when they write their next letter.

## Have a Try

Invite the students to talk with a partner about one of their own reader's notebook letters.

> Take a look at one of your letters. What makes it a strong letter? Are there parts that could be improved? Share these thoughts with a partner.

When students have finished sharing with their partners, ask a few to share their thoughts with the class. Add new ideas to the chart.

## Summarize and Apply

Summarize the learning and remind students to refer to the checklist when assessing their own letters.

> Today you thought about the qualities of a strong letter. Look through the letters that you have written. Which one shows your best thinking? What makes it strong? Bring that letter with you when we come back together.

## Share

Following independent reading time, gather students together in the meeting area to talk about their letters.

> Turn and talk to a partner about the letter you chose. What parts show your best thinking? What made this a strong letter?

## Extend the Lesson (Optional)

After assessing students' understanding, you might decide to extend the learning.

 ◗ Have students write a few sentences or a paragraph telling why they think the letter they chose is a strong letter.

 ◗ Use the form called Assessment of Letters in Reader's Notebook (p. 53) to assess your students' letters (visit resources.fountasandpinnell.com to download the resource).

---

December 4

Dear Ms. Hsu,

I read Better Than You by Trudy Ludwig. At first, I felt sad for Tyler. All Tyler wanted was for Jake to act like a good friend, and Jake made sure to let Tyler know he was never going to be as good as him. It was hard to read about when Jake made Tyler feel bad.

Uncle Kevin helped Tyler understand why Jake bragged so much. Tyler learned a lesson in this story—the way Jake was treating him had more to do with Jake than with himself.

I think the author wanted me to know that I don't have to spend time with someone who keeps putting me down.

From,

Jack

---

### Qualities of a Strong Letter

✓ Is enjoyable to read

✓ Includes information about the book: title and author

✓ Makes sense

✓ Uses letter format: date, greeting, and closing

✓ Shows thinking about the book with evidence from personal experience or the book

✓ Provides responses to the teacher's questions

✓ Is neat and easy to read

✓ Shows best spelling and punctuation

---

Section 4: Writing About Reading

## Assessment

After you have taught the minilessons in this umbrella, observe students as they talk and write about their reading across instructional contexts: interactive read-aloud, independent reading, guided reading, shared reading, and book club. Use *The Literacy Continuum* (Fountas and Pinnell 2017) to guide the observation of students' reading and writing behaviors.

▶ What evidence do you have of new understandings related to writing letters about reading?

- Do students write a letter about their reading each week?

- Do they include evidence from the text or personal experience to support their thinking?

- Are they making their letters interesting by writing with voice and including genuine thoughts and reactions to the text?

- Are they consistently responding to questions in their letters?

- Can they identify the qualities of a good letter?

- Do they use terms such as *voice, quality, evidence,* and *respond* when they talk about their letters about reading?

▶ In what other ways, beyond the scope of this umbrella, are students writing about books?

- Are students using other forms of writing to share their thinking about books?

- Are they writing about longer chapter books over the course of several letters?

Use your observations to determine the next umbrella you will teach. You may also consult Minilessons Across the Year (pp. 59–61) for guidance.

## Reader's Notebook

When this umbrella is complete, provide a copy of the minilesson principles (see resources.fountasandpinnell.com) for students to glue in the reader's notebook (in the Minilessons section if using *Reader's Notebook: Intermediate* [Fountas and Pinnell 2011]), so they can refer to the information as needed.

**The Idea of Home**

## Minilessons in This Umbrella

| | |
|---|---|
| **RML1** | Use a diagram to show cause and effect. |
| **RML2** | Use a topic outline to show the main topic and its subtopics. |
| **RML3** | Use a grid to organize, analyze, and compare information. |
| **RML4** | Use a web to show how ideas are connected. |
| **RML5** | Use a Venn diagram to compare and contrast books. |

## Before Teaching Umbrella 4 Minilessons

Graphic organizers can reveal the structure of a piece of writing and assist in examining the content. Before you teach these lessons, students should be familiar with using a reader's notebook (see the first two umbrellas in this section). The minilessons may be taught in any order that coordinates with relevant literary analysis minilessons. The lessons in this umbrella each provide one example of how to use a graphic organizer; however, the lessons can be used in a multitude of ways, some of which are mentioned in Extend the Lesson.

The students should think and talk about the concepts before they write about them. Use the books from the complete *Fountas & Pinnell Classroom ™ Interactive Read-Aloud Collection* text sets Series: Vanishing Cultures and Genre Study: Fairy Tales as well as the titles listed below. Or, choose high-quality fiction and nonfiction books from your classroom library.

**Taking Action, Making Change**

### The Idea of Home

*My Name Is Sangoel* by Karen Lynn Williams and Khadra Mohammed

*The Lotus Seed* by Sherry Garland

*Grandfather's Journey* by Allen Say

### Taking Action, Making Change

*The Promise* by Nicola Davies

*Follow the Moon Home: A Tale of One Idea, Twenty Kids, and a Hundred Sea Turtles* by Philippe Cousteau and Deborah Hopkinson

### Cinderella Stories

*Sootface: An Ojibwa Cinderella Story* by Robert D. San Souci

*The Persian Cinderella* by Shirley Climo

*Yeh-Shen: A Cinderella Story from China* by Louie Ai-Ling

*The Rough-Face Girl* by Rafe Martin

**Cinderella Stories**

As you read aloud and enjoy these texts together, help students

- notice how information is organized in fiction and nonfiction books,

- talk about ways that ideas from one or more books are connected, and

- compare and contrast multiple books or multiple ideas from one book.

### Reading Minilesson Principle
## Use a diagram to show cause and effect.

## Using Graphic Organizers to Share Thinking About Books

### You Will Need

▶ several familiar fiction books that have clear examples of cause and effect, such as the following from Text Set: Taking Action, Making Change:

- *The Promise* by Nicola Davies

- *Follow the Moon Home* by Philippe Cousteau and Deborah Hopkinson

▶ two pieces of chart paper prepared with cause-and-effect diagrams

▶ baskets of short fiction and nonfiction books that have clear examples of cause and effect

▶ a copy of a cause-and-effect diagram for each student (optional)

▶ To download the following online resource for this lesson, visit **resources.fountasandpinnell.com**: Cause and Effect

### Academic Language / Important Vocabulary

▶ reader's notebook

▶ graphic organizer

▶ diagram

▶ cause and effect

### Continuum Connection

▶ Notice and write about an author's use of underlying structural patterns to organize information and sometimes apply the same structure to writing nonfiction texts: description, temporal sequence, question and answer, cause and effect, chronological sequence, compare and contrast, problem and solution, categorization (p. 197)

## Goal

Use a diagram to show cause and effect.

## Rationale

When you teach students to use a diagram to show cause and effect, they better understand the concepts and can think deeply about how one action causes a variety of other actions to occur. This lesson provides a model for teaching students to make graphic organizers to show other structural patterns. Students will benefit from understanding underlying text structures in nonfiction books before you teach this minilesson [see Umbrella 16: Noticing How Nonfiction Authors Choose to Organize Information in Section Two: Literary Analysis].

## Assess Learning

Observe students when they make diagrams to show cause and effect and notice if there is evidence of new learning based on the goal of this minilesson.

▶ Are students able to determine cause and effect in books they read?

▶ Are they using the terms *reader's notebook*, *graphic organizer*, *diagram*, and *cause and effect*?

## Minilesson

To help students think about the minilesson principle, use familiar fiction texts to help them think about cause and effect. Here is an example.

▶ Display one of the prepared cause-and-effect charts.

> What do you notice about this graphic organizer? How might it be used?

▶ Show the cover of *The Promise* and briefly review the page that shows the girl trying to steal the older woman's purse.

> Think about the event in this book that caused the rest of the events in the book to happen. How would you describe that event in just a few words?

▶ Add student responses to the *Cause* section of the chart.

> What are the events that happened because the girl tried to steal the older woman's purse full of acorns?

▶ As students provide responses, help them form their thoughts into just a few words that will fit in the *Events* boxes on the chart.

> In what ways might this cause-and-effect graphic organizer be helpful?

## Have a Try

Invite the students to talk with a partner about using a graphic organizer to show cause and effect.

▶ Display a blank cause-and-effect chart alongside *Follow the Moon Home*.

Turn and talk to your partner about how to fill in a graphic organizer for *Follow the Moon Home*.

▶ As needed, review a few key pages from the story to highlight cause and effect before students turn and talk.

▶ After time for discussion, create a cause-and-effect chart using students' ideas.

## Summarize and Apply

Summarize the learning and remind students to think about how to use a graphic organizer to show cause and effect.

You learned that you can use a graphic organizer to show cause and effect.

▶ Add the principle to the chart.

▶ Provide baskets of fiction and nonfiction books that have clear examples of cause and effect. Provide a Cause and Effect graphic organizer for students to glue in the reader's notebook, or have them make their own.

With a partner, choose a book from the basket to read. Work together to fill in your cause-and-effect graphic organizer. Bring your notebook when we meet so you can share.

## Share

Following independent reading time, match up sets of partners to make groups of four.

Share with your group the cause-and-effect chart you made.

## Extend the Lesson (Optional)

After assessing students' understanding, you might decide to extend the learning.

▶ **Writing About Reading** Once students have completed a Cause and Effect graphic organizer, have them use it to write about the book.

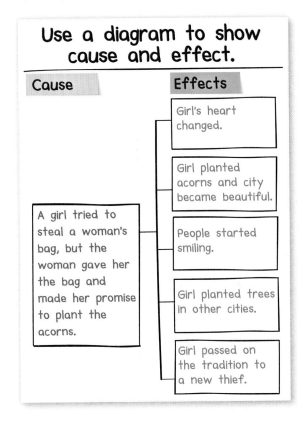

**Use a diagram to show cause and effect.**

| Cause | Effects |
|---|---|
| A girl tried to steal a woman's bag, but the woman gave her the bag and made her promise to plant the acorns. | Girl's heart changed. |
| | Girl planted acorns and city became beautiful. |
| | People started smiling. |
| | Girl planted trees in other cities. |
| | Girl passed on the tradition to a new thief. |

Section 4: Writing About Reading

**Reading Minilesson Principle**
# Use a topic outline to show the main topic and its subtopics.

### Using Graphic Organizers to Share Thinking About Books

#### You Will Need

- one or more familiar books that can be used to create an outline, such as the following by Jan Reynolds from Text Set: Series: Vanishing Cultures:
  - *Frozen Land*
  - *Sahara*
  - *Himalaya*
  - *Amazon Basin*
  - *Far North*
- chart paper prepared with first section (I) of an outline
- markers
- basket of nonfiction books, some of which are organized by related topics

#### Academic Language / Important Vocabulary

- reader's notebook
- graphic organizer
- topic outline
- main topic
- subtopics

#### Continuum Connection

- Recognize that informational texts may present a larger topic with many subtopics (p. 63)
- Outline the main topic of a book and its subtopics (p. 197)

## Goal

Create an outline with headings and subheadings that reflect the organization of a text.

## Rationale

When students learn to use an outline, they learn to identify the main topic and subtopics of a nonfiction book or books they are reading and to display information to see the organization of the text.

## Assess Learning

Observe students when they talk about and create outlines and notice if there is evidence of new learning based on the goal of this minilesson.

- ▶ Can they use and create a topic outline?
- ▶ Are they using the terms *reader's notebook, graphic organizer, topic outline, main topic,* and *subtopics*?

## Minilesson

To help students think about the minilesson principle, engage students in an interactive lesson about how to make an outline. Here is an example.

- ▶ Before teaching this lesson, students should have read a variety of nonfiction books and discussed different nonfiction text structures, especially categorical (i.e., topics and subtopics). Depending on the experience of your students, you might want to adjust the number of entries to vary from those shown in the example.

- ▶ Show the covers of the related books you are using for the outline, such as those from the text set Series: Vanishing Cultures.

  How are all of these books related?

  If we want to think about the big ideas about vanishing cultures in these books, one way to do that is to create an outline. I made one about *Frozen Land* before class. Let's take a look at it.

- ▶ Show the topic outline you started before class. Engage students in a discussion of the outline. The following prompts may be helpful.
  - *How do you think I decided what to write on the outline?*
  - *How does this outline help you think about vanishing cultures?*
- ▶ Show the cover of another of the books in the series.

  If we want to add this book to the outline, what could I write?

- ▶ Using students' ideas, fill in the next section of the outline (section II).

## Have a Try

Invite the students to talk with a partner about using a topic outline.

> Turn and talk with your partner about how the outline is organized.

▶ Guide students to understand that topics are listed from larger to smaller and that information is listed very briefly, not in complete sentences.

## Summarize and Apply

Summarize the learning and remind students to use an outline to show the main topics and subtopics.

> Today you learned that a topic outline is useful to show the main topics and subtopics from different books. Sometimes a book has headings. How might headings help you outline a book?

▶ Add the principle to the top of the chart.

> Today when you read, choose a nonfiction book or set of related nonfiction books to read with a partner. Work together to create a topic outline that could be added to your reader's notebook. Bring your outline and the books you used when we meet.

## Share

Following independent reading time, match up sets of partners to make groups of four.

> Share the topic outline you created with your group. Talk about the decisions you made about what to include on the outline.

## Extend the Lesson (Optional)

After assessing students' understanding, you might decide to extend the learning.

▶ Use different nonfiction examples to create more expanded outlines with students, including the various outline subsections.

▶ **Writing About Reading** Encourage students to create a topic outline in a reader's notebook to show the main topic and subtopics within one book, such as a biography or other nonfiction book.

---

**Use a topic outline to show the main topic and its subtopics.**

### Vanishing Cultures

I.    Frozen Land
  A. Inuit
  B. Travel
    1. dog sleds
    2. caribou herds
  C. Way of life
    1. homes
      a. igloos
      b. tents
    2. food and clothes
      a. fish
      b. caribou
      c. rabbits
      d. wolves
II.

*Section 4: Writing About Reading*

# RML3
## WAR.U4.RML3

**Reading Minilesson Principle**
## Use a grid to organize, analyze, and compare information.

### Using Graphic Organizers to Share Thinking About Books

#### You Will Need

- several familiar books with clearly identifiable themes and messages, such as the following from Text Set: The Idea of Home:
  - *My Name Is Sangoel* by Karen Lynn Williams and Khadra Mohammed
  - *The Lotus Seed* by Sherry Garland
  - *Grandfather's Journey* by Allen Say
- chart paper prepared with a grid that has the headings *Title, Theme[s] and Message[s]*
- markers
- a reader's notebook for each student
- basket of fiction books
- a copy of the Comparison Grid for each student [optional]
- To download the following online resource for this lesson, visit **resources.fountasandpinnell.com**: Comparison Grid

#### Academic Language / Important Vocabulary

- reader's notebook
- graphic organizer
- grid
- theme
- message

#### Continuum Connection

- Write about connections among texts by topic, theme, major ideas, authors' styles, and genres (pp. 193, 196)

### Goal

Use a grid to organize, analyze, and compare information across texts.

### Rationale

When students learn how to use a grid to write about their reading, they learn a tool that will help them make connections and recognize important characteristics across texts. This lesson provides a model for how you can teach students to use a graphic organizer to organize, analyze, and compare ideas.

### Assess Learning

Observe students when they talk about and use grids and notice if there is evidence of new learning based on the goal of this minilesson.

- Are students able to use a grid to organize, analyze, or compare information from different books?
- Do they understand the terms *reader's notebook, graphic organizer, grid, theme,* and *message*?

## Minilesson

To help students think about the minilesson principle, use familiar texts to demonstrate how to use a grid to organize, analyze, or compare information. Here is an example.

- This example uses a grid to compare themes and messages. Other suggested options for teaching students how to use a grid are listed in Extend the Lesson.
- Before teaching this lesson, students should have read a variety of fiction books and understand how to identify the theme and message of a story.
- Show the grid that you started before class, along with the covers of *My Name Is Sangoel* and *The Lotus Seed*.

  What do you notice about this grid?

  What do you think I can use this grid for?

- As students respond, engage them in a discussion about grids so that they understand what should be written in each section of the grid and how the grid will help them consider the themes and messages from several books.

  Can you help me fill in this grid for these two books?

- Ask volunteers to make suggestions. Briefly revisit any pages necessary to help students identify the multiple themes and messages from the books. As students provide ideas, fill in the sections of the grid for the two books.

## Have a Try

Invite the students to talk with a partner about adding *Grandfather's Journey* to the grid.

> Turn and talk to your partner about what would go in the grid for *Grandfather's Journey*.

▶ After time for a brief discussion, ask students to share. Add to grid.

## Summarize and Apply

Summarize the learning and remind students to try using a grid in a reader's notebook.

> You can use a grid like the one we made on the chart to think about several books together.

▶ Add the principle to the chart. Then provide a copy of the Comparison Grid graphic organizer for students to glue into a reader's notebook, or have them make their own.

> Choose a fiction book to read today. Label two columns *Theme(s)* and *Message(s)*, just like on the chart, and then fill in one row of the grid about your book. Bring the book and your reader's notebook when we meet so you can share.

## Share

Following independent reading time, gather students in small groups.

> Share the grid you started in your reader's notebook. Did anyone in your group have a similar theme or message?

## Extend the Lesson (Optional)

After assessing students' understanding, you might decide to extend the learning.

▶ **Writing About Reading** Have students return to the Comparison Grid to fill in the other rows as they encounter books with similar themes and messages.

▶ **Writing About Reading** When students have completed a grid, have them write about what they notice.

▶ **Writing About Reading** Encourage students to create grids (see resources.fountasandpinnell.com) to compare other information in fiction and nonfiction books, such as the following: versions of folktales, fiction and nonfiction books on the same topic, main ideas and details, distinguishing fact and opinion, and external and internal character traits.

### Use a grid to organize, analyze, and compare information.

| Title | Theme(s) | Message(s) |
|---|---|---|
| *My name is SANGOEL* | • fitting in<br>• identity<br>• change<br>• home | • Be confident about who you are.<br>• Be proud of your heritage.<br>• You can be yourself, even in a new place. |
| *THE LOTUS SEED* | • home<br>• change<br>• memories<br>• courage | • You can take memories with you when you move to a new home.<br>• Items we keep from the past can be very special. |
| *Grandfather's Journey* | • home<br>• change<br>• differences | • You can feel at home in two different countries.<br>• New experiences help you grow as a person.<br>• Different cultures have different things to appreciate. |

**Reading Minilesson Principle**
# Use a web to show how ideas are connected.

## You Will Need

- several familiar books that have connected ideas, such as these from Text Set: Genre Study: Fairy Tales:
  - *Beauty and the Beast* by Jan Brett
  - *Rumpelstiltskin* by Paul O. Zelinsky
  - *The Dragon Prince* by Laurence Yep
  - *The Twelve Dancing Princesses* by Rachel Isadora
  - *Brave Red, Smart Frog* by Emily Jenkins
- chart paper prepared with a blank web graphic organizer
- markers
- a copy of a web for each student (optional)
- To download the following online resources for this lesson, visit **resources.fountasandpinnell.com**: Web

## Academic Language / Important Vocabulary

- reader's notebook
- graphic organizer
- web
- connected

### Continuum Connection

- Write about connections among texts by topic, theme, major ideas, authors' styles, and genres (pp. 193, 196)
- Use graphic organizers such as webs to show how a nonfiction writer puts together information related to the same topic or subtopic (p. 197)

## Goal

Learn how to use webs as a graphic organizer to connect information within a text or across texts.

## Rationale

When students learn to create a web as a way to connect ideas within or across texts, they learn to pay attention to common ideas both in books and in their own lives. This lesson provides a model for how you can teach students to use a graphic organizer to connect ideas.

## Assess Learning

Observe students when they talk about webs to connect ideas and notice if there is evidence of new learning based on the goal of this minilesson.

- Do students participate in creating a web to connect ideas within or between books?
- Are students using the terms *reader's notebook, graphic organizer, web,* and *connected*?

## Minilesson

To help students think about the minilesson principle, use familiar texts to help students create a web to connect an idea that connects several books. Here is an example.

- Display the blank web.

  You have read many fairy tales. One element of a fairy tale is magic.

- Write the word *Magic* in the center bubble.

  What fairy tales do you know that have magic in them?

  What would be an example of magic from this fairy tale?

- As needed, show a variety of familiar fairy tales, such as *Beauty and the Beast, Rumpelstiltskin, The Dragon Prince, The Twelve Dancing Princesses,* as well as several from *Brave Red, Smart Frog.*

- As students provide examples, begin to build the web by writing the title of the story and a few words about the example of magic into one of the web bubbles. Help students revise their wording so as to include only a few words to represent the idea of magic in the story.

## Have a Try

Invite the students to talk with a partner about creating a web to connect ideas.

▶ Show the cover of *Brave Red, Smart Frog*.

What other elements of fairy tales could you use a web for? Turn and talk about that.

▶ After time for discussion, ask a few volunteers to share ideas.

## Summarize and Apply

Summarize the learning and remind students to think about how to use a web to connect ideas.

Today you learned that you can use a web to connect ideas in different books.

▶ Add the principle to the chart. Then provide a copy of a web that students can fill out and glue into their reader's notebooks, or have them draw their own.

You talked with a partner about other elements of fairy tales you could write in a web. Choose one of those ideas and fill in a web about that. Bring your web when we meet to share.

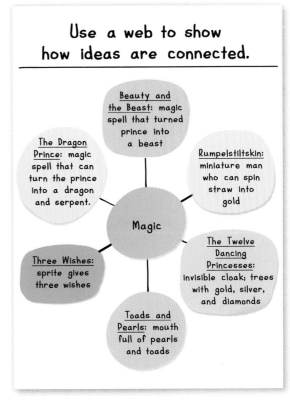

## Share

Following independent reading time, gather students in the meeting area. Ask a few students to share.

Who would like to share the web you made?

## Extend the Lesson (Optional)

After assessing students' understanding, you might decide to extend the learning.

▶ **Writing About Reading** Encourage students to use webs in other ways to show how ideas in fiction and nonfiction books are connected (e.g., connect nonfiction topics or subtopics in one or more books, create a character traits web, use a web to connect themes across several texts).

▶ **Writing About Reading** Once students have completed a web, have them write about their noticings of how the information is connected.

Section 4: Writing About Reading

**Reading Minilesson Principle**
# Use a Venn diagram to compare and contrast books.

### You Will Need

- several familiar fiction books that lend themselves to comparing and contrasting, such as the following from Text Set: Cinderella Stories:
  - *Sootface* by Robert D. San Souci
  - *The Persian Cinderella* by Shirley Climo
  - *Yeh-Shen* by Louie Ai-Ling
  - *The Rough-Face Girl* by Rafe Martin
- chart paper prepared with a blank Venn diagram
- markers
- a copy of a Venn diagram for each student (optional)
- To download the following online resources for this lesson, visit **resources.fountasandpinnell.com**: Venn Diagram

### Academic Language / Important Vocabulary

- reader's notebook
- graphic organizer
- Venn diagram
- compare and contrast

### Continuum Connection

- Write about the connections among texts by topic, theme, major ideas, authors' styles, and genres (pp. 193, 196)

## Goal

Use a Venn diagram to compare and contrast books.

## Rationale

When students create a Venn diagram to compare and contrast books, they notice similarities and differences across texts. This lesson provides a model for teaching students to use a graphic organizer to compare and contrast ideas.

## Assess Learning

Observe students when they create a Venn diagram and notice if there is evidence of new learning based on the goal of this minilesson.

- ❯ Are students able to compare and contrast two books?
- ❯ Can they create a Venn diagram to compare and contrast two texts?
- ❯ Do they use the terms *reader's notebook, graphic organizer, Venn diagram,* and *compare and contrast*?

## Minilesson

Provide an interactive lesson to help students learn how to use a Venn diagram. Here is an example.

- ❯ Show the prepared blank Venn diagram.

  **What do you know about this type of graphic organizer?**

- ❯ As students respond, ensure that they understand that a Venn diagram is used to compare and contrast two things.

- ❯ Show the covers of *Sootface* and *The Persian Cinderella*. Add the book titles to the Venn diagram.

  **Think about these two Cinderella stories you know. How are they the same and how are they different?**

- ❯ Revisit a few pages of each story as needed to prompt the conversation.

  **What information is the same in the two stories?**

  **Where does the similar information go on a Venn diagram?**

- ❯ Add similar ideas to the center of the Venn diagram.

  **What information appears in *Sootface*, but not in *The Persian Cinderella*?**

- ❯ Add responses to the left side of the Venn diagram, under the *Sootface* heading.

## Have a Try

Invite the students to talk with a partner about creating a Venn diagram.

> Turn and talk about what information could be written on the right side of the Venn diagram, under *The Persian Cinderella*.

▶ After time for discussion, ask students for ideas. Add ideas to the chart.

## Summarize and Apply

Summarize the learning and remind students that they can use a Venn diagram to compare and contrast ideas.

> Today you learned that a Venn diagram can be used to compare and contrast ideas in two books.

▶ Add the principle to the top of the chart.

▶ Show the covers of *Yeh-Shen* and *The Rough-Face Girl*. (If students are able, they may self-select two books to compare and contrast.) Provide students with a Venn diagram that they can glue in a reader's notebook, or have them make their own.

> Think about what is the same in these two Cinderella stories. Work with a partner to fill in your Venn diagram. Bring your notebook when we meet so you can share.

## Share

Following independent reading time, match up sets of partners to make groups of four.

> Share the Venn diagram that you made. If you learn any new ideas from other people in your group, you can add those ideas to your Venn diagram.

## Extend the Lesson (Optional)

After assessing students' understanding, you might decide to extend the learning.

▶ Encourage students to use a Venn diagram to compare and contrast other ideas, such as the way a topic is presented in a fiction and nonfiction book, comparing and contrasting two characters in a fiction story, or using information from an expository text to compare and contrast two animals.

Use a Venn diagram to compare and contrast books.

| Sootface | The Persian Cinderella |

Ojibwa people / mom dies / Persia

invisible mighty warrior / mean stepmom and stepsisters / Prince Mehrdad

old moccasins and clothes / hard work / star on face

ashes on face / old clothes / magic blue jug

wigwam house / handsome guy / wrinkled woman / happy ending

Section 4: Writing About Reading

## Assessment

After you have taught the minilessons in this umbrella, observe students as they talk and write about their reading across instructional contexts: interactive read-aloud, independent reading, guided reading, shared reading, and book club. Use *The Literacy Continuum* (Fountas and Pinnell 2017) to guide the observation of students' reading and writing behaviors.

> ▶ What evidence do you have of new understandings related to graphic organizers?
>> • Are they able to use a diagram to show cause and effect and other underlying text structures?
>> • Are they able to create an outline to organize ideas from fiction and nonfiction books?
>> • Can students use a grid to represent ideas from books?
>> • Can they create a web to show how ideas from books are connected?
>> • Do they use a Venn diagram to compare and contrast books?
>> • Do they use academic vocabulary, such as *reader's notebook, graphic organizer, grid, outline, web, Venn diagram,* and *cause and effect*?
>
> ▶ In what other ways, beyond the scope of this umbrella, are students using a reader's notebook?
>> • Are students thinking about other ways to use a reader's notebook to write about fiction and nonfiction?
>> • Do they use a reader's notebook to share opinions about their reading?

Use your observations to determine the next umbrella you will teach. You may also consult Minilessons Across the Year (pp. 59–61) for guidance.

## Reader's Notebook

When this umbrella is complete, provide a copy of the minilesson principles (see resources.fountasandpinnell.com) for students to glue in the reader's notebook (in the Minilessons section if using *Reader's Notebook: Intermediate* [Fountas and Pinnell 2011]), so they can refer to the information as needed.

## Minilessons in This Umbrella

**RML1**    Your writing about your reading shows your thinking about it.

**RML2**    A short write shows your quick thinking about a book.

**RML3**    A storyboard shows the significant events in a story.

**RML4**    A summary of a book gives the important information.

**RML5**    A recommendation for a book or series encourages others to read it.

**RML6**    A sketch shows your thinking about something important in a book.

**RML7**    A written sketch of a character is a short description of his traits with supporting evidence.

**RML8**    Two-column writing shows your response to a phrase or quote from a book.

**RML9**    A persuasive poster is designed to persuade others to agree with your opinion.

## Before Teaching Umbrella 5 Minilessons

Students should be familiar with using a reader's notebook (see Umbrella 1: Introducing a Reader's Notebook in this section). Students should be thinking and talking about concepts before they write about them, so consider teaching these minilessons alongside relevant literary analysis minilessons.

Use these texts from the *Fountas & Pinnell Classroom ™ Interactive Read-Aloud Collection* or choose high-quality books from your classroom library.

**Illustration Study: Craft**

*Dingo* by Claire Saxby

**Genre Study: Memoir**

*The Scraps Book* by Lois Ehlert

**Figuring Out Who You Are**

*A Boy and a Jaguar* by Alan Rabinowitz

**Empathy**

*The Boy and the Whale* by Mordicai Gerstein

*The Crane Wife* by Odds Bodkin

**Telling a Story with Photos**

*Wolf Island* by Nicholas Read

*The Seal Garden* by Nicholas Read

*A Bear's Life* by Nicholas Read

**Exploring Identity**

*Imagine* by Juan Felipe Herrera

*Be Water, My Friend* by Ken Mochizuki

**Genre Study: Historical Fiction**

*The Buffalo Storm* by Katherine Applegate

*Dad, Jackie, and Me* by Myron Uhlberg

**Taking Action, Making Change**

*Emmanuel's Dream* by Laurie Ann Thompson

*One Hen* by Katie Smith Milway

**Illustration Study: Craft**

**Genre Study: Memoir**

**Figuring Out Who You Are**

**Empathy**

**Telling a Story with Photos**

**Exploring Identity**

**Genre Study: Historical Fiction**

**Taking Action, Making Change**

**Reading Minilesson Principle**

## Your writing about your reading shows your thinking about it.

### You Will Need

- chart paper and markers
- a reader's notebook for each student

### Academic Language / Important Vocabulary

- reader's notebook
- brainstorm

### Continuum Connection

- Compose notes, lists, letters, or statements to remember important information about a text (p. 193)
- Write a note, card, friendly letter, invitation, or email with a specific purpose in mind (p. 274)

### Goal

Brainstorm a list of the different types of thinking you might share about books.

### Rationale

When you teach students to think about the many ways they can write about books, they learn how to use writing as a tool to think more deeply about their reading. They reflect on common themes, messages, settings, and similar characteristics of literature. These understandings help them apply ideas and messages to their own lives, and they develop their understandings of writer's craft in in a variety of genres.

### Assess Learning

Observe students when they think and talk about writing about reading and notice if there is evidence of new learning based on the goal of this minilesson.

- ▷ Do students participate in generating a list of ways they can write about their reading in a reader's notebook?
- ▷ Are they able to select an idea from the list to use for writing about a book they are reading?
- ▷ Do they use the terms *reader's notebook* and *brainstorm*?

## Minilesson

To help students think about the minilesson principle, engage them in brainstorming ideas for writing about reading in a reader's notebook. Here is an example.

- ▷ Each student should have a reader's notebook to use during this lesson. If students have been keeping notes about reading or about minilessons in a reader's notebook, they can refer to those notes during the brainstorming portion of the lesson.

  When you talk about books, you share your thinking about your reading. You can also share your thinking by writing about what you read. Turn and talk to a partner about the many ideas you have for the kinds of things you can think about and write about in relation to books you read.

- ▷ Allow students a few moments to think or to refer to any notes they have about minilessons.

- ▷ As students share ideas, begin a list on chart paper.

- ▷ As needed, prompt the conversation to generate new categories of ideas. If you are using *Reader's Notebook: Intermediate* (Fountas and Pinnell 2011), the Writing About Reading section has suggested ideas to help with the brainstorming session.

## Have a Try

Invite the students to talk with a partner about the list of ways to write about reading in a reader's notebook.

> Look at the list of ideas for writing about your reading. Which ideas will you use? Do you have any ideas we didn't list? Turn and talk about that.

▶ After time for a brief discussion, ask a few students to share. Add any new ideas to the chart.

## Summarize and Apply

Summarize the learning and remind students to use writing about their reading as a way to reflect on their books.

> Today we made a list of different ways you can write about your reading in your reader's notebook.

▶ Review the ideas on the chart.

> Today write about your thinking about the book you are reading. You may want to use some of the ideas from the list. Bring your reader's notebook and the book when we meet so you can share.

▶ If you are using *Reader's Notebook: Intermediate* (Fountas and Pinnell 2011), have students write in the Writing About Reading section. If students are using another notebook, have them use a dedicated section of the notebook.

## Share

Following independent reading time, gather students in small groups.

> Share with your group what you wrote in your reader's notebook. Did you use one of the ideas on the list, or did you write something different?

## Extend the Lesson (Optional)

After assessing students' understanding, you might decide to extend the learning.

▶ Keep the list posted and add to it as students experience new minilessons or as they generate new ideas for writing about reading. Encourage them to try new ideas from the list instead of repeating the same types of writing responses. Your feedback to their writing will also expand the possibilities.

▶ Have students create a list in a reader's notebook of ideas for writing about reading.

---

### Ways to Share Your Thinking

- describe character traits
- tell how a character changes
- tell what you learned about a topic
- make a timeline to show events
- discuss the writer's message
- make a drawing about the book and write about it
- write a letter to your teacher or a peer
- list wonderings you have while you read or after reading
- describe the high point of the story
- describe the setting and why it is important
- make a list of books to recommend
- relate a story's message to your own life
- select a quote from the book and give your response

Section 4: Writing About Reading

---

**Reading Minilesson Principle**
## A short write shows your quick thinking about a book.

## Introducing Different Genres and Forms for Responding to Reading

### You Will Need

- several books that are good examples for doing a short write, such as the following:
  - *The Scraps Book* by Lois Ehlert, from Text Set: Genre Study: Memoir
  - *Dingo* by Claire Saxby, from Text Set: Illustration Study: Craft
- chart paper and marker
- document camera (optional)
- a reader's notebook for each student

### Academic Language / Important Vocabulary

- short write

### Continuum Connection

- Understand writing as a vehicle to communicate something the writer thinks (p. 285)

## Goal

Use a short write to share and deepen thinking about a book.

## Rationale

When you teach students to do a short write, they learn how to share their thinking about a variety of aspects of their reading quickly.

## Assess Learning

Observe students when they write to share their thinking and notice if there is evidence of new learning based on the goal of this minilesson.

- ▷ Can students do a short write to share their thinking?
- ▷ Do they use the term *short write*?

## Minilesson

To help students think about the minilesson principle, provide a demonstration of how to do a short write. Then have students talk about what they notice. Here is an example.

▷ Show the cover of *The Scraps Book*. On chart paper, begin a short write about the book. Write the title and author. Show the pages before the first page and model your thinking as you write.

> One thing I really loved about this book was the way the author caught my attention right away and made me want to read. I think I will start by writing about that quickly and for a short time.

▷ Show a few more pages of the book.

> I really loved these creative illustrations. I am going to write about that next.

▷ Continue with the short write, modeling your thinking and writing aloud.

> What did you notice about my short write?

▷ Guide students to notice that a short write is quick thinking in response to something they have read and that it can be about anything, though it should have a clear point.

## Have a Try

Invite the students to talk with a partner about doing a short write.

▶ Show the cover of *Dingo*.

If you wanted to do a short write about *Dingo*, what might you say? Turn and talk about that.

▶ After time for a brief discussion, ask a few volunteers to share.

Did you hear any new ideas you might like to use to do a short write about a book?

## Summarize and Apply

Summarize the learning and remind students to share their thinking as they write in a reader's notebook.

You can do a short write to share your quick thinking about any book.

Today, do a short write about *Dingo*. Bring your notebook when we meet so you can share.

## Share

Following independent reading time, gather students in small groups to share their writing.

Share your short write with your group. Take turns reading to each other.

## Extend the Lesson (Optional)

After assessing students' understanding, you might decide to extend the learning.

▶ **Writing About Reading** Encourage students to use the Writing About Reading page in the reader's notebook for other short write ideas (also available from resources.fountasandpinnell.com). Examples include how the author builds suspense, what the dialogue reveals about a character, how the author uses time in the story, or what could be changed about the book to make the story more interesting.

---

### Short Write
(Your quick thinking about a book)

The Scraps Book by Lois Ehlert

The author made me interested in reading even before the first page. An entire page says, "DON'T READ THIS BOOK" in large capital letters. Then, below that, it has in parentheses, "unless you love books and art." I think that is such a clever way to capture a reader's interest. The other way the author made me interested is by the many photos and creative drawings. She used scraps of paper to show her different memories. The drawings almost look 3-D and they look like you could grab them right off the page.

*Section 4: Writing About Reading*

## RML3
**WAR.U5.RML3**

**Reading Minilesson Principle**
# A storyboard shows the significant events in a story.

**Introducing Different Genres and Forms for Responding to Reading**

### You Will Need

- an example of a comic book, graphic novel (e.g., *Robin Hood* by Aaron Shepard and Anne L. Watson from *Independent Reading Collection*), or other book written in storyboard format (optional)

- several familiar books that have easy-to-follow events, such as the following:

  - *A Boy and a Jaguar* by Alan Rabinowitz, from Text Set: Figuring Out Who You Are

  - *The Boy and the Whale* by Mordicai Gerstein, from Text Set: Empathy

- chart paper and marker
- document camera (optional)
- a reader's notebook for each student

### Academic Language / Important Vocabulary

- storyboard
- panel
- plot
- events

### Continuum Connection

- Make notes or write descriptions to help remember important details about plot (p. 194)

## Goal

Create a storyboard to represent the significant events in a plot.

## Rationale

When students identify the most important events in stories and write about them in a sequential way, they recognize the pattern in narratives and are able to think deeply about the elements of plot. Storyboards provide an opportunity for students to use images to communicate their thinking about a book.

## Assess Learning

Observe students when they create a storyboard and notice if there is evidence of new learning based on the goal of this minilesson.

- ❱ Are students able to identify and sequence the most important events in a plot?
- ❱ Can they create a storyboard that shows the events from a book they read?
- ❱ Are they using the terms *storyboard, panel, plot,* and *events*?

## Minilesson

To help students think about the minilesson principle, guide them in creating a storyboard to show the plot events from a familiar book. Here is an example.

- ❱ If you have a comic book, graphic novel, or other book written in storyboard format, show a page.

  What do you notice about the format of this story?

- ❱ As needed, assist with the conversation so that students notice that each event is in a box (panel), there are pictures and just a few words, and the events go in order.

  This is similar to what is called a storyboard. A storyboard shows pictures of the important events in a story and has just a few words for each panel. Storyboards are often used to plan how to film a movie because they tell something about each main event that the director wants to show.

- ❱ Show the cover and revisit a few pages of *A Boy and a Jaguar*. As needed, guide them to think of which main events to show in a storyboard. The following prompts may be helpful.

  - *Which events from this story should be included in a storyboard?*
  - *How would you show the first event?*
  - *What could go in the next panel?*

- ❱ As students provide ideas, begin sketching the first few panels.

## Have a Try

Invite the students to talk with a partner about how to create a storyboard using a familiar book.

> What would go in the first few panels of a storyboard to show the action in *The Boy and the Whale*? Turn and talk about that.

## Summarize and Apply

Summarize the learning and remind students to think about the most important events as they read.

> Today you learned how to create a storyboard of the important events in a story.

▶ Add the principle to the chart.

> Make a storyboard for the last fiction book you read. Bring the book and your storyboard when we meet so you can share.

▶ To make the drawing easier, you might want to give students an unlined sheet of paper the size of the page in the reader's notebook so they can glue it in when finished.

A storyboard shows the significant events in a story.

## Share

Following independent reading time, gather students in pairs.

> Share your storyboard. If you are not finished, tell your partner what you will put in the next few panels, or ask for ideas if you are unsure about what to draw next.

## Extend the Lesson (Optional)

After assessing students' understanding, you might decide to extend the learning.

▶ Have the students use other types of books that have a narrative structure to create storyboards (e.g., biography, memoir, narrative nonfiction).

▶ The class can work together to create a large storyboard mural for a favorite book to display in the hall.

Section 4: Writing About Reading

**Reading Minilesson Principle**
# A summary of a book gives the important information.

## Introducing Different Genres and Forms for Responding to Reading

### You Will Need

- several fiction books that are good examples for writing a summary, such as the following from Text Set: Empathy:
  - *The Crane Wife* by Odds Bodkin
  - *The Boy and the Whale* by Mordicai Gerstein
- chart paper prepared with a book summary
- a reader's notebook for each student

### Academic Language / Important Vocabulary

- reader's notebook
- summary

### Continuum Connection

- Select and include appropriate and important details when writing a summary of a text (p. 193)
- Write summaries that include important details about setting (p. 194)
- Write summaries that include the story's main problem and how it is resolved (p. 194)
- Write summaries that include important details about characters (p. 194)

## Goal

Write a brief summary of the most important information in a fiction text, including the characters, setting, and the problem and solution (when applicable).

## Rationale

When students write a summary, they learn to think about the elements of fiction stories or nonfiction books and the big ideas in them. This is different from a retelling that gives most of the information. Prior to teaching this lesson, students need a good understanding of plot and summarizing (see Umbrella 25: Understanding Plot in Section Two: Literary Analysis and Umbrella 5: Summarizing in Section Three: Strategies and Skills).

## Assess Learning

Observe students when they write summaries and notice if there is evidence of new learning based on the goal of this minilesson.

- Can students write a concise summary of a book they have read?
- Do they use the terms *reader's notebook* and *summary*?

## Minilesson

To help students think about the minilesson principle, engage them in an inquiry-based lesson about writing a summary. Here is an example.

- Display the prepared summary and the cover of *The Crane Wife*.

  I have written a summary of *The Crane Wife*. What information do you notice included in the summary?

- As students respond, prompt the conversation as needed so they notice the typical contents of a summary of a book: title and author, main characters, setting, problem, resolution, and possibly the author's message, theme, or big idea.

- Record responses on chart paper.

  In what order did I write the information?

  What are some things from the book that I did *not* include in my summary?

  Why do you think I did not include that information?

  What is the difference between a retelling and a summary?

## Have a Try

Invite the students to talk with a partner about writing a summary.

▶ Show *The Boy and the Whale* and turn through a few pages.

What would you include in a summary of *The Boy and the Whale*? Turn and talk about that.

▶ After a brief time for discussion, ask students to share ideas.

## Summarize and Apply

Summarize the learning and remind students to think about how they would summarize what they are reading.

▶ Review the chart about summaries.

Try writing a summary of a book in your reader's notebook. You can write a summary of *The Boy and the Whale*, or you can write about a book you recently finished reading. Bring your reader's notebook when we meet so you can share.

## Share

Following independent reading time, gather students in pairs to share their summaries.

Share with your partner the summary you wrote. As you listen to your partner's summary, look at our chart and notice whether the summary includes all the important information and has *only* the important information. Then talk about that when your partner is finished.

## Extend the Lesson (Optional)

After assessing students' understanding, you might decide to extend the learning.

▶ Guide students in writing a summary for a familiar nonfiction book. This will be challenging since they must focus on the big ideas with only a few very important supporting facts. Create an anchor chart for a nonfiction summary.

---

### A Summary
#### (only the important information)

The Crane Wife by Odds Bodkin is about a poor man named Osamu, who wants a wife. One night, he helps an injured crane. Afterward, a beautiful woman named Yukiko shows up and they marry. Yukiko secretly works to make a magic sail, which makes a lot of money. Osamu is greedy and demands that she make more. Finally, he realizes that the woman is actually the crane in disguise, who is harming her own wings to make the sails. She flies away and is never seen again.

---

**A summary of a book gives the important information.**

A summary of a fiction book contains . . .

- Title and author
- Main characters
- Setting
- Problem and resolution
- Author's message, theme, or big idea

A summary . . .

- Tells information in order
- Has only the most important information

---

*Section 4: Writing About Reading*

## Reading Minilesson Principle

# A recommendation for a book or series encourages other to read it.

**Introducing Different Genres and Forms for Responding to Reading**

### You Will Need

- several familiar books or books in a series, such as the following by Nicholas Read from Text Set: Telling a Story with Photos:
  - *Wolf Island*
  - *The Seal Garden*
  - *A Bear's Life*
- chart paper prepared with a book recommendation
- highlighters in several colors
- a reader's notebook for each student

### Academic Language / Important Vocabulary

- reader's notebook
- book recommendation

### Continuum Connection

- Form and express opinions about a text in writing and support those opinions with rationales and evidence (p. 194)
- Form and express opinions about a text and/or an author or illustrator in writing and support those opinions with rationales and evidence (p. 197)

### Goal

Express an opinion about a book in the form of a book recommendation.

### Rationale

When students learn to write a book recommendation, they express their opinions about books and provide support for those opinions. They begin to develop their reading identities and preferences and improve writing skills. Written book recommendations are similar to book talks, so before teaching this lesson, it would be helpful for students to have experience listening to and giving book talks (see RML2 and RML3 in Umbrella 3: Living a Reading Life in Section One: Management).

### Assess Learning

Observe students when they write a book recommendation and notice if there is evidence of new learning based on the goal of this minilesson.

- ❯ Are students able to write a convincing recommendation for a book or series of books?
- ❯ Do they include the title, author, something about the book, and why it is recommended?
- ❯ Do they use the terms *reader's notebook* and *book recommendation*?

## Minilesson

To help students think about the minilesson principle, engage them in a discussion about the characteristics of a book recommendation. Here is an example.

- ❯ Display the book cover(s) and read the prepared recommendation for a series of books.

  Take a moment to notice the series of books I have displayed and what I have written.

  What do you notice about what I have written?

  Turn and talk to a partner about the information you notice I have included in this book recommendation.

- ❯ After time for a brief discussion, ask students to share what they notice. As they do, use different colors of highlighters to highlight and then label the text of your recommendation to show the elements that you have included, such as series name, book titles, author, audience, interesting facts, and reason you recommend the book.

  Look at the information that is in the recommendation. Why is this information important to include when writing a recommendation for a book or series?

## Have a Try

Invite the students to talk with a partner about information to include in a book recommendation.

> Think about a book you have read or are reading now and that you like a lot. What would you say to recommend it? Turn and talk about that.

▶ After time for discussion, ask a few volunteers to share.

## Summarize and Apply

Summarize the learning and remind students of what they would write in a book recommendation.

> Today we talked about what to include in a book recommendation. How are book recommendations helpful to you?

> Write a recommendation in your reader's notebook for a book you have read recently and think others would really enjoy. Before writing, think about the information you want to include.

> Bring your reader's notebook and the book you wrote about when we meet.

## Share

Following independent reading time, gather students in a circle to share their book recommendations.

> Who would like to share the book recommendation you wrote?

## Extend the Lesson (Optional)

After assessing students' understanding, you might decide to extend the learning.

▶ Provide examples of book recommendations from a variety of genres. Consider finding examples of recommendations or positive book reviews online.

▶ Encourage students to list books they hear about in book recommendations that they would like to read. Suggest that they make the list on the Books to Read page in the reader's notebook.

---

### A Book or Series Recommendation
(encourages others to read the book or series)

| | |
|---|---|
| I love learning about animals in nature. Do you? If so, you will love the My Great Bear Rainforest series by Nicholas Read: <u>Wolf Island</u>, <u>The Seal Garden</u>, and <u>A Bear's Life</u>. These books are about animals in different habitats. For example, some photos show wolves and bears fishing for salmon. Another photo shows a seal so close up that you can see every whisker on its face. I loved this book because it made me appreciate the beautiful places where these animals live and how important it is to protect their land. I would love to travel there someday, and I think you would, too, after reading this book. | who should read the books series name, titles, author<br><br>what the book is about interesting part<br><br>why you liked the book |

---

Section 4: Writing About Reading

## RML6

**WAR.U5.RML6**

**Reading Minilesson Principle**

# A sketch shows your thinking about something important in a book.

### Introducing Different Genres and Forms for Responding to Reading

#### You Will Need

- several fiction books that lend themselves to sketching something significant about the setting or message of the book, such as the following:
  - *Dad, Jackie, and Me* by Myron Uhlberg, from Text Set: Genre Study: Historical Fiction
  - *Imagine* by Juan Felipe Herrera, from Text Set: Exploring Identity
- chart paper prepared with a sketch that shows the setting or message of a familiar book
- a reader's notebook for each student
- drawing materials

#### Academic Language / Important Vocabulary

- reader's notebook
- sketch

#### Continuum Connection

- Draw or sketch to represent or remember the content of a text and provide a basis for discussion or writing [p. 193]
- Draw or sketch to assist in remembering a text or to represent its content [p. 196]
- Use sketching to capture detail that is important to a topic [p. 284]

### Goal

Use sketches to share and expand thinking about books.

### Rationale

When students create sketches showing their thinking about reading, they express ideas about setting, big ideas, themes, or messages of a book with images instead of words. Before teaching this minilesson, students need a good understanding of the concepts of setting (see Literary Analysis Umbrella 24: Thinking About the Setting in Fiction Books) and big ideas related to messages and themes (see Literary Analysis Umbrella 8: Thinking About the Author's Purpose and Message and Umbrella 9: Thinking about Themes).

### Assess Learning

Observe students when they draw sketches to share their thinking about reading and notice if there is evidence of new learning based on the goal of this minilesson.

- Can students respond to their reading by creating a sketch?
- Are students using the terms *reader's notebook* and *sketch*?

## Minilesson

To help students think about the minilesson principle, engage them in noticing how sketches or quick drawings communicate meaning. Here is an example.

- Show the cover of *Dad, Jackie, and Me* and the prepared sketch.

  A sketch is a quick drawing that helps me show my thinking or remember something about what I have read. Turn and talk about what you notice about this sketch about *Dad, Jackie, and Me.*

- Provide time for discussion and then ask students to share. Support the conversation with several prompts, such as the following, to encourage them to think about your choices.
  - *Why did I choose to make this sketch look like a newspaper?*
  - *Why is it important that I chose the colors that I did?*
  - *How is the year important to the story?*
  - *What is important about the words I added to the bottom of my sketch?*
  - *How is a sketch about a book a helpful way to show your thinking?*

- Guide the conversation so students understand that sketches can be a way to show important aspects of a story, such as setting, theme, or message.

## Have a Try

Invite the students to talk with a partner about making a sketch about a familiar book.

▶ Show the cover of *Imagine* and revisit a few pages.

   **What would you draw to show your thinking about *Imagine*? Turn and talk about that.**

▶ After time for a brief discussion, ask a few volunteers to share. Ask students how their sketch idea shows something important about the story.

## Summarize and Apply

Summarize the learning and remind students to think about what they would sketch to show something important about their reading.

▶ Review the chart.

   **Today, create a sketch to share your thinking about a book. You can use the idea you talked about from *Imagine*, or you can use an idea from a different book you are reading. Bring your reader's notebook when we meet so you can share.**

▶ To make drawing easier, you may want to give students an unlined sheet of paper that can be glued into a reader's notebook.

## Share

Following independent reading time, gather students in small groups to share their sketches.

   **With your group, share the sketch you made about your book. Explain how you decided what to draw and the choices you made about what to include.**

## Extend the Lesson (Optional)

After assessing students' understanding, you might decide to extend the learning.

▶ **Writing About Reading** Share other ideas for making sketches as a response to a fiction or nonfiction book and encourage students to try them out (visit resources.fountasandpinnell.com to download a list of ideas).

---

### Sketch
(shows your thinking about something important in a book)

— April 1947

**BROOKLYN DODGERS SIGN JACKIE ROBINSON**

Jackie Robinson fought discrimination and taught other people to do that too.

---

**Reading Minilesson Principle**

# A written sketch of a character is a short description of his traits with supporting evidence.

Introducing Different Genres and Forms for Responding to Reading

## You Will Need

- several familiar books that have a well-developed character, such as the following:
  - *The Buffalo Storm* by Katherine Applegate, from Text Set: Genre Study: Historical Fiction
  - *Be Water, My Friend* by Ken Mochizuki, from Text Set: Exploring Identity
- chart paper and markers
- a reader's notebook for each student

## Academic Language / Important Vocabulary

- reader's notebook
- character sketch

## Continuum Connection

- Make notes or descriptions to help remember important details about characters (p. 194)

## Goal

Write a sketch of a character.

## Rationale

When students write a sketch of a character, they have to think about how the author portrays the character. Sometimes creating a drawing of the character first can start their thinking. Before teaching this lesson, be sure students have learned about characters (see Literary Analysis Umbrella 26: Understanding Characters' Feelings, Motivations, and Intentions, Umbrella 27: Understanding a Character's Traits and Development, and possibly Umbrella 14: Studying Biography).

## Assess Learning

Observe students when they write a character sketch and notice if there is evidence of new learning based on the goal of this minilesson.

- ▶ Can students write a character sketch that accurately reflects how the author depicts the character?
- ▶ Are students using the terms *reader's notebook* and *character sketch*?

# Minilesson

To help students think about the minilesson principle, engage them in thinking about what information to include in a character sketch. Here is an example.

- ▶ Show the cover of *The Buffalo Storm*.

  A character sketch is a brief paragraph that helps someone get to know the character. Think about what you know about the girl in *The Buffalo Storm*. Turn and talk about what she is like and how she does things.

- ▶ Provide a moment for discussion to refresh students' memories about the character.

  Let's work together to write a character sketch of the girl. What information should be included in the paragraph?

- ▶ As students provide ideas, write a brief character sketch. As you write, help students stay focused on the traits of the character and evidence of those traits.

- ▶ Read the character sketch. Then, engage students in an analysis of the character sketch. Prompt students to understand that a good character sketch will tell not only what Hallie's physical traits are but also what her personality is like.

  This is just one example of a character sketch. When you write your own character sketch, you will make your own choices about what to include.

## Have a Try

Invite the students to talk with a partner about information for a character sketch.

▶ Show the cover of *Be Water, My Friend*.

You can also write a character sketch of a real person. What might you include in a character sketch of Bruce Lee, using what you learned about him in *Be Water, My Friend*? Turn and talk about that.

▶ After time for a brief discussion, ask students to share ideas.

## Summarize and Apply

Summarize the learning and remind students to write a character sketch in the reader's notebook.

▶ Review the character sketch.

Today, write a character sketch in your reader's notebook. You can use the fiction character from *The Buffalo Storm* or Bruce Lee from *Be Water, My Friend*. Or, you can choose someone from a book you are reading. Bring your reader's notebook when we meet so you can share.

## Share

Following independent reading time, gather students in small groups to share their character sketches.

With your group, share the character sketch you wrote. Talk about the choices you made.

## Extend the Lesson (Optional)

After assessing students' understanding, you might decide to extend the learning.

▶ Have students make a drawing of the character to go with the written character sketch. Encourage students to show details in the drawing beyond just physical traits so a person looking at the drawing can determine other qualities about the character.

---

### Character Sketch
(a short description with supporting evidence)

The main character Hallie in <u>The Buffalo Storm</u> is a small girl with brown hair and a big personality, who set off on the Oregon Trail with her family. She did things that girls didn't usually do, like help drive the oxen team. She was brave, which she showed by saving a trapped buffalo colt all on her own. Hallie loved and admired her grandma. When a herd of buffalo came past, she shouted with joy and laughed the way her grandma would have done. After arriving in her new home, she held her baby sister close and promised to care for her just like her grandma did when she was a baby.

The Buffalo Storm
by KATHERINE APPLEGATE · illustrated by JAN ORMEROD

# RML 8
### WAR.U5.RML8

## Reading Minilesson Principle
## Two-column writing shows your response to a phrase or quote from a book.

## Introducing Different Genres and Forms for Responding to Reading

### You Will Need

- several familiar books that have memorable phrases and/or quotes, such as the following:
  - *The Buffalo Storm* by Katherine Applegate, from Text Set: Genre Study: Historical Fiction
  - *Be Water, My Friend* by Ken Mochizuki, from Text Set: Exploring Identity
- chart paper prepared with two columns and a quotation in the first column (*The Buffalo Storm*, p. 18)
- marker
- a reader's notebook for each student
- document camera (optional)

### Academic Language / Important Vocabulary

- phrase
- quote

### Continuum Connection

- Draw and write about connections between the ideas in texts and their own life experiences (p. 193)

### Goal

Use two-column writing to respond to a phrase or quote from a text.

### Rationale

When students learn to respond to a phrase, quote, or question from their reading, they learn to express their responses to reading in a clear, organized way and to think deeply about language they encounter while reading.

### Assess Learning

Observe students when they write responses to phrases, quotes, or questions and notice if there is evidence of new learning based on the goal of this minilesson.

- ▶ Can students write a response to an important phrase or quote?
- ▶ Are they using the terms *phrase* and *quote*?

## Minilesson

To help students think about the minilesson principle, provide an interactive lesson about responding to phrases, quotes, or questions that students come across as they read. Here is an example.

> Sometimes when you read, you find a phrase or quote that stands out to you in some way and that makes you think. You might want to write about it in a way that helps you explore your thinking. Here's a sentence from *The Buffalo Storm* that I think is beautiful and interesting.

- ▶ Read aloud the first sentence on page 18 from *The Buffalo Storm* and show that you have written it in the first column.
- ▶ In the second column, write a response to the phrase, reading aloud as you write.

> Turn and talk about my writing. What do you notice?

- ▶ After a brief moment for discussion, ask a few volunteers to share.

> If you were writing a response to this special phrase, what would you write?

> Responding to this sentence helped me appreciate the author's writing even more. Writing about something is a way to think about it.

## Have a Try

Invite the students to respond to a phrase, quote, or question from a book.

▶ Show or project page 19 from *Be Water, My Friend*. Write on chart paper or project the quote: "Gentleness . . . I think I understand."

> Think about this quote by Bruce Lee. How does it show something about Bruce Lee? In your reader's notebook, write a quick response to this quote.

▶ After students have had a few minutes to write a response, ask a few volunteers to share.

## Summarize and Apply

Summarize the learning and remind students to use a reader's notebook to write responses to phrases and quotes.

▶ Review the idea of creating two columns to respond to phrases or quotes.

> Today, choose a phrase or quote that you like from the book you are reading. Make a two-column chart in your reader's notebook. Write the title of the book and the author at the top. Write the phrase or quote in the first column and write your response in the second column. Bring your reader's notebook and the book you used to our class meeting.

## Share

Following independent reading time, gather students in pairs to share what they wrote.

> Share your quote or phrase and your response with your partner.

## Extend the Lesson (Optional)

After assessing students' understanding, you might decide to extend the learning.

▶ **Writing About Reading** Encourage students to respond to other types of language they notice (e.g., words they like, other memorable phrases, beautiful language, descriptions) in a reader's notebook.

---

### Two-Column Writing
#### (your response to a phrase or quote)

#### The Buffalo Storm
#### by Katherine Applegate

| "Weeks wove together and faded in the sun." (page 18) | I picture a very long journey when I read this sentence. I remember when my family drove three states away, and it felt like a very long time to me, too. The journey for the family in the book was even longer because it took weeks and weeks. The way the author writes that they wove together and faded in the sun shows that each day started looking like the day before. It was a very long trip. |
|---|---|

Section 4: Writing About Reading

### Reading Minilesson Principle
## A persuasive poster is designed to persuade others to agree with your opinion.

**Introducing Different Genres and Forms for Responding to Reading**

### You Will Need

- several familiar books that encourage the reader to develop an opinion about a topic, such as the following from Text Set: Taking Action, Making Change:
  - *Emmanuel's Dream* by Laurie Ann Thompson
  - *One Hen* by Katie Smith Milway
- chart paper prepared with a persuasive poster
- markers
- a reader's notebook for each student
- drawing materials

### Academic Language / Important Vocabulary

- reader's notebook
- persuasive
- opinion

### Continuum Connection

- Understand that argument or persuasive texts can be written in various forms: e.g., editorial, letter to the editor, essay (p. 277)

### Goal

Make a persuasive poster based on an opinion developed through reading.

### Rationale

When students create persuasive posters that show their opinions, they begin to develop their voices and realize that their opinions about reading gain value when shared with others.

### Assess Learning

Observe students when they make a persuasive poster and notice if there is evidence of new learning based on the goal of this minilesson.

- ▌ Can students create a persuasive poster based on an opinion developed from reading?
- ▌ Are they using the terms *reader's notebook, persuasive,* and *opinion*?

## Minilesson

To help students think about the minilesson principle, engage them in a discussion about how to create a persuasive poster. Here is an example.

- ▌ Show the cover of *Emmanuel's Dream* and the prepared persuasive poster.

  Think about *Emmanuel's Dream* and notice the way I shared an opinion I have after reading this book. Turn and talk about what you notice.

- ▌ After time for discussion, ask students what they notice about the poster. As they identify what you included, add labels for the different parts of the poster. Prompt the conversation as needed. For example:
  - *Does my poster make my opinion clear? Why or why not?*
  - *Is my poster persuasive? In other words, does it convince you to agree with my opinion?*
  - *Would you choose to make the persuasive poster differently than I did? What would you do?*
- ▌ Provide time for students to share a variety of ideas so that they understand that it is a personal choice about how to create a persuasive poster.

## Have a Try

Invite the students to talk with a partner about creating a persuasive poster.

▶ Show the cover of *One Hen*.

> Think about *One Hen*. If you want to make a poster that persuades people to agree with your opinion about an idea in the book, what would you include? Turn and talk about that.

▶ After time for discussion, ask a few students to share.

## Summarize and Apply

Summarize the learning about how to make a persuasive poster.

▶ Review the chart.

> Choose a book that you have read and would like to use to make a persuasive poster. Think about the opinion you have after reading the book and about what you want to include. You can choose one of the books we used in class, or you can choose another book you are reading. Bring your reader's notebook when we meet so you can share.

▶ Give students unlined paper to use for the poster. Posters can then be glued into notebooks or, if large, displayed in the room.

## Share

Following independent reading time, gather students in small groups to share their writing.

> Show your group the persuasive poster you made. Talk about the choices you made.

## Extend the Lesson (Optional)

After assessing students' understanding, you might decide to extend the learning.

▶ Encourage students to think about opinions they have after reading and to create persuasive posters for display in the classroom.

### Persuasive Poster
(designed to persuade others to agree with your opinion)

One person is enough to change the world.

Inspire others to do good in the world, like Emmanuel in <u>Emmanuel's Dream</u>.

## Assessment

After you have taught the minilessons in this umbrella, observe students as they talk and write about their reading across instructional contexts: interactive read-aloud, independent reading, guided reading, shared reading, and book club. Use *The Literacy Continuum* (Fountas and Pinnell 2017) to guide the observation of students' reading and writing behaviors.

▶ What evidence do you have of new understandings related to responding to reading?

- Are students brainstorming ideas for writing about reading?

- Can they do a short write about a book?

- Are they able to create a storyboard to represent significant events in a story?

- Do they write concise summaries of fiction and nonfiction books?

- Can they write a book or series recommendation?

- Do they make sketches to share thinking about books?

- Are they able to write a character sketch?

- Can they respond in writing to an important phrase, quote, or question from a book?

- Can they make a persuasive poster to convince others to agree with their opinion about a book?

- Are they using the terms *reader's notebook, brainstorm, short write, storyboard, summary, recommendation, sketch, persuasive,* and *opinion*?

▶ In what other ways, beyond the scope of this umbrella, are students responding to reading?

- Are students using a reader's notebook in a variety of new ways?

Use your observations to determine the next umbrella you will teach. You may also consult Minilessons Across the Year (pp. 59–61) for guidance.

## Reader's Notebook

When this umbrella is complete, provide a copy of the minilesson principles (see resources.fountasandpinnell.com) for students to glue in the reader's notebook (in the Minilessons section if using *Reader's Notebook: Intermediate* [Fountas and Pinnell 2011]), so they can refer to the information as needed.

**adventure/adventure story** A contemporary realistic or historical fiction or fantasy text that presents a series of exciting or suspenseful events, often involving a main character taking a journey and overcoming danger and risk.

**affix** A letter or group of letters added to the beginning or end of a base or root word to change its meaning or function (a prefix or suffix).

**alphabet book/ABC book** A book that helps children develop the concept and sequence of the alphabet by pairing alphabet letters with pictures of people, animals, or objects with labels related to the letters.

**animal fantasy** A modern fantasy text geared to a very young audience in which animals act like people and encounter human problems.

**animal story** A contemporary realistic or historical fiction or fantasy text that involves animals and that often focuses on the relationships between humans and animals.

**assessment** A means for gathering information or data that reveals what learners control, partially control, or do not yet control consistently.

**beast tale** A folktale featuring animals that talk.

**behaviors** Actions that are observable as children read or write.

**biography** A biographical text in which the story (or part of the story) of a real person's life is written and narrated by another person. Biography is usually told in chronological sequence but may be in another order.

**bold/boldface** Type that is heavier and darker than usual, often used for emphasis.

**book and print features** (as text characteristics) The physical attributes of a text (for example, font, layout, and length).

**categorization** A structural pattern used especially in nonfiction texts to present information in logical categories (and subcategories) of related material.

**cause and effect** A structural pattern used especially in nonfiction texts, often to propose the reasons or explanations for how and why something occurs.

**character** An individual, usually a person or animal, in a text.

**chronological sequence** An underlying structural pattern used especially in nonfiction texts to describe a series of events in the order they happened in time.

**closed syllable** A syllable that ends in a consonant: e.g., ho-*tel*.

**compare and contrast** A structural pattern used especially in nonfiction texts to compare two ideas, events, or phenomena by showing how they are alike and how they are different.

**comprehension** (as in reading) The process of constructing meaning while reading text.

**concrete poetry** A poem with words (and sometimes punctuation) arranged to represent a visual picture of the idea the poem is conveying.

**conflict** In a fiction text, a central problem within the plot that is resolved near the end of the story. In literature, characters are usually in conflict with nature, with other people, with society as a whole, or with themselves. Another term for *conflict* is *problem*.

**consonant digraph** Two consonant letters that appear together and represent a single sound that is different from the sound of either letter: e.g., *she*ll.

**cumulative tale** A story with many details repeated until the climax.

**dialogue** Spoken words, usually set off with quotation marks in text.

**directions (how-to)** A procedural nonfiction text that shows the steps involved in performing a task. A set of directions may include diagrams or drawings with labels.

**elements of fiction** Important elements of fiction include narrator, characters, plot, setting, theme, and style.

**elements of poetry** Important elements of poetry include figurative language, imagery, personification, rhythm, rhyme, repetition, alliteration, assonance, consonance, onomatopoeia, and aspects of layout.

**endpapers** The sheets of heavy paper at the front and back of a hardback book that join the book block to the hardback binding. Endpapers are sometimes printed with text, maps, or designs.

**English language learners** People whose native language is not English and who are acquiring English as an additional language.

**expository text** A nonfiction text that gives the reader information about a topic. Expository texts use a variety of text structures, such as compare and contrast, cause and effect, chronological sequence, problem and solution, and temporal sequence. Seven forms of expository text are categorical text, recount, collection, interview, report, feature article, and literary essay.

**fable** A folktale that demonstrates a useful truth and teaches a lesson. Usually including personified animals or natural elements such as the sun, fables appear to be simple but often convey abstract ideas.

**factual text** See *informational text.*

**fantasy** A fiction text that contains elements that are highly unreal. Fantasy as a category of fiction includes animal fantasy, low fantasy, high fantasy, and science fiction.

**fiction** Invented, imaginative prose or poetry that tells a story. Fiction texts can be organized into the categories realism and fantasy. Along with nonfiction, fiction is one of two basic genres of literature.

**figurative language** Language that compares two objects or ideas to allow the reader to see something more clearly or understand something in a new way. An element of a writer's style, figurative language changes or goes beyond literal meaning. Two common types of figurative language are metaphor (a direct comparison) and simile (a comparison that uses *like* or *as*).

**flash-forward** A literary device in which the action moves suddenly into the future to relate events that have relevance for understanding the present.

**flashback** A literary device in which the action moves suddenly into the past to relate events that have relevance for understanding the present.

**fluency** In reading, this term names the ability to read continuous text with good momentum, phrasing, appropriate pausing, intonation, and stress. In word solving, this term names the ability to solve words with speed, accuracy, and flexibility.

**folktale** A traditional fiction text about a people or "folk," originally handed down orally from generation to generation. Folktales are usually simple tales and often involve talking animals. Fables, fairy tales, beast tales, trickster tales, tall tales, realistic tales, cumulative tales, noodlehead tales, and pourquoi tales are some types of folktales.

**font** In printed text, the collection of type (letters) in a particular style.

**form** A kind of text that is characterized by particular elements. Mystery, for example, is a form of writing within the realistic fiction genre. Another term for *form* is *subgenre*.

**fractured fairy tale** A retelling of a familiar fairy tale with characters, settings, or plot events changed, often for comic effect.

**free verse** A type of poetry with irregular meter. Free verse may include rhyme, alliteration, and other poetic sound devices.

**friendly letter** In writing, a functional nonfiction text usually addressed to friends and family that may take the form of notes, letters, invitations, or emails.

**genre** A category of written text that is characterized by a particular style, form, or content.

**graphic feature** In fiction texts, graphic features are usually illustrations. In nonfiction texts, graphic features include photographs, paintings and drawings, captions, charts, diagrams, tables and graphs, maps, and timelines.

**graphic text** A form of text with comic strips or other illustrations on every page. In fiction, a story line continues across the text; illustrations, which depict moment-to-moment actions and emotions, are usually accompanied by dialogue in speech balloons and narrative description of actions. In nonfiction, factual information is presented in categories or sequence.

**haiku** An ancient Japanese form of nonrhyming poetry that creates a mental picture and makes a concise emotional statement.

**high-frequency words** Words that occur often in the spoken and written language (for example, *the*).

**humor/humor story** A realistic fiction text that is full of fun and meant to entertain.

**hybrid/hybrid text** A text that includes at least one nonfiction genre and at least one fiction genre blended in a coherent whole.

**illustration** Graphic representation of important content (for example, art, photos, maps, graphs, charts) in a fiction or nonfiction text.

**imagery** The use of language—descriptions, comparisons, and figures of speech—that helps the mind form sensory impressions. Imagery is an element of a writer's style.

**independent writing** Children write a text independently with teacher support as needed.

**infer** (as a strategic action) To go beyond the literal meaning of a text; to think about what is not stated but is implied by the writer.

**infographic** An illustration—often in the form of a chart, graph, or map—that includes brief text and presents and analyzes data about a topic in a visually striking way.

**informational text** A nonfiction text whose purpose is to inform or give facts about a topic. Informational texts include the following genres: biography, autobiography, memoir, and narrative nonfiction, as well as expository texts, procedural texts, and persuasive texts.

**interactive read-aloud** An instructional context in which students are actively listening and responding to an oral reading of a text.

**interactive writing** A teaching context in which the teacher and students cooperatively plan, compose, and write a group text; both teacher and students act as scribes (in turn).

**intonation** In speech, the rise and fall in pitch of the voice to convey meaning.

**italic** (italics) A type style that is characterized by slanted letters.

**label** A written word or phrase that names the content of an illustration.

**layout** The way the print and illustrations are arranged on a page.

**legend** In relation to genre, this term names a traditional tale, first handed down orally and later in writing, that tells about a noteworthy person or event. Legends are believed to have some basis in history, but the accuracy of the events and people they describe is not always verifiable. In relation to book and print features, this term names a key on a map or chart that explains what symbols stand for.

**limerick** A type of rhyming verse, usually surprising and humorous and frequently nonsensical.

**limited point of view** A method of storytelling in which the narrator knows what one character is thinking and feeling. The narrator may relate the actions of many characters but will not move between the points of view of different characters in a given scene or story.

**lyrical poetry** A songlike type of poetry that has rhythm and sometimes rhyme and is memorable for sensory images and description.

**main idea** The central underlying idea, concept, or message that the author conveys in a nonfiction text. Compare to *theme, message*.

**maintaining fluency** (as a strategic action) Integrating sources of information in a smoothly operating process that results in expressive, phrased reading.

**making connections** (as a strategic action) Searching for and using connections to knowledge gained through personal experiences, learning about the world, and reading other texts.

**meaning** One of the sources of information that readers use (MSV: meaning, language structure, visual information). *Meaning*, the semantic system of language, refers to meaning derived from words, meaning across a text or texts, and meaning from personal experience or knowledge.

**memoir** A biographical text in which a writer takes a reflective stance in looking back on a particular time or person. Usually written in the first person, memoirs are often briefer and more intense accounts of a memory or set of memories than those found in biographies and autobiographies.

**mentor texts** Books or other texts that serve as examples of excellent writing. Mentor texts are read and reread to provide models for literature discussion and student writing.

**message** An important idea that an author conveys in a fiction or nonfiction text. See also *main idea, theme*.

**modern fantasy** Fantasy texts that have contemporary content. Unlike traditional literature, modern fantasy does not come from an oral tradition. Modern fantasy texts can be divided into four more specific genres: animal fantasy, low fantasy, high fantasy, and science fiction.

**monitoring and self-correcting** (as a strategic action) Checking whether the reading sounds right, looks right, and makes sense, and solving problems when it doesn't.

**mood** The emotional atmosphere communicated by an author in his or her work, or how a text makes readers feel. An element of a writer's style, mood is established by details, imagery, figurative language, and setting. See also *tone*.

**narrative nonfiction** Nonfiction texts that tell a story using a narrative structure and literary language to make a topic interesting and appealing to readers.

**narrative text** A category of texts in which the purpose is to tell a story. Stories and biographies are kinds of narrative.

**narrative text structure** A method of organizing a text. A simple narrative structure follows a traditional sequence that includes a beginning, a problem, a series of events, a resolution of the problem, and an ending. Alternative narrative structures may include such devices as flashback or flash-forward (to change the sequence of events) or multiple narrators.

**narrator** The teller of the story of a text. The term *point of view* also indicates the angle from which the story is told, usually the first person (the narrator is a character in the story) or the third person (the unnamed narrator is not a character in the story).

**nonfiction** Prose or poetry that provides factual information. According to their structures, nonfiction texts can be organized into the categories of narrative and nonnarrative. Along with fiction, nonfiction is one of the two basic genres of literature.

**nonnarrative text structure** A method of organizing a text. Nonnarrative structures are used especially in three genres of nonfiction—expository texts, procedural texts, and persuasive texts. In nonnarrative nonfiction texts, underlying structural patterns include description, cause and effect, chronological sequence, temporal sequence, categorization, compare and contrast, problem and solution, and question and answer. See also *organization, text structure*, and *narrative text structure.*

**open syllable** A syllable that ends in a vowel sound: e.g., *ho*-tel.

**oral tradition** The handing down of literary material—such as songs, poems, and stories—from person to person over many generations through memory and word of mouth.

**organization** The arrangement of ideas in a text according to a logical structure, either narrative or nonnarrative. Another term for *organization* is *text structure.*

**organizational tools and sources of information** A design feature of nonfiction texts. Organizational tools and sources of information help a reader process and understand nonfiction texts. Examples include table of contents, headings, index, glossary, appendices, about the author, and references.

**peritext** Decorative or informative illustrations and/or print outside the body of the text. Elements of the peritext add to the aesthetic appeal and may have cultural significance or symbolic meaning.

**personification** A figure of speech in which an animal is spoken of or portrayed as if it were a person, or in which a lifeless thing or idea is spoken of or portrayed as a living thing. Personification is a type of figurative language.

**perspective** How the characters view what is happening in the story. It is shaped by culture, values, and experience. See also *narrator* and *point of view.*

**persuasive text** A nonfiction text intended to convince the reader of the validity of a set of ideas—usually a particular point of view.

**picture book** An illustrated fiction or nonfiction text in which pictures work with the text to tell a story or provide information.

**plot** The events, actions, conflict, and resolution of a story presented in a certain order in a fiction text. A simple plot progresses chronologically from start to end, whereas more complex plots may shift back and forth in time.

**poetry** Compact, metrical writing characterized by imagination and artistry and imbued with intense meaning. Along with prose, poetry is one of the two broad categories into which all literature can be divided.

**point of view** The angle from which a fiction story is told, usually the first person (the narrator is a character in the story; uses the pronouns I, me) or the third person (an unnamed narrator is not a character in the story; uses the pronouns he, she, they). See also *narrator*, *limited point of view*, and *third-person-omniscient point of view*.

**pourquoi tale** A folktale intended to explain why things are the way they are, usually having to do with natural phenomena.

**predicting** (as a strategic action) Using what is known to think about what will follow while reading continuous text.

**prefix** A group of letters placed in front of a base word to change its meaning: e.g., *pre*plan.

**principle** A generalization that is predictable.

**print feature** In nonfiction texts, print features include the color, size, style, and font of type, as well as various aspects of layout.

**problem** See *conflict*.

**problem and solution** A structural pattern used especially in nonfiction texts to define a problem and clearly propose a solution. This pattern is often used in persuasive and expository texts.

**procedural text** A nonfiction text that explains how to do something. Procedural texts are almost always organized in temporal sequence and take the form of directions (or how-to texts) or descriptions of a process.

**prompt** A question, direction, or statement designed to encourage the child to say more about a topic.

*Prompting Guide, Part 1* A quick reference for specific language to teach for, prompt for, or reinforce effective reading and writing behaviors. The guide is organized in categories and color-coded so that you can turn quickly to the area needed and refer to it as you teach (Fountas and Pinnell 2012).

**punctuation** Marks used in written text to clarify meaning and separate structural units. The comma and the period are common punctuation marks.

**purpose** A writer's overall intention in creating a text, or a reader's overall intention in reading a text. To tell a story is one example of a writer's purpose, and to be entertained is one example of a reader's purpose.

**question and answer** A structural pattern used especially in nonfiction texts to organize information in a series of questions with responses. Question-and-answer texts may be based on a verbal or written interview or on frequently arising or logical questions about a topic.

**reader's notebook** A notebook or folder of bound pages in which students write about their reading. A reader's notebook is used to keep a record of texts read and to express thinking. It may have several different sections to serve a variety of purposes.

**readers' theater** A performance of literature—e.g., a story, a play, or a poem—read aloud expressively by one or more persons rather than acted.

**realistic fiction** A fiction text that takes place in contemporary or modern times about believable characters involved in events that could happen. Contemporary realistic fiction usually presents modern problems that are typical for the characters, and it may highlight social issues.

**repetition** Repeated words or phrases that help create rhythm and emphasis in poetry or prose.

**resolution/solution** The point in the plot of a fiction story when the main conflict is solved.

**rhyme** The repetition of vowel and consonant sounds in the stressed and unstressed syllables of words in verse, especially at the ends of lines.

**rhythm** The regular or ordered repetition of stressed and unstressed syllables in poetry, other writing, or speech.

**searching for and using information** (as a strategic action) Looking for and thinking about all kinds of content to make sense of a text while reading.

**self-correcting** Noticing when reading doesn't make sense, sound right, or look right, and fixing it when it doesn't.

**sequence** See *chronological sequence* and *temporal sequence.*

**series** A set of books that are connected by the same character(s) or setting. Each book in a series stands alone, and often books may be read in any order.

**setting** The place and time in which a fiction text or biographical text takes place.

**shared reading** An instructional context in which the teacher involves a group of students in the reading of a particular big book to introduce aspects of literacy (such as print conventions), develop reading strategies (such as decoding or predicting), and teach vocabulary.

**shared writing** An instructional context in which the teacher involves a group of students in the composing of a coherent text together. The teacher writes while scaffolding children's language and ideas.

**short write** A sentence or paragraph that students write at intervals while reading a text. Students may use sticky notes, notepaper, or a reader's notebook to write about what they are thinking, feeling, or visualizing as they read. They may also note personal connections to the text.

**sidebar** Information that is additional to the main text, placed alongside the text and sometimes set off from the main text in a box.

**small-group reading instruction** The teacher working with children brought together because they are similar enough in reading development to teach in a small group; guided reading.

**solving words** (as a strategic action) Using a range of strategies to take words apart and understand their meanings.

**sources of information** The various cues in a written text that combine to make meaning (for example, syntax, meaning, and the physical shape and arrangement of type).

**speech bubble** A shape, often rounded, containing the words a character or person says in a cartoon or other graphic text. Another term for *speech bubble* is *speech balloon.*

**stance** How the author feels about a topic; the author's attitude.

**story** A series of events in narrative form, either fiction or nonfiction.

**story about family, friends, and school** A contemporary realistic or historical fiction text that focuses on the everyday experiences of children of a variety of ages, including relationships with family and friends and experiences at school.

**story within a story** A structural device occasionally used in fiction texts to present a shorter, self-contained narrative within the context of the longer primary narrative. See also *plot.*

**strategic action** Any one of many simultaneous, coordinated thinking activities that go on in a reader's head. See also *thinking within, beyond, and about the text.*

**stress** The emphasis given to some syllables or words.

**structure** One of the sources of information that readers use (MSV: meaning, language structure, visual information). *Language structure* refers to the way words are put together in phrases and sentences (syntax or grammar).

**style** The way a writer chooses and arranges words to create a meaningful text. Aspects of style include sentence length, word choice, and the use of figurative language and symbolism.

**subgenre** A kind of text that is characterized by particular elements. See also *form.*

**suffix** A group of letters added at the end of a base word or word root to change its function or meaning: e.g., hand*ful*, hope*less.*

**summarizing** (as a strategic action) Putting together and remembering important information, disregarding irrelevant information, while reading.

**syllable** A minimal unit of sequential speech sounds composed of a vowel sound or a consonant-vowel combination. A syllable always contains a vowel or vowel-like speech sound: e.g., *pen-ny.*

**tall tale** A folktale that revolves around a central legendary character with extraordinary physical features or abilities. Tall tales are characterized by much exaggeration.

**temporal sequence** An underlying structural pattern used especially in nonfiction texts to describe the sequence in which something always or usually occurs, such as the steps in a process. See also *procedural text* and *directions (how-to).*

**text structure** The overall architecture or organization of a piece of writing. Another term for *text structure* is *organization.* See also *narrative text structure* and *nonnarrative text structure.*

**theme** The central underlying idea, concept, or message that the author conveys in a fiction text. Compare to *main idea.*

**thinking within, beyond, and about the text** Three ways of thinking about a text while reading. Thinking *within* the text involves efficiently and effectively understanding what it is on the page, the author's literal message. Thinking *beyond* the text requires making inferences and putting text ideas together in different ways to construct the text's meaning. In thinking *about* the text, readers analyze and critique the author's craft.

**third-person-omniscient point of view** A method of storytelling in which the narrator knows what all characters are thinking and feeling. Omniscient narrators may move between the points of view of different characters in a given scene or story.

**thought bubble** A shape, often rounded, containing the words (or sometimes an image that suggests one or more words) a character or person thinks in a cartoon or other graphic text. Another term for *thought bubble* is *thought balloon.*

**tone** An expression of the author's attitude or feelings toward a subject reflected in the style of writing. For instance, a reader might characterize an author's tone as ironic or earnest. Sometimes the term *tone* is used to identify the mood of a scene or a work of literature. For example, a text might be said to have a somber or carefree tone. See also *mood.*

**tools** As text characteristics, parts of a text designed to help the reader access or better understand it (table of contents, glossary, headings). In writing, references that support the writing process (dictionary, thesaurus).

**topic** The subject of a piece of writing.

**traditional literature** Stories passed down in oral or written form through history. An integral part of world culture, traditional literature includes folktales, tall tales, fairy tales, fables, myths, legends, epics, and ballads.

**trickster tale** A folktale featuring a clever, usually physically weaker or smaller, animal who outsmarts larger or more powerful animals.

**understandings** Basic concepts that are critical to comprehending a particular area of content.

**visual information** One of three sources of information that readers use (MSV: meaning, language structure, visual information). *Visual information* refers to the letters that represent the sounds of language and the way they are combined (spelling patterns) to create words; visual information at the sentence level includes punctuation.

**wordless picture book** A form in which a story is told exclusively with pictures.

**writing** Children engaging in the writing process and producing pieces of their own writing in many genres.

**writing about reading** Children responding to reading a text by writing and sometimes drawing.

# Credits

Cover image from *Able to Play: Overcoming Physical Challenges* by Glenn Stout. Copyright © 2012 by Houghton Mifflin Harcourt Publishing Company. Reprinted by permission of Houghton Mifflin Harcourt Publishing.

Cover image from *Action Jackson* by Jan Greenberg and Sandra Jordan, illustrated by Robert Andrew Parker. Text copyright © 2002 by Jan Greenberg and Sandra Jordan. Illustrations copyright © 2002 by Robert Andrew Parker. Reprinted by permission of Roaring Brook Press, a division of Holtzbrinck Publishing Holdings Limited Partnership. All Rights Reserved.

Cover image from *Amazon Rainforest* by William B. Rice. Copyright © 2012. Reprinted by permission of Teacher Created Materials.

Cover image from *Attack of the Bullfrogs* by Therese Shea. Copyright © 2017. Reprinted by permission of Gareth Stevens Publishing.

Cover image from *Barbed Wire Baseball* by Marissa Moss, illustrated by Yuko Shimizu. Text copyright © 2013 Marissa Moss. Illustrations copyright © 2013 Yuko Shimizu. Used by permission of Abrams, an imprint of Harry N. Abrams, Inc. New York. All rights reserved.

Cover image from *The Barefoot Book of Earth Poems* by Judith Nicholls, illustrated by Beth Kromes. Copyright © 2003 Judith Nicholls and Beth Kromes. Image used by permission of Barefoot Books, Inc., Cambridge, MA.

Cover image from *Beauty and the Beast*. Text and illustrations copyright © 1989 Jan Brett Studios, Inc. Reprinted with permission of Clarion Books, an imprint of Houghton Mifflin Harcourt.

Cover image from *Be Water My Friend* by Ken Mochizuki, illustrated by Dom Lee. Copyright © 2006 Ken Mochizuki and Dom Lee. Permission arranged with Lee & Low Books, Inc., New York, NY 10016.

Cover image from *The Bicycle Man*. Copyright © 1982 by Allen Say. Reprinted with permission of Houghton Mifflin Harcourt.

Cover image from *A Boy and A Jaguar*. Text copyright © 2014 by Alan Rabinowitz. Illustrations copyright © 2014 by Catia Chien. Reprinted with permission of Houghton Mifflin Harcourt.

Cover image from *The Boy and the Whale* by Mordicai Gerstein. Copyright © 2017 by Mordicai Gerstein. Reprinted by permission of Roaring Brook Press, a division of Holtzbrinck Publishing Holdings Limited Partnership, and Raines and Raines Literary Agency. All rights reserved.

Cover image from *A Boy Called Bat* by Elana K. Arnold. Text copyright © 2017 Elana K. Arnold. Used by permission of HarperCollins Publishers.

Cover image from *Brave Red, Smart Frog*. Text copyright © 2018 Emily Jenkins. Illustrations copyright © 2018 Rohan Daniel Eason. Reproduced by permission of the publisher, Candlewick Press, Somerville, MA.